Testament of a Russian Fascist

TESTAMENT OF A RUSSIAN FASCIST

KONSTANTIN RODZAEVSKY

TRANSLATED BY DANIEL MONTOYA

ANTELOPE HILL PUBLISHING

Translation Copyright © 2023 Antelope Hill Publishing
Biography Copyright © 2023 Daniel Montoya

First edition, first printing, 2023.

Translated by Daniel Montoya, 2023.

Testament of a Russian Fascist is a translation of *Zaveshchaniye russkogo fashista*, compiled and published in Russian by FERI-V, 2001. The contents of this compilation are as follows:

Contemporary Judaization of the World, or The Jewish Question in the Twentieth Century: published as *Sovremennaya iudaizatsiya mira ili yevreyskiy vopros v XX stoletii* by the Russian Fascist Party, Harbin, 1943.

The ABC of Fascism: originally compiled by G. V. Taradanov (with the participation of V. V. Kibardin); edited and annexed by K. V. Rodzaevsky; published as *Azbuka fashizma* by the Russian Fascist Party, 1935.

"The Party Program of the All-Russian Fascist Party": approved by the Third Congress of the Russian Fascists in Harbin, 1935.

"All-Russian Fascist Party Documents": approved by the Supreme Council of the RFP in Harbin, 1936.

"Supreme Court of the Russian Federation Ruling No. 043/46": released 1998.

The two closing articles by Aleksey Shiropaev from the 2001 edition were not translated for this edition.

Publisher's note: Note that the spelling of the names of minor figures may not be accurate due to the difficulties caused by transliteration and that such minor figures cannot all be independently found and the spelling of their names verified. The spellings given here are a transliteration of what was given in the original Russian.

Cover art by Swifty.
Edited by Harlan Wallace.
Layout by Margaret Bauer.

Translator, Daniel Montoya | ducealexandrovich@gmail.com

Antelope Hill Publishing | antelopehillpublishing.com

Hardcover ISBN-13: 978-1-956887-60-0
EPUB ISBN-13: 978-1-956887-61-7

The New Russia is a Russia without Jewry
and Freemasonry, a religious Russia,
a national Russia, a labor Russia,
a Russia of the Orthodox faith.

Konstantin Rodzaevsky

CONTENTS

A Short Biography of Konstantin Rodzaevsky by the Translator .. xvii

Volume I
Contemporary Judaization of the World, or the Jewish Question

Introduction 3
Preface from 1943 9
Part One: A Journey Around the World
  1. Starting with the British Isles 11
  2. England and the Kings 12
  3. The New Aristocracy 13
  4. Eighty-Year-Old Lady Fitzgerald's Return to Judaism 14
  5. The History of the Jewish Takeover of Great Britain 15
  6. Talmudic Wanderers at the Forefront of the British Empire 18
  7. England and Judea 28
  8. London as One of the Capitals of International Judea 30
  9. Judas Invades France 32
  10. The Freemason Brothers 37
  11. French and Jewish! 39
  12. The French Republic or the Rothschild Brothers? 40
  13. The Fruits of Philosemitism in Spain 42
  14. "The Most Devout Community in the World," or the Jews in Gibraltar 45
  15. For Three Thousand Years Judas Tormented Italy 48
  16. Jews in Switzerland 53
  17. Jewish Boasts Over Conquered Germany 54
  18. Jews in the Glorious Belgian Police 57
  19. The Dutch "Asylum for the Persecuted" 58

20. "Great Jews" in a Small Denmark 63
21. Jews in Sweden and Norway 68
22. Jewish Limitrophes 71
23. Poland, the Great Fortress of Jewish "Culture" 77
24. The Lost Czechoslovak "Paradise for Jews" 79
25. Austria Before the Anschluss 82
26. Jews in Hungary 85
27. Romania Under the Heel of the Redheaded Lupescu 86
28. Bulgaria Is Being Cleansed 87
29. "A Country That Knows No Anti-Semitism" 88
30. The Greek King and the Synagogue 90
31. Russia Under the Red Star 92
32. Jews in the Soviet Government. 94
33. Kaganovich 97
34. Jews Are Being Introduced to East Asia 100
35. Jews in the South Seas 105
36. The Center of Jewish Life Moves to America 109
37. Jewish Population Growth in Overseas Countries 112
38. Roosevelt and World Jewry 113
39. The Judaic Rulers of the US 114
40. Landmark Rulings in Montevideo 117
41. Following the Journey Around the World—To the Time Machine 118

Part Two: Excursion into History
42. Where Did They Come From 121
43. Purim 123
44. The Birth of the Sanhedrin 123
45. Anti-Semitism in the Ancient World 124
46. Judas Rejects God 126
47. Jewry as a Nationality 128
48. Jewry as a Religion 132
49. Jews and the Talmud 134
50. "Shulchan-Aruch" 137
51. The Foundations of Judaism 137
52. The Significance of Religion for the Jewish Nation 140
53. Jewry as an Inter-Nation 142
54. Judaism and Freemasonry 146
55. What Is Freemasonry? 150
56. The Organization of Freemasonry 152
57. How the Secrets of Freemasonry Came to Be Known 154
58. Historical Exhibitions in Paris and Tokyo 160
59. The Unity of World Freemasonry 165
60. Freemasonry and the French Revolution 165
61. The French Revolution and Jewish Equality 167
62. The Fatal Significance of Jewish Equality for All Mankind .. 169

Contents | ix

63. Jewry and Liberalism 171
64. Jewry in Democracy 173
65. Jewry in Capitalism 175
66. An Age of Great Jewish Preparation 175
67. The Century of Great Jewish Achievements 178
68. Jewry in Socialism 181
69. Socialism and Palestine 185
70. A Letter from a Friend of Marx 188
71. Jewry and the World War 188
72. The League of Nations 191
73. The Various International Organizations 192
74. Judas and the Revolution 195
75. The Victory of Jewish Equality Over Russia 199
76. Judas Financed the Red October 200
77. Judas Takes Over Russia 202
78. The Harbin Proof 204
79. Revolutions and Jewish Enrichment 204
80. Jewry in Communism 206
81. Communism and Jewry in Jewish Confessions 209
82. Another Stack of Jewish Confessions 214
83. Some More Facts of the Same Kind 215
84. The Ways of Judaization 217
85. Hypocrisy 219
86. Under All Sorts of Masks 223
87. Espionage 226
88. Bribery and Corruption 228
89. Winston Churchill and the Silver Coins of Judas 230
90. The Love of Money of Politicians in the Jewish Orbit 232
91. In the Networks of Grand Scams 233
92. Politics and the Jewish Woman 234
93. Jewish Terror 236
94. Massacre of Hostages 238
95. Detours of Jewish Terror 242
96. Jewish Terror in the Name of Power 243
97. By Don Basilio's Recipes 245
98. "Herem" and "Quarantine" 247
99. Judas as the Inventor of Torture 248
100. The Organizers of the Red Terror 257
101. Women! Beware of Jewish Sadism 263
102. The Picture of Jewish Terror in Russia 265
103. Figures of the Jewish War with Russia 272
104. The Destruction of a National-Strong-Willed Elite 274
105. The Jewish Poisoning of Nations with Debauchery 277
106. Judas Storms the Family 288
107. Jewish Drug Poisoning of Nations 293

108. Judas vs. the Nation 294
109. Ultimate Goals 298

Part Three: The World Jewish Inter-State, Its Internal Organization

110. The Results of Judaization 301
111. Jewry as an Inter-State 304
112. The Community as the Basic Unit of the Jewish Inter-State 305
113. Functions of the Jewish Community 308
114. Jewish Councils as an Amalgamation of the Communities into the State 313
115. Parties and International Jewish Organizations 314
116. International Jewish Organizations 316
117. B'nai B'rith 319
118. World Jewish Congresses 320
119. The Jewish Super-Government..322
120. The Scheme of the Jewish Inter-State.................................325
121. World Jewish Population..326
122. The Hidden Armies of World Jewry.....................................328
123. The Jews Are Taking Over Our Cities 329
124. The Jews Are Taking Over Our Capitals 331
125. Jews Take Over the Centers of Our Capitals......................332
126. Jews Take Over the Center of Russia..................................333
127. The Inter-State Wants to Conquer the Whole World 335

Part Four: The Solution to Our Destiny, or the Decoding of Contemporary Events, Their Hidden Drives, and the Latest Jewish Policy

128. Judaism and Fascism 341
129. The *Zarnitsa* of the New Order..343
130. Mobilization of the Forces of Darkness 348
131. The Jewish Struggle Against Fascism 352
132. Parallelism...354
133. Against the Idea of Selection, the Idea of Unification 356
134. Kosher Fascism 358
135. The Jewish War Against Fascism 359
136. The Jewish Takeover of World Diplomacy 364
137. Bullitt, a Typical Representative of the Judaization of Diplomacy 367
138. Count Potocki Exposes Jewishness and the US...................370
139. Jewish Preparations and Anti-Jewish Warnings 374
140. "Hands Off Japan!"—From England 380
141. "Hands Off Japan!"—From the US 383
142. Will America Go to War? 384
143. Under the Smoke Screen of the German-Soviet Pact..........387
144. The Secret UK–USSR Axis...389

145. The Anglo-Soviet Pact, World Jewry's Greatest
Achievement 391
146. The German–Soviet War 392
147. For Whom Does the Red Army of the USSR Fight? 393
148. The Jewish Appeal to Stalin 396
149. Jewish Speeches at the Second Congress of the Jewish
People in Soviet Moscow, 1942 399
150. The Judeans in the War for Judea 401
151. Dr. Goldman Exposes the Secrets of Politics 404
152. The Jewish Aims of War 408
153. The Three Swords in the Hands of Israel 417
154. Recent Maps 424
155. Japan's Historical Mission 426
156. The Historical Mission of Russian Emigration 428
157. A New Order 431
158. A New Russia 432

Volume II
The ABC of Fascism, The Party Program of the All-Russian Fascist Party, All-Russian Fascist Party Documents, and Supreme Court of the Russian Federation Ruling No. 043/46

The ABC of Fascism
Introduction to the First Edition 437
Introduction to the Second Edition 439
Part One
Chapter I: General Idea of Fascism
1. Causes for the Emergence of Fascism 441
2. What Is Fascism as a Global Movement? 441
3. Where Does the Word "Fascism" Come from and What
Does It Mean? 441
4. Where and When Did Fascism First Arise? 441
5. Examples of Fascist Movements in Different Countries ... 442
6. What Does Fascism Bring That Is New, and What Does
It Keep That Is Old? 443
7. What Is the Nation? 443
8. What Is a Class from the Fascist Point of View? 444
9. What Is Labor and Who Is the Worker from the Fascist
Point of View? 444
10. What Is Capital and the Attitude of Fascists Toward
It? 445
11. What Does Fascism Bring in Place of Class Struggle;
in What Way Does Fascism Reconcile Labor and Capital? ... 445
12. How Does Fascism View State Power? 445
13. What Kind of State Are the Fascists Trying to Create? .. 446

14. What Is a Party in General and What Is a Fascist Party? 446
15. Who Are the Fascists Fighting? 447
Questions to Review: 447

Chapter II: The Enemies of Fascism
16. Main Directions of Socio-Political Thought 449
17. What Is Liberalism and What Are Its Dangers? 449
18. What Is Democracy and What Is Its Lie? 450
19. What Is Capitalism and What Does It Lead To? 450
20. What Is Socialism? 451
21. What Is the Cause of Socialism? 452
22. Fascism as a Substitute for Liberalism and Socialism 455
23. How Does Fascism Differ from Liberalism and Marxism? 455
24. Why Are Fascists Hostile to the Jews? 456
25. Why Are Fascists Fighting Freemasonry? 456
Questions to Review: 457

Chapter III: The Situation in Russia
26. Why Are the Russian Fascists Fighting the Existing Power in the USSR? 459
27. What Is the CPSU? 459
28. Tell Us Briefly the History of the CPSU 459
29. What Is the Comintern? 460
30. What Is the USSR? 460
31. Tell Us Briefly the History of the USSR. 461
32. What Is a Five-Year Plan? 461
33. What Is Total Collectivization and What Are Its Results? 462
34. Describe the Actual Situation in the USSR 463
35. Describe the Mood of the Russian People. 463
Questions to Review: 464

Part Two
Chapter I: Causes and Main Objectives of Russian Fascism
36. What Is the Ideology, Program, and Tactics of Russian Fascism? 465
37. What Does the Failure of the White Movement Mean? ... 465
38. What Does the Experience of Italy and Germany Teach? 466
39. The Situation in Emigration Before the Emergence of Russian Fascism. 466
40. The Causes of Russian Fascism 467
41. What Is Russian Fascism? 467
42. Why Is the Claim That Russian Fascists Copy Italian and German Fascism Unfounded? 468
43. The Unique Elements of Russian Fascism. 468

44. The Connection of Russian Fascism with the Russian Historical Past. 469
45. Why Do We Call Ourselves "Fascists"?............................ 469
46. What Is the All-Russian Fascist Party? 470
47. What Is the Russian National-Labor State? 470
48. What Is the Russian Nation? 471
49. Why Should the Russian Nation Include All the Peoples Inhabiting Russia? 471
50. The Task of the Russian Fascists in Relation to Russia. 472
51. What Does Russian Fascism Bring to the Individual Peoples of Russia? 472
52. The Situation of Jews in the National-Labor State. 472
53. Obligations of Every Russian Citizen in Relation to the Russian National-Labor State.. 473
54. What Will the Russian National Labor State Give to Every Russian Citizen?.. 473
55. The Role and Significance of the Family in the Future National Labor State. 474
Questions to Review:... 474

Chapter II: What Kind of State System Are the Russian Fascists Going to Build for the Russian People
56. Basic Principles of the State Structure of the Future Fascist Russia... 477
57. What Is the Slogan "Russia For Russia"?......................... 477
58. How Will the Corporate System Be Implemented in Russia? 478
59. What Are National Unions and Their Differences from National Corporations?... 478
60. Who in the National Labor State Will Be Considered a Worker?... 479
61. Objectives of the National Union. 479
62. What Is the National Council? 480
63. What Is a National Corporation? 480
64. How Will the Supreme State Power Be Organized? 481
65. The Role of the All-Russian Fascist Party in the State Life of the Future Fascist Russia. 481
66. The Attitude of Fascists to the Form of Government. 482
67. What Kind of Court Should Exist in National-Labor Russia? 482
68. What Goals Will the Russian National-Labor State Pursue in the Matter of National Education and Enlightenment? 483
69. What Does the Slogan "Make Way for Abilities and Talents" Mean?.. 483
70. Religion in the Russian National Labor State. 484

Questions to Review: 484
Chapter III: The National Economy and the Situation of Individual Classes in the Russian National Labor State
    71. The Economic Policy of Russian Fascism. 487
    72. The Fascist Attitude Toward Private Property. 488
    73. The Role of State Power in the Economy of the National-Labor State..488
    74. How Will Private Entrepreneurs Be Attracted to Participate in the Economic Life of the National Labor State?...489
    75. On What Grounds Will the Financial System of the National-Labor State Rest?..489
    76. Trade in National-Labor Russia. 490
    77. The Role of Individual Classes in the National Economy. 490
    78. What Does Russian Fascism Give to Russian Workers? .491
    79. What Does Russian Fascism Bring to Russian Peasants?...493
    80. What Does Russian Fascism Bring to the Intelligentsia?494
    Questions to Review: 495
Chapter IV: Tactics of the All-Russian Fascist Party
    81. Stages of the RFP's Work..497
    82. What Is Our General Line and Our General Plan?..........497
    83. Ways to Implement the Three-Year Plan. 498
    84. What Are the Basic Principles of Our Revolutionary Work?..498
    85. The Tasks of the Party During the Implementation of the Fascist Three-Year Plan 499
    86. What Is the Meaning and Role of Our Annual Tactical Slogans?..500
    87. The Attitude of Fascists Toward Intervention. 500
    88. The Attitude of Fascists Toward Japan 500
    89. The RFP's Attitude Toward Other Organizations............501
    90. The Task of Each Individual Fascist.................................501
    Questions to Review: 502
Chapter V: Organization of Russian Fascism
    91. What Is the Organization of Russian Fascism?................503
    92. Territorial Distribution of RFP...504
    93. Who Does the RFP Consist Of?..504
    94. How Is the RFP Managed and Built?................................505
    95. Tell Us Briefly About the History of the Emergence and Development of the All-Russian Fascist Party................506
    96. What Is the Meaning Behind the Party Symbolism?.......508
    97. What Composes the Party Uniform?.................................508

98. What Is the Party Badge and the Religious Sign of the RFP, What Do They Consist Of, and What Is Their Symbolism? 508
99. What Does the Fascist Party Greeting and the Party Flag Mean? 509
100. What Does the Fascist Battle Hymn Call For? 509
Questions to Review: 510

The Party Program of the All-Russian Fascist Party
1. What Kind of State Does the All-Russian Fascist Party Fight For? 511
2. What Does the RFP Bring to the Individual Peoples of Russia? 512
3. What Kind of State System Does the RFP Seek to Establish? 513
4. What Does the RFP Seek to Accomplish in Industry and Agriculture? 514
5. What Does the RFP Hope to Achieve in the Area of Finance? 515
6. What Is the RFP's Program in the Field of Trade? 516
7. What Will the RFP Accomplish in Education? 516
8. What Does the RFP Seek for Religion? 516
9. What Does the RFP Bring to Russian Workers? 517
10. What Does the RFP Bring to the Russian Peasants? 518
11. The Army of the Future Russia 518

All-Russian Fascist Party Documents
On the Party Greeting 521
On the Party Flag of the RFP 522
On the National Flag and National Anthem 523
On the Party Icon 525
On the Party Banner 526
On the Party Uniform and Hierarchical Signs of the RFP 527
On the Religious Icon 530

Supreme Court of the Russian Federation Ruling No. 043/46 533

A SHORT BIOGRAPHY OF KONSTANTIN RODZAEVSKY

By the Translator

Russia is a country with a rich and complicated history. Ravaged by the forces of Bolshevism for almost a century, the words "Russian" and "fascism" put together would almost sound like an oxymoron to most Russians. There was one man, however, who sought to make this fusion into a reality and manifest it into a concrete political party.

The founder of Russian fascism, the creator and the Head of the All-Russian Fascist Party, a brilliant publicist, orator, and propagandist, Konstantin Vladimirovich Rodzaevsky was born on August 11th, 1907 in the far eastern city of Blagoveshchensk to a family of an almost extinct Siberian bourgeoisie. His father was a notary by profession with a higher legal education, while his mother dedicated her life to her children: Konstantin, his younger brother Vladimir, and his two sisters, Nadezhda and Nina. Rodzaevsky is often described as being tall and attractive, yet of "ordinary" appearance. He was 5 foot 11 with a weight of only 140 pounds, possibly due to poor nutrition, having lived his entire life with scarce resources. His face was pale and thin, with a patched growing beard, dark auburn hair, and unblinking pale blue eyes. This at first glance ordinary appearance did not impede him from capturing the attention of those around him. He is described as radiating a powerful aura and energy; he was able to turn the most meaningless of discussions into bursts of fiery passion. Constantly active, whenever he was moved by something or simply in a certain mood, he would rush to the nearest piano and sing in the aria of Prince Igor.[1] Being an idealist at heart, Rodzaevsky had a deep knowledge of European history, and an insurmountable will that would propel him, unlike some other minor self-described "Russian Fascists," to become

---

[1] John J. Stephan, *The Russian Fascists: Tragedy and Farce in Exile, 1925–1945* (London: H. Hamilton, 1978), 51.

the true *Vozhd* of Russian Fascism. This ardent idealism did not come without its flaws. Rodzaevsky's close confidants describe impulsiveness and gullibility as his main weaknesses, some even calling him impractical.[2]

Rodzaevsky's life would change forever in 1925, when the young graduate fled from the USSR to Manchuria as a member of the Komsomol. Little is known about the circumstances of his unexpected exodus. His mother, upon discovering his whereabouts, went to Harbin and urged him to return. But she had no luck, as her son was determined to stay. This meeting would turn out to be the last time the two saw each other.[3] His father and brother later followed him to Harbin, but his sisters Nadezhda and Nina soon after were captured by the OGPU. Nadezhda eventually returned to Moscow, while Nina's fate remains unknown.

Manchuria was no stranger to Russian visitors. There were more than one hundred fifty thousand Russians living in Manchukuo.[4] Most of them lived compactly in the city Harbin, it being one of the largest hotspots for the Russian diaspora following the Revolution. From there the legal and political career of Rodzaevsky began. He enrolled in the juridical institute and later on obtained a degree in law. It was during this time that he fell under the influence of prominent nationalist and anti-Communist figures, in particular G. K. Gins, Nikolai Vasilyevich Ustryalov, and N. N. Nikiforov, whom he met and whose lectures he attended. It was also at this time that he began cultivating and developing his ideological movement into fascism. Gins, being a former member of the White Omsk government, expressed admiration for Benito Mussolini during his lectures and convinced the students that the corporate state was the best remedy against the disease of class struggle and the dictatorship of the proletariat.[5] Alongside other law students, Rodzaevsky became fascinated with the figure of the *Duce* and the Blackshirts; their discipline and their philosophy of direct political action would become their main inspiration for countering the Soviets back in their homeland. In particular, the will to action and strength of the Italian *squadristi* was a formative influence, so much so that Rodzaevsky would end up adopting black uniforms as the party's official garb,[6] and Mussolini's message as a direct inspiration for his future speeches, party, and even gestures.[7]

---

[2] Ibid., 52.
[3] Ibid., 49.
[4] Ibid., 37.
[5] Ibid., 50.
[6] Ibid., 76.
[7] Ibid., 52.

In 1925, having just arrived as a student, Rodzaevsky joined the Russian Fascist Organization.[8] Soon after, he also joined Nikiforov's Union in 1927. It did not take long for Rodzaevsky to partake in anti-Soviet demonstrations, which would get him suspended from the law faculty in 1928, only managing to get his diploma reinstated in 1929. On May 26th, 1931, in Harbin, the Russian Fascist Party (RFP) was founded, with the sole and main goal of achieving the "National Revolution." General V. D. Kosmin was elected as the formal leader of the party, while Rodzaevsky took the post of General Secretary of the Party. Even though Kosmin was the supposed formal leader, the real power remained with the members of the RFO.[9] From here Rodzaevsky proved his leadership skills, considerably strengthening the influence of the party in the Far East. After merging with the All-Russian Fascist Organization of A. A. Vonsiatsky in 1934, the All-Russian Fascist Party was officially created.[10] The organization quickly became the largest political organization among White emigrants in the Far East. In addition to the RFP, more "classic" White émigré organizations scattered around the world were also present in China at the time, such as the Russian All-Military Union (ROVS), the Brotherhood of Russian Truth (BRP) and the Union of Cossacks in the Far East.

Scholars often dispute the fascist influence of the White emigrants generally, but it is without a doubt that the lack of ideological cohesion is something the émigrés retained from the White movement. This would not come without its troubles. Rodzaevsky and the party line avoided discussing openly the issue concerning monarchist pretentions and rival pretenders to the throne.[11] Trying to avoid the same lack of ideological cohesion of the White movement and at the same time not alienating the undoubtedly largest faction of the White émigré diaspora, monarchists. Nonetheless, Rodzaevsky wanted to "learn from the mistakes of the White movement" and was rarely willing to compromise on ideological grounds, and made it clear that the fascists rejected the old system's birth titles, privileges, and landowners as much as the destructive Communist collectivization policies.[12]

Russian fascism was in a unique situation, having peculiarities few fascist movements had back in Europe. Being composed of mainly Russian émigrés in exile across the world, Russian fascism diverged in many ways from its European counterparts. It goes without saying that, unlike their ideological counterparts in Europe, the Russian Fascists were facing a Stalinist regime from foreign exile. As such,

---

[8] Ibid., 51.
[9] Ibid., 57.
[10] Ibid., 142.
[11] Susanne Hohler, *Fascism in Manchuria: The Soviet-China Encounter in the 1930s* (I. B. Tauris & Company, 2017), 59.
[12] Ibid., 55.

Rodzaevsky sought to establish a common ground in the global struggle against liberalism and Judeo-Bolshevism with other fascist movements around the world. Although the Western influence on Rodzaevsky is obvious, constantly praising the brilliance of Mussolini, the genius of Hitler, and the great conquests of Franco in Spain, as well as many others in the party's official press *Nash Put' (Our Way)* and *Natsiya (Nation)*, Rodzaevsky sought to create a unique movement that adapted itself to the Russian historical and national context. The Russian fascists in fact repudiated Western culture, seeing in it the decadence that poisoned their homeland, and instead venerated the great Russian nation and its autochthonous culture.

Russian fascism was explicitly and staunchly Orthodox Christian. With the slogan "God, Nation, Labor," Russian fascism proclaimed the union of church and state for the moral and religious rehabilitation of the Russian people. Russian fascism wanted to reconcile and develop a new and unique solution to the destructive forces that were haunting Russia since well before the Revolution. Moreover, the (perhaps ironic) influence and adoption of Communist lexicon was noticeable and even acknowledged; from the insistence on the party being the "vanguard of the (National) Revolution," to terms such as "general secretary," "central committee," "three-year plan," and the "Supreme Soviet." The RFP had many songs that were originally Communist songs with their lyrics changed, something that the Communists themselves did with Russian tsarist and imperial songs. They refused, however, to use the term comrade, instead adopting *soratnik* as the official party address, which has a similar meaning but with a more militaristic connotation.[13]

Rodzaevsky was a committed ideological fascist, a Third Positionist, a corporatist, and a staunch anti-Semite. As such, he sought to implement this strict vision which would contrast with other figures such as the pragmatic Matkovsky or the American based showman Vonsiatsky. Rodzaevsky advocated and dedicated his life to the overthrow of the Communist regime in Moscow. To do this, Rodzaevsky announced several three-year plans. The plan to achieve victory consisted of five points: strengthening fascist propaganda, uniting all emigrants in Manchuria under the auspices of the RFP, close cooperation with Germany and Italy, strengthening ties with Japan, and infiltrating the USSR to establish contacts with anti-Stalinist elements. The corporate state was to unite the *Narod* under a single national consciousness by creating national unions made up of people sharing common occupation. The corporate state envisioned by the fascists as a prototype could be traced back to Tsar Alexey Mikhailovich, with the entire state apparatus at the time representing a prototype of

---

[13] Stephan, *The Russian Fascists*, 58.

a modern corporate system: the entire population of Russia was organized in ranks (classes) and corporate associations (syndicates). The Zemsky Sobor (assembly of the land), which expressed the people's will, was an assembly of representatives of individual ranks and classes, making it into a prototype of the modern body of representation in a corporate state.[14]

Following the party structure of other fascist parties in Europe, he created subsidiary organizations under the (RFP); the Russian Women's Fascist Movement (RWFD), the Union of the Vanguard, the Union of Young Fascists, and the Union of Fascist Little Ones. It also had sections spread across the world ranging from Australia to South America and the United States. Under the leadership of Rodzaevsky, an international organization of White emigrants was created with its headquarters in Harbin, which had connections in twenty-six countries and collaborated with many fascists across the world, notably Arnold Leese and Willian Pelley.[15] Being scattered around the world, and faced by a Communist superpower with global reach, the RFP had to depend on foreign powers for its subsistence. At first, Rodzaevsky and his peers were allowed to operate by a passive Chinese rule in Manchuria. A turn of events however would give the new RFP opportunities they could have never dreamed of: Japanese patronage. When the Kwantung army occupied Manchuria, it wasn't long before Rodzaevsky and his party welcomed with grace the new Japanese rulers and began their collaboration.

The Japanese sought to legitimize their rule and maintain the cohesion between all the different ethnicities located in Harbin, although the Russian diaspora was generally considered as a foreign minority and were never considered to belong to the five founding races of Manchukuo.[16] The Japanese were nevertheless more than willing to exert their influence on the Russian community. Under the patronage of the Japanese, Rodzaevsky was appointed head of the second department (cultural and educational) of the Bureau for Russian Emigrants in Manchuria (BREM).[17] This allowed the All-Russian Fascist Party to extend their propaganda machine by sponsoring lectures, running schools and clubs, broadcasting radio programs, and maintaining branches overseas. Moreover, it allowed the control of Manchukuo's White Russian minority. This came with a number of benefits, such as pecuniary and legal support, although at the expense of having to go through Japanese censorship and political maneuvering, and having to

---

[14] Ibid., 57,
[15] Central Archive of the Federal Security Service of the Russian Federation. Investigative case N-18765 against Semenov, Rodzaevsky, and others. T. 10, p. 187–188.
[16] Hohler, *Fascism in Manchuria*, 32.
[17] V. A. Bobrenev, et al., *Executioners and Victims* (Military Publishing House, 1993), 193.

collaborate with problematic individuals and rivals such as the ataman warlord Semenov. This would lead to splits and internal rivalries within the party, but Rodzaevsky was willing to comply. Personal and party rivalries were not uncommon either. When the RFP was formed and Rodzaevsky assumed the *de facto* leadership position in the party, another individual who had deep influence on Russian fascism during the interwar period followed suit, Mikhail Alexievich Matkovsky.[18] Matkovsky throughout his career proved to be the leader of an unapologetically realist and pragmatist wing of the Russian Fascist Party; if Rodzaevsky led the party, Matkovsky is said to have sustained it. Although they both sensed a natural rivalry between each other, they both set aside their differences and worked together for the next twenty years. It would be a mistake however to attribute the rise of the party solely to Japanese support; it is doubtful that the RFP had any substantial support from the local government to conduct its activities, limiting itself to being as one of the many other civil societies present in Harbin at the time. The party was never particularly well-funded and there is little to no evidence of substantial financial support, having most of the party's funds coming from fundraising campaigns and donations.[19]

The party at some point in 1935 reached thirty thousand members in Manchuria according to Rodzaevsky. From here the Fascist Party carried out several sabotage operations in the Far East of the USSR. The Japanese at this time did not desire to instigate a conflict with the USSR, however, and limited the party's activities and numbers. Some academics like J. Stephan stress the illegal activities committed by the RFP, and it is without doubt that Japanese patronage did not come for free, as the Japanese frequently used the party for their own purposes, ranging from sabotage and scouting missions to the USSR (missions from which few returned) to alleged illegal activities involving extortion, narcotics, and even kidnapping. Rodzaevsky, though far from confirmed or clear, might have been involved in the famous Kaspé affair involving the abduction and murder of a wealthy Jew. The evidence however is scarce and does not match the testimonies of Rodzaevsky, who is described as someone who "shrank from violence," a man who was many things but "not a criminal,"[20] making the charge most likely an unsubstantiated rumor due to the party's obvious stances on Jews. In fact, if one thing might be said about the RFP, it is that it sought to involve itself in the rising anti-social behavior within the Russian community in the dire times of exile in Harbin. With crumbling unemployment, drug abuse, and high vandalism rates, the RFP

---

[18] Stephan, *The Russian Fascists*, 52
[19] Hohler, *Fascism in Manchuria*, 67.
[20] Stephan, *The Russian Fascists*, 86.

offered assistance, promoting virtue and reintegration into the community,[21] as well as the idea of "Russianness."[22] Regardless of what individual fascists might have been involved in, the alleged behavior of the Russian Fascists is at odds with the party line and philosophy. Far from being just a political party, the Russian Fascist Party was a true civic society, involving itself in the building of the Russian community and way of life, ranging from the promotion of schools and churches to providing aid, fighting poverty, and offering resources and men in times of crisis. Famously, after floods ravaged the households of Harbin, boats with the letter *F* and men dressed in black and wearing swastikas came to the rescue. The party gained influence and notoriety with their cultural activities and interactions with other communities. The RFP also organized numerous debates, lectures, and conferences (often having Rodzaevsky giving they keynote speech), influencing the public and political discourse of the community.[23]

The Russian Fascists had a cultural and ethnic conception of the nation, and this conception demanded that young Russians be instructed in it.[24] They believed firmly in the power of education and the formation of the youth. By forming organizations and monitoring schools, the fascists ensured that a new generation of national revolutionaries would arise. This wasn't exclusive to just ideological or religious teachings, but was conducted to inculcate the youth from an early age with the values of Russian fascism and especially for the cultivation of a fierce warrior spirit capable of retaking the fatherland from the forces of Judeo-Bolshevism. As such, it wasn't just about being a true Russian, but about becoming a true Russian fascist, a warrior ready to give up his life for his nation. The Russian Fascist Party was not just a political organization, but a social and religious one. To cultivate this spirit, party members had mandatory readings and had to become acquainted with the history of Russia and that of the party. This included many cultural activities, such as meetings in the "Russian club," bringing together all Russians, regardless of political affiliation, under a common identity and culture by promoting vocational and cultural activities; free access to the club's library, vocational and technical training, etc., and despite the party having scarce means, it made membership fees affordable for all Russians.[25] But it wasn't just about cultivating a powerful mind. A true fascist was to be able to embody his ideals. Activities for this purpose included:

---

[21] Hohler, *Fascism in Manchuria*, 89.
[22] Ibid., 82.
[23] Ibid., 98.
[24] Ibid., 82.
[25] Ibid., 99.

sports, intense military discipline, and even combat training.[26] But cultivating a powerful body and mind wasn't enough either. Faith and spirit were to be above everything else; stressing the importance of the Orthodox Church and religious virtues, the party collaborated with multiple churches and parishes in Harbin, and had multiple priests in its ranks.[27] This was not exclusive to boys or even Russians either, as fascists viewed the nation as a cultural and spiritual phenomenon, allowing non-Russians (mainly Tatars and Muslims) to join its ranks as well as women; for if men were to be in charge with retaking the fatherland, women would oversee spreading the party propaganda work and the administration back home.[28] Here we see another unique characteristic of Russian Fascism, it's focus on Eurasianism.

During this time, Rodzaevsky proved his talent as a propagandist as the chief editor of the RFP newspaper *Nash Put'* and in the magazine *Natsiya*. Rodzaevsky published a number of anti-Semitic brochures and books such as *Judas on the Edge* and the *Modern Judaization of the World, or the Jewish Question in the Twentieth Century*, which are both now classified as "extremist material" in the Russian Federation. To Rodzaevsky, the USSR and the "Russian" Revolution was entirely orchestrated by Jews, Freemasons, and other international forces. Jews co-opted the Soviet message and cause and used it to implement a tyrannical Judeo-Masonic regime that brought the Russian people to its knees. Jews were not only an outside people, but an outside people that sought to destroy the Russian nation from within with their satanic influences.[29]

By spreading antisemitism, the Russian Fascists were able to direct emigration into one single direction and target. Rodzaevsky admired the figure of Adolf Hitler and maintained his support even when this caused backlash among other White emigrants or even fascists. But even members close to Rodzaevsky, and to some extent the *Vozhd* himself, expressed indignation at the "grave mistake" that was the Molotov–Ribbentrop Pact.[30] His hopes were restored however when he wholeheartedly welcomed the German invasion of Russia, calling it a battle for national liberation.[31] In June 1941 Rodzaevsky was awarded the Badge of the Main Bureau of BREM for his diligent labors. Rodzaevsky personally became friends with General Araki and other prominent Japanese anti-Communists,[32] who had sympathies with the Russian fascists and as such vouched to help the party to retake its lost

---

[26] Ibid., 79.
[27] Ibid., 163.
[28] See "The ABC of Fascism" question 48.
[29] Hohler, *Fascism in Manchuria*, 108.
[30] Stephan, *The Russian Fascists*, 204.
[31] Ibid., 310.
[32] Ibid., 143.

homeland. Another notable supporter was Tōyama Mitsuru, the *kuromaku* of the Black Dragon Society, who once sent Rodzaevsky a katana as a token of his esteem and sympathy for the anti-Soviet struggle. The Russian fascists however never gained much influence in what they saw as their national allies and ideological brothers, the Axis powers. Rodzaevsky managed to get a representative in Rome and in the Third Reich, but it was mostly symbolic, and didn't stop the Gestapo from making several arrests and supplying damming intelligence to the Japanese.[33]

When Germany invaded Russia in 1941, Rodzaevsky was eager to join the war, seeing this as an opportunity to revitalize the party struggle. The party from here engaged in various attempts to sabotage the Soviet Union during the war, but they were limited by the Japanese. Soon however, some of the *soratniki* would have the opportunity to prove their might in combat, only not against the Soviet Union. As Sino-Soviet relations worsened, the Kwantung army found an opportunity to finally test the might of the *soratniki*. In May 1939, the first shots rang out near the Khalkhin Gol River, foreshadowing the coming clash between the Soviet Union and the Empire of Japan. Although at first unwilling, the Japanese made the Russian *Vozhd* collaborate with the Manchukuo imperial army by forming the Asano brigade. The Russian soldiers of the Japanese army planned to inflict a blow on the Red Army, but instead they were drawn into a long (by the standards of a local conflict), bloody, and senseless massacre. As a result, both sides suffered heavy losses, and Japan's position near the Mongolian border became even more precarious. The Asanovites, according to various sources, had both successes and failures in this clash. Despite this, some members of the brigade performed feats that even the Kwantung samurai did not believe to be possible. Despite all the heroism of the Russian-Japanese troops, the Khalkhin Gol conflict was a catastrophic defeat, especially with the Nomonhan Incident. By 1940, Russian–Japanese cooperation in Manchuria was reformatted due to the change in leadership of the Japanese military mission.[34] Now at the head of the JVM in Harbin stood the adamant General Genzo Yanagida, who called on the White Guards to become "Russian samurai."[35]

Despite Rodzaevsky's enthusiasm, at some point it became clear that the Communist regime wasn't showing signs of collapse. After Rodzaevsky's prediction of the USSR collapsing by 1938 was proven wrong, the party membership began to fall, and inner splits emerged. It was during this time that the party began to collapse. It wasn't the

---

[33] Ibid., 318.
[34] Erwin Oberlander, "The All-Russian Fascist Party," *Journal of Contemporary History* (1966): 166.
[35] Peter Harmsen, *Storm Clouds over the Pacific 1931–41* (Havertown: Casemate, 2019), 112.

first time the party experienced internal splits, with the former head of the RFO, Anastase Vonsiatsky, leaving the party (he later resumed collaboration only to leave again and form his own organization in the US) due to his quarrel with Rodzaevsky's anti-Semitic stances and the incorporation of some individuals in the party by the pressure of the Japanese, mainly Semenov. Others left due to the apparent anti-Slavic sentiments of the Third Reich, which caused them to side with their fatherland. Rodzaevsky however always assumed that the Germans did not have any intentions to make Russia into a colony, and that they would place the emigrants in Manchuria in high positions.

Despite calls for war between the USSR and Japan, the Japanese started suspecting Rodzaevsky of possible Soviet ties and his yet to be resolved mysterious escape from Russia after being supplied with Gestapo intelligence. The party was then banned by the Japanese controlled Manchuria in 1943 with little explanation.[36] The Russian Fascist Party had met its downfall, not by the Soviets, but at the hands of what they thought to be their patron saint, Imperial Japan.

In 1945, due to the approaching Soviet army and occupation of Manchukuo, Rodzaevsky was forced to leave for Shanghai, leaving his wife and daughter behind. Here Rodzaevsky understood that some of his so-called *soratniki* were never ideologically committed to the cause, and some of them possibly outright spies; many of them now waved the Soviet flag. According to some sources, due to the betrayal of his peers and the apparent defeat of his cause, Rodzaevsky's mental state deteriorated, and he started to yearn deeply for his abandoned family, wife, and children.[37] Not just the Russian Fascist Party, but the entire Russian diaspora in Harbin, was in a dire trap, with the Japanese withholding any travel documents, and rumors spreading like wildfire that the Japanese would force the Russian community to either fight the Reds or face the firing squad. The Russian emigrants in Harbin were at the mercy of the encroaching Red Army and a Stalin eager to punish all the White traitors.

With the war ending, a broken and disgraced Rodzaevsky published an article entitled "The Week that Reforged the Soul," where he outlined his mental state, emotional breakdown, and regret for his past activities. He recognized the USSR as the rightful continuation of the Russian Empire and proclaimed Stalin as the true leader and "fascist" he was looking for—the once archenemy was the true (fascist) *Vozhd* he sought all along.[38] The letters were so damning that his first wife and a few others doubted its veracity. He concluded that the USSR under Stalin had become nationalistic by reconciling the Orthodox

---

[36] Stephan, *The Russian Fascists*, 320.
[37] Ibid., 337.
[38] Ibid., 338.

Church and the Soviet state and having purged from the party the "Internationalist Leninists" who called for a world revolution. He also made the extraordinary claim that Stalin had solved the Jewish Question, making the Jew a member of the Soviet nation by stripping him out of his Talmudic environment. Whether this sentiment was genuine or not, after being persuaded by some of his peers and a charismatic Soviet diplomat, he felt confident enough to return to the USSR. Rodzaevsky was given promises of immunity and a position as a journalist. He moved to Beijing to live in a Soviet embassy for a few weeks, and until the very end he had doubts of how necessary it was to return at last to Russia. After being discouraged one more time by one of his peers, at last Konstantin replied[39]:

"No, the door behind me is now shut, there is no going back. My family might have to pay for my past decisions of running forward and back again, there's just no way I can let that happen."

Upon returning, Rodzaevsky was detained by the Soviet authorities. He was put on trial, alongside other Russian émigrés such as Grigory Mikhailovich and Semenov. Rodzaevsky was accused of active anti-Soviet activities after fleeing from the USSR, in particular the creation and leadership of the "Russian fascist organization," the conduct of anti-Soviet propaganda among the White Guards in Manchuria, the compilation of leaflets, brochures, and books of anti-Soviet content, and terrorist activities on the international stage with the creation of similar organizations and groups in Manchuria, China, Europe, and the United States.[40] In addition, according to the verdict, he was involved in preparing an attack on the USSR together with a number of Japanese generals, organizing and personally participating in a number of provocations carried out by Japanese intelligence as a pretext for the occupation of Manchuria, as well was organizing and training from among the members of the RFU spies and terrorists used against the USSR.[41]

All defendants admitted their guilt. Rodzaevsky didn't plea, didn't ask for clemency, did not try to bring up any excuses. He had accepted his fate. On August 30th, 1946, at five in the morning, Ulrich began and at five thirty finished reading the verdict. Rodzaevsky was sentenced to death and shot on the same day in one of the basements of the USSR MGB building on Lubyanka.[42]

Nowadays, Rodzaevsky's family is scattered around the world, with some still in Moscow, while others have moved to the United States. On March 26th, 1998, the Military Collegium of the Supreme

---

[39] Ibid., 351.
[40] Ibid., 352.
[41] Central Archive of the Federal Security Service of the Russian Federation. Investigative case N-18765 against Semenov, Rodzaevsky, and others.
[42] Stephan, *The Russian Fascists*, 354.

Court of the Russian Federation reversed the convictions of K. V. Rodzaevsky, Lev Okhotin, and others under Articles 58-10 Part 2 of the Criminal Code of the RSFSR (anti-Soviet agitation and propaganda), terminating the criminal case for lack of corpus delicti.

Aside from the case resurfacing in the Russian courts, few remember the figure of Rodzaevsky, and even fewer mention him by name. Rodzaevsky lived a tumultuous and tragic life, with a deep love for his nation and homeland. He took it upon himself to fight what he thought were the forces of darkness haunting Russia that had taken everything from him and his people. Despite Rodzaevsky's name gaining slight popularity on the internet in recent years, the sad truth is that Russians, his own people, see him as a puppet pulled along by the Japanese and the anti-Slavic Germans; at best a foolish demagogue, at worst a traitor lusting for power and a tool of anti-Russian and generally anti-Slavic politics. Regardless of any objections, this is the sad reality of his tragic legacy. With him the last vestige of true Russian Fascism died, vanishing forever into obscurity.

Daniel Montoya

VOLUME I

Contemporary Judaization of the World

OR

The Jewish Question in the Twentieth Century

INTRODUCTION

1

It's early in the morning. . . . You open a newspaper, skim through the news, read an article by your favorite journalist. . . . Of course! You are already wearing tinted lenses. You are looking at the world, at politics, at the needs of your people through Jewish glasses. Your newspaper, to some extent, is owned by a Jew, and the news itself compiled by a Jewish telegraph agency. Don't believe it? Read the following pages, as they contain all the facts. That's how you get an orientation for the upcoming present day. And even the tea that you drink, especially if it is the highest grade of Lipton tea, is most certainly supplied by a Jewish company, the sugar for the tea is refined in a Jewish factory, and the bread was delivered by a Jewish bakery.

You are in a rush to get to work, to the office, to the factory, to the institution. At the top of your leadership there is a smug, well-fed Jew. He is a manager, he is an entrepreneur, he is a financier. You get sick. . . . Won't your good friends refer you to a Jewish doctor, celebrity, or healer? You are forced to ask for the protection of the courts, and a popular Jewish lawyer is at your service. All day long you are faced with Jews, and all of these encounters take on such a constant, everyday character that you begin to forget that they are outsiders, that they are a distinct people living their own separate lives, having their own specific interests. You smile skeptically again.

But wait, we will show you the essence of Jewry, it being separate from all other peoples. We will tear off all the veils and show the Jew for what he really is, naked and predatory.

The Jewish question, whether we want it or not, surrounds us from all sides every day, if not every hour. Everywhere and all the time we are faced with Jewish interference in our lives, with the process of Judaization.

But here in the evening, tired from a hard day of work, you lose yourself within a book that a Jewish advertisement has helpfully recommended to you. Most certainly this is a Jewish erotica, designed to arouse the unhealthiest instincts within you, to ruin and destroy your family.

Not enough romance in your life? Go to the dance hall! Once you're in the cabaret, Jewish jazz will inflate your sensuality to the absolute limit, and a Jewish singer with a painted face will be seen laughing at love and all your ideals! In theater, in music, in cinema, Jews are everywhere. They drug you with fairy tales, and under the whisper of these fairy tales they drag you down the wrong path, they draw you into the anesthetic state of their Judaized civilization, which is coming to replace our Christian culture, and destroy you.

"Goyim." That's what they call us. "Akum" is how they designate a non-Jew. The Talmud warns us of the "Akuma seed being worse than the seed of cattle." (The Talmud is the Jewish faith and law, the quintessence of Judaism. It is a mandatory instruction manual for the practices of every Jew.)

And finally, the power that you believed in, that you hoped for, whether democratic, covered with the almighty mantle of popular elections, or monarchical, based on the hoary tradition of the past centuries—this power in reality is subject to a strong Jewish influence.

Judas crawled into the bedrooms of kings, into the offices of prime ministers, and into parliaments. Again, don't believe me? In this book, this reality from Jewish and anti-Jewish sources alike will show it to you.

Where was this striking picture I just drew taken from, if not from the teaching of history in our days? If not from the current reality of any of the modern states in the first half of the twentieth century?

For these states, this seemingly bygone reality still persists. This is why my book will be of great use, and a timely warning for them. But for those other states where Judaization is something of the past, it is crucial to get acquainted with the dangers that unfolded before humanity in our century, tracing the dominance of Judas in the government, culture, and economy. This is in order to reveal the internal and external organization of the forces of darkness, but to reflect on the possible cure for this poison surely won't be a waste of time either.

Our time is one of great transition and reconstruction. New generations, alongside the brightest minds and visionaries of their elders, are called upon to build a new way of life. The youth move into a great avant-garde for a world scale improvement, a new national revolution. As such, this book is dedicated to the youth of all nations and, above all, to our Russian youth. Once we have learned the mistakes of the past, we shall never repeat them in the future.

Knowledge of the Jewish question is the key to freedom.

Freedom of the National State from international and supranational influences. Freedom of the national conscious individual from international pressure, whispers and intrigues.

2

"The Jews are a people who always distinguish themselves from others, isolate themselves, avoid contact with other peoples, persecute others with a kind of bestial malice, and are justly despised by them in turn," says the immortal Italian philosopher Giordano Bruno.

"Money and revolution are engraved on the sacred tablets of these despicable people," the emperor Vespasian says from Ancient Rome.

"Jews are a perfect manifestation of the egoistic will to live; they are a calculative, cunning kind of beast. They are the incarnate triumphant demon of human degeneracy," the German composer Richard Wagner espoused.

"Cursed race! With neither a fatherland nor a king, living parasitically in a foreign nation, pretending to obey the laws, but in reality, obeying only their God—the God of bloodshed and malice. They spread hatred wherever they are, hiding in the shadows like a spider in its web and trapping its prey to suck their blood to the last drop," says the French writer Émile Zola. "Have you ever seen a Jew work? No! Work dishonors them, their religion forbids them to work. They can only exploit the labor of others."

"'*Cherche de Juif* (look out for the Jew)!' breaks out involuntarily, as soon as public opinion is outraged by some still unheard-of trickery," exclaims A. S. Shmakov.

"*Cherche de Juif!*" the court adjudicates when a complicated, immoral, shameless and treacherous crime is especially oblivious.

"*Cherche de Juif,*" the financier guesses, wondering about the collapse of a Christian bank or a sudden drop in interest rates that turned the market upside down.

"*Cherche de Juif!*" exclaims a statesman, when national events are being spread with satanic lies in the supposedly liberal, supposedly non-Jewish press, and on the other hand perverted by some hypocritical underground force.

"*Cherche de Juif,*" the diplomat repeats to himself, at the sight of someone's political chess moves being skewed and directed to his own detriment.

"*Cherche de Juif!*" the great thinker is finally entitled to exclaim, once the eternal laws of reason and the very idea of justice are ridiculed and frozen in midst of the stock market chaos that is seizing the vital forces and the most important centers of the social "organisms" before our very eyes.

"We are a one-of-a-kind people," asserts the founder of modern Zionism, the late Jewish leader Theodor Herzl. "When we go bankrupt, we turn into revolutionary proletarians, providing non-commissioned officers to all revolutionary parties, while our monetary power increases at the top. In a difficult moment, we all unite and suddenly discover our strength."

"Children of Israel, the hour of our victory is near! We stand at the verge of global domination," cries the French minister, the head of the Masonic Grand Orient of France, and a faithful son of his "persecuted" people, Adolphe Crémieux.

"The pinnacle of Jewry reigns over humanity stronger and firmly and is striving to make the world mirror its own image and essence," F. M. Dostoevsky warns.

Quotes from the works of a large variety of authors, greater and lesser, Jewish and non-Jewish, we could keep citing indefinitely.... Let's stick to the facts.

3

In the governments and city administrations, in parliaments and in central committees of the most important and largest political parties, in the boards of directors of banks, in concerns, trusts, and syndicates, on the stock exchange, in wholesale and universal trade, in import and export, in the press, radio, theater, and cinema, in law and medicine, music and singing, anywhere you look you find an insolent, grinning, hook-nosed face.

Our whole civilization is becoming the prey of "the eternal wanderers of the Talmud," whom Titus, through the destruction of Jerusalem and Judea in AD 79, cursed the two-thousand-year-old *golus* to wander endlessly around the globe.[43]

For those who were cursed by Our Lord Jesus Christ (John 8:44), the colors and joys of life are mansions, cars, and champagne. But for the remaining billions of other people—"humanoid creatures"—they were purposely created by Jehovah, to serve the God's "chosen people" (that's how the Talmud describes all non-Jews) and their gradual destruction and enslavement, a type of slavery gloomier than the slavery of the builders of the Egyptian pyramids.

From two opposite ends and in different ways, Jewish capitalism and Jewish communism threaten to reduce us to a "primitive equality," to deprive us of our families, property, and the state. An international dictatorship and the rule of the "proletariat," which translates to a

---

[43] Meaning "exile" in Hebrew; outside of the land of Israel; away from a vibrant Jewish community; the time period since the destruction of the Second Temple at Jerusalem. (Translator's note.)

group of Jewish politicians, the dictatorship of the invisible sages of Freemasonry, a dictatorship of international capital—does it make a difference under what disguise the Jewish "inter-nation" rules us over?

WAKE UP, PEOPLE! WAKE UP, PEOPLE! HERE IS THE SAD FINALE OF THE GREAT CHARIOT OF PROGRESS: ABYSS, ABYSS, ABYSS!!!

Judas in government, Judas in culture, Judas in the economic system. These three pillars form the greatest problem of our century, the Judaization of the modern world. A close examination of these images of Judaization leads us to the World Jewish Organization. This awareness of the forms that Judaization takes will give us countermeasures. It is these countermeasures that must be indispensably applied to each individual person, to each individual people, to each nation, state, and to humanity as a whole.

One day, an *International Congress of National Forces of the World* will indeed gather and solve the Jewish question on a global scale. But until then, let some nations be freed. And may my people be freed, to whom I shall dedicate all my strength and thoughts until my last breath.

Mask off, many faced Judas! Russian folk! Build your Russia without the Jews, without corrupt opportunists, Shabbos goyim, and without any hidden Judaization.

Nationalists of all countries! Expel the Jews and their lackeys—the Freemasons and Shabbos goyim—further away from the spheres and pedals of politics, economy, and culture. Destroy England and the US—the main bases of militant Israel! For an exclusively New Order in which each nation has its own destiny and each nation has its own state and peaceful cooperation in all aspects. A New Order such as the one being implemented in East Asia and declared at the first Conference of Representatives of East Asian Peoples in Tokyo, which will bring people true freedom from the greatest intellectual and material slavery, freedom from the chains of world Jewry!

PREFACE FROM 1943

The work at hand of the Head of the Russian Fascist Union is based on long years of study and research of the Jewish question. It is the most detailed review in Russian of the influence of Jews on the political, cultural, and economic life in modern states, exposing the internal and external organization of Jewry, as well as the ways and means of Jewish expansion.

Why was our Head able to deal with this grandiose and truly vast topic, while being overwhelmed by the current leadership of the Russian Fascist Union during the most difficult years of its development? Because fascists and other Russian people from all countries sent to our central organ all sorts of materials: their observations and considerations, the most interesting revelations of the Jewish press, extracts from Masonic sources, and along with them an extensive anti-Jewish and anti-Masonic literature periodically and quite literally in all languages.

Several dedicated patriots translated the most interesting of these publications and helped K. V. Rodzaevsky to define the essence and work of Judaism. This is how a real collective collaboration was formed.

We know that its publication will stir up a storm in world Jewry. Provocations against our movement and the counteractions to it will increase. But we take this risk in full awareness of the danger to which we are exposed, and having taken our own sufficiently reflected upon and systematic countermeasures.

The Russian people, more than any other people, must reflect on the Jewish question, realize its dimensions, and take measures to free themselves from Jewish control and Jewish influence. But other nations also face the same problem to a certain degree or other. As such, this book is dedicated to the Russian nation and to nationalists of all countries as a Russian contribution to this cause of world struggle against Judaism, as well as a contribution of the RFP to the cause of Russian liberation.

Everyone who is interested in the destiny of his nation and state should be interested in this publication, for the Jewish question is the question of our common human freedom and life: will we be prisoners of Judaism, or will every nation have control over its own destiny?

Japan is currently fighting Britain and America—the main forces of world Jewry in our time. Japan is building Greater East Asia on the principle of a union of independent nation-states, and thereby freeing a huge region from world Jewry. Regardless of temporal and subjective goals, Japan seems to have been entrusted by Providence itself with the task of delivering a decisive blow to the strongholds of Judaism. We would like this book to be translated into Japanese, and read by the future leaders in charge of building a new life.

PART ONE

A JOURNEY AROUND THE WORLD

1. Starting with the British Isles

Unroll a large geographical map. A geography lesson awaits. Try to tell this lesson in school and you will immediately be expelled.

But it is indispensable, indeed vital to supplement political geography to the modern list of subjects being taught in education, so that the younger generations comprehend the Jewish Question from the point of view of Jewish involvement in the day-to-day governance of different countries, and to have a better grasp of the dangers of Jewry.

In fact, this subject is even more useful for adults than it is for children, and it will not be irrelevant for politicians, parliamentarians, and even ministers.

We shall see who truly rules the New and the Old World, once the empty husks of official narratives are cast aside. To be more precise, who *used* to rule. For just as this very book is being written, Judas is losing ground. Perhaps much of what is being outlined here will only be of historical interest once this book comes to light, a thing of the past. That said, for the edification of our descendants, it is useful to get acquainted with this recent past in more detail. For posterity, this will be a good edification, and for contemporaries, the most necessary of warnings!

Let's focus not on any specific instance or individual event, but on the general picture of the first half of the twentieth century.

Let's look at individual states and world Jewry in their interweaving during the period approximately from the 1900s to the 1940s, mainly in the period of time following the First World War of 1914–1918 where, through the Bolshevik Revolution in Russia, the Versailles Peace Treaty, and the League of Nations, world Jewry achieved world domination and hastened the downfall of the previous order.

Let's start an imaginary journey around the world on a map of both hemispheres from the far west of Europe, the British Isles.

"On our way!" Mephistopheles sang in Gounod's opera, with the difference that our traveling companion this time will not be Mephistopheles. On the contrary, let us ask the Almighty God to help us distinguish gold from mere gilding, to see Judas in the complex and ever-changing web of social and political life of different states.

2. England and the Kings

King Edward VII of Great Britain had a crucial role in the spread of Freemasonry. While still the Prince of Wales, he joined Freemasonry in 1868. In 1871, he became Patron of the Grand Lodges of Scotland and Ireland. Following the resignation of the Marquess of Ripon's title of Grand Master of the Grand Lodge of England in 1875, the prince took his mantle as Grand Master. King Edward VII is known to be one of the main actors behind the Great War of 1914–1918.

His successor, King George V, was also a Freemason. In 1910, he received the title of Grand Patron of the three royal Masonic institutions, and his wife, Queen Mary, was elected as the Grand Patroness of female Freemasonry.

Edward VIII, the current Duke of Windsor, while still the Prince of Wales, was initiated on May 2nd, 1919, in lodge No. 2614, called "Household Brigade Lodge." In 1924, he was appointed Grand Master of the provincial Lodge of Surrey.

The current King of Great Britain, George VI, received his Masonic initiation on December 3rd, 1919, into the Naval Lodge No. 2612. In 1934, he became the Grand Master of English Freemasonry.

"We are reading about this in the *Prince Hall Masonic Digest*, a Masonic magazine published in Los Angeles in the United States. No. 7 for July 1939," adds the *World Service*.[44]

---

[44] The *World Service* was founded in 1934 by Lieutenant-Colonel Ulrich Fleischhauer in Erfurt and reported on Judaic-Masonic influence around the world. It issued newsletters twice a month in eleven languages. In 1939, the MS center moved to Frankfurt and was run by a former assistant to Fleischhauer. (Translator's note)

3. The New Aristocracy

The official Judaic reference guide *The Jewish World*, published in Russian by the Union of Russian-Jewish Intelligentsia in Paris in 1939, provides an instructive list: a stunning list of Jews in the upper and lower houses of the English Parliament. The following list of kikes assuming the form of English lords currently sit in the House of Lords:

1. Michael Alfred Rufus Isaacs, 3rd Marquess of Reading
2. Colonel Walter Horace Samuel, 2nd Viscount Bearsted, head of the oil company Sheley & Co.
3. Herbert Louis Samuel, 1st Viscount Samuel, former High Commissioner of Palestine
4. Joseph Duveen, 1st Baron Duveen
5. Herbert Merton Jessel, 1st Baron Jessel
6. Arthur Michael Samuel, 1st Baron Mancroft
7. Henry Ludwig Mond, 2nd Baron Melchett, head of the Chemical Trust 1. S. 1., Zionist activist
8. Nathaniel Mayer Victor Rothschild, 3rd Baron Rothschild
9. Julius Salter Elias, Baron Southwood, head of the media conglomerate.

In the House of Commons, the same source lists:

1. Sir Leslie Hoare-Baelish, Minister of War
2. Sir Percy A. Alfred Harris (from London)
3. L. P. Glickstein (from Nottingham)
4. Dudley Joel (from London)
5. A. M. Lyons (from Leicester)
6. T. Levy (from London)
7. James George Rothschild (from London)
8. Sir Arthur Michael Samuel (from London)
9. Samuel, Marquess of Wentworth (from London)
10. Sir Isidore Salmon (from London)
11. Sir Philip Sassoon (from London)
12. Sydney Silverman (from Liverpool)
13. Eduard A. Strauss (from London)
14. Lewis Silkin (from Peckham)
15. Harry Nathan (from London)
16. Daniel L. Lipson (from London)

Yes, Jews for the time being demonstrate their belonging to English society without revealing their masked Jewish identity. However, as soon as the time for "playing with the English" arrives (as we can see in all other countries of the world), the masks are instantly thrown out so that the Jewish lord disguised as a "one-hundred-percent Englishman" once again turns into a true representative of his people.

The Harbin *Jewish Life* cites many such enlightening biographies, such as one we found in one of the issues of this magazine about "The most prominent representative of the English aristocracy, Lady Fitzgerald."

4. Eighty-Year-Old Lady Fitzgerald's Return to Judaism

It was one of those cloudy London mornings. The secretary of the Jewish National Fund was familiarizing himself with the morning mail that had just arrived, as per usual, when suddenly, a check fell out of one of the envelopes . . . and having picked it up and examined it, the secretary was astonished: the check was written for five thousand English sterling pounds and signed by "Lady Fitzgerald."

This was Lady Fitzgerald's debut in the Jewish community. No more than a year had passed since that incident, and in that short time she had become one of the most energetic activists and an irreplaceable champion for the interests of English Jewry. And we must not forget that Lady Fitzgerald is no longer young, she is eighty years old. Her deceased husband was an English aristocrat, a Christian, and her children profess the Anglican faith. But in her old age, Lady Fitzgerald has returned to her people and gives them all her love and loyalty, as if yearning to make amends for the sin of moving away from her people in her youth.

Lady Fitzgerald belongs to the highest caste in England. She is on friendly terms with Prime Minister Chamberlain, who very often visits her in her castle, located sixty miles away from London. Moreover, the royal couple of England is friends with the old lady and often spends time in her company.

Recently, under the initiative of a restless eighty-year-old granny, a foundation under the name of the Golden Foundation was established. The main thrust of this effort was to make Jews in England give up all the precious belongings they were able to spare for the resettlement of Jewish victims from Germany to Palestine.

Lady Fitzgerald got to work energetically and personally sent tens of thousands of letters to Jewish women across England, urging them to donate to the Golden Foundation. And the call was immediately answered: A golden stream of various valuable items from all over the country arrived at the Keren-Kayemeth Bureau.[45] "Mail parcels with silverware, silver and gold vases, candlesticks, silver cup holders, paintings, engravings, crystal, bracelets, watches and various other gold items arrive all the time, and all this with no end in sight."

This little note is instructive in many regards. First of all, it shows one way of Jewish integration into a foreign national organism: the marriages between Jewish women and prominent people of the country that hosts them. The note goes on to recount how a Jewish woman or a Jew who has converted to Christianity remains true to the religion of its ancestors in her or his heart and returns to it at the first opportunity. The piece also testifies to the global unity of the Jewish people: "English" aristocrats helping Jewish refugees from Germany. At last, the article also exposes the British aristocracy, the government, and even the royal house by showing its friendly ties with the Jews.

"No one like one's own," says folk wisdom. Later on, we will see fascinating revelations of Jewry drawn from the Harbin *Jewish Life*— an official publication of the Jewish Far Eastern National Council, published by the KHEDO. This is the Harbin Jewish Spiritual Community under the editorship of Dr. Kaufman, a Far Eastern Jewish leader who is truly incessant in his verbal frankness. Thank you, Abram Iosifovich!

5. The History of the Jewish Takeover of Great Britain

What led to England being overrun by the Jews? For the sake of painting a picture that is unfolding before you of the Jewish conquest of this country with the utmost of objectivity, we will give the floor to a Jewish historian.

> In 1320, the English government expelled the Jews from their country [why were they expelled, the Jewish historian, of course, does not say].[46] There have been no Jews in England for three hundred and fifty years. During Cromwell's time, a Jew from Amsterdam, Menasseh ben Israel, sent a petition to the British government to allow Jews entrance from overseas. In 1655, England was at war with the then powerful Spain and the wealthy merchant power of the Netherlands.
> During these wars, England was in great need for knowledgeable and well-established Jewish financiers, even if these were natives of the same Spain, Holland, and Portugal they

---

[45] The Jewish National Fund. (Translator's note)
[46] This and all subsequent bracketed statements are interjections by Rodzaevsky. (Editor's note)

were at war with. But how will the English populace react to the government granting Shylock's brother permission to enter the country? The English rulers of course found a typical English way out of the situation: although the government did not give explicit permission for Jews to enter the country, they decided that according to the current English legislation there were no explicit indications in the law of the country to prevent Jews from entering England either!

The essence behind this ruling consisted in Jews being allowed entrance in the country, but it had to be carried out without making much noise and almost unnoticed. A year after the aforementioned decision of the English government in 1655, a group of Portuguese and Spanish Jews were allowed to purchase minor land plots for a cemetery and a synagogue. At the same time, they advised in the form of an order that "service to God in the synagogue should be performed absolutely modestly and reserved." And for almost two hundred years there was a migration of Jews to England. It was mainly Portuguese and Spanish Jews that resettled, and it was followed by a migration of Jews from Italy and France in the eighteenth century.

But in 1850, the Jewish population in England only amounted to 45,000 people.

A large wave of Jewish immigrants from Eastern Europe flooded England after the pogroms in Russia: in 1881, 16,000 Jews settled in England, 47,696 in 1891, and from 1891 to 1906, 310,000 Jews.

In contrast to the Jews of Eastern Europe, English Jewry actually achieved real rights and, over the years, formal equality. After the Napoleonic Wars, the political and especially the economic life of the country began to progress greatly. Jewish financiers and bankers, both in the metropolis and in the English colonies, greatly contributed to the flourishing of England.

In 1847, Baron Lionel Rothschild was elected to the English Parliament of the City of London. In 1855, Sir Solomon was elected Lord Mayor of London. And in 1866, for the first time in the history of England, Baron Rothschild was granted the title of lord. Disraeli's Jewish background did not prevent him from being prime minister, either.

Sir Isaac Rufus was appointed Viceroy of India in 1919. Lord Samuel was a minister in the cabinet in 1915, and Hore-Belisha was Minister of War in Chamberlain's cabinet.

This is how Jews gradually took over England and made it the "Sword of Israel" in the twentieth century. However, the Jewish historian is modestly silent about the many Jews who stand at the pinnacle of British life, whose names we have given above.

It is all the more instructive to bring forth these excerpts from the biographies of famous and outstanding "Englishmen" cited by the Jewish press. From them, the unenlightened can learn that, for instance, one of the main English parties, the Liberal Party, was even led by a Jew for a long time!

"Sir Herbert Samuel, the first High Commissioner of Palestine, is now sixty years old," the *Jewish Life* politely reported in 1931.

> He was born in Liverpool. He is the youngest son of Edwin Samuel, brother of Stuart Samuel, president of the Union of Jewish Communities of England.
>
> As a student, Herbert Samuel was an adherent of liberalism [of course!]. In 1902, he was elected minister of the English Parliament. For a long time, he was the president of the Liberal Party.
>
> He is considered one of the best theorists of liberalism [noted!]. In 1905, Samuel took the position of Interior Vice-Minister [Judas considers England's home affairs his own!]. Since then, he has held various high positions in all liberal cabinets. From 1918 to 1920, Samuel was Chairman of the Royal Statistical Commission.
>
> In 1920, he was appointed High Commissioner of Palestine and held this post until 1925 [Poor Arabs!]. Recently, Samuel was considered the most relevant candidate for the position of Viceroy of India [Poor Hindus!]. Herbert Samuel occupies a very prominent place in the governmental life of England [we can see that!]. He is also an ardent Zionist."

And here is yet another "Great Englishman":

> "Alfred Mond, Baron Melchett, who was known in England as the Field Marshal of British industry, has died.... Lord Melchett was a staunch supporter for the rationalization of the Imperial Chemical Industries with a capital of £54 million, of which he was chairman.
>
> He was the chairman of twelve other companies, and in general was listed [was he really only listed?] in thirty different boards of directors.
>
> He was a member of the British Parliament from 1905 to 1928. Then he was elevated to the Peerage.
>
> During the last war, he was the government's commissar of factories, then the Minister of Labor, and later on the Minister of Health.

He was rightfully called the "Chemical King of England."

He was an ardent supporter of the Zionist movement, as the chairman of the Zionist Federation in England, Chairman of the Council of the "Jewish Agency."

He is buried in his family crypt at a Jewish cemetery. "Kalish" said his eldest son Henry, who inherited the title of Lord.[47]

And behind the coffin of the deceased were standing: a representative of the government, a representative of the House of Lords, representatives of the World Zionist Organization, "Jewish Agency" political parties, many prominent state and political figures, large industrialists and financiers, and a huge crowd of people.... The King and Queen of England sent a telegram with their condolences to Lady Melchett. After the funeral, a solemn *azkorah* was held in the synagogue on Berkeley Street."[48]

6. Talmudic Wanderers at the Forefront of the British Empire

This picture of a national state funeral for a deceased Jew, in which the government and the people are trailing along his coffin, with the king and queen, mourning—an image too impossible to capture. This was the bright and vivid scene showcasing the true power in England; it illustrated well why the head of the British Imperial Fascist League, Arnold Leese, once called London "the New Jerusalem" and predicted that "the Future of England was either fascism or DEATH."

We could also cite an instructive biography of a small Jewish apothecary's student, Rufus Isaacs. He, with the encouragement of his fellow Jews, became the Lord of Reading and Viceroy of India, virtually the autocratic ruler of five hundred million Hindu slaves as the Jewish newspaper *Today* reported in 1936. But to spare both the reader's time and nerves, we will limit ourselves to just excerpts of it:

"The son of a poor Jewish broker. From a ship's cabin boy to the Viceroy of India, an English Marquess, and King George's closest friend" reads the boastful subtitle of *Today*."

And then follows a "colorful" biography:

---

[47] "Kaddish": A memorial prayer. (Translator's note)
[48] From Hebrew *azkorah*, a commemoration. (Translator's note)

The Marquess of Reading, formerly known as Rufus Isaacs, was born to a poor stockbroker in London's Jewish district of Whitechapel.

He was fourteen years old when, unable to stand the stifling atmosphere of his parent's home and commerce school, he set out on unknown adventures that his youthful dreams long ago had called for. Filled with the desire to have a say in the affairs of soldiers and generals who had conquered the world, Rufus Isaacs, a pale, puny boy, became a ship's cabin boy.

The first paycheck on the ship seemed to him like a free pass to all the countries of the world.

These romantic adventures, however, did not last long. Two years after the first voyage, Rufus Isaacs returned, disappointed and heartbroken, to the East End where his father was an orange merchant. He started attending college, but again couldn't stand it any longer [What?! Dare we ask?].

Then he tried his luck on the stock exchange, but even there he failed. Then Rufus Isaacs again settled for science and ... achieved a Doctorate in Law [not without difficulties, apparently].

His wits, his energy and his organizational talents paved the way for a brilliant career as a lawyer. To make a name for himself, he defended poor people who could not afford the luxury of hiring a lawyer [and just like that, it turns out, that is the reason for Jewish charity, to make a name for oneself!]. Fruit vendors in Covent Garden repaid him with apples, merchants in Soho, with roots.

Isaacs' rare wits quickly gained fame. He began to gain prominent clients, and quickly rose to the forefront of London's law offices.

As a representative of the Vickers military industrial factories, he played a leading role in the war industry prior to the World War.

By 1904, a brilliant lawyer and champion of liberal ideas [of course!], he had first entered the House of Commons. However, the attacks that made a splash in the courtroom did not impress the House of Commons.

Now a politician, Isaacs remained in the background for a long time until he received a seat in the House of Commons as the first Jewish attorney general in English history.

The sensational scandal with the shares of the Marconi Company seemed to have put an end to Isaacs' brilliant political career [it would be interesting to know the extent of the venerable Isaac's participation in this scheme]. He alongside his friend and fellow government official David Lloyd George seemed to have been badly compromised, but he somehow succeeded in completely justifying himself before the select committee investigation. Isaacs' position was strengthened once again.

A few months later he became a Lord Chief Justice and, as the Baron Reading of Erleigh (Earley), he joined the House of Lords.

A new stage in his life. His debut on the path of aristocracy was initiated by several major trials at which he presided. As the supreme judge, he ordered the judicial review of most trials, commuted the sentences of previous instances, and became the ideal of the people, who deeply revered a humane, God-fearing, and fair judge.

Lord Reading's twenty-five years in office did not change his character. Once a ship's cabin boy, he achieved the highest levels of prestige after the World War. He held the highest office possible after the English king, becoming the Viceroy of India.

During his rule in India, the British government fought hard against rebellious tribes, against the Gandhian boycott movement, and against the predatory raids of the Muslims.

The day Lord Reading welcomed the Prince of Wales to India was the most disturbing and restless day of his life. The English heir to the throne was constantly threatened with assassination, and Lord Reading was personally responsible for his safety. As an opponent of Gandhi, who was then at the height of his fame, Lord Reading again displayed the diplomatic skills that he had already shown during the World War, when he secured a loan for the Allies in America. He gave Gandhi the ability to act as long as Gandhi did not openly commit a crime against the law. Only then was the leader of the Indian revolutionaries arrested and neutralized for several years [so the Jews admit that their Viceroy provoked Gandhi].

Nine years ago, Lord Reading, after a five-year long reign in India, returned to London. He was one of the most famous and significant viceroys to ever rule the greatest part of the British Empire in the name of the King of England and the Emperor of India.

The English King has awarded Lord Reading the title of Marquess. Until his last day, he was one of the king's confidants and friends. Despite being the youngest of the twenty-seven Marquesses of the British Empire, he was one of the most influential advisers to the Crown.

Lord Reading was seventy-one when he remarried. This wedding was a sensation in London [no wonder: a seventy-year-old wreck marries his secretary!]"

The newspaper *Today* was being published in Riga by the Hoffman Jews in Russian as the largest newspaper of Russian emigrants in Europe.

"India under the boot of the Jews" might as well be the title of the Lord's reign, as well as all the subsequent viceroys. But finally let us summarize the list of members of the British government, at least since 1936. Alas, from this list we learn that the second leading party in England, the Conservatives, was and still is led by Jews.

"Founder of the New Economic Policy, a prominent Jewish figure, and head of Marks & Spencer, Moses Schiff is now playing the same role in England as Judah Frankfurter did at the height of the New Deal in America," wrote the English *Fascist* in 1936.

The dependence of Prime Minister Stanley Baldwin on the Jews comes from his intimate relationship with the Jew Robert Bernard Waley-Cohen, director of the locomotive company Baldwin Ltd.[49] Baldwin's two sons-in-law are in a close relationship with the banking executives of the Jewish firm Wagg & Co., which, in turn, is in a kind of joint venture with the Jewish firm Bonn & Co. Moreover, Baldwin's third son-in-law is legally married to a lady whose maiden name was Cohn. A prominent Jewish agent, G. S. Frey has been working for Baldwin for fourteen years. MacDonald's personal secretary has been a Rosenberg, a Jew, for a long time.[50]

Secretary of State for the Colonies J. H. Thomas' own son is employed in the Jewish office of Beilisha & Co. The wife of the Secretary of Aviation, Swinton, has just inherited the fortune of the Jewish millionaire Joseph Meyers. While his closest aide and second-in-command is none other than the infamous Philip Sassoon of the Far East.[51]

The Earl of Halifax's heir is engaged to the granddaughter of the Rothschilds. Joseph Chamberlain's own brother was strongly supported by Jewish business and, in gratitude, provided the Jews with valuable territory in East Africa. Joseph's aunt by blood belongs to the Andrade Jewish family.

The wife of the Home Secretary, Lord Simon, has long maintained an intimate relationship with the Zionist movement.

---

[49] Prime Minister of Great Britain from 1923–1924, 1924–1929, and 1935–1937. (Translator's note)
[50] The leader of the Labour Party, in 1924 and from 1929–1931, later prime minister, who established diplomatic relations with the USSR. (Translator's note)
[51] Sir Philip Albert Gustave David Sassoon, 3rd Baronet, (December 4th, 1888–June 3rd, 1939) was a British politician, art collector, and socialite. (Translator's note)

Jeff Cooper was named godfather of one of the sons of Otto Kahn, co-owner of Kuhn, Loeb & Co., who spent millions on the Bolshevik revolution in Russia. R. V. Grimston has a full-blooded Jewish wife, and Neumann was her maiden name.

The Marquess of Zetland, the Secretary of State for India, is a Grand Master of the Masonic Order and director of the National Bank of Scotland. His assistant is Cecil Kish, a Jew, and the de facto leader is another Jew, Henry Strakosch.

The brother of the Minister of Commerce, Sir Walter Runciman, married with his father's blessing a Jewish woman by the name of Lehman. While the Parliamentary Secretary to the Ministry of Agriculture and Fisheries, Herwald Ramsbotham was married to a Jewish woman by the name of de Stein.

Even the admiralty in England is surrounded by Jews, ever since the fellow naval minister Stanley married one of the Rothschilds. Another Stanley, by the name of Oliver, is the chairman of the Supreme Council for Public Education and is also the son-in-law of the same prolific Rothschild family.

"The true British government is organized by the Finintern," *The British Fascist* published in 1937.[52]

The power of this financial elite is realized through the obedience in all matters of the official representatives of the visible government of Neville Chamberlain. The change of Baldwin to Chamberlain, as we see, did not change the situation in the British Empire at all.

"Some of the ministers are real Jews, others are Aryans who serve the interests of Jewry, and others have already become tightly related to Jewish families," the *Fascist* sums up and reports. "In fact, rule of England is now concentrated in the hands of the informal organization of the PEP, also known as the Political and Economic Planning organization," founded and led by the most powerful Jew in the UK right now, Israel Moses, owner of the banking firm "Marks & Spencer Co."

The purpose of this organization roughly coincides with that of the American "think tank." It boils down to strengthening Jewish control over British industry, as well as to instill in the minds of ordinary Britons the extremely dangerous idea that the causes of the economic depression are reducible to the unsatisfactory organization of business, and that only through the slag efforts of Jewish financiers can the desired Germany be restored.

---

[52] The word *"Finintern"* is an abbreviation for "Financial International." It describes the elite as a cabal of international, rootless, transnational financial elites ruling over nations. More often than not, the members of this elite are Jewish. (Translator's note)

"We call on His Majesty King George VI," Arnold Leese exclaims:

to put an end to all of the diabolical triumphs of the Jewish dragon, so that Britain can once again live its own self-fulfilling life and, in its international orientation, follow its own voice, and not the commands of Jews that are now pushing London to destroy and meddle with Hitler's Germany. We call on His Majesty in the hope that he will condemn Freemasonry instead of supporting it, and that his actions will prove him worthy of the unanimous greeting that was given to him by the entire English people at his coronation, based on the hope that the British monarchy would be under a truly English and not Jewish leadership, which, alas, has been observed in recent times too often!

The following catalog provides detailed information about British Ministers:

Prime Minister Chamberlin: His father owes his career to Jewish support; in return for this, he strongly insisted on giving the Jews a vast territory in East Africa as a "National Home." This was at a time when the English emigrant could barely obtain free land and had to show and prove to owning substantial sums of money to qualify for entry to the colonies.

The aunt of Joseph Chamberlain was a true Jewish woman named Andrade.[53] There is, however, every reason to believe that her mother also had Jewish blood running through her veins, her maiden name being Harbets.

Neville Chamberlain's brother Austen was rightly regarded by Jews themselves as the true leader of world Jewry. The current prime minister's son holds a prominent position in the chemical industry, which Jewry has completely monopolized. All evidence suggests that the Chamberlains, just like the Churchills, have placed themselves entirely at the disposal of world Jewry.

Sir John Simon, Chancellor of the Under-Treasurer of HM Exchequer: Stubbornly suspected of being of Jewish origin, Sir Simon for some reason deemed it necessary to deny it outright, claiming that he "belongs to a purely Aryan family without any Jewish admixture." His wife for some odd reason also denies her Jewish origin, although for many years she has been organically connected with the Zionist movement and even once expressed in the press to Jewish delegates who had visited her that "in the great cause of Zionism, Jews can consider her as one of their own." Sir Simon was personally present at the synagogue for the wedding of Jewish banker Le Franklin (Kaiser &

---

[53] The brother of Neville Chamberlain. (Translator's note)

Co.) with an Aryan girl who was seduced into Jewry. It is also significant that the Soviet ambassador in London, the Jew Maisky, held a special people's banquet in honor of Sir Simon on February 22nd, 1935. Sir Simon's life revolves so much around Jews that he himself resembles a typical Jew in his manners and appearance, to the point that many Englishmen find it shocking.

Lord President of the Council of Ministers, Viscount Halifax: His closest heir recently married to one of the granddaughters of the Rothschilds. Any further comments, as they say in such cases, are superfluous.

Lord Chancellor Viscount Hailsham[54]: His own brother, Sir Malcolm Hoag, is married to the daughter of the Jewish tycoon Gohmert, and his Permanent Secretary is a full-blooded Jew, Sir Claud Schuster.

Home Secretary Sir Samuel Hoare: Coming from a Quaker family, in his book *The Fourth Seal* he made it clear that he was aware of the magnitude of the Jewish danger. We leave it to him to say for himself as to why he warns his colleagues in the ministry in this regard. His personal secretary is V. V. Astor, a nephew of the owner of the Jewish bank Hambros. His mother is the sister of banker Brande, managing director of the "Lazar Bros" banking house in London.

State Secretary for Foreign Affairs Anthony Eden: He is directly descended from a "certain Polish citizen," F. Schaffalitzky. He has an intimate friendship with the Rothschild family and with Sir Philip Sassoon. His personal secretary is the son of a full-blooded Jew, Sir Maurice Hankey. His closest associate as a fellow minister is Viscount Cranbourne, who is married to the granddaughter of the prominent Jewish figure B. Osborne. Cranbourne has also a particularly intimate relationship with the Jewish Soviet ambassador Ivan Maisky.

Dominion Minister Malcolm MacDonald: Ramsay MacDonald, his father, had a Jewish woman named Rosenberg working as Permanent Secretary for many years. Both MacDonalds are closely associated with the already mentioned Jewish organization PEP owned by the Schiffs. It was Ramsay MacDonald himself who called on the British workers in 1917 to follow the example of the Russian Revolution.

The Marquess of Hartington, associated with the powerful insurance organization of the Rothschilds, Bearsteds, and Rosebery Jews, is a comrade of the minister MacDonald. A Freemason of the Scottish Rite,[55] he was one of the most active leaders of the 1936 exhibition organized to enrich the Jewish National Fund.

---

[54] Viscount Hailsham. (Translator's note)
[55] A member of a Masonic lodge working according to the Ancient and Accepted Scottish Statute. (Translator's note)

The Marquess of Zetland, Secretary of State for Indian Affairs: He is one of the most prominent Masonic figures. It was none other than his wife who introduced a Jewess, Madame Judas, to His Majesty's coronation reception. His closest associate is Lord Stanley, whose sister recently married one of the Rothschilds. His closest second-in-command is the Jew Sir Cecil Kish, while the other Jew is Sir Henry Strakosch, who sits on the council of this ministry.

Colonial Secretary William Ormsby Gore: He is an avowed enthusiast of Zionism. His closest relatives, Viscount Cranbourne and the Marquess of Hartington, have already been mentioned. He is a particularly typical representative of the "ruling class" that is completely subordinate to Jewry.

First Lord of the Admiralty Alfred Duff Cooper: His closest assistant is H. B. Kepp, an ardent supporter of Shiff's PEP and a prominent Freemason of the Scottish rite Y. Llewellyn.

Minister of Health Sir Kingsley Wood: On February 23rd, 1937, in Manchester, he delivered a significant speech, where, in particular, he emphasized that "Jews are a race that the country should value and always want among us." Not only that, in practice Mr. Wood carries out the same ideas that he announced in his Manchester speech. It is quite understandable, then, why the Jew R. H. Bernays is his secretary, and the Jew L. Infeld is his deputy.

Secretary of Commerce Oliver Stanley: His own sister married one of the Rothschilds. It was Stanley who gave a speech in January 1933 at the consecration of the portrait of Ernest Schiff, a Jew from the Schiff family, co-owners of the banking house Kuhn, Loeb and Co. His deputy is Captain D. E. Wallas, who is married to an ardent supporter of everything that is Jewish, Lady Lutence. His main economic adviser is the most mysterious man in Great Britain, Sir F. W. Leith-Ross, who is closely associated with the Finintern. He was recently sent to China to survey its economic situation. A prominent Freemason of the Scottish Rite, Captain F. S. Crockebank was appointed head of the mining department.

Minister of Labor G. E. Brown: He was particularly hospitable to the Soviet ambassador Maisky. His most trusted secretary is Humbert Wolf, a Jew by nationality.

Minister of War Leslie Hore-Belisha: A real Jew! The most unfortunate of choices, as the cabinet in charge of dealing with the deepening antagonism with Hitler's Germany. His deputy is Lord Strathcona, whose brother is a director of the Jewish Trading Investment Co. The personal secretary of the Minister is R. B. Grilston, who is married to a Jewish woman named Neumann.

The Minister of Aviation, Viscount Swinton: Fortune smiled upon him, not long before marrying Baroness Masham, who inherited a significant part of her inheritance from the Jewish millionaire Joseph

Meyers. He graciously extended hospitality not only to the Sassoons, but also to the Zionist leader Naum "Sokolov" himself. His second-in-command was until recently the Jew Sir Philip Sassoon, who had just been replaced by Colonel Mirkhel.

Minister of Public Works Sir Philip Sassoon: A true Jew who inherited the blood of the Rothschilds from his mother's side.

Minister of Pensions Herwald Ramsbotham: He is married to a Jewish woman named de Stein. His Permanent Secretary is Sir Adair Hore, the stepfather of the Jewish Minister of War Hore-Belisha!

"It goes on and on, all in the same spirit," Arnold Leese concludes in his review.

> We invite you to draw the appropriate conclusions yourself. We expect all the good Englishmen of this country to support us in the struggle we are waging. Especially now that we are needed more than ever before, for our enemy is strong and mighty and once we speak the truth about the Greatest Evil that has ever threatened Great Britain, we are constantly under the risk of ruin and prosecution. England has become the NEW JERUSALEM. It's time for all Englishmen to figure it out![56]

"So that's who the colonies of the British Crown belong to—Israel!" we add with reference to this purely English review!

As for the British government during the Second World War, the Jewish influence in it was even stronger. In particular, in the 1940s, Harbin's *Jewish Life* wrote:

> The British government has new ministers who are representatives of the parliamentary opposition, and almost all of them have recently spoken from the parliamentary rostrum as ardent opponents of the "White Paper," opponents of emigration restrictions and prohibitions on the purchase of new land by Jews. These parliamentarians are the leaders of the Labour Party: Atlee, Greenwood, and Morrison, Liberal leader Sir Archibald Sinclair, and opposition from the Conservative Party's Jeff Cooper[57] and Emery. Almost all disputes concerning the Palestinian problem are always addressed by the aforementioned deputies.[58]

---

[56] The English *Fascist* No. 98 for June 1937. The British fascists were so in need that they could only produce a small monthly newspaper. With the outbreak of the Anglo–German War, Arnold Leese disappeared into the dungeons of an English prison.
[57] Meaning Alfred Duff Cooper. (Translator's note)
[58] English *Fascist* No. 12, 1938, London.

Cooper's parliamentary speech last summer against the White Paper and his speech at the Zionist Conference in Washington made his name widely known in public circles as an ardent advocate of pro-Zionist policies and the creation of a Jewish state in Eretz Israel.

> Less known however is Emery, who was Minister of the Colonies in the Baldwin administration (1924–1929). On one hand he is a supporter of the development of the Jewish National Home on the principles of Ahad Ha'am (the creation of a spiritual Jewish center and a binational Arab state). On the other hand, he ardently defends the integrity of the Balfour Declaration.[59] Being personally an outstanding expert on the colonial problem and an ideologue for British imperialism, he considers that it is, under any means necessary, an absolute imperative to strengthen the construction of the Jewish National Home in Eretz Israel, which for Great Britain is not only a political necessity, but also a moral duty. Pasfield's long-forgotten "White Book" was sharply criticized by him at the time. Together with Baldwin and the already dead Austen Chamberlain, he openly addressed *The Times* on October 23rd, 1930, with a letter in which they admit that the White Book contradicts the mandate and the Balfour Declaration. Not content with just talking with the press, on November 17th, 1930, he delivered a thunderous speech in Parliament, which served as the end for the White Book. Now Emery has been appointed Minister of India, but the power that he will yield will impact the Middle East.[60]

The last Prime Minister of the British Empire, Winston Churchill, is frequently called by Jews "a supporter of political Zionism and a friend of the Jewish people." His brother, Jack Churchill, is a member of the Jewish brokerage firm Vickers, his daughter married the Jew V. Oliver, and his son Randolph is listed among the honorary members of the presidium of the Jewish youth organization Maccabi. Winston himself has a close friendship with the American Jewish billionaire Bernard Baruch, on whom US President Franklin Roosevelt is dependent.

---

[59] The public statement issued by the British Government on the establishment of a Jewish "national home" in Palestine, published by the Foreign Minister Balfour. (Translator's note)
[60] *Jewish Life*, 1940, No. 26.

7. England and Judea

It is not surprising that a country with such a government, with such a Judaized elite, and with such kings mired in Freemasonry, was and is the champion of all Jewish endeavors.

At the end of the World War, having ignored its promises to the Arabs, Great Britain gave Palestine to the Jews and has ever since repeatedly acted as the patroness of the Zionist movement, supposedly to establish a Jewish state in Palestine. Jewry "touchingly" pays England in the same coin, cares about England as its "promised" land and, apparently, considers it quite its own, often declaring their shared interests.

As such, with the outbreak of the Anglo-German War in 1939, the Jewish Agency published: "His Majesty's Government has declared war on Hitler's Germany. This is our war. We will provide assistance to the Government and people of Great Britain by all means at our disposal."

"Nothing will stop us," responds the representative of this very Jewish Agency, Dr. A. I. Kaufman in the Harbin *Jewish Life*, and another Harbin Jewish magazine, *GADEGEL*, frankly reported in the middle of 1940:

> In this hour of great upheaval, the Headquarters of the New Zionist Organization is implementing new projects and plans. Over the course of the past two months, this activity has been limited to the cardinal problem of preparing a propaganda campaign for the creation of the Jewish army. A memorandum was drawn up clearly setting out the assumptions for the formation of a military unit, which has already been discussed with prominent members of the British Parliament. Preliminary Negotiations already began in London by the end of 1939, and as a result, one of the arbiters of Britain's fate helped us get in touch with members of the war cabinet."

At about the same time, the *Jewish Life* published on its front page, in bold type, a telegram from Gavas in London under the eloquent headline "The Jewish Legion," in which it said:

> The Zionist Federation has stated that its proposal, made from the very beginning of the European war to organize a Jewish army has now been realized. The Zionists vouched for full cooperation, and stressed that 50,000 Jews have already signed up to serve in the Jewish Legion.

The next issue reported on a hundred-thousand-men Jewish army, which allegedly is being formed by a certain Colonel Paterson in America.[61] At the same time, the leaders of the Shanghai Jewish community, Witker and Topaz, issued an appeal to the Jews of Shanghai to form a Jewish battalion with the aim of preserving Renkong for England, which is currently under threat by Japan.

At the large Jewish meeting in New York, which was attended by two thousand delegates from all over the country, the first Lord of the British Admiralty D. Cooper delivered the most Zionist speech of all Zionist speeches ever delivered by a British statesman over the past twenty years.

D. Cooper began the speech with sorrow, expressing how "his old friend," Dr. Weizmann [president of the World Zionist Organization] was absent. He then moved on to the great mission of the revival of Zion, "a dream that met realization with the publication of the Balfour Declaration."

"No race has given more to humanity than the Jews," declared this Judeo-submissive minister.

The Union between England and world Jewry was formalized and made official in June 1940 by the signing of a formal agreement between the British government and the Jewish Agency. The British government was represented, of course, by Churchill, and the Jewish Agency was represented by Chaim Weizmann and Movsha Chertok. The British government recognized the Jewish Agency as the highest body—the Executive—as the Ruler of the future Jewish state of Judea, which was to become part of the dominion of the British Empire. The government of the new dominion, in turn, recognized the English King as the King of Judea.

The agreement was reproduced by the London correspondent of the American World Press Union and, of course, is not limited to the above article. Even we are aware of the existence of a number of other articles showcasing this, not to mention articles that we are not aware of. The British government guarantees the implementation of this treaty by all means at its disposal.

This begs the question: how many Jews currently reside in England, which they so firmly hold onto?

This number turns out to be ridiculously small compared to the indigenous population of the country. If we take into account that forty-

---

[61] John Henry Patterson (November 10, 1867–June 18, 1947) was a British military man, hunter, and writer. He served as the commander of the "Jewish Legion" during World War I. (Translator's note)

two million Britons live in the British Isles (England and Ireland), the number of Jews is quite modest.

According to Jewish sources, only 333,200 Jews live on the islands (London 234,000, Manchester 37,000, Leeds 30,000, Glasgow 15,000, Liverpool 7,000, Birmingham 6,000, Ireland 4,200).

If we take the entirety of the British Empire, which has the largest population of any country in the world (about 600,000,000), an even more interesting comparison will come to light. There are, in addition to the ones already indicated: in Canada 156,720, in Africa 102,000, in Australia 23,000, India 8,000, New Zealand 3,000, Rhodesia 38,000, Aden 2,500, Jamaica 2,000, and in addition, a small number in Gibraltar, Malta, Cyprus, and other British possessions. In total, this is only 350,000 Jews. Together with the Jews in the metropolis, this figure only amounts to about 683,000 souls. These 683,000 rule a population of 600 million people, exploiting and enriching themselves with impunity at their expense. Half a billion in slavery to half a million—such is Great Britain, the British Empire and Judea!

8. London as One of the Capitals of International Judea

It was in London where Karl Marx lived and wrote his famous *Capital*. It was there where the First International was founded and first gathered, just as it was also there where the uprising of the Paris Commune and the subversive Jewish revolutionary work in Russia were inspired from. Also in London, the second congress of the newly born "Russian Social Democratic Labor Party" was held—the same one that eventually split into the Bolsheviks and Mensheviks (the first congress was in Minsk, in the Pale of Settlement).[62]

The London police knew about this, but they turned a blind eye! The wealthy in London generously helped the "poor" Russian, German and French revolutionaries. Since then, the unnatural cohabitation of the "deniers of all foundations" with the most unscrupulous intelligence service in the world—the British intelligence service began.

The largest international Jewish groups, including the Executive World Zionist Organization, have settled in London. The former has scattered its "city committees" in all countries of the world, and the Executive of the powerful international Jewish Agency that unites Zionists and non-Zionists alike and entangles the whole world with the tentacles of its agents is also headquartered in London. This Executive,

---

[62] The Pale of Settlement was a western region of the Russian Empire with varying borders that existed from 1791 to 1917, beyond which permanent residency by Jews was mostly forbidden. (Translator's note)

as the Jews themselves inadvertently report, is in constant contact with the British government.

Chaim Weizmann, the current leader of the Jewish people, lives in London, and his predecessor, Nahum (Naym) "Sokolov," lived there for a long time. Another "Russian emigrant" lives there too, although not from the USSR, but from Imperial Russia—Professor Brodetsky, president of the World Maccabi Club. He has access to the highest spheres of English society. He is the elder head of young athletes who disguise themselves as "Maccabees," while simultaneously being chairman of the Jewish National Council in England and president of the Board of Deputies—the "Parliament of English Jews." And these English Jews, being loyal subjects of the King of Britain and the Emperor of India, at the same time always remember their belonging to world Jewry.

It is not for nothing that Lord Beaconsfield (Disraeli), the head of English politics at the end of the last century, returned to Judaism before his death.[63] Hore-Belisha, according to his relatives, belonged to the most devout family in Gibraltar.

At the end of all these revelations, the *Jewish Life* testifies:

> At the center of public activity of English Jewry is the synagogue. Each synagogue has its own cultural and charitable institutions. Some synagogues offer evening courses in which Jews learn Hebrew, Tanakh, and Jewish history. All charitable and cultural work is supervised by the synagogue's rabbi. At the head of English Jewry, on one hand, is the chief rabbi of the Ashkenazi and Sephardic communities. On the other the Parliament of English Jewry—the Board of Deputies—with delegates from each community and organization, carries out the public legal representation of English Jewry.
>
> The Board of Deputies first assisted in a high-profile case in Damascus that accused Jews of partaking in ritual murder. The current president of the Board of Deputies is Professor Brodetsky, the first Zionist and Russian Jew in this highly respected post, and this serves as an indicator of the new mood of English Jewry.

So modestly they write about their deeds. But modesty is not always inherent in the "damned race," as we shall see more than once.

---

[63] Beaconsfield-Disraeli, Prime Minister of Great Britain in 1868 and from 1874–80. Minister of Finance from 1858–59 and 1866–70. (Translator's note)

9. Judas Invades France

Begone Foggy Albion![64] We crossed the English Channel, and here it is, beautiful France! Half a century ago, the great Frenchman J. Drumont called it the "poisoned France." Let's see how far Judaism has progressed over the past half-century.

A. S. Shmakov dramatically conveys the vicissitudes of fortune of the "last and decisive battle" between the international nation and national France—details of the Dreyfus affair, which were once roared all over the world, the case of the espionage of a puny French Jewish captain.

"Twice convicted by military courts for treason, Captain Dreyfus, after all, still had the privilege of a special pro-Dreyfus ministry. Eventually, according to the report of the Jew, the Minister of War, Breeches, he was pardoned by the Rothschild lawyer and by the president of the Republic of Loubet—shame!

After having disgraced the generals, tarnished the army, humiliated France, the Qahal still did not hesitate to demand the complete rehabilitation of this traitor.[65] However, despite the efforts of the Jews and the complicity of the authorities, there was no possible grounds which would make the case eligible for a judicial review. In order to avoid mistakes, the court was rigged in its composition, but it was not possible to bribe the proceedings either, due to the evidence of treason. So there was nothing else to do but to acquit Dreyfus, against the law and without trial, although ostensibly on appeal. This is exactly what the court did. He simply overturned on appeal, without hearing the prosecution on July 12th, 1906, the second Dreyfus verdict, which was pronounced by the Court of Rennes back on September 9th, 1899.

As a consequence of this crime on the part of the Court of Cassation, the condemned man who confessed to his crimes was pardoned and restored to the rank of major. The Jew-traitor acquired, as an acquitted man, the right to disgrace the French army by his presence in its ranks. But the saddest thing is that the enraged parliament did not hesitate to sanction an act insulting to France.

This was preceded by mysterious deaths.

---

[64] "Foggy Albion." Used commonly by Russians to refer to Great Britain, "Albion" being the oldest known name for Britain. It comes from the Latin word for "white," and may refer to the white cliffs of Dover, or due to the constant fog that used to cover the isles not long ago. (Translator's note)

[65] "Qahal." In the broad sense of the word, an (often secret) community of Jews. In the narrow sense, an administrative form of self-government of Jews in Poland and other countries of Eastern Europe in the sixteenth through the eighteenth centuries, in the Russian Empire from 1772–1893. (Translator's note)

First of all, Colonel Sandherr, a zealous patriot, very capable and knowledgeable head of the counterintelligence bureau, who mysteriously died. Poisoned after rejecting Jewish money.

Soon after followed Major Attel, the warden of the military prison, who was present at the very moment of Dreyfus' demotion and personally listened to him admit his guilt, was soon killed. He was naturally a very inconvenient man, and on October 1st, 1895, he left Triel in perfect health by train. Less than an hour later, at the Somane station, he was found in the compartment of the wagon already wheezing and green. The poison was in his very eyes, but they decided to not look for the culprits.

Deputy Serignet received information from Captain Lebrun Renault on Dreyfus' admission of guilt and in 1898 published it in the newspaper Entrand-Sizhan. Only a few weeks later, on June 15th of the same year, near Mons, where he was traveling, he was found crushed to pieces on the railway line. He was undoubtedly thrown out of the wagon. The door was found closed again, and the only attendant present fled the scene.

The excellent social position of the murdered man, his character, and his prudence excluded the notion and possibility of suicide or accident. The atrocity was obvious, but it was decided that it was not necessary to examine it and expose it.

The death of Colonel Anri, however.... We do not say that the Dreyfusards killed him, because suicide seems likely, but we do say that they drove him to take his own life, since this is the peak of the Jewish art. Here we see something even more disgusting than just murder.

Everything makes one come to the conclusion that a false friend, one of those sneaky "brothers" whom ghettos and lodges send to all the strata of society, incited this honest warrior and ardent patriot to commit not even a complete, but a popular rendition of a document that for now must remain confidential. While regrettable and dangerous, this atrocity was, moreover, of dubious usefulness, for at this point the traitor had long since been condemned. And this fact was known to the Dreyfusards much earlier than it was reported to the Minister of War. Thus, with Anri left to choose between dishonor and suicide, he was generously allowed to choose his fate.

Lorenzo, an honest patriot, prefect of the northern department, who pointed out the existence and tricks of the Dreyfusardian conspiracy which transferred huge amounts of money from Brussels. He was summoned to Paris by Minister Dupuy where he presented irrefutable evidence. But he did not have time to return to the Hotel Terminus, as he suddenly died in his room. He was too curious, and he had to be taken out, especially since Anri's widow called him as a witness to her case.

Fedes, the former head of the search team, managed to dig far into the plans of the Dreyfusard plot. Suddenly, he too died on August 4th, 1900, on the same day as Lorenzo.

Being fully aware of Fedes' and Lorenzo's whereabouts and knowing everything thoroughly, but not being afraid of these two deaths, Minister Dupuy declared in the Chamber of Deputies that he knew nothing about the existence of the "syndicate." Death spared him, but another terrible event occurred in Laisborn no later than March 5th.

On March 4th, Dupuy received a gift from the Qahal in the form of the death of both his assistants—Lorenzo and Fedes. It was no later than the next day, on March 5th, in the dead of night, that 185 thousand pounds of gunpowder exploded in a state-owned factory near Toulon. The explosion shook the whole district and was heard over thirteen miles away. The building, like everything else that was in the area, was turned to dust, littered with the remains of hundreds of human bodies. A little further in the vicinity were located many more laboratories of smokeless gunpowder and melinite, which fortunately were not caught up in the explosion. Otherwise, i.e., if they would have produced a chain reaction, as the authors of the villainy calculated, the arsenal and the fleet could have vanished as if a cyclone had passed by.

Not satisfied with these results, the Jews again sent six anarchists (bribed by them) to blow up railway stations on March 7th. Pursued by the authorities, the Shabbos goyim fled, but managed to plant sixteen dynamite charges at the place where the assassination attempt took place.

Less prudent than Dupuy, but equally aware of the intrigues of the "case," Minister Kranz valiantly testified before the Chamber of Deputies of his conviction of the "martyr's" guilt—the very next day, June 22nd, himself, his wife, and their children were poisoned. And if they were somehow rescued from the clutches of death, it was only through extreme effort and after severe suffering.

Detective Genach, who was deeply familiar with the case and had followed Dreyfus for a long time in France, Belgium, and elsewhere, was called to provide evidence at the trial in Rennes. However, someone made sure to take care of him and prevent him from doing so, as he suddenly died on July 5th, 1899.

On another note, it is necessary to consider separately and in more detail the murder of Felix Faure on February 16th, 1899, and Sibeton on December 8th, 1904.[66]

Here, without further commentary, is the main evidence:

a. The testimony of Faure himself, who said a month before his death: "Do you really think I don't know how my death is waited upon?"

---

[66] President of France from 1895–1899. (Translator's note)

b. A month before the murder, the housekeeper of the German embassy in Paris heard one of the interlocutors say: "We must eliminate Faure."

c. Other evidence—newspapers, telegrams—suggests that a certain number of individuals in Judeo-Masonic circles were warned of the imminent murder of Faure, because some let slip about the upcoming event: one of them in a week, another after a few days, and the third not even after few hours.

d. The importance of his death. Only Faure's patriotism was an obstacle to the Jewish conspiracy, and prevented the flood of treason from ravaging everything in its way.

e. Seeing himself pinned down and deceived, the president prepared a stern rebuke—an "Appeal to the People," where he pointed to the gaping abyss that had opened up in front of France, and to the Jewish conspiracy as a constant threat to its national security. It was necessary at all costs to prevent the publication of this great government act ... and so they did. And for this, they took advantage of Faure's close associates. The president had an official reception that lasted until six o'clock. It was then when the Jewess Shteingel arrived. It was at this one-on-one meeting where the crime was committed. The guards came running to the screams, but the killer was put in a car and sent home the moment when they began to crowd around the poor president, who was already in agony.

f. The nature of the measures and concerns that were taken up by doctors, in particular by Professor Lenelog. Doctors applied specific remedies for poisoning. In other words, they diagnosed the patient as being "poisoned" and acted accordingly. This is not contradicted either by the medical certificate issued the next day on the death of Faure that diagnosed a brain hemorrhage—there are poisons that produce such a hemorrhage.

g. But the crime is established not by the actions of the doctors alone, but even more obviously by the absence of an autopsy, which was not performed to accurately determine the cause of death. It is often the case that precautions designed to mask an event cause the opposite effect. Having eliminated the autopsy, they anticipated that the poison would cause rapid decomposition of the corpse; they then hurried with the embalming ahead of time. At eight o'clock the following morning, ten hours after the death, the embalming was already completed, and again, contrary to custom, without any protocol. And as this haste did not stop the process of early decomposition, they put the body in a coffin and buried it immediately.... As if out of fear that he might come to life and expose their evil deeds.

h. By the Dreyfusards own admission. The most interesting of these is an article by a prominent Dreyfusard published in a Jewish leaflet on the day following Faure's death. Here is what we find there:

"Earlier, the shocking news of Anri's death had already rattled their thick skulls. Now the death of the president of the republic becomes more significant and frightening. It overthrew the conspiracy that had been woven around him with his help against the truth and freedom. When your motivation is forced, under the pressure of necessity, the logic of things requires that the blows against you increase until your perseverance is finally crushed. If you had rendered justice a year ago, the course of events would probably have changed, and among the subsequent chain of events, the accident in which the head of state himself died, perhaps, wouldn't have taken place."

How else do you interpret this use of language, but that Faure would still be alive if he had submitted a year earlier and reinstated Dreyfus back with his uniform of a major in the French army?

As soon as Faure was buried, the Dreyfus case went up for review by a courier.

The election of a proxy of the sons of Judas such as Loubet;[67] the formation of a deliberately pro-Dreyfus ministry with the help of a Rothschild lawyer—the Shabbos goy Valjean Rousseau as prime minister or Galliffet for the post of Minister of War; the sudden promotion to brigadier general and then general of division of Picquart, who, on the contrary, should have been tried by a military court; the extreme efforts of Galliffet to rig the military court in Rennes to acquit Dreyfus, along with a written order for him, from the same Galliffet, to conclude, that Dreyfus was innocent; the order then being transmitted to the prosecutor of the court by a messenger from Waldeck-Rousseau; a solemn proclamation of the President Loubet that "the verdict in Rennes will no doubt reveal the truth, and that no matter what it was, all must obey without question"; the scandalous revelation, however, and the new conviction of Dreyfus was followed by anger, curses, fury throughout the Dreyfusard camp, and Dreyfus' "pardon" through Loubet on the Galliffet report, as well as Dreyfus' acceptance of this pardon and his withdrawal of his second appeal, i.e., a double admission of guilt.

The direct consequence of this situation is the seizure by the Jews of all government functions, the offices of the Ministers of War and Navy. As well as the systematic persecution of patriotic army officers by the Qahal through the establishment of a whole system of espionage and special "conduit lists," the creation of an apotheosis—Syveton's subsequent slap in the face in the very session of the Chamber of Deputies. Then the poisoning of Syveton, and then, as the final chord of this symphony, the complete rehabilitation of the traitor Dreyfus by parliament.

Syveton's trial for slapping Minister Andre in the face was scheduled for December 9th, 1904. In his defense and to uncover the Qahal

---

[67] President of France 1899–1906. (Translator's note)

conspiracy against France, the accused called out witnesses, notably Colonel Ninet and other officers who were aware of the satanic tricks of the Qahal. Thus, this process is not so much a matter of Syveton himself, but rather a test for Dreyfus, Andre, and their instigators, the Judeo-Masons. Their vileness was to be exposed in all its nakedness to the world. Unfortunately, Syveton had apparently forgotten the fate of Felix Faure.

Among other things, everyone who knew the situation was saying: how does the Qahal expect to get out of this? It was necessary to destroy Syveton or else remove his witnesses, since such a trial cannot be allowed and obviously cannot take place. It indeed did not.

On December 8th, on the eve of the trial, MP Syveton was found dead in his office. They say that after dozing off and lying down, his face was against the gas burner, which he had forgotten to close.

But this was no more than a pathetic simulation of a suicide. Since everything looked like the case was going to end up in a victory for Syveton, there was no point in taking his own life, but along with the other deaths, this death was not something special.

Once Syveton had perished, then, in accordance with Jewish custom, it was decided to desecrate his memory. Hoping to confuse the ignorant crowd, they invited those who wanted to trash it with disgusting slander, spewed by the lackeys of the Qahal on the unfortunate hero.

Such is the fate of ascetics in the course of history. . . .

France must remember that neither his death, nor that of Felix Faure, were ever avenged.

However, such a triumph did not come cheap for the "chosen people." "Up to 200 million francs were collected by the Qahal for the Dreyfus case in both hemispheres, and in September 1899 alone, the second court in Rennes demanded, it is said, about 4 million francs from the Qahal." (A. S. Shmakov "The International Secret Government," Moscow 1912.)

10. The Freemason Brothers

A. S. Shmakov wrote in 1912: "After that, a lot of water flowed away . . . and even more Jews were washed ashore." In 1939, *La Vita Italiana* was able to publish a list of Jewish generals in the French army. The French army was the only army in the world with a large number of Jews in high commanding positions. The seizing of the army was preceded by the continuous filling of government leadership with Jews and Freemasons.

Next is the French government of 1937, according to the French newspaper *Free Voice*, founded by Drumont and published until 1939 (in its last years it was published in Algeria, after it was exiled from metropolitan France by the forces of democratic "freedom"):

- Prime Minister Leon Blum[68]: A socialist-capitalist, author of the disgusting doctrine of free love and incest. His book *Marriage* is banned in many countries because of its record-breaking pornographic content.
- Secretaries of State: Francois de Faisant, a Frenchman. As well as a certain Mumber,[69] a Jew. Ahh, equality....
- Ministers without portfolios: French, but very reliable rest assured, from the Jewish point of view that is, including Shabbos goyim and Freemason-socialists such as Camille Chotan, Paul Faure, and Maurice Bayolet.
- Minister of War Edouard Daladier: [The same one who pushed France against Germany and brought his country to the brink of destruction.]
- Minister of Marine Francois Blanchot.
- The Minister of Aviation, a Jew and Freemason, Pierre Cotte. [Before the end of the war with Germany, he managed to execute many outstanding representatives of the French air force and was killed by the younger officers for this.]
- The Freemason Minister of the Interior Dormua, his assistants: the Jews Behs Solomon and Kagel Salvador—the police are, of course, in Jewish hands.
- The Minister of Foreign Affairs is the Jew and Mason Delbos, one of the leaders of the "philanthropic" League for Human Rights.
- The Jewish Minister of Public Education Khan Zey.

This latter ministry is particularly Judaized (*Free voice* was forced to move from Paris to Algeria in 1937, where it continued its bold denunciations of world and French Jewry, including the local administration, and was closed in 1939).

Le France Enchaîné, year 1936, tells us:

> One of our friends recently visited the Ministry of Public Education and wanted to see the minister. Since the Jewish Minister Khan Zey was absent, the visitor was received by the Jewish Deputy Minister-Chief of Cabinet M. Abraham. But he could not give the required information himself, so he sent our

---

[68] Head of the Popular Front government of 1936–1938.
[69] Surname typical among merchants that began to spread in the eighteenth century in Russia.

friend to the head of the press department at the Ministry of National Education. It turned out to be the Jew Miris.

Free Voice concluded: "Of the ninety members of the Blum administration, forty are Jews and forty-five are Freemasons!"

"Compatriots." These are the masters of France! They call themselves the "Popular Front." Front of what people?

11. French and Jewish!

Leon Blum himself, the head of the Popular Front government, achieved, among other things, a legislative ban on anti-Semitism during his rule in France. He once said this about himself:

> I am a French Jew, and I can honestly say that I am a good Frenchman. I was born in France, in the very heart of Paris. My parents and grandparents lived in Paris, and since the history of my humble surname lends itself to research, I believe that my great-grandparents were Alsatians, which also means French. I was brought up as a Frenchman, attended French schools, my comrades being French, and I have held French posts.
> I believe that French culture has become a big part of me. I speak French without the slightest trace of any foreign accent. Even my facial features are free of particularly prominent racial traits. And I am sure that there is no element of the French spirit, of French culture, that is alien to me. And yet, even though I feel like a real Frenchman, I feel like I'm Jewish at the same time.

Duly noted! And a year before that, the Harbin *Jewish Life* explained:

> Many believe that the current French Minister-President Leon Blum, as a Marxist, should have a negative attitude towards the Zionist idea. Yudishe Rundsha points out that this is far from the case. Leon Blum, being a fiery French patriot, at the same time never forgot his Jewish origin, emphasizing this on many occasions.
> At the same time, he feels a deep sympathy for the Zionist cause and is a member of the French Palestinian Committee. At the end of 1924, at a banquet given by "Keren Hesodom" in honor of Professor Weizmann, Blum gave a speech in which he vigorously advocated the construction of Palestine.

He was no less enthusiastic in welcoming the opening of the University of Jerusalem the following year.

In 1949, Blum was elected to the Council of the Jewish Agency as a representative of French Jewry. On the opening day of the expanded Agency, Blum delivered a speech in Zurich on the challenges of Jewish construction in Palestine. And later, he repeatedly spoke out in the interests of the Zionist cause, especially Keren Hayesod.[70]

Quite revealing isn't it?

May every nation that allows a Jew into its leadership know that said Jew will use his position for specific Jewish causes and interests.

12. The French Republic or the Rothschild Brothers?

And here's the finale:

Having talked once with Rothschild, Clemenceau, the then-prime minister of France, somewhat disparagingly, spoke about the Jewish people. Rothschild jumped up from his chair, pounded the table with his fist, and shouted, "Be quiet, Clemenceau, more respect for Jewry! The Jewish people are the greatest in the world.[71]

"R. F.—*la République française*? Or R. F.—*le Rothschild Frères*, the Rothschilds brothers?" asked Shmakov back in 1907.[72]

And in 1942, the Jews indulged in such melancholic memories:

"The symphony that is Paris has more than once had a peculiar Jewish melancholic tone," is the title of an essay by Rabbi Dr. Simhoni, sent from Shanghai to Harbin.

To the wonderful mosaic which was once called Paris the Jew gave a lot of its color. A Jewish street took its place in the labyrinth of streets. Some specific features were added to the picture of "Paris": the Jewish makeup, the Jewish language created a dissonance, the opposite of what Paris was supposed to be different about. The Jew in Paris was not hidden in a corner. His name could be seen at every turn. A foreign tourist

---

[70] Also called the United Israel Appeal, it is the national building fund for the Land of Israel, the central financial agency of the worldwide Zionist movement, and of the Jewish Agency for Israel. It was founded by a decree of the Zionist executive committee in London, in 1920, and was constituted as an association in 1921. (Translator's note)
[71] *Jewish Life*, No. 5, 1939.
[72] A. S. Shmakov, *Freedom and the Jews*, Moscow 1907.

could be looking for the Jewish quarter just as he would look for the Latin quarter.

Likewise, you are used to seeing Jewish names at the political forefront. Their words resounded loudly and echoed in many thousands of hearts.

You've seen more than one Hebrew name on Mount Parnassus. Andre Maurois was a favorite among the French. He was read and understood. Every couple of months, he blessed us with a book—a book that the entire literary world discussed, and marveled at his great talent. His last book appeared in the days of the war. The book is written with Maurois' true talent, but tanks are just stronger. The French, the elite, the top ten thousand that carried Maurois in their arms, put him in the French Academy with honors and made him immortal.

Charles Maurras, the brilliant anti-Semite, protested: his artistic pen seethed with malicious pamphlets against the Jew as a politician, against the Jew as a member of Paris, but free thought won, the principle of equality prevailed, for this is what it is . . . France.

The Jewish poet-playwright Edmund Flug had a great triumph. On the French stage, his dramas were very successful. Andre Sapir, also Jewish, had great success with his novel *Jacob's Well*.

More than once the Jew has been a priest in the temple of arts. Who does not know the Jew Pascin in Paris?[73] Who did not admire his tender, sensitive paintings? From each picture, one could see that Pascin's art came from his very soul—a confession of the soul. No wonder he made his debut illustrating the works of Heinrich Heine. "Pascin the Jew was among the few who understood Heine's lyrical irony, the deep pain hidden under a slight sneer," so wrote the great art critics about Pascin. I am not here to talk about Pascin. But I remember the inspiring words spoken after his tragic death: "The poet, the artist, has left. Everything was there for him: elegance and grace; everything about him is thrilling: his blue velvet, his ethereal line—everything from him has taste."

At the gates of the Temple of Arts, you come across the son of the universal "sefer," Lasar Segall, who was said to have discovered the great mystery of art.[74] He chose man as his

---

[73] The "Prince of Montparnasse" was a Bulgarian artist known for his paintings and drawings. (Translator's note)
[74] *Sefer Refuot* ("The Book of Medicines") is the earliest-known medical book written in Hebrew. (Translator's note)

ultimate goal; without refinement, without decorative embellishments, he showed us man for what he really is.

So much beauty was created by Jews in Paris.

Where is the Jew from the Pletzl now—there the Jews spoke to the French in Hebrew![75]

Where is the Jew from Belleville now—where the Jews worked fifteen hours a day, so that they could then call their relatives here!

I know all these Pletzl and Belleville Jews. Without knowing them, I know their history. After all, these are mostly people who have never had a youth, nor a home. Cold was their home, and hunger was their night. Unhappy, persecuted, they came to Paris. Over time, they worked together, and by the sweat of one's brow, the sun began to shine over them. Twenty years ago, they were running for bread. Paris accepted them.[76]

And they made Paris their own—until the catastrophe of European Jewry in 1940.

13. The Fruits of Philosemitism in Spain

Spain.... Again, the word itself belongs to Jews themselves. "Since the time of their expulsion in 1342, the first legal Jewish community has now been established in Madrid," *Jewish Life* told us in 1927.

> The French banker Bauer, the Finnish Consul General in Spain, was elected chairman of the community [on Spanish soil, the French banker and the Finnish consul general still feel Jewish above all the rest]. Bauer has a close relationship with the royal court—in fact, the community owes its legalization to the personal intervention of King Alphonse. The synagogue of the new community is located in the very center of the city.

Not ten years after the opening of the community, their beloved king lost his crown. Spain was bathed in blood. Monasteries and palaces burst into flames, gunshots rang out, and the Cheka began its work. In Spain began the "red terror," familiar to us Russians, especially the savage treatment of religion and women, as Satan burned out the love

---

[75] The Pletzl ("little place" in Yiddish) is the Jewish quarter in the fourth arrondissement of Paris. (Translator's note)
[76] *Jewish Life*, No. 45, 1942

of Heaven and the love of beauty—of heavenly and earthly beauty. Goebbels sums up these terrible results:

> Spain had 71,353 churches, chapels, and monasteries before the Civil War. Of this number, 20,000 have now been destroyed, of which 2,201 are in Madrid alone, in which churches are closed and most have been robbed. According to Soviet statistics, 42,000 priests were murdered in Russia. In Spain, 27,000 priests and monks and 11 bishops suffered the same fate before February 2nd, 1937.

We have at our disposal the original check with the following signature: "Check of Comrade Juan Palomec for ten nights of his choice. Toledo. August 1st, 1935." Similar checks were found in large numbers in Toledo, Malaga, and the Cordovan front.[77]

> The suffering of women and children in Judeo-Bolshevik Spain is terrible, unspeakable. A Spanish refugee tells a Parisian newspaper how his seven-year-old child was killed in front of him by Red policemen, thrown from the fourth floor into the barracks courtyard, his lifeless corpse left dead like litter. In "Echo de Paris," March 29nd, 1937, a Belgian volunteer who escaped tells of the shameless molestation of twelve- and thirteen-year-old girls by the Reds. In the town of Granja de Torrehermosa, two bodies of murdered girls—one aged five and the other aged nine—were found. The medical examination discovered that the youngest's cause of death was being beaten on the ground or against a wall, while the nine-year-old was raped.[78]

The *New York Sun* cites a letter dated July 23rd, 1937, written by a student at the American Welsh University based on eyewitness accounts. The author of the letter informs us that the personal experiences of the interviewees are so terrible that they can only be conveyed in print with extreme discretion.

Crucifying their opponents and burning them alive was an everyday occurrence. Girls were stripped naked and gang-raped in the street. Pregnant women were slashed open with knives by savage mobs. There was a case when in place of a weathervane, a severed head of a girl was stuck on a car. Many times, people were simply thrown

---

[77] One of these checks, in particular, was shown at the anti-Communist exhibition of the Russian Fascist Union in Paris and Brussels in 1937.
[78] "The Truth about Spain," a speech of German Minister Dr. Goebbels at the congress of the National Socialist Workers' Party of Germany in Nuremberg in September, 1937.

into boilers and burned alive. Priests and nuns were tied together naked and led through the streets.[79]

Who was responsible for this? The Jewish "Marranos" who have retained their hatred of the Catholic Church and of national Spain since their forced baptism in the Middle Ages. Evidence of the malevolent role of the Marranos in Spanish Bolshevism is provided by *Der Stürmer* (No. 5 and No. 33 for 1936). Among them are the leaders of the Spanish troubles Del Rios, Maura, Zamorra, and others. It also notes the preparation of the Spanish Revolution by Lev Trotsky-Bronstein, who spent a long time preparing for the Spanish Revolution, lived in Spain and right next door to the famous Bela Kun, who came to the Spanish "proletariat" on the orders of the Comintern.[80] Not only *Der Stürmer*, but the Jews themselves acknowledge their authorship of the Spanish troubles, fanned and supported by Judaism around the world, and yet suppressed by the heroic army of General Franco:

"No Jew can and should remain indifferent to the Spanish war," said the Jewish newspaper *Haynt* in Warsaw. "Every Jew must fight on the side of the red republic. This is our republic."[81]

"I know for certain," Companys, the president of red Spain, announced, according to the same *Haynt*, "that the Jews who have come to us are now the most reliable and loyal of Republicans."

> *Riga, June 5th. Jewish circles in the Baltic States have received news that a Lithuanian Jew, Isaac Brauer, the son of a coal merchant in Kauna, has been appointed Deputy Minister of War in the new Valencian government.*
>
> *Brauer went to Spain eight years ago to study, intending to become a rabbi. During his stay there, he changed his mind, abandoned his studies, and gave himself up to politics. After becoming one of the most influential members of the Spanish Comintern, he is now called upon to represent the Communist Party in the new red government.*

Finally, the Jewish *Yudishe Review* in Carpatho-Russian Mukachevo published in its December 1937 issue No. 12 a pure Jewish boast by Kurt Ninzover with the headline "Jewish Heroes in the Spanish Civil War." It said, verbatim, "The young, enthusiastic Jews fought heroically."

"Jewish heroes," bewildered the *World Service*, where we borrow this message from. It sounds bizarre and comedic. The reader easily

---

[79] *World Service*, No. 17–18, November 15th, 1937.
[80] For more on Bela Kun and the Hungarian Communists, see Cécile Tormay's *The Outlaw's Diary*, reprinted by Antelope Hill Publishing in 2020. (Editor's note)
[81] *Haint*, March 14th, 1937, Warsaw.

has a slight doubt: *Jews*? *Heroes*? To get further into the truth, one reads on and finds the following list of young enthusiastic heroes: "Former Austrian Minister of War Julius Deutsch holds the rank of general, Egon Kisch is a brigade commissar, Kontorovich is a company commander." But we know all these gentlemen. They are not young at all. Deutsch and Kisch are well into their fifties! If they are inspired, it is only by the economic benefits they receive. They are not to be confused with heroes, but that they are Jews is true. The realest of Jews! And where did these young, enthusiastic heroes fight? Of course, both Deutsch and Kisch only occasionally saw hand grenades, bayonets, and flamethrowers.

They fought the defenseless population, releasing their satanic sadistic anger on the unfortunate women and children.

14. "The Most Devout Community in the World," or the Jews in Gibraltar

On Spanish soil, in the far south-western point of the Iberian Peninsula, lies one possession of the British, which holds the world's attention. Gibraltar is the first link in the grand chain that the British have encircled from southern Europe and Asia. This is the beginning of the skeleton of the British Empire, the first point of global power, followed by Suez, Aden, Singapore, Hong Kong. What can the Jews tell us about Gibraltar?

They will brag, albeit vaguely, but still quite clearly about the extent of their influence in this vital primary node in the western gate of the Mediterranean Sea and the Mediterranean world.

> A city with just one street.... Gibraltar has only one street—Main Street—which is noisy and very wide. A tall fire tower with the strongest reflectors in the world.
>
> This marine lantern shows the way for steamships passing by at night on the road between the two hemispheres of the world.
>
> Gibraltar is a city that in many ways has no equal. It is the busiest, most expensive, and most populous of cities. Any piece of unoccupied land was built up and crowded. You can't get seats in cafes and hotels. Even an Englishman finds it difficult to get into the city. To settle in Gibraltar, English citizens must obtain a special permit from the Gibraltar governor, for there is literally no place left to settle. No new homes can be built anymore, and only as many people are allowed in as leave there.

Many people want to settle in Gibraltar, it is a city of eternal progress and prosperity. There are virtually no unemployed, no crises, because the main consumers are sailors, who regularly receive their normal salary and easily spend money.

Beautiful Spanish dancers come there. Many of the cafes and bars along Main Street feature mostly all-female bands, singers, and dancers of all colors and races, singing in all languages, even in Hebrew.

In the famous "Universal" restaurant, a beautiful black-eyed girl was singing the famous Russian song "Volga, Volga" and dancing a Cossack dance in red boots when she suddenly started singing Jewish songs from various operettas, and the sailors sang along with her. She is a Jewish actress and singer in Riga. She used to sing on stage in Morocco, and from there was invited to Gibraltar.

Gibraltar's Jewish community has about 2,000 members, all devout Jews. It is perhaps the most devout community in the world. In this city of barracks, where the civilian population is minimal, it being either a Jewish holiday or the Sabbath, their presence is clearly felt. You notice this on Main Street, where the biggest shops are owned by Jews.

On Friday evening, when the sun sets behind the cliffs of Gibraltar, the shops on Main Street close and remain closed until Saturday evening, after the "gavdolo."[82]

"Shabbos" is felt very strongly in this fortress of a city. The sailors already know the customs of the Jewish inhabitants of Gibraltar and wait patiently for the first stars to appear in the Sabbath sky—the time when the Jewish merchants reopen their shops. The sailors then buy everything they need for Sunday.

Synagogues and houses of worship, of which there are many in Gibraltar, are always crowded, and they pray with enthusiasm the Sephardic way. All the worshippers sing along during the entire service.

Gibraltar is home mainly to Sephardic Jews who were resettled from the neighboring Morocco. There are also Jews who came here from England, and a couple of dozen Polish Jews who have already been in all parts of the world and finally reached Gibraltar, where they have already settled. These Polish Jews, mostly Galician Jews, set up their own "Hasidic Stack" houses of worship.

There are very rich Jewish merchants in Gibraltar who conduct international trade. The name Belisha is very popular

---

[82] A prayer that is read at the end of the Sabbath. (Translator's note)

there, the family of the former Jewish Minister of War Hore-Belisha. As Minister of War, Hore-Belisha often visited Gibraltar, stayed with his family, and went to pray at the great synagogue on the Sabbath. He was always called to the Torah (Shishi).

This small but very devout Jewish community is full of riches, and there is a universal solidarity for every Jew who goes there and asks for help.

The Jews there give generously to Eretz Israel, to various yeshivas, etc. Gibraltar does not use any other matzo during Passover, except for "shmuro-matzo," from the Palestinian matzo factory in the famous city of Safed. Not to mention the wine, which must only be exclusively Palestinian.

On weekdays, synagogues and houses of worship are transformed into *cheders,* where four hundred boys are taught.[83] Gibraltar even printed its own "siddur," which was compiled by their rabbi. This devout community has produced many sailors who currently serve in the English Navy. There are also several senior officers who have particularly distinguished themselves in various naval operations.

Gibraltar is now, of course, in a permanent state of martial law.

It is a possibility that Gibraltar will have to undergo large-scale naval battles in the future. But this city is so prepared that at the first signal of an enemy attack, the entire population will move to underground fortresses, where they can comfortably and normally withstand a siege for even a whole year without suffering the slightest lack of food and water. The most modern underground city has been built in the rocks of Gibraltar, which is capable of providing strong resistance against both land and sea attacks."[84]

This is how the Jews opened up about Gibraltar in 1940. Subsequently, they had to repent for this frankness. But, as they say, "what is written with a pen cannot be cut down with an ax."

However, should we move, reader, on to Italy?

---

[83] A traditional elementary school that teaches the fundamentals of Judaism and Hebrew. (Translator's note)
[84] *Jewish Life* No. 33, August 16th, 1940.

15. For Three Thousand Years Judas Tormented Italy

About three thousand years have passed since the first Jews settled under the sunny skies of the Apennines, first as merchants, and then forming the first Jewish community in Europe.

They did not attain Roman citizenship until the second century AD. However, then they managed to entangle the entire economy of the country with their financial tentacles and easily pass the "law on equality" in Roman institutions. But by using their usual methods on the people who had once sheltered them, the Jews soon awoke a terrible hatred against themselves.

> And it was not easy for the ancestors of the Italian Jews in ancient Rome, for although they lived quite tolerably financially, they did not feel in need of anything. They were engaged in trade, various crafts, and later even farmed and owned huge estates.[85]

And so the Jews themselves write. If the reader imagines Italy, where even now, after the grandiose irrigation works already under Mussolini, every piece of land suitable for cereal cultivation is valued above all, it will become clear that the Jews, who once had possession of the entire land in Ancient Rome, could not be tolerated.

"The surrounding Roman population," the Jewish historian frankly admits, "has repeatedly expressed its hostility to Jews." Nor was the hatred of the Jews confined to Ancient Rome: all the lands subject to the Romans did not tolerate the sons of the "God-cursed race," as the Jews were called by their contemporaries. The Jewish historian is now trying to present the persecution of the Jews as a result of some intrigue. "Roman writers and politicians spread various accusations against Jews and the Jewish creed throughout Italy and across the countries of the cultural world embracing all the lands of the Mediterranean Sea. There are various accusations against Jews and the Jewish faith," he writes. However, he also lets it slip by mentioning these "various accusations" directed against Jewry and their faith. What these charges were, he does not say. He doesn't speak because he doesn't dare to. It is undesirable for Jews to remind modern humanity of the nature of these accusations. It is undesirable, because everyone who reads them will see that, just as three thousand years ago, the accusations thrown at them still remain the same, and, therefore, they are thereby confirmed. But we'll leave the floor to Mr. Isser for further narration:

---

[85] *Jewish Life*, No. 28, 1940, article "Jews in Italy," M. Isser.

In the Middle Ages, Italian Jewry had a much easier life than their fellow brothers in other countries. The papal authority in Italy sought to attract as many Jewish souls as possible to the bosom of the Christian Church. The popes were convinced that sooner or later Jewry, especially Italian Jewry, would convert to Christianity. And their policy had only one goal: to open the eyes of the stubborn, rebellious Jewish people to the true faith as soon as possible. . . . In regard to this endeavor, the popes used cultural means: propaganda, and scientific and religious disputes. But when these means had no effect on the Jews, more drastic measures were applied, the purpose of which was to isolate Jews from their environment and break their stubbornness and self-confidence.

To achieve this goal, a number of church orders were issued towards Italian Jewry: Jews were forbidden to keep Christian servants, treat Christian patients, own estates, build new synagogues, etc. . . .

And all these ecclesiastical orders were not applied in everyday life in Italy, since Italian Jewry was under the protection of papal authority. In Italy, Jews were very rarely persecuted during this period of time. Jewish medics and major financial figures often occupied court seats in the princely courts of Italy. Pope Alexander III had the Jewish rabbi Iechel as Minister of Finance, the nephew of Reb Nosov, the author of the famous scientific work *Georukh* in the Middle Ages.

In the second half of the Middle Ages, Italian Jewry experienced its golden age. The Italian republics and cities became the centers of world trade and finance. The advent of the Renaissance and humanism brought Christianity and the Jewish intelligentsia closer together. A number of departments for the study of the Jewish discipline were established in Italian universities. *The cardinals studied Jewish law with Jewish scholars* [emphasis added by Isser]. Italian universities widely opened their doors to the world. Due to the admission of Jewish students to medical faculties, it was not long before Jews took a prominent and dominant position in the medical world of the age. The influence of Jewish doctors was so strong that a well-known Italian anatomist in his scientific work gave not only Latin names for individual parts of the human body, but also Jewish ones. The rector of the University of Leipzig in 1518 suggested that students study Hebrew, since "there are many valuable works on medicine in this language."

From Venice, the famous doctor Leon was sent to Moscow, who, by order of Grand Duke Ivan Vasilyevich in 1540, was executed for treating his son Grand Duke, unsuccessfully. The

Italian Renaissance also had a great influence on the spiritual life of Jews. Emmanuel of Rome, contemporary Dante introduced many secular motifs into the Hebraic literature of the time. Leon Ebro, the son of Yitzhak Arbarbanella, became known in Italian literature for his "Dialogues of Love." The Venetian Rebbe Yehuda-Leib Modena is the founder of Jewish philosophical thought. At the request of one of the English lords, he wrote a book in Italian for King Charles I, *On the Jewish Testaments*. Many Christians and even clergy came to listen to his sermons. One Sabbath a French prince was passing through Venice, and when he learned that the famous Reb Yehuda of Modena could be heard preaching, he went to the synagogue with his entire retinue.

The Jewish historian has blabbed enough. He said very little about the role of the Jews in the Middle Ages, but outlined the extent of the Jewish influence that decayed the entire medieval Italian life quite prominently. It is quite natural that these activities of the Jews could not but cause a reaction:

For Italian Jewry, the horrors of the Middle Ages came in the second half of the XVI century. Italian Jewry was the first victim of the Catholic reaction. At Rosh Hashanah in 1553, in Rome, Venice, Anchin, and Cremona, the Talmud and its commentaries were burned. The Marranos from Spain and Portugal who had found refuge in Italy were driven into ghettos, into the narrow streets on the other side of the Tiber River, and a high brick ghetto wall was erected around these streets. A large cross with sayings from the prophets was installed at the gates of the ghetto. Catholic monks made speeches in the synagogue every Saturday, holding a "Sefer Torah" in their hands and having a large gold cross on their chest. At first, the Roman community was sending deaf Jews as listeners to these sermons. But the monks found out about this trick of the Jews, and the papal authority ordered the mandatory presence of all Jews at these sermons. And Jews came to their synagogue to listen to the sermons of Catholic monks with their ears filled with wax.... The residence permit in Rome was renewed annually. On the first day of the carnival, the Jewish delegation had to appear in the Senate and, bowing to the senators, the head of the delegation presented a gift from the Jewish community—a bouquet of flowers with twenty *scudias* and a request to extend the right of residence of Jews in the Roman ghetto. One of the Jews presented a gift, and then one of the senators, touching the forehead of the Jews who had come, declared: "We will continue your right of residence for another year. And you must always know that we do this out of charity." Under such conditions, Italian Jewry lived until 1848, when Pope Pius IX ordered the destruction of the walls around the ghetto.

Where are these so-called "horrors of the Middle Ages" that the Jewish historian promised to show us?

Despite all his efforts, he could not find any evidence to prove that the legitimate protective measures of the papal authority and the Roman Senate involved any inhumane treatment of the Jews. However, the Jewish historian does not report some of the harsh measures to which some of the Jews of Italy were subjected during this time. He does not report that many Jews were burned at the stake for outrageous crimes against morality, nor does he say that many Jews were executed in the squares on the premises of egregious crimes. Reports that almost every year the Italian government executed Jews for acts against the state, especially for espionage in favor of one or another enemy of the Italian state, especially in favor of Turkey, which by that time had fallen under strong Jewish influence. On all this M. Isser prefers to remain silent, because by pointing out the punishments, he would have to at least touch on the crimes committed generally. But Jews do not talk about Jewish crimes or Jewish criminals. This is a "taboo"—forbidden!

From Judea's point of view, no crime against a "goy" constitutes a crime at all. But to justify some egregious act or to talk about the precepts found in the Talmud, they would similarly rather avoid bringing that up. For that reason, they have to keep quiet. In that case, let them remain silent, and we will get back to the testimony of M. Isser:

> The new Italy granted all rights to its Jewish citizens. King Victor Emmanuel of Italy, when meeting Dr. T. Herzl in 1904, said: "In my government, no distinction is made between a Jew and a Christian. Jews are given the right by law to achieve anything: in the army, in public service and in the diplomatic field. There are eighteen Jewish deputies in the Parliament, and almost every Cabinet has a Jewish minister. Now Luzzatti, and in the recent past, Generals Otolonga and Wallenberg."

Further into his writing, the classic Jewish arrogance breaks out in M. Isser in the most outrageous way possible: "And if this conversation," he writes, "would have happened ten years later, the King Victor Emmanuel would have noted with an even greater pride that the Jew, Luigi Luzatti, became the prime minister of the Italian government."

What the reign of Luzzatti and his fellow Jews did for Italy is well known to the whole world. The shame of the defeat at Caporetto, the inglorious end of the war in 1918, the poverty and hunger, the flow of the Communist movement. Fortunately, all this caused the act in self-defense of the newly awakened nation—the victorious emergence of fascism. And M. Isser sadly sums up the situation of Italian Jewry before fascism:

> Until a few years ago, there were about 70,000 Jews living throughout the Italian Empire: 40,000 in Italy, 26,000 in Libya, and 5,000 in the islands of Rhodes and Dodecanese. Jews in Italy lived mainly in big cities: 12,000 in Rome, 4,000 in Milan and about 3,000 in Turin and Florence. Jews played a prominent role in the country's trade and industry. There was also a significant number of Jews among professors, and a large number of Jews occupied the highest civil and military posts in the country.

The Jewish historian then admits that before fascism, Italy owes the shameless system in place of exploitation of the state and its people brought about by its rulers to all the Jews who stood at the heights of Italian life and created the defeat of the country. When from among the people the redemptive and swift reaction of fascism arose, then, according to the Jewish historian, "Italian Jewry took a lively part in the creation of fascist Italy." In other words, the Jews tried to get their hands on Fascism as well!

> Sarah Sorf was one of Mussolini's earliest and closest collaborators and the one who published a biography of the Duce for the first time. Jews took part in the "march of Rome," and held a number of senior positions ... in the Fascist Party [even there!].
> The late Chief Rabbi of Rome, Dr. A. Satcherdoti, was a member of the Fascist Party and an intimate friend of Mussolini. The colony of Italian Jews in Egypt, with its Italian-language schools, and the Jewish-founded rabbinical seminary in Rhodes, were both carriers of Italian culture and a major political factor in their local communities. The faithful followers of the new Italy were Jewish students who were warmly welcomed to Italian universities. And when Mussolini called on the people of Italy during the war with Abyssinia to sacrifice gold and other valuables on the altar of the fatherland, a Jewish student from Latvia was the first to help Mussolini in Milan, donating to the Italian state all of his meager inheritance—a silver cigarette case.

What cynicism! The whole world knows that it is precisely to the Jewish onslaught that Italy owes the brutal "economic sanctions" that were carried out during the Abyssinian campaign at the behest of England and Freemasonry through the Judeo-Masonic League of Nations! Everyone remembers the fact that the "king of kings" Haile Selassie was fully supported by world Jewry, and this played a role in delaying the Abyssinian campaign.

However, the Jews are accustomed to always aid both sides of the war. They earn money in the war by mocking the naive "goyim" who see such "allies" as their friends during the war.

But the Jews did try to do their work with all their might in Fascist Italy also because they had to prevent an alliance between the fraternal movements of Italian Fascism and German National Socialism. During the meeting in Brenner over the issue regarding the "Austrian inheritance"—the solution to the remains of the old Habsburg state—the Jews still hoped to bump the heads of the new Italy and the new Germany against each other.[86]

But the leaders of fascism chose the right and only right path: the unity of the fascist countries in the struggle for the happiness of their peoples. And, when finishing the history of Italian Jewry, the Jewish historian was melancholically forced to write:

"This was the case in the recent past. At present, there is a racial law in Italy: Jews are expelled from the army, from various positions, from the liberal professions, from universities, etc."[87]

Unfortunately, the purge was insufficient and delayed—the Jews had poisoned the Italian public to such an extent that it did not survive the military tests in 1943. Jewish influence was also found in the Supreme Council of the National Fascist Party, in the family of King Victor Emmanuel. And the king himself, in the tragic last days of Italy, ended up being on the side of world Jewry.

16. Jews in Switzerland

In Switzerland, as in other countries, Jews in the Middle Ages preferred to engage in medicine and usury. In 1348 and 1349, a wave of persecution of Jews swept through Switzerland. Bern expelled its Jews in 1427, permanently, as it was said at the time. By the time of the Reformation, the Jews had completely disappeared from the Swiss cities. The French Revolution improved the situation of Jews in

---

[86] Several territorial disputes that took place since the War of the Austrian Succession and still continued to the days of Hitler and Mussolini. (Translator's note)

[87] In the same place (*Jewish Life*, No. 28, 1940, "Jews in Italy," M. Isser). (Translator's note)

Switzerland as well as everywhere else. In 1798, Jews were granted civil equality and freedom in Switzerland. Under the pressure of France, England, and the United States, which concluded trade agreements with Switzerland, the situation of Jews in Switzerland steadily improved during the second half of the nineteenth century. This is evidenced by the *Historical and Biographical Dictionary of Switzerland*, compiled by M. Gede and G. Gurler, the directors of the National Library and Archives in Bern, in which the *World Service* is referenced.

In the twentieth century, Switzerland became the formal center of European Jewry. Zionist congresses gather in Bern and Zurich, all kinds of Herzls, as well as Lenins and Trotskys. In the immediate vicinity of the Jewish Convention Bureau, in 1915, in the village of Zimmerwald, the nucleus of the future Third Communist International is established. The future capital of the League of Nations, Geneva, becomes a transfer station on the Jewish communication highway composed of New York, London, and Red Moscow.

17. Jewish Boasts Over Conquered Germany

Germany, which we are now getting closer to in our journey through Switzerland, is now in the vanguard of the global anti-Jewish liberation movement. But no more than twelve or fifteen years ago the situation in Germany was very different. There is a reason why you should get acquainted with it, because then the solemn colors of the Jewish victory will fade, and the reader will see that even from the bottom of the deepest abyss you can climb to the top of the highest mountain. Yes, the liberation of Germany serves as a clear proof of the temporality of Jewish rule for every viable nation that is able to select strong leaders, the national spirit and its bearer—a strong elite that draws the masses of the people behind it.

For perhaps nowhere in the world has Jewish domination been so strong, dense, and comprehensive in recent times after decades of gradual Judaization as it was in Weimar Germany.

The Jews themselves boasted grandly and serenely:

"No amount of anti-Semitic efforts will stop the growing power of German Jewry," declared Zionist activist M. Grossman in the pages of the Berlin magazine *Dawn* in 1929. "It is almost impossible to find a single aspect of German life in which Jews do not take a more than prominent and dominant part," he says.

> Most of these thriving enterprises, in which Jews were the initiators, managers, or financiers, by their very nature are constantly in the public eye: in the world of politics, literature, theater, film, etc.

Literature is the area in which Jews are most strongly represented, but it is far from the only area of Jewish intellectual activity. For instance, in theater, you will meet Jewish directors, actors, singers and dancers at every turn.

Director Max Reinhard is a theater innovator and trendsetter. His three Berlin theaters are recognized as the peak of contemporary dramatic art. Three conductors of the State Opera—Bruno Walter, Erich Kliver and Otto Klemperer—are the favorites of the entire musical world.

Four famous artists: Elisabeth Bernger, a tragic actress who Berlin goes crazy with in *Joan of Arc*. Gretta Mostlame, a twenty-four-year-old character actress. Ilsa Vois, a cabaret star and impersonator. Fritz Massari is a diva of musical comedy and a favorite of both German capitals, Berlin, and Vienna. They all have something in common, they're all Jewish.

The most prominent drama artists of modern Germany, Siegfried Arnault, Fritz Koertner, Max Pallenberg, Ernst Deitsch, are also all Jews.

We'll go over editorial offices, bookstores, theaters, the Reichstag, and the offices of major humanitarian movements in Berlin, Frankfurt, and Munich. Look at the books displayed in the windows and the posters displayed at the intersections. You will be surprised to see how many well-known faces and names that you thought were purely Aryan belong to Jews.

Take the press with its six thousand newspapers. The owners of two of the largest publishing houses in the German capital, the firms of Rudolf Mosse and Ultstein, are Jews. Two world-renowned editors: Theodor Wolf of the *Berliner Tageblatt* and Georg Bernhard of the *Fossische Zeitung* are also Jewish. Then there is the famous *Frankfurter Zeitung* and dozens of weekly and monthly magazines that set the tone in the German public square. Numerous publications of the pacifist movement (of course!) and human rights leagues are also produced by Jews, who are the most active champions of peace and freedom in Germany.[88]

"The Jewish bard has walked through only a small part of the Jewish possessions in Germany," notes the magazine of Russian monarchists, showing the confession of the Jewish *Dawn* I have just quoted.

If he wanted to, he could just as much show that almost all German trade and banking, and through the banking industry and agriculture, is at the mercy of the Jews. He could also

---

[88] *Dawn*, No. 33, 1925, Berlin.

please the Jewish hearts of his readers by pointing out that the most expensive restaurants, hotels, resorts and bars are occupied not by Germans, but almost entirely by German and foreign Jews. That Jews sit in first-class carriages and in the front rows of theaters and concerts. That most of the best houses in German cities belong to Jews, and that Jews occupy the most luxurious apartments in Germany.[89]

All of this happened recently, like a dire nightmare. "Germany, wake up!"—a fire call sounded, being picked up by individual units, then tens, hundreds, thousands, millions, the whole then awakened, united and as an organized nation. Germany has finally awakened. At last, it escaped ... and became free. And greater than ever before! What an inspiring example for others in deep slumber and in slavery.

The ardent descriptions of an enthusiastic Zionist confirm the dry data of German functional statistics published after Hitler came to power in a small pamphlet, "What the Numbers Say about Jews." Just a few days after the November Revolution of 1918, the Austrian Jew and Minister of War Deutsch wrote: "Now we Jews are at the top, at the very top. Now we are the masters. Our fiery dreams are finally fulfilled!"

Indeed, the members of the first revolutionary government of Germany were Jews: Haase, Kautsky, F. Kohn, Hertzfeld, Schiffer, Bernstein, Preis, Kahen, Dr. Freund, Loewald, and others. At the state conference of November 25th, 1918, the individual provinces were represented by Jews: Prussia (Hirsch, Haase, Herzfeld); Bavaria (Kurt Eisner); Saxony (Lipinski, Gradnauer); Wurtemberg (Gaiman); Baden (Haau); Austria (Herman).

The army represented by Ludendorff was also tried by Jews Kohn, Katzenstein, Sinzheimer. From 1918 until the National Revolution, other Jews who held senior positions in Prussia included: Rosenfeld (Justice); Simon (Finance); Hirsch (Internal Affairs); Brown (agriculture); Gerlach and Furtan (education); Patan (press affairs); Wurm (food industry).

In the Bavarian government sat: Kurt Eisner (Minister-President); Jaffa (Minister of Finance); Fechenbach (Minister of Education).

Later Ministers of State were: Dr. Dernburg, Dr. David Landberg, Dr. Hilferding.

Eighty percent of all the important posts in the state, provinces, and communities were taken over by Jews, this dispassionate statistic states, drawing a truly hopeless enslavement.

The Jewish locusts have entangled the German people hand and foot. As of May 16th, 1925, out of 1,000 people in Prussia who were

---

[89] *The Double-headed Eagle*, No. 37, 1930, Paris.

earning their living in one of the three following fields, this was the breakdown of Germans compared to Jews in various positions[90]:

		Senior Positions	Mid-Level Positions	Workers/ Low-Level Employees	Helping Family Members
Industry	Germans	51.4	46.5	305.3	6.2
	Jews	107.5	77.8	59.7	13.4
Trade And Transport Routes	Germans	37.8	71.6	49.7	12.0
	Jews	314.9	207.8	11.6	53.6
Public Administrations, Justice, and Liberal Professions	Germans	5.5	37.1	5.8	0.1
	Jews	7.8	29.8	1.7	0.1

The chief of the Berlin criminal police force for a long time was a certain Jew Weiss, who openly patronized Jewish criminals and severely punished Germans for the smallest offenses. Having "a lot on his plate" in the fight against the criminal element, Weiss took on political "criminals." Who he meant by the latter will be clear by his own words, which he said after being transferred from the post of chief of the political police to the high post of police president of the German capital:

"In the span of the more than four years that I served as the head of the so-called political police, I often took action mainly against right-wing and anti-Semitic groups," he told reporters.[91]

From these little references, it is clear that the Jews left only menial labor to the Germans, taking over the organization and leadership in all branches of life, and even took over the police. Notwithstanding, the German people were liberated.

God willing, other nations will also be freed!

18. Jews in the Glorious Belgian Police

At the very least, Belgium, for example, is already free. And now it looks back with horror at the recent past. But still can't find the will to start a new life.

"Judaizers"—this is what the chairman of the Belgian anti-Semitic league "Protection of the People" Lambricht called those who, in one way or another, out of a weak will or due to sheer ignorance, are still supporting the Jews, B. L. Solonevich said in Berlin's *New World* on

---

[90] "What the numbers say about Jews." From official German Statistics, Shanghai 1934.
[91] *Jewish Life*, No. 1–2, 1936.

April 6th, 1941. Lambricht delivered a speech to a vast audience focused on the Jewish question and Jewish "occult forces." For Russian listeners, references from the Talmud or naming the characteristics of Jewry were not new. All that was new was the latest data on Jews in Belgium and their dominance since 1919.

It is interesting to note that, as it turns out, the directorate of police of Surtay was completely under the influence of Jews and supported them very persistently. The head of the Department for Combating Unemployment was a Jew. He also chaired the committee for the admission of refugees. One can imagine the kind of "objectivity" that prevailed there.

Although this report is a first sign of success, it is impossible not to admit that almost nothing is being done in the fight against Jewish dominance in Belgium!

19. The Dutch "Asylum for the Persecuted"

"Holland has always been known to the world as a refuge for the persecuted," notes the *Jewish Observer*.

Since the sixteenth century, Holland cordially held tens of thousands of Spanish-Portuguese Marranos fleeing the Inquisition. In the seventeenth century, Holland sheltered tens of thousands of Polish Jews who were forcibly expelled from their homes by Khmelnitsky's pogrom gangs. And since 1933, before our very eyes, a flood of refugees from Germany has rushed to Holland.

Dutch Jews have prospered much more in the last four hundred years than their brothers in other European countries. Ever since 1651, when Dutch Jews were recognized as citizens, they have occupied a leading place in the economic life of the state, and later on, from 1797 onwards, in political and administrative life. Spanish and Portuguese Jews with great commercial knowledge and connections greatly contributed to the development and consolidation of Dutch-Flemish maritime trade, which had to withstand heavy competition and struggle against the growing economic power of England. Dutch Jews played a prominent role in the East India Campaign, which effectively won them the Dutch colonies in the East. It was the same in America after the conquest of Suriname (Dutch Guiana). In 1664, Dutch Jews and a group of exiled Jews established a large sugar plantation in the new colony called Yond-Dori, which had its own administrative center in the Jewish village of Yond-Dori with its own Jewish police. This land still belongs to the Jews of the community in Paramaribo, the main metropolis of Dutch Guiana.

Dutch Jewry is represented in all professions. You can witness in Holland Jewish politicians, judges, professors, bankers, directors of large trading firms, merchants, high- and low-level municipal officials. On the streets of The Hague and Amsterdam, you often run into Jewish flower sellers and so on.

Spanish and Portuguese Marranos planted in their newest homeland a Judeo-Spanish tradition—a deep love for secular culture. Since the sixteenth century, there have been cultural threads between Dutch Jews and the non-Jewish world around them.

It is enough to mention names such as Spinoza and Uriel da Acosta. It is enough to mention Rembrandt and his versatile artistic attitude towards Amsterdam's Jews.

The long-term synthesis of Jewish and general education rendered unnecessary for Dutch Jewry the continuation of an internal struggle, the duality of the soul between Jewry and humanity, which was reflected in the life of two whole generations in Eastern Europe. The best proof of the national-religious feeling of Dutch Jewry is the fact that all attempts to transfer the religious movement to Holland failed.

Sephardic synagogues have had the same structure since the sixteenth century. Dutch Zionists have always taken an active and distinctive position in the world Zionist movement. Under the leadership of Jacobus Kahn, they were among the most energetic fighters for political Zionism in the post-Herzl period. At the same time, they provided many ideas and tools that are valuable for the practical construction of Eretz Israel. During the last World War, the Central Office of the Jewish People's Fund was located in The Hague under the leadership of Nehemiah de Lieve. Among the most prominent economic figures in Palestine, the recently deceased Van Friesland is worth noting. A descendant of immigrants from the Netherlands, the former director of the Anglo-Palestinian bank, S. Goofaen—the Dutch consul in Tel Aviv.

There are very cordial relations between Dutch Jews and their queen [so they remark indeed: "THEIR!"]. The queen is always extremely interested in the Jewish communities and their charitable institutions. She is a frequent guest at Amsterdam's Moishe-Zekeinim and the Home of Jewish Invalids. Dutch monarchs and ministers have always been loyal and kind to their Jewish fellow citizens [not loyal subjects, but on the contrary monarchs and ministers!]. Since the appearance of the first Jews in Holland, they were treated with the greatest of hospitality and were immediately given equal rights.

The current Dutch queen Wilhelmina I remained true to the tradition of her ancestors [that's why she lost her crown!]. In our time, when all around is raging anti-Semitism and the terrible persecution of the Jews, the Dutch queen showed so much warmth and affection to their Jewish citizens [so much so that alongside with them, she left the Netherlands]. The old tradition of faith and freedom and the denial of any racial distinctions between groups is something the Dutch queen kept during all the forty years that she has governed the country, in recent years especially. She has always strongly condemned anti-Semitism.

In the field of philanthropy for Jewish citizens, the Dutch queen also remained true to the tradition of her parents and the dynasty. She frequently donated, and quite heavily, to various Jewish causes: hospitals, orphanages, homes for the elderly, and other Jewish philanthropic institutions.

The Jewish population of Holland thanked the Dutch people and country by devoting all their energy and resources to the development of trade and industry, and contributed to the transformation of Holland into an important commercial maritime center.

Everything written in this Jewish article (strange as it may seem!) is absolutely true. But even when telling the truth, the Jews can't help but lie, hide something, or distort something.

So, this time, upon giving a true picture of their life free of trouble in the country they have enslaved, they did not report the hatred that has long been observed in this country towards them. Where, one wonders, did this hatred come from then? Why would the Dutch hate their "benefactors"?

"Until very recently, Jewish influence was a monopoly in our country," says Mussert, the leader of the Dutch National Socialists.

The Jews systematically undressed all the Dutch in the most merciless way, using their usurious methods. Not only have they taken over all the old Dutch banks, but they have taken over almost all our historical firms, taking advantage of the new joint–stock law, and most importantly, they have recently taken over almost all agriculture, turning our farmers into farmhands. In order to make the Jewish takeover of our country transparent, I will give exclusively raw figures: in 1939, out of 24,800 more or less large enterprises, 22,320 were either in the hands of Jews or completely dependent on them.

The picture Mussert has drawn is complete if we add that Queen Wilhelmina, about whom the Jewish magazine speaks so laudably, has long been involved as a partner in many Jewish enterprises.

"If the queen wanted to get out of the Jewish Kabbalah," wrote the German Explorer V. Frank before the queen even fled to England,

> she would instantly lose all the property of her entire dynasty accumulated over three hundred years, especially over the past decade after the start of heavy usage Dutch colonies. Which was largely owned by the Royal House until 1911, and since that time, it has gradually been incorporating more and more Jewish capital.

How did it happen for the queen of the Netherlands, one of the richest queens in the world, to become so dependent on Jews?

It turns out to be quite simple. As soon as the queen approved a new industrial plan for the development of her colonies, she immediately needed huge funds. Then she had to invest most of her free capital in the business. When the requirements for new appropriations began to grow with the development of enterprises, only one path seemed possible—the path of loans. But it was also impossible to get loans constantly. Loans must be repaid with interest, and repaid on time. There was no money for all this. Only one option remained. This course was immediately suggested by the Amsterdam bankers, who became the queen's partners in all her colonial and other endeavors.

But who so "successfully" dragged the unfortunate queen into such a confusing mix?

The most interesting thing is that the initial financial plan for the development of the Dutch East Indies was drawn up by none other than the adviser to the Royal Palace and an honorary member of the committee of the Ministry of Finance of the Netherlands, Abraham Levi, V. Frank reports.

> This Levi calculated strategically that the sixty million guilders that the queen had as spare funds would be enough for the entire plan. But someone managed to turn the plan around so that three years later they had to send another twenty-one million guilders to the South Pacific to assist some "very profitable additional enterprises." And these enterprises, two years later, made it "absolutely necessary" to open other enterprises with the same colossal allocations. And, as a result, Koroleva found herself entangled from head to toe in the Jewish financial network.

Of course, due to the entry of Jewish capital as an associate of the queen in the East Indian enterprises, a mass of Jews flocked to the Dutch Asian possessions. Just as in the metropolis, they manage to capture all the heights of life, not allowing the Dutch to come to their senses. More and more often we hear about how the richest Dutch firms in Java and Sumatra passed into the hands of Jews.

The same pattern is observed in other Dutch colonies. In order not to return to the ill-fated Dutch, we will give here a reference from a Jewish magazine about how Jews live in the Dutch West Indies.

> Among all the colonization proposals currently in question, Suriname is the only West Indian colony to have had a rich Jewish past. To this day, it still contains the richest Jewish properties, such as sugar plantations, oil springs, etc., which belong partly to the small Jewish population that still lives in this colony, as well as to well-known Dutch-Jewish families. There was a time when there was a large Jewish community in Suriname that flourished and grew, and served as a role model for the indigenous population.
>
> This was several centuries ago, when some of the Portuguese Jews who migrated to Holland later moved to Suriname, and contributed their share of cultural development to this country, itself rich in natural resources.
>
> The great commercial talent and export connections that the Portuguese Jews brought with them to this country not only enriched the local population, but also were beneficial for their native country—Holland.
>
> The Jews of Suriname lived their own Jewish life and had an autonomous community for themselves, which they founded in those days and which still exists today. There is also a huge, beautiful synagogue, which celebrated its bicentennial anniversary last year.
>
> In the capital of this country, Paramaribo, there is a separate section called "Jewish savanga," i.e., "Jewish quarter," which still exists to this day, and reflects the entire spiritual Jewish life of the then community of Portuguese Jews. In this "Jewish quarter" there are synagogues, baths, schools, and a cemetery of the famous Jewish-Portuguese faces of those distant times that are still buried there."[92]

Where did the Jews of Suriname go for several centuries, the Jewish author does not say. But it is clear from his words that, following the previous period, Jews are now again filling the Dutch colony. And it is

---

[92] *Jewish Life* No. 20, 1939, article by Goldreyzin.

understandable: they are driven away from Europe, so they rush wherever they can. The Jews can do very well in the Dutch colonies, which so far recognize the power of Queen Wilhelmina's pro-Judeo government, which has fled to London.

20. "Great Jews" in a Small Denmark

Denmark. . . . Alas, the "eternal wanderers of the Talmud" did not leave her without their favorable attention.

"Great Jews in Little Denmark" is the pretentious and arrogant title of an article in a Jewish magazine. These great Jews are: Georg Brandes, Carl Eduard Brandes, Mendel Levi Nathanson, Henry Nathanson, Moritz Melchior, Isaac Glinstadt, Meir Goldschmidt, Jacobson, a whole bunch of Henricuses.[93] Journalists, editors of major newspapers, parliamentarians, financiers. . . .

One of them, with the help of little Denmark, it turns out, dared to put pressure on Great Russia. That man, Moses Melchior, according to the Jewish magazine, was a frequent guest at the royal palace. Thanks to his efforts before Frederick VIII, he allegedly influenced his nephew, Tsar Nicholas II, so that the Jewish pogroms would cease, which were expected in 1907, so the Jews write. And it is then when they reveal the secret of Moses' possible influence on the Danish king: Moisha Melchior's brother, a member of the Upper House, a big financier, also founded a "private bank that had branches all over the country"

The boastful Jewish author cannot resist the temptation to add that this Melchior was supposedly very friendly with Hans Christian Andersen, who even lived in his house and died there. Even the fairy tales, cute children's tales, they wish to take away for themselves. Even into this magical land, the foul Jewish spirit is headed to poison all living things and stain all that is pure.

But let's give a chance to the Jewish source. Let the Jews tell us again about their life in Denmark:

> Not only Germany, but also little Denmark can serve as an example of how much the Jewish mind and genius can flourish and show everyone their miracles when it is not hindered by legal distinctions made between a Jew and a non-Jew.
>
> It is simply amazing that such a small group of Jews has produced so many great people in all fields, art, literature, science and finance, as we see in the country of King Christian H.

---

[93] Jacobus Henricus Kann was a Dutch Jewish banker and partner of the Lissa & Kann banking house. He was among the main leaders of the early Zionist Movement. (Translator's note)

A little more than 125 years have passed since Jews achieved full civil rights in Denmark, and already you can name a whole list of exceptionally famous Jews who are the pride of the entire country.

Georg Brandes, a Danish-Jewish critic, made his country's name famous all over the world, in no lesser way than the Danish fairy tale author Hans Christian Andersen. From Jewish parents, with the real Jewish name Con Georg, he was born in Copenhagen. However, his adopted name Brandes did not free him from Jewishness and, of course, from his Jewish way of thinking. One of his famous works, "The Main Currents of Nineteenth-Century European Literature," caused a storm against him as a Jew. It was believed that because of Brandes, Jews could be suspected of hatred of Christians, and he had to leave Denmark for a while and live in exile. His attitude towards Jewry was representative of the character of his worldview. For Brandes, Jewishness was just a religion. His old friends in Copenhagen tell us that Pepper Smolensky, with whom he became close friends while in Vienna, made Brandes a complete Jew and a semi-Zionist. Brandes even became an employee in the "Hashacher of Smolenskin," in which he published a story in the *Hasidic Life* in Galicia.

He had always been a member of the Copenhagen Jewish community, and thus his Jewish identity was formally recognized. Later, in 1910, he left the community due to what the community did to the then chief rabbi of Denmark, Dr. Levinstein, whom it dismissed and gave a large compensation sum. The incident between the congregation and the rabbi occurred because Dr. Levinstein did not want to recognize mixed marriages.

This case indicates that Brandes sided with the rabbi and also believed that mixed marriages should not be recognized. This case, by the way, is also very characteristic of the demands that were made thirty years ago to the spiritual leaders of the Jewish community.

G. Brandes, especially in the last years of his life, showed a lot of sympathy for Zionism. He also showed a fatherly attitude towards the Eastern European Jews who settled in Denmark. . . . Georg Brandes once said: "Hatred of Jews stems from two things: from the number of Jews in the country and from their influence. Since the number of Jews in Denmark is small and they do not have power, anti-Semitism is still nonexistent here. Music is the only international language, and those who work with it are not hindered by any national obstacles." There is no grave for Brandes, as according to his will, his body was burned in the crematorium after his death. But his works on Lassalle and Disraeli, Shakespeare and Goethe, Michelangelo and Voltaire, and Julius Caesar have remained masterpieces of world literature. And Danes, like Jews, remember his name with great pride. Georg's brother, Karl Eduard Brandes, was the founder of the largest and most popular Danish newspaper, *Politikan*. He was also at various times a member of both houses of the Danish Parliament (Folketing and Landsting) and even served as the Minister of Finance in the Kingdom of Denmark.

Another Jew also had great achievements in Danish journalism. He was Mendel Levi Nathanson, a representative of the famous Danish surname Nathanson, which gave rise to many great people. He was for a long time the editor of the largest trade newspaper, *Berlingske Tirende*, which he turned from a small leaflet into a very large newspaper. He is rightly called the "father of Danish journalism" in Denmark.

The recently deceased Henry Nathanson was a famous playwright and director at the Royal Theater in Copenhagen. He also wrote on Jewish themes, and the staging of his drama *Beyond the Wall* about Jewish life in the ghetto prepared him a place among those immortalized. The Melchior family name is no less famous for its talented children. One of them, Moritz Melchior, was a member of the upper house (Landsting) and a great financier. He was the first Jew in the State Chamber of Commerce, and founded a "private bank" with branches all over the country. Moritz Melchior was also for many years chairman of the Jewish community in Copenhagen and was a generous supporter of artists and scholars. He was very friendly with Hans Christian Andersen (who even lived in his house and died there as already mentioned).

His brother, Moses Melchior, was a great philanthropist and a frequent visitor to the royal palace. M. Melchior created workers' colonies in Copenhagen and there is even a monument dedicated to him at the entrance.

In the Danish Trade and Shipping Museum, located in Hamlet's Castle Kronborg in the city of Helnsberg, a huge portrait that occupies the entire wall stands out. An energetic face stares at you, you can recognize it as a Jew. This is Isaac Glanstadt, a big investment banker. He also held the honorary position of chairman of the Jewish community. He was one of the greatest minds in the country. The old Sephardic surname Henricus has also paid its own tribute to Danish culture. From said family these individuals are known:

Pini-Voldemar Henrikus, a conductor and composer; Maria Henricus, famous Danish artist; Nathan Reuben Henricus, another famous artist; Robert Henricus, a composer; Solomon Reuben Henricus, a physicist.

In a quiet and beautiful location of the Danish capital, on a street located on the edge of a wide Frederick Park, among trees and flowers stand the busts of many honored personalities, many of them in fact Jewish.

It is here where the name "Meir Goldschmidt" is engraved in one of the tombstones. A politician and writer, his first novel is called *The Jew*. But even in his later works, he did not fail in using Hebrew: *Avremel the Nightingale*, *Reb Elizer*, *Homeless*, and many works in Danish about Jewish themes. Meir Goldschmidt is considered one of the Danish classics and is still very widely read by the public.

Until recently, the only Danish university in Copenhagen, which has a long and illustrious history, had a Jewish rector, Carl Julius Solomonson. Of course, there was no shortage of famous professors and scientists, the name of the Jewish naturalist and physician Ludwig Jacobson is one that stands out.

The Jacobson family is also generally well known. It has produced great art collectors and patrons.

Carl Jacobson founded the world-famous Copenhagen sculpture museum "Glipstek" and bequeathed all the profits of his company for the maintenance of the museum and for the acquisition of new objects. (The museum is also called "Ny Carlsberg Glyptotek.")

Carl Jacobson also presented the Danish government with a beautiful villa with a park on the condition that one of Denmark's most distinguished people should always have an honorary apartment in it. Now a famous philosopher lives there. Jacobson presented the city of Copenhagen with other products.

In the center of Copenhagen, on the wide, amazingly beautiful City Hall Square with its beautiful City Hall building, there is a statue fifty feet tall. These are two people in ancient Danish robes with old national instruments (pipes "Lur") in their hands. These trumpeters were created by none other than the Danish Jewish sculptor Siegfried Wagner. Wagner visited Eretz Israel a few years ago, from whence he returned inspired. He creates sculptures on Jewish themes ("At the walls of Jericho" and others). A famous doctor and philanthropist was Ludvigisrael Brandes, author of many medical works: he was a professor at the University of Copenhagen and chief physician of the city hospital. He also founded a large "Moschen

Zneikin" and unions for the protection of children. The name of the Jewish artist Balin is also widely known.

The list of great Jews on Danish soil is far from complete. One could keep naming them endlessly in all fields. But it is more than enough to see what the Jewish mind and genius has created in little Denmark, to see the enormous Jewish contribution to Danish science, art, and economy.

The number of Jews in Denmark is small. But everywhere you look you find a Jew: a professor, an artist, a conductor, a director, a sculptor, a composer, a musician, a doctor, a writer, a researcher.

And this Jew, without an impediment to his rights and opportunities, creates and brings rich gifts to Danish and world culture.[94]

"It is simply breathtaking that such a small group of Jews has produced so many great people in all fields of art, literature, science, and finance!" the Jewish author wonders (hypocritically, of course). But who can do all these listed professions? In order to learn music, you need funds. Moreover, they are needed in finance.

"The first generation of Jews who settled in Denmark," Christian Hoffmann reports in an article on Jewish influence in northern Europe,

> were all moneylenders. The sheer amount of funds these families were able to provide for their youth in order to pursue an art career. For these "prodigies," it was easy to achieve fame.
>
> They occupied the pages of the most influential newspapers and magazines at their disposal. For the publication of the "literary works" of Jewish poets and writers, special publishing houses were created or Danish publishing houses that were ruined by their moneylender fathers were bought up for next to nothing.

In short, the flip side of the coin is the same here as in other countries. Therefore, it is not safe for Jews to brag about their "cultural achievements," because behind these "successes" lies a sea of tears shed because of them; the ruin, misery, hunger, and shame of the used "goyim."

---

[94] *Jewish Life* of August 23rd, 1940, No. 24.

21. Jews in Sweden and Norway

Fjords, snow, ice, and wind! The all-consuming world-spiders crawled here, to Scandinavia and settled down quite firmly. At least, the same Jewish source, the brazen *Jewish Life*, tells:

> Among the Scandinavian countries, Sweden has the largest Jewish population. Up to 150,000 Jews live in the Swedish capital, Stockholm, while a significant proportion of Jews live in another large Swedish city, Gothenburg. The rest are scattered in various other cities across Sweden.
> Jews began to move to Sweden under King Gustav III (in 1771). The first among them to emigrate, named Abram-Aron Brody, wrote his notes in Swedish. This diary is in the Royal Library of Stockholm. Despite the insignificant percentage of the Jewish population in Sweden, they occupy a prominent place in the country's trade and industry. Most of the jewelry retail companies are in the hands of Jews. Similarly, in the leather industry and the manufacture of ready-made dresses, Jews occupy the first place. Even the Jews who moved to Sweden not so long ago settled down to various kinds of affairs quite satisfactorily. Most of the Jews who have recently arrived in the country practice small-scale trade while the rest occupy other professions.
> And in the political life of the country, Jews occupy a prominent place. There are Jews holding from the highest to the lowest of public positions. There are also several dozen prominent Jewish journalists who have become so assimilated that they themselves do not know nor wish to know of their Jewish identity. The only anti-Semitic newspaper in the country almost daily reminds of the Jewish origin of one or another prominent person in the country, and it very often includes native Swedes in this list just because they are socialists or liberals. This newspaper publishes a special column called "Alarm Clock," which exclusively deals with the disclosure of trading firms owned by Jews and trading under an anonymous name. But this anti-Semitic newspaper agitation has no effect on the masses.
> The second largest Jewish community in Sweden is located in Gothenburg, which has the busiest steamship connection point with Libava. Emigrants from Libava arrived in this city by small steamboats and boarded the large overseas steamboats in Gothenburg, but some of the emigrants remained in

Gothenburg. Those who stayed in Gothenburg gradually settled down and called their relatives from Russia. Thus, within a short time, a community consisting of Eastern European (Russian and Polish) Jews was created.

In each of the Swedish cities inhabited by Jews, there is a synagogue and all the other communal institutions. The leadership of the Jewish community in Sweden is composed mostly of Eastern European Jews.

The Jewish community in another Swedish town, however, Lunda, is an exception in all of Sweden. The whole community consists of Polish-Russian Jews, and the Jews of this community lead a lifestyle similar to the one they had before in the towns of Russia. This community has a "mikveh," a synagogue, a "beis midrash," and it imports brides, calendars, prayer books, Reb Meir-Baal-nesa mugs and all other items related to Jewry to this town to then distribute to other Swedish cities. It should be noted that brides from Lunda enjoy a certain positive reputation in Sweden. . . .

The Jews of this city have peddling as their trade, and they carry their goods to peasant farms scattered throughout the country, whose owners welcome them kindly. In this community, the whole week passes in silence and tranquility. It is only on Saturday that the heads of families return to their "penates," the synagogue is filled to maximum capacity with a dressed-up audience, and everyone indulges in conversations on topics of concern to everyone.[95]

Lund is a big university city. It is located in the south of Sweden, not far from Germany. On one occasion several anti-Semitic students tried throwing attacks against their Jewish colleagues. Their venture however was not marked with success.

Swedish Jewry provided considerable material aid to German Jewry, with many of the German Jews even finding refuge and shelter in Sweden, thanks to the efforts of local Jewry.

It is crucial to note the vigorous activity and the name of chief rabbi Dr. Ehrenpreiz, a well-know. Jewish scientist familiar to all Jewry and in all of Sweden. He is the spiritual leader of Jewry and occupies a prominent place in Swedish literature, and Swedish critics speak of him as the most brilliant stylist of the Swedish language.

---

[95] In Roman mythology di penates or penates were protective deities of the household storehouse. Subsequently, they became household gods providing protection for the entire households, or even the entire state. (Translator's note)

Aside from his original works, he has also translated many of the best works of Jewish writers, both from Hebrew and Yiddish, into Swedish."

This is a candid account of his "achievements" in Sweden by a Jewish source. Pay attention to this candor:

In the political life of the country, Jews occupy a prominent place. There are Jews who hold from the highest to the lowest of government positions. There are also several dozen prominent Jewish journalists. The only anti-Semitic newspaper keeps reminding us of the Jewish origin of different faces across the country [here Jews fall into an understatement: even we, far from Sweden, know about the existence of at least three anti-Semitic newspapers there]. This newspaper publishes a special segment called "Alarm Clock," which exclusively deals with the disclosure of Jewish trading firms that trade under anonymous names.

This is a favorite Jewish protective shade! Pay attention, for everyone wishes to seriously and practically address the Jewish Question in a modest but real scale of the city or province where they live.

Norway obviously had a similar, if not worse situation. For at least, after the occupation of Norway by the German army and the formation of the Quisling government, a series of anti-Semitic events began to erupt there, exposing the deep penetration of the Jews into the Norwegian state organism. Telegrams from Stockholm in November 1942, cited in the Shanghai *Nash Put'* (No. 77), in particular reported:

In Berlin and Oslo, there have been arrests of Spanish Jews and former members of the Spanish International brigade. Also arrested are all members of the former Communist Party and red volunteers who fought in Spain before, as well as the senior rabbi of Oslo and several other prominent Jews.

After the murder of customs official Hvam at the hands of Jews on October 22nd, a fierce anti-Semitic campaign began throughout Norway. The crime was committed by two Jews on a train. About the murder, the Norwegian Minister of Public Affairs said: "The Norwegian people have not yet understood the real role that Jews play in Norway."

The Quisling government issued an order to confiscate all property belonging to Norwegian Jews and Jews who entered Norway. All Jewish property would go to the state, meaning it will be returned back to the Norwegian people, to whom it actually belongs.

There are currently several thousand Jews in Norway. All these hereditary parasites, spies, and traitors will be expelled from the country!

22. Jewish Limitrophes

From Sweden, we will go down again to the south, to Lithuania, Latvia, Estonia.

Numerous Jewish settlements have been concentrated between the meridian of the Dnieper in the east and the Oder in the west over the past centuries.

As such, these areas have long been the center of the most complex and permanent strife in both foreign policy and social life.

But humanity in the nineteenth century could not yet understand the true reason behind these phenomena. It could not yet sufficiently grasp the full significance of the dark machinations of the Jews and the influence of the men of the accursed race under their many disguises. Imperial Russia, Germany, and Austria-Hungary were too confident in their own power and looked at the Judean tribe as a harmful, but not dangerous element for the state foundations. But the Jews knew their real meaning and despite all the restrictions and imperial controls, they were able to circumvent both obstacles and laws before them.

By the beginning of the First World War the Jews gained a monopoly of influence over various areas of life in all regions of their Central European "inuva." However, the events of the World War, during which the Jewish mass was subjected to various hardships alongside the rest of the population of these places. As it became the main stage of the war, it brought new opportunities to the Jews. Taking advantage of the war, the Jews seized a lot of different enterprises and then became complete masters of the economy of this entire territory.

It is the Jews themselves that boast about this being precisely the case, and that all these "independence movements" were essentially movements directed by Jewish brains.

For example, a Jewish author writes in the article "The Role of Jews in the restoration of the Lithuanian State":

> The well-known Lithuanian-Jewish celebrity R. Rubinstein wrote in the pages of *The Yiddish Time* in connection with the re-election of President Antanas Smetona, referring to the merits of Jews in Lithuania: "It might be the case that someone has forgotten what Jewry has given Lithuania at the time of its rebirth. Very possibly, for apparently, such forgetfulness is desirable, since new winds 'blow' from nearby neighbors. But

we should still remind those who have forgotten about it, and especially Molodeja Vu, who knows little about the struggle of the Jews side by side with the Lithuanians, who shed their blood for a Free Lithuania!"

That is why, when we celebrate any events related to our independence, it is also necessary to remember the Jewish fighters who took part in the restoration of the Lithuanian state.

Since the days of tsardom in Russia, Jews have maintained close ties with the Lithuanians in the struggle for Lithuanian independence, creating a Lithuanian-Jewish bloc in Vilna to run their candidacy for the State Duma.

During the famous conference for the Lithuanian people held in Vilna between September 18th and 22nd, 1917, when independence was proclaimed, Lithuanian Jews took an enthusiastic and active part with prominent Jewish figures such as: Yakov Vidgorsky (who recently celebrated his eightieth birthday), Dr. Tsemmach Shabad (who died in 1935), and Dr. Rosenbaum (who died in Tel Aviv in 1935). Dr. Rosenbaum took an active part in the Lithuanian diplomatic delegation to the Versailles Conference in Paris.

Dr. Rosenbaum, taking part in the discussion on the issue of returning to Vilnius to Lithuania at the Lithuanian-Soviet peace conference on December 6th, 1920, showed that he was an experienced diplomat and a dedicated fighter for the freedom of Lithuania.

The Foreign Minister of the time, Dr. Purimis, speaking of Dr. Rosenbaum, called him the greatest of Lithuanian imperialists, mainly because at the Lithuanian-Soviet peace conference his demands for "borders" crossed all boundaries. Thanks to Dr. Rosenbaum, Vilna Jews did not participate in the Jewish plebiscite. Subsequently, Dr. Rosenbaum served as the Lithuanian Consul General in Tel Aviv until 1935. . . .

Another notable figure of the time was Dr. Max Soloveitchik, the Minister of Jewish Affairs.

Dr. Soloveitchik similarly took an active part in the reconstruction of Lithuania. In October 1920 he was a member of the Lithuanian delegation to the Brussels Financial Conference, where he encouraged Western European countries to recognize Lithuanian independence.

Dr. Rachmilevich played a huge role in strengthening the power of the resurgent Lithuania, being in 1920 a comrade of the Minister of Finance, and from 1935 to this day he has been the Lithuanian Consul General in Tel Aviv (after the death of Dr. Rosenbaum).

When speaking about the trio, Rosenbaum, Soloveitchik and Rakhmilevich, one cannot ignore other Jewish figures who took part in strengthening the independence of the Lithuanian state.

These include R. Rubinstein, editor of the Yiddish-language newspaper *Di Yidishe Shtime*, which is well-known not only in Lithuania, but also in the entire Jewish world.

At the time of the promulgation of the Declaration of Lithuanian independence, lawyer R. Rubinstein was in Russia and upon the opening of the Lithuanian consulate in Moscow, he was invited to serve in the Ministry of Foreign Affairs of the Republic of Lithuania.

From 1920 through 1923 R. Rubinstein held prominent posts in the department of the Ministry of Foreign Affairs.

He was the vice-chairman of the advisory board under Baltrušaitis. Since 1923, upon his return to Kaunas, he has been actively involved in the organization of Lithuanian Jewry and is a member of the editorial board of the newspaper *The Yiddish Time*, of which he remains editor to this day.

The diplomat Henry (Ganukh) Rabinovich is very popular among the employees of the Ministry of Foreign Affairs. He was among the first diplomats to work in the Ministry since 1918. From 1920 through 1923 he was secretary of the Embassy in Washington, from 1930 to 1935 in Moscow, and from 1935 to this day in London.

The Lawyer Gr. Rutenberg was an assistant at the Ministry of Foreign Affairs. A well-known publicist, he participated in the Hague Tribunal on the Vilna issue. He published a wealth of materials on the history of Lithuania, introducing European and other countries alike to Lithuanian history and its literary features.

The Lawyer Leiba Garfunkel in 1918 was among the representatives of Lithuania during the reception with the former territories annexed by the occupying German force, serving as the first secretary of the Kauna City Duma.

According to the order of President A. Smetona of 1922, L. Garfunkel, together with Professors Lesnas and Vzizhevsky, held elections in the Grodno Seima, was spokesperson of the Jewish community and representative of the Jewish population in the Seima's first, second and third convocation.

Lawyer Yakov Robinson took an active part in the drafting of the Klaipeda Constitution and in the activities in the Sejm.

Among those who have performed great services to the country are brothers M. and G. Wolff.

Dr. M. Wolf was for a long time the head of the Kauna City Council and chairman of the Jewish community, where he was a member in the prewar period, together with former Justice Minister Šilijasz, lawyer Hapodski, F. Filkenstein, Friedman (former deputy of the State Duma, now deceased), Rosovsky (chairman of IKO, former vice-president of Vilnius), and others who took active part in strengthening the young Republic of Lithuania.

In a newspaper article, it is difficult to list in detail not only the merits but also the names of persons who shed their blood for the Motherland in battle.

General Grigamanos-Golovetsky writes in his memoirs that Jews were among those who helped to build the foundation of Free Lithuania, who helped to build their homeland, giving an opportunity to improve the life of the army.

At the moment when the liberation war was going on, Jewish women, along with Lithuanian women, overwhelmed by patriotism, did everything possible to ease the fate of the fighters at the front. In particular, Madame Lenig (awarded the badge of military distinction) distinguished herself.

Jews served sanitary institutes. Among them are Dr. Dembovsky, Dr. Goldschmidt, Dr. Golombek, Dr. Gutman, Dr. Vregovsky, and others.

Sixty young Jewish lives were lost on the battlefields, aside from the wounded and shell-shocked.

We are also happy to state that, in contrast to those "evil winds" blowing an anti-Semitic "stench" from their close neighbors, the Lithuanian intelligentsia, represented by its best members, actively participates in the rapprochement of the Lithuanian and Jewish peoples, who have both lived on Lithuanian soil for hundreds of years.

Recently, an evening of rapprochement between the two peoples took place in Kaunas. Numerous speeches were made by: The chairman of the association, Lithuanian writer Ludnaus Giro, famous Lithuanian critic Korsakas Radzvilas. This first step towards familiarization with the cultures of the two peoples, presumably, will serve as a foundation for the eradication of the wretched western winds of anti-Semitism in the future.[96]

Speaking about the "evening in Kaunas" (Russian Kaunas), the Jewish author characterized it as "the first step" to get acquainted with the cultures of the two peoples. This evening was arranged in 1939, on the

---

[96] *Jewish Life* of May 5th, 1939, No. 19.

eve of the outbreak of World War II. Where were the Jews during all those twenty years before the war? Why didn't they try to get closer to the Lithuanians then, whose independence they so strongly advocated? The answer is obvious: it wasn't necessary. What do the Jews care about the culture of some Lithuanians, inasmuch as they carry out the spread of their own culture in all directions, carrying out the process of Judaization.

From art, to the press, to radio and to schools, the whole "independence of Lithuania" was imbued with Judaism.

Here, for example, is a factual reference from a Jewish source about the number of Jewish schools in tiny Lithuania:

> A report at the Fifth Conference of Jewish Language Teachers revealed that in 1938 there were 109 Jewish public schools and 26 sixth-grade gymnasiums in Lithuania. Lithuanian public schools have 48 departments for Jewish children.
>
> There are currently 383 Jewish teachers. There are 17,942 children studying in these public schools, and 1,064 in Lithuanian schools. There are also 32 preparatory schools with 940 children under the guidance of 46 Froebelics.[97] All schools are fully subsidized by the Lithuanian government.

In the same issue of the Jewish magazine we also find the following:

Jewish Teachers' Seminary in Vilna

The Minister of Education in Lithuania has authorized the opening of the four-year teacher's seminary "Garbus" in Vilna.

About Peretz on the radio

The Lithuanian radiophone in Vilna broadcasted a half-hour program dedicated to the famous writer on the 25th anniversary of the death of I. L. Peretz. Many gave their speeches: lawyer P. Kan, chairman of the community Dr. Ya. Vidgorsky, Rector of Vilna University, Professor M. Birzhizhka and Professor S. Dubnov.

When Lithuania was incorporated into the USSR, the Red Army troops and the Communist government were greeted with great delight. Of course! Their "own" government came, which immediately began to

---

[97] A teacher of preschool children that followed the pedagogical method of German educator Froebel. (Translator's note)

demonstrate its Jewish essence. Here, for example, is what happened exactly one month after the Red Army joined Lithuania:

Streets in Vilna named after Jewish writers

> The Vilna City Council has decided to name four streets in Vilna after Jewish writers and public figures: I. L. Peretz, Mendeleh-Moher-Sforim, Meir Dik and Dr. Shabad.

We can observe the same pattern of Judaization in other limitrophes.

The Jewish dominance in Latvia was vividly manifested especially in the capital of its ancient Riga. There, the center of Judaization for the entire Baltic States was concentrated. In Riga, back in 1920, the largest Jewish publishing house was created. In which, by the way, the largest shareholder was Leon Trotsky himself. This publishing house has published a number of publications in Hebrew, Yiddish and Russian. Owned by this publishing house, the newspaper *Today* reached record circulation figures of more than 250,000 copies, more than any other Russian publications published outside the USSR and *was the only "emigrant" newspaper allowed into the USSR*. The arrogance of this newspaper in connection with Lord Reading Rufus Isaacs has already been cited in the chapters on England.

How quickly the Judaization of Latvia took place is shown by the fact that by 1924 about 70 percent of all households in Riga belonged to Jews. And in 1925 a Jewish rabbi became Prime Minister of Latvia! Here is what the Jewish newspaper Segodnya had to say about this event:

> The Cabinet of Ministers in Latvia has resigned. The President of the Republic of Lithuania has instructed Seimas Deputy Rabbi Dr. Nurok to create a new government. Rabbi Dr. Nurok accepted this mission and began to negotiate with parliamentary groups.[98]

Harbin's *Jewish Life* cheered this extraordinary event:

> Rabbi Nurok, PhD, is a well-known public figure. Dr. Nurok is a prominent member of the Seimas, a defender of the rights, an active participant in national minority congresses and a speaker on the rights of national minorities. In 1918, Dr. Nurok was elected in Harbin and the Far East as a delegate to the All-Russian Jewish Congress from a list of the Jewish community

---

[98] *Today*, March 10th, 1925.

and Zionists, among four other delegates: S. I. Ravikovich, Dr. Kaufman, Dr. Nurok, and Dr. Kissin.

A rabbi as the head of the government!!! This is the apotheosis. . . . This explains why, for example, Jews here in Harbin prefer citizenship of all these limitrophe countries and why any Jew could easily buy a Lithuanian, Latvian, or Estonian passport. When genuine nationally conscious and essentially fascist movements appeared in these Judaized baby states—Perkonkrust (Cross of Perun), Union of Liberators, Union of Nationalists—some dark forces inspired these pseudo-fascist coups with the help of armies and governments. A kind of "totalitarianism" has now been established in place of the former "democracy," an ideological military dictatorship based on English capital and led by Freemasons.

23. Poland, the Great Fortress of Jewish "Culture"

With reference to the upcoming death of Poland the Jews wrote:

A great fortress of Jewish culture has collapsed. Poland supplied the entire Jewish world with a large and rich cultural and educational national material. In Poland, more than anywhere else in the world, the Zionist ideology and Hebrew came to life. Poland was the best of the "halutz."[99]

The Polish newspaper *The Self-Defense of the People* published a list of the dictators of the Polish economy in its December 25th, 1938 issue (No. 52). Poland was ruled over by the following twenty personalities:

1. Czeslaw Kaarner—former Minister of Agriculture, then President of the Warsaw Chamber of Industry and Commerce. Manages a capital of 252,066,000 zlotys.
2. The Jewish Simon Lyandau, capital of 66,425,000 zlotys.
3. The Jewish Ippolit Gliwacz, capital of 636,760,000 zlotys.
4. The Jewish Alfred Falder, infamous in Upper Silesia.
5. The Jewish Tadeusz Epstein, capital of 9,210,000 zlotys.
6. The Jewish Eduard Nathansen, banker, capital of 70,000,000 zlotys.
7. The Jewish Leopold Welkisch, capital of 49,665,000 zlotys.
8. Freemason Piotr Drzewiecki, capital of 30,862,500 zlotys.
9. Freemason Boris Freris, capital of 60,900,000 zlotys.
10. The Jewish Felix Wislicki, capital of 36,000,000 zlotys.

---

[99] Ibid.

11. Andrey Verbitsky, capital of 219,600,000 zlotys.
12. Marian Szydlowski, capital of 31,930,000 zlotys.
13. The Jewish Nahum Eitington, capital of 250,000,000 zlotys.
14. Raphael Shereshevsky, a Jewish banker, capital of 17,000,000 zlotys.
15. The Jewish Fyodor Vainshank, capital of 14,620,000 zlotys.
16. The Jewish Andrey Rotvand, capital of 24,647,000 zlotys.
17. Antony Wieniawski, married to a Jewish woman, capital of 62,000,000 zlotys.
18. Josef Zyukhlinski, capital of 35,525,000 zlotys.
19. Viktor Hlasko, capital of 75,000,000 zlotys.
20. Victor Pedpelski, capital of 30,000,000 zlotys.

"Such then, are the real lords of Poland: Jews, Masons, and those who depend on them!" the *World Service* commented on this list.

"All Polish ministers, the minister-chairman and the president of the Polish Republic were all Freemasons." On the other hand, the *Newsletter* of the Bulgarian Department of the R. F. S. testifies that Minister Kostelovsky's wife is a Jew who converted to Catholicism and appropriated the name of Sofia Tarkovskaya. In reality, she was born Sonka Wallach-Finkelstein, the sister-in-law of Finkelstein-Litvinov.[100]

> In Poland there was an institution called the Supreme Control Chamber. It was an institution whose leader had few secrets unknown to him. Not even the contents of the minister's desk drawers were unknown to him, and even the president of the republic was under his grasp. And it was here, at this responsible post that General Klemensky turned out to be, in fact, not even a fully baptized Jewish "Friedman," a former colonel of the Austrian service. Klemensky-Friedman was the head of the Polish "B'nai B'rith" and the unofficial grandmaster of the Polish Masonic lodges.

Is it to anyone's surprise, then, that Poland perished? The Jews understood what they were doing and where they were leading Poland. But it was important for them to start a new European war, knowing in advance that the Poland they had chosen would be a redemptive sacrifice.

Now Jews everywhere are working furiously to help Polish anti-German groups in England, in the Middle East and in the USSR.

---

[100] A famous Soviet figure, People's Commissar of Foreign Affairs. (Translator's note)

The Jews even "promise" their active assistance, threatening to send their Polish Jews to the front against Germany. However, for a diversion, maybe they will send some battalions to brag about it for a couple of centuries, to demand afterwards compensation for their "aid." At the very least, a Jewish source writes the following:

Jewish front-line soldiers call for a struggle to liberate Poland

"Polish Jews will shed their blood in the struggle for the liberation of Poland," an organization of former Jewish soldiers in Poland said in its manifesto.

"The misfortune that has befallen Poland is a tragedy for Jews," the Manifesto says. Jewish soldiers have fulfilled their duty to protect their homeland and will continue to fight for a free and strong Poland, which will be a mother, a kind mother for all her sons without distinction of religion and race. In the New Poland, Jews will have equal and full civil rights. Common suffering and common struggle will unite the citizens of Poland. The manifesto calls on all Jews to join the New Polish Army in France.[101]

24. The Lost Czechoslovak "Paradise for Jews"

Czechoslovakia. . . . "It was a paradise for Jews," the Jews of Harbin remember sorrowfully in 1941. The Palestinian Jews in 1937 were moved:

"Although Czechoslovakia is surrounded by states dominated by hatred and enslavement of other peoples and anti-Semitism, it stands firm as a rock and gives the world an example of a free state."[102]

"Equality of rights" in Czechoslovakia led to similar results to all other countries where it was applied. The *World Service* from April 14th and May 1st, 1939 tells:

On Graben, the busiest street in Prague, there are huge bank houses in which the general headquarters of the Rothschild big banks operated throughout Czechoslovakia.

Here is a list of directors of the Czech Bank Union, which controlled a large number of enterprises and various industries. Although the name of this bank sounds national, its leaders were the following Jews: the first general director was Aron Goldstein, who was evicted from Lithuania; the director

---

[101] *Jewish Life*, No. 22.
[102] Ibid., No. 11.

of the main central office was Eklig Man Moizel, who was expelled from Russia by the Moscow police in 1913; the first chief director was Max Hecht, who arrived in Bohemia and Moravia as a fare evader.

The second chief director is Baruch Bondi, a migrant from Odessa; the director of the exchange department is David Federer; the director of the pawnshop department is Lerk Spitzer, a migrant from Finland; the director of the securities department is Nathan Klyahold, born in Vienna; the director of the currency department is Salis Verkovich, his nationality is still unknown; the director of the bill branch is Imrich Stein, born in Tarnow in Polish Galicia; the director of the motto department is Oscar Pollach. . . .

The director of the coal department, Mazko Finer, apparently comes from Arad. The director of the sugar department is Vlad Lustig, this is his fourth name; the director of the distillery department Otto Guthartz had no Czechoslovak citizenship certificate at all; the director of the textile department, Isaac Doble is from Hungary; the manager of the lottery department, Rico Mordecai, comes from the east; the manager of the woodworking department, Max Krakauer, arrived to Czechoslovakia with a fake passport; the manager of the metal industry department, Max Zonenstein, was expelled from Belgium before the World War; the manager of the paper industry department is Arthur Rozenblum, native of Estonia; the manager of the export department is Ebenek Moravek, his real name is Zeis Marmshe; the manager of the import department, Jan Elbogen, was smuggled into Czechoslovakia by one of the former rulers; the manager of the press department, Ralph Kopetsky, aka Kauders; the manager of the department for the export of sensational literature to Japan, Yare Stransky; the manager of the political department, Chaim Kugelberger, a Jewish immigrant from Berlin. The meeting manager is Erantz Bauer, who fled to Czechoslovakia from Austria; the technical department manager is Felix Moisevitz, who secretly moved abroad near Eger; the manager of the department for the production of national Czechoslovak vodka, Alexey Spinde, comes from eastern Galicia and used to live in Paris and Vienna.

Such were the leaders of the seemingly national "Czech Bank Union."

Similar facts about Jewish dominance in Czechoslovakia can be found in many other areas of Czechoslovak life, but we will limit ourselves to Lord Winterton's statement in the British House of Commons on May 11th, 1934:

"Czechoslovakian land is not in the hands of the peasants at all, but in the hands of Jewish moneylenders."[103]

The following message from the *World Service* from Marienbad shows how much the Jews were convinced than Czechoslovakia was in fact their paradise:

> During the mourning ceremony held by the local Jewish religious community in memory of the deceased old President Massarik, the Czechoslovak national anthem was sung in Hebrew. Chief Cantor Levin of Marienbad took the trouble to translate the national song of the Jewish-friendly Prague system into Hebrew.[104]

The short history of the independent life of the Czechs is inextricably linked with names that are dear to the Jewish heart: the names of Massarik and Benes.

> On March 7th, 1930, Massarik turned eighty years old. At the conference of the Zionist Federation, it was decided to plant a forest named after Massarik and write his name in the golden Book of the Jewish National Fund. Massarik's jubilee was solemnly celebrated in all schools and... synagogues of the Czechoslovak Republic.

Why such favors you ask? Oh, Professor Masaryk was an old friend and agent of world Jewry! Back in 1889, he led a fierce campaign against anti-Semitism in Austria over the accusation of L. Gilzner of ritual murder in the town of Poland on the Moravian border.

The bloodthirsty murderer was sentenced to death, which Emperor Franz Joseph modified with life imprisonment. In 1907, the tireless Masaryk again raised this issue in Parliament. Not for free, of course. How much he was paid for this process, history will never say.

In 1913, Massarik once again got involved in the history of ritual crimes by protesting against the Beilis trial in Kiev.[105] Why did this little "Czech brother" care about some Kievan Jew? But of course, the whole Jewish world, Masaryk included, rose to the defense of Beilis once the Jewish press wrote about this case:

---

[103] *World Service*, No. 8–9, 1939.
[104] Ibid., No. 1–2, January 15th, 1938.
[105] Menachem Mendel Tevievich Beilis was a Jewish burgher in Kiev accused of the ritual murder of the Kiev boy Andrei Yushchinskiy (1911) in a high-profile trial known as the "Beilis case." (Translator's note)

The Russian government has decided to launch a decisive war against Jewry in Kiev. One would think after such a titanic warfare launched, the fate of the Jewish people would seem to be at stake. No, by no means: the Jewish people are invincible. And therefore, it is the fate of the Russian state that is at stake. . . . Remember this well.[106]

In 1918, the revolutionaries released Gilzner from prison. Masaryk even here is true to himself, or rather to his masters: he has been providing monetary assistance to the freed man for several months. At whose expense and on whose behalf? History is silent, leaving us to guess.

This was the first president of Czechoslovakia and its creator. The second president and her destroyer, Dr. Benes is known as an active friend of political Zionism. He is the author of the famous phrase: "The Jewish people are the greatest in the world."

Benes' surname is featured in the Jewish press all over the world and in all international Jewish events. "Benes is a high-level Freemason," notes the *World Service*, who was also the grand master of the Czechoslovak Grand Lodge and is an influential member of the International League against Anti-Semitism, headed by the famous Jew Lenash Lifshitz.

25. Austria Before the Anschluss

The author of the report in the reference book *The Jewish World* of 1939 gives eloquent data on Austrian Jewry:

> The Viennese community has always been one of the wealthiest in Europe. It had nineteen synagogues, maintained a number of Talmud torahs and primary religious schools and subsidized the teaching of the Jewish Law of God in state and private educational institutions. Her library is one of the richest in Europe—over 350,000 volumes, her museum is also one of the best.
>
> Up to thirty Jewish newspapers and magazines have been published in Vienna recently, more than anywhere else in Europe.
>
> All directions of Jewish social and political thought had their own organs here. The daily Jewish newspaper *Wiener Morgan Zeitung* was published here.

---

[106] See *Gammar* No. 74

In the history of our national Renaissance in the last half of this century, the role of Austrian Jewry is one of the most honorable: In Austria, Pepper Smolensky, a native of Russia, published his magazine *Gashahar (Dawn)*, the first Palestine-Philistine organ (1883–1884). The Jewish student organization "Kadima" immediately arose from the ranks of which Herzl's closest collaborators came from. His book *The Jewish State* was published in Vienna in 1897.

The Committee of the new organization, elected at the first Zionist Congress of Akonon, met in Vienna and its organ *Die Welt* was created.

The estimate of the Vienna Community for 1938 accounts for 6,687,810 shillings of expenditure and 6,335,360 shillings of the parish income. It was supposed to spend 665,570 shillings for education, 2,871,000 shillings on the special assistance department, 120,000 shillings for winter assistance. Large sums were also allocated to help refugees from Germany.

The number of Jewish enterprises in Vienna reached 207,000. Compared to the 188,000 owned by non-Jews.

Isn't this enough?

We will not give a list of the owners of the most luxurious Viennese mansions; we will limit ourselves to just one picture. It'll tell you everything.

"Behind the Grave of a Great Man" is the title of a 1925 article in *Jewish Life*. The "great man" is the leader of Austrian Jewry, Haides. So, the Jewish magazine reports that tens of thousands of people, including many Christians, were trailing behind his coffin. Along the trail, where the procession took place, Jewish students held a guard of honor, and electric lanterns on the streets were covered with a black crepe. All shops were closed for half an hour as a mourning sigil. And in the synagogue, among those present were: the president of the Republic of Austria, Dr. Heinisch, the chief of police, ministers, burgermeisters, etc.

The Evangelical Church Council and the Catholic Church, according to *Jewish Life*, were also represented by special delegations both in the synagogue and at the open grave, where fifteen speakers spoke.

The last census, noted the January *Stürmer* in 1937, showed that Jews currently make up 9.4 percent of the total population of Vienna. But what is completely disproportionate to this percentage is the influence that has been developing over the past decade in this city by Jewry in the most important areas of life.

For example, 51 percent of all doctors in Vienna are of Jewish nationality. The Jewish dominance on the front of the legal profession is even more felt there, since over 85 percent of lawyers are Jews. The shoe trade is 75 to 80 percent concentrated in Jewish hands.

Even among the ordinary peasantry in Austria, the undeniable fact of Jewish dominance in banks and banking offices has become a "byword" for everyone.

The situation with the Vienna press is also extremely bleak. There are only seven daily Viennese newspapers out of sixteen that are not entirely in Jewish hands. All the rest are purely Jewish publications that serve the interests of world Jewry to a much greater extent than the interests of the Republic of Austria.

The number of Jewish dentists in Vienna has reached 70 percent. A similar percentage is reached by Jewish fur traders and various kinds of materials up to and including cloth.

Needless to say, the film industry there is almost entirely in the tenacious hands of Jewish entrepreneurs. In 1935, according to precise statistics, there were 166 cinemas in Vienna, 106 of which were owned by Jews, and over time this ratio has changed somewhat in favor of the Jewish element.

And at the same time, the largest cinemas are concentrated in the hands of Jews, which can be noticed since of the 72,583 seats that Viennese cinemas have in total, Jews control 50,799 seats.

It is characteristic to note that, as a general rule, Jews show the greatest interest in large-scale enterprises, while the "small fries" are kindly left to the Aryans. In order to drive the point home, it is enough to mention that out of the six major cinemas in Vienna, five are owned by Jews.

In order to extort money from the population, Jews do not shy away from the most horrendous ways: taking advantage of the freedom prevailing in Vienna, Jewish cinemas showed a number of vile films, indulging in the lowest of instincts, causing moral damage to the population of the Austrian capital.

Bakeries and laundries in Vienna are over 60 percent Jewish owned, as is the trade in lumber and stationeries being over 70 percent Jewish-owned.

The Jews of Vienna have achieved an absolutely exceptional position in the junk trade. In particular, the trade in old iron and scrap metal was completely monopolized by the Jews, 100 percent, in their tenacious hands.

Just from these examples, which are far from claiming to be a complete picture, one can judge what a powerful position Jewry occupies in Vienna. What vast wealth, far out of proportion to their numbers, they managed to concentrate in their own hands!

The good-natured Viennese are completely powerless to fight this close-knit Jewish front, and are forced to content themselves for the time being only with sincere indignation at the sight of their beautiful

Vienna becoming more and more alien to them, more and more stained with tasteless and obsessive Jewish advertising, disfiguring the very appearance of the Austrian capital.

The ordinary citizen of Vienna is increasingly coming back to the idea that this cannot continue, that there must be a limit to the further progressive movement of Jewry, but no one yet knows where to start. And on the table of the Austrian, who is pondering these vital questions of his very existence, probably lies another catalog of some Jewish trading house, slipped to him by a swift Jewish salesman.

26. Jews in Hungary

The Jews in Hungary are so deeply ingrained in Hungarian daily life that even after repeated cleansing and cleansing, it can't quite get clean. Already in 1939, Hungary had passed a new law on Jews, classified as anti-Semitic just for reducing Jewish participation in public life to a ratio of 20:80. After all, Jews in Hungary make up only 5 percent of the population. At the same time, the press (for example, the Berlin *New Word* of October 23rd, 1938) commented on the new law:

> The changes the new law will bring in the economic life of Hungary can be seen from the participation of Jews in the economic life of Hungary now.
>
> Of Hungary's 324 banks and banking offices, 223 are under Jewish control, Jewish editors and publishers make up 67 percent of the 21 daily newspapers in Budapest, 14 of which are, mostly or entirely, in the hands of Jews. Of the four leading publishing houses in Hungary, three are Jewish. 25 Jews have the title of baron and 290 have the title of nobility. There are 105 Jews among the 126 millionaires in Hungary.
>
> The participation of Jews in some industries is instructive: in Budapest, 90 percent of all zucchini production is in Jewish hands. 75 percent of jewelers are Jews. Hotels are also 47 percent Jewish owned. Among the merchants, of whom there are 83,671 in total, 38,072 are Jewish.

"There are one million Jews in Hungary who seek to create panic and spread dissatisfaction and distrust in the population," *Havas* reported From Budapest on October 12th, 1942, quoting the statement of the Hungarian Minister of Agriculture Margene at a meeting of Hungarian farmers.[107] Wherever rumors of economic misfortune appear, and

---

[107] The name of the *France-Presse* news agency until 1944. (Translator's note)

where such an appearance deepens, grows and expands—indeed, look for the Jews!

27. Romania Under the Heel of the Redheaded Lupescu

Through Hungary to Romania! The Jewish power in Romania is characterized by the statement of the recent Romanian king when he was still the Crown Prince:

"I'm a friend of the Jewish people and I will not allow any anti-Semitism in my country. There will be no Jewish problem in Romania while I am on the throne," King Carol said, according to *Jewish Life* on August 7th, 1930.

In Romania, the Jews applied their ancient technique known since the time of the biblical Esther, whose bloody "feat," as is known, is remembered annually by Jews of all countries as "the most cheerful of Jewish holidays"—Purim.

The Esther of our days was played by the red-haired Magdalene Lupescu.

The temperamental Jewess, who was, perhaps, really charming in her youth and studied in depth the ways of seduction, managed to enslave not only the body, but also the soul of the king when he was still crown prince. For the sake of Lupescu, he abandoned his wife and family, renounced the throne, went abroad, squandered all his personal fortune. But this was not enough for the modern Esther and the modern Mordecai standing behind her! They needed power and blood. And we can see the results of this restoration: with the return of the king to his homeland, we see him on the Romanian throne, surrounded by Jews.

The country is suffocating under Jewish economic and administrative shackles. It is so unbearable that it causes terror. The sounds of the shots fired by the avengers of the people, crushing the Masonic minister Duka and his accomplices. The nationalist Iron Guard, especially hated by Lupescu and her relatives, is now outlawed. As years pass in a hard-exhausting struggle, Young Romania, in the grip of the most brutal police terror, does not give up.

The fateful year of 1938. . . . After the short–term reign of the famous anti-Semite Octavian Goga of forty-four days, the black Jewish night comes again.

"Israel, you have won!" the pale Goga shouts, leaving the power in accordance with the royal command. A few months pass and a lonely Goga mysteriously dies, rumored to be poisoned.

The long night is thickening over Romania. The Iron Guard has been outlawed again. Its leader, the fiery Corneliu Codreanu, was arrested. Codreanu and fourteen of his closest associates were killed, allegedly, while trying to escape. As a later investigation showed, they were severely tortured, on the orders of the bloodthirsty Lupescu. Young people shoot back at the government of the Freemason Calinescu. But then a real pogrom begins, reminiscent of the Persian actions of the biblical Esther.

This is how the Jews acted in Romania. And the criminal king who tied his fate to Jewry lost his throne and almost lost his life. Only then Romania was set free.

28. Bulgaria Is Being Cleansed

The extent to which the Jewish plague has spread in Bulgaria is evidenced by the activities carried out by the Bulgarian government over the past few years.

For example, a telegram from Sofia dated December 10th, 1942, given in the Shanghai *Nashem Puti* No. 77, reported:

> The Ministry of Internal Affairs of Bulgaria is developing measures to concentrate a significant part of the Jewish population of Bulgaria in one of the districts of Thrace, which will be the initial step in the adoption of a number of legislative measures, aimed at limiting the activities and influence of Jews.
>
> All Jews inhabiting Bulgaria will be required to have the sign of a red circle on the left side of their clothes. The same sign should be on all commercial and other enterprises in which persons of Jewish nationality are a part of. All landed property in Jewish hands will be bought by the state. Intermarriage with Jews is wholly prohibited.

The next telegram: "On October 13th, the Bulgarian Minister of Justice demanded from Parliament that the measures recently adopted by the Government concerning the new status of Jews be immediately put into effect."

On October 15th, a telegram from Sofia reported that forty-eight Jews were fined one million leva each by the Bulgarian Ministry of Finance for real estate speculation.

Bulgaria is being cleansed! Slowly, maybe too slowly even, but gradually nonetheless.

29. "A Country That Knows No Anti-Semitism"

From the point of view of the Jewish question, frankly, we have little data regarding Bulgaria. As for Yugoslavia, "a country that knows no antisemitism"—so the Harbin *Jewish Life* describes. From this widely used source we learn:

> In this country with 70,000 Jews, there is no such thing as the Jewish question. . . . Jews live peacefully and happily, starting from the Royal Court and government spheres up to the broadest grassroots of the people.
> Prime Minister Stoyadinovich, despite his pro-German orientation, repeatedly expressed his sympathies for Jewry making large donations to various Jewish causes.[108] Prime Minister Cvetkovic and his cabinet colleagues are not only friends of Serbian Jewry, but more importantly, friends of the Jewish people.
> This is how the Jewish magazine described Yugoslavia on the eve of world events in this country. Considering, obviously, their seizure of European states as an already established reality, the Jews also make the most outspoken confessions in relation to this country. These confessions give us a lot of data in order to understand why our fraternal Yugoslavia unexpectedly committed suicide by entering the war. . . .
> It should be noted that with the departure of Stoyadinovich's cabinet, the only anti-Semitic minister that the country has ever had in its government, the Slovenian priest Anton Koroshec, has vanished into oblivion. The danger of restrictive laws being established under a Stoyadinovich government was avoided, but some trade restrictions have still been introduced. A government agency was founded, whose duties were to export raw materials abroad, such as wool, fruits, etc. which dealt a heavy blow to private firms. And in this government institution Jews were not given any positions. On the other hand, imports decreased due to the introduction of currency laws which caused the liquidation of most of the Jewish firms importing foreign manufacturers into the country. In institutions with close trade relations with the Germans, Jews were barred from various positions.
> It should be noted that the above restrictions apply only in Croatia, Slovenia, and in the rest of the Hungarian provinces

---

[108] Prime Minister and Minister of Foreign Affairs of Yugoslavia from 1935–1939. (Translator's note)

which are saturated with non-hatred of Jews since the days of the Austrian Empire. In the rest of the country's provinces, Jews enjoy all rights and even hold a number of positions in the administrations. Even in the army, Jews holding lower officer positions are encouraged by the Serbs to take exams in special subjects in order to get promoted to an even higher officer rank. This is done at a time when in other regions of the country Jews have no access to any officer position at all.

Foreign anti-Semites have repeatedly tried to plant anti-Semitism among the administration or within the Serbian people, but their attempts were unsuccessful. It is known for certain that Prince Regent Pavel categorically refused to debate the so-called "Jewish question" with diplomats from one of the Central European states. Prime Minister Cvetkovic, whose party is backed by most of the Serbian Jewry, categorically refused to grant permission to subsidize the only pogrom leaflet in the country called "The Balkans," despite external requests.

There were cases when Jewish manufacturers, fearing for their future, ceased making large transactions and even began to close down their factories in some places. The government press immediately began to publish ardent articles calling on Jews not to lose confidence in the people and in the authorities. That hostility or injustice towards Jewry would never be allowed in the country, and that racism is suicide for a country like Yugoslavia, in which over half a dozen different nationalities live, including Serbs, Croats, Slovaks, Muslims, Germans, etc.

And confidence in the authorities was restored, especially since there was not even a hint of anti-Semitism at the head of the entire country's press. Of course, even in Yugoslavia, you can find a couple of dozen anti-Semites who can't wait for "their final hour." The typical "hurrah-patriots" however will not risk meeting "their final hour," and if they dare to speak out against Serbian Jewry, they will find themselves in quite a pickle even in front of their close friends, as can be proved by the Talmud trial, which recently spread all over the Jewish world press.

This story is connected with the publication of a newspaper by M. Milic in the small Serbian town of Petrograd. Filled with various pogrom articles against Jews with excerpts from the Talmud, Bible, and prayers by the "expert in Jewish science" M. Milic.

This "newspaper business" however could not last long. The Council of United Jewish Communities in Serbia initiated proceedings against the ignoramus. The Court invited some professors of the Faculty of Theology of the University of Belgrade to give opinions on the accuracy of the conclusions and sayings from the holy books of Judaism given by M. Milic. The trial lasted several months, and the college of professors passed the following resolution: "The articles and readings published by M. Milich from the sacred books of Jewry are false from beginning to end and the quotations quoted by M. Milich are not even present in the Talmud, M. Milich has no idea about Judaism, and even Hebrew is not familiar to him." The "scientist" was convicted by the court with a large monetary fine, prison and his newspaper was permanently closed."[109]

This is how Yugoslav Jewry showed its strength. Milic was put in jail, some were poisoned, and some were forced to leave Yugoslavia. And when no one was hindering them in the land, the Jews were set loose. They forced the Serbs, against their national interests, to start a brief struggle for Anglo-Jewish interests. The Jews destroyed a country that did not know anti-Semitism.

30. The Greek King and the Synagogue

And next to Yugoslavia is yet another country that has long been captured by the Jews, which has also experienced a bloody tragedy and was used by the cursed race for its own purposes and benefit. This is little Greece.

In this country, as in neighboring Turkey, Jews have recently played a prominent role, seizing financial control.

Thanks to the Jewish influence of Disraeli, who so patronized the Greeks, it was possible to establish a de facto Anglo-Jewish protectorate in Greece in the middle of the nineteenth century, which then brought up a wave of Masonic figures, such as the sad memory of Venizelos and others.[110]

After the famous "republican period," Greece once again became a kingdom. The king was put there by none other than the Jews. George II, who now fled to London, was closely associated with Jewry.

Here are some notes from a Jewish source:

---

[109] *Jewish Life* from July 26th, 1940, No. 30, Harbin.
[110] Prime Minister of Greece from 1910–1915, 1917–1920, 1924, 1928–1932, and 1933. (Translator's note)

The King of Greece expresses sympathy for Zionism.

During his visit to Thessaloniki, King George II of Greece received the Chief Rabbi of Thessaloniki, Dr. Zvi Koretz, and had a long conversation with him about the situation of Jews in Greece, as well as in Palestine. The King showed great interest in the cause of Jewish revival in Palestine and expressed his sympathy for the Zionist movement.[111]

The Greek King at the synagogue prayer service.

The Greek King George II, while in Thessaloniki, attended a solemn prayer service in his honor in the synagogue.... The Jewish population gave the king a standing ovation. The King thanked the leaders of the Jewish community.[112]

But the question is: why do the Jews in Greece need a king again? Obviously, it was needed because the republican system turned out to be a tool with dangerous features for Jews.

At least from the same Jewish source, we can see that not everywhere Jews lived happily after their "freedoms" were granted.

This is what happened in northern Greece and Macedonia, for example:

> As soon as you arrive in the glorious city of Macedonia-Thessaloniki, which until recently was called the "Jewish republic" with its mobile eighty-thousand Jewish population, with its Sabbath rest for everyone, for both Jews and Christians. Such a sight surprises you and keeps you amazed.
>
> Where did all the Jews go with their signs in Hebrew, their typical faces, which were almost the only ones in the *golus* constantly glowing with pride and happiness? And with great sadness you state that there are no signs of Jewry at the moment in Thessaloniki! Everything is Greek: signs, newspapers, huge advertisements on the walls of houses. But listening to the conversation of a group of people, you will make sure that they are not talking to each other in Greek, French, or even Italian. It turns out that it's them, our native brothers, the Hispaniola Jews. And if they had not spoken the language of the Inquisition among themselves, which they have not forgotten despite the four hundred and forty years that have passed since

---

[111] *Jewish Life*, September 4th, 1925, No. 1–2.
[112] *Jewish Life*, August 7th, 1936, No. 22.

then, you would under no circumstances have found a Jew in the largest Jewish center in the Balkans.

What do Hispaniola Jews currently possess? Is it possible to come across specific Jewish attractions in this city?

I asked this question to a group of Hispaniola Jews and received an extremely curious answer: "We have as our rabbi not a Hispaniola Jew, but a native of Poland. This case is the only one in the entire long, extremely turbulent period of the Salonika community's existence and the fact that our community has an Ashkenazi German Jew as its spiritual leader is our pride. We have never had such an educated and secular person in a rabbinical position before."

So the Jews say.

And it was with "such an educated and secular man"—a fugitive from Poland, Dr. Zvi Koretz, that George II had a long conversation during a visit to Thessaloniki

These conversations cost Greece, and George II, dearly.

31. Russia Under the Red Star

And here before us are the vast fields of our homeland, Russian villages and towns. Collective farms and industrialization, concentration camps, five-year plans, socialist construction on top of the piles of bones of the Russian people.... "The most perfect democracy in the world," "the freest people in the world," the Union of Soviet Socialist Republics.

Yes, this "democracy" is indeed well organized. The "free" citizen knows beforehand who he should elect. The candidate was already chosen by the party unit, authorized by the GPU. Here the simple mechanics of Soviet power are exposed: the ladder of the "freely elected Soviets," rural, urban, district, regional, and republican, is crowned by the Supreme Soviet of the USSR, allocating the Sovnarkom (sovereign Soviet government). Parallel to it, holding it in chains, its controlling ladder of committees of the ruling party of the CPSU, primary party organizations in villages and cities, factories and collective farms, institutions and enterprises, district and city committees, regional committees, the Central Committee of the Communist Parties of the "union republics" and, finally, the all-powerful Central Committee of the CPSU—the true master of the country.

Elsewhere, I describe the history of the emergence and development of this party and the Jewish state in Russia (in my "Criticism of the Soviet State," in the essay collection *Jews in Russia*). From the very beginning, the RSDLP (Russian Social Democratic Workers' Party), divided into Bolsheviks and Mensheviks and subsequently renamed the RCP (Russian Communist Party) and the CPSU (the All-Union Communist Party), was a predominantly Jewish party, guided and inspired by Jews, supported and upheld by Jews.

It is not for nothing that this party acted as a representative and propagator of Jewish Marxism in Russia—the disgusting evil teachings of the German Jew, the "evangelist of hatred" (as the scholar on Judaism Melsky accurately designated him), Karl Mordechai Marx and the conductor of the triumphal march of the Jewish intelligentsia to replace the Russian one it exterminated.[113]

With diabolical dexterity the Jews used the idea of soviets, which has nothing in common with Marxism, and has its roots deep in the Russian past, and in 1905, Trotsky tied her to the short program of the Bolshevik Party of Leiba, and in 1917 Steklov-Nakhamkes recalled it. According to the recipe of deputies, in the very first days of the February Revolution of 1917, a "sovdep" was formed with an executive body—the "executive committee," and the first executive committee, according to historians and a participant in the revolution, the Jew Sukhanov-Gimmer, included Georgians Chkheidze, Russians Lebedev, Skobelev and Peshekhonov, Jews Bogdanov, Kachelinsky, Franko, Grenevich-Shechter, Sukhanov-Gimmer, Ehrlich, Steklov-Nahamkes, Roman, Braunstein, and Sokolo of unknown nationality. Out of fourteen—three Russians, one Georgian, one unknown and nine Jews!

"We can state with no exaggeration that the great Russian social revolution is the work of the Jews," the Zionist Kogan declared in April 1919 in the New York newspaper *The Communist*.

"Would the dark, oppressed masses of the Russian workers be able to throw off the yoke of the bourgeoisie?" asks this New York comrade. And he responds: "Certainly not." The Jews were the ones who gave the Russian proletariat the dawn of the International, and they not only gave it, but are still carrying on the Soviet cause, which is firmly in our hands. The symbol of Jewry became the symbol of the Russian proletariat, which adopted a five-pointed star, very close to the six-pointed star of our Zionism. Under this sign is our victory and death to parasites: for the tears that the Jews shed, they will pay with blood.[114]

"We cannot deny that individual Jews did and still play a major role in the entire Bolshevik movement," admits Pasmannik, a White Jew from the "opposite camp" of the anti-Communists who wrote a book filled with falsehoods specifically for the rehabilitation of Jews.

---

[113] A. N. Melsky, *The Evangelist of Hate (Karl Marx)*, Za Pravda Publishing House, Berlin, 1937.
[114] See Henry Ford, *International Jew*, New York, 1927.

"There is no doubt that Jews in the USSR have many opportunities and chances that they did not have before the revolution, and that they do not have even in some democratic states," Ivanovich-Portugues in the article "Jews and the Soviet Dictatorship." "They can be generals, ministers, diplomats, professors, the highest-ranking nobles.... The Russian ways of world Jewry have been and will continue to be the most significant, and we will not escape Russia, just as Russia will not escape us." And finally, Moses Gaster, a well-known Anglo-Jewish scholar, on his return from a survey trip to the USSR, announced joyfully to world Jewry, Zionist and non-Zionist:

"I do not fear for the Judaism of Russian Jews. They have it deeply ingrained, deeper than anywhere else in the world."[115]

32. Jews in the Soviet Government

Take the composition of the Soviet government for any given year of Stalinist socialism.

Take the year 1934 for example:

Chairman of the Council of People's Commissars of the USSR Molotov-Scriabin (Russian, married to a Jewish woman), People's Commissar for Military and Naval Affairs Litvinov (Jewish), People's Commissar of Foreign Trade Rosenholz (Jew), agriculture—Chernov (Jew), state farms—Kalmanovich (Jew), education-Bubnov (Russian), finance—Grinko (Jew), heavy industry—Ordzhonikidze (Georgian), light industry—Lobov (Russian), health care—Kaminsky (Jewish), supply—Mikoyan (Armenian), transport—Andreev (Russian), Chairman of the All-Union Central Council of Trade Unions—Shvernik (Jewish), Chairman of the State Planning Committee Mezhlauk (Latvian), Chairman of the State Bank Mariyasin (Jew), Chairman of the Committee on Grain Procurement under the Council of People's Commissars Kleiner (Jewish), People's Commissar of Internal Affairs (GPU) Yagoda (a Jew).[116]

Or year 1937:

1st Chairman of the Council of People's Commissars of the USSR Molotov, People's Commissar for Foreign Affairs Litvinov Finkelstein, People's Commissar of Internal Affairs Yezhov, People's Commissar of Defense Voroshilov, People's Commissar Khinchuk, People's Commissar of Internal Trade Weitzer Israel Yakovlevich, People's Commissar of Heavy Industry Kaganovich Lazar Moiseyevich, People's Commissar of Light Industry Shestakov, People's Commissar of Defense Industry

---

[115] D. Pasmanik, "The Russian Revolution and Jewry," Paris, 1928.
[116] G. Fest, *Bolshevism and Jewry*, Riga, 1934.

Rukhimovich Moses Lvovich, People's Commissar of Mechanical Engineering Mezhlauk, People's Commissar of Food Industry Mikoyan, People's Commissar of Forest Industry Ivanov, People's Commissar of Local Industry Vakhrushev, People's Commissar of Railways Bakulin, People's Commissar of Water Transport Pakhomov, People's Commissar of Finance Chubar, People's Commissar of agriculture "Chernov," People's Commissar of State Farm Yurkin, People's Commissar of Communications Burman Matvey Davydovich, People's Commissar of Justice Krylenko, People's Commissar of Education Bubnov, People's Commissar of Health Boldyrev, People's Commissar of Public Utilities Komarov, Chairman of Gosplan Smirnov, Chairman of the Soviet Control Commission Antipov, Prosecutor of the USSR Vyshinsky, Chairman of the State Bank's Management Board Levin Reuben Lvovich, Chief Central Management of national economic accounting Kraval Borukh Antonovich, Head of the State Reserves Department Rosengolts, Deputy People's Commissars for Finance Grichman, for Heavy Industry Ingerrman, Food Industry Gilinsky Abram Lazarevich, Minister of Health Pronner-Gerashchenkov.

This is who represents the Soviet Union abroad at this time (Litvinov-Finkelstein, as People's Commissar of Foreign Affairs, did his best for his beloved relatives).

In Germany—Plenipotentiary of the USSR Suritz (Jew), in England—Maisky (Jew), in France—Potemkin (Russian), in Italy—Galfand (Jew), in Austria—Petrovsky (Jew), in Greece—Kobetsky (Karaite), in Poland—Davtyan (Armenian), in Lithuania—Bratman-Brodsky (Jew), in Estonia—Ustinov (Russian), in Finland—Stein (Jew), in Norway—Bezdaktyan (Armenian), in Turkey—Karakhan (Armenian), in America—Troyanovsky (Jew), in Persia—Brenev (Jew), Consul General in Moscow Manchukuo—Slutsky (a Jew).

This is who represents the USSR in the League of Nations: Litvinov-Wallach-Finkelstein the Jew, Hosenberg is a Jew, Stein is a Jew, Markus is Jewish, Breners is a Jew, Gershfeld is a Jew, Galfand is a Jew, Svanidze is a Georgian.

Of the eight, seven are Jews and one is Georgian!

Fest, giving the longest of lists, counts:

The Council of People's Commissars consists of 24 people: 8 Russians, 12 Jews, and 4 other non-Russians.
The Central Committee of the party consists of 71 members and 68 candidates: 32 Russians, 27 Jews, 10 other non-Russians, 2 unknown nationalities; candidates: 31 Russians, 32 Jews, 5 other non-Russians. The party control commission consists of 61 members: 22 Russians, 35 Jews, and 4 other non-Russians. The Soviet control commission has 70 members: 30 Russians, 35 Jews, and 5 other non-Russians. The Revision

96 | Testament of a Russian Fascist

Commission of the CPSU has 22 members, including 7 Russians, 11 Jews, and 4 other non-Russians.

The Committees of the Communist Party, exercising de facto power on the ground, by 1935 show a picture of complete Jewish leadership. *Nash Put'* No. 293 lists the names of the secretaries in charge of them, according to the administrative division of the USSR, alphabetically:

1. Abkhazian ASSR—Lakozi (Jewish).
2. Adjarian ASSR—Guria (Georgian).
3. Azerbaijan SSR—Polonsky (Jewish).
4. Azov-Black Sea region—Borukh Sheboldaev (Jewish).
5. Armenian SSR—Hayan (Armenian).
6. Bashkir ASSR—Moisey Bykin (Jewish).
7. Byelorussian SSR—Gikalo (Jewish).
8. Buryat-Mongolian ASSR—Yerbanov (Buryat).
9. Voronezh region—Ryabinin (Russian).
10. East Siberian region—Razumov-Sakovich (Jewish).
11. Gorky region—Reuven Pramnen (Jewish), chairman of the regional executive committee—Yuri Kaganovich (Lazar's brother).
12. Georgian SSR—Lavrentiy Beria.
13. Dagestan ASSR—Tsekhher (Jewish).
14. Far Eastern Region—Lavrentiev-Lippman (Jewish).
15. Western region—Rumyantsev-Rubinchik (Jewish).
16. West Siberian region—Eikhe (Jewish).
17. Ivanovo region—Naum Nosov (Jewish).
18. Kazakh SSR—Mirzoyan (Armenian).
19. Karelian ASSR—Apollonik (Jewish).
20. Kirghiz ASSR—Belotsky (Jewish).
21. Kirov Region—Joiner (Jewish).
22. Crimean ASSR—Semenov-Solomonsky (Jewish).
23. Kuibyshev Region—Miron Shubrikov (Jewish).
24. Kursk region—Ivanov (Russian).
25. Leningrad region—Zhdanov (Russian), deputy-Pevsner (Jewish).
26. Mari Autonomous Region—Shanvari (Jewish).
27. Moldavian ASSR—Bulat (Jewish).
28. Moscow region—Khrushchev (Russian), deputy-Kogan (Jewish).
29. Omsk region—Butkevich (Jewish).
30. Orenburg region—Gorkin (Jewish).
31. ASSR of Volga Germans—Kurz (Jewish).
32. Northern region—Koptarin (Jewish).
33. Stalingrad region—Vareikis (Latvian).
34. Saratov region—Kripitsky (Jewish).

35. Sverdlovsk region—Moisey Kabakov (Jewish).
36. Tatar ASSR—Poppok (Jewish).
37. Turkmen SSR—Leza (Jewish).
38. Ukrainian SSR—Kosior (Jew). Its constituent areas are:
    a. Vinnytsia—Trilissky (Jewish);
    b. Dnepropetrovsk—Khatayevich (Jewish);
    c. Donetsk—Sarkas (Jewish);
    d. Kiev—Boris Kaganovich (Jewish);
    e. Odessa—Golub (Jewish);
    f. Kharkiv—Shelekhes (Jewish);
    g. Chernihiv—Markitan (Jewish).
39. Chelyabinsk region—Gyndin (Jewish).
40. Yakut ASSR—Pevznyak (Jewish).

Total: Jews 41, Russians 4, Armenians 2, Georgians 1, and Buryats 1. This is the so-called "Russian" power!!!

33. Kaganovich

Kaganovich at this very moment is reaching the zenith of power. He is Stalin's Assistant General Secretary, Second Secretary of the Central Committee of the CPSU and the de facto manager of the Secretariat, he is a member of the Politburo and the Organizational Bureau of the Central Committee of the CPSU, he is the People's Commissar of Railways and chairman of the party control Commission. He is managed and controlled only by himself. His brothers sat in the leadership of other people's commissariats, and his daughter Rosa Kaganovich became Stalin's beloved wife.

The foreign Jewish press enthusiastically publishes:

In the Jewish-written newspaper *Moment* published in Warsaw, V. P. Goldberg, who is currently on a trip to the Soviet Union, gives the following description of Kaganovich, Stalin's deputy (translated by a Russian Jew).

Remember this name: Lazar Moiseyevich. He is a great man. He may someday rule over the land of kings. Lazar Moiseyevich is Kaganovich, Stalin's deputy. When Stalin leaves, he takes his place. When Stalin turns 120, Lazar Moiseyevich will be the new Stalin, being ten years younger. "Lazar will be Stalin's heir," one Jew assured me, who is nothing less than Kaganovich's brother-in-law. This brother-in-law is not just anyone either: he is a prominent Communist with a rather big name, although he does not hold a high post. In passing, I immediately hear from the Communists: "What a clever man he is, this Lazar Moiseyevich, how practical he is, he won't say a single superfluous word, and how intelligent he is, and how straight he goes along the road of Marx, Lenin and Stalin." So, I began to believe that he was the real Crown Prince. There is another point here: the practical goals of the Bolsheviks are a quintet, namely: Marxism should be transmitted from one great man to another. Marx inherited Marxism from the dialectics and passed it on to Engels, Engels to Lenin, Lenin to Stalin, and now Stalin is passing it on to Kaganovich. Yes, yes! He's already passing it on!

Just now Stalin is on vacation, he takes baths in the vicinity of Sochi and lives there in a secluded hut in the forest. When Stalin is resting, he is resting completely and does not want to be bothered about anything. Who will replace Stalin then? Lazar Moiseyevich!

There was a parade of military airplanes.... Who was replacing Stalin at the parade? Lazar Moiseyevich! There was a congress of writers.... Who gave a banquet in honor of foreign writers led by Gorky? Again, Lazar Moiseyevich. And there was Lazar Moiseyevich in Odessa, treated as if he was Stalin himself, and everything confined within the party spheres, without much noise, as Stalin likes it. Kaganovich is a native of Rybna (a small town in the Kiev province). If you remember Sholem Aleichem, then you know about Rybna. His father was a clerk for a landowner on the estate. His father has been dead for a long time, his mother died recently, she was just a common Jewess who went to the synagogue to pray. She was buried not in the Jewish cemetery, but in Mariinsky Park, [where] the heroes of the revolution are buried. There are four Kaganovich brothers and three sisters in total. Of the brothers, one of them is Lazar Moiseyevich, the secretary of the Central Committee and Stalin's deputy, the second Kaganovich is Ordzhonikidze's deputy, the third is the secretary of the regional party committee in Nizhny Novgorod, now Gorky, the fourth runs a block of shops in Kiev ... consisting of fifteen food shops. All three sisters are married. One lives in Moscow, the other two in Kiev.

Lazar Moiseyevich is forty-three years old. His daughter, who is turning twenty-one, is Stalin's current wife. Such are family matters.

What is Kaganovich's greatness? Of course, he is not a major scientist, [but] he is not at all such a simpleton as he is presented. True, he was just a sewing machine operator, but he was adaptable, he studied and knew Marx, Engels, and Lenin. He cannot be called a great speaker either, although he does not speak poorly, he speaks clearly, strongly, and to the point. He is a good organizer, like Stalin, and most importantly, he serves as a bulwark of the party, and the party is always right. In his conscience there are no deviations either to the right or to the left. "Stalin is Marx," Kaganovich's brother-in-law categorically declared, and [himself] Kaganovich strictly adheres to the Stalinist road.

When Ukrainian nationalism surfaced (the Skrynnikov scam) and they realized that the Communist Party in Ukraine was chauvinistically Ukrainian and wanted to even separate from Moscow, Kaganovich was sent to rebuild the party, and he did it. He knows how, he was an employee of the Cheka in the worst years.

He is kind to the Jews. When they wanted to close the Rybinski synagogue, the Rybninsky Jews ran to Kaganovich, and he gave them the opportunity to pray in the synagogue for three years.

You see how good it is to have one of your own among those in power.

Indeed, Kaganovich openly patronized his relatives, as evidenced, for example, by the composition of the council at the NKPS, transcribed by *Nashim Putem* from the Soviet press on February 4th, 1936:

Kaganovich Lazar Moiseyevich (Chairman), Livshits Yakov Abramovich, Vilik Pavel Borisovich, Mamendos Lev Arsentievich, Kostanyan Gaikaz Arkadievich, Shikhgildyan Vagan Pirumovich, Amatuni Polayu Karapetovich, Rutenburg Arkady Mikhailovich, Rosenzweig Maximilian Arnoldovich, Paverman Vladimir Lvovich, Nolod Naum Pavlovich, Kavtaradze Georgy Davidovich, Gorshin Joseph Borisovich, Petrosyan Georgy Stepanovich, Gaister Semyon Israilevich, Arnoldov Aron Markohiv, Filov Viktor Grigorievich, Teumin Yakov Abramovich, Belenky Boris Natanovich, Hartman Bentsian Natanovich, Gramko Andrey Isaakovich, Kopp Ilya Mikhailovich, Revin Solomon Lazarevich, Rosenthal Yakov Davidovich, Goltsman Yuri Mikhailovich, Bukhovsky Yakov Markovich—19 Jews, 3 Armenians, 2 Georgians, and not a single Russian!

The OGIZ (association of state book and magazine publishers of the USSR) calendar directory calmly reports in the biographies of the red leaders for 1939:

Lazar Moiseyevich Kaganovich, member of the Politburo of the Central Committee of the CPSU, deputy chairman of the SNK of the USSR, was born on November 22nd, 1893. Before the revolution, he engaged in underground work in Kiev, Yekaterinoslav, Melitopol, and Yuzovka.

In 1917, L. M. Kaganovich was a member of the All–Russian Bureau of Military Party Organizations under the Central

Committee of the RSDLP, as chairman of the Polessky Party Committee. In 1918, he was commissar of the All–Russian Board for the Organization of the Red Army [in other words, one of the actual creators of the Red Army]. From 1918 through 1921, he led party and Soviet work in Nizhny Novgorod, Voronezh, Tashkent. At the Twelfth Congress of the Party, Comrade Kaganovich was elected as a candidate member of the Central Committee of the CPSU, and since the Twelfth Congress as a permanent member of the Central Committee of the party. From 1921 through 1925 he was Secretary of the Central Committee of the CPSU, from 1925 to 1928 he served as the First Secretary of the Central Committee of the CP of Ukraine. From 1928 to 1929, Kaganovich was secretary of the MK and MGK of the CPSU.

From 1935 to 1937, L. M. Kaganovich was People's Commissar of Railways. In 1937 he was the People's Commissar of Heavy Industry. In 1938, he was again appointed People's Commissar of Railways and approved as Deputy Chairman of the USSR Council of People's Commissars.

For outstanding services in the leadership of socialist construction, Comrade Kaganovich was awarded the Order of Lenin and the Order of the Red Banner of Labor.

Bolshevik principles, deep knowledge of the case, careful cultivation of personnel, the ability to infect people with pathos in work are characteristic features of L. M. Kaganovich, an outstanding political figure, a faithful disciple, and one of Comrade Stalin's closest associates.

Comrade Kaganovich is a deputy of the Supreme Soviet of the USSR.

"Where we were humiliated and persecuted, we are now overbearing and merciless persecutors," sums up the Jewish writer Israel Zangwild in the book *Now and Always*.

34. Jews Are Being Introduced to East Asia

To put an end to the Old World, it remains now for us to take a cursory look at the introduction of Jews into East Asia, China, Japan, Manchuria, and the countries of the South Seas of the Pacific Ocean. Jewish snakes crawled here from Russia, around Asia, and from the opposite side of the Pacific Ocean. Anglo-American imperialism here, as indeed everywhere else, was predominantly Jewish imperialism. And when its collapse began, Jews from all over Germany, Austria, Czechoslovakia, and Poland rushed here.

In another section of this book, we talk about the conquest of China with the help of British troops by the Jewish dynasty of the Sassoon opiate pushers, who sucked all the juices out of China and made billions in fortune here. Due to a certain reason, we will not touch the Jewish Question in Manchuria.[117] As for Japan, thanks to its 2,600-year isolation, it has remained aloof from Judaization. In recent years however, according to some prominent Japanese, the Jewish threat has also begun to be felt here.

So, on July 7th, 1941, the Tokyo newspaper *Hochi* published the article "The Japanese Sword," in which it indicated that a country in which there are 3,000 Jews can already consider itself conquered, and in Japan the number of these "guests" is already approaching these figures.

For Japan, the Jews came up with a special theory that the Japanese are one of the lost tribes of Israel. This theory, insulting to the Japanese nation, was developed (without any success however) by the late Duzi Nakada, a Methodist bishop, author of the book *The Mysterious Nation*. But Japanese patriots stand guard over their country—the teachings of the Methodists and of other agents of world Jewry are neither influential nor widespread in the Land of the Rising Sun.

But in Shanghai, thanks to the invasion of a huge number of "refugees" from Europe, the situation became so unbearable that the Japanese newspaper in Russian *Far Eastern Times* published a wonderful article that our readers should get acquainted with in full:

"Shanghai is a fetid nest of Jewish hatred, malice, vindictiveness, and greed."

The cold-blooded Jewish viper spreads its deadly poison among the peoples of East Asia. A nation cursed by God and humanity for their criminal work in the struggle against the New Order, against laws and legality: black-hearted ingratitude for hospitality is the economic undermining of Japan and the New China.

There is no nation more vindictive than the Jews. Getting revenge against someone is all they have ever done in their lives. Once they were persecuted by the Jesuits in Spain, but now for example, they are taking revenge on Japan, the people who sheltered them.

And no sooner had the articles appeared in the *Far Eastern Times*, the stench, the supposed innuendos, the cries about how miserable the Jews are and how they are all oppressed, began.

One Jew had foam coming out of his mouth yelling that he knew this Mr. Matsuoka and he would personally tell him that there would be no trace of the "little Jap."

---

[117] As outlined elsewhere, the RFP was not the only émigré group active in Manchuria, some of them being hostile. (Translator's note)

Another shouted that they had so much money in Shanghai that they could load a steamer, immediately send it to Tokyo, and end this newspaper and whoever was behind it.

The third one in the Jewish Club shouted that he had a CAPTAIN (captain, captain, smile!) and such a great captain and such a great patron of the Jews that everyone would tremble.

Why were the Jews so worried? Is it because they have built a nest in Shanghai, at a time when there is a life-and-death war; when the greatest cities in the world are crumbling and tens of thousands of innocent victims die every day from bombs? Here, in Asia, the blood of the Japanese soldiers is being shed, and all the while they have created a central base in Shanghai for their speculative purposes and to take advantage of the fact that Shanghai is a state without sovereigns and parliament, to do their *geshefts* as they please, not shying away from inflicting economic damage to Japan.[118] Moreover, they take the most lively part in the harassment and provocation that is being conducted around Japan and the Japanese imperial representatives in China, in the army, in the navy, etc.

Before making our accusations, we want to acquaint the Jewish gentlemen with the situation that exists in Japan.

First of all, what has Japan done to you? Why do your newspapers, your journalists, be they English, American, German, Russian, or Polish—there are hundreds of them in Shanghai—why do they conduct systematic harassment of Japan and the New Order?

Beloved Jews, there are no racial prejudices in Japan. This was even discussed by prime ministers in Japan. This is exactly the reason you are here now; in Shanghai, in Harbin, in Dairen, in Kobe, in Tokyo. Wherever the power of the Emperor of Japan is, you live freely, like nowhere else. Could you live like this, for example, in the USSR? To be able to speculate, merge, make millions without paying either the state or anyone else for that matter? And how about in old Russia, in Germany now, or in Italy and, finally, in your beloved England, which has been promising you Palestine for fifty years already? It is you, gentlemen, who fought for her in that war, and it is still you who fight for her now.

What have the Japanese done to you to poison them from all the pages of your magazines, newspapers, and through all the telegraph agencies? All the foreign correspondents in Shanghai, in most cases Jews, not only distort the facts, but come up with such propaganda, such malicious fabrications that could only come out of the devilish mind of a Jew, having received thirty pieces of silver from his Qahal in London or Washington.

---

[118] A German word meaning business, which comes from the Yiddish slang for a business deal. (Translator's note)

Is Japan's policy in Asia directly or indirectly directed against Jews? Of course not! But if it is directed against one state or another, then isn't it time for them to ask themselves if you are doing the right thing by taking revenge on Japan? For what? For taking refuge?

Let's start with the basics. D. V. Paul, the editor of the *China Weekly Review*, is Jewish. His malicious assistants Buchman, John Allers, Glatz, and dozens of others besides him work for various American and English newspapers in Shanghai and are correspondents to London, New York, and San Francisco. Aren't these the ones who make up the gang that heads the anti-Japanese front? It is impossible to imagine everything that these vile Jews write in pen and draw in caricatures, all in order to defame Japan. They, you see, protect China.

What do you, gentlemen, care about the internal struggle between Japan and China? But of course, after all, the conflict in China was created artificially and, once again, the hands of the usual gold dealers and brokers like Sassoon and Co., Arabic Jews, and bankers, who created this conflict with the help of American Jews, are involved just as much here.

And who are those senators in America and various ministers in England who shouted about the evil Japanese demon, who urgently needed to be embargoed? Aren't these your fellow compatriots? The ones behind the anti-Japanese articles in the *China* Press and the *Irving Post*, not to mention scum like the Lonovs, and the ones higher up. Aren't they your blood?

And that is when you got hurt a little, you wailed and screamed. You, at the rear of the Japanese army, dare to raise your voice, threaten, because somewhere, some newspaper in Russian hurt you, made you feel unpleasant, offended you. And isn't it monstrous that you, who can be crushed at any time and arranged a Hitler purge against you at any time, you still dare to make mischief day after day, every hour, every minute? What's the matter, why are you interested in this? It just seems to us that you dream of destroying the throne and foundations of all states in order to take the reign for yourself. You are gravely mistaken: this will not occur! Time is against you.

What kind of talk is this, what kind of threats are these to pressure someone, to displace someone? Behold, gentlemen, behold the backstage rulers!

You underestimated, gentlemen, one thing among Asians, among the Japanese, namely that in Japan everyone can say what he wants, if it is for the good of the Emperor and the Fatherland. In Japan, everyone can profess any religion and any doctrine, just so that it would be for the good of the Emperor and the Fatherland. Therefore, did you really have the preconceived notion that, say, for offending a bunch speculators, agitators, spies and foreigners, that would make someone be hit in the head, to cause someone to be displaced? Hilariously stupid.

We advise you to come to your senses and instead of sending a steamer with money to someone, use it for a good cause, not for yourself, but for others.

Even those refugees who came here from Europe and who owe their lives to Japan for letting them in here, since the British do not allow all of you to enter your promised Palestine, even they, having settled in different newspapers, conduct the most vicious propaganda against the people who sheltered them. Various gentlemen like Hamburg, Hubert Frank, Ginzburg, and others continue the anti-Japanese campaign, becoming more impudent and angrier in their articles; you know who they are and what they write, you do not need to explain. You have repaid your hospitality with a dagger to the back.

Do you remember how you ran away with your money from the Bolsheviks? You have found salvation in Asia. You fled Europe and found salvation in Asia.

What have you been doing until now, and especially lately, during these four years of war between Japan and China? We can tell you.

Jewelry was illegally exported from Japan, bought and smuggled. There are hundreds of such cases, and they are all registered. Counterfeit money was imported. Yes, this was the case, and it continues to be. We will give you a little fact: when the son of a Jew got caught with a fake check, he immediately sent his father an ultimatum through Russian detectives (out of youth, out of stupidity) that, allegedly, if dad doesn't pay, he will explain in court how he and dad distributed fake yen last year. We know this father, and dozens of other businessmen who have so far managed to evade the long arm of law called justice.

You have exported tens of millions of yen and American dollars and are still exporting them. According to the closest calculation, the economic damage caused by you in two years is equal to more than one hundred million yen. True, your wives are flooded with diamonds, they flaunt black and brown foxes and arctic foxes, you have now acquired plots of land and fourteen-story apartment buildings here, and you are also busy with American papers for yourself, but all this is known, and so is every one of you known. You will have to answer for all this in time. We warn you that America is a utopia, and nowhere can there be such an acute social crisis, nowhere else will the foundations be shaken so much as in America. Above all, you will try nowhere like in America, and for that you will have to pay. Yesterday's beggars made millions during the conflict, and all this on Japanese blood. You know yourself; they are among you; they are everywhere.

Would you have been allowed in Europe and the USSR to buy furs and goods, travel all over China and Japan, spend time at resorts, and transfer money to America?

After all, you manage to lead a luxurious life legally, to make a gratuitous profit without giving anything to the state, and at the same time to conduct a terrible and sabotaging work in word and deed in as many forms as you possibly can. What is the point?

After all, you have everything in Shanghai in your hands. But it can't go on like this, and there will be an end to it.

We are not giving you a warning, but rather an order: come to your senses. We repeat that this is not a case of Judeophobia, not anti-Semitism, no, it's just tolerance of Asia. You should warn your relatives here and in America and in England that everyone knows about you, everyone knows that it's time to stop doing evil to those who sheltered you, and most importantly, stop sticking your nose in, interfering, in that great struggle called the New Order. For now, you stand on the sidelines, but the time will come, and when it does you may be required to pay the price.

The stock exchange, hotels, cinemas, banks, loan offices, jewelry and its trade, restaurants and cabarets, brothels, pharmacies, lawyers, doctors, newspapers and the press in general, art, shops, import–export—everything, everything, everything is in your hands. You are strong in this oasis that is called Shanghai, you have a thin network of threads in all directions of the world. There is one nest of cobwebs here, but what is on your mind will not succeed.

You will not break the strength of the peoples of Japan and China, because these people have a homeland and their own culture, which is older than yours and who have always been at home, and have not been scattered around the world like you. You cannot undermine the foundations of those who have millennia behind them, and this is Asia. You can't outwit Asians!

35. Jews in the South Seas

In Singapore, in Hong Kong, in French Indochina, the Dutch East Indies, and further in Oceania, priceless gifts of nature before the outbreak of the Great War in East Asia were almost exclusively in Jewish hands. The vast majority of the administration there was represented by Jews, and those who are not Jews, those pure-blooded Englishmen or Americans, are certainly Freemasons—that is, ultimately, servants of the Jews. The Russian *New Journal of Foreign Literature, Art and Science* by Bulgakov and Suvorin provided us with terrible pictures of the conquest of the Philippines by the Americans back in 1902. For example, under the heading "From the Annals of Crimes" we read there such fascinating documents:

> In March 1901, a North American newspaper printed in Massachusetts published letters from Sergeant Charles Billy from

the 26th Volunteer Regiment. It described the way the war was waged in the Philippines:

"Gordon's scouts were waiting for us in Gwimble. There were about forty of them, all on horseback, and we immediately saw that fun was to come. Arriving in Igbaras at dawn, we found quite a peaceful population in it, but we were not slow to discover that 'we are on rocky grounds.'

"The president (the chief of the tribe), a priest, and a notable were brought to a large village square and interrogated. The president didn't want to answer. They tied him up and began to torture him with water. He was thrown to the ground, turned over on his back and dragged to the well. Then they began to pour water into his mouth forcibly, while another pressed on his stomach so that he would not die from the operation. This loosened his tongue. The old 'sly man' soon asked for a pardon and confessed. When they began to interrogate him a second time and demand more precise information, they had to treat him with a second portion of water before getting a confession. Salt was added to the water to make it work more successfully."

This letter from Sergeant Billy went all over the American press. The events to which it referred took place on November 25th, 1900. The president who was tortured was a Tagalog from the island of Panay. He enjoyed the general respect of the tribe. They wanted to find out from him and tried to torture out of him the number of indignant natives, what weapons they had and what positions they occupied. The president was an old man, and his advanced years must have seemed to instill in the American soldiers a sense of respect and compassion. He was tortured by water for not wanting to betray his brothers and send them to their deaths. Sergeant Billy does not say whether he was among the executioners. But be that as it may, he finds this way of waging war not only natural, but also useful. And instead of feeling sorry for the noble, dedicated president, he calls him an "old cunning man."

Another letter, written by Mikhail Sni from the 9th regiment of the Regular Army, fully confirms the message of Sergeant Billy. Here's what he writes:

"From the very moment of our arrival in Samar, we were sent on an expedition to the mountains surrounding the city. The instructions did not order to expel the insurgents, who, according to the instructions of the native police, hid in the gorges. The natives were ordered not to leave the mountains. All those who fled to the mountains risked their lives. Every two days, Lieutenant Schiffel sends a detachment of soldiers to reconnoiter in the mountains under the command of an officer. I participated in these detachments several times. We were given definite and strict orders: 'Whoever we capture in the mountains, we kill.' 'To stab the dogs and pigs,' was our order, 'regardless of age'; but I must say that we did not have to shoot children, because we never came across any. We were also ordered to take from the prisoners all kinds of testimonies about the uprising and, in order to get them, we resorted to waterboarding. For many of us, and even for all of us, perhaps, it was unpleasant, but we had to obey under the threat of the most severe of punishments. I have seen over twenty Filipinos being waterboarded. We tortured them in the gorges where we came across them, but there were also numerous cases in the village where our detachment was stationed.

"The method of torture was cruel. At first, the soldiers tried to find out from the prisoner everything he knew about the insurgency. If he refused to talk, they tied his hands behind his back, put him on the ground facing the sky. After that, they put a bottle with a broken bottom in his mouth and used it as a funnel to pour a lot of water into it. I have seen two or three buckets of water poured in this way into the stomach of one or another native. The body was plump and took on dimensions two or three times the normal size. Then the man was rolled on the ground to force him to regurgitate all the swallowed water, after which the torture resumed. The native, of course, resisted, and the soldiers again stuffed a bottle with a broken bottom into his mouth, tearing his flesh. When the waterboarding was over, the prisoner was shot and killed. If the execution took place outside the city or in the mountains, then the dead body was thrown to the dogs."

Corporal John Barnett of the 2nd Infantry Regiment, in turn, told what he saw:

"On the evening of September 16th, 1900, waterboarding was carried out in my presence over the president of Tassi, a city of 1,200 inhabitants: he was taken to a bamboo hut, and there officers of the United States Army interrogated him. Following orders, the soldiers dragged him away from the wall of the hut and bent his head backwards. A bamboo was inserted between his teeth, which did not allow him to close his mouth, and then they began pouring buckets of water on him. Water fell on top of him, flowed down his forehead and penetrated into his nostrils and mouth. The slightest effort to breathe through his nose should have fatally suffocated the poor soul, so he continuously swallowed water with his mouth. Then the interpreter said to him, 'Hebla,' which means 'talk.' The man stammered weakly: 'I know absolutely nothing about the insurgent forces in the vicinity of the city.' The torture resumed, but even more severely, as soap was added to the water. When he almost choked, he gave a sign that he would speak. The torture was suspended. He fainted on the ground. He was brought to his senses."

What was being done by American troops on the Philippine Islands is now known as "American atrocities." The hair stands on end, and the blood literally freezes within your veins when reading the horrors that were coldly committed by soldiers and officers of a country that considers itself civilized and enlightened. Positively, the so-called "Turkish atrocities" pale in comparison to what was happening on the Philippine Islands. Every moral sense has been extinguished in the conscience of people who commit unheard-of cruelties and resort to medieval style torture in order to loosen the tongue of the natives and get them to betray their fellow citizens. Military justice in America tried to drown out these cases when it was entrusted with the investigation.[119]

Naturally, the Jews acted, for the Jews, according to Jewish instructions.

Note that these incriminating facts of American expansion are not cited by a Japanese or German source when the war is boiling, but by a pre-revolutionary Russian magazine—they are forty years old. He tells us by what methods the Philippines was conquered. And for whom, as the Shanghai Jewish magazine explains, which tells:

Jews in the Philippines (correspondent from Manila)

The Philippine Islands are now at the center of the world. Despite the thousands of miles separating them from the United States, their economic, cultural, and political ties with the metropolis are far stronger than with any neighboring country in the Far East.

The indigenous population of the Philippines numbers thirteen million people, and they speak different dialects. Spaniards, of whom there are a lot on the islands, also live separately. Catholics, divided into many sects, still represent a great force to this day. Many pagans still live in the interior of the country.

On the island of Mindanao, where the President of the Philippines Manuel Kenzon intends to settle ten thousand Jews in

---

[119] *New Journal of Foreign Literature, Art and Science*, 1902, vol. 11.

ten years, there is a wild tribe of "Mora" living there. American civilization has penetrated so deeply into the life of the country that the Filipino youth speak English well.

As for the Jewish population of the Philippines, there are currently only 1,300 Jews living in the entire country. Over the past three years, about 500 Jews from Germany and Italy have arrived on the islands. 90 percent of the entire Jewish population lives in the capital of the Philippines, the city of Manila. The Jewish population of the Philippines can be divided into four groups.

In the first place are English and American Jews. Among them are the largest planters, bankers and industrialists and several millionaires. The leader of Filipino Jewry is the largest cigarette manufacturer.

The sugar, coconut and rubber industries, as well as the production of other items that are exported to America, are in Jewish hands. It is interesting to note that 80 percent of the income of the entire industry of the Philippines goes to America and only 17 percent to other countries, and only 3 percent remains for their own needs.

In second place are Sephardic or Baghdadi Jews; the weasels engage in export and import from all ports of the Far East and South Asia.

In third place are our Russian and Polish Jews arriving in Manila from Harbin and Northern China. They make up the middle class in terms of wealth. Finally, German refugees are in last place.

With the exception of this last group, all Jews are well-off. The peso is highly valued, there is no ban on the export of money from the country, and people with a business can work well in the Philippines.

We have given these frank statements almost completely, because they vividly illuminate the essence of the colonial policy of the United States and Britain: that's why the American beasts tortured the unfortunate Filipinos!

36. The Center of Jewish Life Moves to America

Our journey is coming to an end. Having crossed the Pacific Ocean, we are approaching the shores of the New World, which, as the Shanghai Jewish *Our Life* declared long ago: "Now, with the destruction of European centers, the center of Jewish life is being moved to the United States."

Indeed, America is becoming the main base of world Jewry. Omitting Central and South America and Canada to save time and paper, we will focus our attention on the United States, where the most important Jewish governing bodies are now located.

Back in 1915, a characteristic series of cartoons emerged in America, almost tragicomic: "An Illustrated History of the US in Three Parts." Firstly, a picture of an Indian on a rock with an Anglo-Saxon sneaking behind him. In the second, an Indian is falling into the abyss, a smug alien is grinning in his place, but a Jew is sneaking up on him from behind. In the third picture, Uncle Sam is the one falling, and a Jew has taken his place and unfurled the star-spangled banner.

And so, the Jew began the conquest of America very modestly. How he started, O. Krainz recounts in his curious book *Judas Discovers America* (1939).

Krainz cites irrefutable evidence of exactly how the Jew corrupted the Indians with "fiery water" and how he seized the entire fur trade in America. Twenty-two distilleries in Newport were producing a ruinous poison that led the Indians to their doom. From the consumption of alcoholic beverages, the once belligerent redskins turned into weak-willed drunks who lost all idea of honor and decency. Because of this, many Whites died at the hands of the Indians. This sad phenomenon did not sadden the Jews in the least, however. They were only concerned about profit. The lack of a laboring class forced the American colonists to import negroes from Africa at one time. At first, however, these Negroes were not slaves, but only temporary forced laborers who had the right to become colonists after a certain number of years. Negroes were, therefore, in the same position as Jews, who also did not enjoy any of the rights granted to citizens.

As the social status of the Jews improved, the craft of the slave trade expanded, which in the end even determined the policy of the United States and led to a civil war. Newport became the world Jewish center of the slave trade. Charleston, however, did not lag behind in this regard.

The Jews bought Negroes in Africa from twenty to forty dollars a head and sold them in America for two hundred dollars. With the help of a widely branched organization, in which many Negro leaders also participated, bribed with rum and low-value gifts, black slaves were driven through the tropical forests from inner Africa. During this painful rut, thousands of unfortunate people didn't make it along the way. It was believed that for every Negro who could endure the unheard-of disasters of this path and, moreover, the painful crossing of the ocean, there were nine who died before him. At the time of the highest development of the slave trade, the total value of slaves was estimated at about a billion dollars, and in 1860 it reached four hundred billion.

When the importation of slaves was finally banned, an extensive smuggling trade flourished. The latter took on such dimensions that the American government declared this trade piracy.

But the unscrupulous Jews managed to get around it: in Virginia and Georgia, they simply switched to breeding slaves. So a new kind of trade emerged. Soon Virginia began to supply up to 3,000 Negroes annually for export to other states. Some Jews went so far as to pay their employees twenty dollars for each Negro woman who got pregnant from them. Because of this, the number of mulattoes has increased enormously.

And so the Harbin *Jewish Life* tells:

> In New York there is an institute headed by Professor Maurice Cohen, who studies the role of Jews in economic life. The institute employs prominent economists and statisticians who collect materials in this field. This institute has now produced interesting studies on the occupations of the two million Jews in New York. Here is the data: two million Jews live in New York. Of the 34,000 factories in New York, two thirds of that is owned by Jews and only a third are workers. The fur industry is entirely in Jewish hands, both for employers and workers; in other dress industries, the situation is different: almost all employers are Jews, but no more than half are working Jews.
>
> In the paper industry, more than half of the entrepreneurs are Jews, and only one fifth of the workers are Jews; in the forestry industry, half of the employers are Jews, and one fifth of the workers. In the food and tobacco industry, the total number of employers is 17,000, of which 830 are Jews, and the total number of workers is 51,000, of which 10,000 are Jews.
>
> In the glass industry, half of the Jews are among employers (200 out of 395), Jewish workers are 1,500 out of a total of 4,113.
>
> In the metal industry, out of 3,000 employers, 1,000 are Jews and one fifth of the workers are Jews.
>
> About two thirds of New York pharmacy businesses are in the hands of Jews. 67 percent of the owners of dress shops, household goods, and furniture are Jews.
>
> An important point is the participation of Jews in the construction industry. Of the 10,000 construction entrepreneurs in New York, 4,000 are Jews.
>
> In two artistic professions, theater and music, 22,000 Jews are employed in New York (7,000 actors, 12,500 musicians, and 2,500 other employees in theaters and concert halls).
>
> Over 100,000 Jews are employed in New York restaurants, hotels, laundries, and other services.

There are 10,000 Jewish teachers in New York, 3,500 writers, 5,000 engineers, 1,000 archaeologists, 12,000 chemists, 7,000 doctors of medicine, 4,000 dentists, and 2,000 photographers.

The new institutions have 7,500 Jewish employees. Of these, 6,000 work in insurance companies. There are 21,000 Jews in public institutions, 18,000 in the city government, and 3,000 in post offices. In addition, 5,000 Jews work at the telegraph, telephone, trams, gas, and electric establishments.

25,000 Jews are employed in the transport industry." [120]

The numbers speak for themselves. They show how deeply Judaism has penetrated into the economic and social, and therefore into the political life of New York. We should not forget that these figures are given in a Jewish journal and compiled by a Jewish professor, a specialist in Jewish statistics. Obviously, these figures are understated rather than exaggerated, but what an impressive picture they paint before us!

37. Jewish Population Growth in Overseas Countries

The frankness of the *Jewish Life* of the old times is supplemented by a table in the same Harbin Jewish magazine on December 1st, 1942. It draws the growth of the Jewish population in countries overseas:

	1800	1880	1900	1933	1938
United States	2,000	23,000	1,000,000	4,500,000	4,700,000
Canada		2,400	16,400	160,000	175,000
Argentina			30,000	245,000	275,000
Brazil			3,000	45,000	55,000
Uruguay				20,000	25,000
Chile				7,000	10,000
Cuba		1,000	3,000	9,000	10,000
Mexico			1,000	15,000	20,000

"America for the Americans!" Alas, in the twentieth century, the Monroe doctrine sounds slightly different: "America for the Jews." The American Secretary of the Interior, Mr. Ickes, depending on the pronunciation, did not hesitate to say this, in different terms, in a speech dedicated to "the great role of the Jewish people in human culture," delivered by him in Baltimore in the summer of 1940:

---

[120] *Jewish Life*, No. 35, 1938, Harbin.

No nation has given so much to humanity as the Jewish one. Anti–Semitism is a cancer of humanity [compare it with Stalin's statement to the correspondent of the American telegraph agency: "Anti–Semitism is the worst form of cannibalism"]. . . . You should gladly accept the flow of refugees, which harbors treasures of energy, knowledge, and high mental capabilities [what treasures are these the example of Shanghai testifies, which has a similar refugee flow, increased crime exactly seven times according to police statistics].[121]

The Jews must have rushed to have Mr. Ickes listed in the *Golden Book of the Jewish National Fund*. But Ickes is not the only one in the leadership of the US. He is one of many other Ickeses. His piety for Jewry is shared first of all by the third-term president of the US, Franklin Delano Roosevelt.

38. Roosevelt and World Jewry

When Franklin Delano Roosevelt was elected president of the US in 1932, Harbin's *Jewish Life*, reflecting the opinion of the Jewish press around the world, wrote:

"The newly elected American president Roosevelt is a sincere friend of the Jews and is very much interested in the Jewish question. Roosevelt is very sympathetic to the Zionist movement."[122]

You bet! His ancestors, as some German sources attest, were Jews themselves. His wife Eleanor also being a pure-blooded Jew and an active Zionist. His children were initiated into the Masonic lodge in 1937, and the president himself, like the English king, has long been at the disposal of the world supranational secret power, occupying one of the highest ranks in Freemasonry.

You bet! Roosevelt's first policies upon coming to power were the organization by him of buying gold in America and around the world, the establishment of the Judeo-Masonic "NRA" or "Restoration Association" to seize control of the economy of America, and then the whole world into the hands of Jewish capital. Additionally, Roosevelt sought to have the United States recognize the government of the USSR, in order to spread the influence of communism in America and all over the world.

With the advent of Roosevelt at the helm of the American ship of state, the world policy of the "great overseas democracy" takes on a defiant character. Two distant countries become targets of Roosevelt's

---

[121] *Jewish Life*, No. 46, 1940.
[122] *World Service*, No. 23, December 1st, 1938.

incessant and diverse attacks, those being Germany and Japan. In both directions, the expansion of Roosevelt is conducted by world Jewry.

Germany, as soon as she freed herself from her Jewish fetters, as soon as she began to revive to a new life and power and went her own distinctive way, became the first target of this expansion. At first one might ask, what do Americans care about the fact that a few Jews were crushed in old Europe? But these Jews cried in pain to the whole world, and their clamors gave a deafening resonance on Wall Street, the street of Jewish billionaires in New York.

Already in 1938, various leagues and committees were organized in America with the aim of boycotting Germany. Roosevelt takes a lively part in most of them, and when he is absent, his wife takes his place. Every year, a propaganda campaign of the Jewish-American press is developed and pushed by the White House and from the American Treasury. One of the most dangerous international Jewish leaders, Henry Morgenthau, a representative of the United Israel World Union, has settled in America until the United States finally moves to engage in direct acts of bringing war to Germany.

Roosevelt acted against Japan for the same reasons. Germany, free of the Jews, was deemed hateful by the "freedom-loving Americans." But Japan has never known the Jewish question. From the Jewish point of view, this is also a crime: because of their characteristics, which create an impenetrable armor against Judaization, the Japanese are inaccessible to the direct effects of Judaism. No longer because of persecution of Jews, but simply because of its inherent national identity and independence, Japan aroused the hatred of world Jewry.

And therefore, back in 1937, one of Roosevelt's main Jewish advisers, Samuel Untermyer, on behalf of the Jewish Congress, proposed through a New York radio station and in the Anti-Nationalist Bulletin: "It's time to extend our boycott of Germany to Japan as well."

And immediately Chiang Kai-shek's overseas loans intensified and all kinds of direct and indirect pressures on Japan were intensified: strengthening naval bases in the Pacific Ocean, colossal allocations for the development of the Pacific Fleet, and provoking a war in the Pacific Ocean, which finally broke out. But contrary to all the calculations of the priests of the Golden Calf, it gives even more unexpected results, just like the war they themselves caused in Europe.

39. The Judaic Rulers of the US

At the same time, when Roosevelt was elected president, that is, in 1932, the Jewish press joyfully reported:

The Jewish Governor of New York.

Herbert Lehman, a Jew, was elected as governor of New York. Lehman is fifty-four-years old; he is a banker and a major industrialist. During the war, Lehman served in the military and rose to the rank of colonel. Lehman is an active Jewish social activist.[123]

Poor New Yorkers! But they were not satisfied with just a Jewish governor and so they elected the new mayor of the city, also a Jew—La Guardia.

The Aryan Cardinal Hal seems to be in charge of America's foreign policy, but even his family is not without Jewish control, because his wife is the daughter of the Jew Isaac Vitz. His ministry is swarming with Jews. Here is Dr. Herbert Feis, famous for his pornographic research, and the resourceful Lev (more precisely, Leiba) Zaslavsky, a native of Russia, and David Salmon; in one of the main chairs rests the highly esteemed Yankel Munzer, in the other the well-fed Joseph Becker. It should also be noted that the department for the Philippine islands is also managed, of course, by a Jew—Joseph Yacoba.

On the military and naval secretaries Stimson and Knox, the American analyst Ben Carter, during their entry into the government in 1940, reported the following:

> Henry Stimson serves as an advisor to Kuhn, Loeb & Co. The law office of the new Secretary of Defense is generally known for its extensive business ties with English and French financial circles along the Jewish line.
>
> Some time ago, the *Chicago Daily News*, owned by Colonel Knox, put a large number of its shares on sale. One of the major buyers of the shares was Kuhn, Loeb & Co., which thus gained a great influence on this newspaper.

The famous "brain trust" of the American president consists in fact entirely of Jewish brains. The main ones, according to R. Commons: Jacob Becker, Morton Wilford, Albert Abramson, David Abel, Lestel Herzeg, Harold Posner, Emmanuel Levin, Louis Kirstein, Heinrich Nathan, David Shatsov, Maycher Levinidr.[124]

---

[123] *Jewish Life*, No. 46, 1932.
[124] R. Commons, *Jews, the Authors of Politics*, Berlin, 1939

The American *Liberation* also adds: Samuel Rosenman, Donald Ringer, David Sannos, Sidney Shilman, N. Strauss, by Bernard Baruch, Samuel Dickstein, Leo Vrilman, Samuel Untermyer, and Jerome Frank.[125]

The famous American fighter against the dark forces, Edward Edmonson, draws a Jewish hexagram (a six-pointed star), in the center of which he places a circle—"The Personal Rule of Roosevelt." Next to Roosevelt is billionaire Bernard Baruch, called by Edmonson "the unofficial president," and Henry Des, whom Edmonson calls "the father of New Deal." The New Deal is, as we know, a kind of planned economy that ruined the American economy.

Further, in the horns of the six-pointed star, Edmonson lists: Rabbi Stefan Wise, Sidney Shilman, Samuel Dickstein, James Warburg, Herbert Lehman, Samuel Rosenman, Lev Stern, Henry Horneyer, Louis Kirstein, Vail Sauros, Goldenweizer, Rabbi Margulis, A. Gohers, Gerard Soupe, Adolf Sabazs, Isidor Lubin, Mordecai Ezequiel, Mossi Holgin, Samuel Untermyer, Ben Carloso, La Guardia, Lev Dubinsky, Jerome Frank, Rob Moses, Goldman, Bullitt, Altemeyer, Steinhardt, Albert Einstein, Rosa Steiderman, Ben Kogan, Nathan Margold, Walter Lippman, David Lilienthal, William Leyerson.[126]

Let's just add to the conclusion that Roosevelt's message appears at all Jewish congresses and that, namely, the American president addressed in 1941 with a special congratulation to the Jewish people on the day of Rosh Hashanah, the Jewish New Year. When the bases of Jewry in Europe collapse, the true overseas base remains the last main fortress of Judaism.

At one time, Pelly, the leader of the American Legion of Silver Shirts, once painted a prophetic picture. A fleet of steamships from all European countries carries Jews to America from Germany, from the former Czechoslovakia, from Poland, from Romania, from France, and from Russia. At Ellis Island, where the quarantine for immigrants is located, there is a warning sign: "No stop is required here." The Statue of Liberty stretches out its arms to heaven in horror, and Pelly himself calmly observes:

"Europe will be liberated, Russia will be liberated, and so they will now all come to us. And then it will be time for the Silver Legion to act."

---

[125] *Liberation*, No. 18 of 14.04.1939.
[126] A leaflet issued by Edmondson and sent to the author of this book from New York.

40. Landmark Rulings in Montevideo

In early July 1941, a large Pan-American Jewish conference was inaugurated in the Uruguayan capital Montevideo. The local press published:

> After receiving the consent of the interested governments, the first All-American Conference will be inaugurated in a solemn atmosphere in the capital of Uruguay on July 9th. Representatives of North, South, and Central America will assist. The conference will be closed and will last three days. The external purpose of the conference is:
> 1. To create a close connection and full cooperation between the Jewish centers of the Western hemisphere and instill in each of them a sense of the common interests of all the peoples living on the American continent.
> 2. Coordination of material and spiritual assistance to the victims of the European tragedy.
> 3. Uniting the entire Jewish population of America to create a Jewish National Home.
>
> The internal goals of the conference are not disclosed. The invitation to the conference was signed by: The Supreme Rabbi of the Jewish Communities of the United States, Dr. Stefan Wise, Louis Lipsky; on behalf of the World Jewish Congress, D. Mek, and Dr. Nahum Goldman.

The Jewish press around the world paid great attention to this conference. In particular, the official journal of Jewish refugees who settled in Shanghai, published (for some reason in two languages, Hebrew and Russian) in *Our Life*, editorial No. 10 of 1941 a dedication about this event, meaningfully entitled "Unification of the Jews of the Western Hemisphere." The editorial states:

> The war destroyed Jewish life in Europe. Even in the event of a successful outcome from the war, the once flourishing Jewish centers of Europe will remain atrophied for a very long time.
>
> The Congress will engage in "preparing for the great historical tasks that the Jewish world will face after the war."
>
> The Montevideo Convention clearly shows that the center of gravity in Jewish life is moving from Europe to America. This has always been the case in our history. Jewish life is eternal."

So they declare. We shall take note!

41. Following the Journey Around the World—To the Time Machine

We started our journey around the world with, so to speak, a horizontal trip on the surface of the globe, with a journey through space.

"Political geography"—we proposed to name a new subject of study, an examination of the political map of the world from the point of view of Jewish participation in state leadership. Of course, we have not given any systematic course. We managed only to photograph individual pictures of the Judaization of individual states of the Old and New World. These pictures belong to different years of the first half of our century, mainly to its middle, and together they paint a general picture, but so much more work needs to be done on them to get the first preliminaries of the science I proposed calling political geography.

First of all, it would be necessary to choose one particular year and show the status of the Jewish question in different countries in this year. We had to take examples from different years, albeit from the same historical period, because we had to proceed from the available material at hand. Only such an accidental circumstance explains the first flaw of our work, clearly visible above all others to its author.

Then we should have given a picture of all the states of the modern world with no exceptions. And we left out Belgium, Portugal, Switzerland, Finland, Turkey, Asia Minor, and even "our own land"—Palestine; we ignored colonies, in Africa, Australia; said nothing about South America. This gap is explained by the same reason as the first one—there were no suitable materials. Finally, we did not intend to write a full encyclopedia on the Jewish question.

A systematic course in political geography requires the availability of numerous statistical, geopolitical, historical, and other types of references. An overview of the Judaization of modern states can be either purely politico-geographical—the number of Jews in each given country, their influence on the apparatus of power, their participation in power, the biographies of the Jewish masters of a given country; or politico-geographical and historical, supplemented by an outline of the emergence and constant spread of Jewry in each given country. Such work, of course, is beyond our power. But it is a vital necessity for every nation and for all mankind. Our task was only to give individual examples, but at the same time it gives a precedent for the creation of political geography, the science of the political Judaization of the world: by countries and continents; by centuries and epochs.

So, from the final remarks about the first section of our work, we quietly moved on to the second. Traveling within space necessitates time travel. In order to understand how the Jews came to be at the head of all modern states, we need to turn to the greatest of scientific books, to human fate, that is, simply put, to history. And if time is the fourth dimension or perpendicular to the plane of our three dimensions of space, then now we need to go back down this perpendicular: to rush into the past on a time machine.

Political geography brings another new sociological Science to the horizon—political history. This grandiose task, the revision of the entirety of world history is coming into existence. And for each individual nation, a revision of the native history of these people is required. What kind of revision? First of all, the cleansing of history from numerous Judeo-Masonic falsifications and forgeries. Extracting many events and names from under the *herem*, from under the taboo.[127] A study of the role of Jewry in the social movements of antiquity, the Middle Ages, and our time. Finding out the hidden engines of modern events, that is, the same Jewish and Masonic conspirators behind the scenes—this is the new history of peoples, ideas, and movements. Doing this from the point of view of the participation of Jews in it will make it possible to find out to the end the most ingenious Jewish strategy and tactics of the struggle for world power, that is, it will reveal the roots of Judaization and along the way its goals, stemming from the history and ideology of world Jewry from the spirit of Jewish faith and morals.

This new political history requires an enormous amount of work by not one, but many institutions of researchers, because it puts a new systematic consideration in connection with Jewish history on the line: world history by centuries and epochs; world history by peoples and states, and in particular; the history of political ideas and movements.

In this book, the second section is devoted to this issue, in which we also have to limit ourselves to fragmentary materials. But let this fragmentary material be the Ariadne's thread, which will help others find more time and more opportunities to uncover the whole labyrinth of the diabolical Jewish conspiracy.

Traveling through time, we will gradually discover the clear and yet somehow unnoticed fact that among the states of the past and present there is one hidden state, unlike others, that does not have its own territory and is ready to consider the entire globe as its territory. The Jewish state that the Zionists declare to want to create in Palestine, it turns out, has long existed, and is operating! The *inter-nation* or the *inter-state*, as we call it, represents the greatest danger for all other states, because it is in a state of continuous war with them and continuously enslaves millions of "subjects" of the goyim, who do not even notice it! The third section of this book will be devoted to the Jewish inter-state. It also comes from more or less random materials and therefore needs further processing. It is necessary to clarify precisely

---

[127] The most severe form of excommunication, used by rabbis in sentencing wrongdoers, usually for an indefinite period of time. (Translator's note)

the "constitution" of the Jewish inter-state, its structure, its organs, its central and local authorities, the rights and obligations of citizens, their aspirations towards its subjects, its internal and foreign policy, its economy and culture. We have taken the first steps in this study and we invite our followers to go further.

Finally, the fourth section will take us from the Jewish inter-state to the world around it, to our world of current events of the twentieth century, in Jewish and anti-Jewish facts and documents. The turning days of the Second World War will pass before us, which turns out to be a war caused by the Jewish inter-state for the final enslavement of the world and in which, on the contrary, the Jewish inter-state suffers defeat after defeat and is subject to complete destruction and annihilation. Judaism collided with fascism; the religious and national aspirations of Jewry collided with the religious and national consciousness of all other peoples; the materialistic order of Judaization created by Jewry—with a New Order of Nationalization.

The New Order wins, and the rising sun and the sparkling swastika from east to west rises into the sky, driving away both Jewish stars, the five-pointed and six-pointed stars. Here is the inspiring fact of our days, designed to resolve the Jewish question once and for all.

We examined Judas in profile and full-face over the states, so to speak, in a static state, in a state of complacent calm. Now consider Judas over states in the dynamics of expansion, in a state of restless movement, following political geography, the lost leaves of world history!

PART TWO

EXCURSION INTO HISTORY

An examination of the origins of Judaism, the use of political ideas and social movements by Jews, or simply put, the Jewish strategy and tactics in the struggle against nation-states.

42. Where Did They Come From

We have consistently gone through almost all the countries of the world: everywhere in the twentieth century, for years and decades, the Jews were at the very top of the state ladder. The history of the first quarter of our century is particularly instructive in this regard, amazingly instructive: in our very faces the smartest people of all countries, kings and presidents, ministers and leaders of political parties, were all in a dense Jewish environment, densely and abundantly layered with Jews. Descendants of Lucifer and Cain rule the Old and the New World, acting in every country as patriots of this or that country and at the same time as patriots of the inter-nation, as faithful sons of their satanic religion, their people forever wandering and migrating. What happened? Why did the Jews end up at the top? To answer this question means to give a correct history of recent political teachings and social movements—a purified history, a history that has not yet been written. A history of ideas and their connection with the history of Jewish inspiration, provocation, and use.

Where did they come from, these Jews, now at the head of humanity in the twentieth century? After getting acquainted with the general picture of Judaization, that is, with the current state of the Jewish question, let's look at this question historically.

Let's trace its evolution on the pages of universal history. Meanwhile, the study of the history of Jewry, along with the study of Ancient

Greece, Rome, the Middle Ages, and modernity, would give a lot of instructive material even to a high school student. Moreover, it is of vital necessity for any politician and citizen. Let us fill this gap in our general education, at least in the most imperfect way—with excerpts.

The history of the Jewish people is lost in prehistoric times. The greatest expert on the Jewish question, Shmakov, viewed it from the struggle between the Semites and the Aryans as an individual yet also the main episode of this struggle. He tells about the clashes of the Aryans with the Semites in the times preceding most ancient history, and then deciphers the Punic Wars as the struggle of Aryan Rome against the Semitic Carthage. Jewish sources on the origins of the Jewish people refer to the Bible. The Bible, as you know, traces the origin of the Jews in a straight line from Adam, then from Shem and Abraham. The Jews consider their ancestor to be Jacob—the Israelite God-fighter who wrestled with God. As Simon Dubnov remarks:

> In remote times, about 4000 years ago, in the Asian countries adjacent to the Mediterranean Sea, the peoples who by their origin and language belonged to the Semitic race, dominated. From the vast steppes of Arabia, the Semitic tribes migrated to neighboring Mesopotamia, located between the Euphrates and Tigris rivers. From Mesopotamia, the Semitic tribes penetrated into the countries located closer to the Mediterranean coast. Some had established themselves in Aram or Syria, others in Canaan or Palestine. In addition to the sedentary Semites, who became permanent residents in various countries, there were still nomadic Semites who were engaged in cattle breeding or shepherding outside cities and moved from place to place. While the settled Semites mixed with other tribes, the nomads lived apart and kept the type (physical and spiritual appearance) of their race in great purity. The tribe of Jews belonged to these pure Semites. Their ancestors used to live in Babylonia, then moved north to Aram (Syria), and then migrated to Canaan.[128]

In the Bible we see how, by being the people chosen by God, the Jews often fell under the power of the opposite forces, refusing divine chosenness, becoming representatives of Satanism on earth, indulging in all kinds of disgusting sin, substituting faith in the One God with faith in Baal, in the Golden Calf, engaging in ritual crimes ranging from human sacrifices and murders of their own children, ritual prostitution, wife trafficking, incest, and all sorts of unnatural vices.

---

[128] Simon Dubnov, *Textbook of Jewish History*, Irkutsk, 1916.

The story of Sodom is no exception in the historical life of biblical Jewry.

And the story of the unfortunate Haman and Esther, in honor of whose crimes Jews still celebrate the Purim holiday, certifies that even in ancient times there were anti-Semitic intellectuals and fighters against Jewish dominance, that in ancient times Jews acted in the same bloody ways as now, and that the mass extermination of the Russian intelligentsia in the USSR has a distant prototype in the mass extermination of the Persian intelligentsia under Artaxerxes. Just as the Bible says about it and the Jews remember it every year in their "annunciation," the most cheerful and joyful of all Jewish holidays—Purim.

43. Purim

Let us remind you of what this is all about. In the fourth century BC, Jews in Persia began to pose a significant threat to the state. Anti-Semitism broke out among the Persian intelligentsia. Its best exponent was Haman, the prime minister of the king Artaxerxes, who developed a draft of restrictions for Jews.

The alarmed Jews in the person of their sage Mordechai slipped to Artaxerxes the she-wolf, Esther—a strange tale that would be mirrored in the temptation of Carol II by Lupescu in Romania. She became the favorite wife of the king, and demanded from the slavish monarch the execution of Haman, his ten sons, three hundred of his relatives and friends, as well as a three-day beating of 75,000 representatives of the elite in all 127 regions of Persia. This bloody pogrom of their enemies is remembered every year and everywhere by the Jews in their Purim. Read the Bible—what horrific and eloquent descriptions. What a fascinating subject for a stunningly dramatic novel!

44. The Birth of the Sanhedrin

In the same biblical, pre-Roman times, the future secret Jewish government in the form of the Sanhedrin was born.

Following the new destruction of the Jerusalem temple (temple of Solomon), the Persians in the fifth century BC freed the Jews from Babylonian captivity, and allowed them to return to their homeland, Palestine. The high priests replaced the ancient kings at the head of the people. "They began to rule with the help of the Supreme Council or the Assembly of Elders," says the Jewish historian Dubnov. "This council was called the Great Council (Knesset HaGedolah) and consisted of legal scholars and the best representatives of the people."

There is no Talmud yet, but there is already a dictatorship of scribes, the future Talmudists. The devil stretches out his long claws to God's chosen people. The most ancient (biblical) period of history ends with the destruction of Persian rule by Alexander the Great in 332 BC. The ancient (non-biblical or Greco-Roman) period of Jewish history begins. Jews penetrate into the body of Ancient Greece and Ancient Rome, and decompose it from within.

45. Anti-Semitism in the Ancient World

Jewish sources cannot hide the presence of anti-Semitism in the Ancient World. Wherever the Jews went, they aroused popular indignation against themselves. This is evidenced by Herodotus, Cicero, and Tacitus. The Jews themselves talk about it, for example, in Lurie's book *Anti-Semitism in the Ancient World* and in the *Jewish Encyclopedia*.

In the second volume of the *Jewish Encyclopedia* on page 638, in the article "Anti-Semitism in antiquity," we read: "Already in Hecatel of Abder under Ptolemy II in 305–285 BC, who is studying the genealogy of the Jews and the history of their expulsion from Egypt, we find negative descriptions of their characteristics."[129] The *Jewish Encyclopedia* names as the first theorist of anti-Semitism the priest Manetho under Ptolemy II Philadelphus (285–246).

> Manetho is followed by Macaeus Patroxius, a disciple of Eratosthenes. Jewish historians claim that Antiochus IV Epiphanes (175–164) engaged in an open persecution of the Jewish religion, which caused the uprising of the Jews under the leadership of Judas Maccabeus. As a result of this uprising, the Jews were expelled in 169 BC from Jerusalem together with the high priest Onias, received in Egypt by Ptolemy VI Philometor (180–145) and a new temple was built near Heliopolis.

Here, the ancient Jewish religion is invaded once again by the dark influences of the ancient magicians of evil.[130]

"This is a turning point in the history of Jewry," observes the *Jewish Encyclopedia*. The fierce defensive war and persecution are developing a tendency to separateness already inherent in Jewry. Since the time of the Maccabean era, when this isolation has reached

---

[129] Ptolemy I Soter (305–283 BC). (Translator's note)
[130] Here, Rodzaevsky is referring to the ancient biblical Hebrews, who had barely anything to do with the Jews he refers to across the book. (Translator's note)

its apogee, a special literature emerges. Moses is called a philosopher, astrology is derived from Abraham, astronomy is derived from Joseph. Jewry declares an irreconcilable war on Hellenism, which is responded to by increasing anti-Semitism. Apollonius Molon of Rhodes, Cicero's teacher, in a special polemical essay accuses Jews of atheism and misanthropy. These accusations are reinforced by Posidonius Anlionus, who then spreads a "legend," as the *Jewish Encyclopedia* says, about ritual murders.

Under the Ptolemies, Jews gain more prominence: "In Alexandria, they formed a huge ghetto," says the *Jewish Encyclopedia*. "Jewish names are found among the highest positions, they enjoyed many legal rights, full internal autonomy, they own many economic assets, monopolies, payoffs; in various branches of trade and state economy they play a predominant role." Under the successors of the Ptolemies, the Roman emperors, the attitude of the government towards the Jews is gradually changing. This change is especially felt under Caligula (AD 37–41).

The ruler of Egypt, Flaccus, issues an edict depriving Jews of citizenship rights and equating them with foreigners. The Jews inspire the murder of Caligula, and his successor Emperor Claudius patronizes the Jews. The Jews then grew impudent to the point of starting an uprising which ended in year 70 with the complete defeat of Jerusalem by Titus Flavius. The temple was destroyed, and the population dispersed.

The presence of anti-Semitism in Ancient Rome proves that anti-Semitism is as ancient as Jewry itself, and that wherever Jews appear, they provoke spontaneous protest against themselves. The causes of anti-Semitism, then, are in the Jews themselves: Haman, Shmakov, Hitler, Rodzaevsky—all "anti-Semites," large and small, are the natural self-defense of nations in the person of people who feel, see, and understand the danger.

"Despite all the anti-Semitism of Ancient Rome, however," writes Shmakov,

> Israel managed to create such a golden era for itself that, according to Mommsen's certificate, the proconsuls and promagistrates of the provinces were forced to treat the local Israelites gently unless they wished to be awarded with outcry or even a criminal trial instead of a reward or a triumph following the expiration of their term.[131] The Jews do not doze off, nor do they forget to "make their own luck" in general. In spite

---

[131] A promagistrate (from Latin: pro magistratu) is a person who acts in and with the authority and capacity of a magistrate, but without holding a magisterial office in Ancient Rome. (Translator's note)

of everything, they maintained their own government a secret at all times, and continued to regard the Jerusalem Temple as their international bank, where they brought stolen gold taken from Italy and the provinces.

The procurators and proconsuls did not dare to object, despite, of course, they saw the dangers that threatened the Roman state through such an accumulation of gold in the central treasury of the Jews.

Only one prefect of Cappadocia, Valerius Flaccus, dared prohibit at least the export of gold to their Jews. As usual, Jewry did not remain "unprofitable" and, having bought a then prosecutor named Lelius, presented Flaccus with a number of shameful accusations.[132] The Jews provided Lelius with false witnesses and false documents, and in conclusion, having gathered at the forum, they began to cause such scandals and hubbub that it seemed there was no salvation for the defendant. But the sons of Judas miscalculated and between them and Flaccus stood Cicero. Flaccus was acquitted. Nevertheless, this episode shows what fate threatens even the highest administrator in the world state if he dares to stand in the way of Jews. Not everyone has Cicero as a defender.

The author of this book has repeatedly experienced similar Leliuses attacking himself and his colleagues. The Jews also brutally dealt with the author of this quote, brutally drowning him in a cesspit a few days after the October Revolution in Russia.

46. Judas Rejects God

The main and most tragic fact of Jewish history, of course, is the fact of the rejection of the Messiah. The history of this fact is well known to all of us from the gospel. The Jews of that time declared that "His blood is on us and our children." At that time, they were no longer Jews, as the latest research confirms that the kingdom of Israel ceased to exist. The Jews of that time were descendants of the kingdom of Judea (Yids, not Jews). The consciousness of the Jews of that time was already poisoned by the Pharisees and various kinds of Chaldean Satanic false wisdom. The Talmud already existed in embryonic form; Kabbalah was passed from mouth to mouth. Along with the Bible, at that time there was already a secret Satanic teaching, which later

---

[132] Decimus Lelius acted as a prosecutor in court on behalf of the Roman cities. (Translator's note)

emerged in Freemasonry. That is why Christ, according to the gospel (John 8: 41–47), defined the Jews of today as children of the devil:

> "You do the deeds of your father." Then they said to Him, "We were not born of fornication; we have one Father—God." Jesus said to them, "If God were your Father, you would love Me, for I proceeded forth and came from God; nor have I come of Myself, but He sent Me. Why do you not understand My speech? Because you are not able to listen to My word. You are of your father the devil, and the desires of your father you want to do. He was a murderer from the beginning, and does not stand in the truth, because there is no truth in him. When he speaks a lie, he speaks from his own resources, for he is a liar and the father of it. But because I tell the truth, you do not believe Me. Which of you convicts Me of sin? And if I tell the truth, why do you not believe Me? He who is of God hears God's words; therefore you do not hear, because you are not of God."

Shmakov deciphers such an assessment from the analysis of the then-triumphant influences of Kabbalah on Judaism in the first century.

The crucifixion of the Son of God is immediately followed by the destruction of Jerusalem by the Roman emperor Titus in AD 70. An attempt to repeat the experience of Esther through the Jewish Princess Veronica was sent to Titus, but fails. Another topic for an amazing drama—who will dare to write it correctly?

"The Jewish nation begins to live as a politically dependent, but internally free nation with its own self-government," says Dubnov, thereby anticipating our subsequent definition of Judaism as an internation with its own secret government. After the destruction of Jerusalem, Judaism founded two centers, one in Palestine and the other in Babylonia. In the era embracing the end of antiquity and the beginning of the Middle Ages (70–1040), the Talmud is created and brought to life: Patriarch Yehuda Hanasi in the year 120 completed the "Mishnah," the first part of the Jerusalem Talmud.[133] At the beginning of the fifth century, the second part of the Jerusalem Talmud, the Gemara, appeared. Finally, in the year 500, the Babylonian Talmud was formed.

Despite the destruction of Jerusalem, the Sanhedrin continues to exist, but goes into conspiracy. There are, however, frequent references to it in world and Jewish history. Only gradually does its trace disappear. The last time it suddenly appears briefly is in the time of Napoleon. The Jews who rejected the Messiah because he did not bring them the kingdom of the earth but the Kingdom of Heaven, having forever separated from the heavenly homeland of all people, forever lost

---

[133] Yehuda ha-Nasi. (Translator's note)

their earthly homeland, their state in the Holy Land, the city of Jerusalem and the Temple at Mount Zion. And so began their endless painful wanderings around the globe.

47. Jewry as a Nationality

The settlement of the Jewish people after the destruction of Jerusalem by Titus goes in several directions. The Jewish colony in Rome is growing. A segment of the Jews goes far to the east and establishes the Khazar kingdom there. Large Jewish bases are being strengthened in Asia Minor. Finally, a strong Jewish colony is being introduced into Spain. Further, through the fall of the Roman Empire, undermined by them from within, the Jews found themselves in France and Germany and spread throughout Europe, penetrating into Russia and Asia. The role of the Jews in the persecution of Christians is well known, since they were the ones who instigated it. Poppea was a Jew under Nero.[134] Julian the Apostate patronized the Jews. The Jews surrounded Charlemagne with a dense ring (eighth and ninth centuries). "The emperor especially appreciated the activity of Jews in the areas of international trade," notes Dubnov. Since then, the Jews have settled in different countries and are beginning to monopolize international trade in their hands.

At the same time, at the beginning of the Middle Ages, the Jews were trying to take over Catholicism. "In Rome, the popes treated Jews with tolerance, and some even patronized them and did not allow church councils to restrict their rights," the Jewish historian notes. "The conversion of Jews to Christianity was encouraged in all sorts of ways," and hence the concealment of Jews under a Christian guise. "A descendant of a Jewish family who converted to Christianity later became pope under the name of Anacletus II (1130-1138)," Dubnov boastfully but carelessly remarks.

Unlike Catholic Rome, as Jewish historians admit, Jews were met with a hostility from the Orthodox Byzantium and ancient Germans. They repaid Byzantium, subsequently contributing to the Turkish invasion of it. The Jews also helped other Semites, namely the Arabs, in their conquest of Spain. In the Cordoba Caliphate (755), the base of medieval Jewry was established. However, the liberation of Spain from the Moors ended this Jewish prosperity.

---

[134] Nero's second wife, Poppea Sabina. There is no data on her Jewish origin, but she was interested in Judaism and patronized Jews, but later promoted the appointment of Hessius Flora as procurator of Judea, who allowed many abuses and oppressed the local population. (Translator's note)

Here we can give another historical example of the vicious Jewish reprisals against non-Jews.

"It was AD 615," says Amadeus Tver:

> This year was predicted by the Muslims and Persians as the last for Christians in the whole area of Palestine. At the end of May, under the command of Rumizan, a capable but inhuman general, a formidable army marched on Galilee and swept along the banks of the Jordan leaving nothing but blood-soaked ruins. Meanwhile, a significant segment of the population, enlightened by the preaching of the gospel, crowded into these places. Following the crushing and destruction of houses by fire and the sword, the crowds of residents bound to each other were dragged by the scourge of the Persians as migrants into the miasma-poisoned swamps of the Tigris and Euphrates. And so, with sacks filled with gold, Jewish merchants in whole gangs began to crowd behind the "victorious" army, buying up everything they could from the mass of prisoners, only not to save them, oh no, but to slaughter them completely. At the same time, the Jews diligently chose people of special importance (recall the 75,000 "strong men" who were exterminated by Mordechai): city judges and other officials, beautiful and rich women and above all nuns and priests. The money paid to the Persian soldiers for the Christians being torn to pieces came from the "folding fee," which was levied on all Jews, in proportion to the condition of each. Over 90,000 Christians died in this way.

The medieval Crusades, slandered by liberal historians, were a great spiritual movement aimed not only at freeing the Holy Sepulcher from the hands of the infidels, but also to liberate Europe from Jewish domination, which had become unbearable by that time. Using the temperament of their women and their usurious abilities, the Jews seized many positions in medieval states. Therefore, the Crusades were accompanied everywhere by sometimes brutal Jewish pogroms. Anti-Semitism, it turns out, is no stranger to the Middle Ages either!

The Jewish historian Dubnov tells us how gradually the Jews occupied Spain by the fourteenth century:

> Jews occupied a prominent place in both kingdoms—in Castile and Aragon. The Spanish kings . . . often attracted the most capable of them to fill positions in the public administration. Almost every king had at his court a tax collector, a finance minister, an adviser, a court doctor, or a Jewish scientist. The Jewish families Benveniste, Vaccar, Abulafia, Pihon, and

Abarbanel appeared in the ranks of the Spanish nobles and courtiers."

This caused an outbreak of popular indignation, in particular the famous Seville massacre of 1391, which resulted in the mass flight of Spanish Jews to the neighboring Portugal and Africa.

From the same year, Spanish Jews began to adopt Christianity for the sake of appearance, but secretly remaining Jews. Such Jews are called Marranos. How dangerous these Marranos are is shown by their atrocities against the Spaniards and especially the Christian clergy during recent Spanish events: hatred passed from ancestors to their descendants even after 500 years!

"In the Middle Ages, Jews tried to make profit from mysticism. People saw the highest wisdom in their innermost knowledge," says Shmakov. With the above conditions, all classes of society gradually began to master: astrology, with its horoscopic stars and prophecies of the future; alchemy, with the philosopher's stone and the elixir of eternal life; oneirocracy, or the science of dreams; necromancy, the art of summoning the dead; witchcraft, or corruption, a supernatural skill with the power to incarnate Satan; thaumaturgy, or the science of miracles; aeromancy, chiromancy, hydromancy, pyromancy, and various other types of herd madness of the human masses. Such was the environment in which the germs of Jewish parasitism were cultivated and from which both twice baptized Jews came out for disputes with the rabbis, and those Talmudic virtuosos who "decorated" with pornography the Gothic buildings of startling monuments of the fiery faith of the Middle Ages. It is on the path of this era under consideration that we notice the penetration of Judaism into such pious communities of architects and stonemasons as those who created the cathedrals of Cologne, Trier, Vienna, Strasbourg, Reims, Paris, and other cities for centuries.

Generally speaking, we must trace the moves of Jewish trickery in the religious strife of the Middle Ages, explain the role of the Yeshivites in such phenomena as the revived Albigensian and Orléans heresies as a clearly Jewish sect, [135] reveal the benefits received by the sons of Judas from the Crusades and determine their sinister role in obscurantism—through alchemy, magic, Kabbalah and various other types of human nonsense, as well as their activities for the corruption and destruction of the Templar Order. As well, their activities to corrupt and destroy the Order of the Templars or to prosper the maritime robberies on the Mediterranean Sea are evident, as is their plan to establish the machinations of the Talmud in the convulsions of the Genoese and Venetian republics on the one hand and the bloodshed of the Reformation

---

[135] Dualist and gnostic heresies. (Translator's note)

on the other, to draw material lines along which the "chosen people" are moving, preparing their current dominion. Such are the important and complex, but instructive and noble tasks of a statesman who would like to understand the real meaning of the Middle Ages.

For their abominations committed in the Middle Ages, Jews were driven into ghettos. They were marked with special signs, they were driven from country to country, burned at the stake, smashed, and killed. They were forced to renounce their faith and nation, their Jewish religion, their Jewish nationality. They changed their appearance, put on different masks, were baptized, renamed, and introduced into the new environment, but still remained Jews. Why? Obviously, because Jewry is a nation and a race at the same time, the enemy of the human race combined in this "chosen" Jewish nation-race, being the sum of organizational features that make Jewry united, strong, and dangerous for other peoples.

In AD 70, when Titus destroyed the rebellious Jerusalem, the capital of vassal Judea, the kingdom of Judea seemed to have ceased to exist. The Jewish people lost their visible center and, already scattered everywhere, began to emigrate to all the countries of Europe accessible on their horizons. The notorious two-thousand-year-old *golus*, as the Jews call their wanderings, began. Were the Jewish people destroyed in these wanderings? No. Over the past centuries of ancient, medieval, and modern history, it has known various twists and turns of its motley fate: ups and downs, disasters and achievements, but with all these changes it has not been destroyed. Exiled from one country, the eternal wanderers settled in another, then went to the third, to later return to the first, and this cycle continues to this day. During their centuries-long wanderings, the Jews have shown exceptional strength of blood and loyalty to their historical covenants, their religion, and their psychology. This gives us the indisputable right to recognize the Jews as a nation. The presence of a Jewish nation among the nations shows that not all nations have a divine origin—some seem to come from the devil.

Be that as it may, by the end of the second millennium of emigration, deprived of their homeland and the state, the "poor persecuted" Jews had achieved a significant impact on the life of all mankind and at the same time retained their national identity, their gloomy isolation, and in the twentieth century even felt like the winners.

"What is the secret of the longevity, vitality and endurance of Jewry? What is the secret of the immortality of this weak nation?" asks an anonymous Jewish author of the essays *The Essence of Judaization*, published under the eloquent subtitle "from the archive of broken tablets" by the Harbin *Jewish Life* at the end of 1941. He answers:

Having come close to deciphering the question of this stubborn fortitude, this mysterious vitality of the nation, which has survived to the present day despite all the laws of human history [laudable recognition!], first of all we need to delve into the essence of Judaism, into the essence of the Torah, which is the brain and soul of the people from the very cradle of its history.

Let us return to this cradle following this Jewish author.

48. Jewry as a Religion

Contrary to the popular view about the gift of the Torah by God to Moses on Mount Sinai, an anonymous rabbi confides: "Our Torah is not an unexpected divine revelation, descended to earth by God's grace and imposed on us from above. No! Our Torah is the flesh and bone of the people themselves, their soul, their nature and instinct." In other words, the Jewish religion is the Jews themselves, the deification of oneself! "These great covenants came out of his very bowels, from the very depths of his soul," the Jew is touched. "For even a few centuries before the Sinai revelations, these divine sparks of our Torah were inextinguishable, smoldering in the popular consciousness." Where, after all, are their origins? Is it not in the rebellion of the day against God? *Jewish Life* narrates:

> Even at the dawn of Jewish history, when Jewry was a nomadic tribe of shepherds, it was imbued with divinity in the creation of the mystery of nature, it feels it anywhere and everywhere with its whole being. And realizing and deeply feeling these omnipresent divine forces on earth [note, not in heaven!], this is how God's descent from the heavenly heights to man on earth is accomplished, and this is how the fusion of spirit and matter, the interweaving of divinity with earthly interests is accomplished. That is why the first voice of God that reached Abraham speaks of the promised land:
> "And the LORD appeared to Abraham and said to him, 'To your offspring I will give this land.'" (Gen 12)[136]

So the Jewish author brought God down to earth and first proclaimed pantheism: God is nature. "So these pronounced national motives, dominating over all religious motives, run like a red thread throughout our holy Torah, throughout our Bible." He takes the next step from pantheism to the deification of Jewry: God is the Jews.

---

[136] *Jewish Life*, 1941, No. 50–52.

"God, the Torah, the country and the nation are the one and only components that make up the whole," to put the last dot over the i. And materialism is finally consolidated further:

> In the still unclouded consciousness of the Jewish tribe, these children of nature, Jehovah appears to be the God of life, the God of the joy of being, a God who descended to earth, and not a God who sat on heavenly heights, despising earthly riches and promising in return an unknown kingdom of heaven.

The Kingdom of Heaven, apparently, does not seduce the Jew at all. He wants the kingdom of the earth. That's how he understands the Bible:

> This exact formulation of the supreme essence and dogma of Judaism is given to us by the holy Torah, where it is said clearly and distinctly: "So if you faithfully obey the commands I am giving you today—to love the Lord your God and to serve him with all your heart and with all your soul—then I will send rain on your land in its season, both autumn and spring rains, so that you may gather in your grain, new wine and olive oil. I will provide grass in the fields for your cattle, and you will eat and be satisfied (Deuteronomy 11)."

To be satisfied—here it is, the vulgar ideal of Jewry.

> In these unambiguous words, which, by the way, are repeated many times and about which it is said: "With all your heart and with all your soul" (Deuteronomy 11), the whole meaning and true essence of our Torah is formulated in these words. Adherence to the Torah covenants is a means to achieve earthly benefits, an abundance of rains, wheat, livestock and other material benefits, [the openly cynical Jew writes]. And Moses on Mount Sinai, who acted as the mouthpiece of the people and felt it with his heart, had only to give these ideas a form and a system. But the basis of these ideas remained the same: national-materialistic ideas.

The Talmud consolidated this materialistic understanding of the Bible in the sense of the Jewish people being chosen for earthly power and enjoyment of earthly goods by a set of rules of life, politics, economics and culture. The vague Torah was not enough for the Jews when they rejected Christ—they needed a concrete Talmud.

49. Jews and the Talmud

Ever since the Sanhedrin went into hiding after the destruction of rebellious Jerusalem by the Roman legions, the cunning Jewish brains concentrated according to the law of natural selection somewhere in the invisible Zion. They have taken care to strengthen the inner-national bonds of the scattered Biblical people. In addition to the Bible, which carries out the idea of the election of Jewry to rule our planet, the elders of Zion came up with the Talmud, consistently tightening the screws of their conspiracy. The written teaching complements the unwritten teaching. Finally, Kabbalah emerges.

The origin of the Talmud, according to the teachings of the Jews, dates back to the time of Moses. It turns out that on Mount Sinai, in addition to the written law (Torah Shebih-tav), the oral law (Torah Shebaal-pe) was taught at the same time. The latter was then passed down by Moses to Joshua, from him to the elders, from them to the great synagogue, and from it to all of the people. Hence the written law itself must be understood only as it is set forth among the traditions and interpretations of the oral law. In other words, the Talmud is higher than the Bible. Anyone who doubts the Talmud is expelled from the face of Israel and should be killed. The legend developed by Maimonides certifies that the sources of the Talmud are hidden in the abyss of the ages. The first part of its oldest edition—the so-called Jerusalem Mishnah—was compiled during the time of the Second Temple and issued by the second century AD. The second part of the Jerusalem Talmud, the Gemara, was formed about a hundred years later. The Babylonian Talmud, the second and more substantial edition of the Talmud, appeared in the time period from AD 200 to 500.

Both the Jerusalem and the Babylonian Talmud were originally written in the Chaldean language. For a long time, both Talmuds were copied by hand. The first and most luxurious edition of the Talmud appeared between 1489–1492, that is, concurrent with the expulsion of the Jews from Spain.

There is no translation of the Gemara in any other language. The Mishnah was translated for the first time and fully into Latin (Amsterdam, 1698–1703), almost entirely into Italian, French, and German, and most recently, only occasionally into English. Its translation into Russian was made at the end of the nineteenth century. In excerpts, some texts of the Mishnah and Gemara are given in Chiarini. A detailed synopsis with important authentic quotations is critically given by Eisenkinger, against whom the Jews tried to initiate a criminal prosecution.

Recently, extracts from the Talmud with commentary have been given by Shmakov, Pranaytis, and Lyutostansky. In emigration, it is not without difficulty that one can get a brochure of the *Jewish Mirror* by Dr. Eckart, where one hundred laws from the Talmud are given, translated into Russian for the first time by Shmakov as an appendix to his famous work *Freedom and the Jews* (see also F. Brenye's *Talmud and the Jews* and Brandt's *Ritual Murder among the Jews* part 1, chapter 3).

Shmakov characterizes the arrangement of the contents of the Talmud as follows:

> First of all, the Talmud is divided into six parts, or formations (sedarim). These "shisha Sidaris," according to the Jewish custom, form from their initial letters the Kabbalistic term "Shas," which the Jews call the Talmud.
>
> The parts are as follows: Zeram ("crops," agrarian laws), Poed (holidays), Ours ("women," marriage law), Kaziki ("damages," civil and criminal law), Kodashim ("shrines," canon law) and Tegarot, "purity" (with the non-pure, from a ritual point of view).[137]
>
> The parts are divided into thiry-six treatises (masekhet). The treatises are divided into chapters (perek), of which there are 524 in thirty-six treatises, and with the addition of five small treatises, 617. Chapters also consist of paragraphs called "misham." There are 3,787 of them in the Babylonian Talmud.
>
> A Talmudist must know all this by heart. It is his duty to be able to quote a whole verse, one word per excerpt, and the entire chapter, one verse at a time. At the age of five, a Jew begins to learn his literacy. At the age of ten, the Mishnah, and at fifteen, the Gemara. Teaching is done by printed sheets and by secret lists. The latter, as a repository of hatred of Christianity, playing no small part in the teaching of the Talmud. Talmudic literature in general is enormous.

Shmakov characterizes the content of the Talmud as follows: "This is a Jewish encyclopedia on theology, law, history, politics, geography, perfumery, medicine, astronomy, astrology, magic and an overall black magic book. The Talmud is the soul of the Jew, and Kabbalah is the soul of the Talmud."

"Everything for the sons of Judea comes down, if you look at it sensibly, to the history, theory and practice of the Talmud. The Talmud is the photographed heart of Jewry," he repeats elsewhere and brings the diversity of Talmudic positions to two main themes:

---

[137] The names of the sections are not accurately conveyed. They are: Zraim, Moed, Nashim, Nezikin, Kodashim, and Theorot. (Translator's note)

In this vale of lamentation, there is only one chosen people—the Jews. Everything else is just part of his property, which Israel received from Jehovah for its circumcision. The gentiles—goyim or akums—are not people at all, but human-like creatures created in honor of the Jews in order to serve them as slaves with great decency in relation to the holiness and greatness of Israel. In harmony with this, a Jew is not able to rob or cheat a goy, just as no master could do the same to his animal. It follows from this, that it is not a Jew, who commits a crime when he takes something from a goy as rightfully his own, but on the contrary, it is the goyim that dare to insult their Jewish majesty, that is, consequently, to commit blasphemy when they dare to lie about how something could even belong to them.... Therefore, it is obvious that property, along with the life of the goyim themselves, is like a commons, that is, it does not belong to any of the peoples in particular. Consequently, any Jew is authorized by Jehovah to cast his nets and catch whatever he pleases. Those who rebel against the divine authority of the Jews—the goyim, of course—should be treated appropriately. But in the name of the sanctity of Jewish dignity, it is required that the goyim do not forget about their boundless insignificance before the "chosen" people. Therefore, they should be held in ridicule, and Jewish *geshefts* should be given such artistic completeness when the glory of Israel would become unattainable and dazzlingly bright.... The vastness of the aforementioned Jewish economy, as well as the irrevocability of the Domination of the Sons of Israel over the goyim, causes not only economic, but moral and mental slavery of the goyim.

Thus, the centralization of Jewish power is logically necessary. This power must be indestructible, and therefore inaccessible, that is, unknown to the goyim, and not even suspected by them. Therefore, it must remain hidden. In its final form, the tragicomedy of history is played out, the tyrannical, hopeless, that is, the unshakable and shameless power of the Jews.

"This thesis," notes Shmakov,

can be proved both theoretically—through the narration of the Talmud in an exact translation into Russian—and practically—by disclosing the data of the Jewish biography. Both, especially in Russia, are a state necessity.... Whether we want it or not is irrelevant, since the decision does not depend on us. We are condemned by fate to such a struggle against

Jewry, before which the Punic wars are child's play. It is clear [what] we must know next, that is, to study the enemy.

50. "Shulchan-Aruch"

Here we should also mention the *Shulchan Aruch* ("set table"), a simplified and abbreviated summary of the Talmud. The first attempts to outline the Talmud due to its enormous size and contradictions were made already in the eighth and ninth centuries. Finally, in 1565, the rabbi of the Palestinian city of Shafeta, Joseph Karo, compiled the most successful, from a Jewish point of view, summary of the Talmud—the *Shulchan Aruch*. This book satisfied everything that it is possible to demand from this legal code: having discarded outdated prescriptions, it alone brought the current laws into a clear presentation, in definite and clear expressions and in brief formulas. This is the great significance of the *Shulchan Aruch* for Judaism and for the study of Judaism.

51. The Foundations of Judaism

Let's get acquainted with some quotations from the Talmud and the *Shulchan Aruch*, which establish the views of the Jews towards us, whom they call "goyim" and "akums." Here the Jews warn menacingly: "To inform a non-Jew of anything about our religious mores is tantamount to killing all Jews, for if non-Jews knew what we teach about them, they would kill us." (B. David according to Pranaitis, p. 122 in Brandt).

"Non-Jews studying the Talmud, or a Jew who teaches a non-Jew the Talmud must be subject to death." (Sanhedrin 59, Hagigah 13, Avodah Zarah VIII, according to Mommert 11, p. 19 in Brandt).

Jewish priests instruct their like-minded people to: "Kill the best of the goyim." (Zohar III, 14, 3, according to Rolling, p. 86 in Brandt).

"It is permitted to kill a denier of the faith." (Pezachim 122, 2, Tosef by Rolling, p. 88 in Brandt).

"He who sheds the blood of Akum brings a sacrifice to God." (Alkut Shimoni).

"The captivity of the Jews will continue as long as the rulers of the Akums are not destroyed." (Zohar I. 29, 2 according to Rolling, p. 89 in Brandt).

"Jews who kill those belonging to other nations (the Akums) will enter the fourth hall of paradise." (Zohar I. 38, 2 according to Rolling, p. 89 in Brandt).

"You should not deceive your brothers, and the Nazarenes are not your brothers, on the contrary, they are worse than dogs." (X. Mishpat, 227 in Rosov).

"When a Jew receives dishes from an Akuma, he must wash them, because one touch of an Akuma stains all dishes."

"The seed of Akuma should be regarded as the seed of cattle." (25 Ketubot).

"The marriage of an Akuma is the mating of stallions and mares." (Tsben-Gaeser 16, 44 at Rosov).

These vile precepts of hatred could go on ad infinitum. This is how they look at our girls:

> It's wonderful that the blood of filthy Klipot virgins (non-Jewish) still represents a fragrant sacrifice for heaven. Truly, shedding the blood of a non-Jewish virgin is as sacred a sacrifice as the best incense, and is a means to reconcile God with oneself and gain God's mercy. This is what Holy Scripture means: it is wonderful that a virgin herself is unclean and a Klip (non-Jewish), nevertheless the shedding of her blood is such a precious sacrifice. (Zefer Halkufek 146,147,156 according to Justus, pp. 94 and 95 in Brandt).

"Deceit in relation not only to one's neighbor, but also to God is the most essential and most characteristic feature of the Jewish religion and the Jewish tribe," concludes Shmakov. In remote times, other peoples were not distinguished by particularly gentle and exalted morals. Nevertheless, the idea of right and wrong, the concept of good and evil, were known to everyone, and therefore the vile and wicked were persecuted by them or at least despised. Yet, even in the midst of the thickest darkness of centuries, we do not find the deification of untruth anywhere. To elevate fraud to the degree of virtue is a task that has been taken on by Jews alone. The Talmud is absolutely unprecedented, and no other history, except the Jewish one, knows anything like it.

Rosov (*The Jewish Question*, Odessa, 1906) gives lessons on Jewish morality according to the Talmud:

> If a dying Jew leaves something in his will to the Akuma, then it should not be fulfilled.
>
> If a Jew finds something belonging to an Akum, there is no need to return it to him, except in the case when this is done in order to encourage the Nazarenes[138] to say: "Jews are very honest people."

---

[138] Christians. (Translator's note)

When a Jew owes an Akuma and he has died, he is not obliged to pay his own.

It is allowed to deceive a goy, but in such a way that the deception is not detected.

During the holidays, it is quite allowed to give the akum money for growth, otherwise the opportunity will be missed, and the Jew will lose his profit.

A Jew is allowed to take a false oath.

To give something good to the share of an Akuma or to give something to an Akuma is considered a great sin.

It is better to throw a piece of meat to a dog than to give it to a goy.

However, you can sometimes give alms to the poor Akums or visit their sick ones so that they can think that Jews are good friends to them.

For Jews, the property of the Nazarenes is considered an asset without a master, therefore it can be seized as much as possible.

Shmakov summarizes: "By humiliating the goyim and even Jehovah in every possible way, sometimes exposing him in a pathetic and ridiculous way and even portraying him as sitting studying the Talmud, the Jews deify themselves and their leadership."

"Israel is crowned with three crowns: the Law, priestly sanctity, and royal dignity," the Tilhat Talmud Torah speaks arrogantly.

"All Jews are princes" (tr. Shabbat), "The Israelites are more pleasing to God than the angels themselves" (tr. Hullin), "The light was created only for the sake of the Jews, they are the fruit, and all other peoples are only its husk" (Shane Luhon Gaberi), "God gave the Jews the whole world for them to own" (tr. Baba Kama, Shulkhan-Arukh, Hoshen Gamishpat, Hagga).

The desire of Judaism for a world dictatorship is openly revealed here.

It is not surprising that, with such views on the people around them, Jews, wherever they appeared, aroused spontaneous hatred against themselves—anti-Semitism. As the Jew Franz Werfel in the Shanghai Jewish *Our Life* of January 16th, 1942, correctly points out:

> In the old days, hatred of Jews had certain boundaries, but now it spreads to our entire planet. There is no need to delude yourself with the illusion that there is at least one place on earth that is not poisoned by anti-Semitism!

And the founder of Zionism, Theodor Herzl, also wrote during in his time in the Jewish State:

> This is an old relic of the Middle Ages, from which cultured peoples even with all their desire cannot free themselves. And they proved this desire by granting us emancipation. The Jewish question exists wherever there is a fair number of Jews. Wherever it doesn't, it is then brought there by Jewish newcomers. Of course, we are heading to places where we are not persecuted, but with our appearance, the persecution begins. This is true even in highly developed countries. So it is and so it will be until the Jewish question is politically resolved.

And elsewhere: "The longer anti-Semitism makes itself wait, the more it manifests itself."

Which we agree with!

52. The Significance of Religion for the Jewish Nation

The importance of the Jewish religion for the fate of Judaism was emphasized by Rabbi A. M. Kiselyov of Harbin when he wrote in his book *The Nationalism of Jewry*:

> And what, in fact, unites Jews scattered across countries, what binds them into one whole, into a single people, if not religion? What other connection exists between Jews living in Asian or African countries—Yemen, Persia, Morocco—with Jews living in Western or Eastern Europe? They speak different languages, are under completely different household, economic, and legal conditions; the surrounding conditions have influenced their way of life; the climate of the country has also affected their appearance. Yemeni Jews bear little resemblance to Lithuanian Jews, even less to Siberian Jews, although, of course, they have some national traits. Why do all Jews feel like brothers, why do the sufferings of Jews in a country far from us resonate in the hearts of all Jews, in all places of their dispersion . . . ?
>
> Thus, it is clear that the unity of the Jewish people cannot be attributed exclusively to origin, but to common origin, together with the community of religion for all Jews, makes them a single people. . . .
>
> So, therefore, we owe the integrity and unity of the Jewish people to our religion. From what has been said, it should not be concluded that the Jews do not currently constitute one people, that the Jews of different countries are only co-religionists, and not a single people. That the Jews living in England are

only the Englishmen of the Mosaic Law, in France the Frenchmen of the Mosaic Law, etc. The falsity of this view is visible even from the fact that we do not have a separate Mosaic law at all. We have the law of Moses and Israel, i.e., without the Israeli people there is no Mosaic law. Further, the falsity of this opinion is proved by practical life. After all, there are many different peoples professing the same religion, and yet they are completely strangers to each other and even often at enmity with each other.

Why does the Jewish assimilator's soul ache at the sight of the suffering of Jews, even of those living in other countries, if, in his opinion, they are mere co-religionists, and not a single people? Russians and Romanians, being co-religionists (they profess Orthodoxy), are yet strangers to each other. Although at present we are united only by religion, we must take into account that our creed embraces all aspects of our people's life, determines every step of a believer from the cradle to the grave: it defines his duties both to himself and to his family, to his people and to the whole of humanity.

This creed created the soul of the people, gave a certain direction to their thoughts and actions, developed the specific properties of our people.

With which we agree! Rabbi Kiselyov notes elsewhere in his book:

Our religion is national in the truest and deepest sense of the word, which cannot be said about the religion of other peoples. Our religion is national already because it is professed only by the Jewish people, while Christianity and Islam are professed by a variety of peoples who have nothing in common with each other.

Even separate branches of Christianity—Orthodoxy, Catholicism, Protestantism—are professed by different peoples, not even belonging to the same roots.

Orthodoxy is professed not only by many Slavic peoples, but also by Greeks, Romanians, and even Abyssinians.

Catholicism is practiced not only by the peoples of the Roman tribe—the French, Spaniards, Italians—but also by many Slavic peoples: Poles, Czechs, and others.

Among the Germans there are Catholics and Protestants; among the Arabs there are Muslims and Christians; among the Chinese there are Buddhists, Muslims, and pagans.

However, although they all profess different religions, they still form one kind.

Consequently, none of these religions can be called the national religion of a given people. There are no Jews who profess other religions. The one who departs from Judaism also departs from his people.

Which we agree with, only if the departure is not made for performance's sake.

The Jewish religion made the Jewish people a nation before many other nations. Both the main factors shaping the nation were at work, the unity of experiences and the unity of consciousness. There is also a third factor, a unity of origin, cementing the spiritual organism with a blood bond; which is why we call Jewry not only a nation, but also a race. The presence of Jewry among nations shows that not all of them come from God—the Jewish nation comes from the devil!

53. Jewry as an Inter-Nation

Yes, Jews often emphasize their essence as a Jewish nation based on the Jewish religion. "Nation and religion are equivalent concepts for Jews," notes Jewish private associate Professor M. Vaintrov in the Jewish magazine Gadalel (Harbin, January 1st, 1942). "Jewish orthodoxy, by smoking incense to religious dogmas with the subordination of national claims to these dogmas in mind, actually subordinates them to national claims."

This recognition is extremely important. It shows that the Jewish religion, embodied in the Talmud, is only the main tool of world Jewry in the struggle for world domination. At the same time, it becomes clear why Jews who have changed their faith still remain Jews, even if they seem to have lost the religious basis of their nationality. They remain Jews because the rejected religion still owns them through their nation. This is why they so often return to Judaism at the end of the day: the voice of blood, the voice of the soul, the voice of the nation!

But the danger of Jewry for other peoples lies not in the fact that Jewry is a nation, but in the fact that it is a special kind of nation—an inter-nation: an international and an internal nation. This nation has dispersed all over the globe among other nations, has penetrated into foreign national organisms, and is decomposing them from within. There is no normal class structure in it, because this nation is a parasite—it exists at the expense of other nations, feeding on their juices, their blood, drinking all their vital forces.

That is the essence of the Jewish question. Jews live at the expense of other people's lives, like a tapeworm, like a vampire; the Jewish nation has become a nation of parasites on the body of other nations! No matter how outwardly a Jew departs from Jewry, pretending to be a loyal subject of another state, the day will come when he reveals his true colors.

The head of English politics in the second half of the last century, Lord Beaconsfield (Disraeli), seemed to many to be a true Englishman. However, before his death, he converted to Judaism. In the book of the Zionist Goldstein, the following kind words are dedicated to him:

> In 1878, Lord Beaconsfield put forward and held at the Berlin Congress demands for full equality of Jews in newly formed states. Those who are more familiar with the Jewish soul of the author of *David Alroy* know how much further Disraeli's dreams about the future fate of Israel went. He dreamed of the restoration of a Jewish Palestine, of the resurrection of his native people to its former beauty.[139]

And England thought that for him the interests of the British Crown were paramount!

No matter how much a Jew pretends to be a patriot of a foreign country, he always remembers his tribe and cares for it. French Prime Minister Léon Blum did not hesitate to publish in 1937:

> Jews in France do not know any suffering, although anti-Semitic winds blew once in the country. As for me personally, I am a French Jew, and I can honestly say that I am a good Frenchman. I was born in France, in the heart of Paris; my parents and grandfathers lived in Paris and, since the history of my humble surname lends itself to research, I believe that my great-grandfathers were Alsatians, which also means French. I was brought up as a Frenchman, attended French schools, my comrades are French, and I held French posts. I believe that French culture has become a part of me to a significant extent. I speak French perfectly without the slightest trace of foreign accent. Even my facial features are free of particularly noticeable racial traits. And I am sure that there is no element of the French spirit, French honor or French culture that is alien to me. And yet, although I feel like a real Frenchman, I feel that I am at the same time a Jew.[140]

Do you hear, you gullible?

And here is another testimony of the same kind from an ordinary Jewish intellectual, sincerely entitled "Thoughts of the Heart":

---

[139] Goldstein, "Our Prospects," Moscow, 1917.
[140] Quoted in *Jewish Life*, Harbin, May 21st, 1937.

We were born in Russia, the Russian language is our native language, we think in it, we feel it. We grew up on Russian culture, and grew together with it. We were brought up on the traditions of Russian literature and the public. Gogol, Pushkin, Lermontov, Nekrasov, Turgenev, Tolstoy, Chernyshevsky, Herzen, Belinsky, Pisarev, Mikhailovsky, and others were the rulers of our thoughts. We imbibe the Russian spirit, the boundless free Radzinsky.[141] We love the boundless plains of Russia, the vastness of its fields, its broad expanses, the endless horizon of its steppes, the dull noise of its dense forests, the aroma of its spring nights and the chants of its noisy and cheerful waters. For us, many Russian holidays are also our holidays. In short, we are Russians.... But we are also Jews.... We have our own religion, our own temples. We have our own national characteristics. We are typical, we are a nation. Religion, nation—nation, religion.

The Orthodox says that a true Jew is only one who lives according to the *Shulchan Aruch*, performs 613 mitzros, etc. In fact, unlike other nations, we cannot draw a strict line between our religion and our national origin and say: this is where religion ends and this is where the nation begins. These are the two main elements of our Jewish organism. Our religion and nation are closely and inextricably linked.

"We are Jews," writes a certain Boris Kader in Harbin's *Jewish Life*.

Jean Zey was the French Minister of Education, but we learn from the Jewish press, for example, that:

The International Congress of Pen Clubs was held in Paris. The first solemn meeting at the Ataka Theater was chaired by the French Minister of Education, Jean Zay. The first speech was delivered by the famous French writer Jules Romain, who considers the Pen Club a defense of the human spirit and fighters against the danger of war everywhere. The Jewish delegation at the Congress consists of the following members: Steinberg, L. Koenig (London), Nachman Meitzel (Warsaw), S. Chernyhatsky (Palestine), Zelman Schneur, and Mrs. Anda Tingerfald. The famous German-Jewish writer Lion Feuchtwanger made a great speech. Congress has passed a sharp resolution of protest against the persecution of Jews.

---

[141] The surname Razinsky is formed from the name of the area Radzin in Poland. Following the annexation and partition of Poland and other regions of the Baltics by the Russian Empire under Catherine II, many Jews only had a first name and patronymic. (Translator's note)

The French minister is a Jew; therefore, he used his position in the interests of world Jewry. At first glance one might ask what does the French minister care about the persecution of Jews in Germany? But the minister feels like a Jew and does not hesitate to get involved in an alien "native business."

Another example: G. Bernhard occupied an important place in the political and economic life of Germany and as the editor of the *Vossische Zeitung* had great influence. He was a member of the Reichstag, a financial adviser to the Republic, and a director of Deutsche Bank. He was also a member of the Jewish Agency and the Jewish Keron Kissada.

Finally, the story of General Grulev, the only Jewish general in the Russian Imperial Army, is particularly instructive. The same Jewish press, in addition to the externally anti-Communist Jewish press, wrote about him in 1935:

> The name of this general is M. Grulev. A Jew, a native of the Vitebsk province, Grulev joined the Russian army in 1877, served three tsars, and in 1909 was one of the first candidates for the post of Minister of War. A few years ago, the sensational book by General Grulev, *Notes of a Jewish General*, was published. The book is of a fascinating interest. The cover reads: "This work is dedicated to the memory of my unforgettable parents and the entire long-suffering people of Israel; all revenues are entirely given to the Koran Kayemet Leisrael." It is clear that in the gloomy era for the Jews of Alexander II and Alexander III, and the last tsar, there was no way for Jews to penetrate into the higher military milieu. Grulev had to make a "transformation," but even after that the general remained a Jew at heart. Before joining the army, he published his poems in Hebrew in *Getspifra*, the newspaper of H. Z. Slonimsky and Nahum Sokolov, and dreamed of becoming a Jewish poet. In his youth, he studied the Talmud, the Hebrew scripture, and was well versed in the wilds of our old literature. . . . All his years he longed for all of Jewry.

How did the Jewish general, praised by Dr. Kaufman, end his life in exile? He poured mud on the army that trustingly let him into its midst, and in 1937 he left for the USSR and placed himself at Stalin's disposal.

54. Judaism and Freemasonry

And so we continue the story of the "long-suffering" Jewish people, which we interrupted for a while to review the Jewish religion itself, to determine the Jewish inter-nation. The Renaissance! The revival of ancient antiquity and the cult of the human personality, tearing the medieval bonds so hated by the Jews. A new story opens with faith in the human mind: rationalism and natural law. An interesting task for historians will be the opening of the channels through which the demands of Jewish equality were poured into the non-Jewish masses. Looking for these channels, historians will inevitably come to Jewry and, of course, to England, to the historical ally of Israel. None other than the Jews and the British came up with the bold idea of using harmless artels[142] of Freemasons—the "frank masons"—to create a global political secret organization. The Jews poured into its lodges the Kabbalistic secrets they had kept since ancient times. And the Jews and the British spread first professional, then speculative and, finally, political "Freemasonry" all over the world. Nowhere else, but it was in London, England, where the first "Grand Lodge" was established, which later on became the "Grand Lodge of England" and the "mother lodge" for the grand lodges of France, Prussia, and Russia. Its ideology came straight from Babylon.

Our brochure *Secrets of World Freemasonry* has been a colossal success, not surpassed by any of the books published so far. This brochure clearly proves that the rituals of the brotherhood of Freemasons are the spiritual brainchild of world Jewry and that all members-employees of the organization of Freemasons are participants in the construction of the Temple of Solomon. Everyone who enters is symbolically transformed into a Jew, the external indicator of which is the symbolic process of circumcision performed on him. Everyone who enters symbolically has to die, that is, to renounce all the qualities of the person he was before joining the Freemasons. A funerary ceremony is performed over him, and then in a magnificent and solemn form he is reawakened (resurrected) to a new life, where the law of Hiram the Jew, the builder of the temple of Solomon, reigns. Further, during initiation to the higher ranks, Jewish blood is ingested, and stored for this purpose in wine. This blood ritual is performed not symbolically, but is very real, that is, the initiate to the highest degree must literally drink from a vessel with wine and mixture of the blood of "brothers" of the same (high) degree, both living and long-dead. This ritual pursues the establishment of a brotherhood with Jews by blood.

---

[142] A traditional Russian association of laborers for collective work, a cooperative craft society. (Translator's note)

In all other respects, the whole spiritual side of the life of Freemasons is also penetrated by a pronounced Judaism. We will talk about this separately, but in the meantime, we note the fact that Freemasons with typically Jewish methods reject everything that is inconvenient for them. They deny the most irrefutable evidence against them not only in front of outsiders, but in front of their own "brothers" in the lower ranks. Therefore, in this brochure we cite the exact sources from which we have withdrawn any given material. At the same time, we do not rely on the materials of the enemies of Freemasonry, but use Masonic sources. For this purpose, we have used almost all the latest publications of Freemasons, as well as the *International Lexicon of Freemasonry* (Yevgeny Lenkhov and Oskaro Posner, ed. "Amalthea"), the drafters of which were, first, a member of the Supreme Masonic Council in Austria, and the second the grand master of the Czech Lodge. We have spared no effort and time to give readers the most accurate information about Freemasonry, and therefore, when establishing a fact, we always refer to the page number of the named lexicon, where the corresponding fact is highlighted by the Freemasons themselves. Thus, all friends of Freemasonry abroad, as well as former Freemasons themselves in Germany, will have all the opportunities to check all our indications and, having checked, be assured of their accuracy.

The German publishing house Aufbau testifies in the brochure *Secrets of Freemasonry* translated by Russian fascists into Russian and published with the mark of the publishing house Masks Down (Brussels, 1938).

The Jewish brother Gustav Carneles wrote in his holiday's message to the Order of B'nai B'rith (a purely Jewish group of lodges) in 1902: "The ideas of Freemasonry originated from Judaism. Their founder is the great King Solomon, who, anticipating the high flourishing of Israel, established part of the rites of Freemasonry."

An eighteenth-degree leather apron of the Knight of the Rose and Cross with a cross wrapped in roses was found in the ancient lodge of the Freemasons, "The Lebanese Under Three Cedars," stored in a glass cabinet. This cross is depicted falling. In the middle of the apron, however, one can see the Tablets of Moses standing. Thus, the picture on the apron symbolizes the victory of Judaism over Christianity.

In the same case was found a print of a painting by the French artist Berand, in which Freemasons are represented as scourging Christ. On the right side of the picture, a Freemason with a high-degree apron, a ribbon of a lodge and a horde is visible. With his words, he excites the crowd to commit a crime, and the criminals are in a hurry to begin the flagellation. This image could not be in the lodge without any significance for the enemies of Christianity, and the fact that this picture hostile to Christianity was displayed in the lodge shows that by this the lodge wanted to confirm its hostility towards Christianity.

The ruler of the Great German Union of Lodges, as well as all the Grand Lodges with the name "national," in 1914 was a Jew, "Zon." The rituals of all lodges of the world are all Jewish.

> The Lutheran priest Habich had to declare before the court: "I must in addition add that in the ritual of our Grand Lodge (one of the so-called German national lodges) the main part of the contents is Jewish. All the secret and hidden words are taken from the Hebrew language. At the initiation into the ninth degree of the Grand Lodge of Prussia, the new brother had to undergo a blood ritual. For this purpose, blood from the thumb of the candidate's right hand was poured into a bowl. Droplets of blood of all the brothers who reached this degree were kept in a glass prism. This blood is dried. Once dissolved in the wine poured into the cup, this blood is to be drunk by the initiate, and in this way, he drinks the blood of the brothers who have reached this degree, both living and dead.

In a similar glass prism, allegedly, the blood of the presidents of the Illuminati, the Jewish organization that instigated the French Revolution, is kept. This is thus done through Jewish influence, to which, in a similar case, the German Freemasons, like all the Freemasons of the world, obeyed. The blood ritual reminds one of the song of the Jewish prophet Joel against the Egyptians. The conclusion of the song reads, "But Judas must live forever, and Jerusalem was and will be, and I will not leave their blood unavenged, and the Lord must dwell in Zion." This hymn is quoted by Freemasons when carrying out the blood ritual.

The leather apron worn by the Masons resembles the clothes of the high priests of the Jerusalem Temple. The Masonic writer Goethe attaches such importance to leather aprons:

> In the second book of Moses, (Exodus 28: 42–43), it appears: "And you shall make for them linen trousers to cover their nakedness; they shall reach from the waist to the thighs. They shall be on Aaron and on his sons when they come into the tabernacle of meeting, or when they come near the altar to minister in the holy place, that they do not incur iniquity and die."

In the Masonic lodge "The Lebanese under the Three Cedars," eighteen out of one hundred members were Jews, although there were no more than ten Jewish families in the city of 31,000 inhabitants. Thus, in order to have a zealous leader of the lodge one must choose only one Jew.

The Masons: the famous Burgomaster of Rome Ernesto Nathan, the Foreign Minister Sonnino, who embroiled Italy in the World War; in Austria, Dr. Karl Ornstein, the Deputy Grand Master Dr. Adolf Capralin, the Great Orator Dr. Gustav Sniller, the Great Archivist Heinrich Glucksmann, and the entire bureaucracy of the Grand Lodge, all were Jews.

How deeply the Jewish spirit had entered the lodge is shown by the use of the Hebrew language. Our readers know that the Jewish influence embraced the lodge the strongest and more terribly the higher its degree. This is literally stated as follows:

> In the rituals of all the Masonic degrees, especially in the higher degrees, numerous Hebrew words and terms appear. The use of Hebrew words increases according to the height of the degree. Thus, the high degree ritual is overflowing with Hebrew words, so much so that Oliver Macay's dictionary that we know of is filled with Hebrew words and texts on many pages. The dictionary confirms the evidence for the existence of the seventy-two letters as the signs of the seventy-two names of God, which are not pronounced in Hebrew. The Hebrew words are common vernacular in the lodges and therefore have a binding significance.

Therefore, Hebrew is made by the lodges a worldwide secret language. Since the ritual and the sign of the words used by the lodges is in Hebrew, the spiritual content is also Jewish.

Aufbau summarizes: "We will say it once more, with the liberation of the Jews, the lodges start to appear. The first lodges were founded by Jews and have Jewish names."

- The main part of the ritual (the legend of Hiram) and the inner content of the lodges are Jewish.
- The passages and identifying words are essentially Jewish.
- The Hebrew language comes into general use more and more as the degree rises, and is established definitively in the highest degrees of the lodge.
- The interior of the lodges is arranged in such a way it resembles Solomon's Temple.
- Masonic brothers are considered the building blocks of the Temple.
- In the high degrees Jews and non-Jews make blood bonds through the consumption of mixed blood.
- The lodges have taken the leading role in all revolts and revolutions in the last two hundred years.

- Lodges destroy the foundations of the state (the church, marriage, the authority of the state).
- Freemasons always firmly seize the place of an overthrown state power.

55. What Is Freemasonry?

However, let us say a few words on the subject of what Freemasonry is.

Freemasonry can nowadays be defined as an international union of secret societies hiding behind various objectives of philanthropy, mutual assistance, brotherly love and even ecclesiasticism and nationalism, but in reality, striving for one destructive goal: to create a godless world state on the ruins of modern religions and states, run by the leaders of Freemasonry. It is easy to see that this goal coincides with the goals of Judaism, and how the Jewish spirit, symbolism, participation, and leadership of Freemasonry completely gives away the Jewish nature of the entire enterprise. Researcher of Freemasonry N. Scrolls counts 26 different versions of the origin of Freemasonry. Shrouded in secrecy and misinformation, it does not provide accurate answers to questions of its history. At the same time, different versions are given for different categories of Freemasonry.

Here we find the Gymnosophists of India, the priests of Memphis and Heliopolis, the mysteries of Elinais and Samothrace, the construction of Solomon's Temple, the cult of the Good Goddess and the Syrians and Romans, and the college of builders founded in 115 BC. Numa Pompilius and the Druid religion, which spread in Britain with Julius Caesar; the Crusader dreams of chivalry; the establishment of German secret trials in the thirteenth and fourteenth centuries; the Quaker mysticism of Cromwell and his partisans (who trusted in God but kept their weapons dry); the plotting of the English royalists, enemies of the Great Protector; and finally, the Templars, before and after the destruction of their order.

Numerous proofs of the Jewish character of Freemasonry are given in our 1937 translation of the official German revelations in *Secrets of Freemasonry*. See also Selyaninov, *The Secret Power of Freemasonry* (Moscow, 1908), Bostunich, *Freemasonry* (Belgrade, 1922) and Markov, *The Wars of the Dark Forces*.

In what way the transition from antiquity to modern Freemasonry took place however, remains unclear; in terms of the connection with the temple there is an official statement of the Freemasons themselves and their Wilhelmsbad Congress in 1782.[143]

---

[143] At Wilhelmsbad, near the city of Hanau in Hesse-Cassel, was held the most important Masonic Congress of the eighteenth century. (Translator's note.)

Hegumen Theodosius (Kulchitsky) summarizes:

The Masonic corporation first appeared in France in the Middle Ages, an era of particularly strong increase in religious sentiment, and with it, church building (in the new Gothic style). From the eighteenth century onward, these purely professional societies of free stonemasons that had spread abroad (Freemasons being stonemasons who were subject to different "liberties") began to accept as honorary members persons of other professions and ranks who could be of use. And it was these new members who quite soon completely transformed the Masonic lodges, turning them from religious and artistic societies into bodies of their contemporary mystical and revolutionary movements.

These artels were a very convenient way to cover up the secret forces of evil that were plotting a world conspiracy. Their alliances at the dawn of the New Age were taken over by secret socialist and mystical organizations that indulged in the cult of Satan and other abominations brought to the Old and New World from Mesopotamia by Jewry. Particularly grim were the remnants of the Knights Templar, who in the fourteenth century became an anti-Christian sect and were annihilated by Philip the Strong. The Templars, in turn, received secret teachings from Jewish Kabbalah, ancient Egyptian and Assyro-Babylonian magicians. Thus, the roots of modern Freemasonry go back to the professional organizations of stonemasons, from which they take their name, the Freemasons; and at the other end, to the time of the betrayal of the Messiah, and even deeper, to the Tower of Babel, and Sodom and Gomorrah.

At the end of the seventeenth century a certain James Anderson organized the first lodge in London. In 1723, the Grand Lodge of England published the Constitution of the Freemasons. It said, among other things, "We belong to all nations, languages, and families," thus establishing the international character of Freemasonry. From London, the lodge crept into the rest of England and crawled over to the mainland. In France, Freemasonry has taken a political character since 1725, when Lord Derwent-Waters came from England, who founded a lodge in Dunkirk on the instructions of the London Lodge in 1717. In Germany, a professional Freemasonry also had time to transform into a political society, also under British influence. It began in Hanover in the middle of the eighteenth century. In 1776, Adam Weishaupt, a professor and then rector of a small German university in Ingolstadt, founded the Order of the Illuminati. In five years, this Order took a leading position in Freemasonry, not only in Germany, but also in other countries. Among the members of the order were such eminent men as the Dukes of Braunschweig, Weimar, and Gotha, the Bishop of Dahlberg, and others. In 1778, thanks to the organizational talent of Weishaupt, the Masonic hierarchy had more than two million people scattered throughout Europe. In Russia, the first lodge was organized on instructions from England by the Englishman John Philips in 1721, and its first Grand Master was the Englishman D. Keith.

"To get a place at home," says Weishaupt, "you must have the appearance of men of serious and moral character. Offer harmless books first, have the appearance of lovebirds, and then gradually wamp up the fools to whatever degree you like." It is not without reason that Pope Clement XII compares Masons to "thieves breaking into a house."

Masonic statistics now number about 6,000,000 Masons living in all parts of the world. "All the world under one republic," demands the Grand Orient of France, and in its bulletins we find, "We must break up the church. Go back, Crucified One! Your kingdom is over. No need for God."

"Freemasonry, to whom history owes many individual revolutions, will also be able to carry out the largest, the so-called international revolution."

"The coming international revolution will be the work of the Freemasons."[144]

56. The Organization of Freemasonry

Among Freemasons we see many outstanding people in different ways. There are statesmen, including kings and presidents, prime ministers of governments, ministers and ministry workers, leaders of political parties, famous orators and journalists, financiers, bankers, merchants and industrialists, leaders of the largest railroads, philosophers, scientists, writers, artists—"the color of civilization," "the aristocracy of the mind," "the largest bourgeoisie," "the leaders of the proletariat." In this conglomerate of resounding names there are many people of high decency and profound nobility, unquestionable patriots and fervent believers . . . amongst a mass of patented liars and destroyers. What happened? Where does this confusion come from? Because Freemasonry is not what it appears to be! The main tools of Freemasonry are secrecy and disinformation. Such a system makes it easier

---

[144] *Collection of Resolutions of the Grand Orient of France*, 1922, 236.

for many gullible and seeking minds to become involved in Freemasonry.

This system consists in gradually revealing to those involved in Freemasonry the true aims, objectives, and methods of Freemasonry. At the heart of all Masonic organizations lies the innocuous so-called "Blue Freemasonry," the task of which is to bear witness to the purity of Masonic vestments and the nobility of Masonic aspirations. It has only three levels or degrees: apprentice, fellowcraft, and master. And these very sincere Freemasons at times may claim that their lodge does not do anything reprehensible and does not receive any orders from above.

But among the lodges sit high-degree Freemasons, who use "Blue Freemasonry" as a smokescreen on the one hand, and as a reservoir for attracting members on the other, and suggestively, to inspire the lodge with their decisions, which then, precisely because "the color of civilization" is involved in Freemasonry, must inspire public opinion. Above the three degrees of Blue Freemasonry stand numerous degrees of "Red Freemasonry." As they ascend, the secrets of Freemasonry are gradually revealed.

From the ninth degree come the secret degrees, of which steps nine through seventeen of the pyramid constitute the "atelier of studies." It is in this degree that Freemasonry makes a bloody alliance with Jewry. The ridiculously melodramatic ceremonies of Freemasonry, at times so wild as to resemble a fairy tale, have a special and profound meaning.

From the eighteenth degree, the Rosenkreuzer[145] degree[146]—the Freemason enters the field of active issues of world politics. Another ritual is for the Mason to extinguish three candles symbolizing the love for God, for his people, and for justice. From the eighteenth to the thirtieth step comes the "areopagus." Here the Mason is explained that his task is to fight against "prejudice: with religion and with nationalism." This completes the circle of the Masonic dialectic—the high aims are substituted for its opposite.

The thirty-second degree Masons form a Supreme Council governing this Masonic system and claiming a share in world domination.

None other than the Jew Disraeli, the head of British politics, Lord Beaconsfield, in one of his speeches in Aylesbury, September 20th, 1876, assured:

> The governments of our age should always reckon with secret societies: secret societies at the last minute can overturn what would seem to be the most settled of matters, they have agents

---

[145] From the Rosicrucian Order. (Translator's note)
[146] Meaning Knight, or Prince, of the Rose and Cross according to the Ancient and Accepted Statutes of Scotland. (Translator's note)

everywhere, agents not ashamed of anything, ready to kill and ready to massacre.

These quotes are cited in a very interesting and thus very rare booklet by Hegumen Theodosius (Kulchitsky), *Who are the masters of this delicious seasoning, who are they?*

57. How the Secrets of Freemasonry Came to Be Known

The uninformed reader may ask: Where did the secrets of Freemasonry come from?

Much has been gained by studying published Masonic documents, meeting reports, correspondence, etc. The general public, unfortunately, does not know that Freemasonry has its own press in various languages. This press is not intended for the "uninitiated," but even we, for all our organizational and financial weakness, have managed to obtain several interesting Masonic journals, such as *New Age*, the official organ of the Supreme Council of Scottish Rite of Freemasonry published in Washington, the *Rosenkreuzer Companion* (*Rosenkreuzer Digest*), the official international Rosenkreuzer journal of the Universal Order of Rosenkreuzer, and some others. Jewish publications, as we have seen, do not always keep secrets either. Most importantly, there are repentant Freemasons who have given the world a number of truly sensational revelations. Their analysis of wars and revolutions, deciphering all modern events, also explains a lot, which at first glance incomprehensible. In many countries, finally, the Freemasons themselves have grown bold enough to make overt and therefore suicidal statements for Freemasonry.

"Show me at least one living Freemason," demand some naive emigrant politicians, even Solonevich, and one of the heads of the Harbin Emigrant Bureau.

"Just look at America!" we reply. Freemasonry exists quite openly, publishing openly its meetings and challenges in the pages of the general press. At last, precisely in Harbin, an instructive incident occurred which is useful to perpetuate here.

In 1929, in the now defunct newspaper, the Harbin *News of Life*, a former citadel of Jews and communism, the following blatant article appeared in No. 111 of May 17th under the title "A Japanese General and the Freemasons of Harbin": "The *Osaka Ji Ji* newspaper published a large article about Freemasons, which we quoted from the *Japan Chronicle*." The article, which occupies two and a half columns, is full of utter childish naivety. For example, the chief of the Ikida police station, Dr. Yoshino, made this revelation to a newspaper correspondent:

We do not consider the question of the Freemasons serious, but it may turn out to be so. The Russian Revolution was started by Freemasons. The Russian Communists have adopted the Masonic system. Moreover, the headquarters of Masonic lodges in Moscow are connected with the Third International.

Next comes this gem:

Major General Shioden studied Freemasonry so thoroughly, while in Harbin, that he was considered an authority on the subject in Japan. And this general discovered that the Freemasons were mostly Jews. It is not difficult to guess who mystified the venerable general in Harbin. Apparently, he fell into the circle of White provocateurs, who convinced the gullible warrior that Harbin was full of Freemasons. Authorities with such baggage, apparently, are the judges of the Russian revolution.

A group of Russian people, despite the presence of abundant Russian émigré presses in Harbin, had no way to come out openly with objections and documents against the printed assurance of the newspaper, formerly an officialdom not only of the USSR, but also local Jewry, about some "non-existent" Harbin Freemasons, and issued a leaflet, placing on it a photograph of the Masons of the Harbin lodge. Immediately all the local Russian national press reacted to this "underground" leaflet by placing the same photographic picture on the pages of their newspapers in extensive articles. And this, incidentally, is what these newspapers wrote in the articles entitled "Harbin Masonic Lodge" and "The Truth about Harbin Freemasons":

The main task of Masonic lodges is to establish a brotherhood among mankind, regardless of nationality and creed.... To ascribe to Freemasonry any selfish purpose, much less evil intentions, can only be due to extreme ignorance and misanthropy, everywhere looking for an opportunity to pit man against man, nation against nation, class against class.... The Masonic lodge organizes a whole network of charitable organizations, such as orphanages, canteens, almshouses, hospitals.... That's all the scary stuff behind this "undeniably pleasant" ... organization and that frightened so much the "nationalist" gentlemen who compiled this illiterate flyer.

And finally, the report of these newspapers is truly a masterpiece:

After our editorial office received this flyer, our employee contacted the local leaders of the Masonic lodge, and they kindly agreed to provide photos of a group of members of the Harbin lodge for placement on the pages of our newspaper and shared information about their activities.

"This simultaneous outburst of the Russian newspapers against the authors of some 'insignificant, illiterate flyers' is very revealing. And it is indicative in particular for what it contains!" commented A. A. Karmilov in my 1933 brochure *Freemasons in Harbin*. And shortly before the publication of this brochure and the preliminary publication of its contents on the pages of *Nash Put'* in the open debates about Freemasonry, journalist S. A. Sergeev announced a list of Harbin Freemasons, which nobody later denied, from which we list members of the Sungar Masonic Lodge; the list proves that during Soviet domination of the CER, credit, finance, import-export, the most important branches of European trade and industry in Harbin were all concentrated in the hands of Anglo-American Freemasons, for this list is entirely of financiers and businessmen:

Honorary Members: Guy X. Holiday, P. M. P., D. G. M., E. W. Fraser, P. M. A., S. G. W. (E. C.)

Members: S. V. Anner, I. A. Brown, S. T. Bitshiner, E. F. Bolito, B. G. Carbonel, I. V. Kartlin, E. M. Kattel, V. M. Kulakov, T. L. Emiston, A. W. Farmer, H. C. Fakson, I. Van-Gorder Gillis, A. Golding, R. S. Rudman, A. B. Gutman, S. Khanin, G. S. Hankinson, V. Gonyak, D. L. Gutchizhko, T. O. Ibsen, N. S. Ivanov, S. N. Jacobson, R. R. Kabalkin, A. M. Korelin, Venerable Pastor S. A. Leonard (HSML), E. H. Mason, W. R. Marshman, W. D. Merehit, H. C. Mason, W. R. Melling, O. I. Musgert, D. A. Weville, H. I. Neville, S. D. Orescan, M. Pikersgill, E. W. Shawkit, E. I. Zurman, F. A. Walden (sworn. ver.), S. T. Woodroof, R. A. S. Vater.

The first case of an exposure of Freemasonry in world history is like a miracle. It was in 1785 that Lanz, a member of the Bavarian Illuminati Masonic organization, was struck by lightning in Regensburg. On his corpse, the police found documents that caused a series of arrests, searches, and a trial. The head of the Illuminati, Weishaupt, disappeared. However, the documents revealed the anti-Christian, revolutionary, and anti-national essence of Freemasonry and for the first time shed light on the greatest of the world's conspiracies. These documents are still kept in the Munich Archive. Long before the revolution of our time, they were reviewed by many researchers who presented the world with a number of scientific works in Russian, German, French, and other languages.

The second documentary exposure of Freemasonry dates back to 1845, when the Vatican took possession of the documents of the High Roman Venta Masonic Society. Thereafter, the popes repeatedly issued encyclicals against Freemasonry, citing exact quotes and facts. The Orthodox Church also spoke out against Freemasonry in the person of the late chairman of the Council of Bishops, Metropolitan Anthony. His *Epistle on Freemasonry*, which every Russian emigrant ought to study and which should hang in every emigrant school, in every emigrant organization and, of course, above all in the governing bodies of emigrants, was shamefully silenced by the emigrant press, even the newspapers which called themselves anti-Communist. Only the press of the Russian Fascist Union introduced the Russian people to this timeless historical document, translated into many foreign languages and particularly included in the most serious studies of German National Socialism.

The third exposure took place in the 20th century in Hungary, when after the fall of Béla Kun (the Jew Kohn), the bloody executioner of Hungary, and before that of Crimea, one of the most prominent figures of the Third International, who briefly seized power in Hungary, the Hungarian government seized the archives of the lodges of Budapest.

The result of this seizure was the following sensational data (we quote from the book by Léon de Poncins, *The Secret Powers Behind Revolution*):

> The book on freemasonry in Hungary which the union of Christian and National councils has just published in Hungary is divided into three parts. The first intitled: *The Crimes of Freemasonry*, by Adorjan Barcsay, contains a great quantity of documents seized when the lodges were dissolved in 1920. The second part written by Joseph Palatinus, is intitled: *The Secrets of a Provincial Lodge*, and exposes like the first the secret masonic work of destruction which led Hungary to the revolution of October 1918 and to communism in 1919. The last part contains the list of the members of the masonic lodges of Hungary, which proves that 90% of the Hungarian freemasons were Jews.
>
> The three first chapters briefly summarize the general history of the masonic movement. Chapters IV to VIII analyse the working methods of Hungarian freemasons: their struggle against the church and religious teaching in schools, their campaign in favour of universal suffrage, their policy regarding nationalities and their international tendencies. Finally, the last chapters, which attract more specially our attention, show how the Jews, grouped in the lodges, systematically prepared defeat and then the destruction which followed upon the end of the war. Chapter XI shows us by means of numerous documents, that in Hungary, freemasonry is eminently a Jewish

work; thus, for example, the book containing the constitution of the grand symbolic Lodge of Hungary, printed at Buda Pesth in 1905, bears the date of the Jewish era 5885. The text of the vows taken by members is in Hebrew. The secret pass-words are in the same language. The list published at the end of the book shows us that 90% of the members were Jews with names such as Abel, Bloch, Berger, Fuchs, Herz, Levy, Pollack, Rosenthal, Schoen, etc. Or Magyarized Jewish names like Hun and Haber. The author of the book quotes on this subject a very characteristic preface which appeared in the work of professor Pierre Agoston (one of the people commissars who shared the power with Bela Kun and who was condemned to death by the Hungarian tribunals last December) a work entitled: The path of the Jews. Among other things one finds the statement that in order to write the history of the Jews in Hungary it is also necessary to write that of Hungarian freemasonry.

Chapter X furnishes the proof that public charity has never been the principal object of Hungarian freemasons as they liked to have people believe. Although they only obtained the recognition of their lodges by the minister of the interior in 1886 at the express condition that they should not deal in politics, charity was for them only a sign-board behind which were hidden the secret intentions of Jewish freemasons for the gradual monopolizing of all political power.

In a report of 24th February 1911 signed Paul Szende, venerable of the lodge "Martinovics," we find passages such as the following.

"We readily recognize that charity such as we now practise does not correspond with our ideas. We must concentrate our attention on the necessity of achieving radical changes in the actual society." In 1916 Charles Szalay, grand master of the lodge Comenius, in a speech made to a full assembly acknowledged that: the spirit which animates all true freemasons has always been revolutionary. Works of public charity are not their principal objects, but simply a means towards attaining their final aim. [147]

On the role of Freemasonry in social movements, de Poncins cites the resolutions of the Basel Congress of Zionists of 1897, convened by B'nai B'rith, of which only Jews are members. He continues:

---

[147] The original English version is given here, not a translation of the Russian version. Léon de Poncins, *The Secret Powers Behind Revolution: Freemasonry and Judaism* (London: Boswell, 1929), 72–74.

As regards their part in the communist revolution in Hungary, this work shows that the freemasons worked above all by the press. By patient and tenacious labour they succeeded in gaining power over the majority of the press organs by means of which they sought to destroy the Magyar national sentiment. The daily newspaper *Vilag* was specially responsible for the weakening of discipline in the Hungarian army; copies of it were distributed by thousands in the trenches.

It was also the Jewish masonic newspapers which always defended the Jewish immigrants from Galicia who ruined the economic life of Hungary by their shameful speculations during the war. They also worked to poison youth in the schools by their anti-patriotic theories. The *Vilag* wrote: "The exaggerated teaching of the Hungarian language and the exaltation of patriotic sentiments by the study of national songs have only one result—the brutalizing of the children." And the *Kelet* the official paper of the Hungarian freemasons wrote: "We must win over the teachers and schoolmasters in order to reach, through them, the soul of the young and prepare the way for non-religious instruction. The teachers must be the forerunners of the most advanced ideas. . . ."

All the Hungarian masonic lodges were dispersed in 1920 and their goods confiscated for the benefit of the state according to the laws of the Hungarian constitution. An inquiry was opened by the ministry of interior in order to know who were the masons directly responsible for anti-constitutional acts and to bring them before the regular tribunals as soon as the inquiry was over.

The Christian societies which formed themselves since the end of the war, all inscribed at the head of their programmes the struggle against freemasons and demanded energetically their prosecution, for Hungarian public opinion held them responsible to a great extent for defeat and above all for the revolutionary troubles which caused so much harm to Hungary.[148]

A great deal of material on Freemasonry came into the possession of the Italian and German governments after the closing of the Masonic lodges in Italy in 1923. These materials were widely used in the Italian and German press and were displayed for all to see at exhibitions held throughout Europe. They were complemented by the seizure of the Grand Orient archives in Paris in 1940, when German troops arrived there.

---

[148] Ibid., 74–76.

58. Historical Exhibitions in Paris and Tokyo

A correspondent of *Nation* managed to attend the Paris exhibition, and sent the following correspondence, published in issue 11 (126) of our newspaper from March 9th, 1941, to Harbin.

In October of last year an exhibition of various Masonic documents and objects of Masonic ritual was held here in the Small Exhibition Palace, consisting of sixteen departments. Posters were displayed at the entrance to the Palace:
"The Greatest Deception of Mankind."
"The Freemasons Were Only a Human Mirror Behind Which Israel Maneuvered."
As is known, there were two major Masonic centers in France: the Grand Orient of France and the Grand Lodge of France. In the depths of these lodges wove international intrigues, which eventually led to the death of France. Now the secrets of Freemasonry are brought into the light.

Numerous showcases contain Masonic documents of extreme importance, drawing the destructive work of Freemasonry. Spectators in the halls of the palace see furniture and furnishings taken from Masonic lodge temples. There are Egyptian-style sarcophagi, armchairs from knightly times, swords with cross-shaped handles, skulls, skeletons, and other Masonic objects "of everyday usage." Here one can also see Masonic aprons—"cufflinks." A collection of such aprons and ribbons found in the possession of one of the Rothschilds, who abandoned them when he fled France in a hurry, attracts general attention. The exhibition reconstructs the Masonic rooms of the ordeal. It is a room covered with black cloth and depicting skulls, skeletons, etc. on the walls. In such rooms, the initiates were tested, and here they signed the terrible vow of silence.

Visitors to the exhibitions can view the frightening attributes with which the initiate is terrified. There is a device for the production of thunder, falling swings, etc. There are halls of the lodge of the "Great East" at the exhibition, where only the chosen ones are allowed—Freemasons of the thirty-third degree. Of particular interest are the objects and documents seized from the lodge of Rouen, where the cult of Adoniram was especially revered.

From the documents presented at the exhibition, it is clear that the study of the Hebrew language was mandatory for Freemasons. In particular, Russian Freemasons studied the

Hebrew language under the guidance of a rabbi. Unfortunately, there is no special department dedicated to exposing Russian Freemasons at the exhibition, but their participation in Masonic work is evident from the documents on display.

A visual illustration of the fruits of Masonic work is the poster that visitors see as they leave the halls of the exhibition palace.

The poster depicts a cemetery with thousands of crosses over the graves of fallen soldiers. Next to them are the impoverished rags of working-class neighborhoods. And next to them are gold-embroidered, jewel-encrusted Masonic cufflinks.

The exhibition of Masonic work makes an oppressive impression. It sheds rays of light behind the scenes of the world. And behind these curtains one can see those who have hitherto ruled the destinies of nations . . . in order to build their power over the world on a golden foundation.

Finally, in early 1943, an Anti-Masonic Exhibition opened in Tokyo. The Japanese government allowed the masses to display the many Masonic objects captured by the victorious Japanese army and navy during their glorious combat operations in China and the Malayas, in Singapore, and in the South Seas. *The Shanghai Dawn*, which can hardly be suspected of any special antipathy towards Freemasonry, said about this exhibition on February 17th, 1943, the following:

The world is indeed enmeshed in secret powers. The world is truly ruled by secret international forces. Wars are created by dark forces. The evil and terrible role of Freemasonry is not an invention, but a very real terrible truth.

These are the slogans of the exhibition of secret rituals, secret objects, and revealing documents on the role and significance of Freemasonry that opened in Tokyo at the Matsuya store, organized by the Central Information Office of the Cabinet of Ministers and the newspaper *Tokyo Asahi*. The numerous pavilions, which required enormous expense, present the secret mysteries and secret objects of Masonic lodges, not in the form of any models, drawings, or even photographs, but as authentic furnishings of all Masonic lodges; garments, symbols, documents and even the individual most interesting secret ritual chambers and lodge rooms, taken by the Japanese authorities from the main headquarters of Freemasons in Hong Kong, from the Masonic Lodge in Canton and from the central Grand Lodge in Canton, and from the central Grand Lodge in Dutch-colonized India. A pamphlet about the exhibition and Freemasonry in general is given with the issue.

Germany and Italy have organized such exhibitions, but the Tokyo exhibition is the first of its kind in human history because it exposes the work of Masonic organizations specifically in East Asia.

The vast room was almost in the dark, and only a dark purple light poured in from the narrow windows, in which we could see that this was the main secret room of the Grand Lodge of Freemasons in Hong Kong, for on the central wall of the room hung the silk and gold-embroidered banner of this lodge, with a square and compass embroidered on a British flag with the British coat of arms and the inscription in English: "Grand Lodge of Hong Kong No. 1236." The central part of the secret room was paved with a mat of black and white squares. In front of the banner was a high black table upon which stood a white marble stone, the symbol of the "free stonemasons," and on its left was a wooden hammer, spade, and a pick. On the right was a tall mahogany column with a globe on it. At the black table were three Englishmen (mannequins) in black civilian clothes, but each of them had a magnificent crown of gold and silver on his head; the central face had a crown, like a royal crown with prongs, and the others had smaller crowns, one of them representing as it were the globe, and the other a flower. On the necks of the three principal Freemasons hung beautiful gold chains and ribbons, to which were attached from below large stars ornamented with precious stones. They all wore beautiful belts and small Masonic aprons with symbols of dark silk on a white background. On each side of the table stood in a semicircle six, twelve in total, of the other Freemasons. Each of them was dressed differently and adorned with different signs and symbols, depending on his degree of initiation. The most distant ones wore simple wide gray-green robes, and deep gray-green hats pushed low over their heads. Next in line were the Freemasons, who wore embroidered robes with beautiful stars around their necks, and oddly shaped hats. Lastly, still nearer the table stood the Freemasons in beautiful, but also full of mystery, uniforms which covered all their figures tightly. On their sides hung swords, and on their breasts were some badges. The whole setting of the secret cabinet and the faces of the Freemasons were surrounded by some eerie mystery. It was a picture of the most secret meeting of the leaders of the Masonic Lodge in Hong Kong, the Freemasons of the highest degree, which considers and makes decisions only on the most important and most secret matters. One couldn't help thinking, looking around this secret cabinet, that if a normal person were to come here unexpectedly, he would either faint from fright or go mad.

In the next pavilion we were acquainted with symbolic objects of Masonic lodges and ritual paraphernalia. Several pictures of the "all-seeing eye," real iron blades, picks and axes, swords, knives, a carpenter's level in a silver frame, several different pictures of the globe and the universe, carpenters' corners and circles, wooden hammers, silver, beautifully decorated six-pointed stars, some mirrors, strange objects made of square pieces of white and black tinted glass, human skulls and tibia bones, gold and silver embroidered inscriptions, models of Chinese pagodas, gongs, incense pots, various banners of Masonic lodges in East Asia, mysterious icons in the form of a flat eel and compass, the all-seeing eye and star, which appeared to help Masons recognize each other at unexpected meetings and which were worn by Masons either as a tie-pin, or on watches and rings, or in a buttonhole, on hats, badges, and even on cufflinks, and much more. All of these items have an indication of which lodge they are taken from.

A separate pavilion is devoted to the Masonic press, where it is especially clear what tremendous power and influence Masons have all over the world, in all nations, over all governments, and over all mankind, since all those newspapers which are in Masonic hands, or where Masons have their representatives in the leadership, are housed there. Beginning with such an influential newspaper as the *Times* of London and practically every American newspaper without exception, many French and others, are all in Masonic hands. Influential magazines and publishers are also at their service. This pavilion shows that the most numerous and powerful Freemasons are in England and America.

The following pavilions show that many radio stations of religious and social organizations, large firms, almost all the largest European and American banks, steamship and railroad companies, the richest mines, factories and plants, the military industry in the form of weapons and gunsmiths, chemical plants, and other factories are in the hands of Freemasons.

A huge poster displays photographs of the most important leaders of the international dark forces.

A separate collection of photographs includes Masonic artists and musicians, dancers, painters, and writers. By the way, among the Masonic artists are Mary Pickford, Charlie Chaplin, and others. In the Supreme Council of International Freemasonry, pictured here, we see in the first place the former Prince of Wales, now Duke of Windsor.

The depiction of the ordeal of a newly initiated Masonic candidate and his attire is particularly eerie. They are dressed in a wide red shirt made of plain paper material, without right sleeves, and wide red pants of the same material, without the left leg. He is blindfolded and led along a narrow road through special dark rooms, where he suddenly finds himself either under an icy shower, or walking along a narrow path over a pit, and then falling into a rather large pit lined with stone, or hearing some strange cries, receiving a sudden and strong blow. The test reaches the point where the blindfolded candidate is given a small but painful wound with some weapon. In such a merciless way, Freemasons test the nerve, will, determination, and firmness of their future fellow-member of the secret organization, who, in the fear of pain and death, must not say a single word about the activities of Freemasonry.

In a separate display case are the insignia of the Freemasons' awards. For their services, they are not only initiated into the highest degrees of the lodge, but also receive beautiful and precious numerous badges on beautiful ribbons, the same as those received by statesmen, ministers, generals and kings. The only difference is that the Masonic Orders have, for the most part, a depiction of the six-pointed star, the eye and other things. They are all decorated with diamonds and other precious stones.

As is evident from the exhibition documents seized from the Cantonese lodge that a Mason is never deprived of a well-paid job, a commanding position in a firm, or the support of a bank for his enterprise. His material well-being is, as it were, guaranteed by the entire international Masonic organization....

The exhibition ends with a special pavilion where almost all the books in various languages of the world are on display, where Freemasonry is exposed.

This exhibition was a huge sensation for everyone. There is no doubt that elsewhere it will become the scandal of the day and the subject of widespread attention by all without exception.

The Shanghai Dawn, however, omitted one essential detail, noted by the *Nation* correspondent, who described this exhibition for our newspaper, no. 5 (208) of March 1st, 1943.

A special niche clearly demonstrates the gradual mastery of the souls of the non-Mason and the power of Masonic power. Before the eyes of the visitors a young man turns into a major financier, then into a Freemason, and finally, in his old age, into a monster with a crooked nose and saggy lips, drinking the blood of mankind.

Nearby is a panorama of a synagogue: gray-bearded Jews praying before tablets, columns, and six-pointed stars. Here on a banner are the warning words "Freemasonry is the same as Judaism, they seek to destroy the world!"

59. The Unity of World Freemasonry

The question of Freemasonry is a vast matter requiring special study. For the sake of economizing place and time, we are forced to confine ourselves to the most general sketch of this Jewish instrument of seizing power over the world. As we have said, modern Freemasonry is an alliance of various secret societies. Outwardly, there is no unified Freemasonry. There are various Masonic organizations, the most important of which are the Great Eastern, the Scottish Rite, the Rosenkreuzers and B'nai B'rith. Each of these rites has its own characteristics, its own hierarchies, and its separate centers. But a common ideology, program, symbolism, and tactics ensure the unity of Freemasonry even without this outward organization, although there are fairly proven claims that all Masonic centers are intimately linked, and above them rises an invisible unified center that coincides with the invisible center of world Jewry.

60. Freemasonry and the French Revolution

Léon de Poncins' book *The Secret Powers Behind Revolution* contains a great deal of documentary evidence to show that the bloody revolution of 1789–1793 in France was inspired by Freemasonry. Those interested in the matter are referred to that book. Here, however, we will cite only a few facts from it.

> None of the great classical histories of the [French] Revolution mentions the part played in it by freemasonry. It is indeed incomprehensible: Here is the greatest event of history for 1800 years, an event which has changed the face of the world; a hidden power plays in it an immense part and this power remains unknown for more than a century! A few persons have known the truth and either from fear or from interest have kept silent. Others, still fewer in number, have spoken and have been treated as visionaries. Many sincere people have felt that the

revolutionary manifestations of 1789 were not entirely spontaneous. They had a presentiment of a secret impulsion without being able to discover its source.

But to-day freemasonry openly acknowledges the French revolution as its work.

In the chamber of Deputies during the sitting of 1 July 1904 the Marquis de Rosanbo pronounced the following words:

"Freemasonry has worked in a hidden but constant manner to prepare the revolution.

"Mr Jumel. — That is indeed what we boast of.

"Mr Alexandre Zévaès. — That is the greatest praise you can give it.

"Mr Henri Michel. — That is the reason why you and your friends hate it.

"Mr de Rosanbo. — We are then in complete agreement on the point that freemasonry was the only author of the revolution, and the applause which I receive from the Left, and to which I am little accustomed proves, gentlemen, that you acknowledge with me that it was masonry which made the French revolution.

"Mr Jumel. — We do more than acknowledge it, we proclaim it.

"It was from 1772 to 1789 that masonry elaborated the great revolution which was to change the face of the world. It was then that the masons gave to the people the ideas which they had adopted in their lodges. (From a report read at an assembly of the lodges *Paix et union* and *la libre conscience*. Orient of Nantes, 23 April 1883.)

"Masonry which prepared the revolution of 1789 is in duty bound to continue its work; the present state of opinion invites it to do so. (Circular sent to all lodges by the grand council of the masonic order to prepare the centenary of 1789.)"[149]

A few pages later, de Poncins says:

Lying and hypocrisy have been characteristics of all revolutionary movements in the world since 1789 up to our time. One thing is said, whilst the contrary is being deliberately done.

"One must lie like the devil," said Voltaire, "not timidly, not for a time only, but boldly and always" (Letter to Theriot).

The general principle according to Collot d'Herbois is that: *Everything is permitted for the triumph of the Revolution.*

---

[149] de Poncins, *Secret Powers Behind Revolution*, 29–30.

This secret power directing the attack knew that certain ideas, lofty and beautiful in appearance, could prove a terrible weapon of destruction. It had, moreover, at its service the real genius of the formula; provided that the telling phrase, full of high sounding words and fine promises, is spoken to the masses, that is the principal thing; the contrary of what has been stated can be done afterwards, that is of no importance. Such are the three words of masonic origin: Liberty, Equality, Fraternity.

We may sum up by saying that the Revolution of 1789 was not a movement of revolt against the "Tyranny" of the old system of government, nor, as we are asked to believe, a spontaneous, sincere, and enthusiastic soaring towards new ideas of Liberty, Equality and Fraternity. Freemasonry was the hidden inspiration, and to some extent the directing influence of the movement. It did not create from the beginning the new social gospel, whose earlier origin dates from the Reformation, but it elaborated the principles of 1789, spread them among the masses and contributed actively towards their realization. . . .

The following is the evidence of the mason Bonnet, orator of the Convent du Grand Orient de France in 1904.

"During the 18th century the glorious line of the 'Encyclopédistes' found in our temples a fervent audience, which, alone at that period, invoked the radiant motto, still unknown to the people, of 'Liberty, Equality, Fraternity.' The revolutionary seed germinated rapidly in that select company. Our illustrious brother masons d'Alembert, Diderot, Helvetius, d'Holbach, Voltaire and Condorcet, completed the evolution of people's minds and prepared the way for a new age. . . .

"It was our brother mason Lafayette, who was the first to bring forward the proposal for a 'declaration of the natural rights of man and of the citizen living in society,' in order to make it the first chapter of the constitution. . . ."[150]

This is what the French researcher says. It is wise to believe him: he cites facts and documents.

61. The French Revolution and Jewish Equality

"The eighteenth century according to the Christian chronology is one of the most interesting centuries in the history of the Jewish people," the Jews tell us. "It marks the beginning of a new era in Jewish

---

[150] Ibid., 32–33. Emphasis in original.

life after centuries of monotonous life in the conditions of the medieval ghetto."[151]

Against the gloomy background of the long Middle Ages, the era of Jewish-Arab collaboration in Spain in the tenth and twelfth centuries stands out with particular clarity, as Jewry, living under more or less normal conditions, promoted from its ranks a whole series of titans of thought, word, and deed. In other European countries, starting with the Crusades, as well as in Spain itself, there has been a long and wide range of different restrictions on basic human rights since the thirteenth century.... Continuous pogroms and massacres alternated with mass expulsions from the most populated Jewish centers. At the end of the twelfth century, one could meet exiled Jews from England, France, and at the end of the fifteenth century from Spain, Portugal, Poland, and Ukraine (Khmelnitsky and the invasion of Moscow and Sweden), and the same regions (Gaida-Matchina) in the second half of the eighteenth century. Thus, since the twelfth century the Jews were forced by the nightmarish conditions of reality to move out of their largest centers and with a beggarly bag on their shoulders to scatter over the immense world in search of refuge.

To what extent these incalculable and immeasurable calamities affected the Jewish people is evident from the following little-known fact quoted by Jakob Leshinkin in his book *The Jewish People in Figures* (1922): "By the beginning of the eighteenth century there were only about one million Jews on the entire globe. But from the eighteenth century begins an ominous turn for the fate of the universe."

Through Freemasonry, Jews inspired the French Revolution. Throughout the world the Jews declare it to be "great." Why? Because in addition to the Declaration of the Rights of Man and the Citizen, it left another "unwritten" monument: the introduction of Jewish equality. Jewish equality, however, derives politically and ideologically from the Declaration of the Rights of Man and the Citizen, from the slogan "liberty, equality, and fraternity," from the foundations of liberalism.

"The first act of emancipation of the Jews was signed by the French Revolution," says Jüd Pasmannik solemnly and respectfully, "the second act was signed by the German Revolution of 1848."[152]

From France, Jewish emancipation spread all over Europe, and in 1917 so it did for the Jews in Russia. There was, however, a country in which Jews enjoyed equal rights even before the French Revolution. This was, of course, the cradle of Freemasonry in England. *Jewish Life* of November 21st, 1941 (No. 46) recalled this event in such warm and at the same time impudent terms:

---

[151] *Jewish Life*, 1941, No. 7.
[152] Pasmanik, *The Russian Revolution and Jewry*.

In 1753 in England a law on the naturalization of the Jews came into force, that is giving them full civil rights on a par with the native inhabitants of this country. This means that the Jews readmitted to England in 1657 by Oliver Cromwell had proven by their actions over a hundred years that they were entitled to the care and protection of a state which benefited from their labors.

It was not just England, though: all the cultivated nations of Europe, as if by magic, stopped the old ways of dealing with Jews, and not only acknowledged their right to work freely, but also recognized their right to enjoy free cultural rights. Jewish participation in the economic and commercial life of Europe brought to the latter an unprecedented cultural flowering and pacification!

Many progressive people of that time were starting to realize a high moral doctrine: the highest aspiration of mankind must be the transformation of humanity into a single fraternal family of nations [is it not Marx who is implied here?]. And this meant that misanthropy was coming to an end.

This is how the Jews of Harbin confessed their sympathy for internationalism and confirmed their Jewish origins.

62. The Fatal Significance of Jewish Equality for All Mankind

Édouard Drumont, the brilliant author of *The Revival of France*, wrote in his truly prophetic work in 1886:

In 1790 the Jew appears at the door; during the First Republic and the First Empire he enters, wanders, looks for places; during the Restoration and during the July Monarchy he takes a seat in the parlor; during the Second Empire he lies in another's bed; during the Third Republic he begins to drive the French out of their own homes or makes them work for himself.

This is France. But not just France, all of Europe during the nineteenth century. For immediately after the introduction of Jewish equality in France and elsewhere in Europe, world Jewry began its ascent to the heights of world power. Having amassed large sums of money, the Jews longed to apply them to other fields of life besides trade and finance. They were beckoned by the power over the goyim the prophets had promised them, and they were attracted by foreign culture. The fateful day when the French Revolution proclaimed the dogma of equality, and specifically applied it to the Jews, opened for them the doors of the front stage, the lodges, the stalls and the front rows. Under the banner of equality, a drastic inequality was established: the organized Jewish rich enslaved the unorganized non-Jewish rich and the proletariat, and along the way drove a wedge between them. Even from a purely logical, ideological, and religious point of view, in the name of justice: what kind of equality of rights can there be between a member of a nation, a son, grandson, and great-grandson of the builders of a common national life, and a Jew, a traveler from a foreign country? A "native" creates a nation-state, fights for it, waters the land with his sweat, blood, and tears, enriches the common economy, extracts wealth from the earth, takes bread from the fields, develops the culture, continues the deeds and labors of countless ancestors, millions of long dead relatives, and here comes an alien beggar, connected with millions of foreigners scattered all over the world. A trickster, sometimes an agent of foreign intelligence, often a swindler, and demanding the same right to participate in the political, social, economic, and cultural life as the master of the country! Yet, the "native" gave himself, his labor, often his life to his country, he fed his fathers and grandfathers, and the foreigners' fathers and grandfathers exploited the work of others for their own interests. Not only because every Jew, by the demands of his religion and the voice of his bloodkin, is a potential present or future criminal against his adopted country, an intruder, unconsciously nurturing or already carrying out insidious designs against the nation, state, class, and individual, but also because every Jew is not a unit, not an individual, but the footsoldier of a single world Jewry—there can be no Jewish equality without harming the independence of the country and its inhabiting people. The achievements of Jewry in the twentieth century, cited in this book, are brilliant proof of that. The Russian, the Japanese, the German, the Frenchman, the Hindu, the Englishman, the Manchurian, each of them bases his life struggle only on his own strength and only in exceptional cases can he count on the support of his national collective, on the action of his people and the defense of his state. The Jew, on the other hand, always has the organized support of his countrymen in his own country and abroad.

The Russian, the Japanese, the German, the French, the Hindu, the English, the Manchurian—it's just him, he alone. Sometimes it is just him plus his family, sometimes just him alongside his friends, sometimes just himself plus the party, the social stratum, the class. The Jew is never alone. The Jew is he plus all his relatives living in a given city (the community), plus all the Jews living in a given country, plus all the Jews of the world. The whole thing is set in motion when it needs to be done: the community at a given point takes care of the individual Jews, but when the communal power is insufficient, the great mechanism is then set in motion. Remember the trial of the French-Jewish captain Dreyfus, denounced as a spy as mentioned above. Or the Beilis case, accused in Kiev of ritual murder of the Russian boy Andrew Yushchinsky. Even supposing there to be a miscarriage of justice in the Dreyfus case, how many people are murdered on this suspicion of espionage, just because they are not Jews! Here an obvious spy, documented and confessed, was finally rehabilitated, while his accusers were all killed. As in the Beilis case, the defendant was rehabilitated, though the conscience of the ordinary Russian people who sat on the jury was unable to agree on the rehabilitation of Jewry as a whole.

In both cases—in the Dreyfus case, as in the Beilis case, the entire world Qahal stirred up. And not just the Qahal, the entire cultural world. Alas, to support the individual Jew, not only his relatives everywhere, but also the "goyim" herds led by them. What equality is there between David and Goliath! David here acts as Goliath, not even Goliath, but a hundred-headed hydra!

Yes, with Jewish equality there is a glaring inequality, to the detriment of the masters of the country. They are alone in their struggle for strength within their nation and state, while the Jews are the terrible force organized on a worldwide scale. Thus, every Jew sees in every Gentile an enemy, while most Gentiles, through their ignorance of the Jewish Question, see these insolent usurpers almost as the benefactors of humanity!

Finally, every non-Jew has his own "good Jew." Some even argue: let's assume that all Jews are bad, but N. is an exception to the rule. And since there are only about sixteen million openly self-described Jews, then almost every one of them has such a kind benefactor! All Jews end up being good Jews! And they take full advantage of it. This is another trick of the world's best tricksters. What a terrible picture: a separate, isolated, disconnected from other native people against a hundred-headed Jewish hydra, mobilizing millions of masses and millions of resources! And to further set people apart, the Jews have spread a beautiful and delicious treat around the world—liberalism.

63. Jewry and Liberalism

Liberalism proceeds from the cult of the individual human personality, detached from Heaven and from the nation, opposed to all other individuals. Liberalism is indifferent to religion, its style is that of religious indifferentism: religion is a private matter, all religions are generally good. To believe in God—what backwardness! At best he accepts pantheism: "God is nature." Liberalism despises "zoological nationalism." "Chauvinism, obscurantism, the black hundred!"—he snorts, erasing national characteristics with his cosmopolitanism. In politics he schemes democracy, in economics he asserts capitalism. He leaves the role of the "night watchman" to the state, powerlessly and unwillingly observing the struggle between political and economic forces.

Think for yourself how beneficial this concept is to the organized and centralized world Jewry as opposed to the disorganized and decentralized "goy herds." The Jews assume the role of organizers and "divide and conquer," grouping the herds into political parties run by bought and paid for leaders.

The French Revolution was crushed by the nationalism of Napoleon, but its ideas, still living as all strong, evil. and good ideas do, did not die, rolled triumphantly across Europe, and spilled over into Russia. The theory of the rule of law that existed in the minds and hearts throughout the nineteenth century emerged as the yeast of this Masonic revolution, reflecting Jewish aspirations. It is a well-known fact that the slogan of the French Revolution, "freedom, equality, and fraternity," the ideological foundation of liberalism, was coined in the silence of the Masonic lodges. Its personal author is unknown; it appeared suddenly and in several places at once. De Poncins categorically asserts Masonic authorship.

Liberal theories are closely associated with the school of natural law and social contract theory. The creators of these theories—Hugo Grotius, T. Hobbes, Voltaire, Diderot, D'Alambert, and other encyclopedists, and finally Jean-Jacques Rousseau—were all Freemasons. Both anti-Masonic and Masonic sources testify to this.

Liberalism penetrated into Russia at the same time as Freemasonry after Captain John Philips, seconded by the Great Lodge of England, established the Great Lodge of Russia in Russia in 1721.[153] The Decembrists' mutiny, on the basis of accurate documents called Gr. Tol's "Masonic action," was the first attempt of armed demonstrations of liberalism in Russia.[154] Most of the Decembrists were Freemasons and subsidized by the Jewish banker Peretz.[155]

Liberalism has declared the supreme value of earthly life to be not God, not the Nation, not the human soul, but the individual, detached from all organic bonds. The "individual," regardless of its qualitative content, good or bad, free and equal, an abstract, mathematical unit, outside religion and outside the nation, free from "prejudices" and seeking all kinds of "freedoms," is at the center of all the conceptions of liberalism. Man is above all! He is the center of all creation! At first glance a proud doctrine, but in reality, what a belittling, debilitating one! Man is no longer the image and likeness of God, not a carrier of

---

[153] See T. Sokolovskaya, "Russian Freemasonry and its Significance in the History of the Social Movement."
[154] See Gr. Tol's *Masonic Action*, St. Petersburg, 1914, 167.
[155] *Jewish Life*, No. 10, 1940.

the immortal soul, not a participant in the higher world, but a miserable product of natural selection, a descendant of the monkey, a machine for the production of his own kind, an animal of the highest order—he disappears without trace and without rest, when death sweeps away his weary eyes.

"When dead, they'll bury you like you were never born / They'll eat herring and drink vodka to it!" reads the true anthem of liberalism, the song of the decay of Russian students, "Days of Our Life." The purpose of life being: To catch a moment before the comedy is played!" "The self-satisfaction of all instincts, the pursuit of all pleasures," some say, making man a slave to the needs of his body; "endless accumulation," some others correct, to subordinate human beings, the creator of values, to the values they themselves create, in addition to artificial and contingent values, to money; "the purpose of life: the endless pursuit of knowledge," define others, enslaving the living man to dry science. Faust! What freedom to cast Jewish fishing rods into this "lake of the free," what boundless liberty to the Jewish Mephistopheles!

Having obtained their coveted equality, the Jews plunged headlong into the maelstrom of political life and, above all, saddled themselves with liberal parties. Previously they had tried to influence the state from the outside, but now the roads to direct participation in public life and clear ways of leading it were open to them. Since the nineteenth century, we have seen how every new political idea is cleverly picked up by Jewish hedge-hunters. They try to make it into a springboard for their next leap, trying to infiltrate every political party, to join every non-Jewish organization, to make sure that every idea, every party, every camp has its Jewish guardian, friend, advisor, ally, comrade, vocal or unvocal leader. This is the Judaization of politics, or Judas in politics: the Eternal Jew in the role of the speculator of ideals in the social movements of modernity.

64. Jewry in Democracy

Jewish politicking was given unlimited freedom by "political liberalism"—democracy. The liberal-egalitarian democracy of our time was, of course, stolen from antiquity by the Jews, who spiced it up with parliamentarianism. Thus was born the theory of the rule of the people, in which the people would rule themselves ... with the help of Jewish swindlers. These masters of politics quickly learned how to exploit political parties in need of material resources. They spared no expense for their triumph.

The "common will" of the people in a democracy is supposedly recognized by the election of representatives. In order for the "blind" people to know who to vote for, various "sighted" politicians are at their service, praising each of their candidates and seducing the masses with programs, one better than the other. But to make their propaganda successful, parties need money: to rent offices, maintain the machinery, publish newspapers and literature, and sometimes to directly bribe the electorate. Thus, political parties depend on various domestic and international capital groups, and their programs become veiled in the interests of these capitalist groups.

The Jews feel like fish in water. The people in a democracy are not a nation, but a mixed people, in which the "equal" Jews can operate unashamedly. The voters and parties are fragmented, while they, the Jews, are organized and their agents and representatives are distributed among the various parties and seek to advance this whole chaos, the division of the nation along party lines and the party struggle. In the end, the "expression" of the "common will"—the party-law—is an assembly of representatives of everybody but the nation, mostly of various Jewish and Masonic groups. Under the national flag of unity comes total disunity! A familiar picture.

"In democratically governed countries there are, for the most part, many more or less significant political parties and splinter groups," says the *World Service*. This is not an accidental phenomenon; it corresponds to the Jewish tactic of "divide and rule." After all, in almost all political parties, the Jews occupy the most authoritative of positions.

This fact, unbeknownst to the Aryans, is admitted by the Jews in all honesty. And so, in the organ of Jewish Freemasonry, "Der Order B'nai B'rith," in the reports of the Grand Lodge for Germany in no. 6–7 of June–July 1926, it was written: "Brothers are everywhere in the most influential places. The Order is proud that its members are, in all camps, officers in charge of the various parties or groups."

This recognition clearly defines the essence of democracy and parliamentarism. The Jews sit in all parties and groups and pull the strings everywhere they are. In this way the Jews dominate all economic and popular life in democratically governed countries. Therefore, when Adolf Hitler came to power in 1933, one of his first acts was to eliminate political parties, destroy Jewish influence, and completely crush the Masonic organizations. Only on this basis was it possible for the powerful rise of the Third Reich that followed.

Specific examples of Judaism in democracies are scattered throughout the previous chapters. Look at the chapters on England or the United States.

Mussolini, in *The Doctrine of Fascism*, deciphered democracy as a plutocracy. Next came Pelli (*Liberation*, 1939), who changed just three letters, whereupon democracy became the "Reign of the Jews," a Judeocracy.

Dr. David Feuchtwanger, the Vienna Chief Rabbi, put it even more accurately: "In general, there is nothing democratic that is not Jewish, for democracy flows entirely from Jewish sources."

Thank you, Rabbi!

65. Jewry in Capitalism

The continuation of liberalism in the economy gave mankind the capitalist order. Up to a certain stage it was a progressive phenomenon, contributing to the formation of the national capital of each country. But in parallel with national capital, international capital also grew and was strengthened. Liberalism demanded freedom of competition, which was transformed into freedom of exploitation. Free competition and equality between Jewish and gentile businessmen favored the former, the more unscrupulous and well organized. Free exploitation facilitated the Jewish takeover of the economy, while at the same time creating mass resentment against the unjust conditions. Finally, liberalism erased economic boundaries and transferred values from one country to another, chipping away at the profit of international middlemen. The Jews have long specialized in international trade. In the age of its development they have become masters of international finance. Liberalism in the economy—the capitalist order—became a form of their domination, although this form soon ceased to satisfy their insatiable appetites.

66. An Age of Great Jewish Preparation

Having its grand opening with the proclamation of Jewish equality in France and then elsewhere, the nineteenth century passes as a century of great Jewish preparation, to be followed by a century of great Jewish accomplishment. Judaism is gaining ground: the nineteenth century shows the progress of liberalism, democracy, and capitalism. Religion, the nation, monarchy, and labor are in retreat. And parallel to the progress of liberalism, democracy, and capitalism, the Jews are getting stronger to an extreme degree, so much so that as early as 1860, Adolphe Crémieux, French Minister of Justice, head of the Masonic Grand Orient of France, and loyal son of his "persecuted" people, founded the Universal Israelite Alliance (*Alliance Israélite Universelle*).

"Sons of Israel, the hour of our victory is at hand! We stand on the threshold of world power!" begins the first landmark manifesto of this first openly worldwide Jewish international organization.

The Union we want to create is not French or English, Swiss or German; no, it is Jewish, it is universal! No sooner will it become the friend of a Christian or a Muslim than when the light of the Jewish faith, the only religion of reason, shines everywhere. Jewish doctrine must fill the world. The network that Israel spreads around the globe will grow day by day, and the lofty prophecies in our holy books will finally be fulfilled! The time is near, Jerusalem will be a house of prayer for all the peoples, and the banner of Jewish monotheism will fly on the most distant shores. The day is not far off when all the riches of the earth will become the property of Israel!

This document is no less explicit than the famous *Protocols of Zion*, although without the methods. It outlines the program of the worldwide Jewish organization, prepared by all the events of the nineteenth century and begun to be realized in the events of the twentieth century.

At the same time, the German Jew Karl Mordechai Marx, grandson and descendant of Orthodox Jewish rabbis by father and mother, in order to penetrate into Christian society, renounces Judaism, converts to Christianity, seduces the flighty daughter of a German Christian count and, having promulgated the *Communist Manifesto*, withdraws to the haven of all world conspiracies—London, where he joins a Masonic lodge and is quickly promoted in it. He attended their meetings and transformed the "free-thinking community" into the International Workers' Association, which at its congress in London became the International Socialist Organization, later called the First International. It is not the workers but the Jews, Freemasons, Englishmen, and international adventurers that are its true founders.

The nineteenth century is marked by the First World Jewish Congress, assembled in Basel in 1897. This congress gave a start to all the subsequent world Jewish congresses, which inaugurated the world unity of the Jewish people. According to the Jewish version, at this congress Theodor Herzl presented his demand for a Jewish state in Palestine, and thus laid the foundations of what is commonly called Zionism, becoming the founder and leader of the Zionists and the external leader of the Jewish people. According to the non-Jewish version, it was at this congress that the resolutions for taking over the world were adopted, formulated in the form of protocols, later called the *Protocols of the Elders of Zion*.

"A fiction! A forgery!" The Jews, after almost a quarter of a century of silence on these protocols, have been bawling out a flood of denials and even entire lawsuits.

At first in Russia, where the ever-immortal thinker S. Nilus published these *Protocols* in his book *There's One Near the Door*, the Jews and their obedient press tried to suppress these *Protocols*.

There were two editions, but they did not reach the masses, secretly being bought up by the Jews. The third edition came out during the untimely government of Alexander Kerensky, Aaron Kirbis.

Kirbis, of course, ordered the withdrawal of the *Protocols*. They were also banned in the White Army by General Denikin. Naturally, it wasn't even worth discussing the prospects of publishing them in the USSR. The Bolsheviks tracked down all the last copies and carefully destroyed them. But the intrepid I. T. Shchelokov in Harbin republished them for the edification of contemporaries and posterity. After that more underground editions appeared. Another active Russian fighter with the dark forces, Colonel Winberg, transported a copy of the *Protocols* to Germany. The Germans appreciated this terrible document better than the Russian people.

It is said, and not without reason, that the *Protocols of Zion* had a great influence on the formation and spread of the forces of German National Socialism. The same beneficent role they played in the formation and development of national liberation movements in other countries.

The *Protocols of Zion* have now been translated into almost every language on earth, from English to Japanese, from Swedish to Hindu, and have produced a vast commentary literature. In Germany they are part of the secondary-school curriculum, and there is probably no cultured person who has not heard or read them.

What are the *Protocols of Zion*? It is the tactic for the execution of Jewish agenda, as outlined by the leaders of world Jewry in the twentieth century. How did these secret decrees come to be known? There is nothing secret that has not become obvious: they were extracted by a talented agent of the Russian political police and, not finding an understanding in the bureaucratic Masonic upper echelons of the police, handed it over for publication to a friend, a prominent Russian nationalist philosopher. The world owes much of its discovery by the Russian police to the freedom from the terrible Jewish web!

Is it necessary to argue about the authenticity of the *Protocols of Zion*? No, because all subsequent events brilliantly confirmed them; and even if they turned out to be a fake, we must admit that their author is a brilliant visionary and prophet!

Until 1920, everything in the world went exactly as it was written in the *Protocols*, which first saw the light of day in 1901. Before the victory of Italian fascism, nothing happened in the world that was not provided for by the *Protocols*. Jewish leaders, Jewish bodies, Jewish organizations, and the entire world Jewry as a whole behaved exactly as it was written in the *Protocols*. Why should Jews spend millions on bribing corrupt "goy" authorities—from Count de Chaillet to Professor Milyukov and the famous whistleblower Burtsev—to produce millions of copies of expensive books, why hire high-ranking officials and learned witnesses, bribe prosecutors and judges, when the greatest of immortal witnesses—history and modernity—confirm the authenticity of the "Protocols of Zion"?

We are proud that our comrade-in-arms B. P. Tedley, the special commissioner of the Head of the Russian Fascist Union for Europe and Africa, spoke at the Bern trial in 1937 about the authenticity of the *Protocols of Zion*, and that we also welcomed the expert of this trial, Lieutenant-Colonel Ulrich Fleischhauer, head of the *World Service*, who had overthrown the Jewish accusation and testified to the truth before the world.

67. The Century of Great Jewish Achievements

Parallel to the spread of Jewish equality and the progress of its manifestations in politics, culture, and economics, and parallel to the progress of liberalism, democracy, and capitalism, there is an internal decomposition of the nation, the state, and the family due to the assertion of the individual: at first complacent, and then frightened and bewildered. The nineteenth century goes under the mark of the individual.

At the same time as Israel, England is strengthened, eventually becoming the world's greatest power, in whose domain the sun never sets. 500,000 Jews hold sway in England. 50,000,000 Englishmen hold the British Empire: 500,000,000 people—White, yellow, and black. Through Gibraltar, Suez, Malta, Aden, Colombo, Bombay, Singapore, and Hong Kong stretches the coveted chain encircling the Old World from the south. And in the New World, other Anglo-Saxons are expanding: Americans and also Jews. On the mainland of the Old World, in Europe and Asia, the agents of British imperialism are in disguise as the Jews, the Freemasons, the Intelligence Service, and in Africa their role is played by ruthless, arrogant English "gentlemen," troops without compassion. On the mainland of the New World, emerge the United States, the USA (North American United States), claiming to be the United States of America (as a whole).

The British imperialists understand the old Jewish saying: "Only Jews are human beings, the rest are humanoid creatures" somewhat differently: "Only Whites are human beings, the rest are humanoid creatures," narrowing the concept of the "White race"—which for some is applicable to Europeans—only to themselves, the English: "Only Englishmen are human beings, the rest must serve the gentlemen!" In addition to the merchant navy and the English island war fleet. The age of the Great Jewish Preparation turns out to be at the same time the most English age of world history—the age of world trade, colonial conquest, imperialism, and the development of maritime travel, the age of the navy. England becomes the mistress of the Mediterranean, the Atlantic, and the Indian Oceans, dreaming of dominating the Pacific, or Great Ocean, so that all the waters of our land, as well as the land and the air, eventually become part of her fiefdom; the fiefdom of world Jewry.

Finally, in parallel with the strengthening of England, Freemasonry is spreading all over the world. The nineteenth century also turns out to be the century of the worldwide spread of Freemasonry, which in the previous century spread across Europe, and in this one is penetrating into the remote corners of the globe.

What cursed times! Civilization seems to be entering its most brilliant period of development, but deep beneath its foundations there is an undermining, and somewhere below there is the deafening murmur of the hungry masses dissatisfied with injustice.

Jews, liberalism, democracy, capitalism, Freemasonry, England; this is how the circle of Jewish expansion in the nineteenth century is drawn. These forces are attacking the independent nations in a tight and scattered formation. The ring is shrinking! And the horror is that the blind, or rather blindfolded nations do not see this encroaching enemy. He is wearing an invisible hat! He has let in so much fog and misinformation that even such a great philosopher as Schopenhauer exclaims with horror:

> What, after all, is our world but a gigantic masquerade, where fruits are made of wax, flowers of paper, fish of cardboard, and where the two there in the corner discussing something so earnestly, one offers fake goods and the other pays with counterfeit coin!

To the extreme Jewish nationalists, however, the liberal pace of goyim enslavement seemed too slow. Not without the permission of the ruling Jewish supremacists, they conjured up new spirits from the abyss: they drove to the aid of liberalism its external opposite, socialism.

When I formerly affirmed the inner organic relationship between capitalism and socialism, arising from their common materialistic and utilitarian basis, one could object to me by contrasting the USSR and the bourgeois world. Now that the "proletarian" USSR, the ultra-capitalist America, and bourgeois England have revealed their secret alliance, always carried out before through the Jews (as it is now being carried out through the Jews), World Revolution and World Finance, even for those who do not want to see, it appears to be two different hands of the same monster.

What of the fact that one hand is shorter, the other one is longer and in a snow-white glove? What of the fact that one hand is armed with one bloody knife, from which blood still drips, and the other generously pours you gold? The same "two-faced Janus" wields these two hands! The same star is burned on its forehead—the star of David, the star of the Jewish inter-nation.

Only for one sixth, the end remains hidden. Lord Weaverbrook and the Soviet ambassadors in London and New York, Comrades Maisky and Litvinov, understand each other perfectly, for they are all Jews.

That is why the dignitary lord probably stands up with special reverence and pleasure at the sound of the "Internationale" when he hears "Arise, you cursed one! He who was nothing shall be everything!" He who is branded with a curse by all the peoples of the earth. He who was nothing in the days of the universe and in the Middle Ages and will be standing in the Final Judgment, and who nevertheless boldly wants to be everything, and in the twentieth century became everything for a while! He understands and understands quite differently from the proletariat, on whose behalf the "dictatorship of the proletariat" of the world, Jewish Finintern, which was opened by the Comintern, is carried out.

The Diverbrooks and Kaganovichs wanted the twentieth century to be a century of great Jewish accomplishments. The class was called in to aid the individual. They wanted the individual to be the symbol of the nineteenth century, and the class to be the symbol of the twentieth century.

Their diabolical plan succeeded for a quarter of a century, and the movement of the Jewish star toward the zenith of heaven continued. But the fall following the rise illustrates the entire historical path of the Jewish people. The night reached the pitch-dark of midnight, when the first tremendous explosion of world Jewry occurred, and instead of the age of the class, the age of the nation began.

But before this, seas of blood, oceans of tears had been shed, revolutions and wars had swept over the great planet in a terrible whirlwind. Along with the overview of socialism, we enter the twentieth century.

Our journey around the world, as the readers have probably noticed, ended in America, where we halted and jumped into a time machine to travel in the fourth dimension, to follow political geography, to deal at least briefly and superficially with political history. To revisit history, to resurrect its forgotten pages under the influence of Jewish *herem*, Masonic silences, and sealed by a censorship more powerful than that of any police. We have learned, very briefly and superficially, the history of Jewry and its instrument of struggle for power, Freemasonry, and the Jews' use of various political ideas in the nineteenth century. Let us now continue this journey into the twentieth century. Let us look at the use of different political ideas in the twentieth century and at contemporary methods of Judaizing politics.

Only then will the contours of the Jewish world-state, which I have called in the title of this book, "Judas over the States," open up before us.

Judas over the States! This was the aim of our century, this was a fact during the first quarter of the century, this is the core of the Jewish Question, which has seized the sphere of politics (there are also cores of the Jewish question which seized the spheres of culture and economy). Zionism is its cover; the International is its essence; the dictatorship of the proletariat, the League of Nations, the union of democratic countries, the old order, are its aliases; and Jewish domination is its goal.

The age of great Jewish achievements had to supplement the invisible power of Judaized public opinion and world Jewish finance with the overt political power of world Jewry, which imagined itself to be "chosen by the people" to rule our sinful land. The Jews wanted unrestricted and unlimited domination over us, and founded a World Jewish Empire in which the Jewish national state in Palestine would play the role of the metropolis, and Jerusalem, as its the capital. Everyone can see what they got. God is not to be scolded! There is world justice, there is Nemesis: the sowing of wind begets a storm. And the storm blows away all the dark clouds of the gloomy night of mankind, as it has already scattered over Western Europe and East Asia.

We feel the Rising Sun, the new life, the New Order!

68. Jewry in Socialism

The extremes of capitalism were bound to provoke the reaction of the working masses, the producers of goods, the creators of value, who were rising to the consciousness of their significance. Just as the bourgeoisie took the leading place of the nobility, the intelligentsia took the place of the bourgeoisie, the workers, and peasants. The workers and peasants themselves rose to conscious life and to the administration of the state. The social question rose as a formidable spectre over the world of lies and injustice. The situation of the masses at large needed radical improvement in all regards. Labor demanded its rightful place in the sun. This, of course, could not escape the acute attention of the Jews. The social question could and should be solved by social reform. Religion was ready to extend its hand to Labor, and in some places it did (the Christian socialism of the Catholic Church). The monarchy, the most "backward" autocratic monarchy of Great Russia, extended its hand to Labor (Stolypin's reform, Zubatov's national trade unions). Alas, only after the terrible experience of the "Russian" Revolution did Labor become the base of the Nation in Italy, in Germany, and in other countries of the new life. Mussolini put forward the immortal doctrine of the union between national labor and national capital. Hitler created a synthesis of nationalism and socialism—National Socialism. In the Great East Asia, the peaceful cooperation between peoples was realized. Russian fascists, from the very beginning, set as their goal in life and struggle the service of a unified triad—Religion, Nation, and Labor. But this all came only after the many lessons taught by the ultimate victories of Judaism.

Before Fascism, before the emergence of the New Order of our ideas, the deceived labor was opposed to religion and nation and the monarchy. It was done, of course, by the same damned "fishermen in troubled waters," the Jews, who decided to use the bankers and politicians. And, the top of the chutzpah: An inter-nation of merchants and exploiters is emerging as the monopolist of social justice. Bankers and their children are becoming leaders of the working class; rabbis and grandchildren of rabbis are launching the slogan "religion is the opium of the masses" among Christians.

Of course, the Jews were quite happy with capitalism: capitalism was leading their Finintern, the international financial international, to power without any upheaval, in an evolutionary manner. The gold of the world, factories and plants, the tools and means of production, banks, stock exchanges, department stores, goods and people, all were accumulated in their insatiable clutches, in the greedy hands of the Jewish priests of the Golden Calf. But "utopian socialism," as the Jews contemptuously called it, was born. Gentile socialism dreamed of overturning the Old World with some kind of New Order. Then the Jews put forward against the noble, though not vital, Aryan socialism of Saint-Simon, Fourier, Owen, and other "utopians" their supposedly "scientific" socialism—a doctrine supposedly based on the exact data of science—the devilish doctrine of Marxism, developed by *gescheftmachers* from other *gescheftmachers*.[156]

Marx's doctrine is thoroughly Judaistic. The natural-scientific, historical, and dialectical materialism underlying it is most in line with the Jewish spirit, it being materialistic and dialectical. Ignoring the qualitative element of labor has always been characteristic of the Jews. The creators of "scientific socialism" attack religion, the nation, the family, the state; this is, after all, a thousand-year-old Jewish campaign against all non-Jewish spiritual and cultural values. The examination of Marxism in terms of the psychology of its creator, a Jew embittered at the whole Christian world, the grandson of many generations of Jewish rabbis, forced to be baptized in order to penetrate into

---

[156] Literally meaning "man doing business" in German (originally came from Yiddish), it is used in Russian to refer to a cunning businessman, speculator or merchant, often pejoratively. (Translator's note)

this alien "world of aristocrats and exploiters," as Melsky so ably undertook in his book *The Evangelist of Hate*, brilliantly exposes Marxism as the "Gospel of Hate" of world Jewry.

Socialism abandoned individuals. It was not about the individual, but the collective. However, in examining the concept of the "collective" in socialism, it is easy to see that the category taken here is not a natural category, a naturally occurring collective, the family or the nation, but a purely artificial category—the collective class, [that is,] a body of people supposedly in the same relation to the means and instruments of production. The artificiality and lifelessness of such a collective is proved by the existence of much stronger communities, which this kind of class psychology attempts to break up. Class boundaries are difficult to delineate because the production process generates an infinite variety of relationships to the means and instruments of production. Very often members of one class can move into another class, becoming, for example, owners in the case of workers and vice versa. These artificial oppositions between classes that do not exist as closed corporations however were necessary to deepen the split in the nation initiated by the party struggle: the nation is being torn into warring classes, with international threads of "international solidarity" drawn between the classes of the same name in various countries.

Socialism appeared as opposed to liberalization and apparently debunked democracy because its ills were too obvious, and if socialism had not exposed them, someone else would have done it (as fascism did in the twentieth century). Marxism opposed capitalism because freedom of competition, having degenerated into freedom of exploitation, had indeed created a social question, an abyss between the producers of wealth—the workers—and the managers of wealth—the capitalists. This abyss had to be liquidated, and it would be liquidated in the way of social reform. But this was disadvantageous to the world's *gesheftmachers*.

In Marxist socialism, the "Gospel of Hate" is opposed to our "Gospel of the Good." The Talmud has received a worthy continuation in *Capital*. The artificial construction of an international proletarian class in Marx's *Capital* is suspiciously reminiscent of the Jews. What is this international "class" but an international-internal "inter-nation"? Consciously or unconsciously, Marx endowed the proletariat, the messianic class, with the traits of a "people-messiah." The "chosen class" was a cover for the desire for the dictatorship of the "chosen people."

The "expropriation of the expropriators" propagated by Marx was directed mainly to productive industrial and commercial capital, leaving alone banking capital, so dear to the Jewish heart. "The dictatorship of the proletariat" is painted as a dictatorship of the international working class, unconnected to a particular nation, but when examining the facts it turns out to be a dictatorship of the Jews. The

Jews in the first place are addressed by Marx's call, which concludes the *Communist Manifesto*: "Proletarians of all countries, unite!" And the Jews are the first to respond to this call. The works of poor Marx, tedious and over many volumes, much like the Talmud, have found Jewish and Masonic publishers, have been translated into every language of the world, and have produced a vast popular and commercial literature, on which millions and billions have been spent in various countries. Who supplied the streams of these pounds, dollars, francs, stamps and full pre-revolutionary rubles? "The proletariat?" Of course not, it is the expropriators of proletarian labor—the Jewish bankers.

Thus began and developed the greatest deception in the history of mankind—a vile conspiracy against God, against every religion except the Jewish one, against every nation except the Jewish one, against everyone's labor except the Jewish one, against any private property except the Jewish one. The execution of this conspiracy brilliantly confirmed the existence of all these exceptions: in the country of "victorious socialism"—in the Soviet Union—the Jewish religion is not persecuted, the Jewish nation is officially honored as existing, while the mention of the Russian nation qualifies as "great-power chauvinism," for which it deserves a concentration camp or execution.

Russian workers are enslaved to tools and machines, peasants are enslaved in the fields and cattle. State property, which Jews dispose of, is declared even more sacred than under the private capitalist system, because even for stealing spikelets from a collective farm field, a Russian hungry peasant faces the death penalty.

It is not surprising: among the leaders of world socialism, apart from Marx himself, there are a great many famous and obscure Jews, starting with Ferdinand Lasalle and Eduard Bernstein. Gaston Crémieux was a member of the First International and the leader of the Commune de Marseille, cousin of Adolphe Crémieux, the French Minister of Justice and founder of the Universal Israelite Alliance (*Alliance Israélite Universelle*). Frenkel is a member of the First International and the head of the Paris Commune, a Freemason of high degree and a relative of orthodox Jewish rabbis. Picollo Tirr is one of the leaders of the Masonic community of the High Roman Venta, an atheist, and a devout Jewish Talmudist. Moses Hess is a theorist of socialism and Zionism at the same time. The founders of Zionism, Theodor Herzl, Usher Ginzburg, Ahad Haam, and their successors, Nahum Sokolov, Vladimir Jabotinsky, Professor Chaim Weizmann. As well as other socialists: Zinoviev-Radomyshlsky-Apfelbaum, Trotsky-Bronstein, Kamenev-Rosenfeld, Ma-Nuilsky, Lozovsky, Kaganovichi and Mehlis will continue this list in our time.

The First International is replaced by the Second, the Second is replaced by the Third, the Third threatens to replace the Fourth. The Internationals and various socialist parties sometimes quarrel with each other, fight with each other, split, unite, split again, but the essence of the matter does not change, for Jews are the ones in charge everywhere.

"Jews always play the most prominent role among socialist politicians," the Harbin *Jewish Life* also notes. "It is only necessary to mention the names of Marx, Lasalle, Paul Singer, Frank, E. Bernstein, Rosa Luxemburg and others."[157]

Marxist socialism, Leninism, and Stalinism turn out to be the most Judaized forms of socialism. While the extreme Jewish nationalists, dissatisfied with the pace of liberalism, rushed to use international socialism in general, then the most extreme of them put on its most extreme wing. From the very beginning the Bolshevik faction of the Russian Social Democratic "Workers' Party" was subsidized by the Jews, and the Jews with this party came to power in Russia.

69. Socialism and Palestine

For some reason the congresses of the First International devoted a great deal of attention to combating anti-Semitism. It would seem at first, what does the "International Comradeship of Workers" have anything to do with the sad situation of one singular nation? Yet national Jewish questions are among the first to be listed at all the congresses of the First International. Nor did the Second International break this tradition, let alone the Third, which, through Stalin, declared anti-Semitism to be "the worst form of cannibalism."[158]

"In Paris, the Poale Zion held a banquet in honor of the Second International," we read in the Harbin *Jewish Life*, tireless in its self-disclosures.

> The banquet turned into a grand manifestation of international socialism in favor of . . . Palestine. French socialists were present: Renaudel,[159] Brock, Lajo (Marx's grandson); Italian socialists: Turati,[160] Morilman, Traves; Russian socialists: Kerensky, Vishniak, Sukhomlin, Tsereteli, Goroninko; Zionist leaders: Nahum Sokolov, Dr. Yakobson, Naidich, and many others.

---

[157] *Jewish Life*, August 12th, 1928, No. 26, Harbin.
[158] Stalin's statement to the American journalist Roy Howard, reproduced in particular by Molotov at the Eighth Extraordinary Congress of Soviets of the USSR in 1936.
[159] Pierre Renaudel was a prominent right-wing socialist, director of the daily newspaper *L'Humanité* from 1915–1918. (Translator's note)
[160] One of the founders of the Italian Socialist Party (1892). (Translator's note)

Blah, blah, blah—what familiar names! I wonder in what language did the meeting of these comrade-internationalists take place? No doubt that all these French grandsons of Marx, Italians, and "Russian" Kirbis and Vishnyaks could speak Hebrew freely, since it was the native language of most of them. But giving the floor to a Jewish magazine reveals even more instructive things and untangles the Jewish web even further:

> "By the end of the banquet, Renaudel, the presiding officer, had read out countless greetings from President Besson, Senators Moriso and M. Godard, deputies Paul Faure, Paul Vonioure, Mistral, Jules Gori, Graumbach, Bolou, Delphine, Balanse; Sellier (president of the Sen department), Professor Olard, Thorez,[161] Severak, and others [Thorez apparently welcomed Zionism on behalf of the French Communist Party and the Comintern].
>
> Renaudel, as leader of the Socialists, thanked the banquet organizers for giving him the opportunity to express his sympathies for Palestine and said among other things: "The work that our people is doing in Palestine is in perfect harmony with international socialism." And Vandervelde, chairman of the Second International, concluded his speech with an appeal to the Russian and Georgian socialists present to help "those peoples who were defeated yesterday to become victors tomorrow."[162]

Which peoples?

More evidence of the Siamese affinity of socialism with Jewish Zionism we find in *Jewish Life* No. 10, 1926

> The president of the Zionist Executive, N. Sokolov was received at an audience by Dr. Heinisch, President of the Austrian Republic [a prominent socialist]. The conversation lasted more than an hour. Sokolov was also received by Chancellor Zenfel [another prominent socialist], with whom he had a two-hour conversation. Both Austrian statesmen expressed their sympathy for the Zionist movement and the cause of rebuilding Palestine [understood].
>
> Chancellor Dr. Zenfel said that he would visit Palestine in August and, knowing the Hebrew language very well [how?],

---

[161] Perhaps referring to M. Thorez, member of the Politburo of the Central Committee of the Communist Party since 1925, General Secretary of the FCP in the years 1930–64, member of the Pres. IKKI in the years 1935–1943. (Translator's note)

[162] *Jewish Life*, August 12th, 1928, No. 26, Harbin.

he would be able to see for himself the cultural and scientific successes of the Jews.

Another issue from the same year:

At the invitation of Poale Zion,[163] a meeting of German socialists was held in Berlin, where Vanderwelde was also present. The purpose of the meeting was to discuss a number of topical Palestinian issues. Vandervelde said in his speech that the socialists should take the greatest interest in the cause. He announced that at the forthcoming Brussels Congress of the Socialist International, there would be a special conference on the Palestinian question, at which forms of assistance for the Palestinian revival by the Second International would be discussed.

Eduard Bernstein, a veteran socialist, and Lebe, president of the Reichstag, attended the meeting as representatives of German socialists.

Jewish Life No. 38 of 1928:

Colonel Wedgwood, an English MP (leader of the English Labor Party), has gone to Germany on an agitation tour . . . on behalf of Keren Hayesod.

On October 14th, Wedgwood spoke in Berlin at a Poale Zion rally. On October 15th, he was received by Reich Chancellor Müller. On the same day in the evening there was a large rally for the Keren Hayesod in one of Berlin's finest halls. Present at the rally were Prussian Prime Minister Dr. Otto Braun, Secretary of State Dr. Weisman, Director of the Department of Minister Dr. Balt, Baron Richthofen (from the Foreign Office), Privy Counselor Kastl (German representative to the League of Nations) and others. Of the most prominent representatives of the Jewish public were present: Dr. Klee, Dr. A. Gentke, the poet S. Czernichowski, Professor Franz Oppenheimer. Representatives in the field of science and art were also present. A number of greetings were received from the German Council of Ministers, Professor Einstein and others.

After Wedgwood, Professor Franz Oppenheimer made an appeal. Then Professor Georg Berngard, editor-in-chief of the *Berliner Tageblatt*, gave a lecture on "the importance of the revival of Palestine for Jews and for the world."

---

[163] Jewish Social Democratic Workers' Party. (Translator's note)

These quotations show how closely the internationalists and social democracy take the interests of the Jews to heart. Doesn't this mean that in the twentieth century Judaism is moving from liberalism to socialism, and that Marxist socialism and Zionism are synonymous?

70. A Letter from a Friend of Marx

"Jewish domination in the world will be achieved as a result of the unification of all other human races, the destruction of borders and monarchies that create the ramparts of particularism, and through the proclamation of a single world republic," reads a letter from Marx's intimate friend Baruch Levy, published by the French magazine *The 1925 Review de Monde*.

In the new organization of mankind, in the absence of any opposition, the people of Israel will be the guiding and governing body, especially if they succeed in placing leadership in the working masses and in the strong hands of their loyal proxies.

In this way all private property will *de facto* fall into Jewish hands, since all governmental institutions will be under full Jewish control, thus fulfilling one of the most important precepts of the Talmud, according to which the Jews, at the coming of the Messiah, will receive into their hands the keys of the wealth of all the nations of the earth.

71. Jewry and the World War

In another book, *Judas on the Edge*, which is a processing of a public report in the garden of the Harbin Railway Assembly in June 1940—a bold prediction that has largely been justified before our eyes—I gave a series of data establishing the culpability of world Jewry and Freemasonry in the World War of 1914–1918.

I recalled the map published under the title "Kaiser's Dream" in the English magazine *Truth* in the Christmas issue for 1890, and reproduced at the end of 1933 in *Nashem Puti* as an already fulfilled prophecy. This map was preserved for mankind by the Russian Colonel Vinberg and recalled in his almanacs "Ray of Light." The three empires that existed at that time—the Russian Empire, the German Empire, and the Austro-Hungarian Empire—were represented in 1890 in London by the Freemason Henry Leboucher on this map as irrelevant.

Germany in the "Kaiser's Dream" is fragmented into separate republics. Austria-Hungary is represented in the form of states that subsequently emerged in the order of the implementation of the Versailles Peace Treaty. The place of Russia is painted over with red paint and is marked as "Russian Desert."

In the corner of the map, three crowned kings—the emperors of Russia, Germany, and Austria-Hungary—dutifully march to the workhouse under arrest, having lost their crowns.

This was the dream of the British Jews and Freemasons in 1890. And in 1914, a World War broke out, pitting the three empires they hated so that Germanism and Slavism mutually destroyed each other for the glory of England and world Jewry.

In the second chapter of the book *Judas on the Edge*, I recall the social events of the beginning of the World War that destroyed the motherland, and give references to historical facts unknown to the general public; documents borrowed from Masonic and anti-Masonic sources. I ask the historians of this war: where are the transcripts of the interrogation of the murderer of the Austrian Archduke Franz Ferdinand and his wife, Princip, and Gabrilovich, who supplied him with weapons, in which they confessed to Masonic inspiration and their membership in Freemasonry?

N.E. Markov II recalls:

Back in 1905, the leaders of Russian liberalism, Freemasons Milyukov, Struve, and Maklakov, sought in Paris to deny Russia a loan for the successful end of the Japanese war, and in 1912 and 1913, not long ago, pacifists and defeatists expressed themselves as ostentatious patriots, they demand the speedy creation of the Black Sea Fleet, they talk about the Straits and Constantinople, they remind of Russia's historical mission in the Balkans.

Just like the Communists during the German–Soviet war.

The two "feuding" emperors, Nicholas II of Russia and Wilhelm II of Hohenzollern, did not want war. But it was coveted by their foreign ministers. The war began and caused an explosion of patriotism on both sides of the front, in which the Jews, who had always been pacifists and cowards, strangely enough took an enthusiastic part. Here the Jews showed an uncharacteristic militancy.

Léon de Poncins gives an instructive account:

English and American Masonic journals have repeatedly stated that the war is a Masonic world war for the sake of the triumph of Masonic ideas. Let us point out, for example, the magazine *New Age* [for] 1918–1919, published in Washington, the Iowa-based *American Freemason* wrote about it as early as

1916, the same for *American Tiger*, the same for the English *Freemason*, and many others.

The Masonic map was fulfilled. The three Christian empires ceased to exist. The principle of self-determination of small nations triumphed: in Europe, in the form of the Balkanization of a large part of it; in Russia, in the form of the Soviet Republics. All these states, as we have seen from our journey horizontally, were ruled by Jewry after the war: he who fought the least won, finance won, Judas won.

This assessment of the results of the World War, although in different words, was made by comrade Chlenov, whose memory the Zionists in Harbin celebrated with such enthusiasm, as if he were their own father, being one of the ideological fathers of Zionism. At the Extraordinary Congress of Russian Jews in Petrograd in 1917, when Russia's northern capital had already become Petrograd, but had not yet become Leningrad, he said:

> I am happy to be able to state that those who direct and influence politics in various countries, including very powerful ones, understand us, our tasks, and aims. The influence of the World War has had an effect here as well. They are ready to support our aspirations, when the proper time comes.
>
> Distinguished members of the Congress!
>
> Three years ago there came a great thunder and a storm which shook the Old World and the New World. Nations and countries have been brutally affected. The great convulsion, however, does not bring grief and death only. Through the agony and the destruction, there are glimpses of rebirth and the rays of a new, free life. And what will remain forever the greatest result of this struggle is that our people will live a national life in their own land, that they will deploy their genius in all its power. The time will arise when he spoke not only for himself, but for all mankind, when he created eternal books and eternal truths. A distant path of light is drawn before us. By this faith we live, by this faith we are inspired in our work, and by this faith we shall prevail!

An infinitely stronger England, the gold of the world migrated to America, the Jews got Palestine, colossal Jewish fortunes grew; that picture of Judaization which is given in the first chapters of this book and is given in the following ones refers precisely to postwar Europe. Whoever won that war, it was really a war for Jewish interests, for Jewish supremacy. With the Treaty of Versailles and the establishment of the League of Nations, the Jews tried to consolidate its results.

72. The League of Nations

In 1936, Arnold Leese, head of the British Imperial Fascist League, who disappeared into the depths of a London cell when the World War began, sent me a leaflet exposing the League of Nations. It reads:

> Britain was represented by Lloyd George, undersecretary Philip Sassoon [later minister, a Sassoon brother, through the Hong Kong-Shanghai Bank and other enterprises, until very recently sucking up both Hong Kong and Shanghai and all of China].
> France was represented by Clemenceau, under Secretary Mindel [subsequently the last "dictator" of the Popular Front, who tried to slaughter more French and Russian émigrés before the German troops occupied Paris].
> The United States was represented by Wilson, surrounded by "advisors" in the form of Baruch, Warburg, Morgenthau, Schiff and Brandeis [see our essays on the US in this book. Baruch is today the master of Roosevelt, Warburg is the founder of the "Jewish Agency" and the head of the Jewish Finintern, Morgenthau is the head of American finance and one of the leaders of the World Israeli Union, Schiff subsidized the Bolshevik revolution, after which he died and went to the underworld, Brandeis emigrated there after him last year, having served as a leader of the World Zionist Organization and also as the Supreme Judge of the United States for decades].
> From Italy came Baron Sonnino, a Jew himself, along with the states, the Jewish delegation took part in the Versailles conference.

"Of all the nations whose interests were involved in the conference," says the Jewish publicist Dr. Dillon in a book published, according to the Liza leaflet, in London in 1924, "the Jews were the most powerful and certainly the most influential. . . . There were Jews from Palestine, Poland, Ukraine, Russia, Romania, Greece, Britain, but the most brilliant selection came from the United States. Jewish questions played a large part in this conference."

The Swiss Masonic magazine *Alpina* in the same year explicitly invites: "Go to the hall of mirrors at Versailles. There you will find an immortal declaration of rights. This is our work. A Masonic symbol adorns the title of the document."

Having dictated to Germany the cruelest conditions of slavery which, incidentally, were very favorable to world Jewry, Versailles gave birth to the "International Authority for Peace," the League of

Nations, about which the Jewish lawyer Dr. Kless is frank in a speech on January 19th, 1936, in New York:

> The League of Nations was by no means the creation of President Wilson. It is essentially a creation of Jewry, of which Jewry has a right to be proud of. The idea comes from our ancient sages. It is a product of Jewish culture.

Much earlier, the late Zionist leader Nahum Sokolov defined at the Carlsbad Congress on January 27th, 1922: "The League of Nations is a Jewish idea. We created it after a twenty-year battle. Jerusalem will one day be the capital of the world. We owe it to the genius of our immortal leader, Theodor Herzl."

Is there any more proof needed? There is enough of it in my book *Judas on the Edge*, in N.E. Markov's *The Wars of the Dark Forces*, and in the works of German, French, and even English researchers.

In every country there were firm and honest people who warned mankind of the danger of international enslavement under the gradually growing power of the League of Nations, the Judeo-Masonic supragovernment. But Yosuke Matsuoka led Japan out of it, and Germany and Italy left the League of Nations as the New Order took hold. The League of Nations will end ignominiously on the margins of history, just as the Third International will one day end.

73. The Various International Organizations

All kinds of international organizations are mostly created or taken over by Jewry. An example of these is the League of Human Rights and Civil Rights.

The Paris newspaper *Au Pilori* tells such a story of this league, which in recent years has often made insolent demands, promoting in every way the privileged position of the Jews and Freemasons:

> As it turns out, the League was founded in 1898, during the Dreyfus trial, by Senator Trarieux with the noblest of aims: the defense of freedom, equality, and justice for all, without distinction of religion, political opinion or social status. Among its founders were Catholics, Protestants, rightists, and leftists. Within a few months, however, the Catholics had to leave, because the organization was taken over by the Jews and the Freemasons. A secret order was given throughout the Masonic line: to take all measures to seize all the leading positions in the organization. The order was carried out. The newspaper printed a long list of the most prominent Freemasons recently

at the head of the League. Suffice it to mention that its president was Victor Basch and its general secretary Émile Kahn, both prominent Freemasons and obvious non-Aryans.

The Freemasons used the League to their full advantage. They organized seventeen branches of the League, including a Russian branch, and brought the total number of League members to 170,000 (in 1939). The League served as an excellent cover, under which the work of Freemasons energetically developed, especially in small and newly formed states, where it was converted into the headquarters for the recruitment of Masonic personnel and helped to handle Masonic business and affairs.

How wide was the scope of the League, as evidenced by the fact that among its members were 307 members of the French parliament, people that, as we know, are very practical and pursued goals that have nothing to do with the protection of freedom, nor with helping the oppressed and offended by human hatred and injustice."[164]

In 1847, the Jews Karl Marx and Friedrich Engels founded the Union of Communists, "the first international organization of the revolutionary proletariat." A third of its members were Jews and more than a third were Freemasons.

In 1848 the Jewish Marx's *Communist Manifesto* was published, establishing the slogan of today's Comintern, "Proletarians of all countries, unite!"

From 1864 through 1872, the congresses of the First International occurred. Same pattern. This intensified the discussion of the struggle against anti-Semitism.

In 1915, the First International Conference of Internationalists in Zimmerwald with Jewish money and Jewish brains.

In 1916, the Second International Conference of Internationalists in Kintal. Same pattern.

In 1918, January 24th. Meeting of representatives of the revolutionary wing of socialist parties in Petrograd under the leadership of Stalin, which played a significant role in the struggle for the creation of the Third Communist International. Behind Stalin's back are his ever-present shadows and leaders.

1918, August. Founding of the Communist Party of Finland—by Jews!

1918, November. Founding of the Communist Party of Hungary—by Jews!

---

[164] *New World*, January 5th, 1941, Berlin.

1918, December. Founding of the Communist Party of Austria—by Jews!

1918, December. Founding of the Communist Party of Germany—by Jews!

1919, the First Congress of the Communist International in Moscow, Russia, which had temporarily become the Jewish capital. Comrade Zinoviev-Apfelbaum comes to the forefront!

1919, April. Founding of the Bulgarian Communist Party. And here come the Jews!

1919, April. Founding of the Communist Party of Yugoslavia. And here they are!

1919, September. The founding of two parties: the Communist Party USA and the Communist Labor Party USA. The unifying congress of these parties was held in September 1920 under Jewish conduct.

1920, July. Founding of the Communist Party of England, by Freemasons.

1920, Second Congress of the Comintern. Delegates from 41 countries were present. They could speak the international language. Four out of five were Jews.

1920, December. Founding of the Communist Party of Italy. Jews are at the head.

1921, April. Founding of the Communist Party of Spain. Jews and Marranos.

1921, May. Founding of the Communist Party of China. By Chinese who had lost their nationality: Freemasons.

1921, May. Founding of the Communist Party of Czechoslovakia. Jews!

1921, May. Founding of the Communist Party of Romania. Jews!

1921, Third Congress of the Comintern. Delegates from 52 countries were present. Forty Jews!

1921, November 5th through December 5th, Fourth Congress of the Comintern. Delegates from 58 countries were present. Forty-five Jews!

1923, June 12th through 23rd. The Third Enlarged Plenum of the ECKI. The struggle against fascism is put on the line, it is proposed and carried out by Jews.

In 1935 came the seventh, hopefully the last, Congress of Comintern. It was attended by representatives of seventy-six countries. Sixty-two Jews. Report of the Jew Pieck on the activities of the Executive Committee of the Comintern. Report by "Bulgarian" Dimitrov, "The Fascist Offensive and the Task of the Communist International in the Struggle for the Unity of the Working Class against Fascism." Report by the Jew Erkoli on the tasks of the Comintern in connection with the preparation by the "imperialists" of a new world war. The report of the Jew Manuilsky "On the Victory of Socialism in the USSR."

Under the Comintern, there is also the YCI—the Young Communist International. Soviet sources trace it to 1907, when the International Conference of Socialist Youth in Stuttgart took place. K. Liebknecht, of course, made the keynote speech at it—"On the Struggle against Militarism."

In 1919, the First (founding) Congress of the YCI in Berlin, organized by Jews.

1921. Second Congress of the YCI. All speakers are Jews and Jewish women.

1922. Third Congress of the YCI. Same.

1924. Fourth Congress of the YCI.

1928. Fifth Congress of the YCI.

1935. Sixth Congress of the YCI. Adoption of a resolution to support any unity of youth, even religious, even national, as long as it is against fascism, proposed by Comrade Bull. There is no need to decipher this surname.

74. Judas and the Revolution

"Money and revolution are written on the tablets of these despicable people," said Vespasian Flavius in ancient Rome. But it is only in recent years that research has begun to delve into the role of Jewry in the revolutions of antiquity as well as our own age. De Poncins investigated the role of Jewry in the French Revolution; Festus and Shulgin, in the Russian Revolution. We have already given the data on the Masonic inspiration of the "French" Revolution, which the Jews called and forced the "goyim" to call the great revolution. Evidence of the Jewish inspiration of the "Russian" Revolution of 1917 is given in plenty of my essays, for instance "The Jews and Russia."

"For almost a hundred years, since the glorious memory of the Decembrists, a preparatory unseen work has been going on, only occasionally showing itself in flashes and explosions," said E. V. Chlenov, the same one whose anniversary was celebrated this year by Harbin Jews at the first open All-Jewish Congress in Russia since 1917.

"How many pure fervent hearts have been sacrificed? How much innocent blood has been shed?! In this blood we are proud to state: there is also our Jewish share."

"In the sixties of the last century Jews took a wide part in literary and public life," said another speaker at the same congress.

The rapprochement of Jews in Russia with liberals and radical social circles was perhaps closer than in the West. The role of the Jewish intelligentsia in the Russian liberal and constitutional movement . . . was very noticeable. The Jews in the most radical positions went with the Russian Narodniks to the "people," with the Social Democrats to the factory.

Eloquent confessions.

Indeed, the Russian Social Democratic Workers' Party was founded in the Jewish Pale of Settlement, in Minsk, by utopian nobles who, as they say, like to "throw their money around," and by Jewish merchants. There was not a single Russian worker in this milieu of founders. Its second congress, at which it was divided into Bolsheviks and Mensheviks, took place in the same center of world conspiracies and intrigues—in London. The true history of this party, though extremely brief, is described in the first chapter of *our Critique of the Soviet State*.

The Jewish Bolshevik and Zionist Refes makes the following confession: "The hatred of the Tsarist regime toward the Jews was justified, for the government in all the revolutionary parties from the sixties onward had Jews among its most active members."

So it was. Beginning with the sixties and especially from the seventies, the Jews really penetrated into the Russian "liberation movement" and gradually seized the leadership of the Russian opposition and revolutionary parties.

The Jew Nathanson organized the first *Narodnaya Volya* parties: the Chaikovsky society, *Zemlya i Volya*, which later gave birth to the *Narodnaya Volya* and the *Cherny Peredel* parties, from which, in their turn, the Social Revolutionaries (SR) and the Social Democrats were born. The same Nathanson founded the People's Right party in the 1890s, from whose wreckage emerged the bourgeois opposition, the Constitutional Democratic Party (Ca-De), from which the so-called "Cadets" later grew. The Party of Socialist Revolutionaries was founded and led by the Jewish capitalist dynasty of Vysotsky. The Party of Social Democrats was created at the initiative of the Jewish socialist organization BUND.

Witness Hermann Fest, *Bolshevism and Jewry* (Riga, 1934):

> Since the nineties of the last century the Jewish mass has also taken part in the Russian revolutionary movement. It is indicative of the message made by the Jewish section of the Communist Party to the Central Committee at the end of 1919:
> "The Jews treated the revolution as a commercial enterprise—in a businesslike way: they invested a lot of money in it, their own and other people's money. Relying on the power of money, they ensured the organizational management of the

parties, in particular the selection of their top personnel, as well as the agitation and propaganda work."

I have repeatedly defined the February Revolution as the Masonic February, because this revolution was led and conducted by Freemasonry, and brought to power a Masonic "provisional government" (Prince Lvov, Miliukov, Kerensky). This government did everything to give Russia to the Bolsheviks.

Very aptly, Fest calls the period from March 12th to November 7th, 1917, "the period of transition." He devotes the following lines to it:

From its first days the Jews were at the forefront of the revolution. In the Tauride Palace, next to the committee of the State Duma, an organ of "revolutionary democracy" was immediately formed—the Executive Committee of the Soviet of Workers' and Soldiers' Deputies. By an agreement with it, the first Provisional Government was formed.

Subsequently, the Executive Committee was gaining more and more influence on the composition and activities of the Provisional Government: in fact, it was the center of power at that time.

The first Executive Committee, according to the historian and participant of the revolution, the Jew Sukhanov-Gimmer, included: Georgian Chkheidze; Russians Lebedev, Skobelev and Peshekhonov; Jews Bogdanov, Kachelinsky, Grinevich-Shakhter, Franco, Sukhanov-Gimmer, Erlich, Steklov-Nahamkes, Groman, Bronstein; and of an unspecified nationality Kerensky and Sokolov.

Of the fifteen, there are three Russians, one Georgian and nine Jews.

In the later expanded Executive Committee, the Jews became even more predominant. In the hands of the Jews was the entire staff of the Executive Committee. At the head of the departments of the Executive Committee were: the Administration of Affairs (the whole organization)—the Jew Bogdanov; agriculture—the Jews Gots and Sukhanov; food—the Jews Groman, Franco, Bronstein; the commission of legislative proposals—Sukhanov-Gimmer, Bramson, Groman, Kolesnikov, Steklov, Franco and one Russian, Tchaikovsky; international relations—Jew Larin-Lurie; economic department—Jew Lieber; agitation department—Jews Ehrlich and Koloskov, Russian Shlyapnikov; financial department—Jew Kosmson, etc.

The first editorial board of the *Izvestia* CEC[165] consisted of Steklov, Tsiperovich, Goldenberg, and Avilov—three Jews and one Russian; the actual leadership of the Executive Committee of the Soviets until the October Revolution was exercised by Chkheidze (Georgian), Bogdanov (Jewish), Goz (Jewish), Tsereteli (Georgian), Lieber (Jewish) and Dan (Jewish). Of the six, two were Georgians and four were Jews.

In the first Executive Committee of the Soviet of Peasant Deputies, out of thirty members seven were Jews. It is interesting to note that in the leadership of the Council of Workers' Deputies there were only two workers and in the leadership of the Council of Peasants' Deputies there were only three peasants.

In such enthusiastic terms tells the Zionist LW Jaffe in his article with the characteristic headline "On the Way to the Future," which should mean "wait, this is just the flowers, the berries will be ahead." In 1917, the Masonic *February* greeted:

A miracle has happened! In a few days, without bloodshed and heavy turmoil, "Russia was free!" In one fell swoop, it easily and joyfully threw off the shackles that had been holding her for centuries! The dream of the best people of Russia, who had prepared for those days with their blood and agony, came true. As in a fairy tale, "all that was once dreamed of, with bliss and a flying song in the dark distance, and like sowing it grew into the soul, like florets, it blossomed."

With great joy, along with the other nationalities of Russia, Russian Jewry welcomes these days. It knows that Jewish blood flowed with a broad sweep into the sea of blood that soaked the soil, on which Russian freedom grew, and that the Jewish sacrifices in the work of liberation were the greatest.

For Jews, these days are especially joyful. The people who brought the ideals of freedom to the world, who celebrated the festival of freedom at the dawn of their lives, the people who have known the horror of enslavement and oppression, love and value freedom above all else. The Jewish people are always on the side of the enslaved and those who fight for freedom. The people of dreams and spirit know how to rejoice. When chains are broken, when dreams are realized, when truth triumphs.[166]

---

[165] Central Executive Commission of the Soviet (now Russian) newspaper *Izvestia*. (Translator's note)
[166] See the collection *Zionism*, Petrograd, 1917.

75. The Victory of Jewish Equality Over Russia

"Only three weeks have passed since Russia achieved freedom," rejoiced Chlenov at the 1917 Congress of the Jews of Russia,

> and the Provisional Government together with the Soviet of Workers' Deputies rushed to wash off from it the shameful stain that had been hanging over it for centuries - the shame of Jewish disenfranchisement. It seems that this stain had fused with the body of the people: the only way to scrape it off is with blood. This is not what happened. . . .

Isn't that what happened?

Indeed, the Provisional Government and the Soviet of Workers' Deputies showed remarkable unanimity: rarely have they spoken so unanimously as in the question of the speedy abolition of the last restrictions on Jews left by 1917. Not surprisingly, on one side were seated Freemasons and on the other Jews. And the faithful disciples of both: liberals and Bolsheviks.

"Yes, a great, immeasurable burden has fallen from the shoulders of Russian Jewry," exulted Chlenov, predicting the near "deepening of the revolution" into the terror of war communism and Stalinism.

> The hands, so long shackled, have been untied, and the scope and horizons have been widened. And it is now that we, the Russian branch of the united people, with all the strength and energy accumulated, will be able to begin nation-building and work on those great challenges that confront us. The tasks are many and major.
>
> The Extraordinary Jewish Congress will have a difficult, large, demanding work ahead of it. But this congress, according to our unshakable conviction, cannot be limited to the resolution of issues concerning Russian Jewry. This is not the moment. It is true that the revolution has touched only Russia—at least, for the time being.

This "for the time being" betrays the desire of Russian and world Jewry for world revolution.

76. Judas Financed the Red October

Even American Jewry rejoiced over the faraway "Russian" course of events. On the day of the arrival of the telegram detailing the revolution in Russia, all of New York City was decked out in American flags, the Russian tricolor, and red and Jewish flags!

Yankel Schiff, the American billionaire and director of the world bank Kuhn, Loeb & Co., sent a congratulatory telegram to the Russian nobleman, Freemason, professor, and liberal P. N. Milyukov. And Shabbos goy Milyukov, as Minister of Foreign Affairs of the Masonic Provisional Government, telegraphed back: "We are united in our hatred."

How could Schiff not rejoice! Léon de Poncins in *The Secret Powers Behind Revolution*, in the part that he did not bother to translate or did not have time to, Professor Nikiforov presents a document certifying Jewish financial authorship of the second stage of Masonic February, the Jewish October[167]:

"The document was compiled by the chief commissioner of the French Republic in the United States in early 1919 according to American secret intelligence. The document was sent to all Entente governments. The document is marked: "7-618-6. Np-912-Sg. 27. 2nd Bureau."

The document reads:

1. In February 1916 it was first noticed that a revolution was being prepared in Russia. It was discovered that the following individuals and banking houses were involved in this destructive work:
   a. Jacob Schiff, a Jew;
   b. Kuhn, Loeb & Co., a Jewish banking house; its director Jacob Schiff is a Jew, Felix Warburg is a Jew, Otto Kahn is a Jew, Mortimer Schiff is a Jew, Jerome X. Zanauer is a Jew;
   c. Guggenheim, a Jew;
   d. Max Warburg, a Jew.
   It is beyond any doubt that the Russian revolution which broke out a year after this information came out was definitely planned and supported by Jewish influences.
2. Indeed, in April 1917, Jacob Schiff issued a public statement signifying that the successful course of the Russian revolution could be ascribed solely to his financial support.

---

[167] This quotation was not found in the English version of *Secret Powers Behind Revolution*, so this is a translation from what was given in the Russian. (Translator's note)

Volume I: Contemporary Judaization of the World | 201

In the spring of 1917, Jacob Schiff ordered Trotsky, a Jew, to organize a social revolution in Russia. *Forward*, a newspaper published in New York, a Judeo-Bolshevik publishing organ, directed its efforts to the same end.

3. The same Trotsky and his comrades received a paid order from Max Warburg in Stockholm. The same order was received from the Rheinisch-Westphalen Syndicate, a large Jewish enterprise; in addition, from other Jews, namely Olaf Ashberg of the Nu Banken in Stockholm and the millionaire Zhivotovsky, whose daughter Trotsky was married to. In this way a connection was established between Jewish super-millionaires and Jewish proletarians. At the same time, the Jew Paul Warburg was discovered to have such a close relationship with the Bolshevik overlords that he was not re-elected to the Federal Reserve System.

4. Among Jacob Schiff's intimate friends is Magnes, a stalwart pillar of international Jewry. Jacob Zilikov, a Jew, once even claimed that Magnes was a prophet. By early 1917, Judah Magnes had founded the first true Bolshevik association in the US under the name Council of the People. Judah Magnes declared publicly that he had become a Bolshevik and fully agreed with the teachings and ideals of Bolshevism. Magnes made this statement at a meeting in America. Jacob Schiff condemned the ideas of Judah Magnes. In order to conduct public opinion, he resigned from this committee. Schiff and Magnes, however, remained as co-members of the executive committee of the Jewish Qahal in the best possible agreement.

5. On the other hand, Judah Magnes, authorized by Jacob Schiff, was closely connected with the World Zionist Organization and was even their leader. Of course, his goal is to establish the international domination of Judeo-proletarian organizations in the Jewish-led workers' parties. In this way the transverse ties between the millionaire Jews and their Judeo-Proletarians were supplemented.

6. A few more weeks passed before the revolution broke out in Germany as well. The Jewish Rosa Luxemburg automatically took over the political leadership there. But the most important leader of the international Bolshevik movement was the Jew Haase. Immediately it becomes clear that the revolution in Germany follows the same Judean leadership as the revolution in Russia.

7. If we do not lose sight of the fact that the Jewish firm Kuhn, Loeb & Co. is in touch with the Rheinisch-Westphalen Syndicate (a Jewish firm in Germany), with the Lazar brothers

(the Jewish bank in Paris), and also with Günsberg (the Jewish banking house of Petersburg, Paris, and Tokyo), and if we further establish, that the above-mentioned banking houses are in close relations with the Jewish banking house Schneier & Co. in London, New York, and Frankfurt, and with the Judeo-Bolshevik bank Nu Banken in Stockholm, then we will be convinced that the modern Bolshevik movement is evidence of a general Jewish movement and that the well-known Jewish banking houses are participating in the organization of this movement.

77. Judas Takes Over Russia

It is impossible to read without excitement the dry reports of researchers devoted to the preparations for the October Revolution. Festus relates:

On October 23rd a historic meeting of the Central Committee took place at which the question of the uprising was decided. This meeting was attended by Lenin, Sverdlov, Zinoviev, Kamenev, Trotsky, Stalin, Uritsky, Dzerzhinsky, Kollontai, Bubnov, Sokolnikov, and Lomov. Of these: two Russians (16.7 percent), seven Jews (58.1 percent) and three non-Russians (24.9 percent). So, almost 60 percent of the participants of this historic meeting, which made the decision to destroy by violence the historically created course of Russian life and impose a new order in the world, were Jews.

The decision of an armed uprising was formulated and made by Lenin. Eight voted for him, two voted against.

To be fair, these two were Jews: Zinoviev and Kamenev. They were afraid, they did not believe in success. But it must not be forgotten that later on and for a long time these two Jews were the central figures of the Bolshevik revolution, they took part both in the leadership and in the implementation of the uprising. Hence, their protest was not of a principled nature....

At that meeting, a seven-voiced "political bureau," the first Bolshevik Politburo was elected. It took in its hands the supreme leadership of the steps which in the coming fourteen days were to determine the fate of Russia. It was the concentrated political brain of Bolshevism. Its members, the elite of Bolshevism, are the principal responsible figures of the Great October Revolution. The composition of this Politburo was: Lenin, Stalin (Georgian), Trotsky (Jew), Sokolnikov (Jew),

Bubnov (Russian), Zinoviev (Jew), and Kamenev (Jew). Only seven, of whom only two were Russians, meaning that since there are fewer of them here, the Jews still have an absolute majority. They have never had such a majority in any leading Bolshevik party body.

On October 25th (October 12th O. S.), the Petrograd Soviet, by that time completely Bolshevized, elects a Military Revolutionary Committee, which is charged with the immediate military preparation for the uprising, the leadership of the Red Guard, and the actual leadership of the Petrograd garrison.

This committee includes: Trotsky (Jew), Podvoiski (Russian), Lenin, Boki (Jew), Ioffe (Jew), Molotov (Russian), Uritsky (Jew), Antonov-Ovseenko (Russian), Mehovshev (Russian), Gusev (Jew), Galkin (Russian), Eremeev (Russian), Dzerzhinsky (Polish), Dybenko (Ukrainian), and Raskolnikov (Russian). There were eighteen or twenty in all, of whom: nine were Russians (50 percent), seven Jews (39 percent), and two non-Russians (11 percent).

On October 29th (October 16th O. S.), the Central Committee singled out a narrower War Center, the concentrated military brain of Bolshevism. Jewish Bolshevik historian Yaroslavsky-Gubelman defines this "Center" as the supreme military leadership of the uprising: this central body, and no other, directed all the military organizations that participated in the uprising: revolutionary troops, Red Guards, etc.

The Center consisted of: Sverdlov (Jew), Dzerzhinsky (Pole), Stalin (Georgian), Bubanov (Russian), and Uritsky (Jew). In total, there are five of them: one Russian (20 percent), two Jews (40 percent) and two non-Russians (40 percent). To the composition of this center we must also add Trotsky, who actually belonged to it as a member of the Politburo and as the head of the Petrograd Soviet, which Yaroslavsky consciously does not mention. Therefore, one more Jew. In none of the decisive organs of the revolution has Russian participation been so negligible as here.

Here we see again a confirmation of the Jewish desire for power and the Jewish tactics of mastering it. Most of all, Jews are always eager to occupy the supreme decisive positions. The greater the importance of this or that body, the greater the Jewish participation in it. This is why the percentage of Jewish participation in the two supreme centers of the revolution, the Politburo and the military center, is so high, and their participation in a body of secondary importance, the Military Revolutionary Committee, is so relatively small.

If we add up the composition of the two supreme centers, we find only ten people in them. They were Lenin, Stalin, Trotsky, Sokolnikov, Bubnov, Zinoviev, Kamenev, Sverdlov, Uritsky, and Dzerzhinsky. Two Russians, six Jews and two non-Russians.

These ten light the world fire of October, in which Russia will disappear first of all. A new era begins.

I had ample reason to exclaim at a Harbin debate on Freemasonry at the Russian Club in 1933: "With all the facts in my hands I assert that Russia was destroyed by Jews and Freemasons!"

It is to Judeo-Masonry that we owe the rivers of Russian blood, the destruction of the greatest spiritual and material values of the Russian people, the transformation of our beautiful Russia into a disgusting USSR, and our hard days of exile in foreign lands.

78. The Harbin Proof

The Jews of Harbin are not hiding who robbed us of our homeland. Here is what a Palestinian Englishman named Easterman writes in the "English" newspaper *Daily Express*:

> My answer to our enemies—Hitler, Goebbels, and Co. One last word: Remember the fate of the persecutors of the Jews; in ancient Persia, Babylonia, Rome, Spain, Tsarist Russia; they were turned to ashes, and remembered with contempt. The Jew, the eternal Jew outlived them all, and so we will outlive you.

This vile phrase was printed in Russian in a Jewish magazine published in Harbin under the editorship of Dr. A. I. Kaufman.[168]

Remember it, Russian people!

79. Revolutions and Jewish Enrichment

But here is another side of the matter that is extremely revealing to the Jews. Revolutions bring the "goyim's" destruction, grief and death. The "goyim" states are ruined. But the Jewish states are mostly preserved. They find themselves temporarily abroad, beyond the reach of the storm of the revolution. But not only are they preserved; they are multiplied.

---

[168] *Jewish Life*, 1933, No. 17.

An example of Russian ruin and Jewish enrichment is, for example, the NEP in the USSR: by the time of this "new economic policy" in the Union of Socialist Republics, a new bourgeois class, the Jewish NEPman class, had grown up alongside the Communist apparatchiks.

And when the NEPmen ended up in the USSR, they found themselves in great numbers in Harbin, under the wing of the Soviet side of the Chinese Eastern Railway. Here Jewish capitalism of the crimson-red convictions blossomed.

Through Harbin to America, many Russian valuables, up to and including the jewelry of the Tsar's crown, were floating along Jewish channels, from the Jewish Chekists of the USSR through their relatives in Harbin.

On the main street of the city there was a rich jewelry store, selling Russian goods looted in the Soviet Union. Russian merchants of the economically and politically Sovietized CER went bankrupt here, while Jewish merchants were getting rich.[169] And the only example in the world of a hitherto unrecorded cynicism: the vast majority of Jewish merchants in Harbin had citizenship of the Soviet country, where capitalism was cursed and capitalists were crushed, they still showed friendship and sympathy for the Communist Party, which once decided to crush capitalism and destroy the capitalists.

Every year on the anniversary of the October Revolution, the local Jewish capitalists closed their stores and hung up red flags. *Our Way* (1936) published a list of them: Arkady Vent, Br. Bent, the "European" silk store, the hat store of G. A. Gurevicha, Aptekovar, Economia, Salon Prima, a children's confectionery, V. Berelson, Kopros, Br. Tismenitsky, Reisin, I. Reifeld's office, Dofado, L. Kaplun's dress store, international company Profese, wholesale warehouse Wolfson (under the American flag), Depot ready-made dresses, Victory, and many more.

The chairman of the Exchange Committee for a long time was Yankel Kayuadkin, a major exporter and manufacturer, who traveled to Soviet Vladivostok with tsarist luxury.

Hundreds of Jewish merchants circulated between the USSR Consulate General, the Soviet Dalbank, and various Soviet espionage agencies. The revelation of a local Comintern resident in 1937 revealed that Gammer was a Jewish merchant. Indeed, nowhere else in the world was the affinity for international revolution and international finance so prominent as in Harbin during the Soviet period of the CER, from 1924 to 1935.

Every international revolution does have the character of a social revolution: values move from one social group to another. Only these

---

[169] Chinese Eastern Railway. (Translator's note)

others are not the proletariat at all. True, there are Jewish proletarians, but it is mainly the Jewish bourgeois who profit. The Comintern, which in place of Russia created a slave-holding state of general poverty and exploitation, turns out to be a gut, pumping gold to the Jewish Finintern.

The organizers of the revolution are the concentrators of finance. We shall return to this problem in the third part of our work.

80. Jewry in Communism

"We cannot deny that individual Jews did play a major role in the whole Bolshevik movement," Pasmannik bashfully admits in his book *The Russian Revolution and Jewry*, written specially to rehabilitate Judaism from accusations of Bolshevism. Numerous facts and arguments are presented by V. V. Shulgin in his book *What We Do Not Like About Them*, which defines Jewry as the backbone of the Communist Party of the USSR. The history of the CPSU-RCP-RSDLP fully confirms this, only not in Stalin's "short course" but at least in my *Critique of the Soviet State*.[170]

"Communism is a Jewish conspiracy," determines the head of the National Unity Party of Canada, Adrien Arcand, in an article for *Nation* of the same name. "Communism is a Jewish plan to enslave the world under Jewish world domination, called a world red republic."

Arcand's argument should be read in full:

> Communism is not a doctrine, it is not a set of principles, it is not a system of administration and management, communism is the negation of all doctrine, the destruction of all that we accept as a principle.
>
> The Jews have been taught from the day they were born, and they will believe until their death, that they are the chosen people, above all other nations; that they alone are the people beloved of God; that they were born to rule; that all other races are soulless cattle, created to serve the tribe of Judas; that all the wealth of the world belongs to them by birthright; that they will soon come into possession of all those riches.
>
> How are the Jews going to achieve world dominion and possession? By implementing the plan set forth by Karl Marx, whom most Jews refer to as the Second Messiah. Karl Marx

---

[170] See names, facts, and figures: K. V. Rodzaevsky, *Critique of the Soviet State*, Harbin, 1934. See also Part I, *Bolshevism and Jewry*, and N.E. Marko's, *The Wars of the Dark Forces*.

teaches other nations to destroy everything that can make individuals and nations strong: their faith, their national beliefs, their traditions, their possessions, their personal initiative, their family life, their morals. Marx and the Jews knew that if they tried to seize the property of other peoples by force, they would be met with forceful opposition. So they tried to persuade us to give up our own property, to abolish the right of private property.

And when the nations get caught up and believe this foolish idea, they themselves, on their own free will, will give away everything they got from their ancestors, which they themselves earned. Who is the one getting the treasures that they are giving away? The government, the state! And who is the state under Marxism? The Jews.

Fyodor Butenko, former Soviet ambassador to Romania, fled to Rome in February 1938 to avoid Stalin's persecution. On the first day of his stay in Rome he gave the following message, which was placed on the front page of the newspaper *Virdinno Gaida Giornale d'Italia* in the issue of February 17th:

"The former Russian bourgeoisie has been replaced by a new bourgeoisie, almost 100 percent of it is Jewish. All Jews in Russia enjoy the special protection of the Jew Lazar Kaganovich, Stalin's closest advisor. All large factories and construction sites, all monopolized production, all military industry, all railroads, all large and small trade, are ultimately in Jewish hands; the Russian proletariat is the "master of the economy" only in abstract, detached theory. Jewish women and families own luxury cars and houses, they spend their summers in vacation homes and resort places in Crimea and the Caucasus, they wear expensive karakuls and other luxury clothing, jewelry, and other luxury items from Paris."

Who better to know this situation than the Soviet ambassador, as was Butenko? His words are confirmed by the Jews themselves.

In the October 1937 issue of the New York monthly, *Jewish Life*, the following was printed in a front article:

"The Communist Party is the party of the Jews, the Communist program calling for a Popular Front meets the needs of the entire Jewish people.... Which party internally represents the interests of the Jews? What party is really fighting for the rights of the Jews as a people? It is the Communist Party, which unwaveringly, invariably offers such a corresponding program and calling the people to struggle! The Jews must therefore regard the Communist Party as their own party."

The great prophets of communism were Karl Marx, Ferdinand Lassalle—Jews. Why are there no Aryans? The big "stars" of Communism are Jews: Kamenev, Zinoviev, Radek, Sverdlov, Kaganovich, Litvinov, Ioffe, Karakhan, Kalmanovich, Parvus-Gelfand, Mekhlis, etc. Why are there no Russians?

Even Stalin married a Jewess, Kaganovich's sister. Why? Because Jews must know everything, even what goes on in the bedroom.

Not only did communism have almost exclusively Jews as its prophets, but it was also financed by Jews, the main "starter" on a large scale being Jacob Schiff, director of Kuhn, Loeb & Co. in New York.

Wherever Marxism is introduced, it elevates the Jews to the top.

In France: Blum, Mandel, Giromsky, Zei, etc. Why aren't they French?

In England: Moses Schiff, Professor JD Lasky, Gallagher (MP). Why aren't they English?

In Mexico: Calles, Saenz, Lieberman, etc. Why aren't they Mexicans?

In Hungary: Béla Kun, Samuel, Agoston, etc. Why aren't they Hungarians?

In Bavaria: Kurt Eisner, Levin, etc. Why aren't they Bavarians?

In Northern Germany: Liebknecht, Emma Goldman, Rosa Luxemburg, etc. Why aren't they Prussians?

In Italy: C. Treves, Nathan, etc. Why aren't they Italians?

In Spain: Maura, Zamora, De Llarisse, Rosenberg, etc.

In Brazil, the US, Canada, Belgium, Scandinavian countries: Jews, more Jews. . . .

Because the Jewish plan for destruction and conquest cannot be safe in the hands of the Aryans.

Aryan peoples of all nations! Open your eyes to reality, to the truth! Throw off the mask of communism, of all Marxist organizations, and you will immediately see the hooked noses and sly eyes of the world's conspirators!

Aryan peoples of all nations! Throw off the mask of the enemy, leave for a moment the silly illusions inspired by the Jews, and look at reality! What does Marxism bring?

The destruction and plundering of your material wealth, your moral well-being!

Communism is a crime against God, against man, against society, against the fatherland. As with any crime, the question must be asked: who benefits from the crime? To find the answer to this question, read again Butenko's statement and look at Russia, a martyr crucified by the Jews.

The Jews began their global offensive only after they seized control of the world's gold, the great instruments of propaganda: movies, newspapers, agencies and telegraphs, the political parties of "democracy" which they secretly financed. They have taken over the markets of the necessities of life, which enables them to put prices on raw materials; precious stones, precious and semi-precious metals, and many other monopolies. They provoke economic crises, crashes and disasters, civil wars, revolutions, and wars in which only they are the winners. We cannot rid the world of malaria unless we first exterminate the mosquitoes. We cannot save people from leprosy unless we first isolate the carriers of the disease. In order to save humanity from all forms of Marxism, socialism (communism, Bolshevism, anarchism), confusion, chaos, we must isolate the carriers of the disease, the Jews. The only place for them is Madagascar!

Christ said (John 8) that they are doing their father's work on earth. When we take into account the prediction of Christ, whom they crucified, and act practically according to that warning, the world will have peace, prosperity, and understanding.

Arcand wrote so in a special article for our *Nation* in 1938, and in 1940 Canadian Jews imprisoned him.

81. Communism and Jewry in Jewish Confessions

Numerous Jewish admissions to the authorship of communism and its leadership in particular can be gleaned from Henry Ford's *The International Jew* and Rudolf Kommos' *The Jews Behind Stalin*, not to mention thorough research such as Herman Fest's book *Bolshevism and Jewry*. Here we will confine ourselves to a single Jewish testimony, but an exceptionally interesting one. It was brought to the attention of the *World Service* by the intrepid Canadian, the same Adrien Arcand who sent the previous exposé to the *Nation*.

1. Place of action: Budapest.
2. Time of action: the reign of Béla Kun and shortly thereafter.
3. Scene details: The action takes place at dinner, and the guests were served not milk, but Tokaji wine.

4. Actors: a) a bank director, a Jew from New York, who had prepared the Bolshevik revolution. b) the French envoy, Comte de Saint-Aulaire, at his side. c) other Jews, other fellow diners.
5. Special note: The persons designated under letters a) and c) were intoxicated by the wine they drank and the victory of their people.

The banker who prepared the revolution was asked: "How is it to be understood that the financial nobility patronizes the Bolsheviks? After all, Bolshevism is the enemy of immovable property, which is the basis of the existence of banks. Bolshevism is the enemy of immovable wealth, which is also of great importance to financiers."

The banker who prepared the Bolshevik revolution, one of the chiefs of the food deliveries to the needy population, drinks a glass of Tokaji, thinks for a while as he lights his big cigar (five gold francs each) and finally answers: "Those who marvel at our alliance with the Soviets forget that Israel is a nation of more national sentiment than any other nation, that it is the oldest, the only, the most exceptional of all nations. You forget that its nationalism is the most heroic, for it has withstood the worst of persecutions. You forget also that its nationalism is the purest, the most spiritual, for despite all obstacles and without the support of its own territory it has survived the ages. It is omnipresent (universal), speaking of an inhabited land, and as spiritual as the papacy. But instead of the past, he is directed towards the future, and his kingdom is here on earth. It is therefore the salt of the earth, which does not prevent it, however, from being, as they say on the boulevards, the least salty and the most purified, the most molded of all forms of nationalism."

Some of the fellow-tempered people laughed implicitly at these last words, which prompted this wise Zionist to clarify as follows: "By saying 'the most purified,' I mean that our nationalism is the most assimilated, the most substantial: other nations take it with the greatest ease, with admiration and without any bitterness. But back to the salt. Do you know the recipe for cod brine? I learned it on Newfoundland. Here it is: over-salting burns the fish, under-salting spoils it. It's exactly the same with the spirit of the people. From this recipe we make a wise use of it as it should be, for salt is the symbol of wisdom. Secretly we add it to the bread of men in destructive doses. We use it only in exceptional cases, when it is a matter of burning the remains of an impure past, such as that of tsarist Russia. From this it should be at least partly clear to you why we find Bolshevism pleasing? It is a marvelous brine for burning, but not that much for conversation. . . . Marxism, you say, is the antipode of capitalism, yet also sacred to us? Precisely because they are antipodes, they represent both poles of the planet, and grant us to be its axis. These two mutually attracting opposites, Bolshevism and capitalism, find their identity in the International. And both these opposites, according to the doctrine of social antipodes, converge in the unity of the same goals, in the renewal of the world from above, that is, through revolution. For centuries, Israel had been cut off from the Christian world and driven into ghettos; this was how the witnesses of the Old Testament were to be exposed, in what was then called, the most profound humiliation before the believers as atonement for killing God. This was what saved us, and through us we will save humanity. In this way we have preserved our genius and our divine purpose. For we are true believers. Our mission is to spread a new law and to create God, that is, to purify the concept of God and turn it into action when the times are fulfilled. We purify it when we equate it with the concept of "Israel," who himself has become his own Messiah. Our final triumph will facilitate his (the Messiah's) appearance, this is our new covenant. Then we will reconcile the kings with the prophets, just as David, the prophet-king or king-prophet, united them in his person. We are kings, so that the prophecies may be fulfilled, and we become prophets, so that we may not cease to be kings."

Whereupon the king and prophet drained a new glass of Tokaji.

A skeptic made an objection: "Are we not in danger of becoming martyrs to this Messiah, by whose prophets and apostles you proclaim to be yourselves, for however far removed your nationalism may be from all outward expression, is yet often plundering other nations? Even if you despise wealth, you are not squeamish about it, if not as a means of pleasure, then as a means of power. How can the triumph of a world revolution that destroys and denies capitalism prepare for the triumph of Israel, which is the holy citadel of that very capitalism?"

The banker who launched the Bolshevik revolution replied, "I know well that Jeroboam introduced the cult of the Golden Calf in Dan and in Bethel, but I know equally well that the modern revolution is the great priestess of that cult, the most adroit for its covenant tabernacle. If the Golden Calf stands firm, its footing is the tomb of the Empire. This happens for two reasons. First, revolution is always a movement, a displacement of advantages, hence also of wealth, not even by use, but above all by mobilization, which is the soul of speculation. The more wealth changes hands, the more of it will remain with us. We are brokers, taking orders for all exchange operations, or, if you like, we are publicans, controlling all the corners of the globe and levying duties on every movement of 'hired and vagrant' wealth, whether it be from one country to another or fluctuations in the exchange rate of money. To the calm, dull, monotonous tune of prosperity we prefer the eagerly excited cries of ups and downs. To awaken these voices, nothing compares with revolution, with war, which is also revolution."

"Secondly, revolution weakens peoples and makes them less resistant to foreign enterprises."

"The health of our Golden Calf requires the illness of some nations, those very nations that are incapable of taking the path of development on their own. Conversely, we are conscious of our solidarity with the great modern nations, such as France, England, and the United States, whose representatives are currently seated at this table. They have proven to us their noble hospitality, and with them we work together for the advancement of civilization."

"But take pre-war Turkey, that 'sick man,' as diplomats called it. This 'sick man' was an element of our health, for it supplied us in abundance with concessions of all kinds: beams, mines, ports, railroads, etc. All his economic life was entrusted to us. We looked after him so well that he died for it, at least in Europe. When the accumulation of wealth becomes a daily occurrence and it is obvious that our mission is accomplished, then we need a new 'sick man.' This reason alone was already enough, apart from the higher considerations, to instill old Russia with Bolshevism. Now Russia has become a 'sick man' for us, far more nourishing than the Ottoman Empire ever was. Besides, it is even less resistant. It is now ripe for a new feast. Soon she will be a corpse, and all we have to do is cut it up."

At the other end of the table sat the speaker's co-religionist; he was just waiting to get a word in and jumped up: "We are considered predators, and we are probably vultures."

"So be it, if you like to insist on this opinion," replied the follower of the new faith, "but you must add that we are vultures only for the good of mankind, for its moral health, like the other birds that destroy carrion for the benefit of the public health in those countries where the animal houses are still organized the old way; also, you must add that our essential dynamism so accommodates the forces of destruction and those of creation that the former feed on the latter. What would become of countries other than the old Turkey, the old Russia? At the very least, the members that constrained all the advances of the world would be fragmented; it would be better to say that for Europe it would be an embolism from which it could die. The blood clots that once blocked the vital blood vessels, when diluted, will be allowed to flow back into circulation for the whole body. If a few drops of blood were spilled during the operation, should we worry about that? It is, after all, a modest payment for extraordinary goodness. In the expedient administration of the New World, we test our organization of revolution and the contents of the destructive work of Bolshevism and the establishment of the League of Nations, which is also our creation. The former is the gas pedal and the latter the braking device of the very same mechanism; the motor and steering wheel of the mechanism being us."

And the goals?

"They have learned from our mission. Israel is a composite and homogeneous nation: it is made up of elements scattered in all parts of the world, but with the fire of our faith in ourselves it is welded together into a single whole. We are a union of peoples, embracing all other peoples. This gives us the right to unite others around us. We are blamed for being the means of dissolving other peoples. . . . We dissolve only the surface, in order to awaken inside the chemicals that have not yet recognized each other. We are the great common divider of peoples only to become their greatest common "connector" (i.e., the connector of all peoples under our rule—*World Service*). Israel is a microcosm and the seed of the coming city."

This is the true story.

The reader will ask: "How did the *World Service* find out about this dinner speech?"

We have taken the text of this speech from a book published at the end of 1936 by the French lord Comte de Saint-Aulaire. The title of the book is *Genève Contre de Paix* (*Geneva Against Peace*).

A courageous and intelligent like-minded *World Service*, Arcand, leader of the National Unity Party in Canada, did the cultural world a favor by drawing our attention to this new edition.

In his newspaper *Le Fascist Canadien*, No. 9 of February 1937, he writes, passing on this speech:

During the last months of 1936 the Plan publishing house in Paris published a new book by the French envoy, the Comte de Saint-Aulaire. In this book, entitled *Genève Contre de Paix*, the French envoy recounts his experiences during his stay in Budapest, the main city of Hungary.

He lived through the time when the murderous Jew Béla Kun led everything there into chaos and established a hundred-day Bolshevik dictatorship, which he later used to model on the Red Terror in Spain.

On page 85ff, the Comte de Saint-Aulaire reports the statements of a Jewish banker from New York: he states, in particular, that he is one of the bankers who financed the Bolshevik revolution.

The statements made by the envoy confirm in almost every detail the plan set forth in *The Protocols of the Elders of Zion*.

It exposes how cunningly and cleverly the Jews take up the cause to achieve world power. The Comte de Saint-Aulaire, who authenticates these statements, is a man of known probity and integrity, not in the slightest suspicion of falsehood or fabrication.

With our friend Arcand, we thank the Comte de Saint-Aulaire for his courageous testimony.

Many diplomats have heard and experienced similar things, but none have had the courage to speak out like this.

82. Another Stack of Jewish Confessions

The *World Service*, June 1st, 1939, No. V/11, analyzes several quotations from Jewish sources.

The Jewish newspaper of London, *Jewish Chronicle*, wrote in its issue of April 4th, 1919: "The fact that there are so many Jews among the Bolsheviks, and the fact that the ideals of Bolshevism are in harmony with the noblest ideals of Judaism—all this really speaks for itself."

On January 6th, 1933, the *Jewish Chronicle* stated, "More than one third of the Jews living in the Soviet Union are in the public sector."

According to *The Defender* (April 1939), the current Soviet minister of foreign affairs, Molotov, said on behalf of the Soviet dictator: "The persecution of the Jews in Germany is clearly the opposite of the reverence we have for this race, which gave us Karl Marx. In the Soviet Union active anti-Semites are not tolerated, they are shot."

I heard Molotov's last phrase myself on the radio, listening to the speech of the formal head of the Soviet government at the Eighth Extraordinary Congress of Soviets of the USSR when the Stalinist constitution was being adopted. It was, thank God, recorded on tape in the USSR. Maybe it even survives history? Here's more: "The Jewish self-government, edifying for all Marxists and Communists," as the following report is correctly titled by the *World Service*.

A Jewish newspaper in Tunis, *La Gazette d'Israël*, published an article by the Jew Rutenberg in its No. 20 of March 3rd, 1939. This Rutenberg, among other things, wrote the following: "In our abnormal times, when the most fantastic chimeras are realized, the plan of the Jewish state must also be realized. But to establish the Jewish State, it is not enough to discuss the question far and wide, or to convene conferences. Our rights will be recognized only through arms, through Jewish arms. Our greatest vices are cowardice and indecision. I am a Marxist, but I confess that I work for Zionism, not socialism. I fight for the creation of a capitalist Judean state."

The engineer Rutenberg, now an ascetic in Palestine, previously "worked" in Tsarist Russia. As one of the leaders of the party of terrorists (socialist revolutionaries, SRs), he carried out the decision of the party committee to "execute" the notorious defrocked priest Georgy Gapon, suspected of being a traitor. After leading Gapon into a trap, the Jew Rutenberg, with the help of a gang of executioners, strangled Gapon with a rope.[171]

83. Some More Facts of the Same Kind

From a large folder of clippings incriminating world Jewry of Bolshevism, we take a few more at random, and end with these illustrations of this side of the Jewish question. From Warsaw:

17 provincial Communist Party delegates were seized in the apartment of the Jew Srul Friedman. Among them were the following very well-known Communists in Poland: Elias, Landau, Yankel Luxemburg, Nucher, Lesher, Mauer, Leiderman, and Aron Streiman.

The leader of the Young Pioneers children's organization in Poland, the Jew Zuskind, was sentenced by the Warsaw District Court to several years of hard labor.

The Polish police have recently carried out extensive actions against destructive Communist work in Poland. In doing so it has again been found that only Jews have been implicated as agents of Moscow. As the Warsaw anti-Communist press agent has established, of the 150 people convicted of Communist subversion in the first half of 1937 by the Warsaw District Court and Appellate Chamber, no less than 138 were pure blooded Jews, which amounts to 92 percent.[172]

---

[171] *World Service*, No. 11, June 1st, 1939.
[172] Ibid., No. V/4, 1938.

The following are the leaders of the Swiss Social Democrats: National Councilor Moi-Sei Dicker; Bruno Grimm, a half-Jew from Olten; Drs. Farbstein, Gurpp, Frank, Witzu from Zurich; National Councilors Huber-Lumberg from Eastern Switzerland, and Moses Silberrot from Davos.

The Communists are led by the National Counselor of Judas Benden Mann-Kirschbaum, the cantonal election was won by the son of a Jewish banker, Pinkum. An ideal representative of the masses.[173]

Nisson Ruda, a Jew from Russia, published a book in Berlin in 1922 entitled *The Revival of the Jewish State*, in which he once again attested to the Jewish origin of Marxist socialism:

The progenitors of the second world religion—socialism—were the Jews Karl Marx and Ferdinand Lassalle. It would be strange if they were not Jews, because the ideas of socialism were put to the Jewish people at the dawn of their historical existence, before they came to the Promised Land.

Ruda refers to the ancient Jews as the first socialists.

This, it turns out, is where Marxism comes from.

On December 15th, a grand banquet was held in Paris in the salon of the Hotel Lutetia in honor of Schwarzbard's defender, Henri Torres. The banquet was given by the Union of Jewish Youth.

More than four hundred persons were present.... At the table of honor, besides Torres, sat the famous Jewish philanthropist "king of pearls," Leonard Rosenthal, the former minister de Monzi, the famous writer Maurice Fex, the former Italian premier Nitga, Senator de Gévenel, the leader of the Hungarian liberals, Count Karolyi, many prominent lawyers, writers, artists and social activists. Torres was given a standing ovation.

As an explanation of the last report, we should add that Schwarzbard, mentioned in it, is the murderer of Petliura, and Torres is one of the leaders of the French Communist Party. At the banquet table this time Communist Jews, Zionist Jews, capitalist Jews, Freemasons, socialists and radicals united.

The Warsaw-based *Russian Word*, which cannot in any way be suspected of anti-Semitism, reported at the end of 1937:

---

[173] Ibid., No. 1/15/16, 1939.

The district court in Ternopil began hearing the case of 50 people accused of belonging to the Communist Party of Western Ukraine (CPWU).

As it turned out during the trial, the Communists in Ternopil covered up their activities with legal organizations: the defendants acted as members of the Jewish youth organization Brit Trumpeldor, etc.

In the Tarnopol Voivodeship there were a number of Communist cells run by the district committee of the CPWU. In addition, in Ternopil there was a local city committee of the Communist Party and a branch of the MOPR.[174] There were also MOPR cells in other towns: in Trembowl, Podhajce, and Brzezny. Komsomol cells were created in the localities.

Some of the defendants were accused of helping the Communists to escape to the USSR through the Zbruch, while others were accused of taking part in a demonstration in front of the District Court in Ternopil. During this demonstration, Communists threw stones at the windows of the court.

More than forty witnesses were summoned to court. The case will continue for several days. At the same time, it is reported that in Zamość, a major Communist trial of forty-five people has ended. Of these, thirteen were found guilty of Communist activities and sentenced to various terms of imprisonment ranging from two to eight years.

A major Communist trial is about to begin in the Rivne District Court.

The reproduction of these clippings could go on ad infinitum. Bolshevism is not a Russian, Spanish, or Chinese disease, but a world contagion spread by world Jewry.

84. The Ways of Judaization

If in the nineteenth century the main faces of Jewish expansion were: 1) "equality" for the Jews; 2) liberalism; 3) democracy; 4) capitalism; 5) Freemasonry; 6) England, then in the twentieth century a few more were added: 7) socialism; 8) war; 9) revolutions; 10) the League of Nations; 11) international organizations; 12) the Comintern; 13) Bolshevism and the USSR; 14) Finintern and the US.

The fourteen paths of representatives of the devil on earth are on their way to power. Here we have compiled, step by step, bypassing the

---

[174] International Organization for the Assistance of Revolutionary Fighters. (Translator's note)

location of the armies of world Jewry in space and time, a fairly detailed inventory of the arsenal of Jewish weapons in the struggle with the rest of humanity.

We have seen that the use of political ideas and the creation of international organizations is the basis of Jewish strategy in the realization of the dreams of the Jewish prophets.

On the basis of this strategy, Jewish operative art squeezes the flowers of the tactics that form the diversity of the various separate ways of Judaizing modern humanity.

The Jews in politics eventually turn into Judas over the states or into the enthronement of world Jewry over all the peoples of our sinful earth. But this is only the first and most conspicuous road map of Israel's ascent to the top of Mount Zion.

There are still other parallel roads, going on in the field of the intellectual and emotional activity of mankind in its work of mastering dead matter. We are not considering Judas' armament to fight on the cultural front or in the economic field, so the scheme of Judaization is incomplete here, since only the scheme of Judaization of politics is analyzed. For now, we ask readers to remember that the modes of Judaization are to be considered on three planes: Judas in politics; Judas in culture; Judas in economics.

These are the three main planes of human life and creativity, respectively. Only then more will be revealed before us. The Judaization of culture and the Judaization of the economy are also called civilization and Finintern (international financial capital).

Judas in Politics is the sad tale of the criminal use of all new political ideas, shamelessly hijacked by world Jewry and used by it for its disgusting needs.

Non-Jewish political parties in the service of world Jewry present the sad spectacle of Jewish victories.

How does this work?

We have already seen the ultimate facts in the pages of this book. We have seen Judas the liberal, Judas the democrat, Judas the capitalist, and Judas the Bolshevik. Now it remains for us to consider how, regardless of his mask, Judas corrupts any social environment in which he appears.

Following the general ones, let us consider particular modes of Judaization, isolated examples of Jewish tactics, and directions of Jewish strategy.

Let history and modernity once again bear witness, and then we shall see, following the artillery of ideas, the infantry and cavalry, regarded here as a kind of auxiliary troops.

Everything is the opposite in this purely Jewish strategy and tactics, because they need a very special and truly limitless victory.

Volume I: Contemporary Judaization of the World | 219

Jewish auxiliary troops in the invisible spiritual war for world power are primarily: 1) hypocrisy or, more accurately, subversion. Thereafter: 2) espionage, which they have taken a fondness for as their favorite pastime; 3) bribery, corrupting the environment; 4) Jewish women infiltrating the bedrooms of rulers and ministers; 5) terror, hidden while it is dangerous, and open and limitless when it is possible; 6) debauchery of all kinds and varieties.

85. Hypocrisy

Deception in general is a distinctive feature of the Jewish people. If in a republic their mask is demagoguery, what mask can they put on in a monarchy? Oh, here, undermining the monarchy with revolutionary work, they know how to pretend to be loyal subjects. They show records of loyalty. And, of course, they get a lot out of it.

The Jewish historian Dubnov praises the Polish governor Boleslaw of Kalish, who in 1264 issued a charter of utmost outrage: its first article says that in legal cases the testimony of a Christian against a Jew is admissible only if confirmed by a Jewish witness. The judicial power over the Jews belongs not to the common city courts, but personally to the prince, his governor, or a specially appointed judge. The identity and property of the Jew is declared inviolable. Accusations of sacrificing Christian blood for religious purposes are forbidden. If any such accusation should arise, it must be proved by six witnesses, three Christians and three Jews. There is, therefore, no way of proving it. If the crime is proven in this way, the guilty Jew is deprived of his life (for ritual murder, of course), otherwise the same punishment befalls the Christian informer. Clever. About this blatant law, Dubnov speaks highly.[175]

The position of the Jews in Turkey was consolidated during the reign of Suleiman the Magnificent (1520–1566), when Joseph Nasi, a Jew, reached the position of Minister of Foreign Affairs and pitted Turkey against the Christian countries. Dubnov testifies, "Joseph Nasi rendered great service to the Turkish government, but he did not forget his fellow countrymen, using his influence on foreign governments. Joseph often interceded for Jews persecuted in other countries."

The Jewish Encyclopedia supplements our little collection with a description of the Jewish intrigues surrounding the late German Emperor Wilhelm II. It says:

> On him [Emperor Wilhelm] the German anti-Semites have long had their hopes pinned. Meanwhile, even before he came

---

[175] Simon Dubnov, *Textbook of Jewish History for Jewish Schools*.

to the throne, Wilhelm II had already spoken negatively about anti-Semitism. In his inaugural address to the Prussian Landtag, he announced his duty to defend all his subjects without distinction of religion. Even more striking was the election speech of Count Douglas (1888), adjutant and intimate friend of the Kaiser, who spoke authoritatively of the emperor's negative attitude towards anti-Semitism. This attitude was later expressed, among other things, in the fact that Stecker was removed from his post as court preacher. Among the Kaiser's closest people there are several Jews.[176]

We know very well how the Jews repaid Emperor Wilhelm—they deprived him of his throne and sent him into exile. *Der Stürmer* adds to the report of the *Jewish Encyclopedia*:

> The Jews exercised their hypocritical cunning with particular fury toward the German Imperial House. So the Jews began to play the "patriots"; they shouted "hurrahs" and sang German patriotic songs for the time being. They raised cheers for the emperor, rich Jews rushed to marry off their daughters to German aristocrats, or mothers bought themselves titles of nobility.
>
> World Jewry surrounded the Imperial Court of Germany with a flock of Jewish secret advisors, court officials, wealthy bankers, and chamberlains. We all remember the names of the Valions, the Friedendorffs, the Warburgs, the von Bleichre-Dorfs, the von Oppenheimers, the Rathenaus, etc., who surrounded Wilhelm II in a tight circle, offering him their services and advice. All of them had political masks on their faces, which helped them to infiltrate the most important offices of the government.

Thus, by means of their favorite weapon, hypocrisy, of which the Jews are so well versed on, they succeeded in luring and infecting monarchical Germany.

One of Germany's most prominent Jewish leaders, Walter Rathenau, acted particularly clearly in the spirit of the *Protocols of Zion*, whose tactics were a living embodiment of the tactics of the *Protocols*. Before and during the war this man appeared as a typical "princely servant." He donated vast sums of money to the imperial government, he infiltrated the court and made the lowest bows to the Emperor, and he made touching friendships with the aristocrats. At the first rumblings of war he placed himself entirely at the disposal of Wilhelm. He

---

[176] *The Jewish Encyclopedia*, vol. 6, p. 570, Moscow, 1912.

organized and rationalized the German military economy. In parallel, he sold and cheated Germany, which had placed its trust in him, in the most shameful way.

When the organized Jewish red power smashed the monarchy to pieces, Rathenau, a "loyal subject" and "faithful servant of the throne," was the first to side with the revolutionaries. The Jewish press at the time exalted him to the skies. He was declared a political "genius." On behalf of the republic he attended international conferences, and conducted the most important negotiations on behalf of the German people. Finally, he was elevated by the Marxists to the post of Minister of Foreign Affairs. And the same Rathenau, who had once showered Kaiser Wilhelm with compliments and made the lowest bows at court, now began to vilify him in every possible way. He published a book, *The Kaiser*, in which he attempts to portray his recent monarch in the most undignified and ridiculous manner, clearly mocking him. He and his tribesmen had already achieved their goal, which was set forth in the *Protocols*: with "force and hypocrisy" they led the non-Jewish German government to its downfall, hurrying to climb onto the overturned throne. Walter Rathenau was known to have been murdered in 1921 by a combat officer.

This example shows that even under the monarchy, the form of government which is most closely associated with the nation, its historical past, its spirit, and its historical traditions, there were still loopholes for Jews to penetrate to the highest levers of power. They take advantage of these loopholes.

As great deceivers, they are able to wear masks so thick that they sometimes deceive the most skillful and discerning people. In East Asia, for example, some Jews hide behind "anti-communism," and under this layer of protection reach deep into the body of the Russian emigrant community to corrupt it from within.

Here they are trying to deceive the Japanese military, hoping that the grateful representatives of a country that has always walked the path of honor and sincerity, the way of *Bushido*, reflecting on the psychology of the Jew, will apply their habits and concepts to this psychology.

The Japanese warrior has historically been brought up in the precepts of valor and justice. That is why it is particularly difficult for him to accept how it is even possible for a person to nestle in such an accumulation of deceit and falsehood as it exists in the Jews.

Here is an example.

The Harbin Jewish "anti-Communist" organ *Jewish Life* No. 44 of November 7th, 1941—on the day of the 24th anniversary of the October Revolution in Russia—instead of any anti-Communist material it brazenly publishes:

The names of General Higuchi and Colonel Yasue are in the Golden Book of the Jewish National Fund [along with various internationalists like Vandervelde, we may add]. A solemn presentation of a diploma.

As you know, the last congress of the Jewish communities of the Far East decided to inscribe in the Golden Book of the Jewish National Fund the names of General Higuchi, Colonel Yasue, and Dr. A. I. Kaufman. General Higuchi (former commander of the Dairen Military Mission) and Colonel Yasue were participants in and speakers at Jewish congresses celebrating the just and humane attitude of the Great Empire of Japan toward the Jewish nation. These dignitaries facilitated the organization of the Jewish Congresses, which played such an important role in organizing national activities and Jewish communitarian life in the Far East. The convention unanimously decided, with rapturous applause from the delegates and the public, to inscribe these glorious names, General Higuchi and Colonel Yasue, in the annals of *Jewish Life* and history for all eternity.

At the end of October, we received three diplomas from the Main Bureau of the Jewish National Fund in Jerusalem—for General Higuchi, Colonel Yasue and Dr. A. I. Kaufman; the diplomas were signed by the late WJC President Menachem Usyshkin.

Taking advantage of Colonel Yasue's three-day stay in Harbin, the National Council, at a banquet table in a very solemn atmosphere, presented Colonel N. Yasue with a diploma of the ENF in a beautiful green frame. Presenting the diploma, the Chairman of the National Council said the words, noting all the kind, humane and just things that Colonel N. Yasue did for the Jewry of the Far East. Dr. Kaufman described Colonel N. Yasue as an exceptionally humane, just and faithful son of the Japanese nation. In his speech, Dr. Kaufman explained to the present representatives of Japanese nationality the significance of the Jewish National Fund as a land fund, a fund pursuing the goal of improving national life. Dr. Kaufman pointed out the significance of the entry in the Golden Book, which contains the most important events of Jewish life and the best names from both the Jewish people and the non-Jewish world. One of these names is the name of Colonel Yasue, a name that has become dear to the heart of every Jew in the Far East.

With applause, the Chairman of the National Council presented a diploma to Colonel Yasue.

In touching words, Colonel Yasue thanked the Jews of the Far East for their attitude towards him. He considers it an honor to be one of the three persons recorded by the Jewish Congress in the Golden Book.

Loud applause covered the Colonel's speech. Among the honored guests at the dinner was Colonel Nakamura.

Among those present at the dinner were the full National Council, representatives of the Presidium of the HEDO (M. N. Kotz) and the National Fund (Y. V. Zyuskind), as well as T. Oyama, Kabasyan, Fusita, etc.

The dinner was held in an exceptionally pleasant and cordial atmosphere.

Harbin's Kaufman, apparently, is not allowed to sleep in the *lavras* of Berlin's Rathenau.[177] Does he really think that the Jews will be able to do to General Higuchi something similar to what they did with Wilhelm Hohenzollern? We do not think so, and understand that only an exceptional humanity and a humane attitude to all the weak and those in need of protection, as the Jews disguise themselves, makes the masters of East Asia accept Jewish diplomas with a kind smile. Maybe even General Higuchi doesn't know that his name was written in the Jewish Golden Book? But the Jews of the East, setting records with their dexterity, manage to infiltrate not only to the Japanese, who did not know them for 2,600 years, but even the Italians, who began to fight with them, and even to the Germans, who are leading the international struggle against world Jewry!

86. Under All Sorts of Masks

Interesting data was announced by the Shanghai *Nash Put'* on February 1st, 1942, as Jews, under the guise of "White Russians," infiltrated the Shanghai colony of Fascist Italy. The note reports:

As you know, the Fascist revolution in Italy, led by the great Duce Mussolini, was marked by the defeat of the strong contingent of Freemasonry in Italy, and the destruction of the Mafia, a secret gangster society with great influence in the south of the country.

Because there were relatively few Jews in Italy (about fifty thousand), anti-Semitic laws were not immediately introduced. This, of course, was immediately exploited by the sneaky Jews,

---

[177] The name of some of the largest Orthodox monasteries of particular historical and spiritual significance. (Translator's note)

who managed to infiltrate the ranks of the Italian Fascist Party, seeking to occupy positions of power within it and thus maintain their influence over the country's public affairs.

In Shanghai, a certain Dr. Oskar Fischer, formerly an Austrian Jew from Trieste, who for a long time was a lawyer of the Soviet consulate and many Soviet institutions, starting with the Central Union, posed as a "devoted fascist." As soon as the Fascist regime established itself in Italy, the so-called Dr. Fischer joined the Fascist Party. Representing Soviet interests in a number of sensational trials and fervently defending Communists and agents of the Third International did not prevent this nimble Jew from even writing touching poems dedicated to the Duce and the Fascist Party. Fischer later became honorary consul to Guatemala, one of the smaller republics of Central America: this gives him social standing and diplomatic immunity.

The alliance with National Socialist Germany and the discovery of the machinations of Italian Jews against the Fascist regime forced Italy to gradually implement a series of anti-Jewish laws ("protection of the nation"). These laws were enforced less harshly, but just as deftly as in Germany. Foreign Jews, who had settled in Italy in considerable numbers after the World War, were firmly told to leave the country immediately.

In Shanghai, Jews had managed to circumvent laws and establish a new practice in Italy: under the guise of "White Russians" they infiltrated the ranks of the Italian Fascist colony as all kinds of victims.

Everyone remembers in Shanghai the brilliant Italian Colonel Grinaderi di Savoia and the giant, handsome combat commander Colonel Andrenni, but few know that the supplier of food, bread, and confectionery to this regiment was Yasha Blinchevsky—a Jew from Yeniseisk. Yasha is notorious for being a vendor in the Russian SHVK regiment, when he witnessed the "unfortunate" robbery of two Russian companies, which led to the dismissal of the first regimental commander.

This dangerous Jew Blinchevsky is neither a baker nor a confectioner, yet he managed to become (it would be interesting to find out how) a supplier of the Fascist Italian Regiment as a "White Russian"! To cover his sinister figure, Blinchevsky seduced an Italian to become his companion. But everyone knows that in fact the business was and is directed by Y. M. Blinchevsky himself, the same one who has a "Wholesale Provision Trade" at 1234 Joffer Avenue, under the signboard of the Welkom Trading Co.

A second specimen of the same order is a Jew known in Shanghai under the name of "Dr. M. Kliachko," a dentist contracted to serve Italian royal marinas. This same Dr. M. Kliachko is also listed as a "White Russian," but is in fact an orthodox Talmudic Jew.

How dexterous and insolent the Jews are in their ability to penetrate impudently into all the crevices of Aryan life, and in particular into Italian Fascist circles, in the guise of "indispensable specialists"—"White Russians"—is vividly illustrated by the following fact. Not long ago, a large secular Italian Fascist wedding took place in Shanghai, about which much was written in the local press at the time. A religious ceremony was held in a Catholic cathedral, followed by a lavish reception at the Italian Fascist Club. The young couple were Lieutenant Commander Marskine and Mademoiselle Itala Chieri, the most popular in Shanghai social circles, the daughter of a famous Italian steamer owner and a local old-timer. Numerous pictures of this fascist wedding were taken by four Jewish photographers who infiltrated the wedding as "White Russians." The young people were photographed in two studios: at the American-Soviet studio of Jew L. Skvirsky and that of the "Russian emigrant" Jew Joseph Schick, who recently donated to the Jewish hospital—exactly where the Sisters of Mercy are now trained to serve the Red Army, which is fighting fierce battles with the Italian regiments on the Dniester!

The wedding had a strictly fascist character: the main witness on the bride's side was Count Ciano, the Italian Foreign Minister and son-in-law of the Duce Mussolini himself, represented by the Italian Ambassador to China, Marquess Taliani di Marchio. On the bridegroom's side the chief witness was the famous Italian minister, Vittorio Tur, represented by Commodore Galetti.

Such facts of the penetration of the impudent Jews into the Aryan environment, masquerading as "White Russians," remind us how in Switzerland before the World War the local population was convinced that the Russians were Oriental people with big hooked fleshy noses, with thick lips and necessarily black, tightly curled hair. And with a strange habit of incredible gesticulation! They are not clean, rather smelly, and consider stuffed pike as their Russian national dish, and majufes as their national dance.

This false impression of Russians was created in Switzerland, because there, on account of Bronstein (Trotsky), Apfelbaum (Zinoviev), and other Communist Jewish leaders, was formed a large colony of Russian revolutionaries, students, and college girls, mostly of Jewish origin. The Jews severely damaged the Russian name, annoying the Swiss with their untidiness, loudmouths, and impertinence, so characteristic of their chosen tribe. When they see a true Russian, the Swiss do not believe that he is really Russian: "Why are you blond or brown-haired," they say, "and why don't you have curly hair like all Russians do?"

Only this lack of experience to figure out who exactly is a White Russian and who is a Jew can explain the penetration of Jews into the Italian fascist environment.

And in Harbin, even in 1943, when Germany was straining all its forces for a victorious onslaught in the world struggle against the Bolsheviks, there existed a German–Russian Hospital. One in which Dr. Friedenstein, vice-chairman of the Japanese–German Society, participates on the German side, and on the other... Dr. Monezon, a Jew, a Soviet subject, a fanatical enemy of Germany, and a propaganda distributor for the Soviet Information Bureau. In the German–Manchurian-immigrant firm Churin, which conducts a lot economic and cultural work, a firm that does much good to Russian emigrants, the chief patternmaker is a Jewish Germanophobe named Ban. While the head of personnel gradually became Wirfel, a German married to the sister of the wife of an "ex-Jew," that is, a Jew who had disguised himself as a Christian—E. S. Kaufman, the owner of the newspaper *Zarya*. Even the nimble Jewish conductor, Stolin, had at one time made his way into the Japanese–German Asia Theater, until he was driven out. But nevertheless, even expelled from Asia, he somehow managed to obtain a "letter of gratitude," as they say, signed by a prominent figure from the local branch of the German National Socialist Party.

Yes, these Jews are unsurpassed masters of trickery—in Asia, in Europe—wherever they are!

87. Espionage

The international dispersion of Jews makes it easier for them to specialize in espionage. Evidence shows that Jewish spies usually cater to both sides interested in the information, and end up cheating them by aligning themselves with the victor and demanding endless reparations from him.

Classic examples of two-way Jewish espionage are given in Shmakov's book *The International Secret Government* in chapters devoted to the history of the Jews of Russia. They date back to the time of Napoleon. It turns out that at that time the Russian Jews had proven their gratitude to the Russian government by conducting mass espionage in favor of Napoleon's troops. When Napoleon rolled back, these same Jews were just as zealous and diligent in serving the Russian troops with "intelligence." Many of them, according to contemporaries, were exposed as working on two fronts.

There are well known facts of bilateral Jewish espionage during the First World War. It is not difficult to suppose that it is psychologically much easier for a Jew, unconnected with the country in which he lives, to become a spy than for a member of the main nation. In the eyes of a Jew, it is not treason, but a job, "business," albeit a dangerous and lavishly paid one. This says it all.

The spirit of espionage is so ingrained in the flesh and blood of world Jewry that in the country they have seized and made their base, in our unhappy homeland, general mutual espionage is elevated to the level of a civil duty. The GPU, which gave birth to this system, is, as we have already established, entirely a product of Jewry.

In the USSR, the Jews force a sister to spy on her brother, a son on his mother, a bride to spy on her bridegroom, a friend on another, one and all to spy on one's fellow-workers and one's acquaintances. The Russian air is saturated with denunciations and treachery, full of blood.

Judas Iscariot is the ideal of world Jewry, an ideal the Jews want to impose on our people, the great Russian people. They want to make everyone a Judas and a Judushka.

In 1934 the head of the Kraypolit sector of the MST, comrade Steingardt, the secretary of the SK Kraykom VLKSM, comrade Tzeitlin, and the chairman of the SK Kraybureau, Y. P. Faytelevich, worked out a memo for the collective farm children and pioneers of the light cavalry unit for the protection of the harvest. This memo is very interesting in content. We must assume that it will be well remembered by the kids, who are entrusted with the honorable role of watching over their relatives. Here is a brief summary of its contents:

> The pioneer must remember that the defeated but not yet finished kulak is the worst enemy of the workers and peasants, trying to destroy the building of socialism by plundering the collective harvest.
>
> The kulak's assistants will not only steal themselves, but also use the backward part of the collective farmers, children, old men, and women to steal the *kolkhoz* bread. Do not trust anyone.
>
> A pioneer must show youthful revolutionary vigilance and the ability to recognize a kulak, a faker, a malinger, and a loafer, no matter who he is pretending to be.

A pioneer must be quick and vigilant, help the outposts to catch the thieves of the *kolkhoz* bread, warn the outpost when and where the kulak-thief can do harm to the *kolkhoz* property.

A pioneer must mercilessly expose thieves, crooks, pests, expose anyone who tries to encroach on the collective farm property.

A pioneer is an example for all the boys.

A pioneer must be an active correspondent.

A pioneer must be faithful to the cause of the working class and the precepts of Ilyich.

Such is the children's "memo" of the USSR. And how many cases have there been of children who, in fulfillment of such "precepts of Illych," betrayed their own relatives, tempted by a prize in the form of a new pioneer uniform or some trinket. The Sidorovs, Petrovs, Karavaevs, Myakishins, working on socialist grub, fight for existence, for a piece of bread, fearing even their children. And the Zeitlins, the Steingarts, and the Faytelevichs are in charge of socialist construction, educating Russian children according to these "memos."

I then commented on the book *Nash Put'*:

The German press calls the famous English secret service a Jewish GPU. The facts support this definition.

Finally, isn't it characteristic that the Jews named their international representative body the Jewish Agency?

Doesn't it seem like there is a Jewish spirit of self-exposure that constantly fails in all Judaic endeavors?

Military and intelligence officers of all nations! Guardians of state and public secrets! Beware of the Jewish spies, no matter what they are called and no matter what they hide behind, beware of the Jewish spirit, spreading the virus of espionage like an epidemic!

88. Bribery and Corruption

But the Jew is armed not only with cunning wits. To our misfortune he is also armed with money. And coin does its work where hypocrisy is powerless.

Under both republics and monarchies, the most popular method of Judaizing political life still is bribery. Judaism studies the weaknesses of public officials, and if there are no weaknesses, it artificially creates them. Beginning with greetings, congratulations, and donations, he moves on to gifts. Gifts are quietly passed on to bribes. All kinds of worldly temptations are created for the incorruptible, and so many traps are set, that only the strongest and most sighted man—strong in the sense of honesty, sighted in the sense of knowing the enemy—can pass over them, carrying out his public, national and social duty.

To cite historical examples of Jewish bribery would be to write a work of an encyclopedic nature, a universal history of the decline of morals—corruption—that eventually corroded the state organism to its foundations. Many nations have disappeared into oblivion because the rust of corruption ate away at the foundations of their state, their local and central administration. For the Jews, who had the bait of gold, the field of bribery was almost limitless, playing on all the kinds of basic passions of mankind: selfishness and vanity, the desire for a luxurious life, egoism and utilitarianism. Jewish merchants operate in the lowlands, corrupting local authorities and officials; Jewish politicians hit high, making their way to politicians, leaders, and ministers. Even some cardinals, as the Jews boast, they have tried to bribe in the Middle Ages. Here is the defender of the Talmud, N. Perferkovich, in his monograph *Enemies of the Talmud*, published by the Jews under the editorship of Dr. S. S. Gruzenberg in St. Petersburg, which tells such stories in the scientific-literary collection *Futurities*:

> In word and deed the Jews were opposed by their own tribesman, the French Jew Donin, who had been excommunicated by the rabbis from the synagogue and had converted to Christianity. He went to Rome and sent the pope a broad note against Jews in general and the Talmud in particular. . . . Immediately letters were dispatched from Rome to the prelates of France, England, Portugal, and Spain, ordering that the Jews, under penalty of death, were to surrender all copies of the Talmud in their possession. A commission was appointed, composed of monks. The commission spoke out against the Talmud, and it was threatened with burning. In order to save their intellectual and spiritual richness, the Jews took extreme measures. At a great cost, they were able to enlist an influential bishop, who had had the confiscated books returned to their owners. The joy of the Jews was unbounded, but alas, it was premature. As luck would have it, the bishop, who had a disposition toward the Jews, died suddenly of a stroke in the presence of the king.

"In view of such an occurrence there was no longer any doubt that God's punishment had befallen the bishop," Pereferkovich tries to ironize about this very timely death indeed.

> A few years later, Innocent IV, who displayed a more humane attitude toward the Jews, succeeded to the papacy. In 1247, this pope issued a bull in which he denounced the accusation

of Jews of blood libel. It urged that the Jews be treated gently, humanely, not stigmatized by false accusations, and that the clergy, nobility, and aristocracy protect them from unjust denigration. It's been a long time since the Jews have heard such speeches.

Pereferkovich adds unexpectedly: "This same pope, two years before, issued a formidable bull against the Jews." It is without explanation, however, how and why the pope so quickly changed his views on the Jewish question.

Pope Julius III issued a decree on the burning of the Talmud. Not surprisingly, as soon as he died, the Jews turned to the new Pope Paul IV with a plea for the return of their literary treasure. But fate played a cruel joke on the Jews. In response to their petition, the pope issued a new bull ordering all Jewish swindlers to surrender all their books within four months, or be punished by death. In desperation, the Jews decided on a last resort: they collected a considerable amount of money throughout Italy and began to "agitate" at the Vatican to be allowed to keep their books. In response to this agitation, in 1559, "the Jewish Talmud with all its glosses, notes, interpretations, and expositions, went into the indexes of forbidden books, and the chief inquisitor was confirmed to watch and burn all Talmudic books. . . . Only from the successor of Paul IV did the Jews obtain a more favorable response. In 1564 the pope authorized the printing of the Talmud, but with the condition that it should not be called Talmud, but Gemara or Shas."[178]

89. Winston Churchill and the Silver Coins of Judas

What is there to say about our time? Let us begin with the personality of the fanatical enemy of Germany and Japan, the perpetrator of the protracted world disasters of modern wars and revolutions, the notorious Winston Churchill. The British prime minister, the same one who once branded the Bolsheviks and then became their most devoted friend and ally. His change of heart toward the Comintern was not without the explicit participation of Jewish gold.

In 1935, *Jewish Life* wrote of Churchill:

---

[178] *Futurities*, vol. 1, 1900, St. Petersburg.

An unusually sharp and passionate speech of the famous English statesman and former minister Winston Churchill against the persecution of the Jews in Germany and the National Socialist regime made a strong impression on the general public. Churchill placed an article in an influential newspaper under the title "The Truth about Hitler."[179]

The *World Service* reports:

This enterprising politician was not always a wealthy man. He wrote about himself that as a young man he led a very expensive life and that the money he earned as a journalist was not enough to cover his large expenses. Being in Parliament also cost him far more than the six hundred pounds he received annually as a Member of Parliament.

Where did Winston Churchill get the money he was lacking? When he was in financial trouble he began to speak with the greatest energy in favor of the Jewish cause, and became the best defender of Jewish interests in the English Parliament. His success was reflected in the fact that very soon he found support from the millionaire Jew Nathan Lasky. In 1905, for example, he fervently fought against the emigration bill, the so-called "Immigration Bill." From this time on, he became a fervent supporter of Zionist ideas and a great friend of the Jews who supported him financially. This was also the reason for his intense hatred of Germany.

Amery—a man who repeatedly stood in the way of fame and never achieved it. Since 1934 he has acted as a fanatical enemy and ardent opponent of the Reich. It is quite remarkable that just at this time he became the director of the Jewish concern of the Marx and Spencer warehouses, owned by the Jew Israel Moses Schiff and the Jew Simon Marx.[180]

And *Jewish Life*, in No. 6 of 1940, adds:

Amery is a proponent of the development of the Jewish National Home on the principles of Ahad Ha'am. Being personally an outstanding expert in the colonial problem and in the ideology of British imperialism, he considers it imperative to strengthen the building of the Jewish National Home in Eretz Yisrael by all means. In all debates concerning the Palestinian problem, he always speaks out.

---

[179] *Jewish Life*, No. 38, 1935, Harbin.
[180] *World Service*, No. 6–17 and 18 of 1–15, XII, 1939.

It is clear from the *World Service* report why.

It is also clear why Amery went from being an opposition leader to a member of the government in 1940 and was appointed Minister of Indian Affairs. "The power he will have to influence," notes the issue of *Jewish Life* just mentioned, "will also have its effect in the Middle East, in particular on Eretz Yisrael, that is, on Palestine!"

In 1943, the Judaized and bribed Amery became Deputy Prime Minister of Great Britain.

90. The Love of Money of Politicians in the Jewish Orbit

A passionate love of money characterizes politicians in the Jewish orbit. One of the most beloved figures constantly quoted by the Jewish press is the late (politically speaking) president of Czechoslovakia, Beneš.[181] The following facts can be pointed out about him:

In Beneš, a man who was the epitome of pseudo-democracy has disappeared from the political scene. The fact that Beneš is half-Jewish, as many have claimed, has not yet been definitely established. At any rate, it is definitely established that Beneš is a high degree Freemason. He is Grand Master of the Czechoslovak Grand Lodge and was, until the voluntary dissolution of the Masonic Czechoslovakia, a member of the "Truth Wins" lodge in Paris, in addition to being an influential member of the notorious International League against Anti-Semitism in Paris, whose president is the Jew Lekash, aka Livshitz.

What is characteristic of the "statesman" Beneš is that he uses his high political position for personal enrichment, and in the most obscene way. Already in September 1938—that is, before the final fall of Czechoslovakia—the right-wing Czech press accused the former president of the republic Beneš of shameful bribery, and the young Czechs even insisted that Beneš be tried for unlawful enrichment.

The *Express* newspaper in Prague reported a typical example of the ways and means by which Beneš made his enormous fortune. The paper points to the purchase of a private villa in Bubunča from a large Jewish landowner, Bondi, nicknamed "the copper Bondi." Beneš bought the villa for CZK 900,000, even though it had sold for CZK 4 million a few weeks before. Beneš, who was then the Minister of Foreign Affairs, insisted that Bondi be paid in Czech crowns on an invoice relating to Austrian supplies. In this transaction, the Jew Bondi received nineteen million crowns of profit.

The Paris newspaper *Lech* attacks Beneš just as sharply. It accuses him of occupying an official apartment in Bourg, which was paid for by

---

[181] Czechoslovak foreign minister from 1918–1935, prime minister from 1921–1922, president from 1935–1938, 1946–1948). (Translator's note)

the state. None of the other ministers had similarly arranged accommodations.

He furnished his second home, the villa in Bubeneč, with such luxury that it is safe to say that no aristocrat before the war lived as Beneš does now.

The wealth of the whole world was collected in that villa. No one asked where Beneš got such money. Among other things, Beneš also used the former imperial palace in Ploščenice. On his orders, the former Czernin Palace was furnished for him with unheard-of luxury. In each of these rooms Beneš kept his own servants, cooks, and valets.

His cook was the same who used to cook for Emperor Franz Joseph, as were the valets who used to dress the Austrian monarchs.

It was characteristic of Beneš' luxury that Mrs. Beneš bought half a million Czech crowns' worth of Persian carpets a few years ago.

The Parisian newspaper *Lech* rightly asked: from what secret sources did the money for such a luxurious lifestyle come from?

91. In the Networks of Grand Scams

Jewish bribery brings terrible corruption into political life. It is no exaggeration to put an equal sign between the Judaization of the state and complete and total corruption. *Der Stürmer* sums up just a few facts of one decade, but what facts they are:

> Especially typical in this respect is France with its series of scandals, at the head of which must of course be placed the swindle of the Jew Lucien Klotz, who for seven consecutive years held the post of Minister of Finance in Paris. During his years at the helm of French finance, a series of cheque and bill of exchange "panams"[182] was accumulated: it was not until 1928 that all these scandals began to come to light. Klotz was sentenced to two years in prison. It was not definitely established at the time that Klotz had been bribed by thousands of government officials and politicians of Aryan descent.
>
> Slightly inferior to the crimes of Klotz was the recent Stavisky affair. The Jew had spent phenomenal sums to bribe hundreds of French politicians, journalists, judges, party leaders and even ministers. The scandal took such gigantic proportions that the cabinet was forced to resign. The French people responded to this triumph of corruption with prolonged riots and demonstrations.

---

[182] The Travancore Fanam (panam) was a type of money that was issued by the State of Travancore, now mainly a part of Kerala in South India. (Translator's note)

No less of a scandal was found in Australia. The case in question was that of the insurance company Phoenix. The chief culprits were found to be the Jews: Dr. Berliner, Bauer, Mosebracher, Stern, Brettmiedter, Rautman, Dr. Regnis, and others. It has been established that the most important government officials, lords, ministers, and a dozen influential party leaders were bribed.

But the vast majority of these scandals developed in Germany before Hitler came to power. The whole world remembers the famous Jewish swindlers Sklarz, Kutiseer, Skarek, and others.

The most typical of these was the Russian Jew Julius Barmat, one of the biggest war profiteers, who bought almost all the most prominent German social democrats. Investigations revealed that the Reich Chancellor Bauer at the time was also bribed with Barmat's money. Another Reich Chancellor, Scheidemann, was bribed in a more subtle way. He was given an extended trip to one of the most fashionable Dutch resorts, and Barmat spared no expense in doing so. Even the president of the German Republic, Fritz Ebert himself, was spotted in all this filth. Not without reason, on Barmat's desk was a portrait of Ebert with his own handwritten inscription: "To my friend Barmat. Fritz Ebert." Barmat also bribed Richter, police chief of Berlin, and Dr. Heffle, Minister of Posts and Telegraphs, who soon afterwards committed suicide in prison, alongside many others.

This is what happens to states that are indifferent to the Jewish question. Governments and nations! Those who have ears, listen.

92. Politics and the Jewish Woman

Finally, when bribes and hypocrisy do not work, when all other means of influencing the "goyim" rulers have been exhausted, Judas calls a Jewish woman to the rescue.

We have already seen the first operation of this kind, when, in the days of gray biblical antiquity, Karl Marx's namesake, Mordechai, sent Esther to King Artaxerxes. The beauty so possessed the body and soul of the voluptuous Persian, that he hanged his faithful and honored minister Haman, allowed the extermination of his entire family, all his associates, and at the same time the entire Persian intelligentsia, his national-willed elite. And so ancient Persia gradually fell into decline, and gradually disappeared under the sands of time. . . .

Characteristically, Jews in all countries annually glorify Esther as a great national heroine, a saint. And the holiday in honor of her exploits, Purim, is a favorite holiday of the Jewish people.

It is also characteristic that the name of Haman became a common nickname for all the major enemies of Jewry. Hitler, for example, they also refer to as Haman.

However, Esther is not alone in Jewish history. There is Judith, the same one to whom the Russian composer Serov dedicated his opera named after her. The same one who snuck up to the grateful, trusting Holofernes, gave herself to him and, after a night of frenzied caresses, coldly cut off his head and brought it to the Jewish camp as a proof of her bloody deed. Judith is also considered a saint by the Jews, and is worshiped by Jews at all times and in all countries.

Titus, the Roman general who destroyed Jerusalem, had a passionate mistress, the beautiful Jewish princess Veronica, sister of Herod. Titus, however, proved tougher than Artaxerxes and more cautious than Holofernes: the charms of the Jewish princess failed to draw him away from his victory over rebellious Judea, and his head, too, remained on his shoulders.

Historians gloss over the fact that the cause of the persecution of Christianity in ancient Rome was the Jews and that, in particular, Nero's favorite wife, who reveled in the torments of the Christians, was Poppaea, a Jewess!

The Jewish historian Dubnov praises the Polish king Casimir (1333^1370), who is called "the wise king" and whom the Poles refer to as Casimir the Great. The king's wisdom is seen in the fact that already in the second year of his reign, he had confirmed the charter of mercy given by Boleslaw of Kalisz, which we mentioned earlier, in Krakow, and extended it to all the regions of the Polish kingdom! Casimir supplemented Boleslaw's charter with new statutes which gave Jews in particular the right to lease the estates of noblemen. Local judges were instructed to hear Jewish cases only with the participation of rabbis and community elders. In 1356, Casimir granted Jews the right to be tried by their own laws. Dubnov recklessly adds that the reason for this "great" Casimir's favoring of the Jews was his love for a certain beautiful Jewess, Esterka! Even the name matches!

Finally, in our own time, we know the bloody deeds of Magdalena Lupescu, the red-haired devil of Romania, who so entangled Carol II with his charms that this modern Artaxerxes flooded his country with the blood of his best subjects, outlawed and physically crushed the fascist anti-Semitic movement of the Romanian people, exterminated Corneliu Codreanu, the leader of the youth, officers, intellectuals, and—justice being not just found in heaven, but also on earth!—lost his throne, and was escorted to flee abroad with shots and curses!

The renegade king fled abroad with Magda Lupescu. And immediately the struggle of Romania with Jewry began. The trick with Esther proved to be dangerous for a Jewess in the tense fascist times.

However, historical experience shows that the Esther trick, or the use of a Jewish woman, often succeeds under monarchies to bribe the otherwise incorruptible. Through the implantation of temperamental Jewish women to unlimited overlords not bound by religious imperialism or the ideology of national servitude, Judas often achieves great results, just as through mixed marriages, when a Christian or a Muslim takes a Jewish woman as his wife, even on condition that she converts to Christianity or to any other religion.

We were introduced to the English Lady Fitzgerald's Golden Fund at the very beginning of this book, and here is another passage from the same opera, or rather, the same operetta:

"Were not the statistics of mixed marriages between Christians and Jews given in print!" exclaims the anonymous author of the pamphlet *The Jewish Question and Anti-Semitism in France*.

> These statistics show that at least three dozen of the most aristocratic surnames in France are related to pure-blooded Jews. Particularly zealous for this matrimonial matter are the young scoundrels of decrepit noble families: all these seedy marquesses, counts, and barons who, with a zeal worthy of a better fate, marry the daughters of Zion in order to cover the faded and crumbling ancestral coat of arms with the new gilding of Jewish millions!

93. Jewish Terror

And so, the ways of Judaization have now been exhausted. The enemy does not yield: there are the honest, the brave, the firm, the incorruptible. "Kill the best of the goyim!" says the Talmud. And reluctantly, not at all out of disgust for blood, but out of fear for his precious skin, Judas embraces terror.

His favorite weapon of terror is poison, the invisible elimination of the enemy. We have seen examples of this kind from the recollections of the Dreyfus affair, when, in describing the "reanimation of France," we cited Shmakov's pages devoted to the mysterious deaths of the leaders of the French state at the time. But sometimes you have to make spectacular noise. Then Judas decides to commit an open act of terrorism.

The chronicle of all revolutions is replete with prior terror, a huge part of which the Jews take part. Thus, in Russia, to prepare for the revolution, as rightly says Herman Fest, the Jews engaged in organized terror; the murder of large and small representatives of state power.

The assassination of Emperor Alexander II was carried out by an organization created by Nathanson.

The head of the terrorist organization of the Socialist-Revolutionary Party was first the Jew Gershuni, then the Jew Azef. With the exposure of Azef's provocative role, the terrorist organization effectively ceased to exist.

Jews are also found among the perpetrators of terrorist organizations. So, in the murder of Alexander II was involved the Jewess Golfand, one of the killers of Minister of Internal Affairs Pleve was a Jew named Sikorski, the murderer of the chairman of the Council of Ministers Stolypin was a Jew named Bogrov.

But it is necessary to notice that in terror the Jews preferred, as elsewhere, leadership roles, while the executions were mainly entrusted to the Russians. It should also be noted that in the acts of terror carried out by the Jews it is always possible to distinguish exactly where the goals of the Russian "liberation" struggle were pursued, and where the goals were purely Jewish. Thus there is reason to believe that the governor-general of Moscow, the Grand Duke Sergei Alexandrovich, was not murdered in the interests of the revolutionary movement in general, but because he had evicted tens of thousands of Jews from Moscow and closed the Jewish synagogue there. "Throwing an explosive bomb at one of the vilest members of the Romanov House," the Jewish historian Dubnov writes unequivocally, "the noble Russian young man Kalyaev hardly suspected that he was an instrument of a historical Nemesis, who punished the Moscow Haman for defaming Jewry."

Haman, there it is again!

Festus' data confirm all other unbiased studies of the role of Jewry in the pre-revolutionary and post-revolutionary terror in Russia. We recommend that our readers become acquainted with this data from the books of N.E. Markov's *The Wars of the Dark Forces* and V. V. Shulgin's *What We Don't Like About Them*.

"Hit the pillars, the pillars will fall down by themselves," the Jewish teachers used to say to their youth. Commenting on the murder of P. A. Stolypin, the last pillar that delayed the fall of Russia into the abyss, Shmakov prophetically warned: "So they (the Jews) will first reach the point of REGICIDE and end up with GENOCIDE!" How cruelly these words were justified!

94. Massacre of Hostages

Political murder, however, due to satanic Jewish cruelty, is often directed not directly at the enemy, not only at hard, brave, and honest politicians and administrators standing across the Jewish road. No, as a kind of warning, they often strike their loved ones as well. Before killing Stolypin, the Jews tore off the legs of his twelve-year-old daughter with an explosive.

And here is what *Der Stürmer* tells about the tragic death of the beloved father of the Turkish dictator in 1936:

> As we reported in the recent past, the head and founder of modern Turkey, Kemal Pasha[183] forbade the further functioning of Masonic lodges within Turkish borders, which automatically led to their total closure. We already noted at that time that with this step the Turkish president aroused the intense hatred of Freemasons and Jews all over the world. We said then that it would not be long before he felt on his own back the weight of the consequences of his courageous step. Our words were now vindicated, and Kemal Pasha really did suffer the vengeance of the forces now hostile to him. Only a few days after the issuance of his anti-Masonic decree an attempt was made on his life. Fortunately, it failed, and the perpetrators were put to death.
>
> When Judeo-Masonry was convinced that Kemal Pasha could not be disposed of so soon, it decided, in the iconic Masonic style, to focus its vengeance on the innocent girl.
>
> Only four weeks after the prohibition of Masonic lodges within Turkish territory, the world press noted the following remarkable fact, which is organically connected with the assassination attempt of the Turkish president himself.
>
> Kemal Pasha's adopted daughter, Ellie, whom he loved as his own, when returning home from London on the Calais–Paris Express, was thrown out of her compartment on the Picquigny crossing.
>
> The unfortunate girl was then taken to the railway hospital in Amiens, where, without regaining consciousness, she took her last breath as a result of internal hemorrhage.
>
> Needless to say, no one, much less the daughter of a Turkish president with a bright future ahead of her, would throw herself out of her compartment window.

---

[183] Ataturk. (Translator's note)

The subsequent investigation established beyond any doubt that the daughter of Mustafa Kemal Pasha had been thrown out of the express train in the most cowardly and nefarious manner by someone else's hand.

Judaism thereby cooled its fierce hatred of Kemal Pasha, while at the same time taking revenge on the innocent victim, the young girl who had still her whole life ahead of her.

The whole bloody incident is a typical reflection of the Masonic ethos, which always prefers to strike from around the corner, even at innocent victims, just to quench the thirst for revenge of the Masonic leaders. In this regard, this whole colorful story takes on special significance and instructive value.

In the Jewish USSR, the families of the Red Army soldiers and commanders who could defect to the side of the enemy, are declared hostages. Wouldn't it seem that the Jews are the creators of the immoral institution of hostage-taking in general?

If in 1940 the Jews were not ashamed to publish all over the world that they were offering a million for Hitler's head, what about their attitude toward individual figures of National Socialism? Individual fascists, too, are a kind of hostage for the next Haman. The Jews were not ashamed to stain the hospitable land of Switzerland with blood by sending an assassin to Wilhelm Gustloff, head of the Swiss branch of the German National Socialist Workers' Party. How unprepared Gustloff was for such a treacherous blow is evidenced by the carelessness of his life. Gustloff's wife let the murderer into the apartment and allowed him to remain in her husband's office awaiting his arrival. This case shows how cautious political workers should be about all private visits to their homes.

And here is a description of the murder of a young poet, author of the German National Socialist anthem during the bitter struggle for power over the fallen Germany of Weimar.

The Romanian *Awakening* tells us how Horst Wessel, creator of the battle anthem of New Germany, died:

> The Berlin Assault Battalions knew very well what it meant to march under the banners of Hitler. Horst Wessel knew it too. He knew better than anyone. He was warned hundreds of times. Even the Communists themselves, who hated the chief of the famous Stürm No. 5 more than they hated Dr. Goebbels. Wasn't Wessel the one who took their best men away from them, turning them into fanatical champions of the Third Reich? Was it not Wessel the one who with his men penetrated into the most secluded corners of the commune to speak and preach about the sacred mission of Adolf Hitler?

His comrades ask him to be careful and to take some time off, to take up his studies again. Caring love finds a thousand motives. "You can fight for an idea, no matter where you are. Get command of the battalion of the town where you are settling in. Work hard Horst Wessel! Much work awaits you!"

He almost hesitated to not yield to his comrades' pleas. But not because of threats of death. Never! The thought of death is a constant companion in assault battalions. Whoever considers himself a political soldier of Hitler must be able to die with a last "Heil Hitler!" coming out of his lips. That is the greatness, the irresistible spirit of the stormtroopers, ready to die for freedom, for the future happiness of the fatherland.

No, Horst Wessel is not afraid of sneaking assassins, at the last moment he decided: "No, I'm staying! This is where I belong! This is where my comrades are fighting. We are constrained by danger and persecution. We have risen together against the lower classes of humanity, we have stood together under fire. And the blood we shed is our bond made strong. I'm staying."

Horst Wessel stayed.

And so, on January 14th, 1930, the tabloids screamed in big headlines: "The Murder of a National Socialist Student," and immediately began whispering what their dirty hopes dictated to them.

On January 14th, a deed worthy of the cowardice of its amoral authors was accomplished.

Horst Wessel occupied a furnished room at No. 62 Frankfurterstrasse, just opposite the restaurant where his Stürm was meeting. His landlady, a Communist who did not speak of her tenant other than as a "Nazi pig," had long been thinking of how he could be "taken out."

She had seen him enter the room, and considered the moment opportune. She ran to the nearest amusement park, where she knew a gang of tried and true red scoundrels and assassins, who had sworn a hundred times already to kill Horst Wessel, had gathered. Soon she found her chosen few. Sixteen men! Ali Geller the Alphonist, Erwin the Convict, Pimel, Jönchen, etc. Sixteen or twenty criminals bought to kill. And someone else was walking with them and taunting them, squinting bloodshot eyes when the men hesitated. It was the Jewess Kogan. Cowardly, like murderers, they kept asking over and over again if the Nazi was really all alone.

"Yes!"

"Well then, long live the red front!"

The landlady, widow Salm, shows the door and nods to them with a twisted smile. Then she goes into the kitchen, whistling the "Internationale."

Sixteen men stand guard in the dark, musty corridor, huddled against one another with revolvers in their hands, and fear distorts their faces. Fear of just one man.

Ali gathers all his courage and knocks on the door. Footsteps can be heard inside.

"One moment!" Horst Wessel shouts. "Come in, Richard!"

He thinks his friend Fiedler came to pay a visit. Then he opens the door himself . . . and the next second a volley of shots rumbles in.

Horst Wessel falls down screaming for his life, and his killers rush out of the house in a frenzy. They run to Karl Liebknecht's house to receive their blood money and a passport with a recommendation to Moscow. To the paradise of the distinguished.

For weeks the victim was tormented. Horst Wessel lies in the hospital with his mouth having been shot through. Struggling against death. Drawing strength from a passionate desire to live to see the rebirth of his homeland. The love of his comrades and leaders helps him in his fight. And it almost seems that his young body overcomes the darkness of death, that he will be the victor here as well. At this prospect the hatred of the red gang of murderers boils up. Their seal foments an incredibly wild, filthy campaign of slander against the dying man. With the twisted pleasure of sadists, they dig into the stinking pus of their own vile souls. And their mercenaries more than once try to finish off the wounded man with poison.

But Horst's comrades are on guard, being wake at his bedside, and woe to any red bandit who in these tragic moments falls into their hands.

Yes, the doctors are hopeful. And the mother and sister send fervent prayers to the throne of the Merciful.

But fate decided otherwise. Blood poisoning eats into the terrible wound.

Horst Wessel is called to a last gathering.

He can still say goodbye. He can still see, once more, his mother, his sister, Dr. Goebbels, and his stormtroopers.

On February 23, at the first flicker of the nascent day, the leader of the famous Stürm No. 5 closed his eyes forever.

And hatred pursued him on the other side of life's edge. She roared and laughed wildly when he was buried. She met the funeral procession with a hail of stones. She wanted to knock the fallen hero's body off the road and tear it apart.

"Why?" you ask. Because he helped his people to cut off the tentacles of the Jewish octopus by the thousands.[184]

95. Detours of Jewish Terror

Sometimes the Jewish terror also chooses very roundabout routes, going not to the loved ones of those who have aroused the fury of world Jewry, but through those loved ones. This way of dealing with enemies is especially vile, immoral and cruel. It is all the more pleasing to the Jewish god, the god of blood and hatred that lives in the breast of every Jew, the god of lies and evil.

An example of this kind of Jewish subversion is the tragedy of the famous French perfumer François Coty, who dared to expose the world's Jewish octopus. This is what happened to the inventor of the world's finest perfumes. Let's listen to the militant French organ *La Libre Pauvre* (*The Free Word*):

> After François Coty had made many millions, which attracted to him a host of friends who turned their backs on him in his hour of need, he died, abandoned by all, in want and despair, a particularly cruel blow being dealt to him by his wife, whom he had always worshiped and literally carried in his arms.
>
> All these blows fell upon this great man because he dared to speak out openly against the Jews, who leave nothing without vengeance.
>
> The morally repulsive Jew Weiner, who for some reason found it advantageous to take the Romanian name of Cotiareanu—after a Romanian province famous for its quality wine—managed to seduce Coty's wife during his lifetime, which dealt a death blow to this great French patriot.
>
> This whore, deserving no other word, already a mature woman, by insisting on a divorce from her ex-spouse, ruined him both financially and morally. The Masonic Court sided with the treacherous woman and ordered François Coty to pay an astronomical sum in cash, immediately placing his flourishing enterprise in difficulty.
>
> By the further cunning combinations of which the representatives of this famous nation are so handy, the entire fortune of Coty and his wife passed into Jewish hands.

---

[184] For more information about Horst Wessel see *Die Fahne Hoch: Three Biographies of Horst Wessel* published by Antelope Hill Publishing in 2022. (Editor's note)

The Anonymous Society of Coty is now run by Madame Cotiatreanu, that is, Weiner, in close collaboration with the Jews Greilsammer, Levi, Bloch-Leninet, and Gesot.

In other words, Coty's world-famous perfumery, the enormous cafés in Paris (the Da Florian and the Coliseum), and all the other enterprises of the great François have now passed into purely Jewish hands.

The only thing left aside was Francois Coty's favorite brainchild—one of the most popular and widely distributed newspapers in France, *L'ami du Peuple (Friend of the People)*, the founder of which managed to defend this fighting organ of patriotic thought, despite the desperate machinations of the Judeo-Masonic clique, which had long been sharpening its grudge against this newspaper.

And so the inevitable finally came to pass.

L'ami du Peuple has just fallen into the grasp of a Jew who has already sat in ministerial chairs several times and even managed to ingratiate himself with the "tiger" Clemenceau, becoming his private secretary during the sad memory of the Versailles Conference.

In the political arena he appears under the assumed name of Mandel. It is precisely this disgusting man, whose repulsive face has already been reported in our pages, who managed to get his hands on one of the best newspapers in Paris.

By the way, we should also keep in mind that Mandel-Rothschild is a Mason of the thirteenth degree, so he had no particular difficulty in acquiring one of the most expensive newspapers in France, the *L'ami du Peuple*.

96. Jewish Terror in the Name of Power

The subversive paths of Jewish terror are sometimes very convoluted and confusing. When a Jew has power in his hands, he ceases to be shy.

The extermination of dissidents then takes on a massive scale, as we have seen and are seeing in the Jew-occupied Russia. There is no limit to the Jewish terror in the heights of power.

In England and the US, all the leaders of the British and American national and anti-Semitic movements are being arrested, some shot, others disappeared. Arrests of the leaders are followed by the arrests of their supporters. Following their own patriots, other patriots are arrested. The fate of Russian nationalists living in these countries raises great fears. Even Vonsiatsky managed to be accused of espionage.[185] Both Pelly, leader of the Silver Shirts in the US, and Mosley, head of the British Fascist Union, are being accused of espionage. In the USSR, all anti-Semitism is punishable by death, according to official statements by state leaders. At the same time, they "expel" not only actual enemies but also any potential enemies: those who, because of past or future, because of social background, because of kinship, or because of acquaintance, could one day become an enemy, could one day become dangerous to some or any degree.

In the law-governed and monarchical Romania, Jewish terror was rampant from the throne, with the bloodthirsty Magda Lupescu, and the shortsighted and self-loving king, at the helm. In 1938, the world was stunned by the reckless murder in prison of Corneliu Codreanu, leader of the anti-Semitic Iron Guard, and thirteen of his assistants, allegedly while trying to escape. A later investigation showed that the heads of Codreanu and his associates had been crushed with iron hammers. Following the Codreanu massacre, Romania was awash in the blood of thousands of nationalists. Young people were shot and intimidated in squares, surrounded by a barbed wire fence, with machine guns, in front of a hooting kike crowd.

"The First Wheelbarrow," the Jews titled their report on Codreanu's death. In the Jewish newspaper *Israël* published in Cairo on January 5th, 1939, on Christmas Eve, the following outrageous lines appeared under the signature of a French Jew, Alexandre Herenger:

> Two powerful blows, peculiarly reminiscent of the old Yahweh's (vengeance) technique, have struck in the past year at the head of Romanian anti-Semitism. Within a month, both of its main leaders went down. Both were executors of Adolf Hitler's commands for the Moldovan-Valanchean kingdom and vied for the honor of becoming the scourge of Israel. Little Goga was deposed in May, immediately after reaching the pinnacle of power. His successor in the klobuk had a memorial service for him to the God of Israel, and decorated his grave with a Hakenkreuz.[186] They placed in the dead man's hand a bouquet of flowers sent by Hitler. It was like a passport to the other world.
>
> Soon it was the turn of his rival, Corneliu Codreanu, a bandit and brigandine, who along with thirteen of his associates fell under the bullets of the gendarmes, who received the order

---

[185] Leader of Russian fascists in the US, a veteran of the White movement, sentenced to five years in 1942 by an American court on trumped up charges. (Translator's note)
[186] A swastika. (Translator's note)

to send the prisoners to the afterlife without any unnecessary formalities.

Herenger laughs at the official *Rador* report of the shooting of Codreanu and his friends while trying to escape. He sarcastically dissects the Romanian government statement and points out numerous contradictions, comments the *World Service*.

The article by Herenger, a Jew, in the Jewish newspaper *Israël*, is important for various reasons. For the first time, Jews openly acknowledged that Codreanu and his followers had fallen victim to a brutal, Jewishly premeditated, and orchestrated by them evil-Jewish murder. The Jew Heerenger openly identifies this murder as an act of vengeance against the old Jewish god Yahweh, on the occasion of which the Jews have every reason to rejoice and triumph. The Jewish title "The First Wheelbarrow" is to announce that more victims among the Aryans, who love their fatherland, will follow suit in the near future. More "wheelbarrows" will carry the bodies of patriots murdered by the Jews to the dustbin of oblivion.

The Jew's article begins with a quote from Isaiah 41: "You shall seek them and not find them."

97. By Don Basilio's Recipes

Besides physical terror, there is also moral terror; besides destroying a person's life, the Jews sometimes try to destroy his good name and undermine his external authority.

A weapon the Jews widely use in dealing with undesirable individuals and groups is slander.

They use the classic recipe of Don Basilio from *The Barber of Seville* with masterful virtuosity: it is often not a simple fabrication, but a qualified slander, a provocation. What is Rossini's Basilio compared to the Don Basilio of World Jewry? A boy, a mere amateur!

We have already cited cases with Flaccus, who was barely saved from the brutal Jewish slander by Cicero. We could also cite the case of the famous Russian writer Derzhavin, who was nearly accused of raping a Jewish woman for his truthful description of the Jewish way of life, but we prefer illustrations from a closer time, the history of our own Russian Fascist Movement.

In the Soviet Union, Jewish Communist newspapers would pass us off to the Russian people as Japanese spies, and in Manchukuo, Jewish Communist agents would try to insinuate to the authorities that we were Soviet agents. In America our associates were identified as German envoys.

In Moscow, *Pravda*, in an article signed by someone named Hamadan, calls me a "tsarist general."

In Harbin and Shanghai, the Jew Arsky Aranovich says: "Rodzaevsky is a Komsomol member, a Soviet provocateur, and the All-Russian Fascist Party is a department of the Harbin GPU."

The ETA (the Jewish Telegraph Agency) in telegrams published throughout the world, in particular in the *New York Herald Tribune* on November 23rd, 1937, defines our organization as a "World Fascist Organization with its center in Harbin."

In London, a certain Vespa, who had escaped from Manchukuo, published his memoirs in 1938, where he gave wild fabrications about how I personally tortured Jews. The Molodaya Gvardiya Publishing House in the USSR translated these memoirs into Russian in 1939 and distributed them throughout the USSR.[187]

Ilya Ehrenburg, the famous Soviet Jewish writer, claimed that I declared myself Japanese. The Russian *Avant Garde* in Shanghai publishes a deliberate falsehood that I once ordered fascists to visit me on Easter Day wearing Manchukuo naturalization papers. At the same time, the Jews of Harbin and Shanghai never tire of attacking the Japanese authorities with petitions in which they spare no effort to paint my supposed harmful anti-Japanese work. Many Russian provocateurs have been diligently assisting them in this over the past ten years.

As an object of Jewish slander, I can be proud: In this respect I have experienced the fate of the greatest men of our time, the fascist leaders. Although Jewish provocations were sometimes very dangerous and threatened considerable trouble, at times even death, I have collected them with interest as recognition of the importance of the work I undertook, of my life's work. Elsewhere we will publish a collection as a cautionary example, as evidence to the contrary of the reality of our struggle.

Adolf Hitler, before he came to power. was portrayed by Jews as a madman. A similar claim made by Arved Aronshtam, by the way, appeared in the pages of the Harbin *Vechernyaya Zarya* in 1924. When Hitler came to power, Jews declared him a "Jew." Similar claims appeared in the Harbin *Jewish Life* in 1933, for example, with reference to the Osterreicher Abendblatt. This is the most vile of all, but in its impudence the Jewish slander is usually self-incriminating. For the evil-spirited devil's chosen people tend to lose all sense of proportionality and minimal plausibility.

---

[187] Organ of the Central Committee of the Komsomol Young Guard, N2, 2–3, 1939, Moscow.

98. "Herem" and "Quarantine"

The *herem* is a curse pronounced on a Jew excommunicated from the synagogue. The herem is also pronounced on us, who do not care about their satanic synagogues—on those who are displeasing to the Jews.

A politician, an organization, a party, who dares to meddle with the interests of Israel, is to be pronounced under the herem.

In this case, herem means, first of all, a boycott.

No Jew would dare to deal with such a "plagued goy"; a "plagued" newspaper will not get any Jewish publicity.

This is only natural, it's a struggle.

But the essence of herem is not the boycott of undesirable Jews by Jews alone.

Through Freemasonry and the Shabbos Goyim, through hundreds of thousands of non-Jews who are dependent on Jews, through hundreds and thousands of scoundrels and fools of various nationalities, the herem tries to create an environment of moral, political, and material isolation around the disobedient "gentiles" not subservient to the Jews—a "quarantine."

An anti-Semite will not find a publisher for his books, not even for his other books, in which he does not deal with Jews. All the doors of the non-Jewish press will be closed to him. He will be feared and ostracized by many who are far from being Jewish, but are neutral and loyal. Even like-minded people will put a spoke in one's wheel for the "sake of the fear of the Jews."[188]

He will be portrayed by some as suspicious, malicious, dangerous, by others as fanatical, blinded, partial, and by some others as narrow-minded, foolish, and even ludicrous.

Such was the fate of the first precursors of anti-Semitism in former Russia and of the Russian fascists in Russian emigration: some stigmatized them, others sneered at them, others murdered them with ridicule, and behind all this whistleblowing stood a smirking Jew pulling the strings.

Remember Nikolai Markov, a thoughtful and profound thinker, who was nicknamed "Get lost Markov," "Markov the Second," and other contemptuous nicknames.

The most "right-wing" of the Harbin émigré newspapers, *Russkoye Slovo*, even called me "Mussolini Hitlerovich Rodzaevsky" in Boris Suvorin's editorial.

---

[188] A saying in the Russian language coming from the Bible (Church Slavonic text). The New Testament (John 19:38) tells of Joseph of Arimathea, who for fear of the Jews ("sake of fear of the Jews") concealed the fact that he was a disciple of Jesus. (Translator's note)

The *Protocols of Zion*, first published in Russia by Nilus, was for a long time simply hushed up by the so-called big press.

For a long time, the émigré press kept silent about the existence of the Russian Fascist Movement. My books—*The Russian Way, Judas on the Edge, The State of the Russian Nation*—were also glossed over.

This is also a kind of herem—to keep silent about any phenomena unpleasant for Judaism, which are nevertheless worthy of mention. And it is not only the implicitly Jewish publications that keep silent, but also the very Russian ones.

Finally, at different times and in different countries, all kinds of people have spoken out against the Russian fascists: from already established Communist agents to my former assistant to the leaders of the administrative life of emigration, including—to the undeniable individual decency and strong anti-Jewish sentiment of the Orthodox priest and leaders of the monarchist association—those with knowledge about Freemasonry! The real question is: who only has not been in the ranks of our temporary enemies? Enemies by misunderstanding! And how these "misunderstandings" interfered with our work!

It can't be helped; such is the power of the Jewish herem!

Whoever wants to fight for truth must be prepared for all sorts of troubles, including blows from friends. This is how the most unexpected Jewish connections sometimes come to light.

99. Judas as the Inventor of Torture

But let us return to the mainstream of Jewish terror, in relation to which slander and herem are only offshoots. Jewish terror is further revealed to us not only as a means of intimidating those in the way, but also as an end in itself—Judas revels in the torment of his victims. And in this sadistic pleasure the Jews derive satisfaction for their satanic malice toward the entire non-Jewish world.

As historical experience shows, the Jews, when they are given the role of executioner, do not only kill, but also they torment their victims. They revel in the moaning and agony. There are sadistic traits found in the Jewish psychology.

Torture is practically a Jewish invention. The Jews invented many of the most cruel and inhumane methods of torture. The history of all Jewish revolutions shows the same pattern. We already saw what Jews did to clergy, women, and children in red Spain.

We shall begin to further illustrate this pattern with the relatively innocuous example of the Jews rushing to kill defenseless people when there is even the slightest opportunity to do so. Colonel Winberg recounts this exemplary case in his famous almanac "Ray of Light," recalling the shot fired by the brave Russian avengers at the well-known traitor Miliukov, which in turn also struck another well-known Freemason, Nabokov, who was standing nearby. Shots which sounded to Judeo-Masonry like a bolt from a clear sky in democratic Berlin in 1924:

> The Berlin Philharmonic Hall. A few minutes had passed since the punishing shots of Szabelski and Taboricki had gone off. Already the police had entered the hall and arrested both mates; they were surrounded by policemen; they were being held; they were handcuffed; they were no longer safe from a frightened Jewish public. And now the Jews crawl out from under the tables, from under the chairs, from under the sofas, and stand up and attack the arrested, who were unarmed and defenseless, in a loud, furious crowd. They shout, the furious Jews, that they want to hold a lynch mob; breaking the resistance of the policemen who are fighting with them in defense of the arrested, they rush on Shabelsky and begin to kill him: in a few moments his poor proud head lies full of blood.
>
> Having risen, one of the last of them from under the sofa under which he was lying, the well-known Jew Barladyan, who was the secretary of the defunct Jewish newspaper *Golos Rossiy*, a socialist-revolutionary, he rushes forward through the crowd of his fellow tribesmen. Barladyan, armed with a stick, raises it and delivers a terrible blow to the head of Shabelsky, who is standing motionless with handcuffs on his hands with two policemen on his sides holding his hands tightly. The fearless eyes of the martyr stare with unspeakable contempt at the vile face of the filthy Jew, twisted with savage malice. Shabelsky shouts to him: "So this is how you scoundrels tortured the Petrograd policemen."
>
> The rage of an angry Jew knows no bounds; he loses his head, forgets his tribe's inherent cowardly caution, and shouts back to Shabelsky literally as follows: "Yes! This is how we used to torment your policemen, and this is how we will always torment you Russian officers."
>
> Barladyan then raises the stick a second time and points the end of it directly into Shabelsky's eye with the clear intention of piercing his eye.
>
> In that moment of great danger Shabelsky never loses his composure: with a movement of his shoulder he loosens the clutches of the policemen and with his leg which was left free he strikes a heavy blow between the legs of the Jew, who falls and lets out a frantic scream, writhing in pain. Having recovered somewhat, but still lying down, he shouts to his fellow

tribesmen the characteristic warning: "Comrades! Be careful! His legs are still free!" With difficulty the policemen snatched the arrested from the hands of the frenzied kike crowd and dragged him away.

Here the Jews wanted to mutilate a defenseless Russian officer in front of the German public, in the presence of the German police. These are the lengths they are willing to go to: to go where there are no bystanders, where their rage is restrained by foreign police, where power is in their hands!

To what extent is the terrible chronicle of the evil memory of the days of "war communism" in Russia, those dark days when Jews finally received, following their "equality," the coveted opportunity to satisfy their hidden hatred of Russian people.

"For those tears shed by Jewry, they will pay with blood," threatened the Jew Kogan of New York in 1919 in the already cited quote in the chapters on the USSR. And indeed: from the Great Russia, which they captured, the Jews have created a kingdom of permanent terror, in which the Russian people are subjected to ceaseless torture by fear and ruthless destruction.

In his capital study, General Golovin (*The Russian Counterrevolution*, chapter 25) summarizes:

> In Kharkov, skulls were scalped and gloves made from their skins. In Voronezh they put the tortured in barrels covered with nails and rolled them around; they burnt a five-pointed star on their foreheads, and wreaths of barbed wire were hung on priests. In Tsaritsyn and Kamyshin they sawed bones with a saw. In Poltava, for example, eighteen monks were impaled and then burned on the stake. At Ekaterinoslav they were crucified and stoned. In Odessa officers were burned in the furnaces of ships and drowned in rotten barges. In Kiev they put them in a coffin with a decomposing corpse, buried alive and then dug out after half an hour."

"Archbishop Andronik of Perm was subjected to particularly cruel torture, to whom his cheeks were first cut out, his eyes gouged out, and his ears and nose cut off," recounts *The Black Book*, published by Russian students in Paris in 1925, "in such a monstrous way he was led around the city of Perm, then thrown into the river. Hermogenes of Tobolsk was sent in winter to forced labor digging trenches and then sunk."

In the Spassky monastery they arrested the abbot, the seventy-five-year-old Archimandrite Rodion, who was led out into the fields the first night and killed there. One of the soldiers of the Red Army boasted that he had killed him by first cutting off the skin and hair from his head and then bending his head and chopping off his neck. Subsequent examination of the corpse confirmed the terrible confession of the Red Army man.

In Izyum county the village priest Loginov was arrested and taken to town. On the way he had his nose cut off and thrown into a river.

In Kherson Province a priest was crucified. In one of the stanitsas of the Kuban Province on Easter night Father Prigorovsky was tortured during his service: his eyes were poked out, his ears and nose were cut off, and his head smashed in. In the same region Father Lisitsyn was murdered after three days of torture. Father Flachinsky was chopped to pieces. Father Boyko's throat was somehow ripped open. Father Gregory Nikolsky of the monastery of Mary Magdalene, who was communing with the faithful at the monastery during the liturgy, was taken from the church outside the fence of the monastery and after all sorts of mockery was killed by shooting a revolver into his mouth, which he was forced to open while yelling, "We are communing you."

Archimandrite Veniamin of Moscow was executed at Chaplino Station in Catherine Province. He was executed for having interceded for the former zemstvo governor who had been sentenced to death at the same station—the weak old man, who could hardly move his legs, was dragged to his execution along Vokzalny Avenue. At the place of execution, he was stripped, and his executioners divided his clothes among themselves. The victim was then beaten with ramrods. The force of the blows was so great that one of them cut off his scythe. The bloodied archimandrite was silent and only prayed, but by blows to his hands the executioners deliberately prevented him from crossing himself. The torture lasted indefinitely, until at last the unfortunate man's head was cut off.

In Bakhmutsky County of the same province, Priest Popov was asked to serve a funeral service for himself, and when he refused to do so, he was immediately shot. Another village priest in the same county had his eyes gouged out and his beard torn out by the Bolsheviks before he died.

In the village of Rozhdestvenskaya in Aleksandrovsky Uyezd, the Red Army soldiers cut off a local priest's arms and legs up to his torso and hung him by his hair from an acacia tree, then shot him and did not allow his body to be removed from the tree for three days.

In the Kamennoe-Ugolny district a village priest, Father Mylutkin, was fictitiously accused of publicly expressing his joy at the passage of a batch of Red Army prisoners through the village. During a long interrogation by the Cheka, he was beaten with ramrods, his leg was wounded, and his scalp was removed. Then, at the request of the local peasants, he was handed over to them on bail, but two hours later he was brought back to the "emergency station," the chairman of which fired a revolver at him and the Red Army soldiers stabbed him with bayonets. The whole floor was covered with blood. The priest's corpse was thrown into the river.

The book by the socialist S. P. Meliunov, documented using mainly the testimonies of the Soviet press itself: first the testimonies of socialists, Jews, and Englishmen, second (and these witnesses certainly cannot be accused of a specific ill-will toward the Soviet power) provides a great many stunning facts about the Red Terror in Russia. This book should have been better titled, the *Jewish USSR*, as we would have clarified.

"It is impossible to count the number of victims," says the investigation of Bolshevik activities in Stavropol from January 1st to June 1st, 1918. "People were killed without trial, on verbal orders from commandants." Memories of the Stavropol province of the former prosecutor of the Provisional Government, Krasnov, published in the *Archive of the Revolution*, confirm these investigations.

He tells of the abuse of Kalmyk women, of children with their ears "cut off," and of the torture of raped gymnasium girls from the village of Petrovsky.

In the records of the Denikin Commission, we see cities named in succession: Kharkov, Poltava, and others. And everywhere "the corpses with severed arms and smashed bones, and severed heads," "with broken jaws, with severed genitals." And everywhere the graves yield dozens of such corpses. In Kobelia there are sixty-nine, in another district town there are twenty, in a third, in Kharkov, lay eighteen seventy-year-old monks. Here is the corpse of seventy-five-year-old Archimandrite Rodion, who was scalped in Kharkov.

Let's take the description of such days in Rostovnadon from another source, from the remarkable book of the social democrat A. Lokerman, *Seventy-Four Days of Soviet Power*, published in 1918 in the liberated Rostov. Here we find the same mass shootings, including those wounded in hospitals.

At headquarters (Siversa) the arrested were undressed, some were left in boots and pants, which were taken off anyway after the execution, others were left only in underpants. In the twentieth century, in broad daylight, people were being chased naked dressed only in underpants down a big city street in the winter snow and, upon reaching the church fence, shot. Many were crossing themselves, and the bullets struck them during their prayers. Bourgeois decorum like blindfolding, summoning a clergyman, etc., were of course not followed.

The Englishman Elston[189] wrote to Balfour on January 14th, 1919:

> The number of innocent citizens brutally murdered in the Ural towns reaches the hundreds. Officers captured here by the Bolsheviks had their epaulets nailed to their shoulders, young girls were raped, civilians were found with their eyes gouged out, others without noses. Twenty-five priests were shot in Perm, and Bishop Andronicus was frozen alive in an ice-hole.

The Russian writer O. E. Kolbasina, while in prison, describes a similar experience in her memoirs: This was already in Moscow, in the All-Russian Extraordinary Commission, that is, in the very center. One woman was accused of having saved an officer by bribing someone with a hundred thousand rubles. Let us convey her story as it appears in Kolbasina's memoirs.

> They took me to the basement to be shot. There were several corpses lying there in their underwear. I don't remember how many. I recall well seeing a woman and a man in socks, both lying on their backs. They were shot in the back of the head, their feet slipping on their own blood. I didn't want to undress. If they wanted something, they could take it themselves. "Take your clothes off!" I was hypnotized. My hands mechanically rose by themselves, like an unbuttoning machine. I take off my coat, I start unbuttoning my dress. . . . And I hear a voice, as if from far away, as if through an absorbent cotton: "On your knees." I was pushed towards the bodies. They were lying in a pile. And one was still moving and wheezing. And suddenly somebody shouted again, very weakly, from far away: "Get up, quick!" Someone pulled me by the hand. Romanovsky (a well-known investigator) stood in front of me and smiled. I know his face, vile and sly, with a malicious smile: "What, Ekaterina Petrovna (always calling me by my patronymic), were you a little scared? A slight shake of nerves. That's alright. Now you'll be more cooperative. Right?"

---

[189] British Foreign Secretary at the time. (Translator's note)

And here is the Ekaterinodar Cheka, where the same methods of coercion were in use in 1920. Dr. Shestakov is taken in a car to the Kuban River. He is forced to dig a grave, preparations are made for the execution and . . . a volley of blanks is fired. The same thing is done several times with a certain Korvin-Piotrovsky, followed by a brutal beating. Worse, he is told that his wife and ten-year-old daughter have been arrested and at night they perform a staged execution of them in front of his father's eyes.

Torture is carried out by means of physical and psychological pressure. In Yekatinodar the torture was carried out in the following way: the victim is stretched out on the floor of the cell. Two Chekists pull on the head and two on the shoulders, thus pulling the muscles of the neck, while at the same time a fifth Chekist strikes the victim with an iron instrument, usually the handle of a Nagant or a Browning. The neck is swollen and the mouth and nose left bleeding. The victim goes through unbelievable suffering.

In solitary confinement they tortured Dombrovskaya, a teacher, whose entire guilt consisted in the fact that she had been found in possession of a suitcase containing some officers' belongings, left by chance by a passing officer who was a relative of hers during the time of Denikin. Dombrovskaya confessed to this guilt, but the Chekists had information that Dombrovskaya had hidden gold objects she had received from a relative of some general. This was enough to subject her to torture. She had previously been raped and mocked. The rape was carried out based on the seniority rank. The Chekist Friedman was the first one to rape her, then the others followed. After this, that they tortured her to find out where the gold was hidden. First they cut her body with a knife, then used iron tongs and pliers to separate her limbs. Enduring unbelievable agony, drenched in blood, the unfortunate woman pointed to some place in the barn of house number 28 on Medvedovskaya Street, where she lived. At 9 p.m. on November 6th she was shot, and an hour later that night the Chekist officers thoroughly searched the place, seemingly finding a gold watch and several rings.

In the village of Kavkazskaya an iron gauntlet was used for torture. It is a thick piece of iron put on the right arm with small nails on it. On impact, in addition to the severe pain caused by the solid iron, the victim suffered the agony of shallow wounds left in the body by the nails, which did not take long to become covered in pus. Such torture included the torture of the citizen Ion Efremovich Lelyavin, from whom the

Chekists extorted gold and money and some of Nicholas' money, which he allegedly had hidden.[190] In Armavir a screw was used during the torture. This is a simple belt with a nut and screw on its ends: the nut and screw are screwed in, the belt then squeezes the head, causing terrible physical suffering.

Torture in Odessa was the subject of a special chapter in a book by the Jew Averbukh. Shackles, confinement in a prison cell, corporal punishment with rods and sticks, torture in the form of squeezing hands with pincers, suspension, etc.—all was present in the Odessa Cheka. Among the instruments of torture, we find sticks "a third of an inch thick and a lash woven from belts, and sh—"[191] In Penza the chairwoman of the Cheka was a woman named Bosch, who was so brutal that in 1918 that she was even called back by central. Similarly, in Tyumen there was also "torture and flogging" with rubber. In the Urals Cheka, they interrogated M. in the following way: "M. was brought to the barn, kneeled against the wall, and felt the shots passing through right and left." Goldin (the investigator) said: "If you do not give up your son, we will not just shoot you, we will first break your arms and legs, and only then we will finish you off." (This unfortunate M. was shot the next day). In the Novocherkassk prison, an investigator put the muzzles of two Nagants in his mouth, the iron sights clinging to his teeth, and pulled them out along with his gums.

In Kiev, in January 1922, the investigator Chekist Remover was arrested. She was accused of the unauthorized execution of eighty arrested, mostly young people. Remover was found to be mentally ill on the grounds of sexual psychiatry. The investigation found that she personally shot not only the suspects, but also the witnesses, who were summoned to the Cheka and who had the misfortune to excite her painful sensuality.

On March 10th and 11th, R. Olekhovskaya, who was sentenced to death for a trifling misdemeanor, which was ridiculous to punish even with prison, seemed unable to be killed. Seven bullets hit her—in the head, in the chest, her body trembled. Then the security officer took her by the throat, tore her blouse open and began twisting and squeezing her neck cartilage. The girl was not even nineteen years old.

Johnston could only have been rivaled in Odessa by a female executioner, a young girl named Dora.[192] People told legends of her tyranny. She "literally tormented" her victims by tearing out their hair,

---

[190] Coins of the Russian Empire, minted during the reign of the last Emperor of All Russia Nicholas II. (Translator's note)
[191] The text ends here. (Translator's note)
[192] A Negro executioner who specialized in skinning people alive. (Translator's note)

severing their limbs, cutting off their ears, twisting their cheekbones, etc. In order to judge her activity, it is enough to mention the fact that during the two and a half months of her service at the Extraordinary Commission she alone shot seven hundred and more people—that is, almost one third of what was shot in the Cheka by all other executioners.

There were many other female executioners in Moscow. S. S. Maslov, as an old worker of the Vologda Cooperative Society and a member of the Vologda Province Constituent Assembly, well versed in Vologda affairs, tells of a local executioner (far from a professional), Reveka Plastinina (Mayzel), who personally shot over a hundred people. "I know of up to ten cases," says the author, "where women voluntarily put holes on the back of skulls."

About the activities in the Arkhangelsk province in the spring and summer of 1920 of Plastinina-Mayzel, the former wife of the famous Kedrov,[193] the correspondent of *The Voice of Russia* reports:

> After the solemn burial of the empty red coffins, Reveka Plastinina's massacre of her old party enemies began. She was a Bolshevik. This mad woman, on whose head hundreds of destitute mothers and wives sent their curses, in her anger had surpassed all the men in the Cheka. She remembered all the little grievances of her husband's family and literally crucified the entire family, and whoever was left alive was morally murdered. She was a cruel, hysterical, mad woman, who thought that the White officers wanted to tie her to the tail of a mare and let the horse gallop. Being consumed by her fiction, she went to the Solovetsky monastery, and there she led a massacre with her new husband, Kedrov.

What the inmates experienced in the basements of the "emergency room" is told by the inscriptions on the basement walls. Here are some of them: "They beat me unconscious for four days and gave me a readymade protocol to sign, and I signed it, I couldn't bear any more torment"; "I suffered about eight hundred ramrods and looked like some kind of piece of meat . . . shot on March 25th at 7 p.m. at the age of twenty-three," "Test Room No.," "He who enters here abandons hope."

Investigator Miroshnichenko, a former hairdresser, and Jessel Mankin, an eighteen-year-old young man, were especially persistent.

An autopsy of the corpses recovered from the graves of the Cheka victims revealed terrible atrocities: beatings, rib fractures, burning with hot objects, scorched stripes on the back, etc. The first corpse recovered was identified as Cornet Zhabokritsky of the 6th Hussar

---

[193] Vologda Chekist. (Translator's note)

Regiment. He had been badly beaten and his ribs had been broken, and in thirteen places on the front of his body had been burnt with an incandescent round object, and on his back had a whole strip burned. He continued: "One man's head was flattened into a one-third of an inch circle. This flattening was done by simultaneous and tremendous pressure of flat objects on both sides." Also: "To an unknown woman seven stab wounds and gunshot wounds were inflicted; she was thrown alive into a grave and buried."

The corpses of those doused with hot liquid, with burns on the abdomen and back, who had been hacked to death with sabers, were found, but not right away: "The executed were deliberately struck first with non-lethal blows, with the sole purpose of tormenting them."[194]

To quote the poet M. Voloshin:

Isn't this dystopian horror enough?
The truth was gouged out from under my fingernails,
Fougasse was inserted into our necks,
Shoulder marks were sewn, lampasse were cut,
One-horned devils were made.
How many lies did it take
In all these cursed years,
To enrage and to raise up to knives
Armies, kingdoms, nations.

100. The Organizers of the Red Terror

Here, in Melgunov's book, there appears to be only glimpses of Jewish surnames, but there are far more of them than there are Russian. They are disproportionately numerous, if we recall the percentage ratio of the Jewish minority to the Russian majority. But what about the individual actors? We have to look deeper: who organized and who leads the Red Terror, a question answered by Festus in his exhaustive and remarkable account of names and numbers in his study *Bolshevism and Jewry*:

The deputy of the first chairman of the Dzerzhinsky Cheka was a Jew named Zaks, then Jew Unschlicht; Menzhinsky's deputy for the OGPU was the Jew Yagoda. Yagoda, as the manager of the OGPU, was the organizer of the entire Chekist apparatus. Yagoda later became the

---

[194] Sergei Melgunov, *The Red Terror in Russia*.

head of the OGPU, later renamed to the NKVD. From Yagoda followed an endless supply of all kinds of Agranov-Sorenzons[195] and Bermans.[196]

The organizer of the Cheka in Petrograd was the Jew Uritsky. The Collegium of the Petrograd Cheka in early 1918 consisted of Jews—Uritsky, Iosilevich, Bokia, and the Pole Vorkhlevsky.

At the head of the Moscow Cheka were Jews: Breslav, then Mantsev. Mantsev was later head of the Extraordinary Commissions of Ukraine and the special department of the Southern Front. With his participation, the Jew Béla Kun (Kon) arranged bloody hecatombs in Crimea.[197] Mantsev, on the other hand, drowned the uprising in Ukraine in blood. Mantsev's successor in Ukraine was again a Jew: Balitsky.

One of the first heads of the foreign section of the Cheka was the Jew Mogilevsky. The organizer of the foreign department in its present form was the Jew Loginov.

The organizer and head of the Internal Intelligence Department was the Jew Katznelson, his assistant being the Jew Kagan. The organizer and head of the "special department" was the Jew Bokiy. The head of Kremlin security and a member of the government was the Jew Belenky. While the personal secretary of Dzerzhinsky is the Jew Zilberberg.

Also known: the head of the department of concentration camps, the Jew Berman and his assistant, the Jew Firin.

Of the Collegium of the Cheka and the MChK, in addition to the aforementioned heads of its departments, the following Jews are known:

Agranov (Sorenzon), Deribas, Yaroslavsky-Gubelman, Rozmirovich, Kizilstein, Shklovsky, Tsitkin, Rutenberg, Pinos, Model, Goldin, Galperstein, Knigissen, Zeitlin, Kronberg, Hakina, Rivkina, Heifetz, Bull.

The doctor of the Cheka was the Jew Hirschfeld.

Of the Cheka investigators, the following Jews are known: Bopk, Rosenfeld, Bykhovsky, Zeitlin, Bull, Delgaz, Rosenblum, Pergament.

Of the representatives abroad: the Jew Stepanov, Yanovich, Blumkin, Goldstein, Jelensky (Vedensky), Berezin, the Friedman brothers.

The local organs of the OGPU were almost exclusively led by Jews and had Jews in their ranks. The most famous leaders of the Cheka in the provinces are:

---

[195] Yakov Saulovich Agranov (Yankel Shmaevich Sorenzon), a native of Chechersk, our countryman. He was a prominent revolutionary, took an active part in the establishment of Soviet power in Gomel, and reached great heights in the state hierarchy of the prewar USSR. (Translator's note)

[196] Soviet security officer and head of the Gulag Soviet prison camp system from 1932 to 1937. (Translator's note)

[197] A solemn sacrifice of a hundred bulls in ancient Greece. (Translator's note)

- Goloshchekin, Yurovsky, Safarov—the organizers of the murder of the Tsarist Family;
- Béla Kun (Kon)—the "executioner of Crimea," another Kon—the "executioner of Kharkov;
- Lander—Cheka's commissioner in the North Caucasus; Tsupko—his successor;
- Katsnelson—commissioner in the Transcaucasus;
- Nakhimson—leading Chekist and military commissar in Yaroslavl;
- Weinberg—head of the Cheka in Saratov;
- Meiskel (Kedrov)—"the executioner of the north."

In the collection *On the Foreign Side* was printed a testimony of someone named Valer, from the materials of a special investigative commission in southern Russia. Valer speaks of the Kievan Cheka:

> During this period the staffing of the Cheka took place; and by nationality we can safely speak of the superiority of the Jews over all others. In view of the fact that the number of the Cheka staff ranged from one hundred and fifty to three hundred, it is impossible to give exact figures here. I am not mistaken when I say that the percentage of the Jews in the staff of the Cheka was 75 percent, and the commanding posts were almost exclusively in their hands.
> Most impressionable and shouty by nature, they created an atmosphere of unchallenged domination by their bustle around the Cheka premises. It is true that I still call this time period Jewish for two reasons: 1) the vast majority (seven out of ten) of the Commissioners were Jews; 2) there was not a single execution of a Jew during this period (with the exception of a Cheka worker Katz).
> This period is rich, but with a special tone in its work (the Union of the Russian people, compiling lists for the Red Terror) and a benign attitude toward Jewish affairs, according to most members of the Commission, who unknowingly, do not understand the revolution and its goals.

Valer also cites the personnel of the Kiev Extraordinary Commission:

- Chairman—Bluvshtein (Jew).
- Dechterenko Peter (Russian)—deputy chairman.
- Shub (Jew)—secretary of the commission.
- Tzvibak Samuel (Jew)—head of the legal department.
- Tzvibak Michael (Jew)—deputy head of the operational department (the head was Yakov Livshits, a Jew).

- Ferman-Mikhailov (Jew)—commandant.
- Katz (Jew)—head of the prison subsection.
- Kagan (Jew)—head of economic affairs.
- Ganiotsky (probably Jewish, although not that likely)—head of the general office.
- Finkelstein (Jew)—commander of a special detachment under the Cheka.
- Motya Grinshtein (Jew)—head of the speculation subdivision.
- Rabichev (probably a Jew)—accountant.
- Savchuk (Russian).
- Shvartsman (Jew)—deputy head of the secret department.
- Mankin (Jew)—deputy head of the legal department.
- Yakovlev (Russian)—Inspector of the secret department.
- Kovalev (Russian)—Inspector of the secret department.
- Loshkevich (not identified)—Inspector of the secret department.
- Rubinstein Naum (Jew)—secretary of the legal department.
- Manteifel (Jew)—member of the board of the legal department.

Valer gives a description of some of the Chekists:

> LUVSHTEIN (aka Sorin) . . . played the role of a great nobleman, knowing his high standing with the Bolsheviks. . . . His participation in the murder of the deposed Tsar Nicholas II and his family created a singular revolutionary aura, encouraging his junior officers to consolidate their revolutionary consciousness by using their own bullets at the Cheka victims, Sorin himself personally participated in shootings.
>
> TSIVAK Samuel, originally from Simferopol. A second-year law student. He is rude and mean. . . . Rude and abusive, took part in the shootings himself.
>
> TSIVAK Yakov . . . his sense of humor and maliciousness made him especially beloved among the Cheka employees. At the same time, this man, probably out of imitation, took part in the shootings of victims. . . .
>
> LIFSHITZ Yakova is a strong orator among working-class circles. Not being a member of the commission, he had a tremendous influence on the affairs of the Cheka. With unlimited cruelty. . . . He takes part in the shootings of Cheka's victims not as a rookie, but as a professional.

FAERMAN-Mikhailov, the commandant of the Cheka.... cruel, cowardly, insolent, self-confident, weak-minded, as a result, being abandoned by all, was shot by the Odessa Cheka (according to rumors), was for a long time the executioner of the victims of the Kiev Cheka.

SCHWARTZMAN Yakov, a member of the Commission.... a major political worker. Brutal. Personally shot, beat and tortured those arrested.

RUBINSTEIN.... diplomat, cunning, voluptuous, very kind in his own twisted way, cruel to the prisoners. Participating in shootings out of amusement, he relished on the agonies of his victims, one of whom he fired upon about thirty bullets in succession.

With the renaming of the Cheka into the GPU, and later the NKVD, the situation, if anything, changed in the direction of strengthening the Jewish position in this hellish apparatus of universal espionage, terror and provocation, which ensures obedience of the Russian people to its present Jewish overlords.

In 1934, for example, the lists of NKVD leaders included: The People's Commissar of Internal Affairs of the USSR and head of the GPU, Yagoda Henry Henryhovich (a Lithuanian Jew), and his deputy Agranov (Sorenson) Yakov Saulovich, also a Jew.

General Directorate of State Security:

- The head of the Special Department, Guy Miron Ilyich—Jewish.
- The head of the Economic Department, L. G. Mironov—Jewish.
- The head of the Perlustrative Department, Arkadiy Arkadievich Slutskiy—Jewish.
- The head of the Transport Department, Abram Moiseevich Shanin—Jewish.
- Head of the Operations Division Pauker Abram Moiseevich—Jewish.
- The head of the Special Division, Veniamin Isaevich Dobrodroditsky—Jewish.
- Head of the Anti-Religious Department Iofe Isay Lvovich—Jewish (former editor of the newspaper *Bezbozhnik*).
- The head of the Main Police Department, Yakov Naumovich Velsky—Jewish.
- Head of the Criminal Investigation Department of the NKVD Leonid Iosifovich Bull—Jewish
- Chief Directorate of Border and Internal Security:
- Chief Yakov Matveyevich Berman—Jewish.
- His deputy and manager of places of exile, Samuel Yakovlevich Firin—Jewish.

- Head of concentration camps in Soviet Karelia and at the same time head of the White Sea camp Kogan Samuel Leonidovich—Jewish.
- Katsnelson S. B., Deputy People's Commissar of Internal Affairs and head of the GPU in Ukraine—Jewish.
- The chief of concentration camps in the Northern Region, Finkelstein—Jewish.
- The chief of the NKVD Department, Pogrebinsky—Jewish.
- The chief of the NKVD of Western Siberia Sabo—a Hungarian Jew, a former employee of Béla Kun.
- The head of the NKVD of Kazakhstan Salin L. B.—Jewish.
- On Solovki, the head of SLON[198] Serpukhovsky—Jewish.
- The chief of the political detention center in Verkhneuralsk Mezner—Jewish.
- Alamson, head of the Moscow "Butyrka" detention center, a Latvian, one of the oldest executioners of the GPU.
- Heads of the NKVD departments:
- Moscow: Regens—Jewish.
- Leningrad: Zakovsky—Jewish.
- Western: Blatt—Jewish.
- Northern: Ritkovsky—Jewish.
- Azov-Black Sea: Frillberg—Jewish.
- Saratov: R. A. Pilyar—Jewish.
- Stalingrad: Rappoport—Jewish.
- Orenburg: Raysky—Jewish.
- Gorki: Abrampolsky—Jewish.
- North Caucasus: Fayvilovich—Jewish.
- Transcaucasia: Goglidze—Georgian.
- Sverdlovsk: Shklyar—Jewish.
- Bashkir: Zelikman—Jewish.
- East Siberian: Trotsky—Jewish.
- Far Eastern: Deribas—Jewish.
- Ukraine: Balitsky—Jewish.
- Central Asia: Krukowski—Jewish.
- Belarus: I. M. Deplyavsky—Jewish.[199]

In the Far East of the USSR, the leadership of the GPU and NKVD has always been represented by Jews, beginning with Deribas and ending with Hersh Lyushkov and Zapadny.

The Jews, represented by Moses Berman, were the inventors of concentration camps, in which ten million Russian people, exhausted

---

[198] Solovetsky Special Camp. (Translator's note)
[199] G. Fest, *Bolshevism and Jewry*, Riga, 1934.

by "blood sweat," had already given their souls to God under the burden of hard labor, and ten million more are waiting to get "blood sweat" in the same re-education. The concentration camps in the Far East were for a long time run by the Jew Martinelli under his aide Zapadny.

We came across a photograph of Comrade Zapadny. A disgusting, typically Jewish, monkey-like face, with barely any human in it. Huge, puckered, carnal lips. Black hair in wild disarray. A gorilla? No, a caricature of man, a typical subhuman. They still depict devils like that in paintings to scare children.

To see what a concentration camp is, see the stunning testimony of Igor Volkov, a recent refugee from Dalag, put into the form of the most tragic novel of our days: *The Sun is Coming Out in the East.*

101. Women! Beware of Jewish Sadism

It being characteristic of them, even where they have no overt power, using their financial power, the Jews set records of vile torture of the defenseless. Again we return to Weimar Germany, to see two examples of Jewish red sadism, this time by Jewish capital. These two examples became well known and went to trial in the end and the guilty were put in prison, even though they should have been mercilessly exterminated, crushed like vipers. Just how many such crimes must remain unknown to the general public, unpunished?

Der Stürmer tells us:

> The Jew Stöse, owner of two factories in Nuremberg, raped and mutilated hundreds of non-Jewish girls. He got them drunk, tied their hands and feet, mocked them, and stigmatized them by burning his name on their bodies with the red-hot end of a wire. The now unmasked Stöse was sentenced in 1926 to many years in prison.
>
> In Nuremberg, the Jew Otto Meyer also got his victims drunk, tied them to wooden crosses, cut into their chests, hands, and feet, and eventually raped them. In 1927 he was sentenced to prison.
>
> This was in Nuremberg, the ancient center of German culture. What were and are Jews doing where there are not hundreds of eyes watching them, where might they be gentlemen!?

Here are the customs of the Kholmogorsk concentration camp, according to Melgunov:

Cooks, laundresses, and servants are taken to the administration from among the prisoners, often choosing intelligent women. Under the pretext of cleaning apartments, the assistant commandants (Skren, for example) invite the girls they are attracted to, even at night time. Both the commandant and the assistants have mistresses from among the prisoners. To refuse to do any work or to disobey the administration is an inadmissible act: the prisoners are so frightened that they are meekly willing to endure all sorts of abuse and insults. There have been cases of protest: one such female protester who dared to openly express her indignation, was executed (under Bachulis). Once they came to make demands to an intelligent student girl from the assistant's commandant at three o'clock in the morning: she abruptly refused to go. What happened? Her fellow students began to beg her not to refuse, otherwise both she and them would end up badly.

In the Special Department of the Kuzbass Cheka, "when women are taken to the bathhouse, the punishment is set not only in the changing room, but also in the bathhouse itself." Remember the teacher Dombrovskaya, who was raped before being shot. Their executioners crowded around the women, throwing a tantrum. Drunken laughter, foul language, dirty jokes, unbuttoning of dresses and searches. "Don't touch them," said the head of the prison, not a Chekist, but a simple prison clerk, in a trembling voice. "I know well that you can't entrust them with a woman before being shot." These are their descriptions of the night of shootings in Saratov on November 17th, 1919.

We read about the rape of two socialist women in Astrakhan in *Revolutionary Russia* (No. 10). That's the way it is everywhere.

Recently, in the *Anarchist Herald* (No. 3–4), one of the exiled anarchists told about a Vologda transit prison:

Upon leaving, the warden warned us to be on our guard: at night, the warden or the manager himself might come to us with clear intentions. That was the custom. Almost all the women who come here are used for that purpose. At the same time, almost all employees are ill and infect the women.... The warning was not in vain.

"You are very interesting, your husband is not worthy of you," the investigator Chekist said to Mrs. G., and at the same time added quite calmly: "I shall have you released, but I will have your husband shot as a counter-revolutionary. I will however release him, if you, when released, become acquainted with me." Agitated, close to insanity, G. told her cellmates about the nature of the interrogation, and was advised to save her husband by all means. She was soon released from the Cheka. An investigator visited her apartment several times, but her husband was still shot after all.

The Chekist offered to release Officer M., who was serving in the Special Section, on the condition that she would live with him. M. agreed and was released, and the Chekist moved into her house.

"I hate him," M. told her acquaintance Mrs. T., "but what can you do when you have no husband and three small children to take care of.... But I am calm now: I am not afraid of searches, I do not worry that at any minute they will break in and drag me to the Cheka."

102. The Picture of Jewish Terror in Russia

We have named the organizers and leaders of the extermination of the Russian people in the USSR, the Jews. Now let us unfold the canvas of this Jewish terror.

Here is our bloody account of Jewry, from Russia and the entire world:

> According to the estimates of a commission established by General Denikin, a commission composed of experienced judicial authorities with representatives from England and France, by the beginning of 1919 the number of victims of the Communist terror had reached a horrifying figure of 1,700,000 people. But this figure refers only to the South of Russia, and if you add to this the murdered and tortured by the Communists elsewhere, in Siberia, in the Urals, etc., you get the terrible hecatomb of millions of victims who died for Russia.[200]

Averbukh, in his appalling book published in Kishinev in 1920, *The Odessa Extraordinary Commission*, counts 2,200 victims of the Red Terror in Odessa over the course of three months in 1919 (the Red Terror was declared by the Bolsheviks in July 1919, when the pre-volunteer troops occupied Kharkov, testifies Melyunov).

The official organ *Odessa News* wrote in those days of terror: "The Red Terror has been set in motion. And it will go wild in the bourgeois quarters, the bourgeoisie will crack, the counterrevolution will hiss under the bloody blow of the Red Terror.... We will drive them out with hard iron, and in the bloodiest way we will massacre them." And indeed, this "merciless carnage," officially declared by the executive

---

[200] *Russian Time* from October 5th, 1941, Shankha

committee, was accompanied by the publication of a number of lists of all the people shot, often without any proof of guilt: shot on the basis of the announcement of the Red Terror.

A lot of facts are given in the book *The Fiery Years* by Margulies.

In March 1919, there was a labor strike in Astrakhan. Witnesses testify that this strike was drenched in the blood of the workers.

The tens of thousands of workers peacefully discussing their plight were surrounded by machine gunners, sailors, and grenadiers. After the workers refused to disperse, rifles were fired. Machine guns roared, aimed at the dense mass of the rally participants, and hand grenades began to explode with a last deafening roar. The rally trembled, crouched down, and fell silent. No one could hear the groans of the wounded or the death cries of those killed behind the machine gun crackle.

The city was deserted, silent: some fled, others hid. At least two thousand victims were snatched from the ranks of the workers. This ended the first part of the terrible Astrakhan tragedy.

The second one, even more terrible, began on March 12th. Some of the workers were taken captive by the "victors" and placed in six commandant's houses, barracks, and steamboats. Among the latter, the steamer *Gogol* stood out for its horrors. Telegrams about the "uprising" were sent flying to Central.

The chairman of the Revolutionary Military Council of the Republic, Leon Trotsky, responded with a laconic telegram: "deal with them without mercy." Thus the fate of the unfortunate captive workers was decided. Bloody madness reigned over the land and waters.

Shootings were carried out in the basements of emergency commandants' offices, and in courtyards. From steamships and barges they were thrown directly into the Volga.

Some of the unfortunates had a stone tied around their necks. Some had their hands and feet tied and were thrown overboard. One of the workers, who survived unnoticed somewhere in the hold near the machine, said that in one night about one hundred and eighty people were thrown off the steamer *Gogol*. There were so many people shot in the city's emergency commandant's offices that they could barely manage to take them to the cemetery at night, where they were dumped in piles as "typhoid patients."

The special commandant Chugunov issued an order that prohibited the carving up of corpses on the way to the cemetery under threat of being shot. Almost every morning people of Astrakhan woke up to find half-dressed executed workers soaked in blood. And from corpse to corpse in the light of dawn the living searched for their dear departed ones. On March 13th and 14th, only workers were being executed. But then the powers that be must have come to their senses. After all, one could not even blame the shootings on the rebellious "bourgeoisie." The authorities decided that it was better late than never. In order to cover up the bluntness of the massacre of the Astrakhan proletariat, they decided to take the first "bourgeois" they could get their hands on and massacre them according to a very simple scheme: every landlord, fish-merchant, small trade owner, and proprietor was to be shot.

By March 15th it was hardly possible to find a single household, where a father, brother, or husband was not mourned. In some houses several people had disappeared.

The exact number of those shot could have been established by questioning all of Astrakhan's residents en masse. At first the number was put at two thousand. Then three thousand. Then the authorities began to publish by the hundreds the lists of the executed "bourgeoisie." At the beginning of April they mentioned the figure of four thousand victims, but the repressions continued. Apparently, the government decided to take revenge on the Astrakhan workers for all their strikes: the Tula, Bryansk, and Petrograd strikes, which in March 1919 had hit like a wave. Only by the end of April did the shootings begin to subside.

A terrible picture of Astrakhan was presented at that time. The streets were deserted. Rivers of tears ran from the houses. Fences, storefronts, and windows of government offices were covered with orders, orders, and more orders.

Let us take Turkestan, separate from the center, where in January 1919 there was an uprising of the Russian part of the population against the despotic regime established by the Bolsheviks. The uprising was suppressed. "Mass searches began," say eyewitnesses. All the barracks and railway workshops were overflowing with those arrested. On the night of January 20th to 21st, mass shootings were carried out. Piles of bodies were piled on the railroad tracks. During this terrible night over 2,500 people were killed.... On January 23rd a court-martial was organized, in charge of which the case of January Uprising was placed and which continued the arrests and executions during the whole year of 1919. Why didn't Latsis count these victims in his official statistics?[201] After all, in the early days at least the Chekists were at work here. At any rate, the "court martial" still was the very same Cheka, even in its composition.

Among the gruesome inscriptions on the walls of the Special Department of the Cheka in Moscow, which were sometimes made by death row inmates before their execution, one can find the following: "The night of abolition became a night of blood." Each amnesty for a prison meant a mass execution. The representatives of the Cheka wanted to finish off their victims as soon as possible. And it happened

---

[201] Russian revolutionary and Bolshevik, one of the most famous Chekists of the Civil War period. (Translator's note)

that in the very night when the announcement of the amnesty was being typed in the printers and was to appear the next day in the newspaper, mass shootings were carried out in the prisons. This should be remembered by those who point to the frequent publication of acts of amnesty by the Soviet authorities.

The Bolsheviks in Ekaterinodar; the prisons are overcrowded and most of the arrested are shot. A Ekaterinodar resident states that from August 1920 to February 1921 about three thousand people were shot in the Ekaterinodar prison alone.

The highest percentage of executions fell in the month of August, when the Wrangel landing force on Kubanya landed. At this point the chairman of the Cheka gave the order: "Execute everyone in the Cheka cells." Kosolapov, one of the Cheka officers, objected that there were many people in custody who had not been questioned properly for having broken the compulsory order forbidding them to go out into the city after eight o'clock in the evening, to which the former replied: "Take these ones away and let everyone else go to waste."

The order was carried out with utmost precision. A citizen called Rakitiansky, who survived the shooting, gives as a picture of the execution:

> Those arrested were taken out of the cells by the dozens. When they took the first ten and told us they were being taken for interrogation, we were calm. But when the second dozen were brought out, we realized they were taking them for execution. They were killed the way cattle is butchered in slaughterhouses.[202]

Since the preparation for the evacuation of Cheka's affairs was packed, Rakitiansky managed to escape. Those summoned to the slaughter were asked what they were being accused of, and in view of the fact that those detained by chance for showing up in the street of Ekaterinodar after the fixed eight o'clock in the evening were separated from the rest, Rakitiansky, being charged as an officer, declared himself also to be detained by chance late in the street and survived. The shooting was done almost exclusively by Chekists, with the chairman of the Emergency Committee at the head. In prison, Atarbekov

---

[202] There are some who claim that the word "cheka" is not only an abbreviation of "extraordinary committee"—*chrezvychaynaya komissiya*—in Russian, but that it also has its origins in Hebrew; meaning "slaughterhouse for cattle," this is in conformity with the Talmud, which considers every non-Jew as an animal and demands killing him. See N. D. Zhevakhov, *Memories*. Moscow, 1993. (Translator's note)

himself conducted the shootings.[203] The shootings lasted for a whole day, causing terror in the vicinity of the prison. All in all, about two thousand people were shot on that day.

Who was shot and why remains a mystery. It is unlikely that the Chekists themselves will give an account of this, because execution, like sadism, was such a common thing for them that it was carried out without any special formalities.

And so the shootings continued. On October 30th, 84 were shot. In November, 1,000. On December 22nd, 184. In January, 210. On February 5th, 94. There are documents confirming these numbers. The Ekaterinodar Extraordinary Commission tried to destroy them before review. "We found packs of verdicts which clearly said 'shoot' in odd places," testifies the same eyewitness. Yes, the Cheka itself often destroyed materials that could serve as evidence in its indictments: this was the case, for example, during the seizure of Tambov by Antonov's peasant rebels.

Here is another picture of the life in Ekaterinodar from the same period:

> From August 17th to August 20th in Ekaterinodar, ordinary life was disrupted by the approach to the city of the Wrangel landing force near the stanitsa Primorsko–Akhtarskaya. During the panic, on the orders of Artabekov, all the arrested, numbering more than sixteen hundred people, as well as those arrested by the Gubchek special section and those imprisoned, were shot. From the Gubchek and the special department the doomed to be shot were brought in groups of one hundred people across the bridge to Kuban and there they were fired upon with machine guns; in the prison they did the same thing against the wall. This was also published. A list of those killed was printed under the heading *Revenge*, only the lists are somewhat shorter than they actually are. While fleeing in disarray, the invaders announced to the workers their duty to evacuate with them, or else they threatened to hang all those who remained on telegraph posts.

Something similar happened during the evacuation of Ekaterinoslav when the danger threatened from Wrangel.

> For months there was carnage. The deadly banging of the machine gun was heard every night until morning. The first night

---

[203] Georgiy Aleksandrovich Atarbekov, member of the struggle for Soviet power in the North Caucasus, of Armenian origin; one of the leaders of the state security agencies and notorious for his cruelty and violence. (Translator's note)

of shootings in the Crimea resulted in thousands of victims: in Simferopol, 1,800 people, in Feodosia, 420, in Kerch, 1,300, etc.

They threw those executed in old Genoese wells. When they were filled up, during the day they took out a batch of prisoners, allegedly for sending them to mines, made them dig common graves in the light of day, locked them in the shed for two hours, then stripped them down to the bone and shot them when darkness fell.

They were stacked in rows. After a minute, a new row was placed on those who had been shot, and so it went on until the pit was filled to the brim. In the morning some of them were finished off by crushing their heads with stones.

How many half-dead were buried. . . .

In Kerch, they organized a "landing force on the Kuban," took them to the sea, and drowned them.

Distraught wives and mothers were chased with rifles and sometimes simply executed. Behind the Jewish cemetery in Simferopol you could see the bodies of women with their infants.

In Yalta and Sevastopol, they were carried out on stretchers from the infirmary and executed. And not just officers: soldiers, doctors, nurses, teachers, engineers, priests, peasants, etc.

When the first supplies of doomed men began to come to an end, the replenishment from the villages began, although there the massacres often took place on the spot. Roundups were organized in the cities. In Simferopol, for example, 12,000 people were detained as a result of a raid on December 19th.

When the fever passed, they began to catch on to questionnaires. They had to be written by the dozens a month, not only by employees, but by the entire population from the age of sixteen. Sometimes the questionnaires consisted of forty or fifty questions. Every year of your life was covered with the most detailed questions. Attention was drawn to the origin of not only the interrogated, but his father, grandfather, children, and aunts. Their attitude to the Red Terror, to the allies, to Poland, to peace with Poland, whether you sympathize with Wrangel, why you didn't leave with him, etc., everything had to be answered.

After two weeks, everyone was obliged to go to the Cheka, where he was again interrogated by investigators, who tried to put him off by casual and meaningless questions. Everyone vouched for the accuracy of the information with their heads. Beyond the Crimea there was Siberia. And behind Siberia there was Georgia. And again, the same picture. There were executions that can't do anything else but to revolt the moral feeling: for example, the execution of twenty-seven gymnasium students in Oryol. We may also add they were children (five persons). In Odessa, after the liquidation of the All-Russian Committee of the Hunger Relief Organization, twelve people involved in this organization were shot (reports *Rulja*).[204]

War communism, you say? Here are the thirties:

The life of seventy thousand Russian villages turned to hell all at once. The fanatical rancor of the little Soviet administrators, the rancor of the local Communists, all these things seemed to have broken off the chain and descended upon the peasantry. The random persecutions to which the peasantry had previously been subjected were now turned into a system; they were legitimized and sanctioned from above. It was (1929–1933) the reign of Red Terror, which established local GPU departments at seventy thousand points all over the country; the local GPU had at its disposal special troops of the GPU and the Red Army. Although no one knew exactly who a kulak was, there never was a shortage of them—they were found everywhere and in great numbers. A population equal to that of Switzerland or Denmark was stripped of all their property, including land, houses, stock and weapons, and even clothes, food-stuffs, and household items, and driven out of the countryside. They were bayoneted like cattle and herded to railway stations, indiscriminately loaded into calf and freight wagons, and then driven for weeks by trains to the northern forest regions, to the steppes of Central Asia. Everywhere where there was a need for free labor.

No one has ever made even a rough estimate of the victims of collectivization, and is it even possible to calculate human suffering by arithmetic? Their sum is beyond the reach of any calculation. The forced collectivization took place in a climate of chaos and confusion. Hundreds of thousands of peasants died in the process of collectivization, people died on the paths, in the deep forests, in the deserts.

Trains carrying loads of agonizing peasants of different nationalities were pulled in different directions under armed guards, human remains were thrown out of wagons, and empty ones returned for a new load.

Thousands of feral, panic-stricken peasants fled in droves to the cities, where they were once again driven behind hedges,

---

[204] Melgunov, *Red Terror in Russia*.

stuffed into broken, filthy wagons, and driven back to the camps. Once again (as during the Communist war years), there were neglected children, boys and girls, often very small children. These were the children of dead, dispossessed peasants, but there were some among the street children whose parents had abandoned them to the mercy of fate, preferring blind chance to the sure death that awaited them in exile.

So testifies a Parisian democratic journal.[205]

103. Figures of the Jewish War with Russia

The figures of the Red Terror in Russia and in the world have not been published anywhere. But even in its pre-revolutionary phase, when this terror was unlawful against the Russian people, it reached large numbers. Purishkevich puts it at 20,000 people. V. V. Shulgin reminds us of this estimate as follows:

> Vladimir Mitrofanovich Purishkevich, a member of the State Duma from the Bessarabian province, who by an evil irony of fate himself later embarking on a peculiar path of terror (the murder of Rasputin), during the first revolution (1905–1907) especially resented the bloody work of the terrorist revolutionaries. These feelings he hastened to transfer to the plane of some real work, which was generally peculiar to his nature. He began to collect the names of the dead, the circumstances under which the acts of terror took place, biographical information, and photographs. To this work Purishkevich involved a number of people. As a result, he published a whole small library in several volumes under the title *The Book of Russian Mourning*. Vasnetsov, Solomko, and other Russian artists made the title pages for these editions. It was a good deed—a debt of respect and gratitude on the part of the survivors to the dead. To our shame, we, the survivors of the Second Revolution, have not yet gathered ourselves to do the same work for the countless victims of the latter, and we pretend that we do not understand a simple truth: if we are alive, it is because they, the dead, made an atoning sacrifice for us.
>
> Purishkevich is far from completing his work. Current politics took too much of his energy and work. But, of course, he tried to establish the total number of victims of the terrorists of the first revolution. Once, during one of his speeches in the

---

[205] *New Russia*, 1932, Paris.

State Duma, referring to the revolutionary terror, Purishkevich, with the help of Duma bailiffs, unfolded a black ribbon, on which the photographs of those killed were stuck closely, one to another: the ribbon was enough for almost the entire width of the hall. At the same time Purishkevich made a statement that, according to his calculations, the number of wounded, maimed, and killed by the terrorists of the "Liberation Movement" is estimated at 20,000 people.[206]

Several times I have tried to summarize the numbers of Communist terror in the USSR. It is difficult to guarantee the accuracy of these calculations, but we can vouch for their approximate accuracy based on simple reasoning: had it not been for the revolution, continuing the rate of growth of the Russian population, by 1937 one would have found 228 million inhabitants in the USSR. Meanwhile, the All-Union census of that year gave a figure of 140 million inhabitants.

True, the Bolsheviks came to their senses and declared the results of the census malicious, and without publishing the results, conducted another census which in 1939 gave a figure of 180 million Russian people. But even if we accept this undoubtedly exaggerated figure, we have to ask: where are the missing 48 million? They do not exist, for they died in the whirlwind of the revolution, in the depths of "socialist construction"—building on the bones of the Russian people, they were not born in part because of the general decline of living conditions, which caused a decline in childbearing. 48 million Russian people—the costs of the Jewish revolution—is a first account presented to world Jewry on behalf of our Russian nation, the first account for the period from 1917 to 1940, to be followed by another account for the subsequent terrible years, for the terrible war provoked by world Jewry.

Consider the components of this astronomical number, this hecatomb of corpses, piled up on Russian soil as a kind of Tower of Babel, through which the murderers of our country are trying to reach the inaccessible sky.

During the years of war communism, during the first waves of the Red Terror, about 2 million people were murdered, tortured and shot in the cellars of the Cheka, the author of this book has calculated in his essays *The Jews and Russia*.

During the years of Stalin's "socialist construction" 3 million people were killed in the NKVD torture chambers and simply "disappeared" somewhere.

A refugee from the Amur region tells us that in early 1938, when the invaders in Russia were terrified of a pan-Russian armed uprising

---

[206] V. V. Shulgin, *What We Don't Like About Them*.

on May 1st, a great many leaders of Soviet and Communist Party institutions, industry, transport, and the Red Army were arrested. In his opinion, and in the opinion of many, a quarter of the entire population of the Soviet Union was imprisoned. This opinion is of course exaggerated because of the frightening impression produced by these arrests, but if we take even one twentieth of that, we get a figure of 8 million people.

The fourth wave of Judeo-Communist terror is crashing down on the Russian people before our eyes. From the very first days of the war, the Soviet government is introducing draconian laws, which cannot be found in any other country.

Not only the NKVD, but also individual security officers were given the right to shoot on sight on the first suspicion—that is, to kill anyone they did not like. The Jewish masters of our motherland are seeing fascist agents, spies, and saboteurs everywhere.

Let us take an approximate figure of 10 million people. These are the last victims of the Red Terror, killed "on suspicion" since the beginning of the German–Soviet war.

23 million Russian lives—the approximate total of the Jewish war with Russia in the twenty-five years of rule over our country by the Jewish Comintern. Add to this 10 million Russian people who died in concentration camps, over 10 million deaths from recurrent famine (in 1918–1921, in 1932–1933, in 1942–1943), 5 million victims due to "total collectivization" policies—and the damage caused to our country by those who today shout about its "defense" becomes clear. No outside war, no outside conquest, no natural disaster can cause such devastation to a living nation as a quarter century of Jewish rule.

104. The Destruction of a National-Strong-Willed Elite

On the tragic example of our homeland, we clearly see the basic aspiration of world Jewry towards any non-Jewish national-strong-willed elite.

Before the seizure of power, this destruction is carried out mainly by cultural means. When power is seized, the masks are off; the national minds are scorched with red-hot iron.

It is "the people" that Judas fools with "equality." He himself knows very well that there is no equality, that there is smart and stupid, good and bad, strong and weak, and it is against the smart, good, and strong in every nation that his sizzling expansion is directed towards, when he can carry out such an expansion.

Modern biology and sociology have proved with exhaustive clarity that the existence of any nation depends on its elite, the selection of an enterprising minority, developed over the centuries. This elite is inspired by the will to power, the will to serve, the will to create, and is a constantly renewing selection of the population. After seeing the pictures of the Red Terror in Russia, it is easy to summarize: how are the Jews destroying the national-willed elite? The example of Russia cries out to heaven and serves as a formidable warning to every nation.

Against whom was the terror of war communism directed? Against the former ruling stratum, against the "elite" of the Russian nation during the old imperial Russia. They killed the clergy, the nobility, officers, the bourgeoisie, intellectuals, crowning it all with the murder of the Tsar and his entire royal family.

Here, for example, in 1921, S. P. Melyunov recalls:

In the fall in Petrograd sixty-one people were shot in the case of the Tagantsev "conspiracy." What were these men shot for? Two examples will give a clear account. Among others, Professor N. N. Lazarevsky, a lawyer by profession, was shot. The official publication (Sept. 1st) of his guilt says: "By convictions: a supporter of the democratic system, by the time of the overthrow of Soviet power had prepared projects on a number of issues, such as: a) the forms of local government in Russia; b) the fate of various kinds of paper money (Russian); c) the form of restoration of credit in Russia."

Or Prince S. A. Ukhtomsky, a sculptor, who delivered information about the museum business and a report on the same issue to be printed in the White press for transfer to an organization abroad. At the same time the poet Gumilev, Kniazkovsky, and others were shot. "Kill the best of the goyim," the Talmud prescribes. "Do not look in materials you have gathered for evidence that a suspect acted or spoke against the Soviet authorities," the *Red Terror* publishes on November 1st, 1918. The first question you should ask him is what class he belongs to, what is his origin, education, profession. These questions should determine his fate. This is the essence of the Red Terror."

The Russian Emperor and his family were killed by the Red Army under the command of the Jew Yankel Yurovsky. The order for the murder of the Tsar was given by the Jewish commissar Shaya Goloschekin. From Moscow, the crime was supervised by the chairman of the All-Russian Central Executive Committee, the Jew Yankel Sverdlov. In honor of Sverdlov, the Judeo-Bolsheviks renamed Yekaterinburg Sverdlovsk.

During the NEP new strong elements of the Russian country emerged, mainly from the peasantry. The sickle of collectivization cut off primarily them.

The three million Russian people who died during the years of "socialist construction," the eight million lives which the Judeo-Bolsheviks took from Russia in reaction to the Fascist three-year plans, and the ten million who live today; this is also an elite, the new elite of the New Russia, which, despite all the Judeo-Soviet barriers, have grown in a country ravaged by the Red Devil in these hard years. They are the flower of the Russian nation, the possible builders of tomorrow's Russia.

Among the few names of the dead which have come down to us, most are Russian names. Four times the Jewish invaders of Russia are scorching Russian minds.

Remember the bloody Esther and the extermination of the Persian intelligentsia. Stalin also has a Jewish wife, Rosa Kaganovich. Let us remember the fate of Persia after the pogrom of the intelligentsia destroyed by the Jewish "holy" heroine. Ancient Persia ceased to exist, while the Jews received Purim for all time. Let us remember, finally, the Masonic map to which we have already referred, where the area of Russia is marked as "Russian Desert." "Remember the fate of the persecutors of the Jews," a certain "Englishman" Easterman addresses in an article entitled "To Hitler, Goebbels, and Co."

> One last word: Remember the fate of the persecutors of the Jews; in ancient Persia, Babylonia, Rome, Spain, Tsarist Russia; they were turned to ashes, and remembered with contempt. The Jew, the eternal Jew outlived them all, and so we will outlive you.

Let these wicked words of the insolent English Jew with the cautionary *memento mori* burn before all of us who do not want to go into captivity to Judas. Those who want to save our nations from destruction, ourselves and our people from enslavement.

But how pathetic and childish seem the so-called "Jewish pogroms" of antiquity, of the Middle Ages and today, and especially the notorious Russian pogroms, in comparison with the Purim and other pogroms of the Jews against the "goyim"! Such pogroms as the Jewish ones are truly unheard of. It is only natural, for they are the Children of the Devil, and they want to fulfill the desires of their father, as Christ said. What Purim will the Jews establish in the future to commemorate the October Revolution that they and their faithful stooges accomplished and failed?

105. The Jewish Poisoning of Nations with Debauchery

The destruction of the national-willed elite is only the first stage on the road to the destruction of the nation and the enslavement of peoples by world Jewry. The second stage can be regarded as the propagation of debauchery, which, as the same historical experience and the experience of our days show, is one of the special tools of world Jewry in the struggle against persistent social organisms, for their decay, dissolution and enslavement.

Again, we will have to turn to the cautionary sad examples of our Motherland, for all that is done in the USSR can be attributed to world Jewry, which there commands and owns not just the economy, not just the culture, not just the state, but the body and soul of every living, enslaved Russian man.

Nash Put', based on research by Soviet authors (by a strange irony of fate, in addition, Jewish), published in 1933:

> Prostitution is terrible everywhere. But nowhere has it acquired such a disgusting form as in the USSR. There it is filthy and pitiful, naked, not even covered in the pathetic rags of poverty.
>
> Soviet hypocrites love to talk about women's organizations, about social patronage—where homeless women, the unemployed, and lonely, abandoned wives, abandoned mothers, and deceived girls can find support, shelter, food, protection, knowledge, and service. In reality, this is not the case. Here is a house on Mokhovaya Street, reserved for girls who came out of orphanages. There's a bedroom, a canteen, and even a "red corner," probably a Komsomol cell.[207] But inside it's filthy, drunkenness is rife, men come here as if it were a brothel, and the girls themselves behave like professional mistresses of love. Here everyone complains of the unbearable boredom. The house is uncomfortable, cold, with nothing to do, and the "red corner" has long been turned into a dating place.
>
> One can understand hunger, boredom, female abandonment as a consequence of prostitution. But the entirely unexpected cause of a woman's downfall is ... marriage. It seems that all over the world this happens only in the USSR. Everywhere, the family shelter and the husband become a woman's support, and only from there do they inevitably prove

---

[207] Red Corner (center of culture)—in the USSR and some post-Soviet countries, a space, part of a room or a special structure (stand), in any enterprise or institution, reserved for the needs of agitation and political education. (Translator's note),

to be detrimental. Statistics show unbelievable numbers. Divorce is on the rise every year.

In 1926 in St. Petersburg twenty-one thousand marriages were registered, and at the same time the number of divorces was five and a half thousand. But in the next year, 1927, there were sixteen thousand divorces for twenty-four thousand marriages. The civil registries found that there were marriages concluded after just one or two days, and in one Moskovsko-Narvsky district there were forty-eight such marriages, in just two days. It is not difficult to find the reason for the increase in the number of divorces. In 1927 an amendment to the marriage code was published, which simplified the procedure. Previously the consent of both parties was required, now the application of one of the spouses is enough to consider the marriage dissolved. A Soviet citizen who went to work as a husband could return as a bachelor by nightfall.

The percentage of divorces to marriages is increasing at a monstrous rate. In 1928, 8,584 marriages were concluded in Leningrad, while during the same period 5,548 couples broke up, i.e., more than half of the families were separated. There were more surprising figures: in one district there were 418 divorces per 547 marriages.

In the end, statistics showed that the average Soviet marriage did not last more than three months. Registration officials even developed a special terminology. There is the "Red Army marriage," which lasts for the period of military service, then there are the "one-day club marriages" that last between two club nights. Of course, all the benefits of the marriage code go to the man, while all the suffering, deprivation, and risk fall onto the woman. Family life is ruined, hunger is at the doorstep, and there is only one way out: the streets. It's not just the wives of yesterday, but it is also the children that are left out in the streets.

Soviet prostitution devours ten-year-old girls. In this bitter fate of women, a special role is often played by the bed. The bed itself becomes a death sentence. From the age of puberty, girls are deprived of their own bed. They have to sleep with whomever they have to, with anyone who will let them lie down: parents, sisters, brothers, strangers, corner owners, temporary lodgers, anyone who owns a bed. Often the girl never knew who it was that first possessed her while she slept. These subpoenas became commonplace and all too familiar there, acquiring the status of an everyday phenomenon.

Prostitution is the inevitable outcome and end of a woman's youth. Neither service nor work saves the day. And then the man demands "payment in kind." In the factory you have to put up with a foreman, in the institution the boss, in life an influential man. You have to choose between surrendering or suicide. So it happened with an actress of the Moscow theater, a young and beautiful woman. Later, two women threw themselves down from the upper floors of a Moscow theater. The exploitation of women is even more evident in the film industry and studios. These are harems. L. Frindlant calls them "a collection of pashas, larger and greater." A supernumerary assistant cameramen and junior assistants of the most mediocre directors lead dozens of young female glory-seekers into their bedrooms.

Mesmerized by the light of Jupiter, the ladies, practically girls, easily jumped into the arms of pimple-faced boys, who were seen clapping on the tripod of the film set, without struggling. It is the same at the different *Posredrabisah*—intermediary acting bureaus. If they take bribes from the men there, then they'll also demand affection from the actresses.

It is even easier at public employment services. You can only get a place through the supervisors of the allocation and registration of the labor force. In order to get a job operating a machine, or at the counter, or at the cafeteria, one has to meekly submit to every demand, to make the most shameful of concessions.

Not long ago the same phenomenon was discovered in the Supreme Court. The petitioners seeking justice inevitably became the secretary's concubines. Other powerholders, including officials of the regional criminal investigation department, did not lag behind the judges. All the time the Soviet public, Bolshevik leaders, and Communist scribes have been chanting the same thing: prostitution is the grim legacy of a fallen regime, the product of bourgeois conditions. Hence the conclusion: prostitutes come from oppressed female workers. But nowhere else are there so many "machine workers" turned into street girls as in the country of the workers and peasants.

The "girls of intellectual labor" also perish, forever cast off into the road. They are thrown out onto this road by necessity, and are corrupted and stupefied by the preaching of the ideology of free love.

"Need a boyfriend? Get one, satisfy yourself. But without any tricks. Look at things soberly," says Gumilevsky's hero.

"The hunt came, and so I gave in. Why bother with all that crap? It is such a simple matter," we read in Brazhnin's *The Jump*.

Indeed, prostitution and venereal disease are more widespread than anywhere else. Forty thousand people were infected in two years in Leningrad alone.

Dr. Rothstein became interested in the sex life of the workers. He collected a wealth of material. Here is his conclusion: with regards to the sexes everywhere in the USSR, only chance rules. Only a third of those surveyed had a single relationship during the year. All the rest had lived with many women at a time, and at least 84 percent had been in a relationship with more than four women.

This is referring to the mature and adult. It's no better among the young.

Everything is casual among students as well: 84 percent of male students are limited to casual hookups. It's the same among the "working youth."

There are almost no supporters of marriage and lasting intimacy—86 percent prefer lightning-fast intercourse. Sexual activity begins before the age of fourteen, when the boys are almost children.

Everything has become simpler, more cynical and accessible. Marriages have become six or nine years younger and more unstable.

Some used to marry at the age of thirty; now they marry easily and without hesitation at eighteen or twenty-two.

Everything in this life is gray, confusing, and fearful. It's wild to read about a Soviet Don Juan who cheated, but didn't break off his relationship with his mistress. Suddenly she filed a complaint against this husband, accusing him of infecting her with a bad disease. She was not lying.

It turns out that he got the disease from his own young wife. It happens before our very eyes—Mr. Seducer, who upon firing her from the factory and then later meeting her at the brothel, saw a prominent official, who was taken in by his buddy to a prostitute named Lucille. This Lucille turns out to be his own wife; dirty and unwashed girls, street women, fancying themselves in the city latrines; filthy bodies, lingerie, and showers; a miserable everyday life; venal love, unadorned even by crappy paint—it stings. And here the hard life has twisted the sores, appearing in its viperous abomination.[208]

This is what the Jews have done to Russia. The debauchery inspired by them in the Soviet Union has become so widespread that even the Soviet authorities were concerned "for the sake of appearances." After

---

[208] *Nash Put'*, No. 64, December 7th, 1933.

1934 some ostensible propaganda and legislative measures against debauchery began. However, in 1936 the Soviet authorities were forced to publish such facts:

A. V. Ivanov, a young engineer at a Moscow electrical plant, had chosen as his first wife a girl whom we shall call conventionally Tanya. When they met, Tanya was sixteen years old and she was still in school. A year later they had a child, and one year later they separated.

When Ivanov was asked about the reason for the divorce, he said: "What else can I do? I do not care about her blood anymore."

They separated, and Ivanov married immediately to Nina, a worker at the electric plant. But again, a year later, another child, and a divorce.

This time the wording is different: he cares about the shared blood, but she is a bad housewife, everything is always overcooked, she is incapable of saving money, and for the salary he gets, she doesn't suit him as a wife. She's just no good. This is a wife on a discount, he needs one that would be within his standards.

A. V. Ivanov immediately enters into marriage for the third time; his wife happens to be Tasha, a copyist from the same electrical plant. But the pace grows, and the relationship lasts only a year and two months. Then, in Ivanov's own words, it turns out that it was only an impulse.

"Love is free," he says upon sending his goodbyes to his wife, "love is like a bird. It has to flutter."

Having fluttered out, he marries immediately for the fourth time. Lida, a teacher and, by Ivanov's textual definition, a "woman of the world," is chosen as his new wife. But the ties of marriage turn out to be tenuous with the "woman of the world." One year after, an abortion, and again she just is "no good."

Why? First, it turns out that she is "thin as a heron"; second, she does a lot of laundry and has ruined her hands; and third, she is too much of an ordinary woman.

He's looking, you see, for the embodiment of his ideals, he longs for spiritual heights, but then all mundane earthly creatures come across.

Once again, a divorce followed, and a fifth marriage is concluded, which is still in the process of registration, but whose outcome, in view of the previous four, is of course not difficult to predict. Moreover, the man has acquired a taste for and sufficiently mastered the technique of the matter, and in case of public or judicial misunderstandings a simple formula of justification is already ready:

"These are just dates, not marriages."

That, at least, is how he put it when talking to the author of these words. Who can possibly be responsible for random encounters?

Thus, in a few years, five wives and two abandoned children.

I think that this seeker of the ideal does not need any comments: too distinct are the traits of a petty and nasty scumbag, seen right through the simple mask of a troubadour of "free love."

However, it would not be quite right to approach the matter from only one perspective. Responsibility in the matter of marriage and the family must be borne not only by the man, but by the woman as well. Ivanov, of course, is a vulgar, cynical, scurrilous, and empty man.

But the girls, the wives, endlessly succeeding each other in his kaleidoscope of marriages, what are they? All of them seem to have been deceived and lured in by him as victims.

They all were blind, and not one saw his true nature. All were abandoned, as the old melodramas would qualify, with broken hearts.

Or could it be that when they got married, they took this step, which should be full of serious and profound meaning and significance, and if not, then, in any case, maybe they did with the same frivolity as Ivanov himself?

We have to admit that this was the case. Ivanov's first wife, Tanya, was the one that divorced him, only to remarry a few months later, and a year later separated from her new husband, with a third one on the pipeline.

The second, Nina, when Ivanov announced his divorce, replied that she was not going to weep at all, for there is plenty of trashy men like him around.

The third, Tasha, who now explains that what captivated her in Ivanov was mainly his handsome mustache, had known him for just one day before the marriage. Real deep feelings aside, what can one possibly learn in a day about a man with whom one is going to share one's life together?

This is reminiscent of a case we all read about recently in the newspaper. A girl got married, and a week later told the authorities that her husband, who later turned out to be a swindler, had stolen from her and ran away. It turned out that, not to mention other finer details, she could not even give the last name of her fleeing spouse. She did not have time to ask.

Ivanov's last name was known to his five wives. But what did they know about him when they got married, beyond this momentary need? About his inner self, for example? About his human qualities and content? About his views, inclinations, habits at least? Nothing.

They did not even try to dig into this area, contenting themselves with a handsome mustache. He was to them what they were to him: an encounter, an acquaintance, a casual companion.

And the children who would then be left fatherless? And their broken families? And the moral ugliness of such a distorted relationship? None of them even thought about this, nor did the Engineer Ivanov himself.

She's a lovebird; she's meant to flutter.

Or another similar case. V. M. Nikitin, a postgraduate student at the Gorky Pedagogical Institute, while on vacation in one of the collective farms of Okulovsky District, meets a girl named Panya.

They meet in the morning and get married in the evening: not a decade, not even five days, but after only ten hours of acquaintance.

Soon Panya becomes a mother, but then it "turns out" that Nikitin is married. He has another family, and they cannot live together. The girl, of course, was stunned, mortified. She is indignant, and she is in the right, of course: such stories often break lives.

But then again, how could she become the wife of a man about whom, when going to court, she found herself unable to tell even approximately where he lived, what he did, or how old he was?

What kind of attitude is that toward marriage, toward family, toward any feeling? On the other hand, everything is not so clear cut either with Nikitin himself: there is an alimony case, his wife finds out about the affair, and all hell breaks loose at home, which will obviously lead to a divorce.

And Nikitin, in addition to his wife, has two children who have to suffer a particularly painful experience in this entire story, on the fragile shoulders of which it lays especially hard.

On the surface, this is also an ordinary case, but when you look behind the scenes, this is how the knot is woven.

A number of additional questions are raised in connection with the discussion of the draft of the new marriage law.

The economist Sholokhov points to the need to connect family law with the right of inheritance. Only a registered marriage can be considered a normal marriage by the state. Parents should have certain obligations to their children in a *de facto* marriage. But only children from registered marriages can formally have the right of inheritance.

Master Grishina declares that strengthening the family is not achieved by words and wishful thinking. "My family lives in a room of 320 square feet with another family. Two families in one room. Don't expect to build comfort and have many children under these conditions."

The students of the main directorate of the automobile industry pointed out a gap in the bill: abortions are banned, while more radical procedures that permanently destroy the possibility of motherhood are permitted.

Petrov protests against the methods of discussing the bill: crowded rallies are called, at which it is impossible to discuss detailed issues, much less those of an intimate nature.

L. Onkova, a student, shares her most intimate experiences with readers:

> I myself have experienced how hard it is when a father abandons his family. My father abandoned my mother with three children, and they were very in need because child support was so low. I have been married for ten years and have a child. I have an abortion every year. My husband doesn't want a second child. Maybe he is planning to remarry, I don't know.
>
> My health has been compromised since my abortions, and my husband doesn't even think it's his fault. He thinks that having an abortion is as easy as going to the bathhouse. If only men knew what a painful procedure it is, not to mention the consequences.
>
> Abortion should be banned. Children cannot possibly interfere with either one's studies or one's work. The only people who can say that children are a hindrance are those who are thoughtless about marriage. That is what the new bill has in mind, and I know some will protest. But they will be in the minority.

"Female workers in the Moscow factories declare that in raising children they encounter many difficulties, the solution of which depends on the state: there are no baby carriages, no pacifiers, it is difficult to get underwear for children; the question of milk for children is almost unsolvable without the help of acquaintances in the markets and in the village: in the state stores there is either no milk at all or no milk to give to a child," sums up the confession of the Soviet press in the fascist *Nash Put'*.

> The whole country groans. It is not enough to introduce laws to strengthen the family, which so recently has been destroyed—we need more housing, a living wage, baby carriages, clothes, milk—in short, the more or less happy life that Stalin promised and which still does not at all exist.

It is not without reason that the peasant from Yelnya (formerly Smolensk province), described by the poet Alexander Tvardovsky, recently addressed the following question to the Soviet authorities:

> Comrade Stalin,
> Give me an answer,
> So people won't argue in vain.
> Is the end in sight, or not,
> Of this whole mess?
> For I can't see it yet. . . .[209]

---

[209] *Nash Put'*, No. 163 of June 28th, 1936.

In that same year, 1936, *Gazeta Polskaia* published an article by its former Moscow correspondent on the new Soviet draft laws prohibiting abortions, giving bonuses to families with more than seven children, combating divorce by substantially increasing divorce fees, etc.

The author of this article, as someone who has been in the Soviet Union for three years, asserts that "in the Soviet Union a man does not belong to himself, but to the state, or rather the authorities, which interfere even in the most intimate areas of his personal life."

Giving a vivid example of this complete dependence of Soviet citizens on the authorities, the author notes:

> Until now, the only area in which Soviet citizens have been presented with complete "freedom," sometimes reaching the point of absurd anarchy, has been in the field of sexual relations. The extraordinary ease of divorce, which in theory could be obtained even on a daily basis; the enormous difficulty in exacting alimony from the "deserter-fathers"; freedom in the field of abortion, limited only by the "arbitrariness" of special commissions on abortion—this is a vivid picture of relations in this sphere that prevailed up to now.

Of course, such a "happy and easy life" was fully enjoyed by a relatively small percentage of the total population of the USSR. The vast majority of it, the peasants, lived as before, according to old customs, and if there have been cases of violation of the seventh commandment in the villages, they have been the result not of loose morals, but of their extreme simplicity.

The author goes on to say:

> [S]exual promiscuity was committed above all by the literary and artistic circles and the masses of the new factory proletariat, ripped out of the rural family life by the revolution. The revolution did eliminate professional prostitution, which was the source of this type of woman's income, but it did not eliminate prostitution altogether.

When it comes to eliminating prostitution, the Soviet administrative authorities have acquired great powers for all sorts of abuses. In the USSR the penalty for clandestine prostitution (in view of the official abolition of explicit prostitution) is fifteen years in exile; up to half of the capital's female population could have been exiled to Murman, or to Siberia, or to Central Asia.

This is how the authorities resolved the issue of supplying Russian military garrisons with "wives" in the Central Asian republics, where "secret prostitutes" from all the big cities of European Russia were sent by the masses during the liquidation of the NEP (1928). Apparently, the Soviet "planned economy" also covers the field of "human husbandry."

Pointing then to the fact that the new bills were given to the masses for debate, the author argues that this was only a pedagogical device, similar to the annual issuance of "internal loans," which is exclusively, as the Soviet government explains, "due to the insistent demands of the population, willing to put their last money into socialist construction." Then he stresses that during the discussion of the new bills many facts came to light which testify to the terrible dissoluteness of morals in the USSR. The author writes:

> Here is the epilogue of the "sexual revolution," undertaken in 1917 by the present Soviet ambassador in Stockholm, Comrade Alexandra Kollontai, an active preacher of "free love," which she no less actively demonstrated by her own example.

The author then cites excerpts from the Soviet *Little Encyclopedia*, which condemns the prohibition of abortion in bourgeois countries in the following words: "This punitive legislation was passed mainly under the influence of the Church and was dictated by the demands of a false official morality under the slogan of fighting 'immorality.'"

The same *Little Encyclopedia* resents the high cost of divorce abroad and boasts that "Soviet legislation introduced complete freedom of divorce, simplifying at the same time the divorce procedure even more."

Based on all of the above, the author asks:

> What is the purpose of the above-mentioned law? It can be safely argued that all Soviet reforms must first be viewed from the purely point of view of the police. The whole Soviet system of management consists in preventing the citizens from having time to think about the grim reality surrounding them, despite the repeated slogans of a "happy life." Previously, this was accomplished by having to stand in various queues for long periods of time, which took up several hours a day. Now these queues are in the process of being eliminated. It is therefore necessary (from the police point of view) to burden citizens with concerns of having a large family and thus protect them from "dangerous thoughts" that can easily arise in a "gray man" when thinking in his leisure hours about the "achievements of the five-year plans."
>
> In addition, the law has another purpose, namely, to attach workers to the factories. A man burdened with a family will, of course, be more compliant and will value permanent service

more. In this respect, the Soviet state, as an employer, is no different from the bourgeoisie.

In the field of "political freedom of thought," the practice in the USSR is to hold family members responsible for "counter-revolutionary crimes" of their breadwinners. It is therefore advantageous for every citizen to have as many "hostages" as possible to serve as a guarantee of his "loyalty" to the socialist motherland.

A divorce law that allows (as in the bourgeois world) only the rich to divorce should, in the legislator's opinion, have the effect of increasing labor productivity.

The military view, along with that of the police, played a decisive role in the promulgation of the law in question. The disciplined division of labor did not require an immediate increase in the number of workers. But the military point of view requires a larger population in the USSR, which could add three hundred million instead of the present one hundred and seventy-six million.

Such a "disproportion" under Soviet conditions of population growth could be exploited by neighbors. Therefore, the Soviet law can be defined without exaggeration as the 'mobilization' of mothers in the event of a future war. This is certainly one of the fronts of the so-called "Soviet struggle for peace."

This is the USSR. But this is what was going on in Weimar Germany, the Germany which, as we have seen from German official statistics in the chapters of our work on pre-Hitler Germany, was also ruled by Jews. A word from the journal of the intrepid Julius Streicher:

Jews make peculiar films. They write theater plays with a certain flavor. They create musical works of a certain style, with an emphasis on all kinds of rousing jazz melodies. They give jazz forms even to such creations as the German anthem, like the Christmas cantata "Silent Night, Holy Night" [the same thing with the Russian anthem].

Especially since the outbreak of the November Revolution of 1918, Germany has been flooded with unnatural and filthy literature up to and including pornography, which has systematically poisoned the youth. And at the same time, it was being just as assiduously corrupted by the filthy strands of Jewish drama: Weil Toller, Zuckmeyer, Unruh, Wolf, and especially Kreneg. The latter went so far as to use the effect of a Negro raping a White woman on the open stage and, in the apotheosis, showing how the black race conquers the White race in its Germany-wide success, *Johnny Plays*.

Jewish filmmakers produced harmful films that glorified free love, abortion, child molestation, criminal offenses, etc.

Among barely mature young Jews, it is considered commendable to rape or defile as many Aryan girls as possible, while, on the contrary, Jewish girls are taken under guardianship.

Jewish merchants and industrialists systematically molest their secretaries and employees, defile their non-Jewish sales clerks, Jewish doctors rape their non-Jewish patients, and so on and so forth.

All this is borne out by the hundreds and thousands of scandalous lawsuits that have enriched Germany in particular.

The director of the High Commercial School in Magdeburg, Albert Gierland, a Jew, who molested or debauched hundreds of his non-Jewish pupils, was imprisoned for ten years.

The Jews succeeded in proclaiming as "science" the so-called "sexual research" of the Jew Magnus Hirschfeld, whose "discoveries" expressed nothing more than the justification of everything in the sexual field, up to and including the unnatural, that he stood up in favor of abortion, that he defended the impunity of intercourse between man and an animal.

The Jew Magnus Hirschfeld, to whom *Der Stürmer* refers, however, is not alone in such justifications. None other than the French prime minister himself, Léon Blum, is guilty of even worse pornography. As head of the French government, Blum suddenly rebelled against virginity and, in his book *Marriage*, demanded that girls begin sexual life at the age of fifteen, supposedly in order to develop an outlook on family life through experience. Blum recommends older men as the best teachers of the "science of love" and argues that husbands will be less jealous of their wives if they know that their wives had lovers before marriage, based on the law and the new good morals with which he wants to replace our traditional morality.

Blum further sanctions incest, recommending, in the absence of a good outsider partner to take a practical course in love, to look to a sibling or a father! Blum's book is banned in all countries except France. It certainly did much to deepen the corruption of French society and the decay of the French nation.

106. Judas Storms the Family

Blum's book and other similar literature betrays the Jewish desire to disintegrate and destroy the family, this basic unit of the nation and the foundation of every solid state. The Judaization of culture goes hand in hand with the destruction of the "Goy" family; here we will point out that the foxtrot, this undoubted "disease of the century," that dehumanizes man not only psychologically but also physically, was not invented by Jews, but at least was spread and approved by them. Here again we have to turn to the example of the USSR. Let us take another Soviet testimony, this time a Soviet novel, a horrible novel depicting the life of the younger generations. The authors are K. Mankovsky and N. Shalashov. The title, *Koska Grachev*. The publisher, USSR Gosizdat. The novel is written in the form of a Komsomol letter.

Here are excerpts from these letters, an unsightly transcript without commentary. This is where the Jewish leadership leads the Russian youth. A word to our friends Mankovsky and Shalashov. Says Komsomol member Grachev:

> Believe me, I often had to make passing acquaintances, and not only in theaters and clubs or at parties, but also in the collective, in the district committee, at serious lectures and even at rallies and conferences. And all the girls, just like Nina (that was the girl's name), would simply, so simply, as if it were the most ordinary thing, go to my place for the night, to me—a random passerby in their lives.
>
> They came without any "tenderness" in their hearts, without warm and friendly affection, and without hot and passionate hugs. All this they called "farce." They just walked in, without any unnecessary words, deftly took off their dress, swallowed a glass of cold tea on the go, said a few apathetic empty words and went straight to the bedroom.
>
> We all love to chit chat about: A new family! A new marriage! A new morality! In one word, everything seems new when put into words, while at the same time quietly doing the oldest nasties.
>
> I'll tell you directly and frankly, how a large part of the Komsomol guys look at women. Do you think they see her as a comrade, as a friend? You tell that to your grandmother. They're just afraid to say it straight out. Now the girls are just the same as the boys: all about "physical training." You may even get punched by your "boxing partner," don't expect to find happiness.
>
> I don't know if you read in *Komsomolskaya Pravda* about our Medvedev dormitory. That's the name of the dormitory at the Herzen Pedagogical University. The Komsomol members and activists here have been up to all sorts of nastiness here.
>
> But still I will say one thing. Now everyone is screaming: the sexes, the problem of the sexes, etc. But is this work? Lectures, debates, reports, discussions, books, magazines,

newspapers—all screaming about the problem of the sexes. But what we don't notice is that all the noise has the opposite effect, and the boys at all the lectures are just sniffing and holding on to the laps of the girls. I know examples when they went straight from the lecture to a prostitute.

And what is especially scary: not only guys, but girls drink, too. I recently had to see a drunken girl for the first time. You can't even imagine a more pathetic sight. Face swollen, red kerchief knocked to the side. This unhappy girl was wandering down the street, flailing from side to side, hugging the streetlamps, and chanting wildly:

> Comrade Malacholny, tell my mother,
> That her son died in the war.
> With a rifle in his hand and a saber in the other,
> And with a cheerful song on his lip. . . .

Some passer-by tried to calm her down, but she swore at him with such stunning, foul language that he preferred to retreat, while she wandered on, performing intricate pretzels with her feet and continued swearing in her song.

Not long ago the boys told me about how the girls gathered together, bought vodka, and drank it dry. They drank it so hard that the crowds could not keep up with them. So much for the unearthly ethereal creatures with a liquor stench seven miles away. . . .

It's not enough that they drink. The main misfortune is that there is no sense of proportion, no, you know, no limit.

Sometimes they catch some passerby and beat him up for a "good living," or they take a girl, pull her skirt up to her head, tie a knot on it and push her naked into the snow, or simply rape the girl, taking turns as if it were a waiting line.

I was curious to see what was going on there, to see how our "class enemies" have fun. I thought, in my innocence, that only the "dispossessed youth" of the NEPmen would gather there.[210]

What kind of audience do you think you will find there? Almost one hundred percent factory and factory youth. I decided to go up to a girl with a lot of makeup on her face: I imagined she must be some kind of *"lishenet"* girl. I went over

---

[210] Referring to the *Lumpenproletariat*, a Marxist term to designate the underclass of criminals and the unemployed, devoid of class consciousness. in contrast to the *Proletariat*. (Translator's note)

to her and asked where she was from. It turned out to be a beggar from the Treugolnik.

I sure saw a whole lot of different things there! Here you find the "monkey foxtrot," the "gymnastic Charleston," the "Boston," the "shimmy"—you can't even mention them all.

A girl there might not know a thing about literacy, but brother, when it comes to the "shimmy" or "Charleston," she's a professor. As such, the atmosphere in these dance classes, too, my brother, is appropriate. A smug maestro instructs the boys in "high society manners" and "fancy man's" body movements, while the suitors, with ceremonial bows, take their ladies under their arms and learn about the "gallant" treatment. And this whole human mass breathes in the smoky air, mixed with the odor of cheap perfume, sweat, and other stenches, which would inevitably give a normal person a headache.

Where does this debauchery, this new "morality" come from? Of course, it comes from Jewish Marxism! If there is no afterlife, if there is nothing higher and holy, if the only thing that's real is matter, the body, then why hold back all its dark natural impulses? If there is no need for the nation, what's the family for? Why the "tenderness"?

Der Stürmer, in 1937, tells two cautionary stories, one of which occurred in Romania, the other in Germany.

> Wherever Jews reside, crime flourishes. There is no country where Jews do not seduce and racially abuse Aryan women!
>
> Just the other day an outrageous incident took place in the Romanian town of Radauti, the victim of which was B. R., an Aryan employee at the brush factory of Nathan Korn.
>
> One tragic day she was detained at the factory under the pretext of having to do some overtime work. Beside her, the factory worker's son Isaiah Korn and four workers stayed at the factory, and all five of them, one by one, committed a heinous act of violence against the miserable woman.
>
> The broken-hearted and badly hurt worker barely made it home, determined to conceal what had happened from her husband out of fear. The consequence of this heinous crime was that the wretched woman contracted a bad disease, which she then infected her husband with.

In this connection the crime was uncovered and to the depths of his indignation the outraged husband rushed to initiate criminal proceedings against these five beasts in human form, namely Isaiah Korn,

Norbert Holder, Levi Gehr, Zeg Bruckner, and another representative of the "chosen people," who all came to the prosecutor's disposal.

> Even more outrageous is the crime just committed in the German town of Frankenthal, when Solomon Weil, a Jewish merchant of forty-nine years of age, committed a heinous assault on his own, but not Jewish by birth, fourteen-year-old stepdaughter, Elfriede M.
>
> The latter's mother, the Aryan Maria M., had a relationship with a German at the age of sixteen, already distinguished by her striking beauty; from this union a daughter, Elfrida, was born.
>
> After her husband's death, her mother had to struggle to earn money to provide for the parenting of her child. Her need finally led her to enroll at the Jewish Union Bar in Mannheim, where, by her own misfortune, she met a Jewish businessman, Solomon Weil, in 1931.
>
> Believing that he was well off financially and tired of working hard at the bar, Maria M. agreed for the sake of her daughter, who was then nine years old, to marry Weil. It soon became clear that Maria M. would have to work even after marriage, and not only for herself and the child, but also for her husband, who exploited her mercilessly.
>
> Taking advantage of her mother's absence, the Jew Weil began to cast more and more predatorial glances at the growing girl, and finally in the fall of 1936 catastrophe broke out.
>
> What did it mean to him that Elfrida was then fourteen years old and that she trustingly called her future seducer "papa"? Weil's sexual appetites demanded satisfaction, and the victim of his Jewish temperament was an innocent German girl whom he took by force, taking advantage of her mother's absence.
>
> In order to silence this violence, he threatened Elfrida with cruel beatings. The unnatural bond between the bestial stepfather and his stepdaughter continued in this manner day in and day out for two months.
>
> But the man-beast was not satisfied with gratifying his Jewish lust and, in addition, he savagely beat the poor child; one day, when he savagely beat her, throwing her to the floor and trampling on her feet, Elfrida screamed so hard that her screams were heard in the street.
>
> The neighbors rushed in and saw an enraged, foaming-at-the-mouth Weil, who bluntly replied to all attempts to intercede for the unfortunate child: "I can do whatever I want with my daughter."

The unfortunate child was so shaken by the experience that she repeatedly attempted to commit suicide; this is all the more disturbing because children are known to be particularly greedy for life, and suicide during childhood is an exceptional event.

On December 14th, 1936, after the first interrogation of the disturbed child, the police intervened and arrested Solomon Weil, who initially refused to confess, but in the face of overwhelming evidence was finally forced to.

A trial followed, at which, despite the best efforts of Jewish lawyers to keep this outrageous case quiet, Weil was sentenced to six years in prison and a twelve-year deprivation of his rights.

How many such and similar cases have been played out in Europe lately, especially in factories, offices, and Jewish homes where Christian girls and women are employed! And where most of these crimes remain hidden from the eyes of the general public!

Such crimes are concealed and suppressed not only through bribery, threats of dismissal, and extortion, but also through false denunciations to the police and false accusations of theft!

It is no mystery that Christian girls in the service of Jewish homes are forced to cohabit either with the sons of their masters or with the master himself.

And in so doing, more and more cadres of innocent beings are morally and physically contaminated.

"Aryan peoples!" *Der Stürmer* concludes its article, "reach out to each other to fight together against Jewish domination in all its forms and manifestations!"

"It's ridiculous to accuse Freud of immorality," the Shanghai Jewish magazine unexpectedly observes. "If he pulls the veil off sexual instincts, it's not a bad thing at all—on the contrary."[211]

107. Jewish Drug Poisoning of Nations

"Jewry carries out an equally systematic contamination of nations with alcohol and all kinds of narcotic poisons," *Der Stürmer* states.

Statisticians in Poland and Romania say that 90–96 percent of all liquor distilleries and related liquor businesses are in Jewish hands.

---

[211] *Jewish Life*, April 19th, 1941.

The wine trade in the vast majority of countries has become a Jewish monopoly.

The police statistics of all countries report that the same is true of the drug trade.

Jews everywhere act as traffickers and smuggle cocaine, opium, heroin, and morphine.

The Jews themselves usually refrain from consuming these destructive poisons, but they are all the more eager to give them to the Aryans.

The great Russian writer and thinker I. A. Rodionov, unheard of in his time, exclaimed in 1912: "The Jews and alcohol are ruining Russia and will ruin it!"

The figures he cites certify that the vodka trade in Russia and the drinking of the Russian people in taverns were mainly in Jewish hands.

It was none other than the Jews who initiated opium smoking in China. Sassoon, a Jewish wholesaler from India, began importing opium into China and made billions from this trade. The Chinese nation began to rot and deteriorate. And when the Chinese imperial government resisted the importation of opium, Sassoon forced the British government to go to war. The historical record was enriched by the unprecedented in its anti-moral justification "opium war," in which British soldiers and officers with fire and bayonets forced the Chinese people to open their customs to the importation of the killing drug!

108. Judas vs. the Nation

The destruction of the elite and the assault on the family betrays the main direction of the Jewish expansion. It targets the nation as the natural, God-given, and historically forged category of the strongest unity of men.

Through the Judaization of culture, Judas diminishes and extinguishes the national consciousness. Through the Judaization of the economy, he is destroying intra-national bonds and enslaving the individual parts of the national body—the classes and the people who compose them.

Through the policies he directs, Judas destroys the nation; through power, when it falls into his hands, he destroys the nation from without, from above. When Judas looms over a state, it means that the nation that makes up the state is soon to face its imminent end. A cautionary example for all living nations is the fate of the Russian nation under the Soviet yoke.

After taking over Russia in October 1917, the Jews hastened to abolish its historical name and divide the unified Russian Empire into separate Soviet republics, to be subsequently merged into the anonymous Soviet Union.

At first there were four such republics, then seven, then eleven, and finally sixteen. Not satisfied with this division, the Judeo-Bolsheviks created more than twenty "autonomous republics" and ten "autonomous oblasts" inside the "union republics," giving rise to a separatism and antagonism that never existed before.

Thus, the Comintern set in motion and actually carried out the dismemberment of Russia, dealing an unparalleled blow to the national-state unity of the Russian people.

It divided the Russian nation into Russians (Great Russians), Ukrainians, and Belarusians, and set up a "separate" state for each of them—the RSFSR, the UkrSSR, the BSSR—and replaced the union of the *Russkaya Natsiya* with the other peoples of Russia, the *Rossiyskaya Natsiya*—a historical fusion of the various peoples of Eastern Europe and Northern and Central Asia—with the fiction of a Soviet federation, where every small nation has a separate language, intense chauvinism, and hatred of the Russians, who in Communist propaganda personified the oppression of the past, and in Soviet practice, were the "exploiters" of the present.

In Soviet textbooks, Russia is still, in spite of its temporary Soviet patriotism, referred to as "Global Policeman" and "the oppressor of national minorities." Soviet schoolchildren are still forced to shed tears over the "suffering" of some Kyrgyz and Uzbeks "under the brutal Russian yoke."

The words *Russkaya Natsiya* and even more so *Rossiyskaya Natsiya* are still forbidden in the USSR.[212] As of late, we can speak of the Russian people, which in the USSR was finally recognized as a great nation, but only because it was the first time that the misanthropic ideas of Marxism were applied in its midst. In the USSR, the Russian people are not valued as such, not for their spiritual giftedness and talents, but only as a servile executor of the Comintern's program.

National feeling is temporarily allowed in the USSR for defense purposes, but it is not allowed to develop into a national consciousness. It is replaced by a Soviet consciousness: Stalinism remains the state doctrine of the USSR, and Marx and Stalin declared nationalism a "zoological prejudice." Nationalism in the USSR is still persecuted under the labels of "great-power chauvinism" or "counter-revolutionary fascism," while Soviet patriotism asserts the existence of a "Soviet people"

---

[212] Here Rodzaevsky makes a clear distinction between the terms *Русский* and *Российский*, which are untranslatable into English; the former (*russkiy*) usually refers to the notion of an ethno-social Russian identity, while the latter (*rossiyskiy*) refers to the nation-state of Russia. (Translator's note)

or even a "Soviet nation," a union of all peoples who embrace communism.

The Bolsheviks are forging the Russian nation into an artificially created "Soviet nation," and it is the fate of all the peoples who accept Marxism and the dictatorship of the Elders of Zion in the form of the "dictatorship of the proletariat" of the Communist party to be dissolved into this nation.

The struggle with the nation in the USSR has been going on all these twenty-five years in various forms: through the denial of the nation and the replacement of its people; through the eradication of nationalism, of love for one's kindred people and its replacement with a surrogate like patriotism, of love for the land; through the destruction of the content of the nation, its spiritual basis, its roots in the past, its consciousness; through the destruction of the national-willed elite and the creation of unbearable living conditions; through the replacement of Russian culture (religious, national, monarchical, artistic) with "Soviet culture"—national in form (only), socialist in content (and content in culture is everything!). The past cultural values of the Russian people were tolerated along with the best works of foreign cultures only for temporary self-gratification: there was no ground for a new Russian cultural creativity in the USSR.

Certain Soviet republics, in which the national feelings of the minor nationalities were awakened, however, had a very illusory "right to self-determination up to secession." No nation falling under the red yoke can secede from the USSR, which in all the years past has tended to continually expand, but never diminish. For all the peoples who fell under the dictatorship of the Marxists are bound together by one chain, the chain of the Communist Party, from which comes the whole system of chains, crowned by the Joint State Political Directorate, which is now called, however, not OGPU, but NKVD. The name is different, but its essence remains the same.

In the USSR, they say, there is a Soviet system. Soviets are elected by the population ("the most perfect form of democracy"). But all elections are conducted by the Communist party, which nominates the candidates, often the only candidate, and pushes people to the ballot boxes. For it is a crime in the USSR even to abstain from voting for a candidate approved above.

This is how the Soviets are formed: rural, urban, provincial, territorial, republican, headed by the Supreme Soviet of the USSR, which in the same order elects the "Soviet government"—the *Sovnarkom*. Each Soviet is governed, at the behest of its central, by the Communist Party authorities of the same name, with the Orgburo, the Politburo, and the Secretariat. The irremovable general secretary is Stalin, his unchanging right hand is Lazar Kaganovich. Inside Stalin's bedroom is Rosa Kaganovich; inside Stalin's brain is Jewish Marxism; inside his inner circle, Lev Mekhlis; first, he was Stalin's personal secretary, then editor-in-chief of *Pravda* (with his former position retained), then head of the PUR—Red Army Political Administration (with his former position retained). Finally, Minister of State Control, and once again Stalin's personal secretary.[213] These secretaries ruled for twenty-five years the currently enslaved Great Russia.

The USSR Constitution enshrines the dictatorial position of the All-Union Communist Party. This party is "the governing nucleus of all state, economic, cultural, and other institutions and enterprises." The statute of the CPSU defines it as "a section of the Communist International." In the Russian Moscow sits the anonymous ECCI (Executive Committee of the Communist International), formerly run by Zinoviev-Apfelbaum and Trotsky-Bronstein, now by the Manuilskys, the Lozovskys, the "Dimitrovs"; and this very ECCI is the highest authority over the RSFSR, the USSR, and the entire Soviet Union, the highest authority which claims to establish its bloody star over all mankind.

"Soviet power," when examined closely, turns out to be an instrument of the "dictatorship of the Communist Party," it is the Comintern's last rope: after the suppression of the nation, follows the conquest of the state! By extending the Soviet Union to the whole world through the global socialist revolution, the Comintern, a gathering of some "representatives" of the Communist Parties of all countries, claims to have absolute power over the universe.

The Soviet state can be defined as a union of peoples who are forbidden to be called and to be nations, as a prison of nations which are dismembered into nonexistent nations and from which a new artificial nation is molded.

This prison of nations is a state-like organization. It is vigilantly guarded against external and internal enemies by several armies of prisoners, of which the main one is formed by selecting Communists into a centralized and disciplined party.

In addition to the party there is also a multi-million-dollar Red Army, an obedient executor of the will of the party, and an even better funded secret police force, formerly called the GPU and now called the NKVD.

It is the only state in the world built on endless control and mutual distrust; Jewish terror lies at its core. And into such a terrible prison-state they want to turn all of humanity, once the Jewish red octopus reigns over it.

These are the four successive stages of Soviet rule: terrorist war communism, externally-liberal NEP (by Lenin's definition "to take one

---

[213] On June 21st, 1941, he again became head of the Chief Directorate of the Red Army, preserving the position of Commissar of State Control. (Translator's note)

step backward in order to take two steps forward"), Stalin's "socialism in one country," and the present NIP (a new ideological NEP, an ideological "step backward to then take two steps forward," a new ideological policy).

The Comintern, in its twenty-five years of power over Russia, has degraded the Russian nation, brought it to the ground, and, having conquered the Russian Empire, led the peoples of Russia into total submission. The USSR is not Russia, but the CJE—the Communist Jewish Empire, the empire of the red conquerors, built in the place of Russia. To this empire the Comintern is trying to annex all neighboring countries and, of course, to extend it to the entire globe. This is where the eyes of Stalin and Kaganovich are set, this is the ultimate plan of world Jewry in the twentieth century.

109. Ultimate Goals

As I summarized in my brochure "The Paths of Expansion of the Comintern" in 1940:

> The Russian experience is an attempt to kill a living nation, a system of artificial "Fellahism," a transformation of the Russian nation into a mummified nation, its culture into a cultural museum of the past, its peoples into fertilizer for foreign expansion.[214]

The USSR is the base of the Comintern, the base of world Jewry in the struggle for a world revolution. Through the destruction of the nations, Judas is marching toward a classless society, destroying the goyim according to the precepts of the Talmud and Marx; through the destruction of "family, property, and state," through the "dictatorship of the proletariat," which turns out to be a dictatorship over the proletariat by Jewish elders and capitalists, Judas is creeping toward infinite power over mankind. World domination was and is the primary goal of Judaism.

Religion stands in the way of this devil's world power—Judas is staging an "assault on heaven." Labor must be enslaved for world power. Judas is setting records of exploitation. The nation stands across Judas' path. Judas degrades it culturally, destroys its economy, and destroys it in the state, as we have just seen.

---

[214] "Fellahism": a term probably borrowed from the German philosopher Oswald Spengler, meaning an uncultured "civilizational residue," which gathers in late megapolitan big cities after the decline of a high culture. (Translator's note)

At the expense of someone else's national life, Judas is building his own nation-state, which wants to become a world-state, under the guise of the notorious Zionism.

This is evidenced not only by the *Protocols of Zion*, but from an overview of all Jewish history and contemporary events.

We can at least say we have been sufficiently convinced of this by now, and we have been introduced to some examples of Jewish strategy and tactics, haven't we? Let us now look at the organization of the masters of this strategy, the world Jewish inter-state, which seeks to become the metropolis of all the states of the earth.

PART THREE:

THE WORLD JEWISH INTER-STATE,
ITS INTERNAL ORGANIZATION

110. The Results of Judaization

And here comes the end: by the end of the first quarter of the twentieth century, the whole world, except the island of Japan, was entirely in Jewish hands:

The State! The Culture! The Economy!

By 1925, Jewry had reached its apex. "Our fervent dreams had finally come true," shouted the Jewish leaders at this time in raptures. It was their time, the time of the Comintern, the League of Nations, and the Finintern.

In 1925 Judas was counting the victories of Judaization, and in this book we have counted the totals of his victories.

These totals, as has already been said, are not complete.

In this first part of our work, we have limited ourselves to considering Judas in politics, but there is also a Judas in culture and a Judas in economics, and we have not yet considered all of his armament for the struggle in the cultural field and on the economic front. Of course, it must be added to the points made above about the various Jewish cannons, shells, and auxiliary troops operating in the ideological, political, state, and public spheres.

These cannons and shells are being used in all the great ideas of mankind of the new age, used by all the international organizations created to unite men; these auxiliary troops are the various cunning and unsophisticated methods of Judaization, and have led to the abnormal situation I have described, where one nation is looming over all other nations, like Judas over the states.

O! but if the situation were otherwise, as it was in 1925, I might have refrained from publishing this book, for it might have the contrary effect—to frighten weak souls with the spectacle of the Jewish triumph.

How is one to struggle against a power so formidable that has taken hold of the world? Isn't it better to submit to it, to work with it, to serve it?

But fear not, for God is merciful.

Let us take three colors to represent the different levels of Judaization.

Let blue, the color of Zionism, stand for countries under Jewish rule.

The color white, the other half of the Jewish flag, shall be chosen for countries with Jewish cultural and economic influence, but where Jewish political power does not yet exist.

And in brown, the color of the Jew-hating "Nazis," we will paint countries that are truly independent, sovereign in the fascist, not pseudo-legal, sense of the word, countries that are free from Judaization.

Let's follow the changes in the coloring of the political map of the world by decade.

1900. Only England and the United States are in blue, but the rest of the world is white, with only Japan being brown.

1910. "Right on our doorstep." The blue spot is spreading, France is already painted with it, as are the French colonies, the British and American colonies, parts of Asia and Africa, Australia, and large parts of Oceania. The blue spots are increasing in the rest of Europe, they also appear in South America, and are getting closer to Japan.

1920. What is this catastrophe? Russia, Germany, and the states formed on the ruins of the Austro-Hungarian Empire, the Balkans, the Apennine and Iberian islands, Scandinavia—the whole world, except Japan, has fallen under the blue paint. Judaization had reached its limit; Judas finally reigns over the states—this was the finale of World War I, which the Comintern and the League of Nations hastened to consolidate.

A world catastrophe for all nations. A world catastrophe for all religions! A world catastrophe for labor and capital, hence also the catastrophe of talent, spirit, and genius.

Has God really given up on this sinful earth? Will the devil really win? Will evil triumph forever? Will there be weeping and gnashing of teeth? Will the "goyim" be deprived of family, property, and state power, as the Talmud taught, as Marx demanded, as the world revolution and world finance sought to do?

The drums of Jewish victory are beating: the League of Nations is no longer enough for them, they talk of an international language, of an international bank, of an international police, of international arms control, of an international body of arbitration between states, of an open supra-governmental, supranational power.

National distinctions are being erased, family distinctions are being erased, distinctions between man and animal, between good and evil, between angel and demon are being erased.

1930. What? The night has turned pale; has the hand of the clock of human destiny gone beyond midnight? The blue spot has drifted and begun to shrink: besides Japan, there is another brown country, Italy. Brown spots have appeared in each country.

1940. Written on the tablets of history as the fateful year of mankind. Fascist Germany struck down the cursed Jewish serpent in Europe. 1940 was the year of Europe's liberation from the dark forces.

In 1926, in the Harbin newspaper *Russkoye Slovo*, I wrote about the coming of a new epoch, when the Nation will oppose the Internationals and lay the foundation of a New Order of State, culture, and economy. In 1933, in debates on Freemasonry, I spoke about the proximity of the world struggle against the dark forces, and at the same time I predicted that Germany would be the vanguard of the world struggle against world Jewry, while Japan would cut the Gordian knot of the Pacific problem and would build a new, free Asia. In 1940—in the middle of the German-Soviet pact—I spoke about the inevitability of the German–Soviet war and about the certainty of the Japanese–English and Japanese–American clash. The New Order has always been pictured to me as the liberation of the world from the Jews. Is not this the direction in which all genuine human progress is now moving towards?

Instead of a global catastrophe for all nations—the disruption and failure of the Internationals. A world catastrophe for Israel! Here is the unexpected result of Judaization: the awakening, the rejuvenation, the unification not of an amorphous universal mass, but of organized peoples and nations, not in the way of an international, but in the way of peaceful cooperation between peoples, nations, and states. Instead of the Masonic "all the world under one republic," the motto of Jinmu Tennō, the founder of the Japanese Empire, "All the World is One House." A house under one roof—under the firmament from which shines the clear sun during the day, the welcoming, not Jewish, but the real godly stars shining in the night; a house in which there are different rooms, with different decorations—God's magical world of bizarre diversity.

Hail the rising sun of a new life—the New Order! Hail the death of the proud Jewish dreams!

The final chapters of this book will tell how the miscalculation of the Elders of Zion, one that turned out to be fatal for the Jews, thwarted the disaster that awaited us instead.

By 1950, God willing, the whole world will be free. The balance of power was not in Judas' favor—the greatest upswing was followed by the greatest downswing.

Light and shadow, however, fill all of Jewish history, showing us continuous falls after rises. Truly, God is not to be mocked!

World Jewry now has three bases—the USSR, England, and the United States—in which it is fortified and desperately defending itself, and from which it threatens the rest of humanity.

But Germany is building a New European Order. Japan has liberated East Asia from the Anglo-Americans. Our homeland, we believe, will also be free. The Judaized British Empire will be crushed to the end, and the USA, the United States of America, will once again become the USNA, the United States of North America.[215]

As this book is being written, there is a war sweeping over Greater East Asia; and the German–Soviet war, in my view and in factual basis, is a war of nation-states against world Jewry, a war of the Nation against the International, the war of the New Order against the Judaized order. May victory go to the nationalists!

111. Jewry as an Inter-State

Earlier we established that Jewry is an international or internal nation, an organized nation within alien national organisms, a parasitic nation, a solitary nation, an inter-nation. This inter-nation has its own state, an inter-state.

Its members, its citizens, are at the same time subjects of other states, but they remember above all their belonging to the Jewish inter-state and, as subjects of the countries that shelter them, regard themselves as citizens of the World Jewish State, and the subjects of the countries that shelter them, perhaps, as subjects of their Jewish inter-state.

In relation to the subjects, the Jews, from their point of view, have only rights. In relation to the Jews, the subjects, who gullibly let them in, have only duties.

The subjects have no rights whatsoever. They should have no family, no property, no state. This is what Jewish Marxism teaches, and this is what Jewish Kabbalah teaches. Each of the non-Jews is assigned to a certain Jew who must then "take care of him." This, I believe, is called meropia.

Every "goy" who is outstanding in some way is entrusted to the care of some dexterous Jew. Thus, is justified the popular wisdom that says that everyone has at least one good Jew.

---

[215] What Rodzaevsky seems to intend here with the phrase "United States of North America" is that, with the advent of a New Order, the United States would cease its internationalist overreaching and return to a concern solely with its native territory, as advocated by the America First Committee and Charles Lindbergh. (Editor's note)

Since there are only sixteen million kikes in God's world and over a billion people, it follows that there are no bad kikes, but only good Jews. The word "Jews," by the way, means "People of God."

They even force us to call them respectfully: not Jews, which corresponds to the tradition of the Russian language and to their name in all other languages—English, German, French, Japanese, and others—but precisely as "People of God"!

That a Jewish inter-state exists is proven by the existence of Jewish communities and the connections between them, Jewish national councils and the connection between them, world congresses, and world governing bodies.

"We the people!" exclaimed with passion in the last century the leader of the Jewish people, Theodor Herzl, in his book *The Jewish State*. "In times of trouble, we unite and then suddenly we discover our strength. Yes, we have the power to build a state, even a model state. We have all the moral and material means necessary for this."

Fifty years have not passed since these words were written—the Jewish state exists, but not in Palestine, where Herzl called for it, but as an inter-state inside foreign states. According to the recipe of the same Herzl, it was founded through the use of two seemingly opposite methods—through the propagation of the world revolution and the concentration of world finance:

"By going bankrupt, we become revolutionary proletarians, supplying all the revolutionary parties with non-commissioned officers, while at the top our monetary power increases."

These frank words of Herzl should be put as an epigraph to all the activities of world Jewry, as a declaration of the entire policy of the World Jewish inter-state.

But the Jewish inter-state does not exist only within foreign countries, but also at their own expense. It is an empire of a very peculiar kind, where the parasitic metropolis hides inside the colonies. And the colonies of the Jewish World Empire are Europe, Africa, Asia, America, Australia, and Oceania.

112. The Community as the Basic Unit of the Jewish Inter-State

The Jewish inter-state is a state organized and composed of a homogeneous element, as we would say in our time, a totalitarian or even fascist state. Only this totalitarianism or fascism, which has infiltrated into foreign organisms, does not give room for the totalitarianism or fascism of all other peoples, which is why national totalitarianism is in irreconcilable contradiction with Judaism, and why true fascism fights it resolutely.

The Jewish inter-state consists of communities, each of which acts as a colony of this state in a foreign one. Characteristically, all the Jews living in a given city are united in a community regardless of their nationality.

Take Harbin, where this book is being written. There are Jews of many different nationalities living here: Russian émigré Jews under the guise of "anti-communism," Soviet nationals, outright Communists, refugee Jews from Germany, and nationals of various countries. There used to be Jews who were subjects of England and America, Jews who were emigrants from Imperial Russia, Jews who were Russian subjects, the old-timers who came here with the first pioneers of the Chinese Eastern Railway. And all of them were and are part of the HJSC, one single Harbin Jewish Spiritual Community. And for several years all had one unchanged chairman, Dr. Abram Kaufman, one unchanged for several years Rabbi Aaron Kiselev, who consistently changed his emigrant citizenship to the Soviet, Soviet to Lithuanian, and Lithuanian to emigrant. It is interesting to note, by mistake, that of all the nationalities, the Jews of Harbin liked the Soviet one best, and in general the richest people of Harbin were Soviet citizens, sympathetic to a country that denied private capital. When the epidemic of conversions to emigrant status began, most of the Jews shifted not to emigrants, but to subjects of the limitrophes.

It is also interesting to note that the citizenship of Finland, for example, for some reason did not attract the Jews of Harbin. But yesterday's Communists and Soviet citizens, today's anti-Communists, the Jewish capitalists of Harbin are overwhelmingly considered citizens of the now defunct Lithuania, Latvia, and Estonia.

The Jewish Religious Community in Harbin has, of course, its own place, its own synagogue, not just one but two temples, a school, a magazine, a club, a theater, a hospital, social service agencies, a funeral brotherhood, a bank, an interest-free society, women's organizations, youth organizations, political groups, a *beth din* court, and even a secret police force. From this example we can judge the organization of communities in general.

Not satisfied with their own temple, the Jews of Harbin reached into temples of all religions, either by adopting another's religion or by securing good relations with foreign clergymen. Not satisfied with their school, the Jews seized control of another "goy" school, not satisfied with their club, they seized the All-Russian Commercial Assembly, monopolized theater halls, and are trying to monopolize the music and singing industry. Not satisfied with *Jewish Life* they now publish another newspaper in Russian, specifically for Russian needs, trying to influence the rest of the émigré press; not satisfied with their hospital, they meddle in other hospitals; not satisfied with their bank, they crushed all the "goyim" banks and for a long time had a situation where no one but a Jew could enter any bank until the authorities opened the State Credit Cooperative. They try to influence all emigrant organizations and even the authorities. The work of any Jewish community in general can be judged by this example.

Of course, their own community organizations are immeasurably closer and dearer to the Jews than those of the "goyim." This is natural, and it would be good if they left ours alone. But since everyone around them is viewed as potential subjects of the community, the Jew cares about everything: our churches, our newspapers, our culture, our sacred places, our life, our livelihood, and the primary sources of our existence.

That the communal organization has long been peculiar to Jews everywhere is evidenced, in particular, by the *Russian Journal* and the faithful son of his "chosen people," Polyakov, in his novel *Sabatai Chain*, where, inter alia, we read about the Middle Ages:

> The bond between the Jewish communities of that time was stronger than state borders. The borders set by kings, dukes, and electorates were a burdensome convention, while the unity of the Jewish people was a coveted and immutable truth. Jews from all countries felt themselves to be one and indivisible. They felt a physical attachment to the place where they were born, to the landscape in which they grew up, to the cemeteries where their forefathers were buried; they sincerely honored good rulers and dealt with the wicked and unjust, seeing in them and in others only instruments of God's will: "the hearts of kings are in God's hands." Their Christian neighbors were treated with indifferent tolerance, paying friendship for friendship and enmity for enmity. It was a foreign thing. The outside Christian world, with its conditions, restrictions, taxes, and passports, was only a necessary sphere of mercantile activity. All this had to be obeyed, for outside these statutes and restrictions one could not move about, go to fairs, make deals, buy and sell goods, stones, metals, money. It was warm, good, and free only in one's own circle, in one's family at the cradle of one's children, in the synagogue.
>
> The Jewish immigrant, from whatever principality, duchy, or kingdom he came from, felt at home among his fellow believers.

This was the case in the Middle Ages and remains so in our time.

And in the twentieth century, the Jewish inter-state speaks openly, openly publishes its goals, its aspirations, its forces.

113. Functions of the Jewish Community

In 1917, when the revolution broke out in Russia, the first All-Russian Jewish Congress was held, which the Jews called "extraordinary"—the very Congress at which Chlenov, who has already been quoted by us many times and who is celebrated as the hero of the anniversary of the of the Harbin Jewish Community in this year of 1943, openly accepted and officially promulgated the Model Charter of the Jewish Community. It should be read in detail so as to understand once and for all the infinitely wide-ranging activities of the community, with the caveat that not everything, by no means everything, that they do could be published openly, in Russian, for all to hear, even in the midst of the drunkenness of the February "liberty."

Community Activities
A. In the cultural and educational field
1. The community is obligated to open public schools and kindergartens sufficient to serve the entire Jewish population of a given area, which must be open to all Jewish children free of charge.
2. The community also opens secondary and vocational schools and, where possible, special schools and institutions of higher learning.
3. The language of instruction in community schools and kindergartens must be Hebrew for all subjects except the national, regional, and other languages.
4. With regard to those educational institutions in which, for local or temporary reasons, it is not yet possible to establish instruction in the Hebrew language, Zionists require the following minimum for Jewish subjects:
   a. Such a level of Hebrew so that the pupils by the end of school can read a Jewish book freely and be able to state their thoughts in writing;
   b. the Bible and the Agenda (the original), and
   c. Jewish history.
5. The community also takes care of extracurricular education of Jews in both general and Jewish subjects, arranging courses for adults, people's houses, libraries, people's universities, etc.
6. The community also takes care of the artistic education of its members by organizing performances and supporting Jewish theater, influencing its improvement and enhancement.

7. Finally, the community also takes care of the physical education of the people, conducting compulsory gymnastic exercises in schools, organizing summer walks for school children and promoting the creation of gymnastic societies.

B. In the field of religious life
1. The community provides for the building and maintenance of a sufficient number of synagogues and prayer houses, open free of charge to all who desire to pray and supplied with a sufficient stock of synagogue memorabilia.
2. The community shall have a rabbi and an adequate number of assistants, preachers, carvers, circumcisers, servants of the synagogue, cantors, and reciters.
3. The community shall maintain the cemetery and form burial brotherhoods.
4. The community has to take care of making matzah for Passover and providing it to the poorest Jewish population at cost price or free of charge, for which the traditional "mose-hitish" has to be maintained, transforming it into an obligatory progressive-income tax.
5. The community takes care of the provision of ritual food for those who wish it in hospitals, detention centers, and soldiers' barracks, reallocating, where possible, the expenses to the appropriate state or municipal treasury.
6. The community stands for Sabbath rights and Jewish holidays, seeking the right for Jews who celebrate the Sabbath and their holidays, as well as to work on Sundays and on Christian holidays.
7. The community takes care that Jews in military service enjoy vacations on high holidays and are welcome in communal dining rooms or private homes.

C. In the field of social and economic aid
1. The community promotes the cooperative means of the Jewish population by adapting to the specific needs of the Jewish economy.
2. The community encourages the development of cooperatives among Jewish workers by providing them with credit in the form of handicrafts or working capital.
3. The community organizes for the poorest part of the population interest-free loan funds, mutual insurance funds in case of death or disability.
4. The community shall have a labor and information bureau.

5. The congregation shall set up a special fund for the unemployed and those in need due to illness.
D. In the field of emigration and resettlement
  1. The community comes into contact with other communities in order to determine the degree to which each one of them is rich in a particular trade or industry, and contributes to the proper distribution of the settling emigrants, giving them the necessary information and facilitating the settling and consolidation of the position of the settlers.
  2. The community takes care to provide its emigrants with cheap travel and preferential fares by rail and by sea.
  3. The community also cares for the support of the families of emigrants until they are settled in their new places.
E. In the field of public health
  1. The community maintains hospitals and dispensaries, organizes free medical aid to the poorest of the population, organizes societies for supplying the poor with medical, sanitary, and food aid and medicines.
  2. The community organizes societies for helping poor women in childbirth and the seriously ill, by supplying them with the necessary enhanced nutrition as well as nurses for night duty.
  3. The community organizes concerns for the health of the Jewish residential districts, undertakes surveys of the health of the Jewish population, organizes lectures for the general public, etc.
  4. The community organizes children's sanatoriums for poor children and promotes physical education by planting gymnastic exercises and sport societies.
  5. The community keeps proper sanitary statistics and informs wide masses about its results for instruction and enlightenment.
F. In the field of social aid
  1. The community makes arrangements for workhouses, night shelters, asylums, alms-houses, crèches, etc.
  2. The community organizes free distribution of bread to the poorest Jewish families, especially on the Sabbath, and maintains cheap canteens where food is provided to every newcomer for several days completely free of charge.
  3. The community maintains a special fund for the homeless and the unemployed, to help them on their way to

their homes. For this purpose the community asks the railroads and steamships for concessionary travel with its certificates.
   4. The community fights begging and street vandalism by means of severe penalties on the one hand, while on the other, providing ample help to those in need.
   5. The community undertakes its concern for pilgrims going to the Holy Land and for the poor living there, by assuming the traditional Reb Meir Baal-haness Circle Fee, bringing it into order in the field, and promoting its proper management in Palestine.
G. In the field of metrics and registration.
   1. In the community proper records are kept of the Jewish population: births and deaths, marriages and divorces, emigration and immigration, conversions from one faith to another, and mixed marriages.
   2. The community produces conscription lists of Jews liable for military service, which it provides to national military units within the specified period.
   3. All certificates of metrical and other certificates are issued by the community to anyone who wishes to do so, free of charge.
H. In the field of nation-building in Palestine
   1. A special "Palestinian Commission" is organized in each community, whose task is to contribute in an organized manner to the success of Palestinian colonization and the national institutions that are emerging there.
   2. The community promotes the organization of special dues among the Jewish population in favor of the Palestinian cause, and supports the general national cultural institutions that already exist and are emerging in Palestine, such as the Bais Ne'eman, the National Museum, the higher schools of Jewish science, the National University, the scientific institutes, the Betzalel, etc.
   3. The community organizes from time to time exhibitions of the Palestinian products and national creativity in Palestine and promotes the distribution of the products of our Palestinian colonies and the work of our Palestinian artisans to the Jewish population.
   4. The community keeps intact the capital, the funds bequeathed to it for Palestinian affairs, and spends them according to the will of the testators.

5. The community places its endowment, if possible, in the bonds of national institutions and institutes working for the success of Palestinian colonization.
I. In the field of political life
1. The community strives to secure the right of an internal Jewish government through the close association of its forces and the strong alliance of all communities with the supreme and elected bodies of self-government.
2. The community and the communal union represent the Jewish population, act on its behalf in communication with municipal and state authorities, protecting Jewish interests.
3. The community also contributes to the development and revitalization of Jewish political and social life by encouraging the emergence of all kinds of societies and unions and providing them with meeting and public lecture rooms.
J. In the field of budgets
1. A budget and finance committee is organized within the community, whose task is to draw up the annual general community budget, to sort out and approve the budget of the community by individual institutions and institutions and to find financial sources to cover the needs of the community.
2. The community keeps the special and inviolable capitals and funds donated and bequeathed to it, using them for the uses intended by the donors.[216]

What does this Jewish document reveal?

First, the exemplary and touching love and care for their people. Each member of the nation, as part of a single organism, is comprehensively cared for by the community, ready to come to its aid in every instance of life. Secondly, the document reflects the will of the community to always take advantage of its environment, even the municipality and the state, to which it seeks to shift some of its expenses. The document betrays the existence of coercive power among the Jews, as long as this power can levy taxes, even as unpleasant for the bourgeoisie as the progressive-income tax. The document even points to the sources of the *kolkhozes* subsequently established in Russia: it turns out that the spirit of cooperation and artels comes from the Jews. Finally, here again we find evidence of the connection between

---

[216] M. B. Kleiman, *The Jewish Community, Essence and Character*, Petrograd, 1917.

themselves and the central Jewish organizations, the world unity of the Jewish people, and the existence of the Jewish inter-state.

114. Jewish Councils as an Amalgamation of the Communities into the State

In addition to Harbin, there are Jewish communities in Hailar, Qiqihar, Mukden, Dairen, Shanghai, Tianjin, Kobe, Manchukuo, China, and Asia, and the mystery has ceased to be a mystery—all these communities acted as a single entity. All these communities acted as one whole, as a kind of autonomous region of the world Jewish inter-state, electing its general governing body—the Far Eastern Jewish National Council, with its executive body (the so-called Executive Committee) in Harbin. The chairman of the council was, of course (as to why—see below), Dr. Abram Josephovich Kaufman.

There are the same Jewish Councils in the USSR (in Birobidzhan), in England, in America, and in other parts of the world. The Jewish Council unites the Jews of a group of countries, singled out according to this or that feature, into a kind of autonomous region of world Jewry.

The Jewish National Council in East Asia does a tremendous amount of work. It not only serves the religious, cultural, legal, economic and national needs of local Jewry as Jewry (that is, as part of world Jewry), it also constantly interferes in the life of the Russian peoples and emigrants under the pretext of protection of Jewish interests.

The existence of the Jewish Councils with the executive committees shows that the whole idea of the Soviets has a Jewish origin. It was not Khrustalev-Nosarbut rather Trotsky who put it into circulation in Russia during the 1905 revolution.[217]

The Jewish councils connect the individual communities to each other in a Jewish inter-state. The next instance is the Jewish World Congresses.

The Zionist M. M. Margolin, in his pamphlet *The National Movement and Jewry*, published in 1917, notes:

> For long centuries, the Jewish people have believed fervently in their national rebirth, they have believed that free, in peace and in truth, they will live in their own land in the future. The

---

[217] Georgy Stepanovich Khrustalev-Nosar (1879–1918), a sworn attorney, in 1905 was one of the initiators of the creation of trade unions; in 1905, he was chairman of the St. Petersburg Soviet of Workers' Deputies. Although both were socialist in orientation, he had quarrels with Trotsky. (Translator's note)

latent national energy living in this faith will, when the moment is favorable, be transformed into kinetic energy, into an active national thought, into a steadfast will for national rebirth.

Life as a Blue Jew was a self-contained world of its own spiritual and cultural values, its own rules of conduct, its own evaluation of the individual, a world with its own ideals and hopes. Abandoned by a hostile environment and constrained by self-discipline, the blue world stood firm for centuries, until some of the world's greatest events dealt blow after blow, shattering its foundations.

The life of a *golus* Jew was a closed, self-serving world, developing for itself its own spiritual and cultural values, its own rules of conduct, its own assessment of personality, a world that lived by its own ideals and hopes. Abandoned from the outside by a hostile environment and shackled by internal discipline, the *golus'* world stood unbroken for many centuries, until a series of the greatest world events began to strike blow after blow, shattering its age-old foundations.

115. Parties and International Jewish Organizations

Passions often boil within Jewish communities, but almost never outwardly. No matter what disputes may be stirred up within the Jewish community, outwardly it acts as a whole. This does not mean, however, that there is not a struggle of opinions and views, notably over tactics for realizing Jewish aspirations, which leads to a multiplicity of Jewish parties. Jewish political parties do exist and fight with one another, but there are values that for all their members are above party politics. These values are the religious and national interests of all Jewish people.

Jabotinsky and his movement were always attacked by another powerful Jewish party, the Zionists. But when Jabotinsky died, all Jewish groups, including the Zionists, were touchingly united in mourning him as a great Jew. This example is very instructive.

There are two main Jewish parties: the Zionists and the Revisionists.

Zionists after the First World War formed the World Zionist Organization, centered in London and forming branches everywhere.

Its leader or chairman of the executive, as its board is called, was first Nahum Sokolov, and after his death Chaim Weizmann, sometimes called the "doctor" by Jews, sometimes "professor." A capable chemist, an inspirational speaker, a brilliant journalist, and a tenacious organizer.

Volume I: Contemporary Judaization of the World | 315

The chairman of the Zionist city committee in Harbin (Communist Party terminology) is the same indefatigable Dr. Kaufman, chairman of the Harbin Community and the Far Eastern Jewish Council. He is also a special commissioner of the WZO Executive for all of East Asia. The goal of the Zionists, according to them, is the creation of a Jewish state in Palestine.

Revisionists call themselves the New Zionist Organization. Their center (in New York) was headed until his recent death by "Vladimir" Jabotinsky, a revolutionary from Russia. They, you see, are dissatisfied with England for its insufficient fight against the Arabs, and prefer to fight the Arabs for Palestine with terror. The Zionists are satisfied with English handouts, while the revisionists demand Palestine "on both sides of the Jordan." If the Zionists in terms of ideology can be called liberals, the revisionists are socialists; if in terms of tactics the Zionists are Mensheviks, the revisionists are Bolsheviks. In applying this phraseology, one must remember that the Jews invented it especially for us "goyim" and that it is totally inapplicable to Jewish life: they have their own ideology, their own program, and their own criteria.

The Zionists have their own women's organizations, such as the WIZO, the Women's International Zionist Organization. The revisionists also have a women's organization.

The Zionists unite their youth in the cultural-sports society Maccabi. The center of the maccabi and the accabi women is, of course, also located in London, where the young Jewish sportsmen and sportswomen are headed by a man who calls himself Professor Brodetsky. An immigrant from Russia (not from the Soviet Union, but from Tsarist Russia), he is directly connected to the British government and the chairman of the London community and the Council of British Jewry.

There is also a Maccabi chapter in Harbin, led by "champion" Lehmanstein, who recently returned from a memorable trip to the United States.

The revisionist youth organization is called "Brit Trumpeldor," in memory of the Jewish terrorist and former Russian soldier Joseph Trumpeldor, who was killed in a battle with the Arabs in the ill-fated Palestine. The "Beitarists" and "Beitaroks" are headed by a man called Abrahams, based in New York; there is also a department in Harbin, headed by a former "Englishman" from Siberia, Comrade Klein.

There are also Jewish parties, openly socialist and even Communist. All of them, it is said, in spite of their mutual ideological rivalry, cooperate with each other in the practical sphere in the public interest.

It is interesting to note that in most communities all available Jewish parties cooperate with each other on a parity basis. On the board of the Jewish community in Harbin, for example, all shades of Jewish political thought are represented, mainly Zionists and Revisionist Zionists.

It is also interesting to note that Jewish political parties have a global reach and function as international Jewish organizations, whose propaganda, education, cultural and organizational work, and connections strengthen the global unity of the Jewish people and the internal life of the worldwide Jewish inter-state.

116. International Jewish Organizations

Besides parties, there are also international Jewish organizations, open and secret, such as the World Israel Union, whose manifesto we have already cited, JOINT, ECO, Zitzem, Keren, ORT, OZE, TOZ, etc.

The Alliance Israélite Universelle was founded in 1860," says the *Jewish World* of 1939.

> As the first article of its charter states, its purpose is: 1) to work everywhere for the emancipation and progress of the Jews; 2) to give support to those who suffer for their Jewishness, and 3) to encourage all kinds of publications of this direction.

Here, of course, only overt aims are indicated, but they, too, are suggestive of much reflection. The *Jewish Guide* continues its story:

> At the head of the AIU is the Central Committee. The chairman of the AIU held his position for a long time (from 1863 to 1866 and from 1868 to 1880), and had a great influence on its development under Adolphe Crémieux, and Narcis Levin (from 1898 to 1915). In some countries the WJC has local committees. One of the main activities of the WJC is to intervene for Jews suffering persecution in different countries, and to appeal on their behalf to European powers and to the public opinion of the civilized world. In the very beginning of its existence, the WJC defended Jews convicted in Saratov of ritualistic persecution. A few years later it worked hard to obtain equal rights for Swiss Jews. The fate of the Jews of Eastern Europe has always been the subject of its chief concerns. From the mid-1860s to, one might even say, the beginning of the Great War, the WJC worked tirelessly to deal with the situation of the Jews in Romania. It convened special congresses on the situation in Berlin in 1872 and in Paris in 1875 and sent a delegation to the Berlin Congress of 1878; Adolphe Crémieux went twice to Bucharest. The WJC also repeatedly advocated for the Jews of

Serbia, Bulgaria, Persia, and the North African countries of Morocco, Tunisia, Algeria, Egypt, and Tripolitania. At the World Conference of 1919 in Versailles, the WJC, among other Jewish organizations, strove to ensure the rights of national minorities for the Jews of different countries. It should be especially noted that any persecution of Jews in Russia—pogroms, ritual persecutions—caused it to react immediately by taking appropriate steps in appropriate spheres and by drawing public attention to this case of religious intolerance.

We all know what this intensified attention by the WJC has led to in our unhappy homeland.

According to the same handbook, the Joint was founded at the beginning of the First World War under the pretext of helping Jewish victims of the war.[218] During the war, the JDC provided substantial funds ro Russian Jews. At the same time, it also provided aid in Russian territories occupied by German troops through the Zollverein of German Jews. In Austria-Hungary and in the Austro-Hungarian-occupied Russia, the intermediary between the JDC and those whom it came to help was the Vienna Committee of the World Israelite Union. In other words, the Jews themselves confirm that the American JDC worked on both sides of the front, and was undoubtedly engaged in espionage.

In Turkey and the Balkans, the North American ambassador to Constantinople, Henry Morgenthau and his successor Abram Elkus, and in Palestine, the American consul, O. Glesburg, took part in the distribution of the funds raised by Joint. Another careless admission: the ambassadors of the United States were Jews, including the father of the current master of the US economy, the Secretary of the Treasury.

"When the United States entered the war in 1917, JDC's direct dealings with Jewish organizations in Germany, Austria-Hungary, and Turkey became impossible," the Paris Jews continue their self-disclosure, "a neutral aid committee was founded in Holland under the direction of Boris D. Bogen and Max Sepior."

All told, JDC spent $14,730,000 during the war years.

But did the Joint end with the end of the war? Even though its direct purpose was to help war victims, it turns out not.

The *Jewish World* nonchalantly continues:

Since 1921, that is, when the most acute period of post-war ruin had passed and what may have seemed an order began to be established, the work of the JDC took on a new character. Direct support to the victims of catastrophes took second place to

---

[218] Jewish Joint Distribution Committee. (Translator's note)

activities that would strengthen the social base of East European Jewry. To carry out this task, the JDC entered into an agreement with the WJC, and both organizations created the JDC of Reconstruction and Funds. To help Jewish agricultural colonies in Russia, Agrojoint was founded (director Joseph Rosen), which did much to develop Jewish agriculture in Soviet Russia and at the same time supported the development of handicrafts. For the same purpose—to develop Jewish craftsmanship and improve its quality—JDC transfers wide financial support to ORT, and in the field of preserving Jewish physical health it subsidizes appropriate organizations: in Poland TOZ, in other countries OZE. It also finances various facilities established to meet the needs of normal child development: crèches, kindergartens, summer homes for children, orphanages, etc., as well as older Jewish school facilities in Poland, Lithuania, Romania and other countries.

From the beginning of its activity, the JDC spent over eighty-four million dollars in some fifty countries it served until 1936. The honorary chairman of the JDC in New York was for a long time the recently deceased banker Felix Warburg, and the chairman was P. Gaiman.

The general director for European countries from the beginning of the JDC was Dr. Bernhard Kahn (succeeded latterly by Maurice C. Tropper), and the director and financial advisor was David Katz. The Main Committee for Europe has been located in Paris since 1933—that is, since Hitler came to power in Germany.

The Jewish Colonization Association (JCA) was founded by Baron Moritz Hirsch in the autumn of 1918 to resettle persecuted European Jews, especially Russian Jews, in the overseas colonies. The society has a charter registered in England, and its capital consists of sums donated and bequeathed by Baron Hirsch. The society is headed by a board, whose chairman is Sir O. D. Avigdor Goldschmidt, and its affairs are managed by the Directorate General in Paris and its subordinate bodies in various countries. Since 1924, Louis Ungre, doctor of law and humanities, has been the chief director. During its existence, it worked in Argentina, Brazil, the United States, North America, Canada, Soviet Russia, Poland, Lithuania, Latvia, Estonia, Bessarabia, Bukovina, Marmoros (former Hungarian province incorporated in Romania), Czechoslovakia, Turkey, Cyprus, and Palestine. It continues to operate in almost all of these countries. It regulated the emigration of Jews from Eastern Europe to overseas countries, the aid and encouragement of savings and loan societies, the founding and support of vocational schools and other forms of professional education, aid to general education, etc.

To the secret Jewish organizations, in addition to Freemasonry, largely administered and controlled by Jewry, should be included the various secret Jewish international unions and above all the Order of B'nai B'rith, which is nothing more than a purely Jewish branch of Freemasonry, controlling all the rest.

117. B'nai B'rith

B'nai B'rith ("Sons of the Covenant") is the Freemasonry within Freemasonry: only Jews are accepted as members.

This is a secret Jewish Masonic organization based on the system of lodges, similar to other Masonic systems.

But the members of B'nai B'rith lodges are usually included in the leadership of Jewish communities, in the leadership of Jewish political parties, in the membership of lodges of all other Masonic systems (such as the Scottish Rite, the Grand Orient of France, the Rosenkreuzers and others), and thus, on one hand, ensuring Jewish unity, while on the other hand ensuring the unity of Masonry and its obedience to Jewry, while simultaneously, through the community and its apparatuses, both directly and through Masonry, governing the non-Jewish environment around it.

Here is the scheme of Freemasonry within Freemasonry.

The Scottish Rite has its own hierarchy and organization, the Grand Orient has its own, the Rosenkreuzers have their own, the individual systems do not mix, the grassroots lodges sometimes even fight, but in each lodge sits, unknown to the others, representatives of B'nai B'rith, and they direct the whole machinery in one direction.

Lodge B'nai B'rith of a given city actually manages the lodges of all Masonic systems in that city.

The Grand Lodge B'nai B'rith of a country effectively directs all the lodges—the "ateliers"—of all the other Masonic systems of that country.

Other Masonic systems are usually crowned "Supreme Councils." Only the Rosenkreuzers, who claim to be Christian, do not have a Supreme Council. Instead, they have an "Emperor." Such is the case of John Lewis in New York. B'nai B'rith also has no collegiality at the very top: B'nai B'rith, like the Rosenkreuzers, is headed by an emperor, with the difference that his name is not published anywhere, no one knows him, and he twists as he wants, the "emperor" of the Rosenkreuzers, the Supreme Councils of all Masonic systems, world Jewry, and perhaps even the entire globe. This "forerunner of the Messiah," a descendant of King David, is the representative of the coming Jewish Antichrist.

Harbin *Jewish Life*, in a fit of candor, once published in 1928:

> The famous prominent Jewish publicist and thinker Ahad-Gaam (Asher Ginsburg), who played a prominent role in the history of the Palestine-Philippine movement, founded in 1890 a circle with a charter similar in many ways to that of the Masonic lodges.
>
> The Union is divided into lodges, and each lodge consists of at least five members.
>
> Every three months, their members contribute at least two percent of their personal and household income to their lodge.
>
> The main lodge is organized to unite and coordinate the activities of all the lodges.
>
> Those who join must pledge to observe and fulfill the statutes, to keep the secrecy of the rite, even the right to leave it.

118. World Jewish Congresses

The external manifestation of the Jewish inter-state are the periodic sessions of the world Jewish "parliament"—the world Jewish congresses.

The first congress was held, as we have already mentioned, in 1897 in Basel.

The last congress took place in New York last year.

Previously these conventions took place mainly in Switzerland. Now they take place in New York.

They are attended by representatives of Jewish councils, major Jewish organizations and parties, and international Jewish leaders.

Some Jewish government or supra-government reports on its affairs and at the same time instructs the Jewish masses, through the ruling elite, to go further.

Jewish Life describes the first Zionist Congress this way:

> In the last days of August 1897, a historic event took place in Basel. Representatives of the Jews of different countries met and expressed their will that a part of the Jewish people should be reborn as a proper nation in its ancient homeland.
>
> Convened under the banner of the "Jewish State," the party congress was supposed to limit itself to proclaiming the conditional national existence of Jewry, depending on its acquisition of its own territory. But even in this form, the

manifestation had historical significance. In the very same Western Europe where, since the Sanhedrin of Paris, Jews had been insisting that they no longer had any claim to the title of a nation, there was now suddenly a call for a national revival.[219] Basel 1897 atoned for the sin of Paris 1807 ninety years later.

On August 29th, the congress opened with two hundred delegates and three hundred guests and newspaper correspondents. Delegates from Russia, representatives of the Hovenay-Zion and the Odessa Palestinian Committee (M. M. Usyshkin and others), had not yet played the active role befitting them at this historic congress.

The delegates were impressed by the imposing atmosphere of the congress, at the opening of which the oldest delegate, Dr. Leppe of Romania, recalled the return of the Babylonian prisoners by decree of the ancient king Cyrus and proposed that a welcome telegram be sent to the Turkish sultan. The proposal, which had a diplomatic purpose, was unanimously accepted, and it seemed to many dreamers that this was the beginning of political negotiations.

In his keynote speech, T. Herzl tried to merge the various currents in Zionism in order to attract all to a common cause. He greatly expanded the scope of his political program with a great aphorism: "Zionism is a return to Jewishness, which precedes a return to the Jewish land." He meant to say that the mere hope of a political revival would lead an assimilated Jew to a national consciousness.

While paying tribute to the pioneers of Palestinian colonization, Herzl argued that the old ways of doing things are of no use to the popular cause; if ten thousand Jews are brought into Palestine every year, it will take nine hundred years to bring all nine million. Meanwhile the Turkish authorities will not admit even this modest immigration, and will resume the repression of those "sneaking" into the country.

Only through a political agreement with the Sublime Porte on the basis of mutual services can a legal mass settlement of the Jews in Palestine be achieved and a lasting national center established there. It is the task of the congress to find such ways and authorize political negotiations accordingly. [220]

---

[219] The Sanhedrin met in Paris on February 9th, 1807. (Translator's note)
[220] *Jewish Life,* No. 7 of November 10th, 1942.

119. The Jewish Super-Government

No one knows where the world Jewish government is hiding. In prehistoric antiquity it emerged under the name of the Sanhedrin. But the last time the Sanhedrin revealed itself was for a brief time in the time of Napoleon, after which it sank into utter darkness.

Only very recently did it appear in *Jewish Life* that land had been purchased somewhere near Jerusalem for . . . the Sanhedrin.

From this we can conclude that the Sanhedrin is hiding in or near Jerusalem.

External manifestation of Jewish supremacist government is an international Jewish Agency, created at the initiative of American billionaire Felix Warburg in 1928 in England, by the union of Zionists and non-Zionists to cooperate with the Jews who remained Jews, and the so-called "assimilated." That is, those who are imbued with the psychology of foreign peoples and nations.

This Warburg is one of those Warburgs, one of which subsidized Germany and as well as the Triple Entente during the First World War. The Warburgs then skimmed revenues from both sides of the bloody world front.

This same Warburg is also one of the owners of the famous Kuhn, Loeb & Co., banking house, one of whose directors—Yankel Schiff—subsidized the Bolshevik revolution in Russia.

The Warburgs are at the head of the American Federal Reserve System, the world's most powerful banking association, controlling the circulation of gold all over the world and causing such financial storms, compared with which the most destructive revolutions are nothing in comparison.

The Warburgs, on the other hand, control the Jewish Joint and all its funds.

In 1928 the Harbin *Jewish Life* published such reports on the construction of the World Jewish Center:

> The members of the Jewish Agency Board are: Bruno Asch (Frankfurt), Dr. Bernhard Kahn, director of the Joint (Berlin), commercial advisor Gershon Simon (Berlin), Rabbi Dr. I. Unna (Mannheim), and director Oscar Wasserman (Berlin).
> Alternates: Prof. Georg Verngard (Berlin), Dr. F. Brodsky or Dreyfuss, Dr. Hahn (Essen), I. Heckscher (Hamburg), ministerial advisor Dr. S. Hirsch (Stuttgart), Rabbi Dr. Horowitz (Frankfurt), B. Israel (Berlin), Dr. Pei Meyer (Munich), Leo Simon, Prof. M. Zoverheim, Dr. Sonderhein, Dr. Ludwig Tip (Berlin), Mrs. Margarita Tietz (Cologne).

Oscar Wasserman gave the first speech at the conference, followed by Rabbi Dr. L. Beck, Alfred Lisser, Kurt Blumenfeld, and Colonel Kisch,

An interesting talk on Palestine was given by Max Warburg, the renowned financial banker. The conference sent greeting telegrams to Professor Weizmann and Louis Marshall.

A meeting of the organizing committee for the expansion of the Jewish Agency was held in Warsaw. Of the non-Zionists, the meeting was attended by Ad. Peretz, Prof. M. Eiger (Vilna), Dr. R. Landau (Jewish community in Krakow), B. Ethington and Jarocinski (Lodz), lawyer Enzel, Trusner (center, Union of merchants), Rabbi Prof. Shor, Rabbi Lifshitz (Kalish), Chairman of the Rabbinical Union, Rabbi David Kaganer (Warsaw Rabbinate) and Dr. Goldfahl. Of the Zionists: Dr. L. Reich, deputies Rosenblat, Levitte, Farvstein, Dr. Tartakover and Dr. Meltzer.

The congress of the Union of Swiss Jewish Communities unanimously decided to participate in the Agency. Dreyfus-Brodsky, the chairman of the Union of Jewish Communities, was elected as a representative on the Board of the Agency.

The National Council of Jews in South Africa elected its representative, S. Refoeli, to represent it on the board of the Jewish Agency.

The Jewish Agency has ambassadors and chargé d'affaires in every country of the world. As *Jewish Life* reported in 1940, the same comprehensive Dr. A. I. Kaufman is a special delegate to East Asia.

The Jewish Agency is in official relations with many governments and in particular, as the same magazine reported in 1940, with the British government. In the same year the correspondent of the American *World Press* published a telegram about a formal treaty of mutual assistance between England and Judea, represented by the British government and the Executive, the board of the Jewish Agency.

This treaty confirms below the definition of the Jewish Agency as the outward manifestation of an invisible Jewish government and super-government for all other countries and nations.

The Harbin *Jewish Life* described the leaders of the Jewish Agency in such pathetic and refined words in 1928.

Well, poor Zionism has moved from its basement into the rich palaces of Jewish millionaires, Jewish lords; Zionism has become a world problem, a political problem, with great potential, a very bold, conscious experiment.

Dr. Chaim Weitzman is flexible and resourceful in his means, but firm and resolute in the main point of his goal of rebuilding Palestine in the Zionist spirit. Full of whimsical, momentary, expressionist sentiments, at the same time he has a much-coveted patience. A real politician, he does everything in his power for Zionism at a given moment, and then lets the Almighty take care.

Alfred Monde is a synthesis of British patriotism, great industrial creative force, and practical Zionism. Monde knows in detail all the trends of our cultural renaissance, and is familiar with all contemporary social problems. An intellectual and practical thinker in terms of long series of numbers and versatile in his attitudes, easily jumps from liberalism to conservatism. An enemy of dead, stiffened formulas. Always driven by the spirit of the times and yet restrained, confined within known boundaries.

James Rothschild was brought up in the Zionist atmosphere of his father Edmund (Nadiv-Giod) and in the true Jewish atmosphere of his mother, daughter of a pious Frankfurt Rothschild. He is a Zionist and a visionary, knows Hebraism, loves Jewish masses, has a connection to literature and the arts, is familiar with all Zionist and Jewish issues and problems in general. He knows perfectly well all the leaders and great minds of modern Jewry. He combines the vagaries of the baron and of bohemia. A patriarch, burdened by the old heritage and thinking freely about the dreams of the Jewish Renaissance and "alrightism." He lives modestly, is reserved, and influences in a Jewish way wherever he can, but not in a shouty, no-showy way.

Yakov Wasserman is one of the directors of the Deutsche Reichsbank (German State Bank). An intelligent mind, he is well versed with numbers. A man with a broad view of modern economic problems. A strictly disciplined mind and yet not without enthusiasm and imagination. Not a Zionist, but a student of Palestine, which he recently visited, alongside the Zionist problems; a man of fresh, entrepreneurial energy. He quickly understood Zionism as a global problem. Cold and measured in his outward attitude, but not without feeling.

Louis Marshall, a conservative, is at odds with the spirit of the times. A veteran in Jewish social work, he is well acquainted with the problems of world Jewry. A leader, a lawyer, with a broad Jewish heart, he has a strong sense of responsibility, is resolute, stubborn in his leadership, with a temper, impulsive and also aggressive, but has lagged behind the progressive Jewish intellectual world.

Felix Warburg—his inner essence is more Jewish than American. An intellectual, thinking, and feeling Jew, with a broad horizon, interested in the reconstruction of Eretz Yisrael, has a keen interest in the cultural aspect of Zionism (as his special interest in the Jewish university in Jerusalem proves). He flirts with philosophical, religious, and social ideas. Easily influenced by well-known circumstances and people. A capitalist romantic.

Dr. D. Frenkel is a man who once made a name for himself as a medical doctor, dealing with sanitary issues and with problems of public health. In his later years, he is one of the vice presidents at the Metropolitan Insurance Society, a position that brings him into daily contact with the masses, and dwells on environmental issues of great magnitude.

As you can see, intellectually and materially, the Jewish super-government has assembled some pretty big figures.

120. The Scheme of the Jewish Inter-State

We can now sketch a diagram of the Jewish inter-state. At its base lies the community, with its governmental, economic, and cultural institutions and its spheres of influence into the social life of the surrounding nations.

Adjoining the community are the local branches of international and political organizations, whose members are members of the community. To simplify the scheme, let's take the two branches of the Zionist and Revisionist parties, with their women's and youth organizations, their propaganda and educational organs, and their influence among the "goyim."

Parallel to the community, let us outline the lodges of the various Masonic systems and draw lines of influence from them to the surrounding society, culture, and economy.

The community is led by the board, the branches of international and political Jewish organizations by the local or city committees, and the Masonic lodges—by their masters. Above all of them hangs, like an invisible six-pointed star, the B'nai B'rith lodge. Their commands of leadership go to the community, to the organizations, to the Masonic lodges of all the other degrees, their direct orders in all directions.

Here is the first row of our scheme. Let's move on to the second. All the communities are subordinate to the Jewish Council. The council heads the executive committee, the branches of Jewish international political organizations are headed by commissioners or special commissioners of "executive-centers," the Masonic lodges of each system are subordinate to their main lodge. From the Jewish Council, the commissioner or special commissioner of the main lodges, the bundles of influence go then in all directions, including the local and centralized authorities of the "goyim" states, while the special commissioner of the Jewish Agency—apparently the main leader of B'nai B'rith—invisibly overhangs the entire structure. Leadership and influence go from them in all directions—including the governments of the "goyim" states.

And here is the third, highest kind of this damned scheme. The Soviets are led by the World Jewish Congresses, Jewish international organizations and political parties by their Central Committee and the Executives, Freemasonry of various systems by individual Supreme Councils (except for the Rosenkreuzers, who, as already mentioned, are led by an "emperor"). Bundles of influence and leadership then go in all directions. And over the third row reigns the invisible "king of kings"—the "emperor" of B'nai B'rith and, apparently, the Jewish Agency Executive. The rest of the scheme is lost in pitch darkness, the very darkness from which all evil, embodied in the hideous figure of the devil, springs.

Among the central Jewish bodies of the present time we must also include the governments of England, the US, and the USSR, the Comintern, and the Finintern, without which the scheme would be incomplete. In fact, despite all their signs, these bodies play a major role in the world Jewish conspiracy.

So, the scheme is ready. It only needs to be supplemented with minor details. We leave this to the readers and researchers. It remains for us to illustrate the scheme with figures.

121. World Jewish Population

According to official Jewish data, published, in particular, in 1939 in *Jewish Life*, the settlement of Jewish internment in that year was given by the following figures.

The total number of Jews in all countries has been estimated to be 15,290,983. Most of these numbers come from the United States: 4,740,048. But with the incorporation of the Jews of Lithuania, Latvia, Poland, and Estonia, the USSR took precedence. Other countries had these numbers of Jews:

Poland—3,028,837;
USSR—3,028,307;
(according to the Russian Fascist Union, this figure is 6,009,000);
Romania—728,115 (according to Romanian data, 2,000,000);
Germany—499,682;
Hungary—444,567;
Czechoslovakia—356,830;

England—300,000;
France—240,000;
Austria—191,408;
Netherlands—156,817;
Lithuania—155,125;
Latvia—93,479;
Greece—72,791;
Yugoslavia—68,405;
Belgium—60,000;
Turkey—55,592;
Bulgaria—28,565;
Asia—785,133;
Africa—501,787;
Australia—25,954.

It is interesting to look at the figures for the Jewish population of the world's major centers. In first place, the Jews choose New York, whose community in 1939 numbered 1,765,000 members, but we are inclined to give the lead to the Red Square, where about 2,000,000 Jews were already living at that time.

Next:
Warsaw—384,354;
Chicago—300,251;
Philadelphia—247,000;
London—231,991;
Budapest—201,301;
Lodz—191,720;
Vienna—178,034;
Paris—175,000.

These figures are, of course, subject to change. Right now, as this book is being written, there are continuous shifts in the statistics. In Europe, for example, there should now be very different figures, which we do not yet have. Already in 1940, the Jewish JDC published such figures on the relocations of Jewish centers and welfare:

Germany—220,000 Jews remain. A quarter resort to aid.

Austria—50,000 Jews left, 25,000 get aid.

Bohemia and Moravia—75,000 Jews, varied rates of aid.

Slovakia—90,000 Jews, 35,000 Polish refugees, many Jewish refugees from Germany, 35,000 get aid.

France—42,000 German Jewish refugees, 12,500 get daily aid; 150,000 Eastern European Jews, most of whom are assisted.

Switzerland—18,000 Jewish refugees, 3,000 get daily aid.

Belgium and Holland—22,000 Jews and 40,000 Jewish refugees; no communication at present.

Poland—500,000 Jewish war victims receive food from JDC, 200,000 receive clothing.

Lithuania—15,000 Polish Jewish refugees in the Vilna and Kauna area. Half of the Jewish population of Vilna, i.e., 30,000, require daily aid. 2,000 refugees from Germany, Austria and Memel also receive daily aid.

Romania—25 percent of the 900,000 Romanian Jews are deprived of their citizenship and the right to work, as well as 1,500 Polish Jewish war refugees and 400 German Jewish refugees.

Hungary—of 600,000 Jews, 200,000 are expelled from service and work because of racial laws, and 1,500 German Jewish refugees and 500 Polish Jewish war refugees have to be taken care of.

These are figures from the second half of 1940. Since then, the situation of European Jewry has changed even more in a worse direction for the former masters of life. And it is getting worse every month. Thank God!

122. The Hidden Armies of World Jewry

When calculating the Jewish forces, one cannot limit oneself to the figure of sixteen million. Moreover, it must be kept in mind that this figure is given by the Jews themselves. This figure is clearly unreliable: it is in fact an understatement. German historians, for example, say there are around seventeen million Jews in the world. The difference in the figures is due to the fact that, besides the openly admitted Jews or the Jews of the Mosaic Law, that is to say the Jews who openly and officially profess their Jewish religion, there are also a great many Jews who remain hidden, who profess to be atheists, are indifferent, or profess other religions. The last trick of the Jews is deciphered by the Russian folk wisdom in the well-known proverb: "A baptized Jew is like a forgiven thief." We have written quite a lot about examples of hidden Jews acting in favor of the open Jews.

The facts of recent history and modern times prove that Jews who are outwardly alienated from Judaism are a great danger. It is the latter Jews, such as Karl Marx, Gersh Zinoviev, and Lazar Kaganovich, who are the greatest criminals on the international stage.

To the hidden Jews should be added half-Jews, quarter-Jews, and all those persons who have Jewish blood in their veins for at least four generations from a Jewish ancestor. It is a very strong blood, and it transmits the harmful characteristics of the Jewish father or Jewish mother, so that after two or three generations their descendant can suddenly feel Jewish and sometimes even openly returns to Judaism.

A classic example of the evil essence of the hidden Jews from today is the story of the so-called Spanish Marranos, whose ancestors outwardly renounced Judaism for fear of the Inquisition in the Middle Ages, and whose distant descendants have been nursing their malice toward Christianity; destroying convents and churches, raping nuns and brutally murdering priests in the Spanish Civil War (see newspaper accounts not only from the German press, but also of the English, French, and American press friendly to the Red Spaniards).

On the basis of this instructive history, we are inclined to call all hidden Jews and descendants of Jews "Marranos," a term which is used to refer to all Jews by origin and not by religion. God knows how many there are around the world, maybe about one hundred million. Summing up the number of Jewish inter-nation, this figure must be added to the sixteen million professed open Jews.

In order to finally establish the number of the Jewish human force, to the sum of the members of the Jewish inter-nation we must add the horde of "Shabbos goy," those non-Jews who foolishly or intentionally serve the Jews. The word "Shabbos goy" is derived from the Hebrew name for the Christian attendant the Jews hired to clean the synagogues on the Sabbath, when the "real people"—the Jews, as ordained by Yahweh—should spend time in complete idleness preparing for the Sabbath. Shabbos goyim include Freemasons and members of the various secret organizations run by Judas, state, political, social, cultural, economic and any other figures who serve Judas, consciously or unconsciously, as well as any human scum and filth that abounds in every country.

The Shabbos goyim increased the armies of the dark forces by many hundreds of millions of two-legged beasts.

As you can see, we are dealing with a great and formidable force.

All of these "Marranos" and "Shabbos goyim" are real subversive units in a worldwide Jewish subversion, sneaking deep into the rear of all nations. Are we talking about detachments? No, entire armies! What kind of detachments are these, with millions of saboteurs in their ranks?

123. The Jews Are Taking Over Our Cities

There is one segment in the statistics of world Jewry that deserves special attention. It is the attraction of Jews to the cities. In *Jewish Life* on January 1st, 1943, in the article "The fate and future of the Jewish people," we found figures for the percentage of Jews in urban areas. It turns out, as the Jews themselves write:

> The percentage of Jews in the cities everywhere is much higher than that of the non-Jewish population. To give you an example of the percentage of urban residents:
> In Germany, in 1933 it was 84.5 percent for Jews and 49.5 percent for Christians.

In Poland, in 1931 it was 76 percent for Jews, 22.1 percent for Christians.

In Romania, in 1930 it was 69.0 percent for Jews and 18.0 percent for Christians.

In Latvia, in 1935 it was 92.6 percent for Jews and 33.6 percent for Christians.

In Hungary, in 1930 it was 79.4 percent for Jews and 40.9 percent for Christians.

In Czechoslovakia, in 1930 it was 50.8 percent for Jews and 21.9 percent for Christians.

In Poland, in 1931, Jews made up almost half of the urban population. In some provinces, such as Polesia, 49.2 percent; in Bolshie, 49.1 percent; in Lublin, 43.7 percent; in Bialystok, 38.4 percent. In no province (except those belonging to Prussia before 1918) did they fall below 24.8 percent of the urban population. In all Polish cities combined, the percentage of Jews is 27.3 percent.

In Soviet Russia there is a continuing strong influx to big cities from the countryside and the backwoods, which began in 1917 and was clearly visible in the census of 1925.

In Eastern countries, Jews live almost exclusively in large cities. In 1931, for example, of the native Jews in Tunisia (25,390 souls) 45.2 percent lived in the capital city. In Armant, with a population of 5,144, the 2,736 Jews were in the majority.

In French Morocco, in 1936, 75,098, or 46 percent of a total of 161,000 Jews, lived in the three largest cities of Casablanca, Marrakesh, and Fez, representing respectively 15.1 percent, 13.5 percent and 7.3 percent of the population.

In Iraq, over 90 percent of the Jews are concentrated in Baghdad, Basra, and Mosab, and in Egypt in 1927, 93 percent of the Jews lived in Alexandria and Cairo.

A similar situation exists in Syria and Iran, Palestine being an exception. The colossal land colonization of the last fifty years has resulted in 24 percent of the Jews living in agrarian colonies.

But some of these colonies have more than 10,000 inhabitants and significant municipal rights.

In Germany and America, the preference of Jews for large cities can be seen in the fact that the percentage of Jews in the population increases as the city grows.

The percentage of Jews was:

	America	Germany
The capital (in America—New York)	30	3.8
Other cities with populations over 100,000 people	5.2	1.2
Places with a population of 50,000 to 100,000 people	4.3	0.7
Places with populations between 25,000 (20,000 in Germany) and 50,000	3.1	0.6
Places with populations between 10,000 and 25,000	1.8	0.4
Places with a population of less than 10,000 people	0.6	0.2
In the whole country	3.5	0.8

So testifies the New Year's *Jewish Life*: look, Aryans, the Jews are taking over your cities.

124. The Jews Are Taking Over Our Capitals

"The influx into the capitals" is the title of the next essay in this series, which begins with an outspoken statement by a Jewish author:

The special attention of the Jews to metropolitan cities is clear from the table.... Masses of hundreds of thousands or even two million Jews in one city, as in New York, something that never occurred in the Middle Ages. The largest communities in Prague, Frankfurt, and Amsterdam numbered a few thousand souls at that time.

Only then were the Jews at the height of their prosperity in Spain. Granada and Toledo had comparatively large numbers of Jewish inhabitants. In the Middle East, such cities included Baghdad, Smyrna, Constantinople, and Thessaloniki. And in 1937 there were twenty-two cities in Europe and America with more than a million inhabitants, a total of fifty-two million citizens, and among them 4,500,000, or 8.6 percent, were Jews.

One in twelve persons in these large cities is therefore a Jew. The percentage of Jews was highest in Warsaw (30.29 percent) and New York (30.0 percent), and lowest in Hamburg (1.5 percent), Glasgow (1.5 percent), Birmingham (0.6 percent), and Barcelona (0.3 percent).

In the twenty-two cities combined, this percentage of Jews was four times higher than the percentage of Jews in the total population of Europe (2.5 percent) and America (1.9 percent). Among the Jews of the world, 27 percent live in cities of more than one million inhabitants. Only Jews have this "metropolitan characteristic."

The table to which he refers is sufficient here:

Country	Capital	Year	Number of Jews in the capital	Percentage of Jews in the country in the capital
Germany	Berlin	1933	160,564	0.8
Hungary	Budapest	1930	204,371	5.1
Poland	Warsaw	1931	352,659	9.7
Austria	Vienna	1934	178,039	2.8
France	Paris	1935	175,000	0.6
Great Britain	London	1937	234,000	0.8
Bulgaria	Sofia	1934	25,863	0.8
Greece	Thessaloniki	1928	55,250	1.2
Holland	Amsterdam	1933	65,558	1.4
USA	New York	1925	2,000,000	3.5
Tunisia	Tunis	1931	25,399	2.3
Argentina	Buenos Aires	1937	140,000	2.0
Brazil	Rio de Janeiro	1937	25,000	0.1
Uruguay	Montevideo	1937	25,000	0.5
South Africa	Johannesburg	1937	40,000	1.0

It testifies: look, Aryans, the Jews are taking over your capitals!

In this table the capital of the USSR is omitted for some reason. Meanwhile in Red Moscow, according to Rudolf Kommos, secretary of the German Anti-Comintern, in 1937 there were already 500,000 Jews.

After parts of Poland, Latvia, Lithuania, and Estonia, filled with Jews, were annexed to the USSR, this number tripled. According to figures from knowledgeable refugees in Moscow, in 1941 there was a concentration of at least 1,500,000 Jews. Think of the horror: every second Muscovite we meet is a Jew. That is half of the population of our ancient capital!

125. Jews Take Over the Centers of Our Capitals

Continuing his essays, Arthur Ruppin, who calls himself Professor Liquid, details in a later issue of the 1943 *Jewish Life*:

> In New York, for example, there has been a steady movement from the poor ghetto on the East Side to Brooklyn and the Bronx, and from there to the glittering and high-society parts of the city, such as Riverside Drive and others.
> Jews made up 10.8 percent of Vienna's population in 1923, but 38.5 percent were in the Leo-Poldstadt area. In Berlin they were 4.3 percent in 1938, but 10.4 percent were in central Berlin; 4.1 percent of the total population of Prague in 1930, but at

the same time 83.3 percent of the population of the Josefstadt district and 16.4 percent of the Altstadt district![221]

"Look, Aryans, the Jews are taking over the centers of your capitals!" the Jewish communal officialdom in East Asia carelessly alarms.

126. Jews Take Over the Center of Russia

In the essays of the Jew Arthur there are words that serve as a formidable warning to the Russian people. It is not Birobidzhan, the Jewish Autonomous Region within Khabarovsk Krai, but the.... I'd rather let Mr. Ruppin have the floor:

Compared to relocations to overseas countries and from Eastern Europe to Central and Western Europe, internal relocations are far less important. The latter took place on a more or less significant scale only in those countries where there were local differences in economic development and where it was profitable for Jews to move from less developed to more developed areas.

This happened in Germany, where Jews moved from the economically backward eastern provinces, mainly Posen and Pomerania, to Berlin and the central and western industrial areas.

The same happened in Russia, where after the revolution there was a large migration from the mainly agricultural areas of Byelorussia and Ukraine to the industrial areas of Ukraine and mainly Central Russia. Some Russian cities which before 1917 had a relatively small Jewish population, now have a large Jewish population: Moscow has 200,000, Kiev has 150,000, Leningrad and Kharkov have over 1,000,000.

In Central Russia, which lay in the Pale of Settlement, in 1897 the Jews numbered 20,000, and in 1938 they numbered over a million. "[222]

This took place in 1938. In 1940, the USSR received "as a gift" another three million Jews from Poland. A large part of them, of course, rushed to Moscow and Central Russia in general.

"The old Moscow had now reached its limit in terms of space: a whole building program had to be developed in order to further expand this administrative center of the USSR," notes Rudolf Kommos in his

---

[221] *Jewish Life*, No. 4, 1943.
[222] Ibid., No. 44, December 10th, 1943.

book *The Jews Behind Stalin*. It is extremely typical that the drafting of this entire program was entrusted to none other than the Jew Lazar Kaganovich. Moreover, the Moscow underground railroad was named after this dark man.

"He now finds himself in the role of that biblical Joseph who holds in his grasp the fate of all his fellow tribesmen in Moscow," says Commos.

The activity of the Muscovite Jews develops, self-evidently, not behind the machine, for all these gentlemen have no inclination whatsoever for menial work. The Jewish journalist M. Suritz, who has visited Moscow, and whose testimony does not have to be challenged, speaks on this subject in the May 13th, 1937 issue of the Jewish newspaper *Moment* in Warsaw, supplying us with very valuable information:

> In the Moscow factories, I was most interested in the percentage of Jewish workers. I was able to ascertain that the total number of Jews employed in Moscow factories, especially among those serving in heavy industry, was extremely limited.
> It was explained to me that among the managerial Soviet circles there were almost no Jewish workers in Moscow at all. The Jewish Moscow consists almost exclusively of the intelligentsia and semi-intelligentsia. The first ones serve numerous government and other official bodies, while the latter work as accountants, employees of firms, clerks, etc.

The Jewish element is now thickly present in Moscow and makes itself felt there at every turn, giving the ancient Russian capital a special character. The atmosphere there is completely different than before, as any tourist who goes there can easily see.

At the Byelorussian Railway Station tourists first of all are met by Jewish interpreters and translators. The Jews make sure that the tourist is taken to a hotel; Jews also keep a close eye on foreign tourists' trips through the "Potemkin villages" of Soviet propaganda.

If a tourist needs to make a more or less large purchase, here again a Jew acts as a salesman in Moscow.

If he has the misfortune to fall ill, he will be treated in Moscow by a Jewish doctor.

If those foreigners who have a chance, be they as foreign correspondents, "specialists," or diplomats, to look behind the scenes of Soviet power, to work with some Soviet official foreigners, or to have a look into the private life of the "red bourgeois," they cannot but agree that the Jewish presence in Moscow is felt at every turn and that all the highest offices of management are entirely in Jewish hands.

The famous American photo reporter James Abbe who published a book *I Photograph Russia*, gives a typical illustration in this regard (the number of which could be multiplied to infinity): "I have closely watched the regular visitors to my Moscow hotel," he writes, "60 percent of them were American Jews; almost all of them are of Russian origin and have come to Moscow now only to see how their countrymen are doing in the new civilization."

It is well established in world Jewish circles that Moscow has become the perfect breeding ground for "our people." Moscow is even better than Palestine itself. It is as good for Jews as New York itself.

And so, in swarms, these kinds of tourists are now flooding Moscow. Dollars don't matter to them anymore, and they willingly leave them for their Soviet counterparts, who are so lacking in foreign exchange.

Already in 1932, the Harbin *Jewish Life* boasted: "Moscow is growing from day to day . . . and the number of Jews in Moscow is growing proportionately. In the last ten years the number of Jews in Moscow has doubled," the magazine smugly notes in a "Letter from Moscow" given to the press by the famous Jewish writer Ben-Zion Katz.

This Katz gives us a picture:

Now the Jews live in the former dacha areas, in all the railway stations: in a place like Elk Island, where no Jew had ever set foot, there are now ten thousand Jewish souls and a synagogue. In Moscow there are even more Jews. Now all suburban railway stations are electrified, trains are running frequently and fast, and all these neighborhoods are like one big city. For Jews coming from Ukraine and Byelorussia, these places around Moscow are paradise.

Jewish World in one place gives the figure of 280,000 Jews living in Moscow, and in another confirms Kommos' figure of 500,000. The Soviet official guidebook *The Whole of the USSR* gives the latter figure. We leave it to our readers to evaluate what happened when parts of Poland, Lithuania, Latvia, Estonia, and Bessarabia were annexed to the USSR.

127. The Inter-State Wants to Conquer the Whole World

The Jewish inter-state poses a significant threat to all nations. The fact is that the Jewish inter-nation, in the name of fulfilling the promises of its prophets, must wage continuous war against all those around it.

Judas hates Christ, so his goal in the realm of religion is to eradicate Christianity.

Christianity is the main enemy, but don't think that the Antichrist will leave other religions alone.

No, he wants all nations to worship him. "Asher Ginsburg dreamed of a temple on Mount Zion, so that all nations would come as pilgrims to this church of eternal peace," observes *Jüdische Rundschau*.

The Harbin *Jewish Life* quotes such "Dreams" of M. M. Usyshkin, one of the most prominent Zionist leaders:

"What will we do with this sanctuary once we are the masters here?" someone suddenly asked, pointing to the Mosque of Omar, towering above Mount Moriah. (The Mosque of Omar is one of the most formidable and beautiful buildings in the world. It was built on the site of the Temple of Solomon. Inside the mosque is Even-Shtia,[223] the place to which, according to the Bible, Abraham brought his son Isaac to be slaughtered.)

"We will turn the mosque into a Jewish temple," answered one. "We have the moral right to do so; it's ours. No one is going to take it away from us. And how many of our temples and synagogues have been turned into churches and mosques over the millennia?"

"No," objected another, "we will turn it into a temple, but not of prayer and lamentation, but one of science and life. A higher humanities school will be established here. Enough moaning, weeping and praying. It is time to teach and learn, to learn and teach. . . ."

"This question was already solved three thousand years ago by the Wise Solomon," said the young writer incredulously.

Staring at Moriah, he solemnly recited the words of Solomon's prayer at the dedication of the temple: "Every prayer, every forgiveness from every man, O You, hear from heaven your house and forgive, and give to man what he asks; for You alone know the hearts of all the sons of men. And also the plea of a foreign tribesman who is not of Your people Israel, a stranger who has come to pray into this house, O You, hear from heaven, your house, and do all that the foreign tribesman asks of You, that all the peoples of the earth may know your name, that they may fear You and know that in your name is called this house which I have built."

His voice, quiet at first, grew louder and louder, and the words of the Stranger-King resounded in the silence of the night like the proclamation of a prophet.

---

[223] The Cornerstone of the World. (Translator's note)

"Yes," he said, "here will rise a temple, but not a synagogue, not a church, not a mosque; it will be a House of Prayer for all nations."

A kind of soul-searching state of mind gripped each of us. Everyone was still long in contemplation and reflection, each realizing that here the mystery of the world's ethics had been solved.[224]

"What was it? A dream or the beginning of reality?" the Jews ask, not noticing what, in fact, they just uttered here.

The storming of the heavens of all religions, therefore, is the goal of Judaism in the realm of the religious.

And in the realm of the national?

Members at the first open Jewish congress in Russia after the revolution explicitly said:

Zionism is the solution to the question of the Jewish people. None of us thinks that the entire Jewish people should be concentrated again in Palestine. At any rate, it is not necessary to solve the problem.

What is necessary and what we are striving for is the creation of a national-territorial center for the dispersed parts of our people, a national metropolis for our national colonies. This center is now established and will continue to be built and replenished by the forces and means of its periphery. The periphery is therefore very important to us [on the other hand, fragments of a nation scattered among other peoples can only be able to lead a healthy life when it has drawn out the juices of the surrounding peoples], stimulation from the metropolis is important. Only thus, in the uninterrupted relationship between center and periphery, in their organic connection, can we imagine the recovery of the Jewish people's organism and the solution to the entire problem of the Jewish people. The work in Palestine and in the Diaspora merge harmoniously for us, one complementing the other, the one flowing out of the other."

Quite a characteristic recognition, isn't it? But there are others.

I am happy to be able to say that those who direct and influence politics in various countries, including some very powerful ones, understand us, our objectives and goals, much more deeply and concretely than they did before. The influence of the

---

[224] *Jewish Life*, No. 42 of October 24th, 1942.

World War has had an effect here too. They are ready to support our claims when the time is right. Distinguished members of the Congress! Three years ago, a great thunder and a tempest broke out, and shook the Old and New Worlds, severely affecting all peoples and nations. The great convulsion, however, does not bring grief and death only. Through the agony, through death and destruction, there are already visible glimmers of revival and the rays of a new, free life. And what will remain forever the greatest result of this struggle is that in it weak and small nations gained the right and the guarantee of a free existence and development.

We believe that when our people will live a normal life in their own land, the national genius will be unleashed in all its might, the time will be revived when he created not only for himself, but for all mankind, when he created the eternal books and eternal truths. A distant, bright path is drawn before us. With this faith we live, we are inspired, and we work, and with this faith we will win.

"At the peace congress, where, I hope, a number of governments will support our petition, or rather our demands, there must be a person who demands it, there must be representation from the Jewish people," said the third Zionist, adding:

The world seeks a federation of peoples, a federation of nations. The great United States has created a united federation of individual states. They have a beautiful multi-star banner, and each state has its own star on this common banner. All of humanity is now moving toward the same banner. Very soon, perhaps, we will see one world banner, a multi-star banner, on which each nation, each country will have its own star. They will all be side by side, big and small, ancient and new.

Gentlemen, shall we allow a people who have lived two thousand years in their own country and dreamed of their own country for two thousand years, shall we allow these people not to have their own star on this beautiful banner? No, gentlemen, we shall have our star, and our star shall burn brightest, for it has passed through the fires of all nations, of all times, of all countries.

"In short, the war has moved Zionism from the realm of utopias and long-term evolutions into the realm of immediate reality. The Russian Revolution acts in the same direction," summed up Chlenov at the time.

That this is so is proved by a simple fact: it was after the revolution that the Russian Zionist Organization grew by leaps and bounds. It is already the most powerful in Jewry. The Zionist response of the Jewish masses to the Russian Revolution is a remarkable fact.

Cantor, released at the same time, in 1917, in a Russia intoxicated with the revolution, a pamphlet called *The War and Zionism*, which added:

And this is already understood in Europe and America by most of the press and many prominent politicians, public figures and journalists. People of different parties and views have converged on it. Here we find the arch-bourgeois conservative *Times* and the officious liberal *Tan*, and the socialists Gustave Herve and Albert Thom, and the minority leader of the French Socialist Party, Karl Marx's grandson Jean Longuet, and the secretary of the International Socialist Bureau, Camille Huysmans, and many others.
The day after the heavy chains of disenfranchisement had fallen from Russian Jewry, large crowds marched through the streets of many Russian cities carrying white and blue banners on which slogans and demands were written: "Freedom in Russia! Land and Will in Palestine!" When a convention of Jewish Socialists in America met soon afterwards, in the last days of March 1917, it was attended by four hundred and one delegates, representing, by a conservative estimate, one hundred and fifty thousand Jewish workers of this country. One after another spoke, old and experienced fighters for the Jewish working class, and called for a struggle for Palestine.

Dr. H. Zhitlovsky said to Cantor:

With the fall of Russian tsarism, the predictions of the Jewish prophets about the liberation of all mankind begin to come true. This will take place on the basis of the complete liberation of small nations, and among them the Jewish people.

Thus, the inter-state seeks to implement:

- The destruction of every nation and the subjugation of every state, the creation of a single Jewish empire in which all the "goyim" would become subjects of the "chosen" people.
- The destruction of every non-Jewish family, since "humanoid creatures" cannot have families.

- The expropriation of all non-Jewish property, since those who are "worse than a dog" cannot have anything of their own.
- The enslavement of every human being into hopeless servitude, if he does not belong to the Jewish inter-nation.

Flip through the Talmud and you will see the aforementioned goals of Judaism. Familiarize yourself with the history of the Jewish people and you will see that the Jews have always pursued these goals; ponder the events and you do not need the *Protocols of Zion* to see the fulfillment of these protocols in practice.

Thus the Jewish question, whether we like it or not, invades our lives with the threat of the destruction of our sanctities, the threat of the loss of our religious, national, social, familial, and personal independence, the threat of the loss of the minimum of freedom that we have, the threat of a terrifying enslavement.

The Jewish question becomes the question of our destiny: do we want to fight for a brighter future or die in a filthy Jewish cage?

"Our freedom is the freedom of the whole world, our wealth will enrich the whole world, our greatness will magnify the whole world," Theodor Herzl concludes arrogantly in his *Jewish State*. "Whatever we undertake for our own good will be for the good of all mankind."

God forbid such "good"!

PART FOUR

THE SOLUTION TO OUR DESTINY,
OR THE DECODING OF CONTEMPORARY
EVENTS, THEIR HIDDEN DRIVES, AND THE
LATEST JEWISH POLICY

128. Judaism and Fascism

Yet, among the bankrupt ideas and corrupt men who were using the state for their own benefit and stealthily asserting the Jewish inter-state over all other states, a new idea and new men inspired by it emerged. Fascism was born. And, staying true to their method of clinging to every new idea, the Jews tried to hijack fascism.

In the chapter on Italy, we cited the testimony of Jewish sources about their attempts to cling to Italian Fascism and the bitter disappointment that resulted from these attempts. Fascism proved to be too much for these vipers. Fascism dealt a crushing blow to Judaism not only because it removed Jews from power through "democracy," but also because it halted Jewish attempts to take over Italy through "communism." But mostly also because it created a new order of life, one under which Jews have no business. Fascism transfers the power of the nation back to the nation, represented by its selection, the national party, which carries out a national dictatorship. The doors of the party are open to active people from all strata of the population, but only for members of the nation—Jews and foreigners will not penetrate into such a party. The fascist dictatorship is not personal, but national in nature: the dictator rules not in the name of birthright, not by capital accumulation, not by virtue of the fact of an accidental seizure of power, but as a representative of the nation, constantly invested in national support, and therefore obliged to act in the national interest. Such a construction guarantees the absence of personal and class influences on power, which the Jews are so fond of using.

Fascism ends Freemasonry by banning all secret organizations. There is no party struggle, no class struggle, whereas the favorite method of Jewry is "divide and conquer." Finally, under fascism, the nation is not only united, but is also organized through a corporate system: the population is united in national unions, but a Jew cannot be accepted as a member of a national union. Consequently, he cannot engage in commerce or politics, nor can he penetrate into the administration: All avenues of intervention in other people's lives, all avenues of influence on other people's power are closed to him here.

In another book, describing the inevitability of the deadly conflict between fascism and Judaism, I wrote:

> Fascism has created a new system in which the nation is not only united, but organized in unions and corporations. And once it is united and organized, the existence of an alien internation within it becomes impossible.
>
> With its state system, fascism wrested the monopoly of political education of the masses from the agents of Judeo-Masonry and made it the monopoly of the nation. Why do we need a unified national-state party? So that the nation is ruled and nurtured not by strangers but by itself—through its organized selection, through its most resolute, ambitious, capable, and talented representatives.
>
> Fascism destroyed the economic position of Judaism with its new economy. Why the need for a controlled economy? To reconcile private interests with the general interest, to harmonize private initiative with state planning, to spiritualize the economy with national service.
>
> Fascism put an end to the pseudo-democracy of corruption and demagogy. Fascism replaced communism and capitalism, liberalism and socialism, with new forms of state, social, economic, and cultural life. Under fascism, there are no more ways to implement the provisions of the *Protocols* of the Zionists: Under this new order, world trade is in the state's interests. The pumping of national capital abroad, the enslavement of national labor by international finance, the concentration of the forces of the Comintern and the Finintern, international propaganda, and world revolution are all impossible.
>
> It is not surprising that Italian Fascism is being emulated in other countries and that similar movements are breaking out all over the world. The powerful need of peoples to arrange their whole life on the natural basis of the nation is manifest, the great instinct of self-preservation speaks.

Mussolini gave mankind the saving formula of the national-labor state, the definition of the state as the bulwark of the nation, the reconciliation of labor and capital in the corporate system, the scheme of internal unification and self-organization of every nation.

Hitler reconciled the contradictions of nationalism and socialism. He overthrew Marxist socialism, and replaced it with real, national socialism.

Hitler freed the greatest country in Europe from Jewry, and launched an open world war against Jewry.

Hitler declared war on Jewry, and liberated Europe from the worst yoke in the history of mankind.

After Europe, it's Russia's turn to be liberated.

After Russia, God willing, the rest of the world will throw off its chains.

The greatest of the world's wars of liberation was initiated by Adolf Hitler, and this will never be forgotten by a grateful humanity.

And the dark powers, of course, are well aware of who robbed them of their world power at the very threshold, not even the "threshold," but when they had already reached Mount Zion. They know who pushed them down that mountain. This understanding determines the attitude of world Jewry toward Hitler, toward Mussolini, toward fascism in general, and toward any fascist movement in any non-Jewish environment.

129. The *Zarnitsa*[225] of the New Order

In early 1926 the author of this book, as a first-year law student at Harbin Law School, gave a lecture entitled "The Meaning of History" to the Historical Circle of the institution. In this lecture, based on a certain change of epochs in the global historical process, he argued for the existence of a certain sequence in this change, a kind of cycle of history, in which, following the era of domination of the body—the era of materialism—comes the era of primacy of spirit over matter—the era of idealism.

It is ideas, not blind economic forces, that rule the world! The individual, not the masses, turns the historical wheel. Strong men, united with one another in organization, give birth to great movements that change the world map, social relationships, and the whole picture of human civilization.

I said then that humanity had reached an impasse, and that the crisis of democracy, parliamentarism, socialism, art, and science, the loss of meaning in life, and pessimism were all part of a crisis of worldview; the end of materialism and utilitarianism—which inspired all these systems—and the beginning of a new age, a new order, and a quest for religious, political, social, economic, intellectual, scientific,

---

[225] Meaning "heat lighting" in Russian. (Translator's note)

and philosophical thought, for new forms of life—new states, a new economy, and a new culture.

To help me in my argument at the time, I called upon quotations from Schopenhauer, Nietzsche, the neo-Kantians, Weininger, Whipper, Carlyle, Novgorodtsev, Lebon, and many other scholars and researchers of various stripes, ending with Spengler.

The Decline of the West predicts the "Renaissance of Asia." However, as I said then, Europe, too, could be saved, if it returns to the religious-national sources of all existence.

At that time, and even earlier, Russian fascists affirmed the need for a new era with the slogan "God, Nation, and Labor," summarizing the demands of religious freedom, national unity, and social justice.

At the end of that year, in "Notes on Fascism" in the Harbin liberal newspaper *Russkoyo Slovo*, describing, partly by intuition, the ideology and constructive work of Italian Fascism, I predicted its worldwide spread.

"In every country a distinctive national fascist movement will emerge, directed both against communism and against capitalism, and a New Order will reign in the world, in which the Nation will be the sole mistress of the State," I wrote in 1926.

I have seen the *zarnitsa* of the New Order in Italy, in Germany, in Japan, and in Yugoslavia. Not all predictions can come true, for then I would not be a thinker, but a prophet! In Yugoslavia my predictions were not realized, but Italy, Germany, and Japan are in the vanguard of the new humanity.

In February 1927, we had a great debate about fascism at the Faculty of Law, in the philosophical circle of Professor Ustryalov.[226]

The venerable leader of the Smenovekhovtsy, who at that time was calling on the Russian emigrant community to reconcile with the USSR (which was supposedly being reborn as a National Russia), allowed this debate in the apparent hope of crushing the young inexperienced ideologues of the New Order.[227]

However, the calculation turned out to be wrong. Despite the fact that we were opposed by the best agitators of the North Manchurian Committee of the CPSU—bespectacled Marxist scribes, Talmudists from the Harbin Jewish community, and even professors—the first ideological battle of the young Russian forces for the New Order was won by us, the fascist boys.

---

[226] He returned to the USSR. On September 15th, 1937, at a closed session of the Military Collegium of the Supreme Court of the USSR, he was sentenced to execution. The sentence was carried out on the same day. (Translator's note)

[227] The Smenovekhovtsy were a political movement in the Russian émigré community that emerged shortly after the publication in Prague of the journal "Change of Signposts" in 1921. . (Translator's note)

Since then, a powerful front has been opened in front of us, the front of Communists, Freemasons, Jews, émigré liberals and conservatives, revolutionaries and reactionaries, but the movement is growing and spreading.

From the beginning this has been a movement for a New Order. How can we not rejoice when we see the victories of the New Order! In 1919, Benito Mussolini, a former socialist who had studied and overcame all Jewish temptations, a blacksmith's son and a non-commissioned officer of the World War, a journalist and orator, a thinker and organizer, convened in Milan a meeting of like-minded people determined to crush all the old political parties for the renewal and reconstruction of the Italian State.

The forces of revolution and capital, communism and liberalism, united against the new movement. But in 1922, after the March on Rome, the Italian king sanctioned the Fascist National Revolution in Italy.

The movement against partisanship, first as a militant alliance, is now becoming a party—a single party—and only for the construction of a new national-labor Italy on the basis of a program reflecting the will and interests of the broad masses of the Italian population and its national elite.

The remarkable restructuring of a backward, liberal and capitalist Italy into an advanced state begins: the boldest social reforms are taking place here. The Declaration of the Rights of Man and of the Citizen is replaced by the Workers' Charter. Everyone must work not only for himself, but also for the nation, for the State, reconciling all contradictions and organizing the economy. The corporate system of Italian fascism provides the now classical formula for resolving the contradictions between labor and capital.

In 1923, the first attempt at a fascist coup in Germany took place. Also a non-commissioned officer, journalist, tribune orator, and organizer, Adolf Hitler and his comrades-in-arms begin to passionately preach the liberation and rebirth of Germany. They do not call their movement fascism, for they have their own name—National Socialism. The dark forces of the world quickly noticed the common basis of German National Socialism and Italian Fascism. It was the Jews and the Bolsheviks who called National Socialism "fascism," and began to call any advanced national-reformist movement, wherever it originated, fascism. It was the enemy who first gave the notion of fascism as a world movement, as a national movement in every country—for a New Order, a New Life!

During the twenty years of our century there has been a spontaneous awakening of the national feeling of the peoples enslaved by Judas. Genuinely progressive men of all countries are helping to develop a national feeling into a national consciousness. In doing so, the Jewish question serves as a powerful means of awakening and reviving the peoples.

Here it is impossible not to mention the timeless merits of Russian researchers of this issue. The names of Nilus, Butmi, Menshikov, Purishkevich, Lutostansky, Markov, and Shmakov must never be forgotten by a grateful humanity.

It is necessary to dig these blessed names out from under the sands of oblivion with which the Jews have sought to bury them. It is necessary to liberate their work from the Jewish heresy. It is necessary to establish monuments to them in our hearts, if only by publishing the biographies of these great heroes and by republishing their books, which have now become bibliographic rarities.

I speak of these intrepid men as heroes, for indeed it took extraordinary courage to stand up against the world's dark forces at the height of their power.

It is not the reckless courage of an impulse that makes the single will of a warrior charge against an outnumbering enemy. It is the persistent, systematic audacity of the explorer who enters a cave teeming with poisonous snakes, a feat all the more striking because the intrepid explorer of Judaism knows what he is walking into, sees the dimensions of the danger, and steps along the narrow path without hope that his dangerous path will ever end: Judas will haunt him all his life for exposing him. The tragic death of Shmakov, martyred a few days after the October Revolution, is clear proof of this. But the old man was, most likely, calm as a child in those last terrible dying hours—his life's work was done, the word of truth had been spoken. He knew that the executioners would never, and in no way, destroy that word. Little did he know that Russian emigrants, once called upon to preserve all his works, would almost erase them from the earth's surface, that he would be forgotten, as they had now forgotten Markov the Second in the cacophony of Jewish ridicule, just as they would have forgotten the author of these pages, had he not taken care to create an organization that swore to continue his work until the last breath of its last member.

But let's not get sidetracked. If the Russian people have not yet appreciated the work of their visionaries, the Germans and all other nations have. The national awakening of the world goes under the banner of anti-Semitism. Almost all the new national-revolutionary and national-creative movements arising in the twenties, thirties, and forties of our century are under the sign of an overt struggle against Jewry and Freemasonry.

Their leaders study Russian works and quote Russian authors. Russia, on the one hand, frightens the world with Bolshevism, and on the other hand, educates the world with materials on the Jewish question.

Consistently, various fascist, National Socialist, and simply national, anti-Masonic, anti-Jewish movements arise in France, Hungary, Poland, Bulgaria, Romania, Belgium, Holland, Sweden, Norway, Denmark, Latvia, Lithuania, Estonia, Finland, Turkey, Spain, Portugal, even in England, even in the United States, in the USSR—under the yoke of Soviet life—and even in Australia, South America, and South Africa.

At this same pivotal time in Asia, new sentiments are growing stronger among the Japanese people, deeply disillusioned with Europe because of all their encounters with the European powers after the first decades of communication following thousands of years of self-isolation. The Japanese do not yet know that these European powers have already lost the two central letters "o" and "p," and have become Jewish powers.[228] After seeing the Jewish machinations and Masonic imperialism, the Japanese are inclined to personify all this in the image of "White barbarians," the arrogant and boastful White race that has conquered the world.

At the Washington conference, Judas, through the Judaized governments of England, the US, and other countries, threw the first noose around Japan by limiting its naval armaments. May the ratio of the fleets of England, the US, and Japan be 5, 5, and 3, Judeo-Masonry demands. Japan is forced to agree, but it's insulted national sentiment only fosters the birth of new movements, a kind of Japanese fascism that combines the best precepts of its ancestral past and the inextinguishable, eternal Japanese spirit with the social forms of the present, with concern for the peasantry—the bulk of the population—of the army, surrounded by general adoration in Japan.

Anglo-American capital is strengthening its position in East Asia, putting up powerful barriers both to Japan's vital southward movement and to Japan's expansion into the neighboring mainland, as is required by the defense and economic interests of a country in need of a raw material base on the Asian mainland. A knot of such contradictions being tied can only be cut through by the sword. Young officers and courageous thinkers are creating organizations that will soon have the final word. At the same time, even before the New Order of Europe, a New Order of East Asia is being formed.

The formation in 1932 of the new state of Manchukuo as a result of the intervention of the Kwantung Army in aid of the Society of Young Patriots of Manchuria in necessary self-defense was the first call to the Judeo-Masonic masters of the old world that Asia was also awakening. Slowly but surely, Asia is coming to the forefront of world history, to a new life, to a new creation.

---

[228] A play on words; by removing the letters о and п from европейские (European) you get the word еврейский (Jewish) in Russian. (Translator's note)

Throughout the world, the New Order's lightning bolts are shining. Judas begins to sound the alarm.

130. Mobilization of the Forces of Darkness

In 1933, the German National Revolution took place. Ten months before, the Jews self-assuredly claimed, "Hitler will never come to power."

"Hitler will never come to power, he will go out like a candle between two Catholic prelates, and he will never be dictator," assured Dorothy Thompson, an American journalist who is now rectifying her sin by creating some kind of "Sympathy Fund" in aid of world Jewry. The words of this old maid just quoted were printed in the American magazine *Cosmopolitan* in March 1932. The "Cosmopolitans" made the same mistake as the Elders of Zion who overlooked the birth and development of Italian fascism.

What the miscalculation here was will be revealed in a future historical study. I personally believe that the Jews overestimated the importance of the material factor. As natural born materialists, they applied the standards of their own psychology to the Aryan world. "I'll buy everything," the gold said. The Jews believed in the omnipotence of their gold, and it was this belief, the belief in matter, the belief in the devil, that doomed them.

Having made use of all forms of government—republics, monarchies, all political ideas—they thought that there could be no new forms of government, just as there could be no new ideas. They were gravely mistaken. They thought they would crush the new forms of government and new ideas with their economic sanctions, and they yet were wrong again. However, the same year Hitler came to power, a general mobilization of the forces of darkness began.

Jewish Life had already published on August 18th, 1933:

> The World Jewish Economic Conference. Thirty delegates from the United States, England, France, Poland, Holland, Belgium, Switzerland, Czechoslovakia, Latvia, Finland, and Palestine attended the opening of the World Jewish Conference in Amsterdam. The conference was inaugurated by the American delegate Dr. A. Coralnik, who noted the various plans for strengthening the anti-German boycott campaign and proposed the establishment of an international secretariat to coordinate this campaign throughout the world.
>
> The American delegate Untermyer was elected chairman of the conference.

At the first session, reports were heard on the boycott campaign in ten states, as well as reports on the organization of national exchanges of goods between the various states, in order to drive out goods of German manufacture.

The presidium of the conference was thus composed of:

President Emeritus Untermyer, President Lord Melchett, Vice-President Dr. Coralnik (New York), Pierre Dreyfus (Paris), Leo Castro (Cairo), Deputy Wischlitzky (Warsaw), Major Friedman (from the Veterans of America).

The resolution of the conference to be submitted to the Secretary General of the League of Nations categorically insists on a decisive boycott of Germany, and rejects any attempt, from wherever it may come, to weaken the boycott movement.

At the same time, in 1933, the International Committee for Assistance to Victims of Hitler's Terror was founded in London. It is quite clear that this "committee" was formed to intervene in the internal affairs of Germany to fight against fascism, for there was, in fact, no special and mass terror at all.

"The tragedy of the German Jews" struck a chord with the world's biggest terrorist state, the Soviet Union. The Harbin *Jewish Life*, following the world's Jewish press, reported at the time:

> Comrade Smidovich, Comrade Chairman of the Central Executive Committee of the USSR, in a conversation with an employee of the Exchange Telegraph, said that the Soviet Union was ready to give asylum to persecuted German Jews.
>
> "If this project is adopted," said Comrade Smidovich, "the USSR is ready to transform the Jewish Autonomous Region of Birobidzhan into a Jewish Republic, an equal member of the Union of Soviet Socialist Republics."

So, in response to their defeat in Germany, world Jewry wanted revenge at the expense of the lands of Russia. Instead of Palestine, how about Kamchatka and Primorye? A new Soviet republic within the USSR, when in truth all the republics united in the USSR already belonged to it.

Why did world Jewry get so agitated? After all, when Hitler came to power, he did not take any steps against Jewry at first. Only the arsonists of the Reichstag building and the moral perpetrators of three hundred and fifty murders were arrested. Then the government discovered that the Communist Party had prepared a series of attacks on the Berlin palace, on the Bismarck monument in Hamburg, on the East Prussian railroads, etc., and therefore a number of Communist Party workers had to be arrested. Among them were many Jewish intellectuals who had for many years culturally and politically contributed to the progress of Bolshevism in Germany.

These measures of the young government against communism provoked a general Jewish outcry in all countries, an open call for a boycott of Germany and for the assassination of the German ruler. On the third day after Hitler's appointment, a Washington Jewish newspaper columnist demanded that the German chancellor be assassinated, adding that very few would regret his death.

As if on cue, articles appeared in all newspapers stating that Hitler was facing the fate of the ancient Persian chancellor Haman.

Romanian newspaper remarks, commenting on these facts:

> Jewry in New York and London began to call for a boycott; hundreds of cars drove around the streets with placards like this: "JUDEA DECLARES WAR ON GERMANY." The protest of the intellectual Jewry in favor of Bolshevism had a very unexpected result for the Jews themselves: world public opinion became interested in the Jewish question and investigated the political events of the last twenty or so years, and discovered a sort of underground connection between world Jewry and the Third International.

An involuntary confession of Chaim Weizmann, the leader of the Zionist organization, came to light. During the war, Weizmann directed the entire Zionist policy towards the conquest of Palestine with the help of Allied troops, and many states accepted it as something natural. After the 1919 victory, Weizmann left London for Palestine, where he gave a lecture highlighting the unequivocal connection between this policy of Jewish nationalism and Bolshevik global destruction. He said in Jerusalem of his relationship to Britain:

> We told the leaders: we will get Palestine, whether you want us to or not. You can speed up our move or slow it down, but it is still better for you if you help us, for otherwise all our creative energy will turn into a destructive force that will lead the whole world into turmoil.[229]

These words show that even a cautious leader like Weizmann lost his composure in a moment of triumph. He confessed that during the war world Jewry had blackmailed Britain and did so with success. From the speech it is clear that Britain was not being helped for British interests, but in pursuit of far-reaching pan-European goals.

---

[229] *Jewish Review*, No. 4, 1920–1921.

Later, when a disagreement arose between world Zionism and the vital interests of England, the same Weizmann declared at the 1921 Zionist Congress in Karlsbad: "The world-embracing England understood better and sooner than other nations that the Jewish problem lay like a shadow over the whole world, and could become not only a gigantic building force, but also a terrible destructive force."

Here, too, the leader of national Jewish world capitalism threatened Christianity with the destructive power of world communism, and in this way reaffirmed the inner connection that he emphasized again the following year. In March 1922, Weizmann said in Oxford about the goals of Zionism:

> The Zionists knew how to proceed and took up the cause with open eyes, conscious of the commonality of interest between the British government and the Jewish people. England knows that not keeping her promise will cost her more than keeping a whole army in Palestine.

The most shameless confirmation of the Communist policy of Jewish imperialism we find in the article of the famous Zionist writer Arthur Yolitcher, who had just returned from a trip to the USSR. He writes in the *New Review* (XI, 1922): "Besides the International of Rome and the International of Moscow, there is only the third International of Zion. It is our world power that has grown out of the roots of religion."

Hitler's great merit is that he put an end to this Judeo-Bolshevik policy and showed the world the way to salvation from the tenacious tentacles of the Pan-European octopus.

In my book *Judas on the Edge*, I summarized the 1930s this way:

> Five years have passed in the tense struggle between Judas and Germany, Italy, and Japan. The air is saturated with tragedies; questions have been raised that require immediate resolution; the specter of a coming war hovers over nations that do not wish to fight at all.
>
> One bandit helps another: if Germany strikes the USSR, France, England, Poland, and all the other nations of Europe except Italy will rush on it; if Japan strikes the USSR, America, England, and China will plunge into Japan. Democratic freedoms are shamelessly being trampled: in democracies, people are arrested for speaking out against Jews. "Israel is in need of a new war as soon as possible!" the Jewish press screams.
>
> The USSR, England, France, and the United States are effectively waging a war with the states of tomorrow without a formal declaration: they fuel the smoldering fire in Spain, support Chiang Kai-shek, do not recognize Manchukuo (despite

the clear fact of its existence), choke Italy with sanctions, and organize the encirclement of Germany.

In 1933, an Exploratory Commission of the League of Nations, headed by the Freemason Lord Lytton and with the participation of the Jew Reichman, its actual leader, arrived in Manchukuo. Harbin Jews supply it with all sorts of lies about Japanese expansion. The Jewish press all over the world organizes public opinion against Japan. But the cries for help are powerless to shake the peaceful cooperation of the peoples of the Manchurian empire and the state building which is going on here in a new way.

In 1937, Japan was forced to start a war with China to free the Chinese people from the dark forces that had chosen the Chinese as their victim and instrument.

Who is setting up China against Japan? The Freemason Chiang Kai-shek is surrounded by Anglo-American Masonic and Jewish advisors.

The fact of the united support of England, the USA, and the USSR for the Masonic Chinese "government" in Chongqing gave away the *de facto* alliance of these three states long before it became manifest, long before the Anti-Communist International Union was created, before the anti-Communist pact was signed between Germany, Italy, and Japan. After Italy and Germany withdrew from the League of Nations, a secret pact was made between England, the USA, and the USSR; an agreement between world revolution and world finance! The organizers of this alliance were Jews and Freemasons—an international mobilization against the impending New Order!

131. The Jewish Struggle Against Fascism

It is clear that the Jews at first underestimated Italian fascism. They regarded it as a purely Italian phenomenon that did not threaten to spread to the whole world. They defined attempts to emulate Italian Fascism in other countries as bad transplants of foreign ideas. The Jews overlooked the beginnings of world fascism and did not notice that since 1922, the year the Italian National Revolution was legalized by the Italian king, the whole history of mankind began to unravel in the opposite direction. Whereas before that year the course of world events had been fully consistent with the diabolical plan for the Jewish conquest of the world through non-Jewish hands, as laid out in the *Protocols of the Elders of Zion*, then, with the victory of fascism in Italy, events went in directions not envisaged by the authors of the *Protocols*.

There are many ways to treat the *Protocols*. You can write hundreds of books disproving them, as the Jews do, or you can hire unscrupulous Jews like Burtsev to do so, as the Jews do. But there is one thing that cannot be disproved: in those decades, when Jews seized power in many countries, world events were exactly as envisaged in the resolutions of the First World Congress of Zionists at Basel in 1897, when the *Protocols* were adopted. Compare Neelu's book and the facts of history in the first quarter of our century—no other proof of the authenticity of the *Protocols of Zion* is required.

Everything went on as written in the *Protocols*, until the rise, establishment, and spread of fascism. Fascism played the Jewish card and ruined the game of Israel. Fascism brought to the forefront of history a new element, not foreseen by the Zionists. The nation had spoken! The Jews thought that they were the only nation, that no other nations could exist: after all, only Jews are human beings, and a nation can only consist of human beings, not of "humanoid creatures."

But the national feeling repressed in the peoples woke up and developed into its own national consciousness.

Fascism develops national feeling into a national consciousness. The Jew can still tolerate with a heavy heart someone else's national feeling, but a national consciousness? Oy, gevalt! That's anti-Semitism! And after a brief period of confusion, Italian Fascism, followed by world fascism, became the object of harsh persecution.

Having missed the birth, growth, and victory of Italian Fascism, the Jews are trying to strangle the growth of the Fascist movements in every country.

In this struggle, they use all kinds of methods, but mostly the most despicable ones.

This includes hidden terror (the mysterious deaths of Primo de Rivera in Spain and Octavian Goga in Romania, the massacre of Codreanu in Romania), overt terror (the assassination attempt on Mussolini in Italy, the assassination of individual National Socialists in Germany and abroad, the publication of the million-dollar reward for "Hitler's head" in the United States, the murder of King Alexander of Serbia in France, the arrests of Mosley, Leese, and their supporters in England, the arrest of William D. Pelly, the Christian Front, and Vonsiatsky in the United States, the arrests of Australian fascists in Australia), and mass terror (the bloody extermination of the Iron Guard in Romania, the shootings of Russian nationalists in the USSR). There are also detours using women (e.g., the trial of Fritz Kuhn, the leader of German American Bund in America, who was seduced into embezzlement by a "platinum blonde"), and slander, provocation, herem (the history of any fascist movement in any country, in particular the history of the Russian fascist movement). What's not to be found here!

The history of any original national movement is at the same time the history of the Jewish struggle against fascism—this is what we must remember.

We have experienced all of this firsthand, through the example of our own national liberation movement. For this reason, we can rely on strictly verified data from personal experience.

132. Parallelism

When Russian nationalists created the Russian Fascist Organization in Harbin, the National Russian Fascist Organization appeared in Europe, and so did the All-Russian Fascist Organization in the United States. When the All-Russian Fascist Party united the political activists of the Russian emigration in Manchukuo, a very similar Monarchist Union appeared in Manchukuo.

All these are facts that occurred before our eyes. And we have seen hundreds of endeavors by Russian émigrés in various countries that failed only because if one proposed a sound plan and began to carry it out, other people, often quite respectable and well-meaning, did not even realize they were being hijacked.

In 1940, the author of this book wanted to create a unified national political organization for all Russian emigrants in Harbin with our Russian Fascist Union as its inner core, hardened by experience in the struggle against the dark forces. The authorities agreed to this undertaking, the public welcomed it, and all circles of the emigrant community agreed to join a common organization. Already a mass demonstration of its establishment in the form of a large public gathering had been held. Suddenly, two participants in all preparations, taking advantage of their administrative position, seized the initiative out of anti-Jewish circles and created the so-called Union of Russian Emigrants.

In 1941, wishing sincerely to help Russian children and young people, I organized a group of well-off, self-sacrificing people and energetic community workers to establish a Youth and Children's Aid Society in Harbin. District conversations were held, and district groupings were outlined. A propaganda campaign in the press aroused general sympathy for this cause, when suddenly a very reliable, intelligent, honest, and serious man, still considered by many to be a fascist, used his administrative means to convene a constituent assembly and arrange the grand opening of this same society. A board was elected, but neither the board nor the society met even once after the inauguration. The initiative, however, was snatched away, and a good, necessary Russian cause was utterly ruined.

In 1942 we called on the Harbin emigrants to establish the Society of Japanese–Russian Cultural Bonding. Immediately two initiative groups were formed, and at the head of the foreign initiative was a professor who had often collaborated with us in the past. For two months there were negotiations about the agreement, and when the agreement was reached, the society was born with obviously shortened tasks, and clearly was not functional.

One of the Russian publicists ideologically close to me planned to arrange an Exhibition of Russian Books in Manchukuo as a powerful manifestation of the emigrant cultural amateurism in the New Order East Asian state that shelters us. To my misfortune, he asked me to head the business committee of the exhibition, and to my even greater misfortune, I accepted. This was enough for the administrators and professors I mentioned above to hasten the announcement that they were organizing such an exhibition.

Finally, last year, we managed to create a new trend of émigré literature—anti-Communist, national-willed, for the New Order. Harbin poets and writers were given new opportunities for creativity by publishing their works in the literary and art almanac *Priboy*. The Union of Russian Writers and Poets of East Asia was gradually formed—anti-Communist, national-willed, and for the New Order. This was enough to immediately lead to a parallel initiative, only not anti-Communist, not national-willed, not for the New Order, but an apolitical one. Its initiator frankly told one of my friends: "Everyone is welcome, except Rodzaevsky."

In Germany, Adolf Hitler's National Socialist German Workers' Party was long rivaled by the monarchist *Der Stahlhelm*.

In England, two fascist organizations polemicized and feuded: Sir Oswald Mosley's British Union of Fascists and Arnold Leese's Imperial Fascist League.

In Spain, for a long time the movement of General Franco was hindered by the discord between the Fascist Falangists and the Monarchist Carlists.

Five similar national movements were active in France: Colonel de la Rocca's Fiery Crosses, Tetanje's Young Patriots, Jacques Dorriot's National Socialist Party. Jacques Dorriault, Maurice Bucard's Francists, and Henri Kostov's Antisemitic Group.

There were five anti-Semitic movements in Romania, and a strong rivalry between two of them, Professor Cuse and Octavian Goga's National-Christian Party and Codreanu's Iron Guard. Codreanu was greatly weakened by the position of Goga's cabinet, the briefly anti-Semitic temporary cabinet of King Karol.

Not five, but almost ten separate organizations represented fascism and anti-Semitism in the United States! What is this? It is a manifestation of another Jewish method of dealing with fascism? Parallelism: whether smacked across or over the head, what difference does it make? It is nothing but a bypassing maneuver. Parallelism means that Jewry is very careful not to expose its protruding ears and instigate the creation of a new national or fascist movement. Seeing the success of the existing national or fascist movement, in order to cause competition, it sows misunderstanding, creates confusion and turns opponents to a mutual struggle against each other, so that Judas and his favored circles and individuals are left alone.

This method, and not without success, is used everywhere in our corrupt world, which is greedy for money, for flattering words, for the game of self-love and ambition and where Judas is a master. Not even a master but a virtuoso, a prodigy who has become the universally recognized star of this operetta!

133. Against the Idea of Selection, the Idea of Unification

Finally, from our own sad experience, we know that Jews like to contrast the idea of national selection with the idea of formal unification, often trying to stifle and destroy fascism by such a universal unification, which reduces the activity of "extremes" in the name of some all-reconciling and all-conquering "middle" ground.

Thus, for example, in many countries, Russian emigration was suddenly seized from time to time by a real fever for "unification." Everyone came together, and in order to make sure no one was left out, a general unity platform was developed: without sharp edges, without new ideas, without principles that might offend or upset anyone. Without anti-Semitism, of course. Without fascism, of course. Anti-Semitism is an extreme, fascism is a "narrow party ideology." This is what the Jews used to preach through their faithful proxies—and widely supported any such unification of emigration.

Emigration was unified, and that was the end of it. There was no serious work to protect its legal or economic interests, no concern for the weak elements of the native blood, no development of the native culture, nor was there the mass anti-Communist struggle in the name of which such unification sometimes took place. But there was undoubtedly a struggle against fascism. Fascism was dissolved in such a union, or rather, they wanted to dissolve it without a trace, and yet it persisted and worked. But the political activity of the emigrant community, so dangerous for Jews and the Comintern, gradually waned: political fighters against the Comintern, devoid of any anti-Semitic spirit, gradually degenerated into philistines.

This whole sad story is still waiting for its unbiased researcher and judgment; there will be a judgment—no one escapes the judgment of man, just as no one escapes the judgment of God. But to make the picture clearer, we will give a few examples from other people's lives that show that every formal association which seeks to suppress fascism ultimately has a Jewish origin.

In 1935, the Seventh Congress of the Comintern met in Moscow. Its main theme turned out to be the formidable rise of fascism. Fascism was declared the chief enemy of the Communists, and the struggle against fascism was the main task of the Communist parties of all countries, thus the fighting task of all Communist agents.

For this struggle, the Comintern adopted the well-known tactics of Popular Fronts, which united the Leninists with social democratic parties, hostile to them up to that time, and even with democratic and bourgeois parties, in order to defeat the despised fascism.

Since then, in all countries unnatural alliances have begun.

In Belgium, for example, against the leader of the fascist Rexists, Leon Degrelle, when he was running for premiership, a truly broad front of "unification" was created—consisting of every group, from Communists to Catholic monarchists—and defeated Degrelle. In Romania, the crowned lover of modern Esther, after the Jewish ultimatum, dictated the resignation of Octavian Goga, created the General National Union, and was led by the patriarch of the Romanian Orthodox Church, Myron Hristo, with the sole purpose of giving the people a surrogate for fascism and suppressing fascism proper.

At the end of 1935, following the Comintern Congress in Moscow, the World Congress of the YCI (the Young Communist International) gathered. And here are the pearls we found in its declaration, published in *Komsomolskaya Pravda* with the comments of Vul. The YCI calls for support of any kind of union of young people! Even religious, even national, so long as it is directed against fascism and against war. "Gevalt, gevalt, gevalt!!!" screams world Jewry, "anything but fascism!" Why? Because only fascism came into open conflict with Judaism, resolving the Jewish question in the direction of freeing all nations from the internal contagion and external dictatorship of the Jewish internation.

No sooner had YCI's directive appeared in *Komsomolskaya Pravda*, than all sorts of "youth associations" began to appear in various countries, including all over the world of Russian emigration. Sharply antagonistic to fascism, which they accused of all the mortal sins, and above all of "narrow partisanship." Clever? What can I say! The Jews are masters of provocation: Jewish decrees are implemented by the most unexpected people, sometimes even those far removed from Judaism.

134. Kosher Fascism

Not the least in the Jewish arsenal of weapons against fascism are various provocative imitations of fascism.

If fascism cannot be overthrown, can we not create our own Jewish-led, kosher fascism? The Jews are attracted to the firm power of dictatorship. But they usually substitute a national dictatorship backed by a nationwide organization for a personal dictatorship, an apolitical military dictatorship backed by blind armed force. This is how Arnold Leese remarkably and clearly defined kosher fascism.

An example of such "kosher fascism" can be seen in the recent "totalitarian" governments of Lithuania, Latvia, and Estonia, which surrendered everything to the Bolsheviks without a fight in 1940. In these small limitrophe countries, after the triumph of fascism in neighboring Germany, their own distinctive national movements began to develop widely, demanding the removal of Judeo-Masonic influences and the renewal of state power. In Lithuania, the Perkonkrusts (Perun's Cross) appeared, in Estonia, the Union of the Liberation Teles, and in Latvia, its own National Revolutionary Movement. Peacefully, winning a majority of voters, the fascists were on their way to power, when suddenly something incomprehensible happened. In 1934, the telegraph consistently announced fascist coups, first in Latvia, then in Lithuania and Estonia. These coups, as it turned out later, were carried out by the democratic governments with the help of the army, led by Freemasons, subsidized by English capital. And the "fascists" who came to power began by arresting the fascists, shutting down anti-Semitic newspapers, and breaking up fascist organizations.

This "fascism" immediately found favor in the neighboring USSR. It was applauded by the anti-fascist press of all countries. Popular movements were banned, their leaders arrested, and their newspapers shut down. But the Jews and Communists gained new advantages, so much so that the takeover of Latvia, Estonia, and Lithuania by the Jewish-Communist USSR that followed a few years later met no resistance.

The same trick was used by the dark forces in Brazil, where the Integralist Action movement was developing widely. All of a sudden, a telegraph announced a "fascist coup," and Brazil began to be governed by a "totalitarian" regime. Who carried out the coup? The democratic president Vargas, with money from the United States of America! The Integralists were then outlawed.

It is interesting to note that shortly after the coup, American newspapers published: "In government circles, the arrest of over a thousand fascist conspirators in Brazil caused great joy." "This is the most decisive victory for democracy in our hemisphere," said one official, as reported by the Communist *Russkiy Golos* of New York with satisfaction. So much for fascism!

The presence of "kosher fascism" shows that not every dictatorship is fascist, and that not every "fascism" corresponds to the true essence of fascism.

Anti-Semitism, the call for the study of the global enemy, defiance of Jews, and a program that sets up a system that guarantees against the infiltration of the inter-nation—these are the things that in our corrupt times can be considered as the main hallmarks of any good organization, of any movement.

Only he who is not afraid to stand up against the world menace, against the greatest enemies of his motherland, of the nation, of religion and labor, only he is a nationalist in the true sense of the word. In other words, in the struggle for national liberation, nationalism and anti-Semitism are synonymous. A real nationalism that strives for religious, national, and social justice, in addition to the anti-Semitism that inevitably follows from this mission—*that* is fascism, not "kosher," but real fascism.

135. The Jewish War Against Fascism

When all the means to curb the escaping energy have been exhausted, Judas decides to take the extreme measure of causing a world war.

He is aware of the risk, but goes for it anyway, seeing in war the last way to drown fascism in blood and cause universal hatred for it.

The proven hypocrites—"pacifists" and "peacemakers"—once again (for the umpteenth time?) act as warmongers. And at the same time, they shift responsibility to the "aggression of fascism"!

"Fascism means war!" Jews, Freemasons, Democracies and Comintern all cry out in one single voice, "Fascism means enslavement!"

At the same time they take care that the war should take universal dimensions, that every country should have people and families affected by the war, that millions of people should associate their suffering with the term "fascism," making the bright and creative idea synonymous with destruction and death.

The instigator of the greatest provocation in the history of mankind is the deceived Poland, whose people's chauvinism had been ignited to the limit by 1939.

The patriots dreamed of a Poland stretching from sea to sea at the expense of all their neighbors—Germany, Czechoslovakia, Romania, the USSR—not noticing that the available Polish lands were not ruled by Poles at all, but by Freemasons and Jews.

The old German city of Danzig, with a population dreaming of reunification with mother Germany, turned out to be the apple of discord around which the global storm was brewing.

Think for yourselves of the absurdity of the "Polish corridor" that cut the living body of Germany into two separate parts!

A great power through which runs a huge swath of foreign possessions, separating East Prussia from the capital and the rest of Germany!

How could the German national consciousness tolerate this kind of blatant absurdity? But the Polish intelligentsia and the army, set up by the Jews and the British, did not notice this absurdity. Europe was heading inexorably toward war, pushed along by the Jews. Aryan attempts to stop the impending threat were thwarted by none other than Judas himself.

Remember, in 1938 there was a Munich meeting of state leaders. It only succeeded because the rulers decided to talk to each other directly, bypassing their ministers and diplomats.

It was an attempt by nations to negotiate without Jewish and Masonic intermediaries.

Here is what preceded it, according to the story of an émigré magazine in Paris:

Already a full month has passed, but the eeriness of this panic-stricken day is not yet dispelled. The whole of Paris was gripped by terrible confusion. All except those who were mobilized, and us sinners, the Russian émigrés. Should we be surprised? We had nothing to lose, we had lost everything. Everything left behind. . . .

But we marveled at the mobilized French. "Suicide bombers," not today, but tomorrow, what calmness, what self-control.

Fear ran rampant among the non-suicide bombers. The wealthy bourgeoisie stormed the banks, emptying their vaults and siphoning off their cash. Hordes of automobiles loaded with people and suitcases were streaming into the provinces, away from the bombs. The mansions died out; the rich apartments died out. Paris died out and lurked ominously.

By evening, when darkness fell on the City of Light, the lights went out, the lights in the windows went out, even we Russians felt uncomfortable. But not from fear, rather from the "mood." It reminded us of things we'd like to forget forever. The depression of Communist slavery came to mind. . . .

And on this night, seemingly full of doom and unbearably oppressive, an evening of extinguished lights, when thousands of bourgeois cars, as if plagued, left Paris, taking away cowards and self-seekers with diamonds and gold, a conspiratorial meeting was held by Bonnet[230] with the former Minister Frossard.

Bonnet's sharply drawn, large face was pale. Outwardly he remained calm. Frossard was also pale, but agitated. . . .

"You see . . . he told you . . . but Poncet. . . .[231] The only person in the world who can influence Hitler. . . . The one and only Mussolini. Call him. Immediately."

With a smile of bitterness, Bonnet shook his head negatively. "That would be a futile, useless humiliation! I am a hundred times ready to go through useful humiliation for the sake of saving France but. . . . You should know how the Popular Front has soured relations with Italy. . . ."

"Then . . . then," Frossard grasps his head in despair, "call Chamberlain. . . . Have him talk to Mussolini at once. Tell him to get an agreement from him. You speak English. . . . How convenient! No need for an interpreter. A secret must be a secret for now . . . and here's the thing, dear friend. Here . . . at the same time I will contact Poncet. . . . Tell him to be on the lookout. . . . And then . . . then a call to the Chancellor's Palace. . . . Hitler will receive him now. . . . One last attack, and if at the same time. . . . No, no, I'm afraid to think. . . . What a blessing that would be. Long ago are the times, a legend now, when the Congress of Vienna took weeks and weeks to organize. Back when emperors, kings and prime ministers all came to gather in Vienna. . . . Long ago are the times when, even at the Berlin Congress, it took entire days for the Chancellors to even exchange dispatches. Now even the telegraph has become legend. . . ."

About a half-hour had passed: the French minister's idea delighted Chamberlain.

"Yes, only he, Mussolini, could dissuade Hitler from invading Bohemia. Will the Duce agree? He, Chamberlain, has no doubt he will! The Duce has remained somehow in the shadows as of late. . . . He must assume such a wonderful peacekeeping role. . . . He must. In a few minutes Bonnet will know exactly."

Indeed, in a few minutes he heard the voice of the British premier:

"I agree, telegraph Hitler. . . . The plan . . . plan . . . to converge, no, to flock to Munich—Daladier, Mussolini, and myself. . . . World peace will be saved. . . ."

---

[230] A prominent French politician, since 1925 he has repeatedly held ministerial posts, and was a participant in the Munich Agreement. (Translator's note)
[231] French ambassador to Germany. (Translator's note)

At the same time, Frossard called Poncet, told him what he wanted to say.... As soon as he hung up, Poncet immediately got in touch with the Reich's Chancellor, he asked to see him, and was invited to come immediately.

And in order to gain time, in the silence and half-light of the deep chancellor's study, Poncet convinces his interlocutor of what he had convinced him of yesterday, and the day before, and a few days before that, and can anticipate, word for word, what Hitler will reply to him.

But just to sit in this office for as long as necessary. And there, there . . . the real man and the politician François Poncet believed in a miracle this time.... Passionately, painfully, with all his being....

And the tale of the "white bull" began:[232]

"So, Mr. Chancellor, is your decision final and irrevocable?"

"Yes, Mr. Ambassador.... A few more hours and thirty of my divisions will launch a concentric offensive toward the center of Czechoslovakia, supported by half a thousand airplanes...."

"This is terrible, terrible, Herr Chancellor! This is the ruin of Europe."

"It's only the triumph of justice, Mr. Ambassador. They're mocking us. But if only it was us.... Are we the enemy? It was you, France and England, our friends who were three months ago insisting: Give Germany the German lands. And what of it? Three months of procrastination, delays, excuses, and evasive answers. A treacherous policy is ultimately fatal for them. My patience had reached its limit.... They would have been much more cooperative if the Soviet Union had not showered them with unimaginable help, as well as some of your own ministers, Mr. Ambassador."

"Mr. Chancellor, it is not for me, the representative of France, to listen to or encourage such accusations."

"Well, let's take a former minister.... Pierre Cott. Your newspapers call him an agent and a Hitler collaborator because he ruined and destroyed your beautiful air force."

"Herr Chancellor...."

"Allow me to finish, Mr. Ambassador. He is to blame for the fact that there are thirty divisions ready to march into Bohemia, and five hundred airplanes ready to take off the moment

---

[232] The Tale of the White Bull is a Russian proverb that means a long, endless story (often boring). (Translator's note)

I order it. Your ex-minister demanded not only general mobilization, not just desperate resistance, but also aerial bombardment of our military bases and industrial centers."

"Mr. Chancellor, I can't allow this."

"Mr. Ambassador, you can't help but recognize Cott's voice. I'm going to play you a disk. I've already shown it to the English and Italian ambassadors. Unfortunately, it's not a waltz by Strauss or a nocturne by Chopin, but something satanic.... No, I must play it for you."

A sharp phone call cut Hitler off at half finishing his phrase. Poncet flinched, as perhaps he had never flinched in his entire life. For a few seconds, he was in a state of oblivion. He woke up and heard:

"Your Excellency, I...."

There was another silence, unbearably tense for Poncet.

"Ah zo bis morgen. Auf Wiedersehen, Ihre Exzellenz...."

Turning swiftly to Poncet, the Führer, still glowing, not having yet managed to "make" another face, merrily said:

"I shall make you happy, Mr. Ambassador. Tomorrow in Munich we will meet with Mussolini, Chamberlain, and Daladier."

This is the record of the historic Hitler-Poncet conversation on the historic night of September 27th. The consequences of this conversation with its finale—a telephone call from Rome—are known to the whole world.

Germany was going for agreements and was willing to limit itself to a minimum of justice. The Aryan politicians were willing to do this. But it was not the agreement of the disputes that the Jews wanted.

Munich, Autumn 1938.

A period of calm ensued. Alas, it turned out to be the calm before the storm. For the Jews, as it turns out, took their own measures against Munich:

"In October 1938, the situation of Jewry was the worst, from a collective point of view," Nachum Goldman, a special commissioner of the Jewish Agency, told the American Jewish Congress in 1940. "After the Munich Treaty, there was a danger that democracies would make final peace with Germany. Had this happened, had France and Great Britain surrendered and come to an agreement with fascism, the Jews in Europe would have been lost, at least for a generation. Their struggle would have remained outside the general problems of life in Europe. They would have remained the only enemies and opponents of fascism without any chance of defeating a powerful enemy."

These words were printed in the Harbin *Jewish Life* No. 13 of 1940, as were further words in which an American Jew directly confessed the failure of the Jews and circles connected with them in their last attempts to pacify Europe:

> All the forces in Europe, standing for a minimum of morality, have risen up against fascism. The struggle we have been waging against it for years is no longer an isolated struggle. We are now fighting together alongside forces, as we have always done in the best moments of our history.

"For the first time in many years, European Jewry is facing not just a terrible present, but a beautiful future!" exclaims Dr. Goldman to a rousing applause from American Jewry and the Jewish press around the world.

When England "stood up" for Poland and opposed Germany in 1939, the Jewish Agency in London, of which Dr. Goldman is the US representative, declared: "His Majesty's Government has declared war on Hitler's Germany. This war is also our war. To the army and people of Great Britain we will give every kind of aid at our disposal."

"Nothing will stop us!" exclaimed Harbin Dr. A. I. Kaufman, specially authorized by the Jewish Agency for East Asia, in the pages of the local *Jewish Life*, signing his full title for the first time under the front page.

The Jews take off their masks for one last time: the Anglo–German war is a Jewish war against fascism.

Look: on the side of England and Jewry are the countries where Jewish power is strongest: Poland, France, Holland, Greece, Yugoslavia, the USA, the USSR! To London, the capital of the Jewish Agency, under the wing of the Masonic king, are flocking the "exiled" governments of Czechoslovakia, Poland, Norway, Holland, France, Greece, Yugoslavia. All these cardboard kings and queens, young princes, corrupt premiers, unprincipled ministers, are densely lined with Jews and Jewish agents. The last masks are falling, the world is split in two, there is no intermediate camp. There is Judaism and its allies, and fascism and its *soratniki*.

136. The Jewish Takeover of World Diplomacy

But why was it during the Munich period that the rulers of France and England wished to speak to Hitler and Mussolini alone, without any diplomats? The answer to this question reveals another side of the political Judaization of the world: the terrible contamination of the diplomatic service of all countries by Freemasons and Jews.

This contamination began long ago. For instance, the influential Jewish newspaper of London, *The Jewish Chronicle*, published in its issue of November 29th, 1901, an article entitled "Some of the Jewish Ambassadors." From this article it follows that Jews have at all times played a leading role in diplomacy.

As the Jewish newspaper reports, the states of the Iberian Peninsula were already using the services of Jewish ambassadors in the early Middle Ages.

In the eleventh century, Alfonso VI, king of Leon and Castile, appointed as his ambassador the Jew Abraham Bon Isaac ibn Shalbiet. In 1005 he sent this Jew to the Caliph of Seville, Almutamid.

A few centuries later, Alfonso V, king of Portugal, sent a delegation to Pope Sixtus IV to congratulate him on his election and to inform him of his victory over the Moors at Arcilla in Africa. At the head of this delegation was the Jew Lopez D'Almeida. Isaac Abravanel, a Jew, tried to get the pope to improve the position of the Jews in the papal dominions.

In the second half of the 16th century, on July 6th, 1574, the then-sultan Selim II sent a Jew, Solomon Nathan Ashkenazi, as the Turkish representative for peace negotiations.

In the middle of the seventeenth century, the Portuguese government decided to appoint Duarte Nunes Da Costa, a Jew, a Portuguese Marrano, as envoy to the city of Hamburg. Da Costa was elevated to the nobility and the office of Hamburg envoy was held by members of the Da Costa family until its abolishment in 1795.

At the same time and in the same Hamburg, two Jews, Daniel Abenzur and Jacob Abenzur, apparently father and son, one after the other, represented the Kingdom of Poland. Jacob Abenzur, who died in 1711, counted the King of Poland himself among his debtors.

In 1780 the Moroccan government appointed Mumbal, a Jew, as envoy to London. His successor at the court of George III was the Jew Mascod Cohen Macnin.

The first Jewish ambassador to the Court of St. James was His Britannic Majesty's ambassador to Madrid, the Jew Sir Henry Drummond Wolf.

At the beginning of this century Italy appointed as its chargé d'affaires to Bulgaria a Jew, Cavallero De Polacco. The Jewish envoys were Senor Isacco Artom and Senor Segre, Italy's envoys to Denmark and Peru.

In the middle of the nineteenth century, the Piedmont government sent Henry D'Avigor, a Jew, to France to negotiate a trade treaty.

D'Avigor was married to the daughter of Sir Isaac Lyon Goldschmidt, leader of the Jewish emancipation movement in England.

As *The Jewish Chronicle* reports, only some of the Jewish ambassadors were involved. What a result we would come to if one day a complete list of Jewish diplomats in all countries and at all times were announced! What backstage would we have to look behind the scenes if all the deeds of these Jewish politicians were subjected to close scrutiny?

When the archives are disclosed, we will find a complete seizure by Freemasonry of the Ministry of Foreign Affairs of the last years of the Russian Empire. There are other examples: during the period of Judaization, the foreign ministries of all countries, empires, and republics were swarming with Judeo-Masonic agents. We will confine ourselves to England and the Soviet Union.

"The power of the Israeli financiers to control British policy is nowhere more clearly revealed than in the Foreign Office, under whose complete control is the entire consular service," observes a 1922 London directory of English anti-Semites.

> The British Foreign Office has been rightly called the Foreign Office, but considering the entrenched patterns of appointments to it, it would seem more correct to call it the Jewish Foreign Office.
>
> Before the war in Sweden, of the thirty-one British consuls and vice-consuls, twenty-four were Jews; in Norway, of the thirty British consuls and vice-consuls, twenty were Jews; in Holland (with the colonies), of the twenty-four, twelve were Jews—that is, less than one in three, or only thirty-four of a total of one hundred and eleven, were British!

So wrote the British themselves in 1922 ("Who is who?"). And here is Soviet diplomacy in 1936. Soviet ambassadors:

1. England—Ivan Mikhailovich Maisky (Steiman), Jewish.
2. Germany—Yakov Suritz, Jewish.
3. Belgium—Evgeny Vladimirovich Rubin, Jewish.
4. Norway—Yakubovich Ignatius Moiseevich, Jewish.
5. Finland—Erik Akmus, Jewish.
6. Latvia—Leon Borisovich Brodsky, Jewish.
7. Lithuania—Alexander Alexandrovich Karski (Breitman), Jewish.
8. Austria—Arkady Ivanovich Lorenz, Jewish.
9. Italy—Boris Yefimovich Stein, a Jewish.
10. Romania—Moses Semenovich Ostrovsky, a Jewish.
11. Greece—Michael Veniaminovich Kobetskyi, Jewish.
12. Afghanistan—Lev Alexandrovich Stark, Jewish.
13. Outer Mongolia—Boris Isaevich Tairov, Jewish.
14. Manchukuo—Consul Slavutsky, Jewish.
15. Japan—Konstantin Konstantinovich Yerenev (Hoffman), Jewish.
16. US—Troyanovsky, by all accounts a Jew, married to a Jewess.

17. Poland—Yakov Khristoforovich Davtyan, Armenian.
18. Hungary—Artemiy Moiseevich Bekzadyan, Armenian.
19. Turkey—Lev Mikhailovich Karahan, Armenian.
20. France—Vladimir Potemkin, Russian.
21. Denmark—Nikolai Tikhmenev, Russian.
22. Sweden—Alexandra Mikhailovna Kollontai, Russian.
23. Estonia—Ivan Ustinov, Russian.
24. Czechoslovakia—Sergeevich Aleksandrovsky, Russian.
25. Bulgaria—Fedor Fedorovich Raskolnikov, Russian.
26. Iran—Mikhail Chernykh, Russian.
27. China—Dmitry Bogomolov, Russian.

Total: Jews sixteen, Russians eight, Armenians three.

The Italian *Regimo Fasciste* provides data on Jewish influence on US politics. According to the data of *Jewish Book* as of 1940, ten US senators and five US ambassadors are Jews.

137. Bullitt, a Typical Representative of the Judaization of Diplomacy

William C. Bullitt, the American ambassador to Moscow and Paris, stands before us at the head of the most fateful diplomats of recent times as a typical representative of the Judaization of diplomacy. He is one of the main instigators of the current world war. The German press reports the sensationalist details of his "efforts for peace":

One of the chief organizers of the war is the American ambassador in Paris, the half-Jewish William C. Bullitt. It was he, as a representative of Jewish big capital, who worked energetically for the outbreak of war.

On October 15th, 1936, the *World Service* published: "Attention! Bullitt in Paris."

> The newspapers announced the arrival in Paris of a new United States ambassador. His name is William Bullitt.
>
> His appointment, under the circumstances, means an immediate danger of war with Germany for France, for Bullitt is a special agent of the Jewish bank Kuhn, Loeb & Co. demanding war against Hitler as soon as possible.

The following can be said about William Bullitt's diplomatic specialty:

> William Christian Bullitt, aged twenty-eight, attended the peace conference at Versailles as a companion of Wilson. His

mother was Jewish. Bullitt left the diplomatic service after being sent by the American government as an observer to Moscow. He became director of a large film society in Hollywood, and also worked as a portrait painter and short story writer.

It was not until 1933, when the National Socialists took power in Germany, that Bullitt reappeared on the political scene.

In 1933 he was appointed as first ambassador to Moscow, and in September 1935 he unexpectedly left that post, settling in Washington and becoming one of President Roosevelt's closest confidants.

In August 1936 he was appointed American ambassador in Paris.

Bullitt contributed on a large scale to Roosevelt's election, gaining the position of Secretary of State.

Regarding the intervention of the United States in the Mexican Revolution, the American people, to their great sorrow, realized the extent to which Roosevelt was a prisoner of the Jewish big banks and an arranger of Jewish and Freemason affairs. All protests and meetings remained unsuccessful: Roosevelt was supported by Bullitt and his Jewish aides.

Bullitt was appointed ambassador to Paris in 1936, apparently with quite specific tasks. He was to incite France to war against the anti-Jewish Germany, so inconvenient to Jewish capitalism. Bullitt, a half-Jew, never concealed the assignment entrusted to him. Already in a time of complete doldrums, he openly admitted to being the mastermind of the war.

On May 29th, 1938, celebrations were held in various places in France to commemorate the American soldiers who fell in France during the World War. At one of these celebrations in Surenne, Bullitt spoke briefly, stating, among other things: "Today, more than twenty years after the World War in which they died, we are not sure that their graves will not soon be mangled by grenades and shells. Americans cannot accept the idea of avoiding war."

Bullitt, a half-Jew, had already spoken publicly with such words fifteen months before the outbreak of war! He has since played a very influential and responsible role among the Jewish-English-French instigators of the war. The outbreak of the present war is for the most part credited to the half-Jewish Bullitt. It was he who again wove his dark threads immediately after the Munich peace accord to continue to stir up the war.

In this connection, let it be mentioned that Roosevelt had direct telephone conversations with Bullitt during the Munich crisis. Even then the American press reported that Bullitt, bypassing the US State Department, very frequently gave Roosevelt direct instructions.

Then came the Polish crisis. In the spring of 1939, the Polish ambassador in Paris, Lukasiewicz, complained to Bullitt about British foreign policy, which, in his opinion, was dictated by internal political circumstances that might lead Poland to a stalemate. Bullitt proposed to the Poles an alliance with England. He even immediately agreed to actively promote this alliance, instructing the American ambassador Kennedy in London to advise Chamberlain on such an alliance. Bullitt, however, went even further. He demanded that Kennedy categorically draw Chamberlain's attention to the responsibility of the British government. To lend the necessary weight to his actions and thereby increase the chances of success, Bullitt pointed out to the Polish ambassador that the United States had the means to exert real pressure on England. He would give serious thought to mobilizing these funds. Kennedy carried out this Bullitt commission with success. As early as March 30th, Chamberlain announced in the lower house that England was ready to guarantee Poland. On April 6th, 1939, the Polish Foreign Minister Beck signed a pact with England in London.

The half-Jewish Bullitt, as the representative of Jewish-American big capital in Europe, had thus in the name of the United States led the political current into a movement leading to war, for Poland now imagined that by relying on an alliance with England and a strong rear cover of France and the USA it could take an absolutely firm stand against Germany, and took in every respect a very defiant tone. Peaceful proceedings thus became impossible. In September 1939 hostilities with Poland began. On September 3rd, England and France declared war on anti-Jewish Germany.

Since this war had been systematically prepared for years by Jewry, it is not surprising that it was the half-Jew and trustee of Jewish-American big capital that was the exponent of forces sabotaging any possibility of settling the situation, any peaceful solution.

But world Jewry has not yet reached the limits of its desires—there are not yet enough countries like the United States on the battlefields.

Here, too, the half-Jewish Bullitt has done his best to drag the US into the European war from the start. That is clear from the telephone conversation on September 17th, 1939, between

Bullitt and the American ambassador in Warsaw, Drexel-Biddle. Drexel-Biddle had left Warsaw at the outbreak of the war, not feeling quite at ease there, and settled in Chernivtsi, then still part of Romania, in the Black Eagle Hotel.

There he received a telephone message from Bullitt, the half-Jew, instructing him to send President Roosevelt urgently with phony information about German atrocities in Poland in order to stir up public opinion in the United States against Germany. Bullitt, a half-Jew, suggested to his colleague that he "put his imagination into the reports" so that the information could be used by the American president and foreign secretary.

By sneaky means of lies and deceit, the half-Jew Bullitt was already trying to draw the United States into the war and make it the executor of the dark plans of world Jewry.[233]

138. Count Potocki Exposes Jewishness and the US

In the wake of Goldman's revelations, he was heavily assisted by Jews and Freemasons in every country. The first note in this caterwaul was played, as it turned out from the seized documents of the Polish Foreign Office, by the Jewish masters of the United States.

When the Germans occupied Warsaw, not all of the archives were burned by the Poles. The sensational correspondence of the Polish ambassador to the United States, Count Potocki, with his foreign minister Beck, for example, who subsequently fled to London, found its way into the hands of the Germans. They published some of these documents in the "White Book" of Sensational Revelations, number three. These revelations confirm Dr. Goldman's candor about the role of Jewry in World War II.

This 1940 edition of White Book No. 3 contains documents that are murderous to American politics and diplomacy, seized from the recent fiefdom of Poland's former Minister Beck, the Brühl Palace in Warsaw. They compromise not only the US ambassadors Bullitt, Kennedy and Biddle, but also Roosevelt himself, making a huge impression even in America.

Let us consider the dispatches of Count Potocki, the Polish ambassador to Washington, to his minister Beck, in which he gives a striking description of the thoroughly Judaized America of our days, including his conversations with Bullitt, confirming once again the strong will of the United States to take a direct part in the war, but only after England and France get resolutely involved against fascism, hated by Roosevelt with all his Masonic heart.

---

[233] *East Asian Observer*, No. 7, Shanghai, 1941.

Moreover, in one of his secret reports, Count Potocki openly claims that Roosevelt, under pressure from his Jewish entourage, considers himself "the champion of democracy and freedom throughout the world" and that the main secret of his policy is "to serve the interests of world Jewry under the pretext of fighting totalitarian dictatorships and the ideas that inspire them."

Count Potocki devoted his top-secret report of January 12th, 1939, as noted in the document, to the domestic political situation in the United States, which inevitably led this conscientious ambassador to touch deeply upon the Jewish power in that country. All those who accuse us fascists of color-blindness when it comes to the Jewish invasion of the world must be silenced by the grim truth of this document, for the ambassador, even if he is from the Polish Republic, surely cannot mislead his minister Beck, and must keep strict objectivity in his report.

"The prevailing mood in the United States," notes Ambassador Potocki, "is characterized by a growing hatred against the fascists, and all propaganda here is concentrated in Jewish hands. One hundred percent of the radio, film and press of all kinds belong to the Jews."

In spite of the fact that all this propaganda is very crudely conducted and consists mainly of demonizing Germany at every turn, with the religious persecutions of Hitler and the camps being the main targets, it achieves its goal to such an extent that the local public remains completely ignorant and has no idea of the present state of affairs in Europe. At this moment most Americans regard Chancellor Hitler and fascism in general as the greatest evil and the greatest threat to the world.

This situation provides an excellent field for all kinds of speakers, especially the newly arrived emigrant workers from Germany and Czechoslovakia, who are generous with their words, using insinuations of all kinds, to inflame the feelings of the local public. All of them praise American freedom, contrasting it with the horrors of totalitarian states.

It is highly revealing that, in all this deeply thought-out campaign, the thrust of which is directed mainly against fascism, the USSR is completely excluded. If it is mentioned in passing, it is done in the friendliest possible way, making it appear as if a Red Moscow is marching alongside the democratic states. As a result of this skillful propaganda, the sympathies of the American people were, in particular, entirely on the side of Red Spain. Along with this kind of propaganda there is an artificial atmosphere of war psychosis: the American people are persistently led to believe that the European world is hanging by a thread, that war is absolutely inevitable. Moreover, it is drummed into the American people's minds that, in the event of an outbreak of war, the US will have to act at all costs and actively defend the slogans of peace and freedom throughout the world.

Roosevelt himself was filled with hatred of fascism and was one of the first to put his feelings into practice. In doing so, he had a dual purpose.

He wanted to divert people's attention from domestic political issues, but above all from the keenly felt problem between capital and labor.

By creating an artificial war frenzy and by whispering about the danger threatening Europe, he wanted to force the American people to come to terms with the gigantic problem of arming America, because the size of these armaments far exceeds the defense needs of the United States. On the first point it can be said that the domestic situation here on the labor market is steadily deteriorating, so that the number of unemployed is now as high as twelve million. The costs of overcoming unemployment are increasing daily. A certain order in the country is maintained only by the billions of dollars spent by the treasury to prevent the crisis.

Up to now the discontent of the masses has only manifested itself in the form of the usual strikes and local disturbances. But now it is difficult to say how long this kind of state support can last. The resentment and discontent of public opinion and the heavy conflicts growing between the giant trusts on the one hand and the working class on the other have created many enemies for Roosevelt and brought him many sleepless nights.

As for the second point, I can only say that Roosevelt, as an adroit political player and as a connoisseur of Yankee psychology, was able to divert the attention of the American public very quickly from the domestic political situation by getting them interested in foreign policy.

The way he learned to do this was very simple: first of all, he had to correctly stage the military threat that Hitler had brought upon the whole world and, in addition, he had to raise the specter of an imminent attack by the totalitarian powers on the United States. Even the Munich Agreement was skillfully used for this purpose, explained here as a capitulation of France and England to militant German militarism.

Here it was even expressed that Hitler put a revolver to Chamberlain's very heart in Munich, after which Paris and London had no choice but to sign the "shameful" agreement for them.

Later Potocki dwells on the growing rage in America against everything connected with fascism, a rage that is artificially fostered and inculcated.

Prominent Jewish figures, such as banker Bernard Baruch, New York governor Lehman, newly appointed Chief Justice Felix Frankfurter, Treasury Secretary Morgenthau and others closely associated with

President Roosevelt himself, are taking an active part in this widely conceived operation. They want him to be a champion of human rights as well as of religious freedom: he is the one destined to punish future peace-breakers.

This whole group of businessmen at the top of the US government hierarchy pretends to be representatives of "authentic Americanism" and the most reliable "defenders of democracy," when in fact they are inextricably linked to international Jewry.

For these Jewish internationalists, who have the interests of their own race foremost in mind, putting a US president in this "ideal" position of defending the rights of humanity is undoubtedly an ingenious chess move. In this way they have succeeded in erecting a dangerous hotbed of hatred and enmity; moreover, they have succeeded in dividing the world into two hostile, mutually exclusive camps.

The whole plan is constructed as well as possible for the interests of Jewry: Roosevelt was given the cards to revive American foreign policy, to build on this ground at the same time enormous military reserves for the war of the future, which Jewry seeks with full conscience. From the internal political point of view, it is very convenient to divert the attention of the masses from the growth of anti-Semitism in America by putting forward the urgent need for all to defend religion and individual freedom against the advance of fascism.

In another report to Beck, Count Potocki details his conversation with Bullitt, who at every opportunity tried to complicate the situation in Europe and in particular to drag Poland into an armed conflict with Germany.

> When I asked him how he envisioned this war, Bullitt replied that above all, France, England, and the United States should arm themselves to the teeth in order to break the neck of German power. Bullitt and the military experts he interviewed estimated that the coming war would last at least six years and result in the total defeat of Europe and the triumph of communism in all countries. There is no doubt that in the end the chestnuts from this clash would go to the USSR, whom Bullitt referred to as the "sick man" of Europe. For the moment, he equated the USSR with the pre-war Ottoman Empire.
>
> When I asked him whether the US would take part in this inevitable war, Bullitt answered: "Without any doubt, yes, but only after France and Great Britain have been drawn into it." In his opinion, the mood in America is so wound up against fascism and Hitlerism, that even now there is a psychosis among Americans, just like in 1917, before America declared war on Germany.

In another conversation, when asked by the Polish ambassador how Bullitt envisioned the coming war, he replied that first there would probably be a military incident between the USSR and Germany. Only then, if Germany was sufficiently weakened in the war, would the democratic states attack the Third Reich, forcing it to capitulate.

> The Russians, then, were to be summoned, according to Bullitt's candid explanation, to a war with the Third Reich, at the end of which was to be the victory of democracy over Berlin and over Moscow! Asked whether the United States would participate in such a war, Bullitt replied, "Undoubtedly yes, but not until England and France move first!"

Bullitt soon spoke even more clearly to the Polish ambassador.

On January 14th, 1939, he again had a conversation with Count Potocki, during which he explained that in the event of war, the United States would side with the European democracies—England and France.

He indicated Roosevelt's aim to strongly discourage any desire on the part of the British and French to collude peacefully with the Axis states, and to direct southeastern Europe against Germany and Italy. This then paid off, at least with regard to Yugoslavia and Greece.

In the pages of the White Book, one repeatedly encounters these passionate efforts by Bullitt to "start a fire" in Europe, for which both he and other Roosevelt associates spared no expense. Now they have achieved their goal: as a result of all their "nudging," the war is breaking out. But it remains to be seen how this whole world cataclysm will end, or whether in the end it will be the "American instigator" himself, acting on the cribs of the Judeo-Masonic directors. So far, fascism is winning. Let's hope the victories of fascism continue until the dark forces are completely defeated.[234]

139. Jewish Preparations and Anti-Jewish Warnings

The above facts expose the Jewish conspiracy. The years 1936 through 1939 show continuous Jewish preparations for that very "last and decisive battle" of which the *Internationale* sings about. The Jews see that a roll-call has begun between the fascist movements of different countries, that various forms of Anti-Comintern are appearing and are able to realize a peaceful cooperation of peoples without the Jewish inter-nation and create the *All-Nationale*, in which there is no

---

[234] Translation of N. A. Ukhtomsky's book in *The Nation*, RFS, No. 35, Harbin, 1940.

place for the "chosen" people. O! at the sight of such a blatant spectacle, Judas must by all means throw all nations against each other.

And so, they used their subservient politicians so that all hell breaks loose!

Shrewd people saw and warned of this Cainian work. 1936 through 1940 is not only the time of Jewish preparations, but also a time of anti-Jewish warnings. From Erfurt and Harbin, from Paris and Berlin, even from London and New York, warnings came from all sides, along with virulent Jewish revelations. It would take too much time to list them all, so we will only give a few samples. The *World Service* wrote in 1936:

> It should have become increasingly clear to anyone who closely follows political events, that peace in Europe hangs by a thread. As it was before, the greatest danger comes from the Jewish-led Soviet Union. Too few realize that the Soviet Union is already at war with the rest of the world. Bolshevization, strikes, disturbances, and uprisings are breaking out with terrifying frequency across the face of the earth, and give eloquent testimony to this. The extent to which the political influence of the Soviets is growing, is the very extent to which a new world war is approaching Europe.
>
> The Judeo-Bolshevik rulers want war to hinder the national awakening of the Aryans everywhere. The super-state powers directed the Soviet Union to facilitate the Jews in their parasitic life, not only in the land of old Russia, but also in other countries. First of all, it is tasked with eliminating all those forces that stand in the way of the Messiah, that is, Jewish world domination.
>
> Mussolini's fascist state idea is subject to elimination just as is National Socialism.
>
> Therefore, Meir Wallach Litvinov-Finkelstein, in alliance with worldwide Freemasonry, the International League of Human Rights, the social democratic parties of all countries, must act as a fierce fighter of the sanction policy against Mussolini.[235]

The *World Service* wrote on July 1st, 1938:

> The Anglo-French-American Entente will very soon become a reality. The preparatory work has apparently gone much further than the democratic statesmen indicate. On December 6th, 1936, one of the fathers of the democracies gave a speech.

---

[235] *World Service*, No. 3–4, February 15th, 1936.

Near and far from the League of Nations, an entente was to be formed, which would temporarily act alone. Subsequently, the entente shall be at the service of the policies of the League of Nations.

Will Judaism succeed in stirring up a new World War?

At any rate it can be seen how quickly the orders of the Jews are carried out. The US-French-English agreement is on the eve of its conclusion, thanks to the systematic subversion of Judaism. Thanks to the Jewish world press there is now more than ever a clamor for war and expectation of war.

Then on July 15th, 1938, the *World Service* wrote:

Every prudent politician who is not bound by the international super-state ties knows in good faith that a new World War can safely be avoided. There is no nation in the whole world which could in any way benefit from a new war. For any peoples, even in the case of a victorious war, the stakes outweigh any possible benefit. This is a fundamental truth well understood by nations and all men of state.

Yet, Europe is nearly bursting with political tension. Nevertheless, the international press is scrambling for war, screaming for war, urging for war. Judeo-Masonic and Communist instigators are at work everywhere, pouring fuel on the flames of high politics. Judas believes that the time has come to light a worldwide conflagration, from which he expects to emerge the only victor, and even to thwart the ever-increasing awakening of tribal consciousness in certain countries. Judas is ready to put everything on the line. Laws and ordinances to guard against Jews in Germany, Poland, Romania, Hungary, etc. are a formidable sign for Jews.

Jewish infestation is under serious threat throughout the world. Only a new World War between the Aryan nations can yet save Judas. A new massacre of non-Jewish peoples could in addition realize the world domination of the Jews.

That is why the incitement to war lasts, that is why the war alarm lasts.

The same cautionary issue of the *World Service* reports:

A prominent New York member of the US Congress, Hamilton Fish, a Republican who belongs to the opposition, clearly aware of the situation, has issued a demand to the American government not to make any more speeches about the situation in

Europe. The statement reads: "Two or three more inflammatory, provocative, hysterical speeches from the President and Cabinet members, attacking other nations, may prove to be the spark that ignites a world conflagration."

Recall, by the way, the brave protest to President Roosevelt from the Militant Christian Federation of America, printed by the *World Service* on March 1st, 1938, which began: "Referring to your recent words in Chicago, the Militant Christian Patriots of America fear that you would probably act on known dark forces to plunge the United States into an overseas war."

The *Deutsche Beckruff und Beobachter*, published in New York, also raises its voice of warning against a new war. It writes on June 9th, 1938:

> No matter how much they try to conceal it, the threat of war that is much talked about comes not at all from Germany, Italy, or Japan, but from the world powers that have entered into the alliance. Behind them stands the global power of the big financiers. The governing influence of the Jews must be restored. If Schiff was willing to spend millions to put Lenin and Trotsky in power in Russia in order to destroy the Christian state, now the big Jewish financiers in London, Paris, and New York are ready to put everything on the line so that the nations will send eight million young people to their deaths again.

Eight million young men. Alas, the Aryans could not even imagine the number of human lives Judas had sentenced to death.

The newspaper of the Jews in the United States, *The American Hebrew*, published an article in its July 3rd, 1938, titled "Will Eli Horst Wessel win?" The article states the following:

> The forces of reaction are mobilizing, the coalition of England, France and the USSR will sooner or later oppose the victorious run of an intoxicated Führer. Accidentally or deliberately, in each of these countries the Jew stands in the most important position!

As early as 1936, *Nash Put'* in Harbin published "Behind the Scenes of the Franco-Soviet Pact," a translation from *Der Stürmer*:

> "The inevitable forerunner of the present in every respect scandalous cabinet of Léon Blum was the Masonic-influenced cabinet of Albert Sarraut, under whom the military alliance with the USSR was ratified 'without a hitch.'" In other words,

the cabinet of Sarraut has concluded a military pact with such serious consequences with the Jews who had settled in Moscow.

Thus, France and the Soviet Union undertook to provide each other with military assistance. At the same time as the conclusion of this last pact, Sarraut gave Moscow a loan of eight hundred million francs, which was intended entirely for the arming and equipping of the Red Army.

The story of this loan is extremely colorful, and the one who did the most work to "secure" it was a man named Kagan, a one hundred percent Jewish man.

This powerful man, even now in France, was then at the very center of both political and financial life, with enormous connections.

Let us begin first of all with the purely familial connection of Kagan, which gave him access to the very heart of the Sarraut cabinet. Kagan married the native daughter of Maurice Sarraut, the brother of Prime Minister Albert Sarraut. He was able to influence him, so to speak, "from behind." In addition, Kagan is closely "linked" to Soviet Jews in the Kremlin and, according to the Paris newspaper *Action Française*, he is even a commissioner of the Soviet government. In particular, he seems to have been entrusted with the delicate mission of distributing Soviet subsidies to the French leaders of communism.

Kagan's third connection opens to him the doors of the big banker's house of the Jew Zeligman in Paris.

This bank is firmly tied to the Soviet government. In other words, the Jews of the Zeligman banking house have long been working hand in hand with the Jews who have become entrenched in Moscow.

At the same time, banker Zeligman has important business connections in French government circles.

Moreover, according to the newspaper *Quotidien*, this bank systematically disburses large sums on the eve of each election to the Chamber of Deputies, giving these abundant "silver coins" to those parties which need to supplement their electoral funds. When the question of providing a loan of millions of dollars to Moscow was put on the agenda, the almighty banker Zeligman made the ratification of the military pact with the Soviet Union a prerequisite.

The demand was met with lightning speed, and the financing of the military apparatus of Red Moscow flowed "as if by magic."

This short but instructive story illustrates better than words the terrifying Jewish power in the Seine River.

Jews and like-minded Freemasons sit in the ministerial seats. Jews and only Jews act as intermediaries and as trusted businessmen. Jews define the very contours of French politics by acting as financial dictators, especially when the Jew Blum is now in the place where so recently Clemenceau, Poincaré, and Doumer were seated.

This makes it clear, even to the uninitiated, that the Jews are now ruling France as if it were their own country.

At the same time, the Jews are now also ruling the fate of the former Russia. The Jews of the Seine River extended their hand to the Jews on the Moskva River and entered into a military agreement, the tip of which is obviously directed against anti-Semitic Germany.

By this clever maneuver the French and Russian peoples are destined, sooner or later, to stand and march against a renewed Germany that did not please the likes of the Qahal.

They will have to shed their blood for the honor and interests of the criminal Jewish gang, which has sworn to reprisal against the disobedient German people.

That this was the intention of the French Jews is best illustrated by the recent outing of the Jew Mandel Rothschild, the only French cabinet minister who tried to open hostilities against Germany after it had occupied the Rhineland.

The sortie was rushed, and the excessively temperamental Jewish minister, who demanded the immediate sending of French divisions across the Rhine, was then left hanging like a fool, not supported by the vast majority of the Ministry.

Thus, it was not the Frenchman who sought to revive the terrible bloodshed, but the pure-blooded Jew.

A man who belonged to the people who, so far, alone had benefited from all previous wars.

The Jew desired a new war with Germany, not at all in the interests of France, but in the interests of Jewish world domination, a path from which a renewed Germany dared to suddenly move away from. This is what Trotsky and all the more far-sighted of the Jewish Communists are eager to do away sooner rather than later.

And for the sake of these selfish goals of world Jewry, French soldiers had to go into battle and die on the battlefields.

To Mandel this hasty sortie was not successful back then; now the Jews are striving more systematically for the same goal. The military agreement between Paris and Moscow against Hitler was concluded by their own hands for this very purpose.

140. "Hands Off Japan!"—From England

It wasn't just against Germany. Jewish provocations were aimed against Japan to the same extent. There was no fascism in Japan, so why did world Jewry try to choke Japan economically and get it involved in the war? Because even without fascism, the Japanese Empire posed a terrible danger to Judaism as the only country in the world which had never experienced the Jewish yoke, and which was ready to carry out its historic mission of liberating and rebuilding the Asian peoples.

This is why the American and British Jews who pitched their countries against Germany did not forget Japan either.

Thus, on January 3rd, 1938, *Nash Put'* had the opportunity to acquaint its readers with a translation of a sensational article that appeared in London's Fascist by Arnold Lees.

"Hands off Japan!" say the British fascists, as reported in *Nash Put'* under the headline "Noble Performance of the British Fascist League: London's Fascist Exposes the Machinations of the Chief Rabbi and the Jewish Soviets."

A timely reminder that could prevent great complications in the Far East. We present this prophetic article in full.

In the last issue of the London Fascist received in Harbin, the official paper of the British Imperial Fascist League, headed by Arnold Leese, there are lines reflecting the British fascists' view of Japan's actions in China.

The Russian Fascist Union sent materials to the Imperial League that illuminate the real aims and objectives of Japan in China. We now have confirmation that the English fascists have read our information and clearly imagine the position which England must hold in the Japan-China conflict.

These statements by official English fascists are a clear indication that fascists all over the world understand each other and adhere to a policy dictated by common sense, rather than by the interests of world Judeo-Masonry. Here is what a fascist writes in the articles "Hands off Japan!" and "Air Bombing" about the efforts of the world Qahal to cause a boycott and economic blockade of Japan:

> In August 1914 a group of bankers and economists decided, to their own satisfaction, that Germany could not continue the war beyond March 1915 because of financial difficulties. How badly mistaken they were, I need hardly remind you.
>
> In 1935, the most progressive "experts" again decided that an economic boycott would very quickly force Italy to abandon the Abyssinian campaign. But despite the sanctions, Mussolini

continued to do his thing until he reached the end he desired. The only result of the boycott then undertaken was a chronic mutual dislike and mistrust between Italy and England that threatened to endure for a generation.

Now we are told again that an economic blockade of Japan by England, France and the US would instantly upset Japan's aggressive policy in China. The Archbishop of Canterbury, who recently revealed his attitude to the Christian faith by voting in favor of the liberalization of divorce, suddenly got up and protested against an attack by one non-Christian church on another, calling for donations for China in its distress. Joining his voice were the British Chief Rabbi, as well as Lord Bierstel (whose interests in China lie chiefly in oil) and Lord McGowan (head of the Jewish-owned Imperial Chemical Industries Ltd., with also a high-net-worth business in China).

Immediately the Jewish German Boycott Council started talking too, which, in a letter in the *Daily Telegraph*, spread the word about how its boycott had put German trade into the hands of England and the other powers, and offered the services of its organization at the disposal of those who were thinking of boycott Japanese goods.

All this is really only a convenient plan to put trade into Jewish hands. This is precisely the result of the boycott of German goods. This was made clear some time ago when a Jew in London refused to cut his ties with the German firms, on the ground that if he had done so the trade would have fallen into the hands of the Aryan firms.

What would have happened in the event of an intense boycott of Japanese goods?

Most international trade would cease at once, because no country but Japan could offer goods at prices that would make it possible to buy them and thereby maintain trade. And this, in turn, would lead to increased unemployment in England, because of the inevitable general decline in trade. Japan would have stopped its purchases of wool from Australia, which would have ruined thousands of Australian farmers and exporters and caused a worldwide wool crisis. And the trade which had been carried on for many years by British firms with Japan would have passed into the hands of Italian and German firms, for it must be borne in mind that Italy and Germany would under no circumstances have joined the boycott.

Moreover, relations between England and Japan would be strained to the point of rupture. We must also take into account the fact that the unfriendly tone in Japan toward England caused by such actions would force us to make a complete reorganization and reinforcement of British naval and other forces in the Far East, which would be very difficult for England, since recruitment and fund raising for our armament had already reached a critical point.

But that is not all. Can we hope that such actions by England, alone or with other powers, will change the present situation one bit? In the present state of affairs, English investments in China are at risk, and our existing and potential markets there are being disturbed. Can we do anything, up to declaring war on Japan, which no normal Briton would even think of doing to stop the war in the Far East?

And if there is nothing to stop the war, then the best we can do is not to interfere, but only to make a demand that British interests be respected; which could have been done before with greater likelihood of success, during the Abyssinian War. It is then for us to be trading partners and, if we are required to do so, to facilitate the earliest possible settlement of the conflict by arbitration or other means.

Where there is no suitable alternative, it is useless to create complications, whether for commercial or moral convictions.

At a time when we are invited to be "outraged" by the fact of Japanese airplane bombing of Chinese cities, it is useful to recall that in 1923 the Japanese representatives at the conference pressed hard for an international law banning airplane bombing altogether, but this Japanese proposal was not adopted because of the opposition of England and France to the measure.

What would have happened if Japan's proposal had been accepted is difficult to say, but we are now faced with the possibility of an aerial bombardment, with all the consequences it entails.

People with clouded minds now wish to "civilize war by prohibiting the bombing of population centers." Such people forget that in every country the most important factories of military industry, the most important railroad hubs, barracks, and other targets, which are usually the objects of attack, are almost always in large cities. To forbid the bombing of these facilities merely because they are in cities would inevitably only prolong the war.

The path to peace lies not in "civilized" war, but in the creation of conditions under which each country can build its life without the interference of international Jewry, when the world government will be in the hands of Aryans, acting in accordance with Aryan principles.

Alas, the English people did not hear the warning voice of Arnold Leese. The Jews in England were stronger. England continued to roll toward its own destruction, to be the "sword of Israel," and to sink into the abyss of war.

141. "Hands Off Japan!"—From the US

"Our Jewish government is provoking us into war with Japan in order to save the Jewish head of the USSR and world Jewry," William D. Pelley, leader of the American Legion of Silver Shirts, published in 1936 in the pages of his magazine *Liberation*. At the same time, *Nash Put'* translated and published what turned out to be a prophetic article:

> The enemies of the world have decided to use the red influence in Washington and make the USA not only a secret ally of the Soviet Union, but also an implacable rear enemy of Japan, which at the right time in the hands of world Jewry would play the role of a destructive battering ram.
> In this way Israel dreams of destroying its enemy without losing a single soldier in its Red Army.
> An analysis of the international situation shows that it would be difficult for Japan, which does not have enough manpower and fighting resources, to withstand a simultaneous struggle with the USSR and the US. Japan will be forced to first turn all its forces against America and, already exhausted, join the battle with the USSR. And of course, it can be foreseen in advance that the greatest casualties and losses in this confrontation will be suffered by the American people.
> This war, waged in the name of patriotism, as the Jewish press screams about it, will only benefit the Baruchs and Warburgs in the end. It will not only enable their compatriots to occupy the highest positions in the official spheres of the country, as they did during the World War, but it will also create a market for the products of the multi-million-dollar war in the Baruch industry and the investment of Warburg millions in war loan bonds.
> The American government, of course, would be forced to issue these bonds. Who will buy them?
> They will be bought by Warburg and his compatriots, who make a profit from war supplies, and the networks of secure credit will braid the American people even more tightly!

This circumstance indicates once more who is interested in the war in the Far East.

Remember also that a rising tide of anti-Semitism, reaching its highest intensity, may solve the damning question: who is responsible for the misfortunes of modern man?

At this moment the enemy of all nations, world Jewry, will be held grievously responsible.

The consequences for the perpetrator will be dire.

One has only to turn over a few pages of history to remember the terrible outbursts of the anger of nations against a common enemy. Fearful of this, Jewry seeks by all means to divert the attention of individual nations from their destructive historical role.

By causing a Japanese–American war, it will, in addition to enriching itself with the blood of heroes, deflect the sword of vengeance of the American people from itself for many years to come.

But let the world know that the American people have no reason to go to war with Japan, and that if this war can be avoided, the bloody government of Jewish murderers who have taken over Russia will soon fall.

And let the Jews of the world remember that before their diabolical plan is carried out, the awakened Aryans will be freed from the shackles of Jewry, and in this last battle between the forces of dark and light, the Silver Shirts will be in the forefront.

142. Will America Go to War?

"Will America go to war?" I asked myself in a report at a public meeting in 1940 in the garden of the Railway Assembly, devoted to the clarification of subversive sabotage by the dark forces of the world. I came to this conclusion: "The answer to this question depends on the degree of determination of world Jewry to risk its last stronghold, and on the degree of resistance of the American people."

It should be noted that the war fever in the US is now much stronger after the visit of the Zionist leader Chaim Weizmann.

Before his departure from London, the most prominent Zionists such as Ben-Gurion, Kaplan, Chertok, Rutenberg, and others came there. Weizmann was introduced to Roosevelt by the British Ambassador Lord Lothian, a Freemason of high rank, and as the Jewish press says, "Lord Lothian left and Roosevelt and Weizmann talked face to face!"

Weizmann then met with the British and French ambassadors in Washington, and in New York he discussed the situation with prominent American Jews, including the Chief Justice of the US Supreme Court, Zionist Louis Brandeis, and the Chief Rabbi of the Jewish communities of America, Stephen Wise. They spoke at dozens of Jewish, American, and Jewish-American rallies and banquets, and departed for England, receiving on behalf of world Jewry the support of England and the Old World, capitalism and Marxism, to the end.

Immediately the alarmist clamor from the American shore of the Pacific intensified to the limit, directed not only against Germany, but also against the Asian bulwark of the Anti-Comintern, Japan. Military cargoes for Chiang Kai-shek once again flowed through the Burmese highway, while in the opposite direction arms transports for Great Britain moved across the Atlantic.

"The US' "defense" budget reached twelve and a half billion dollars in 1940. How could the industrial strength of the United States withstand the enormous burden of supplying arms to Britain?" So asks the Japanese publicist Tokeo Imamura in the Tokyo newspaper *Hochi*. This question is at this time the enigma of the whole world.

"In 1940 the expansion and strengthening of US naval forces reached the limit, revealing something unprecedented yet in the history of naval weapons planning and startling the whole world," notes another Japanese, a well-known publicist on naval issues T. Saito in the Dyrena *Eastern Review* in 1941.

> Vinson's Third Bill, passed in January 1940, as well as Admiral Stark's draft immediately following it, which received congressional approval in June, provides for such a gigantic expansion and enhancement of US naval power that it raises doubts about the normality of the authors.
>
> Vinson's project presumes at an expense of $652 million to increase the naval power of the United States by 11 percent, that is, to build 21 more fighting ships with a total water-capacity of 165,000 tons, auxiliary ships of 75,000 tons, 45,000 planes, and 12 airships, while Stark's project would increase the fleet at once by 77 percent, that is, the tonnage of fighting ships would increase by 1.3 million tons, and auxiliary ships by 100,000 tons. To carry out these projects within five to seven years would require an astronomical sum of $4.6 billion, or between six to twenty times Japan's naval budget for 1940.
>
> According to Stark's design, a total of 1.25 million tons of warships is to be built, viz. battleships 385,000 tons, aircraft carriers 185,000 tons, cruisers 420,000 tons, submarines 70,000 tons, and auxiliary ships 100,000 tons; the execution of this project would at once increase the fighting power of the

American fleet two and a half times against the present: 26 battleships, 1 million tons; 418 destroyers, 478,000 tons; and 185 submarines, 172,956 tons, for a total of 732 units, 3,129,500 tons.

"Such a gigantic fleet, unprecedented in the history of the world, arousing doubts about the sanity of Americans, should appear in just seven years in the eastern waters of the Pacific," T. Saito observes. At the expense and under the command of the Jews, we will add. It is not for nothing that Admiral Bloch, the only Jewish admiral in the world, was appointed commander of the US Navy.

What is the USA going to do with such a huge fleet? According to Harold Stark, Chief of Operations of the Department of Naval Operations, this fleet is nothing more than the implementation of ideas about the necessity of having two independent fleets, one in the Atlantic Ocean to counter Germany and Italy and the other in the Pacific Ocean to attack the west. The link between the two fleets is the Panama Canal. If the USA is to defend its continent from an outside attack or to defend its principles, it does not need such a large fleet. . . . The American fleet is intended solely for an offensive aimed at an expedition to the Far East across five thousand nautical miles of water. This is also evident in the composition of the fleet and the location of naval bases. It is not only the desire of the United States to eliminate all Japanese efforts to establish a great East Asian bloc, but also the non-recognition of the coming New Order in Europe.

"Japan has only one path before it," wrote M. Miata, a prominent Japanese public figure and statesman, in 1940. "The position of third countries must have no influence on it. Therefore, whether the Pacific Ocean remains truly pacific or becomes a raging abyss will depend solely on what steps the US will take toward Japan."

Japan should not succumb to the US policy of procrastination. It should not cease its active efforts to establish the East Asian Peoples' Bloc on the principle of shared prosperity, a bloc that will open the way for the development of East Asia's historical destinies. For the hundred million people of Japan, celebrating this year the glorious anniversary of the twenty-sixth anniversary of the Empire, this is both an honorable and a very responsible task!

Our Life of Shanghai on October 1st, 1941, published an appeal by the President of the United States to Jewish World War Veterans.

From New York it is reported: The annual convention of Jewish World War Veterans was held in Buffalo. In an address to the convention, President Roosevelt said: "Now that much of the world is involved in the war, we should take special satisfaction in coming together and being free to discuss the problems that interest us. We must be united and strong to guard our free democratic form of government."

One of the speakers at the convention described Jewish veterans as the brightest and liveliest symbol of American-Jewish patriotism. There are now three Jewish generals in the American army.

America took the risk of war. Well, Jewish history will repeat itself in Europe: He who sows the wind will reap the whirlwind; he who wants another one's destruction will perish himself!

143. Under the Smoke Screen of the German-Soviet Pact

In 1939 Germany signed a non-aggression pact with the Soviet Union. From the beginning of this pact, as opposed to the misled press around the world, we wrote that this was an unnatural and insincere alliance on both sides, a temporary respite for Germany to defeat its opponents in the West and for the Soviet Union to wait until Germany was weakened to strike it suddenly from the East.

In public reports and in the pages of *Natsiya* we have asserted the existence of a secret Anglo-Soviet and Anglo-American treaty, based on the simple reasoning that such treaties are inevitable where essentially the same evil force rules.

"The USSR is preparing to march on Germany" is the title of A. Vinogradov's article in *Natsiya* on January 4th, 1940. "The salvation of both Germany and our Motherland is that Germany, today's ally of the USSR, should liquidate the modern Communist nest, in place of which will rise National Russia, a faithful friend and ally of the German people," ends the RFU article in *Natsiya* on January 28th of that year. Finally, *Natsiya* on January 29th, printing my report on "The World Catastrophe of Israel," gave the following forecast:

> Naturally, fascist Europe and original Asia cannot exist peacefully, if between them the citadel of the Third International spreads seas of blood, the center of all kinds of troubles and conspiracies. If the National Russia is between them, one can be secure in the rear, one can come to an agreement with it, to establish lasting economic cooperation and mutual aid, and one can include it in the common struggle against the world enemy,

which has taken refuge in America, but a lasting pact is unthinkable with the Soviet Union, which is owned by the Jewish Comintern.

Finally, on the very day of the outbreak of hostilities between Germany and the Soviet Union, when news of the war had not yet reached Harbin, my article in *Natsiya*, written the day before, appeared, in which I directly stated: "The German–Soviet war is not only inevitable, but close." Only when the newspapermen distributed the printed issues of the paper did we receive telegrams in Harbin announcing the outbreak of war.

Where did our awareness come from? From a very simple source: the Harbin *Jewish Life*.

Throughout 1940, the honeymoon year of the peaceful spread and "prosperity" of the USSR, this remarkable source of ceaseless Jewish self-disclosure published such messages as:

> Will Moscow follow the example of Mussolini, Telica,[236] and other gentlemen? This question can be answered by the exceptional data at our disposal, coming from American sources well-informed about Moscow's political situation and the plans of the Soviet government. This data shows that Stalin intends to maintain his independence in the Jewish question by pointing out in the Soviet government newspaper *Izvestia* and broadcast on Moscow radio that the Soviet doctrine concerning the Jewish question is sharply at odds with the views of the German and Italian governments.
>
> The article said: "We cannot tolerate the spirit that oppresses people and deprives them of their liberty just because they are born Jews, people of another, so-called 'inferior race.' The peoples among whom such a barbarous spirit reigns are wicked, for they deny the humanity of others."[237]

In March 1941 was published an even greater frankness: the story of a Jew who came from the Soviet Union on the "religious-national rise" of Moscow's Jews ends unexpectedly: "In Moscow everyone knows that the Soviet–German pact was concluded for a time and only to divert attention. The Communists hate the Germans."[238]

---

[236] Prime Minister of Hungary from 1920–1921 and from 1939–1941. (Translator's note)
[237] *Jewish Life*, No. 22–23, 1940.
[238] Ibid., No. 10, 1941.

144. The Secret UK–USSR Axis

The British fascists, led by Oswald Mosley, fought to end the Anglo-German war in late 1939 by exposing in their organ *Action* the real secret aims of the war and Britain's connection with the USSR.

"Britain can and must be strong enough to defend herself against attack by any nation of the world, but must not interfere in foreign quarrels which have no relation to England or to the whole British Empire," read the main of the four theses of this struggle for peace, carried out under the slogan "England First."

From issue to issue in his official newspaper, *Action*, Sir Oswald Mosley, with countless facts, quotations from newspapers, and extracts from parliamentary speeches, reveals to his readers all the senseless contradictions in which the leaders of British politics have become entangled.

Action never tires of highlighting the countless statements by Churchill, Chamberlain, Greenwood, and Sinclair that the war is being waged to overthrow the national regime.

Having gathered all the facts about this, Sir Mosley addressed the British government through *Action*, where he writes in passing:

> To the war cry of "saving small nations" has been added the cry of "destroying Hitlerism."
>
> Now, in order to remain faithful proclaimers of their principles, governments should throw out a new slogan—"to destroy Stalinism."
>
> But we do not hear from the press and parliamentarians demands for war with the USSR. We ask: why then? Aren't the Soviet Union and Germany allies? There can be only one answer.
>
> Those elements which have a tremendous influence on capitalism in Great Britain have an equally tremendous influence on communism in Russia.
>
> There is no need to explain why the USSR is absolved of its sins but not Germany: because the USSR sinned only against the principle of the protection of small nations, while Germany sinned against the most important citadel of world capitalism: Jewry.

This internal connection of the forces driving both the USSR and British rule is even more vividly emphasized in the last issue of *Action*, before its closure, where, under the headline "Refusal to go to war with the USSR deprives war of all meaning," the British fascists write:

A week ago, we asked: does Britain contemplate launching a war against "Stalinism"?

The answer to our question is our government's tacit sympathy for the activities of the USSR.

In spite of the fact that the USSR acted in the same way as Germany, in spite of the fact that Poland cried out for help in exactly the same way as when Germany aggressed, not a single party said that a war should also be raised against the USSR. On the contrary, both the press and the parties are vying against each other to find all sorts of arguments for allowing the USSR to act exactly as it does.

"Another power has joined in aggressive action," Greenwood said in the House of Commons, and offered no plan to influence this "other" power (the same Greenwood who had rushed from parliament to the editorial office advocating war with Germany). He only admitted that she was so flawed that she had committed "an act of aggression."

Readers will have no difficulty in figuring out why capitalism in Britain, like the British Labour Party, is more sympathetic to communism in Russia than to German "Nazism." Readers of *Action* already know that both capitalism in Britain and communism in the USSR have unusually many elements in common.

Thus the absurdity of a war for the British people against the political creed of another country just because the parliamentary parties do not like it for some reason is even more striking!

Remembering the partition of Poland, the paper sneers at the "Soviet apologists" in the British government.

Comrades have recently gone through quite a bit of trouble. Having started a war for "brave little Poland" and for the rights of the small powers, they were suddenly horrified to see Comrade Stalin stabbing the little thing in the back, while just at the same time the 'comrades' were telling us that Poland was winning. As the situation soon changed, we were told that the Polish cause was lost, but that Comrade Stalin had acted to save the Belarussians and Jews living in those areas.

The Soviet Union was instantly disguised as the savior of the Russian minorities in Poland from the German aggressor. But before the ink of these defensive lines could dry out, another blow awaited the comrades: Russia peacefully negotiated with the very aggressor from which it had saved "the Belarussians and Jews," and wonderfully reshaped little Poland, brushing off the lion's share, without asking the opinion of millions of Poles.

Bad luck for you, comrades. First, it was the "holy war against the aggressor," then the USSR became the aggressor, but made itself look like a savior. This "savior" then took a bite from the kind Poland.

It is international capitalism and its owners, the Jews—that is who drive the governments of Britain and the USSR. These are the secret forces that make Stalin and Chamberlain similar, this is the secret England-Soviet Union axis!

145. The Anglo-Soviet Pact, World Jewry's Greatest Achievement

The Harbin *Jewish Life* exposes those who cooked up the Soviet-English alliance. The London Jewish Agency exposed Jewish authorship definitively in 1941. The Harbin papers, of course, in the smallest print and under the smallest headline, were forced to publish such a telegram from Ankara:

> ANKARA, September 11th. According to a report received in Ankara from Jerusalem on Wednesday, Shertick, chairman of the Zionist Committee in Palestine, declared at the annual meeting of that organization that the conclusion of the Anglo-Soviet Pact marks the greatest achievement of Jewry.
>
> Shertick further stated that for many months the competent Jewish circles have been working energetically in Great Britain, the United States, and the Soviet Union to achieve this agreement.

This telegram was very modestly and imperceptibly published in the September 12th issue of the *Harbin Times*, and did not manage to be seen in the pages of the Harbin *Zari*.

This sensation fully confirms everything that *Natsiya* has written during the past two years, asserting that world Jewry is as equally strong in the United States, Britain and the Soviet Union and seeks to unite these countries in a military, political and economic alliance.

Predictions of this kind in particular were made at an open meeting in the garden of the Harbin Railway Assembly on June 11th, 1940, when the head of the RFU gave a talk entitled "Causes and Prospects of Modern Events," and were the basis for the book published in Shanghai by the RFU Central Office, "Judas is on the Edge. The World Before Liberation."

The significance of Schertik's speech is further compounded by the fact that Schertik is apparently not Schertik, but Movsha Chertok, one of the greatest leaders of world Jewry. A Russian Jew from Odessa, an emigrant not from the USSR but from Imperial Russia, who became a prominent international "loyal subject" of the King of Britain and the Emperor of India.

Movsha Chertok is the head of the political department of the World Zionist Executive, branches of which are scattered everywhere, particularly in East Asia.

This position he combines with the post of chief of the political department of the same Jewish Agency, which was established in London in 1927 at the initiative of the American-Jewish friend of the USSR, billionaire Felix Warburg to bring together the Zionists and non-Zionists, Jewish nationalists, Jews assimilated in each country, and just Jews.

Chertok was one of the representatives of world Jewry who last year signed the famous Jewish Agency agreement with the British government on all-dimensional aid to Jews in all countries of England.[239]

146. The German–Soviet War

The German–Soviet War, which drenched our homeland in blood, was caused by the same damned Jews. The German–Soviet Pact was Adolf Hitler's great appeal to the Russian elements to switch to nation-building, to enter a New World free of Jewish capitalism. In the Soviet government and in the bedroom of Stalin, the Jewish elements are stronger than the Russian. That is why, from the very beginning of the Soviet–German pact, the Soviet side showed complete insincerity at every step of the way.

And here are typical reports of various telegraphic agencies of April through June 1941 which certify that the Communists and Jews knew in advance about the impending war and were preparing for it:

LONDON, 04/29 (United Press). The British Minister said, "The critical period for England in terms of the possibility of a German invasion will continue from now until July."

ANKARA, 04/23 (HAWAS). The evacuation of the entire population living in the thirty-mile zone along the German-Soviet border is now undertaken by the Soviets.

---

[239] *The Nation*, No. 8–38, 1941.

VICHY, 04/23. (GAVAS). One hundred and eighty-seven Yugoslav airplanes safely descended on Soviet territory, mainly at Kiev and Vinnitsa, after flying over Romania.

According to Yugoslav sources, the pilots of the downed airplanes will not be interned, and they expect to join the fight against Germany again.

HELSINKI, 06/17 (United Press). The Soviet government is now sending its troops to all the Baltic states. Backward Soviet railroad trains are going deep into the USSR packed to the brim with Estonians, Lithuanians, and Latvians, who, as unreliable, are being hastily deported from the Baltics to Siberia.

BERLIN, 06/26. (United Press). Reports that Stalin knew as early as May 6th that war between Germany and the Bolsheviks was inevitable, but he kept trying to pretend that he was pursuing a conciliatory and friendly policy toward Hitler.

At a banquet in the Kremlin to celebrate the graduation of the junkers with respect to Hitler, Stalin declared on May 6th that he was raising a glass not to "Stalin's conciliatory policy, but to the victory of the heroic Red Army over Nazi Germany."[240] Although an account of this banquet in the Kremlin was given in the Soviet press, nothing was reported about Stalin's "toast." Only now are those arriving from the USSR reporting this characteristic Communist detail.

Note the dates: April 29th, April 23rd, April 23rd, June 17th, June 26th, with a reference to May 6th. . . . and the German–Soviet war began "suddenly," on June 22nd. Judas' second front!

147. For Whom Does the Red Army of the USSR Fight?

As soon as the German–Soviet war began, Jews all over the world began to show already open sympathy for the Soviet Union, and especially for its Red Army. Assuring, on the one hand, the Russian people that the Red Army was the Russian Army, the army of the Russian people, the Jews held a Jewish convention in Moscow, where they proclaimed, printed in all Soviet newspapers, and trumpeted through all Soviet radio stations, their menacing incantations.

The voice of the spilled Jewish blood demands not fasts and prayers, but vengeance. Not memorial candles, but a flame in which the executioners of humanity must be destroyed. Not tears, but hatred for the monsters and cannibals. Not in words, but in deeds. It's now or never!

---

[240] Junker is a military rank in the Russian Guard and Army. (Translator's note)

So reads the address "to the Jewish people" of a rally of Soviet Jews in Moscow on August 24th, 1941, delivered by TASU, the Telegraph Agency of the Soviet Union.

"In the Soviet Union the Jews found the complete flowering of their national culture."

"In the face of the USSR, the Jews found their motherland, the Motherland that gave them freedom and happiness," the Jews shouted from this rally.

> In the fat fields of the Soviet Union, a Jewish plowman sat behind the wheel of a tractor for the first time. Jews began to work in factories and plants. The doors of universities opened for Jews, they joined the army, the mines, the laboratories. The Jewish people found their place in the family of nations.
>
> Jewish brothers throughout the world! The Red Army is fighting for us. The brown plague is creeping over the other side of the ocean as well; as long as fascism exists, all of humanity is in danger. Let our every moment be filled with readiness for action. Undermine fascism by all means, paralyze it at all costs. Spread everywhere a broad propaganda for solidarity with the Soviet Union against fascism.

Barely a Jewish cry from Moscow is heard, followed by a response from London.

The foreign press published a sensational telegram by Reuters, the official Anglo-Jewish agency, from London on September 17th, in which it appeared that Jews of all countries openly confessed their solidarity with the Comintern.

This position was at least declared by Brodetzky, President of the World Maccabi and one of the top leaders of the World Zionist Organization and the Jewish Agency.

Here is the full text of the telegram:

JEWS—IN THE STRUGGLE AGAINST THE FASCISTS. London, September 17th.

> "The Jewish public in Britain as well as, of course, the Jews of all free and freedom-loving countries have been particularly encouraging of the Jewish public in the USSR joining the struggle against barbarism."
>
> Professor Zelig Brodetzky, President of the Board of Deputies of the British Jews, stated this in response to a telegram received from the Jewish Congress held in Moscow.

The Russian fascist press wrote at the time:

Brodetzky is acting as chairman of the Jewish National Council of England and closely connected with the chairmen of similar councils in all other countries, including the USSR, as we have repeatedly written. He is an emigrant not from the USSR, but from Imperial Russia, an old socialist, at the same time one of the important figures of the World Zionist Organization, which has branches everywhere, including in East Asia. He is one of the supreme leaders of the Jewish Agency, the central Anglo-Jewish body in London.

In addition, the "professor" is president of the World Maccabi, the main Jewish youth sports organization, which has branches everywhere, not excluding cities in the Far East.

Brodetzky's statement about his organization and the solidarity of all Jews with the Jews of the USSR, with the forces defending the USSR and the Comintern, confirms all our forecasts and evaluations.

The Shanghai Soviet newspaper, *News of the Day*, publishes numerous responses from Shanghai Jews to this call of the Jewish congress in Moscow to defend the agonizing Comintern.

These statements followed exactly two days after the radio address from Moscow and Khabarovsk, and they are worth reading.

It begins anonymously:

Jews of Shanghai! I urge you all, whatever your political affiliation, to respond to my appeal. The Jewish colony counts among its ranks many rich and wealthy people. Let them spare no expense and thus show their solidarity with Jews in the Soviet Union and with those unfortunate people who are now at the mercy of the evil fascists.

So declares an unknown Judas in the *News of the Day* of September 26th, 1941.

"Citizens of the USSR are fighting for us, for our well-being and our ability to live," declares another Jew.

No longer anonymously, the famous Jewish capitalist C. Ioffe says: "Jewish brothers! Do not forget that a victory for the Soviet Union means a victory for us." It could not be said more frankly. What will the "Russian Defenders" say after this Jewish bluntness?[241]

Finally, another anonymous person explains frankly why Shanghai Jews are forced to appear in a Soviet newspaper without surnames

---

[241] The Defenders were Russian émigrés who had declared their solidarity with the Soviet regime during WWII. One such defenseman was General Denikin. (Translator's note).

and at the same time exposes the supposed "anti-Communism" of *Jewish emigrants*.

Here is this characteristic document:

> I understand that many would like to help, to donate, but do not do so, not wanting to get involved in 'politics' in view of the difficult international situation in Shanghai. But who is forcing this to be done publicly? After all, one can donate both goods and money without having his name published in the newspaper.
>
> You can give just the initials of your first and last name, you can just use a pseudonym. You don't even have to bring donations yourself; you can send them through a boy or in some other way.
>
> Means are many, and can always be found if one is very willing. Since I have no doubt that all my fellow relatives share my opinion, I allow myself to make appeals to the local Shanghai Jewish community. . . .

There is no signature on this "authoritative" Jewish statement in a Shanghai Soviet newspaper, but there is no doubt that a prominent "yeshivot" is hiding under it.

Shanghai Jewry, in spite of their difficult situation in East Asia and despite their limited numbers, is not shy about laying bare its position on the great struggle going on in the world.

As the Russian fascist press wrote at the time:

> We have always been aware of this position emanating from the unity of world Jewry, and have warned everyone. Now our warnings, following the Soviet and English Jews, following the president of the World Maccabi and the representatives of the World Zionist Organization Executive, are confirmed by the Shanghai Jews as well!

148. The Jewish Appeal to Stalin

"Dear Comrade Stalin!" was the title of yet another "Address to Stalin" of the Second Jewish Congress in Moscow in 1942.

> In the difficult year of the peoples' trials we have gathered for the second anti-fascist rally of the representatives of the Jewish people, and the first word of greeting and love we address to you, dear Joseph Vissarionovich!

Over its centuries-long life, the Jewish people have experienced a lot of grief and suffering, persecution, and humiliation. All the horrors of the past, however, pale before the dark deeds of the enraged fascist beast.

While the bloody pogroms of different times caught our people helpless and committed massacres against our ancestors with impunity, in the days of our Great Patriotic War the enemy found us in the ranks of the Red Army, armed and ready for battle. The best sons of the Jewish people, soldiers of the valiant Red Army, are full of courage and bravery, increasing day by day the family of heroes of the Patriotic War.

That is what they are, the heroes of the "second patriotic war." Here she is, this "patriotic" war. But let us give the floor to the Jewish leaders:

In ancient times, Hitler's and Mussolini's predecessors deprived us of our homeland. After countless wanderings, we have found our homeland again. A quarter of a century of Soviet life has not only healed the wounds of many centuries, but has instilled in the soul of our people new strength, youth, and creative power.

The Soviet country is our motherland. We are proud of the right to fight for its freedom, for its inviolability, for peace and happiness of the peoples. We have been given the great honor to defend it against our enemies to our last breath. For the first time in two thousand years, the great road of courage and exploits has opened for the sons of our people. Our brothers and sons streamed onto this road.

The Jews of all countries look with joy on their Soviet brothers who have the right and the honor to build a life of freedom. Lawlessness and pogroms have passed into the realm of tragic legends. And whoever tries to bring this terrible past back will be swept off the face of the earth.

So the Jews write to their Stalin. And they say the same thing in an appeal to the Jewish people of the world.

As one, the Jews stood up to defend our great homeland. The enemy of humanity, bloodthirsty fascism, for the first was met with a worthy repulse on Soviet soil. . . . The time of decisive battles is coming. And we, the representatives of the Jewish people, say to Jews all over the world: "To arms!" There is not a Jewish family in the Soviet Union that would not send its sons to the front.... We call on the Jews, fighters and commanders of the Red Army, to fight with even greater fury against the hated enemy. Jewish fighters, be snipers! Jewish fighters, aptly throw your grenades! Jewish pilots, destroy the equipment of Hitler's hordes! Jewish tankers, go forward, reclaim your native Soviet land!

Are the guard units of the USSR staffed primarily by Jews? The Jewish appeal states: "Every month the ranks of Jewish guardsmen multiply."

The address seeks to appeal to Jews abroad and gives them disgusting instructions for provocation, sabotage and even terror. "Strike a decisive blow against fascism!" it demands. "The Red Army is the hope of all mankind," Moscow Jews declare. "Jewish brothers of all countries!" reads the closing lines. "We Jews, citizens of the great Soviet Union in the capital of our sacred motherland, solemnly say to you: fight to the last drop of blood! Under the banner of freedom!"

This petition is signed by the USSR People's Artist, professor, and martyr Solomon Mikhoels, writer Shakhne Epshtein, Jewish poet and playwright A. Kuchner (who presents himself as a volunteer, a fighter of the Red Army and decorated with a medal "For War Merits"), S. Marshak, who was awarded with a laureate of the Stalin Prize, the academician Frumkin (also a laureate of the Stalin Prize), the composer A. Kreino (also a laureate of the Stalin Prize), the chairman of the Jewish collective farm in the Kuibyshev region, the man of orders D. Shchupak, Colonel F. Mihlin, Major Veprunsky, the head of the syndical department of the defense industry, with honors, S. Neimark, director of the Jewish State Publishing House "Der Emes" I. Stroyan, an architect and Stalin Prize laureate B. Ilya Ehrenburg, the film director Sergei Eisenstein, Professor David Oistrakh, laureate of the international violin competition, Emil Gilels, winner of the international piano competition, the historian S. Greenberg, the painter Nathan Altman, Jacob Flyer, winner of the international piano competition, the actress Clara Jung, the poets Hana Levina and R. Korn, and many other names that bear witness to the terrible Judaization of Russian culture in the USSR. The newspaper of the Russian Fascist Union wrote at the time:

> Look at this list: who represented the USSR at the international pianist and violinist competitions? Emil Gilels and David Oistrakh. Here it is, Soviet culture, "national in form and socialist in content!"
>
> We recommend quotations from the appeals and the list given in the picture described above to everyone who wants to understand what is going on, who wants to understand his

duty before the Motherland, who wants to fulfill his life's destiny!

149. Jewish Speeches at the Second Congress of the Jewish People in Soviet Moscow, 1942

Devoting an entire page to an account of the Jewish Congress, the *Pravda* of May 25th, 1942, had to quote, of course, much careless talk, for which the Jewish world leaders must have reprimanded their Moscow counterparts.

> The best sons of the Jewish people, fighters of the Red Army, famous artists, writers, scientists, gathered on May 24th in Moscow for a meeting, in order to once again call on their brothers all over the world to strengthen the struggle.

So says the official Communist newspaper. The second meeting of the Jewish people is "opened" by the chairman of the Jewish Anti-Fascist Committee in the USSR (such committees exist in the USSR, England and in all parts of the world)—the artist, professor, as the Bolsheviks call him, Solomon Mikhoels. Addressing Jews abroad, this artist exclaimed:
"My heart is full of a thrilling pride, for I am a representative of that segment of the Jews which has a homeland. This homeland . . . is our Soviet country!"
"Death, death, death to the fascist dogs!" he cries out further in satanic malice and says:

> The Jewish poet went to fight for our Soviet Motherland! My brother Sergeant Bexelman! I remember your oath—to fight for Moscow to the last drop of blood, you, not sparing your life, fulfilled your oath . . . ! A glorious son of my people, Major Za-Lman Onersi! Only a few days ago I stood before your grave at the battlefield! Jewish brothers all over the world! Let there be no indifferent people among you who stand aside from the fight against fascism! Surround with love those who fight in the ranks of the anti-fascist armies! Fire and steel on the heads of the enemy!"

Behind the professor-artist is Pinhos Sabsay, sculptor, Stalin Prize winner, Honored Art Worker of the Azerbaijan SSR, as Pravda calls him (this is who governs art in Azerbaijan), calling for sculpture to fight fascism. Then the Jewish writer David Bergelson, then "the famous poet," again a laureate of the Stalin Prize, Samuel Marshak, and finally Shakhno Epstein, a Jewish literary critic and publicist, Executive Secretary of the USSR Jewish Anti-Fascist Committee, editor of the Jewish newspaper *Einikait*. He certifies:

> In the heroic struggle that the Red Army is waging against the fascists, many sons of our people have distinguished themselves. Hundreds and thousands of Jews, fighters of all kinds of weapons, in the ranks of the Red Army and in partisan detachments are awarded orders and medals by our government. Many of them were awarded the title of Hero of the Soviet Union.

Grigory Tsifrinovich, a military doctor of the second rank, who was awarded the Medal for Combat Merit, calls on foreign Jews to donate medicine and bandages.

Alexander Frumkin, a famous Soviet physicist and, of course, also a Stalin Prize winner, attacks Tsarist Russia and contrasts it with the Soviet paradise for Jews:

> In Tsarist Russia, science was forbidden to Jews; the Soviet authorities opened the doors of scientific institutes and universities to us. The names of such Soviet Jewish scientists as the physicists Mandelstam and Landau, mathematicians such as Bernstein, Gelfond, and many others are now known all over the world.

The academic admits: "We hate fascism not only as citizens of the Soviet Union, we hate it also as Jews for the suffering it brought to the Jewish people. . . . We appeal to the Jewish intelligentsia of all countries."

Another Jew speaks on behalf of the Ukrainian Academy of Sciences. This is Ilya Spivak, corresponding member of the Ukrainian Academy of Sciences and at the same time director of the Cabinet of Jewish Culture:

"The Jewish people has revived and grown stronger in the free family of nations of our motherland," he exclaims, "his back is straightened, his hands are getting stronger and stronger, the creativity of Jewish writers, scientists and artists is flourishing wildly in the country of the Soviets. There is nothing more valuable, nothing more sacred than the Soviet motherland!"

Semyon Neimark, "an award-winning worker," head of the shop at Plant No. 220, speaks:

"And only one thought, one feeling inspires us: to work for the front! There can be no life for us on earth as long as fascism lives!"

Faina Buckler, a Red Army nurse, appeals to the "Jewish women of America, England and all countries" to remember "our heroic foremothers" who chopped the heads of the enemies of our people, and in particular our "mother in Israel Deborah"!

David Shupak, chairman of the Jewish collective farm in Kuibyshev Oblast, which embraced the best lands of Samara Province, cries out:

"I come from a Jewish collective farm on the bank of the famous Russian Volga river. More bread, meat, vegetables, and oil for the soldiers—this is our sacred duty before the motherland, before the Jewish people!"

The Red Army Colonel (probably for the NKVD troops) F. Mikhlin, who correctly pointed out, put the final dot over the i:

"Jews! There is no choice for you! The fate of the Jewish people is decided in the Soviet fields!"

And it is not decided in favor of Jewry, we might add.

"At the rally, welcoming telegrams are read from the Committee of Jewish Writers and Artists of the United States," *Pravda* concludes, "from the German [!] writer Leon Feuchtwanger, from the editorial board of the religious magazine *Protestant Leslie*, from Uruguay and Argentina."

The final touch is also characteristic: this is who the religious freedom in the USSR was introduced for: it was for them, along with the satanic persecution of Orthodoxy and Islam.

150. The Judeans in the War for Judea

Not only in the Red Army, but also in the British and American armies, Jews are now taking a direct part, probably in despair having put aside their natural cowardice.

International Jewish bodies are seriously discussing the creation of a Jewish army. The Harbin *Jewish Life* reported in the spring of 1940:

> In response to a question about the creation of a Jewish legion, the head of the political department of the Jewish Agency, M. Chertok [the same one who rejoiced over the Anglo-Soviet alliance, as we have already reported] said that Jewish Agency immediately after the outbreak of war declared its agreement to participate in it to the British government. In December the Executive Jewish Agency approached the British government with a proposal to create a legion of Jews living in Palestine, Europe and America, which the Allies could fully dispose of at

their discretion. The Jewish community also offered the services of Jewish industry to supply the Allied training centers.

The next issue speaks of an army of one hundred thousand Jewish men, allegedly being formed by the Jewish colonel Paterson in America. At the same time the leaders of the Shanghai Jewish community, Bitker and Topaz, appealed to the Jews of Shanghai to form a Jewish detachment to keep Hong Kong under English rule.

"In this hour of great perturbation, the Headquarters of the New Zionist Organization is carrying out projects and plans," another Harbin-based Jewish magazine, the revisionist organ of the *Gadegal*, reported in mid-1940.

> During the last two months this activity has been reduced to the cardinal problem of preparing a propaganda campaign for the creation of a Jewish army. A memorandum was drafted, clearly outlining proposals for the formation of a military unit, which had already been discussed with prominent members of the British Parliament. Preliminary negotiations [what a great-powerful tone!] began in London at the end of 1939, and as a result, one of the masters of British destiny helped us to get in touch with a member of the military cabinet.

Jewish Life on June 28th, 1940, quotes a telegram from London by "Gavas":

> The Zionist Federation declared that its proposal, made since the beginning of the European war, to organize a Jewish army, has now come to fruition. The Zionists vouched for total cooperation and stressed that 50,000 Jews have already enlisted as volunteers to serve in the Jewish Legion.

A few!

The next issue of *Jewish Life*, in 1940, published photographs of Jews in the British army. Fat and smug warriors!

In the spring of 1941, a triennial convention of Jews and Freemasons of B'nai B'rith organization was held in Chicago. The convention was also attended by representatives of the World Zionist Organization, headed by its president, Chaim Weizmann, who came to America especially for this event, and the official leaders of the United States, led by Vice President Henry Wallace (reported in the twenty-first issue of the Harbin *Jewish Life* in 1941). *Natsiya* then wrote:

As you know, B'nai B'rith is a special Masonic organization, into which, unlike all other Masonic systems, only Jews are accepted. In most countries (and there are branches of B'nai B'rith all over the world), B'nai B'rith lodges exist and operate in deep secrecy. In the United States, where Jews and Freemasonry feel themselves the masters, B'nai B'rith do not think it necessary to hide and exist quite openly, just like in Shanghai.

The B'nai B'rith Center is located in New York City, where its leader, called "the emperor," who is considered a descendant of King David, resides. This organization has at its disposal enormous sums of money and the keys to world politics.

B'nai B'rith controls all other Masonic systems, is their internal cement, and actually directs them. Members of the B'nai B'rith lodge in each city are also necessarily members of the lodges of all the other systems: the Scottish Rite, the Grand Orient of France, the Rosenkreuzers, etc. And thus, the B'nai B'rith lodge is aware of the work of all other Masonic organizations, being a "Freemasonry within Freemasonry," as "Red" Freemasonry is in relation to "Blue" Freemasonry of the first three degrees. B'nai B'rith members are also part of the leadership of all Jewish communities and Jewish parties and direct the day-to-day work of Jewry. Since 1933, the leadership of B'nai B'rith has established an especially close connection with the Executive of the World Zionist Organization in London, effectively subordinating it.

The United States government is also in fact subordinate to B'nai B'rith, which, in particular, could be clearly seen at the last congress.

Weizmann put forward at the congress a project of Jewish mediation between the British and the Arabs, so that after the victory of the democracies there would be an alliance of all Arab countries from the Euphrates to Libya. The Jews would support the establishment of the Union of Arab States under the protectorate of England, if the Arabs would clear Palestine for them. A lot of money was thrown at promoting this idea among the Arabs, Weizmann said.

After Weizmann, US Vice President Henry Wallace spoke and said: "The Nazis seek to eradicate the Jews throughout Europe. Their methods are inexhaustible, but I am deeply convinced that everyone who is worthy of the title of American will never take the path of hatred of the Jews. A glorious future awaits only those peoples who can best satisfy the rights of the Jewish people."

This Shabbos goy speech was broadcast by all US radio stations and translated into Spanish—specifically for South

America. President Roosevelt's congratulatory message was also read at the convention.

The specific decisions of the congress are kept in deep secrecy. All that is known is that they are directed against Germany and Japan and incite America to war. The warmongers of the world do not need more blood than has been spilled and is now flowing—they need a world conflagration.

Jewish leaders are in constant communication with the governments of England and the USA.

The Jewish *Our Life* in Shanghai publishes, for example, October 10th, 1941:

> Dr. Weizmann is conferring with English ministers. London reports: Chaim Weizmann, back from America, is in constant contact with representatives of the English government. The other day he had long conferences with the Minister of the Colonies, Lord Mayne, the Foreign Minister, Anthony Eden, and the Information Minister, Br. Grecken.

Weizmann races from London to Washington and back, reinforcing the unity of England and the USA.

Lord Weaverbrook travels the London-Moscow-Washington route, reinforcing Soviet allegiance to the Judeo-Anglo-Americans.

"Do you know who Lord Weaverbrook is?" asks the Shanghai *Russian Times* No. 109 of October 17th, 1941, and replies:

> I know what one might know from the newspapers, that is, that he is rich, owns a considerable part of the English press, a member of the cabinet and Churchill's right-hand man, an energetic dictator of the aircraft industry, very influential, etc.
>
> That's not all. I know him quite well personally. His real name is Max Aiken. He is a Jew from Canada, where he made a lot of money. After building up an enormous capital, he moved to England, where he finally became rich, was bestowed the title "Sir Max Aiken," and later became Lord Weaverbrook. He is an extremely clever, cunning and experienced businessman.

151. Dr. Goldman Exposes the Secrets of Politics

However, let us return to Dr. Goldman's report to the American Jewish Congress of 1940, reproduced by the Harbin *Jewish Life*. It will lead us closely to an understanding of the Jewish aims of the last bloody war.

Goldman rushes first of all to declare the priority of American Jewry, to which the leading role in all subsequent world events apparently passes.

> What are the implications of this situation in the world in general and for the largest Jewish community in the world—the Jews in the United States in particular? The answer to this question will be decisive for the future of the Jews, because the Jewish community in the United States will have to play a major role in any reconstruction of a new Jewish future. Seven or eight million Jews in Europe are unable at this time to contribute their share to the reconstruction of their future, while approximately five million Jews live normal lives politically, economically, and morally in the United States. It is obvious and elementarily simple that world Jewish leadership must pass to the American Jewish community.
>
> American Jewry is ready to promote the idea that the broad masses of the Jewish population of the US dare not limit their interference in world politics to philanthropy.
>
> In consequence, let me emphasize a few elementary principles on the attitude of American Jewry toward the Jewish problem in Europe.
>
> The supreme necessity is to help. Millions of Jews must be fed and clothed; children must be rescued, emigration must be organized, much larger sums than have hitherto been possible will have to be put at the disposal of this work. I do not wish to go into any detail about the beautiful work which American Jewry has done in the field of relief work, and I certainly do not intend to criticize some of its methods. But I would like to say two things about relief work.
>
> First: aid must be organized and based on the basic idea that it is not alms given by rich Jews to poor relatives, but a work of social welfare organized by the Jewish people for those segments of the Jewish people who are in need of it.
>
> Second, the work of relief in time of war must be united and coordinated.
>
> Relief work is very important, but it is not the decisive factor. This is because the major issue on the agenda of Jewish history today is not the life or death of Jewish individuals, but the future and destiny of the Jewish people.
>
> Many parts of American Jewry, if not most, have become accustomed in recent years to viewing the entire Jewish problem from the sole perspective of refugees and aid. This is a very

dangerous point of view. Its first consequence is that the whole world is beginning to think of the Jews in these terms. I have said on another occasion that sometimes the attitude shown toward us by our non-Jewish friends in recent years is more insulting to us than the struggle organized against us by our enemies.

Once the problem of a living people, a great historical community, has been downgraded to a problem of refugees and a problem of charity, such a people is dead. How can we expect the Gentiles to understand the historical importance of the Jewish problem when the Jews themselves think about it and act solely in terms of aid and charity! The separation of aid from political work is artificial and unjust! No aid can be organized without the political struggle and work that creates the conditions in which organized aid is made possible.

Take the problem of the German refugees of France, interned at the beginning of the war and freed in large part thanks to the intervention of the World Jewish Congress. To intervene on their behalf, is this aid or political work? Fighting for the status of tens of thousands of refugees in various countries, interceding with the government when they are expelled, interceding with the government for work quotas for them - is this relief work or political work? Both are connected together. More importantly, relief work is always a last resort to help the Jews, and everything must be done before you allow a situation to arise that necessitates relief work. In many cases you may have foreseen this situation by intervening at the right time and by political work.

The Jewish leader specifically dwelt on a significant example of Jewish meddling in another's affairs. It is an example we should also dwell on.

Some of us know, for example, the history of the struggle which the World Jewish Congress organized two years ago against the Romanian government, which sought to introduce in Romania anti-Jewish legislation along the lines of Germany, which meant the immediate ruin of one million Jews. Had the Jewish organizations of the world limited their activities to aid, the government would have done what it was about to do: One million Jews would have been ruined in one day, and then American Jewry would have been called upon to raise millions of dollars to help the Romanian Jews. By organizing a worldwide struggle against the government of Goga, openly and publicly, by gaining the support of the governments of England and France, by bringing the matter to the attention of world public opinion, the World Jewish Congress succeeded in defeating the government of Goga.

You may have heard of the famous scene that played out when the King of Romania summoned Goga and asked him to resign in the wake of this world campaign, and when Goga, broken and enraged, left the palace and told the journalists around him, "You win, Israel!" With this intervention, the ruin of the Jews of Romania was averted, with far less waste of money than relief efforts would have demanded. Romanian Jewry was saved and allowed to get on with its life, free from dependence on charity and aid.

This example is repeated daily, because in many other countries political work and intervention are helpful and necessary, and must be done daily.

Notice the repeated word: "daily."

Is the "case of Goga" really a daily recurrence in international politics?

Suppose Dr. Goldman has gone overboard here. Has he not here spoken of the thousands of influences to which the lives of peoples and nations are subjected by the supranational power of internal Jewish intervention, the international Jewish inter-state?

How did the Jews influence Romania and, according to Goldman, intervene daily in the lives of other states? Part of the answer is given by two telegrams published by *Nash Put'* on January 4th, 1938, when Goga was still in power in Romania.

"The brazen frankness of the Jewish International" is the title of one of them:

> A fund of 500,000,000 pounds is being set up to fight the nation-states. *Poka* begins military action against Germany, Poland, Hungary, Romania and Austria.
>
> LONDON, January 2nd. The *News Chronicle* reports that a group of international Jewish financiers has set up a special fund of five hundred million pounds for stock operations directed against anti-Semitic states.
>
> The details of this financial campaign, which will be conducted on the main stock exchanges of the world, will, according to the newspaper, be agreed at a conference to be held at "some place near Geneva" next week.
>
> The exchange operations of the Jewish group will be primarily directed against Germany, Poland, Romania, Hungary, and Austria.

Commenting on this report, the *News Chronicle* opines that Britain, France, and other nations sympathetic to the Jews will benefit from the outcome of this exchange campaign.

"Through 'His' League," reads the headline of another:

> BASEL. January 2nd. The Geneva correspondent of the *Baseler National Zeitung* reports that the World Jewish Congress intends to protest against the anti-Jewish measures taken by the new Romanian government to the Secretary General of the League of Nations, as well as to the governments of Britain and France, which signed a pact guaranteeing the rights of national minorities living in Romania on November 9th, 1919.
>
> In this connection, a serious conflict could be expected between Romania and the League of Nations, especially since the USSR would probably try to intervene.
>
> Jewish circles in Geneva are making efforts to have the question of the Jews in Romania discussed at the forthcoming session of the League's Council.

152. The Jewish Aims of War

"The time has come when the leaders of American Jewry must understand the importance of political work," says Dr. Goldman at the conclusion of his interesting and frank report. He continues:

> The last issue is the most important of all. The world is at war and ready for peace. Peace may come later; it may even come soon. But anyone who understands the political situation in Europe must realize that arranging a future peace will be even more difficult than crushing Nazism and winning the war for the Allies now. If Europe gets a peace like the one concluded after the last war, it would mean another war in ten years and the end of European civilization. Everyone agrees that a new political life in Europe must be organized, and the best minds and heads of democratic countries, both belligerent and neutral, are already working for peace.

How do Jews imagine these "problems"? The outspoken Dr. Goldman lightly answered this question as well:

> We Jews must do the same. I warn you against the illusion that our only task is to feed the starving Jews, because, supposedly,

when Nazism is defeated, the Jewish problem will be automatically solved by the victory of democracies. This is a dangerous illusion. The Jewish problem existed in Europe long before Hitler.... Nor will equality of rights solve the problem. Today I do not deal with the Zionist aspect of the problem. I am dealing with its European aspect. Do not believe that the democracies will solve this problem for the Jews: no people in history has ever been saved by another people. They may have the friendliest of views toward us, but the salvation of a people is entirely up to them.

We need to become aware of the complexity and difficulty of the Jewish problem, to learn from the experiences of the twenty years since the Treaty of Versailles, why the solution to the Jewish problems included in the Treaty of Versailles was violated earlier, some years after the end of the First World War, long before Hitler. We must find formulas and programs for a new sustainable solution to the Jewish problem in the various countries of Europe, a new system of guarantees and safeguards for Jewish rights; we must find a position for the Jews based on the concept of a new organization of Europe in general.

So, then, there it is! "Equality" is no longer enough. The Zionist aspects—that is, the creation of a Jewish national state in Palestine—the Goldmans are no longer interested in. They want the "European aspects." Or maybe world aspects! "Formulas and programs for a new sustainable solution to the Jewish problem in different countries"—remember these demands, peoples!

Remember, European and Asian nations, Goldman's words: world Jewry needs a new system of guarantees and safeguards for Jewish rights. The Judaization of politics, outlined in this book, which took place even in the Versailles period of human history, when Judas sat over the states, no longer satisfies Goldman. World Jewry needs a "position" for the Jews, based on the concept of a new organization of Europe in general!

Clearly, Europe is taken here only as an example. The whole world is meant! Remember this demand, people of Europe, Asia, Africa, America, and Australia!

What is the Jewish "concept"? About it none other than Chaim Weizmann, the President of the World Zionist Organization himself, let it slip—apparently, to make his statements more official, this time as president of the Jewish Agency. His declaration is quoted in particular in the pages of the Shanghai Jewish *Our Life* on July 18th, 1941. One headline explains what it is all about: "The Bible or Mein Kampf." Mankind, it turns out, is being offered a choice between the Jewish religion and Hitler's book—in other words, between Judaism and fascism. Should the Anglo-Americans and the USSR win, humanity would be obliged to recognize the Bible as the common religion of mankind—in other words, to bow down to Judaism. In Weizmann's words:

> We foresee a new just order at the end of the present war. There will be an era of better understanding between peoples. The world today is given a choice between the Bible and My Struggle. No bridge can be built between these two opposites. Our path may seem long and difficult, but we would rather die than stray from the path. For us there is no compromise between the Bible and *Mein Kampf*. There is one path laid out for us: the struggle for the victory of the Bible.

Don't be fooled to think that this is a victory for the Christian Bible, no: the Jews are referring to the Torah, which, apart from the Christian Bible, has been circumcised, cleaned, and falsified. It contains a description of the exploit of the wicked woman Esther and other abominations. If fascism is defeated, the Jews promise to make all the nations of the earth worship Purim, after they have been "Purimized" to the last one of them.

Understood.

The *World Service* wrote on November 15th, 1940.

> *The New York Post* reports on October 2th, 1940, that the British government has made certain promises to American Jewry in the event of a British victory. The author of the solemn statement, which was read at the American Jewish Congress and which, according to Rabbi Stephen Wise, is far more important than the Balfour Declaration, is Greenwood, Minister without Portfolio in the British War Cabinet. In his declaration he expressed the firm hope "that the British victory will bring about a New World Order, with the conscience of civilized mankind demanding that the Jewish people be compensated for any injustice directly inflicted upon them. The transmitter of this statement, the details of which are not yet known, was the chairman of the British section of the World Jewish Congress, Dr. Mauritius Perlzweig.
>
> *The New York Post* calls this message from the British government the first official British statement on the Jewish question since the beginning of the war.
>
> As is well known, the declaration of the former British Foreign Secretary, Lord Balfour, in 1917 promised international Jewry the formation of a national Jewish state in Palestine. It

is characteristic of the duplicity of English policy that the English promised Palestine to the Arabs at the same time, in order to get their armed aid.

Thus, by Greenwood's declaration, England confirms formally that she is fighting a war for the sake of the Jews. But the declaration is interesting in another respect. It indicates that England's own situation is bleak. Just to avoid losing their last ally, other than Greece, the English rulers have turned to the Jewish International with a government statement in the spirit of the Balfour Declaration and with all sorts of promises. But this does not help the English. All indications are that Judaism is preparing to surrender the English bastion, which cannot be held anyway, and move to the United States of North America. America is now chosen by Judaism to serve as the future world center of Jewish power.

"The question of our future is inextricably linked to the victory of democracies, and our fate will determine itself with the outcome of this grand battle of nations," declares Shanghai Jewry in its magazine *Our Life* on October 17th, 1941.

> We now identify fascism with anti-Semitism. The destruction of Nazism does not yet mean the elimination of anti-Semitism, and the position of the Palestinian administration, the tactic of silencing our victims by the British administration, is evidence of anti-Semitism even among democracies. Anti-Semitism can survive Hitlerism as well, for its cause is our abnormal situation, our landlessness and statelessness. We must not be carried away by words and slogans, we must be able to look at the root of things, and should we, who lived through the French Revolution with its slogans of freedom, equality and fraternity, should we, who lived through the infatuation with civil liberties in Germany, close our eyes to the reality of the situation?
>
> The Nazi plan to annihilate and exterminate the Jewish people, or to evacuate them to some tropical island, which amounts to annihilation, must be confronted with our own plan and our demands can only be those of the Zionist organization.

The present situation of the Jews, despite their ruin in Europe, is defined as "between destruction and rebirth!" That is the title of an article in the *Jewish Life* of July 12th, 1940, subtitled "The present situation of world Jewry." It directly states:

> In the long history of our people, it has happened more than once that the destruction, the demise of the old Jewish branch

has led to the creation of a new spiritual and economic center in a neighboring or distant country. This is how, after the great destruction of Eretz Yisrael, a powerful Jewish center was established in Babylonia.

After the Jews were expelled from Spain and Portugal, a flourishing Jewish yishuv was established in Turkey and Asia Minor. There are many such examples where destruction and creation, destruction and construction occur almost simultaneously in Jewish history.

Terrible destruction befell the old and deeply rooted Jewish center in Eastern Europe. The era between the two World Wars, with Jewish suffering and trials over the last twenty-five years in Germany, Poland and many other countries is one of the darkest chapters in Jewish history. A future historian will label this period as the destruction of the largest Jewish yishuv in Europe.

But, fortunately, during the same period, two great new Jewish centers grew up in other parts of the world.

In the last twenty or thirty years, the Jewish yishuv in North America has doubled: there are about five and a half million Jews in the United States and Canada. In Eretz Yisrael, from barely fifty thousand Jews before the First World War, a Jewish yishuv of half a million had grown. However, one must remember that in agriculture, industry, and everything that pertains to both economic and cultural life, the strength of Palestinian Jewry did not increase tenfold, but many times over.

It is therefore possible to regard the present period in Jewish history as an epoch "between destruction and rebirth." Dr. Herman Frank, the author of a new book with this title, discusses the present moment in the life of our people. In his work he has two aims: first, he tries to prove that there is a connection between the terrible political and economic crisis throughout the world and the modern Jewish Destruction. Second, he wants to analyze and describe life in Eretz Yisrael and in America, where large and strong Jewish yishuvs have blossomed.

The *World Service* cites interesting data about the Jewish occupation of the USA. As Europe cleansed itself of Jewish filth, the United States of America became increasingly inundated with a flood of Jewish immigrants. Having lost faith in the victory of England, the Jews are gradually turning the United States into a Jewish fortress. America has now become the world center of Judaism. This is openly acknowledged by the Jews themselves.

Thus, the Paris-based newspaper *Wochenblat Israelites*, on November 29th, 1940, in its article "Jews in America," wrote:

> The United States has become the most important center of Jewish culture.... The stories of Jewish fugitives from Europe, with which the newspapers are full, the interviews, the reports of the World Jewish Congress, and the articles of well-known Jewish leaders and journalists in America, all point to the demise of European Jewry, unless help follows at once. The most important help would be the facilitation of resettlement.

The *World Service* comments:

> The *Wochenblat Israelites* thus insist on the relocation of millions of Jews to the United States. The Jewish fortress of England is to be surrendered. It is already about to be dismantled in stone. World Jewry is also counting the loss of the Jewish center in Palestine. For this reason, the Jews intend to flood the United States with their masses, to take ultimate power there and turn it into a Jewish kingdom. If Americans don't figure out how to defeat the Jewish plans, they will soon find out for themselves what it will cost them.

So prophesied the *World Service* in 1941.

The famous pilot Charles Lindbergh kind of concretizes his exposé when, in the same 1941, he says:

> I will point you to one of these groups and trace their methods and actions. In doing so I will speak frankly, for in order to break their efforts it is necessary to know who they are.
>
> The three most important groups pushing the country toward war are the British, the Jews, and the Roosevelt administration.
>
> Among these groups are an equally important multitude of capitalists, Anglophiles, and those thinkers who believe that the future of their humanity depends on the continued dominance of the British Empire.
>
> Add to that the Communist groups, who were against intervening in the war until a few weeks ago. I think I've already named the main agitators in this country.
>
> I'm only talking about the agitators here, not those serious but directionless people confused by disinformation and frightened by propaganda, following the ringleaders and military agitators.

Further, if America goes to war, it is improbable that an Allied army could conquer Europe and defeat the forces of the Axis powers.

England has and will continue to devote every effort to drawing us into the war.

The second important group I named was the Jews!

It is not difficult to understand why the Jewish nation wants to destroy Nazi Germany. No honest and sighted person can fail to see the danger they pose to us and to others in their provocative policy.

Instead of agitating for war, Jewish groups should oppose it in every possible way, for they will be among those who would feel it the most.

A few farsighted Jews understand this and rebel against interference in the war. But the majority still do not understand this.

Their greatest danger to the country lies in the importance of their values and their influence on our motion pictures, our press, our radio, and our government.

The Roosevelt administration is a third powerful group pulling the country into war. They have used this theme to get a third unprincipled re-election of a president.

They used the war to add more unlimited billions to a debt that was already higher than it had ever been. They used the war to justify the infringement of Congress and the increased dictatorial rights of the president and his appointees. The strength of the Roosevelt administration depends on the wartime environment.

Its prestige depends on the success of Great Britain, to whom the president entrusted his political future at a time when most believed that England and France would easily win the war.

So said Charles Lindbergh, not noticing at the same time that his three groups were all clowns pulled by the same force.

At the first peace conference after the end of the ongoing war, world Jewry will present its bill to the victors and the vanquished. About this future bill in the Harbin *Jewish Life* in 1940 we found these revelations:

"A clear program designed to create a base for the restoration of Europe after peace has been adopted by the American Jewish Congresses. More than four hundred delegates, representing seventy-three congregations from twenty states, attended the session."

The essence of the "program" is not reported, but big names have pledged to support it:

The program was adopted in an atmosphere of statements by the most eminent figures of America, representatives of other governments [obviously Soviet and English]. The first person in this statement was Eleanor Roosevelt, wife of the president of the United States. She was joined by Senator W. Warren Barber of New Jersey, British Ambassador to the United States Lord Lothian, Czechoslovak Ambassador Vladimir Hurban, Ambassador of Finland Yalmar Prokone, and Ambassador of Poland Count D. Potocki. The next day Senator J. M. Mead of New York and Bishop C. Freedman of Washington promised all kinds of help.

Gentiles of all nations! Remember these patented traitors! Americans, Englishmen, Czechs, Finns, Poles, get your ropes ready—each nation must deal with its own traitors.

The World Jewish Congress has decided to establish a special Institute for the Study of the Goals of Peace. This Institute shall be administered by experts in ... Jewish international law, of course. "This Institute will be an instrument of the entire Jewish people in all countries to achieve our goals of peace, as well as a united Jewish front in the struggle for the rights for our people everywhere."

Palestine is no longer enough for them, those insolent, self-righteous Jews from Judaized America. In Palestine they only want to create a spiritual and material center, a power center, to house the government and the brain of the entire Jewish state. This is why the Jews need Palestine: for representation. To explicitly mark the conquest of mankind!

Chamberlain declared, according to Goldman, as *Jewish Life* printed enthusiastically, that one of the aims of British post-war policy would be the creation of a new European federation, not after the example of the United States, but according to a new principle. This "new principle" was not explained by Chamberlain or Goldman, but was exposed by Clement Attlee, first a leader of the opposition in the British Parliament, then a member of the coalition government, and finally Churchill's Deputy Prime Minister.

As leader of the parliamentary opposition, Attlee chose as the theme of his opening speech in 1940 the conditions for a possible peace with Germany, that is, with fascism. While he acknowledged that specific terms were premature, he believed it was not only possible, but even necessary to formulate the principles which would underlie a future peace as understood by international diplomats, to use Attlee's original expression.

What kind of principles are these? Oh, they do more than just resemble the *Protocols of Zion*!

The smaller powers, along with the great powers, must be chained to cooperate in the formulation of a new world order. The right of freedom to all nations, races, and religions! The recognition of a single international responsibility over the individual nations! A European federation and a world economic organization! General disarmament and . . . the creation of a single international military force capable of resisting any possible attack!

General disarmament and arming the international powers are exactly what Karl Mordechai Marx, Lenin, Wilson, the Second International, the Third International, Trotsky, Stalin, international Freemasonry, and international Jewry dreamed of!

Studying the Jewish aims of the war according to Goldman, according to Attlee, according to the Harbin *Jewish Life*, we must remember that as early as June 1917 a congress of Freemasons of the Allied and neutral countries met in Paris, one of whose main tasks, according to its chairman, was to prepare the United States of Europe, to create a supranational power whose task would be to resolve conflicts between the nations. The message of this congress in particular was published in the magazine of the Russian Supreme Monarchical Council in France, *Double-Eagle*, 1927, No. 35. There it was also pointed out that Freemasonry had taken it upon itself to promote this "concept of peace and the general welfare."

The bulletin of the Grand Lodge of France for October 1922, on page 235, details:

> The federal organization of nations presupposes the establishment of a super-state with tripartite powers—executive, legislative, and judicial. The international power must be sanctioned by an army or an international police force.
>
> To disarm the non-aligned states of our League and to arm a federation of states are two phases of the same process.

A concluding quote from *Jüdische Rundschau* No. 83 of 1921:

> It is not Geneva or The Hague that should be the seat of the League of Nations, but Asher Ginsburg dreamed of a temple on Mount Zion, where representatives of all nations would form a church of eternal peace.
>
> Only when all nations come as pilgrims to this church will eternal peace be made a reality.

This says it all. Here is the briefest exposé of the Jewish purposes of the present war, of Jewish purposes in general, and of Judas' immediate purpose over the states.

The purpose of Judaizing politics is here revealed almost to the end.

153. The Three Swords in the Hands of Israel

There is no doubt that, apart from Freemasonry and the ideas and movements it controls, listed in this book, Israel is waving three swords right now. They are England, the USSR, and America.

It once had another sword, the League of Nations, but now that organization helplessly and unwillingly lives out its days somewhere on the margins of history. It also has another sword, the Comintern, but it already has a new sheath prepared to convince the simpletons that it no longer exists. So instead of the League of Nations, we say "the United States," instead of the Comintern, we say "the USSR." England, the USSR, and America are a solid block, which can only be broken by a national revolution or a military defeat. The name of this block is the Finintern, the Financial International, the desperately resisting kingdom of Jewish capital.

One of the many proofs of the existence of the Jewish inter-state is the existence of a unified Jewish policy. The Zionist Pasmannik, in his book *Jewry and Revolution*, directly says: "The basic question is: Is there a distinct Jewish policy? Undoubtedly. And it would be ridiculous to deny this fact. This policy has undergone tremendous evolution, especially in the last one hundred and fifty years."

This book notes the individual stages of this evolution, from liberalism to Bolshevism and back to liberalism, but with the keys of politics, economics, and culture firmly grasped by Jewish hands. There may even be a monarchy established, headed by a king from the house of David. Judas wants unlimited power over mankind.

And here is more proof of the unity of Jewish interests and aspirations throughout the world: look how the Jews of all countries, even in East Asia, even in the days of war, are friendly to England, the USSR, and the USA. No other proof of the executive role of the governments of these nations with respect to world Jewry is really needed, but in this book, in all the relevant chapters, there is indeed a great deal of evidence.

This book answers unequivocally the question of who is in power in aristocratic Britain, in the Communist Soviet Union, in ultra-capitalist America—Jews, Jews, Jews, the priests of the Golden Taurus.

"God Save the King," "The Internationale," and "Yankee Doodle" in our day are expressed in a couple of phrases of blasphemous praise for Mephistopheles, which is truly the Finintern's anthem:

This golden idol
The will of heaven is scorned.

Mocking, cheating
He is the holy law of heaven.
To please the God of gold
The land is on the brink of war
And human blood flows
Pouring down the ground from the bulat.[242]
Men die for metal,
Surrounding the pedestal.
Satan leads the dance.

The Englishman Hilaire Belloc, in *The Jews*, sort of sums up our evidence when he says: "The British came to an alliance with the Jews of their own accord and were the first nation ever to do so."

Now a new "Soviet nation" is marching alongside the British, into which the Bolsheviks are hastening to recast the Russian people. A nation subservient of world Jewry, it was artificially created with the blood and in place of the Russian nation.

The war between the Jews and the Russians for our enslavement began long ago, and in my essay collection *The Jews and Russia* this is traced in detail. A. S. Shmakov in 1907 in his book *Freedom and the Jews* warned:

> Quite like last year, the Russian people, reading the newspapers, followed day by day the development of our unfortunate war, going through Liaoyang, Mukden, Port Arthur, and finally Tsushima, only to conclude with Portsmouth and receive what then began the same campaign, and receive the same kind of news! The Russian people were hardly as ashamed then as they are now. We had before us a formidable military and naval force, which by our negligence, we just failed to foresee or identify.
>
> Now there is another war. Here we see defeat after defeat! But it is inflicted not by a madly brave, animated, and powerful enemy, but by a miserable, cowardly, parasitic tribe among mankind that like a plague has been eating away at Russia ever since we absorbed our historic sister Poland. Since then, six million Jews have been waging a merciless war against the great hundred-and-something million Russian people! Before our eyes the struggle is escalating, and the victory is clearly on the side of the enemy.
>
> But this victory of the Japanese is from a very different nature.

---

[242] A kind of Russian steel. (Translator's note)

What was Japan fighting for? For its legitimate dominance in Asia. It fought to push us back, who had gone too far, who had taken too many foreign lands, and who had not measured their strength against their appetite. The Japanese victory was a terrible blow to our egos and our prestige in the East, in Asia. Russia however is still independent and great, and tomorrow, standing only on its national foundations, can once again become mighty and formidable.

The Jewish war and Jewish victories are quite a different story.

Six million foreigners come at us, not in the name of equality—that being a mere mask—but in the name of domination over the Russian people. The Jews, limited in their rights, confined within the Pale of Settlement and despised by everybody, managed to become virtually the masters of Russia. Having seized the main economic centers of the country with the help of land and commercial banks, they put a heavy hand on all the productive forces, and captured the main liberal professions: medicine, law, the press, not having the right of residence, and have infiltrated everywhere. They have tried to take or enslave all the main trades. Relying on their international organization, the Jews have seized Russian state credit and will take our state by the throat any minute.

These are the supposed powerless and oppressed! What would happen under equality, that is, under the right of free residence everywhere, free purchase of land, free education, without rationing, in public schools?

And here comes the war, and the government of a great power suffers defeat after defeat. "Surrender!" cries Israel. "Further resistance is futile! We will ruin you materially, we will exhaust you morally, we will create such internecine strife in Russia that everything shall be bombed out of existence. We will put your government in an impossible position, as we will exterminate one statesman after another by the hand of the revolutionaries. Surrender!"

Were not these terrible words of our great visionary vindicated? Of the former Russia, not a single stone was left unturned! A new country—the Soviet Union, and in the future the United States of Eastern Europe—is now located in place of Russia! In 1912, commenting on Stolypin's assassination, in another of his books, *The International Secret Government*, A. S. Shmakov wrote these prophetic words:

What does this ultimately mean? It shows the ardent desire of the Jews and the Shabbos goyim to achieve their goal, to do in

Russia no longer a quick and unsuccessful revolt, as in 1905, but a huge bloody pogrom like the Great French Revolution, with hundreds of thousands of tortured victims and with a complete overthrow of our historical system.

A thinker like Drumont testifies that as a result of the French Revolution "a hundred thousand Jews became masters of the great Catholic state."

They want to do the same with the great Orthodox kingdom. "They began with regicide; they will end with genocide!" "Russia, for the millions of Jews who inhabit it, is not an accidental stop on the historical wanderings of the Eternal Jew" assures a Portuguese Jew, known under the pseudonym "Ivanovich" as a White emigrant journalist, in the collection *The Jewish World*, published by the Association of Russian-Jewish Intelligentsia in Paris in 1939. He goes on:

Russia for them and for us is the homeland of our distant and near ancestors and near and distant descendants. No matter how the fate of world Jewry turns, these fates will never turn their backs on Russia. Russian paths of world Jewry have been and will be historically the most significant.

These words contain an ominous threat to the Russian future.

It turns out that even after the liberation of Russia, the Jews will not leave us alone unless we ourselves take care of it. Ivanovich the Portuguese promises:

In the commonwealth of all the other peoples of Russia, the Russian Jews will fight for Russian freedom, for the liberation of man, for equality in full rights, for the primordial ideals of social justice. No matter how long and painful the path of Russia to its lost freedom was, Russian Jewry will follow this path to the end. And when this path will be traversed to the end, Russian Jewry will then be able to rebuild the spiritual and social hegemony, which once deservedly belonged to it.

The well-known public figure, Zionist scholar, and colonialist Dr. Ruppin, according to *Jewish Life* Nos. 1–2 for 1927, visited the USSR and upon his return to Palestine told the staff of the newspaper *Haaretz*: "Jewish equality in Russia is complete, self-consciousness is much stronger now than before the revolution. The Bolshevik government is absolutely against anti-Semitism, and it persecutes officials who are inclined to it."

"Under the conditions of socialist construction in the USSR, the Jews have been given the opportunity to become a nation," the Comintern's organ, *International Beacon* No. 10, argued in 1940. A. J. Ehrenburg in *Pravda* on November 12th, 1942, in the article "The meaning of Russia" says: "We can now say that the future historian will begin to describe the Great October Socialist Revolution by saying that it saved Russia and allowed it to carry out its historic mission."

This historical mission, according to Ehrenburg, is the fight against fascism. In 1917, Russia, in his words, was exsanguinated: "ignorance and inhumanity of the rulers drove the people to despair, October breathed faith into Russia." This is how history is falsified, and how the scandalous and terrible role of serving as the defender of Jewish interests is imposed on our great country.

In the lands of Russia, under the red flag of the USSR, even if it were replaced by another flag, the Jews are forming a Soviet quasi-slave, a concubine, and at the same time protector of world Jewry. Until the whirlwind of the popular storm sweeps away this torture castle, this will be a laboratory of cruel vivisection, the modern island of Dr. Moreau, where Russian people are transformed into golems to save world Jewry.

The Jews make no secret of the Soviet government's concern for them. In the midst of the brief German–Soviet friendship, for example, they did not hesitate to publish in their Harbin magazine on June 21st, 1940, "Life in Soviet Poland."

The plan for the resettlement of the Jews was developed in Moscow with the participation of the highest Soviet military, political, and party circles, and the leadership of the commission for the resettlement of the Jews from Poland to Birobidzhan includes representatives of individual Commissariats as well as Party organizations, with the leadership of this commission being entrusted to Commissar of Internal Affairs Frumkin. Stalin appointed former People's Commissar for Foreign Affairs M. M. Litvinov, who is known to be acting advisor to the Politburo of the Party, as "right hand" deputy chairman of the commission."

Who is subject to "resettlement" in Birobidzhan? In answer to this question, the Soviet government issued a special instruction in which it stipulated:

Men and women from eighteen years of age to fifty-five are subject to resettlement in Birobidzhan.

> The first to be resettled with their families will be: a) the unemployed; b) persons of non-proletarian origin; c) persons who worked in agriculture.
>
> In addition, cadres of Jewish doctors, specialists, and engineers will be used for resettlement to Birobidzhan, if for one

reason or another they will not be used by the Soviet institutions. As for the use of Jewish laborers and craftsmen, the Soviet government reserves the right to use these cadres for the USSR and in other areas of the Soviet Union. Qualified cadres of Jewish workers are not subject to resettlement in Birobidzhan, but can be used either locally or for other areas of the USSR.

Persons over fifty-five years of age are not subject to evacuation.

Transportation will take place at state expense.

Polish officers were shot by the NKVD. Jewish capitalists from the seized part of Poland at this very time traveled freely and comfortably across the USSR and freely left outside the Judeo-Red paradise, heading mostly to another "promised land" overseas.

In 1943, *Jewish Life* published an astonishingly cynical description of one such traveler, "From Kauna to Shanghai" by A. Berkovich.

This one spared no effort to describe the "happy, well-fed Stalinist life":

> Moscow at last! A huge train station. Many trains stand on the tracks. Masses of people are streaming in from all directions.
>
> Intourist representatives greeted us at the train station in a friendly manner, like foreign guests.[243] They took us in special Intourist cars to the hotel.
>
> Silver-white snow lay in the streets of Moscow. A light frost tickled the nose. A strong movement of people on the streets, everyone was in a hurry somewhere, almost running.
>
> Cars drove into the center of the city.
>
> Our hotel is called Novomoskovskaya. We had already been asylum seekers for seventeen months, had gone through all the hells of refugee life, all kinds of horrors and deprivations, at best lived a life of poverty, and suddenly—we were in a big, huge hotel! We were ushered into a large hall-restaurant and seated at a table. It had been seventeen months since we had sat like this. Starved to death, we ate with gusto under the accompaniment of a jazz orchestra.
>
> The Moscow guests, probably the "specialists," were dancing their hearts out.
>
> Our devout religious refugees, rabbis, and yeshivites could not use the Novomoskovskaya kitchen; they sat in the restaurant hall and did not touch a thing.

---

[243] Intourist is the oldest Soviet and Russian travel company. (Translator's note)

At first, when the Muscovites saw these strange guests with hats on their heads, they were amazed—it was the first time they had seen people in such costumes. . . .

The hotel manager's eyes darkened. "Who are these people? What an assault!"

His face was whiter than lime. With good and evil, the director begged the rabbis and yeshivotniks to go away, to leave the hall—he would be lost because of them. The guests in little "hats" and "shtreimels" didn't give a damn. And as if it wasn't bad enough, new guests arrived every hour, all wearing little "hats." Every train from Lithuania brought a large number of rabbis and yeshivots.

The Muscovites had to get used to these guests. The director spasmed. The hall was noisy and lively. The jazz orchestra was working at full throttle. And the rabbis and yeshivniks were sitting at the tables. A young Soviet officer walked past these tables, stopped in amazement and said: "I haven't seen Jews like those."

In the morning and afternoon, we went to see Moscow, Moscow streets, Moscow people, museums, monuments.

But the USSR is dying in the fire of a war storm, a war that he himself caused, or rather, was called by his masters. And Jewry, just in case, hurries to strengthen its position across the ocean:

"European Jewry is broken and destroyed," whined Lazar Kaganovich in No. 46 of *Jewish Life* in 1941, continuing:

> Millions of Jews from Eastern Europe, who before the war constituted the conscious national element of our nation, lie as if tied up, ready to be slaughtered. But the Jews on the other side of the ocean must take the place of the European Jews and stand for the Jewish National Home.

And so they did, driving America into a war with Japan and Germany and making New York the capital of the Jewish Congresses instead of Geneva.

Here we recall the already cited statement of the Shanghai Jewish *Our Life* that said the center of Jewish life is moving to America, and the landmark resolutions of the Montevideo Convention. From here we draw a long, fat line which means that with the expulsion of the Jews from the mainland of the Old World the war is not over—far from it. Only with the destruction of the three swords of Israel, only with the reduction of the Jewish British Empire to a nation-state on its own island, only with the replacement of the USSR by an anti-Jewish, Freemason-free, truly independent New Russia, and only with the confinement of America to an effective Monroe Doctrine and the expansion of the United States confined within limits of the USA, can a final, complete, and just solution to the Jewish question, disturbing humanity, in the interests of all the peoples of the earth, be possible.

154. Recent Maps

And so, witnessing failure after failure and the total collapse of the world conspiracy seen on the horizon, the Jews are throwing their last cards on the table. They want to get the Russian people on their side.

The Soviet press recognizes that Germany is intensifying its propaganda campaign against Bolshevism. The *Komsomolskaya Pravda* newspaper of February 25th, 1943 reports:

> During the days of the battle for Stalingrad, the German vultures pelted the Red Army with propaganda leaflets.
> In these leaflets, the German fascists tried to convince the Red Army that they were fighting not against the Russians, but against the Jews. But the Soviet army did not fall for the fascist deception.

German propaganda directs its main blow to the sore spot of the Soviet power—to Jewry. Hitler not long ago said: "I will punish the Jews in Moscow" The propaganda against Jewry in Russia is undoubtedly successful. Anti-Semitism is growing among the masses.

And so, the Bolsheviks try to counteract with their own red propaganda. The newspaper *Komsomolskaya Pravda* makes an attempt to explain why the fascists dislike the Jews so much: "The Jews are the best patriots of the Soviet homeland. Jews love Russia more than anyone else. The Jews want Russia to always be free. That is why the fascists do not like the Jews more than anyone else." The newspaper goes on to cite the many exploits of Jewish fighters on the Eastern Front.

Before the war, on the pages of Soviet newspapers we read articles by Jewish writers I. Ehrenburg, Zaslavsky, Sheiman, Yaroslavsky, Lifshitz, and others, entitled: "Marxism Won on the Soviet Land," "Fundamentals of Dialectical Materialism," "Socialist Industry," "The Twentieth Anniversary of the Union of Militant Godless People is Approaching," and "The USSR is the Homeland of the World Proletariat." Before the war, Jewish writers placed articles mainly of an internationalist nature, expounding and commenting on Marxist doctrine.

Now we read articles by Ilya Ehrenburg, entitled: "Russia," "Our Russia," "The Glory of Russia," and others. In these articles the Jew Ehrenburg exclaims: "Russian native land," "Dear Russian air." In the article "Our Russia," Ehrenburg writes: "I am a Jew, but I am a Russian Jew. For me there is no city dearer than Moscow. I love Russia and will not give it to the fascists."

Jewish writer David Zaslavsky, in his article "Russian People," exclaims: "The smoke of the Russian hut is dearer to me than anything else in the world." "The sea of Russian wheat ripples—this is Russian land. This is our land." "The ashes of our ancestors are buried in Russian soil. A Russian man will not allow his ashes to be desecrated!"

The Jewish writer Raskin writes:

> Russian people lived happily under the sun of the Stalinist constitution. The Soviet system gave such joy to Russians, Ukrainians, Kazakhs, Jews, and other peoples of the Soviet Union. The fascists want to take away our happiness. But we will not give up that happiness!

The Jewish writer Sheiman (formerly known as the editor of several anti-religious textbooks), in his article "Barbarians" (*Pravda* of January 21st this year) wrote: "Fascists destroy monuments of Russian antiquity—what is dear to Russian people is despised by the fascist barbarians.... They destroy historical and religious monuments." The lies of the Soviet Jewish writers are evident in every line.

One can see right through the vile methods they use to save their skins, pretending to be Russian patriots and Russophiles. The Jew Ehrenburg, for more than twenty years, scolded everything that is Russian and praised the International. Now he praises what is Russian and is silent about the International. His patriotic articles are disgusting falsehoods.

Scheiman, the most prominent leader of the militant atheists, tries to pretend that he is a defender of religion. Who can possibly believe this unscrupulous clownery! Who can believe that Jewish internationalists, the Comintern employees, suddenly fell in love with Russia? Of course, no one will believe them.

With their propaganda, Red Moscow is trying to protect the Jews. Other measures are used to stop the increasing anti-Semitism.

We see how the Bolsheviks are temporarily hiding the most prominent Jewish figures behind the scenes.

Anti-Bolshevik propaganda has often targeted the Jewish Mekhlis, the head of the Purcka, who often lead the soul of the Red Army in his broadcasts. The Jews then removed Mekhlis, gave him a post of responsibility in Leningrad, while putting Shcherbakov in his place.

Anti-Comintern propaganda lashes out at the Kaganoviches. The Bolsheviks hide Kaganovich temporarily and replace him with Russians.

Anti-Soviet propaganda hits Smushkevich (a Jew who led the air force in the USSR). He is then hidden to the rear, and a Russian man is put in his place.

This does not mean, of course, that Jewish influence has diminished in the Kremlin. No! We certainly know that in the headquarters of the armies, in the Sovnarkom, in the Political Administration, in radio, cinema, and the press, there is an overwhelming number of Jews. Jews have long been masquerading behind Russian backs and hiding under Russian pseudonyms. We know that if we were to remove Jewry now, the USSR would not even last a day.

But there will come an hour of reckoning. Soon the guilty will pay for their heinous deeds.

So wrote the Bulletin of Internal Information of the Russian Fascist Union, № 36 of March 23rd, 1943. But it is not only the Russian people that the international Jews are trying to deceive. Another of their latest cards is an attempt to deceive the Japanese, so that they can remain in East Asia and begin to spread throughout Asia after Europe is cleansed of them.

In 1937, in Harbin, a book was published in Russian by Duji Nakada, *The Mysterious Nation*, in which Nakada insulted the Japanese nation by saying that the Japanese were the lost tribes of Israel. This book was published in Japanese and distributed throughout Japan. And it turned out that Nakada-san, though Japanese, was a Methodist bishop and, therefore, had ties in America.

After this came a series of books on Jewry, written in Japanese and clearly in favor of Israel, convincing Japan that anti-Semitism is a harmful European disease, that Jews have much in common with the Japanese, and that it is necessary to give the "poor persecuted West Asian people" a place under the sun as well.

155. Japan's Historical Mission

But all these attempts to deceive the Japanese are defeated by the self-sacrificing Japanese patriots, who have published a number of books to the contrary.

Lieutenant General Nobutaka Shiōden, recently elected vice-chairman of the Japanese parliament, made the statement, "I have decided to sacrifice myself for the purpose of the nation, especially to drive the Jewish influence out of Japan."

Toshio Shiratori, former Japanese envoy to Italy, also publicly expressed his opposition to Judaism. The well-known Japanese diplomat said: "The ideal of the Jewish people is to establish world hegemony by bringing about the decline of other nations and to realize a form of oligarchy, which may be called a theocracy."

Declaring that the ideals for which Japan fights are the same as those of Germany and Italy, General Toshio Shiratori, in an article published in *Yomiuri Hochi*, argues that "Japan must consider the Jews its main enemy." The Japanese dignitary writes:

> It must not be forgotten that the present military conflict is a direct consequence of the Jewish desire to own the world and that this conflict is created by the Jews, who direct the fate of Britain, America and the USSR. France would not have entered the war if it had not been for Jewish politicians. The real war," continues Mr. Shiratori, "is essentially an uprising of the peoples oppressed by the Jews. Fighting with Britain and America, Japan is fighting against Jewish tyranny.

These golden words demonstrate full understanding of the situation. But the Jews also fail to take advantage of Japan because there is no greater antithesis than the one between Shintoism and Judaism.

Shintoism represents the highest form of idealism, while Judaism represents the most repugnant form of materialism.

The Japanese ideal, the *hakkō ichiu* ("All the world under one roof" and "Every nation has its own destiny"), means the peaceful cooperation between peoples, each nation subsisting on its own resources, means, and land, not allowing one nation to dominate the others through exploitation, exhaustion, and enslavement.

We take the liberty to argue that Japan's historic mission of freeing East Asia from alien influences and forces is to free East Asia from Jewry, and that there is no place for Jewish parasitism in the mutual prosperity of the East Asian peoples. There is also no place for Jewry in the spread of *hakkō ichiu* (Canopy of Peace). Japanese ideals bring an end to the Ahasverus.[244]

For almost three thousand years Japan did not know of the Jewish question, because it did not know of the Jews, and during this time of lifesaving self-isolation it has accumulated such a storehouse of spiritual strength and moral concepts that this treasury is enough to save Asia, our homeland, and all of humanity!

All hail to the Rising Sun!

A new life! A New Order!

---

[244] From Latin, *Ahasverus*, meaning "The Wandering Jew"; a mythological figure in Western Christian anti-Semitic art and literature, it depicts a Jew who haunted Jesus on his way to the crucifixion. He was then cursed to wander the Earth until the Second Coming. (Translator's note)

156. The Historical Mission of Russian Emigration

Russian emigration represents the only mass exodus of intellectuals from their own country in the history of the world. This was not desertion and betrayal either, condemning the country to spiritual death, for the Russian people were leaving Russia to continue to fight for it. The preservation of the cadres of the national-willed Russian elite for the Russian future justifies the Russian emigration, if such preservation takes place and succeeds in replenishing the former elite with new generations, grown up outside its homeland, albeit faithful to it. In any case, the exodus of three million voluntary exiles from Russia, overrun by the Red devil, is reminiscent to a certain extent of the exodus of the Jews from Palestine—should not these two exoduses, inspired by directly opposite origins, eventually collide?

At any rate, Russian émigrés around the world spread the truth about the Comintern and exposed communism in the newspapers of many nations. But along with the truth about the Comintern, Russians have carried across the world the truth about the worldwide Jewish conspiracy against God, against all religions, against all nations and states!

There is a well-founded claim: Germany owes to a few unknown Russian immigrants to the waves of anti-Semitism that cleansed the country of world Jewry. For example, the venerable German commander-in-chief Ludendorff declared shortly before his death that, had the *Protocols of Zion* been known to Germany before the First World War, the war would never have happened. The *Protocols of Zion* were brought to Germany after the revolution by Colonel Winberg, a Russian Jew, and there they were translated into German, printed in multiple copies and, by spreading throughout the country, greatly assisted Adolf Hitler's movement. From Germany, the *Protocols of Zion* spread throughout the world, bringing about a saving revival everywhere.

In Munich in 1923 there was a Russian fascist newspaper, *The Russian Tribune*, published by young officers, members of the White struggle, Shabelsky-Bork and Taboritsky. They subsequently shot Milyukov and killed another Freemason, Nabokov. They, together with Colonel Winberg, introduced the German people to the unrecognized works of Russian anti-Semites in the homeland.

At the same time, the German publishing house Aufbau, which means "Renaissance," was established in Munich, where some Russian anti-Semites also took part. To this day, the international anti-Jewish exposé center *World Service*, which operated first in Erfurt and then in Frankfurt-am-Main, employs as head of the Russian department N.E.

Markov, contemptuously called in his homeland "Get lost Markov" and ironically "Markov the Second."

This is the real mission of Russian emigration—to open the eyes of all the peoples of the earth to the lurking Jewish serpent on the basis of what has been experienced, felt, and thought over, and thereby to bring about a world liberation movement that is already thundering through the world in the victorious march of the armies of the New Order.

To collect data on Jewish work in different countries, to uncover events from the point of view of their hidden motives, to find out the strategy and tactics, the organization, the program, and the ideology of the world Jewish intervention and the world Jewish inter-state—what could be more valuable than this work for the countries that shelter us, and for the Russia of the future, to which we must arrive armed with the experience of decoding all demagogy, with the experience of knowing the exact causes of the Russian catastrophe, and the ways of the new Renaissance, overcoming all temptations!

Fifteen years ago, while researching the causes of the world crisis and pondering the necessity of a New Order that would give man a purpose in life and the opportunity for creative work in all the planes of being—spiritual and material—the author of this book first became interested in the Jewish question, and came to the conclusion that it was necessary to seek the root cause of all evil. I have always believed in the existence of the Devil, the antipode to God, the one who dares to rebel against the Light: surely then there must be representatives of evil on earth! As I pondered the facts of history and of the present times, I came to the conclusion that God's chosen people had turned away from Heaven and, like Dennitsa in his day, had surrendered to the Devil and had become the Devil's chosen.[245] Subsequent reading and reflection strengthened me in this ominous discovery.

In building the Russian national movement, I encountered Jewish opposition at every turn, even when I did not have yet the seal of "herem" on all my activities for anti-Semitism. I never had an "instinctive anti-Semitism," and in my school years I even fell in love with a Jewish girl, though "assimilated." I became anti-Semitic consciously, because I saw that Jews were interfering with the struggle for my

---

[245] In Slavic mythology, Dennitsa (meaning dawn) acts as a mother, daughter, or sister of the sun, and is usually associated with its Roman equivalent Lucifer. In the Church Slavonic and synodal translations of the Bible (Isaiah 14:12), the word "Dennitsa" appears as a synonym for the morning star, occurs only once, and refers to the king of Babylon, in order to show his glory and brilliance, similar to the radiance of the morning star. In the biblical text, the prophet Isaiah exclaims: "How you have fallen from heaven, morning star, son of the dawn! You have been cast down to the earth, you who once laid low the nations!" However, the early Christian interpreter Tertullian and some others believed that this phrase referred to the fall from the sky of Satan himself. (Translator's note)

homeland and were on the side of the Comintern that enslaved my people.

Only later did I realize that in fact there is no Comintern, that the Comintern is just one of many facades, a facade that will fall off in time. What there is instead is a Jewish power over our unfortunate Russia. There is a Jewish world organization trying to extend that power to the entire world, and a secret Jewish center, located somewhere either in red Moscow or in aristocratic London, or in the super-capitalistic New York.

In Harbin, I encountered Jewish domination at every turn, and when it was not hiding its colors, it was red. This power strangled and crushed the Russian emigration, the Russian people that share my faith and blood, devastated materially, humiliated spiritually, and impoverished intellectually. Step by step, not at once, but gradually, I realized that the Jew is the enemy—cunning, despicable, and ruthless—and that Jews are the greatest enemies of the Russian people and all peoples who want to live an independent existence and have their own national state.

Jewish opposition to the kind of fascism I believed in at the dawn of my conscious life strengthened my disgust and hatred for world Jewry.

In all countries of the world, the Russian National Liberation Movement, which I founded, encountered the most varied kind of Jewish opposition. From all over the world my comrades-in-arms and allies sent me documents and facts about the criminal Jewish activities, books on the Jewish question, both old and modern, in Russian, in German, in a wide variety of languages.

Thus it was by the will of fate that I corresponded with various foreign centers of international action against Jewry and became acquainted by correspondence with the greatest visionaries of our days, with anti-Semitic scholars and experts on the Jewish question—German, Japanese, French, Italian, even English, American, South African, and even New Zealand scholars!

I found the vocation of the Russian emigration: to act as a neutral stratum and organize a roll-call and connection of anti-Semites of all countries, as an organizer of an international anti-Jewish front, a front of self-defense of peoples. But the war that broke out and was clearly instigated by the Jews frustrated the movement of peaceful cooperation between peoples for a bloodless resolution of the Jewish question on a global scale.

The Russian emigration in East Asia can now set itself a limited task in the Jewish question: to warn the Japanese people and the peoples of Asia led by them to build a new life and to help save Russia and Germany. Then, God willing, our feeble efforts to educate public opinion in East Asia will bear some good fruit.

Japan has never known the Jewish question or the Jews—herein lies the great danger. The peoples of East Asia are just emerging and are not always able to distinguish falsification of the truth from the truth itself. So a major effort must be made to clarify the essence of the Jews. The noble efforts of the Japanese leaders need the support of Russian researchers.

On this ground, we will do our best! A true Japanese–Russian bond will be established, a sincere Japanese–Russian rapprochement will begin, and cooperation will deepen. For people who understand the root causes of war and revolution will be able to agree on a common struggle against a common enemy, to build a better future.

157. A New Order

Perhaps this book should not have been written, for it may frighten the weak with images of a world Jewish power.

But it is always better to overestimate the power of the enemy than to underestimate it. In every patriot this book should arouse a holy awe of indignation and a thirst to fight for true freedom—to free the world from the threat of the most terrible enslavement!

Moreover, the world is at a turning point. One after the other, years of fire are coming, crushing the worldwide Jewish inter-state like a house of cards.

Germany turned against England and then against the USSR in the name of self-defense against the Jews, and liberated Europe from the Jews. Japan opposed England and the US in the name of a new life for the Asian peoples, and will free Asia from the Jews. America will remain when the New Order triumphs over the entire continent of the Old World, and this triumph is not far off—it will follow the crushing of the Jewish USSR.

The New Order, regardless of the declarations of its creators, means the liberation of the world from the Jews.

The New Order means the end of the hegemony of England and America. And we have seen that it is precisely these countries that are the ones conducting the Jewish hegemony of the world.

The New Order means the end of liberalism and its external opposite, communism, the end of democracy and capitalism, the end of utilitarianism and materialism. And we have seen that it was the smirking Jew who was hiding behind these ideas and ideologies all along.

The New Order means the death of the League of Nations, Freemasonry, and the Internationals; what other tools will be left to the world Jewish conspiracy in the end?

Finally, the New Order goes under the banner of the nation, religious freedom, national wholeness, social justice, the peaceful cooperation of peoples, the division of the world into natural regions toward the final triumph of the ancient Japanese ideal, *hakko ichiu*—"all the world under one roof" and "every nation has her destiny." What purpose is left to Judas in his intrigues and provocations?

This is why I say that the New Order naturally resolves the Jewish question. By disrupting the world Jewish conspiracy, it shows every nation its natural way, the road to rebuild one's father's home on the land soaked by the blood, sweat, and tears of his father and grandfather—his fatherland

The Jewish people also need to find their way to such a building of a national state, if they are able to give up their claims to world leadership, if they can beg the builders of the New Order for forgiveness for their crimes, if they are able to.

The New Order means world justice: to each according to his work, according to his merits, according to his abilities, according to his needs. To each—meaning both in the sense of the individual and in the sense of the nation and the state. God's judgment!

158. A New Russia

Precisely because the New Order is an order of religious, national, and social justice, and brings such a restructuring of the world, in which there must be no place for new Jewish machinations and schemes, I also say that in the New Order there must be a place for Russia! Otherwise, the Russian people will be pushed into an unnatural alliance with world Jewry, will perish itself, the world with it—and this will lead to a global catastrophe.

Hakkō ichiu means "Every nation has its own destiny," a place under a common roof. It is to hope that, under the firmament of a new life, there will be a place for the Russian people, our millennial place for self-development of the Russian nation, the youngest nation in the new history.

We regard the New Russia as a necessary and inevitable component of the New Order of the Old World, a bridge between a New Europe and a New Asia, the continuation of the European New Order eastward, and the continuation of a New Asian Order westward, for the sake of the complete destruction of the Comintern and its consequences over the space of one-fifth of the earth's landmass. This destruction brings to the people of Russia liberation from Jewry and the opportunity to build a new Russian state, taking into account all the mistakes, trials, and ambitions of the past.

The New Russia lies before our generations as the historical task of our ancestors and the unspoken demand of our descendants; a Russia free from the ideas, people, and forces of the Old Order, that is free from Anglo-American, Jewish, and Masonic influences, from communist internationalism, from the Communist Party, from Jewish Marxism, from Judaized democracy, from the power of all kinds of Shabbos goyim who do not understand the greatest problem of our day.

The New Russia is a Russia without Jewry and Freemasonry, a religious Russia, a national Russia, a labor Russia, a Russia of the Orthodox faith and social justice—a State of Russian Truth and of the Holy Rus, which our people have always striven for at all stages of our way of the cross.

I will end this book with a call to fight for a New Order and a New Russia, to fight against world Jewry, against all its open and hidden forces.

VOLUME II

The ABC of Fascism

*The Party Program of the
All-Russian Fascist Party*

All-Russian Fascist Party Documents

*Supreme Court of the Russian
Federation Ruling No. 043/46*

THE ABC OF FASCISM

Introduction to the First Edition

Liberalism and socialism no longer attract followers. Their ideological and practical bankruptcy is becoming more obvious every year. Two worldviews are now entering into a "last and decisive battle," just these two, without any intermediates. Socialism in its last and most extreme form—the worldview of Stalinist communism; the last outgrowth from all previous political teachings of the old world and the first declaration of the emerging new world—the worldview of a young fascism.

That is why *The ABC of Communism* should now be presented in opposition to *The ABC of Fascism*. It is *a collection of answers to elementary questions that arise in the mind of every thinking Russian person with the word "fascism" in mind*.

Every fascist should know this alphabet, just as firmly as the letters of his own native alphabet. For the free reading of this alphabet will give us and all Russian people a homeland, one that is currently under dreadful Jewish captivity.

The one hundred questions that form the basis of this book are provided by me, and the answers to them are written by the deputy chief of the Higher Party School RFP Associate G. V. Taradanov. V. V. Kibardin has also been very helpful in this project. Their excellent work, which is destined to become a historical piece, has been reviewed, annexed, and edited by me in order to give members of our party and sympathetic Russian people a more or less exhaustive manual that clearly outlines the essence of fascism in general, the difference between fascism and other tendencies in political thought, and the main contours of the Russian fascist movement.

This book has been written for more than a year, but nevertheless, it needs corrections and additions, which will be made as Russian fascist thought develops in subsequent editions. The same edition is the first test textbook experience of Russian fascism—I strongly recommend it to those who do not want to go blindfolded in life, those who want to take part in the struggle against communism and in the future national construction, those who want to know the specific plan and take part in its implementation.

All fascists—for fascist studies! Prepare the cadres of agitators and organizers. The builders of the future Fatherland, the new Russian state! Hone our weapon, an idea that glows like a steel blade under the bright beams of the spring sun!

Harbin, Summer 1934
K. V. Rodzaevsky

Introduction to the Second Edition

The first edition of *The ABC of Fascism* completely sold out without leaving a trace. The incessant demands for the release of the *ABC* forced us to hurry with the second edition.

The ABC of Fascism played a huge role in the ideological training of party members, introducing into this training a specific system of thought and plan. *The ABC of Fascism* was a short textbook of Russian fascism, according to which our comrades studied its doctrine. With its help they became conscious fascists who know what they are fighting for, in the name of what ideals they are marching for.

The first edition of the *ABC* had a number of drawbacks. Among them, one can point to the difficulty in some cases to understand the language of the *ABC*, the vagueness of some formulations, etc. All these shortcomings have been eliminated as far as possible in the new edition.

The ABC of Fascism, in its new edition, has undergone a change in the system of the arrangement of its questions and answers. The first edition had three parts. The second edition of the *ABC* is divided into two parts. The first part is devoted to: 1) The general idea of fascism; 2) Enemies of fascism; 3) The situation in the USSR. The second part is devoted to Russian fascism, the concrete disclosure of its ideological, tactical program, and organizational attitudes.

The number of issues related to world fascism has been significantly reduced. Only the general basics are formulated here, and special attention is paid to Russian fascism: The concept of a corporate state, its basic principles, organization, the economic policy of fascism, etc., in relation to the Russian condition. The chapters on tactics and organization are set out by taking into account our general plan—the fascist three-year plan.

By releasing the second edition of *The ABC of Fascism*, we take the opportunity to call our comrades to maximum attention in the matter of our ideological training. Every colleague must strive to study the ideology, program, and tactics of our movement—to become a conscious fascist.

Only a *soratnik* who not only knows, but can also explain the reasons for his presence in the party, who therefore clearly understands the responsibility imposed on him by the title of a Russian fascist, can be a real national revolutionary, a real fighter for the good and happiness of his homeland, a soldier of the coming national dawn.

G. Taradanov

PART ONE

Chapter I: General Idea of Fascism

1. Causes for the Emergence of Fascism

Fascism was born out of the disillusionment with all previous political and social systems, which proved their complete failure and bankruptcy. Fascism emerged from the search for new ways with a decisive reassessment of all these bankrupt values.

2. What Is Fascism as a Global Movement?

Fascism as a world movement strives for the reconstruction of modern liberal-democratic (capitalist) and socialist (Communist) states on the principles of: the rule of the spirit over matter (religion), the nation, and labor (social justice). Fascism is a religious, national, and labor movement.

3. Where Does the Word "Fascism" Come from and What Does It Mean?

The word "fascism" comes from Italy, where the fascist movement first arose. It comes from the Italian word *fascio*, which literally means "bundle" or a "sheaf." Then, like many words in the political dictionary, it was carried over into all the languages of the modern world.

4. Where and When Did Fascism First Arise?

Fascism first appeared in Italy. The founder of Italian Fascism was the son of a blacksmith, the former socialist Benito Mussolini.

Being at first a member of the Socialist Party and the editor of the socialist newspaper *Avante* (Forward), he, under the influence of an awakened national consciousness, resolutely breaks from it and proceeds to create his own newspaper, *Popolo d'Italia* (The People of Italy). In 1919, shortly after returning from the army, to which Mussolini volunteered during the Great War, seeing the imminent death of his homeland from the growing threat of communism, he founded the Fascist Party. Relying mainly on former war veterans, young people, workers, and peasants, Mussolini achieved tremendous success in a short period of time.

Under his skillful leadership, the only four-year old Italian Fascist Party, previously only a small clique, turned into a powerful organism and became regimented like an army, with an iron discipline at its base. It crushed the all-destructive forces of communism, which almost led Italy, like our homeland, into catastrophe. He then came to power in 1923, and finally steered the Italian state to a healthy path of national-labor construction.

At present, Italy has turned from a backward country, both economically and culturally, into an advanced, strong country in all respects, bringing prosperity to the Italian people.

5. Examples of Fascist Movements in Different Countries

The phenomenon of Italy caused widespread reaction.

Fascism, which originated first in Italy, began to spread all over the world with lightning speed. *Currently, there is not a single country that has not produced a fascist movement.*

German fascism, which bears the name of National Socialism, is triumphant in Germany. The leader of the German fascists is Adolf Hitler. The German National Socialist Workers' Party emerged in 1920. In 1933, the German Nazis came to power after a long, persistent, and hard struggle against Communists, democrats, and Jews.

The fascist regime provided Germany, as well as Italy, with the rebirth of the state, and made Germany a great power by bringing prosperity to all the people, especially to its working masses.

In France, there are a number of fascist organizations that have not yet been united into a single party, such as the Francists, Genes Patristics ("Young Patriots"), Croix-de-Feu ("Fiery Cross"), etc.

In England, fascism is represented by two organizations: The British Fascist Imperial League and the British Union of Fascists (led by Oswald Mosley).

Fascism is beginning to win the sympathies of the broad masses of Japan, where the fascist principles of religion, nation, and labor are especially popular in the army, being the foundations of the Yamato.

There are a number of fascist organizations in Japan, of which the most noteworthy are the Union of Young Officers of the Army and Navy and the Koku-Honsha (Association of Patriots). The main exponent of "Yamatoism" is General Araki.

Fascist organizations also exist in Austria, the Baltic countries, Romania, Spain, Portugal, Poland, Ireland, Switzerland, Czechoslovakia, the United States, and throughout South America. There is currently no country without a fascist movement.

6. What Does Fascism Bring That Is New, and What Does It Keep That Is Old?

Fascism is a union of the best of the past, dictated by new existing conditions, and what is necessary for the future.

Fascism takes from the past everything that is dear to the heart of man. It preserves the religion bequeathed by its ancestors and the spiritual family of man—the nation. On the basis of a historically formed nation, on its roots, it creates a new special order and remains faithful to the traditions of the past, carefully preserving them. At the same time, it provides the possibility of constant perfection of socio-political forms, applying them to the last necessities of life.

Fascism creates a new social order based on the principle of reconciliation of class interests through the corporate system. Fascism reconciles labor and capital. It provides each citizen and each class individually with the opportunity to improve their personal well-being, and provides them with healthy development within the nation. Fascism brings about the establishment of complete harmony between the individual and the class, on one hand, and the nation, on the other.

7. What Is the Nation?

A nation is the spiritual unity of a people based on the common consciousness of a shared historical destiny in the past, a common national culture, national traditions, etc., and the desire to continue its historical life in the future.

The life of the nation reveals itself in the national spirit, the national consciousness—a sense of patriotism that unites all members of the nation. The strength of the nation depends on the strength of its national spirit. The strength of the national spirit in many respects depends on the richness of the national culture and the strength of its national traditions.

The nation, first of all, is a spiritual unity. But the formation of the nation is also attributable to other factors: racial and tribal affinity, as well as a common language, territory, religion, etc.

A normally developing nation should be closely connected to the state. A nation is always born on the insides of the state, at the beginning of its existence it is always directly connected with the state.

In the process of its historical life, a nation may lose this direct connection with the state. One and the same nation can split up, fragmenting into several states (for instance, the Polish nation in the nineteenth century). This however always damages the strength and spiritual unity of the nation and leads the nation into decay. Therefore, the first assurance for the healthy existence and prosperity of the nation is the creation of a national state that unifies all members of the nation, consolidating its spiritual unity with a real, close, political bond.

The understanding of the nation as a spiritual unity, however, has not been assimilated by all fascist movements. Some fascist movements (for example, the German National Socialists) adhere to a racial understanding of the nation, believing that the most important role in the formation of the nation is played by biological elements, a racial bloodline, which already determine the spiritual makeup of a nation.

8. What Is a Class from the Fascist Point of View?

A class is a certain group of people who share the same social conditions and are united by common economic interests.

Classes complement each other. Their common cooperation in economic life is necessary for their own well-being and the flourishing of the nation and the state. From the fascist point of view, classes represent separate organs of a single organism—the state. A person's belonging to a particular class is determined by his profession, living conditions, and a certain sense of class solidarity which originates in his effort to defend his class interests.

Fascism does not seek to kill common class interests, but it demands that the manifestation of these class interests does not contradict the interests of the national whole. *First the nation, then the class.*

9. What Is Labor and Who Is the Worker from the Fascist Point of View?

From the fascist point of view, labor has to do with *the creation of spiritual or material value*. The worker is the creator of these values.

"The workers," therefore, does not just include manual labor, but also refers to intellectual labor—the intelligentsia, the peasantry, entrepreneurs who bring their organizational talent and their entrepreneurial initiative into production, the merchants who serve the exchange of goods among producers, and the clergy who create a prayerful communion between the faithful and the creator of all things, etc.

10. What Is Capital and the Attitude of Fascists Towards It?

Capital is the wealth necessary for the production of new wealth. Capital can be expressed in money, movable and immovable property, goods, factory equipment, etc.

Fascism distinguishes between two types of capital: *a healthy, productive capital and parasitic capital*. Parasitic capital is the anonymous financial capital, expressed in stocks, bonds, etc. Its danger lies in the fact that, breaking away from national production, it very easily falls into the hands of representatives of the financial international, the Jewish capitalists, and will lead to the establishment of the reign of international Jewish financial circles over the economy of individual countries, enslaving them into Jewish hands.

11. What Does Fascism Bring in Place of Class Struggle; in What Way Does Fascism Reconcile Labor and Capital?

Instead of class struggle and class oppression, fascism brings about *class peace and cooperation between classes based on healthy competition*.

Fascism organizes the living forces of the country by forming the people into self-governing national groups—unions and corporations. It reconciles labor with capital through a corporate system in which workers have their own associations of workers and employers have their own. Moreover, these homogeneous associations of workers and laborers unite together, resolving all disputes and all conflicts within such unions by means of *inter-class arbitration* with the participation of representatives of all interested parties.

12. How Does Fascism View State Power?

From the point of view of fascism, state power should be *national, above class, and independent of any individual influences*. Only the government, relying equally on all elements of the population, on all classes, can ensure the healthy development of the nation as well as the integrity and unity of the state.

State power must express the will of the nation. Fascism demands state power, so that its policy fully meets the historical national objectives, the spirit of the nation. The supra-class essence of state power under fascism directly follows from the need to establish complete class solidarity in the fascist state, for only then will this solidarity be achieved in practice; relying equally on all classes of society, rather than relying on one single class. State power cannot be an instrument of one individual class or group of society; its purpose is to lead the organized service of the nation (through the state).

13. What Kind of State Are the Fascists Trying to Create?

The fascist state is an organized association of the members of the nation, the actual manifestation of the spiritual unity of the nation. The fascist state represents the formalization of the nation, it is inextricably linked with the nation.

The fascist state strives for the organized service of the nation.

Since its task is to ensure the strength and unity of the nation, it must create a social system in which all the organs of the body, all classes of the population are in a closely knit united national family. Therefore, the fascist state seeks to destroy class antagonism, reconcile class interests, and replace class warfare with class cooperation for the good of the nation. The fascist state requires every citizen to fulfill all the obligations imposed upon him by being part of the nation; only by fulfilling these duties can one claim to deserve certain rights. First duties, then rights! Rights in the fascist state stem from the duties performed.

Individuality and class are in the service of the nation! This is the main slogan of the fascist state. Only the fulfillment of all one's national responsibilities can ensure each individual citizen's own personal well-being.

The fascist state is a national labor state.

14. What Is a Party in General and What Is a Fascist Party?

A political party is an association of politically like-minded people who set themselves the goal of coming to power or influencing the establishment in a particular direction of socio-political life.

The difference between a political party and other organizations lies in the fact that a political party always strives to participate in state power to one degree or another, in the leading of the general political life of the state.

The fascist party is by no means an ordinary political party, since it seeks not only to establish a certain political (state) system, but also to radically reorganize life as a whole. It brings about a new social system and a new content of life, both individual and social.

The fascist party differs sharply from other parties in that its activity is based on the principle of service. The fascist party is not an association of politicians, i.e., persons who have made a profession out of political activity for themselves (as we see in all other parties), but an association of people who have set themselves the goal of a sacrificial service to the national state. "Do not expect honors or personal material benefits from us, people come to us to serve and obey." These words from Mussolini, characterizing the essence of the Italian Fascist Party, can be seen as characteristic of all other fascist parties.

The fascist party always relies on all the healthy forces of the nation, on all classes of society equally, striving to become the select group of the nation's best, its leading vanguard.

The fascist party is against all partisanship, the existence of many parties fighting among themselves, believing instead that in every nation there should be one leading selection, one national-state party, the bearer and the embodiment of the state idea.

15. Who Are the Fascists Fighting?

Fascists of all countries are fighting those who explicitly or implicitly oppose God, the nation, and labor, those against fascism, these being its ideological and factual enemies.

The enemies of fascism are socialists of all shades, especially Communists, as well as international capitalists, liberals, the plutocracy without a fatherland, and the Freemasons and Jews standing behind them all.

Questions to Review:

1. Why did fascism arise?
2. What is fascism as a world movement?
3. Where does the word "fascism" come from?
4. What does it literally mean?
5. Where did fascism first originate from?
6. Who was the founder of Italian Fascism?
7. What did fascism bring to Italy?
8. What countries other than Italy adopt fascism?

9. What are the names of the fascists in Germany and who is their leader?
10. List the fascist organizations of France, England, and Japan.
11. What does fascism preserve from the past?
12. What does it bring that is new?
13. What is a nation?
14. How does a nation arise?
15. What is the relationship between the nation and the state?
16. Why should the nation be closely related to the state?
17. How do racialists understand the nation?
18. What is a class?
19. How do fascists view class?
20. What is labor from a fascist perspective?
21. Who are the workers from the fascist point of view?
22. What is capital?
23. What types of capital do you know?
24. What is the danger of parasitic capital?
25. What do fascists bring instead of class struggle?
26. How do fascists reconcile labor and capital?
27. What should state power be from a fascist point of view?
28. Why should state power under fascism be above class?
29. What is the fascist state?
30. What is the role of the individual and the class in the fascist state?
31. What is a party?
32. What is a fascist party?
33. What is the difference between the fascist party and other parties?
34. Who do fascists fight against?

Chapter II: The Enemies of Fascism

16. Main Directions of Socio-Political Thought

There are currently three main strains of socio-political thought: *liberalism, socialism, and fascism*. In addition to the doctrines that have a pronounced liberal, socialist, or fascist character, state systems, and political parties, there are a number of others that represent a blend of these three main directions: liberalism and socialism, liberalism and fascism, etc.

17. What Is Liberalism and What Are Its Dangers?

Liberalism (from the French word "liberté"—freedom) proceeds from the recognition of each person's inalienable rights to his individual freedom and the inviolability of his private property. The main value for liberalism is the individual. The state in the liberal understanding is represented as an aggregate of these individuals, having only one goal: to safeguard their own private interests.

Liberal principles were first proclaimed in America, and then in France during the French Revolution, and were set out in the *Declaration of the Rights of Man and of the Citizen*, which proclaimed separate formal freedoms: freedom of speech, assembly, press, unions, economic freedom, etc.—the foundations of a liberal state. Previously, they were worked out in the hiding places of Masonic lodges.

Liberalism, proclaiming the individual as the highest value, leads to people forgetting their duty to the nation, the state, and to each other, and leads them to care only about their personal well-being. The domination of liberal principles leads to the disintegration of the nation and the state through the state apparatus built on its foundations—democracy—alongside its economic system, capitalism.

18. What Is Democracy and What Is Its Lie?

Democracy comes from the Greek word "demos," meaning "the people," and "kratia," meaning "rule of"—as such meaning "the people's rule," i.e., a democratic state is formally a state where the people rule.

How is the rule of the people carried out according to democratic theory? Through so-called people's representatives expressing the "common will" of the people. It does this through the aggregate of people's representatives, which forms the people's representation, or through the *parliaments*; people's representatives being elected by universal, direct, equal, and secret ballot (the so-called democratic four-tailed system). A democratic state recognizes liberal principles as one of its foundations, which are expressed in the recognition of a person's right to separate formal freedoms: freedom of speech, the press, assembly, economic freedom, etc. A democratic state strives to protect these freedoms.

Since the people in a democracy do not know who to vote for, political parties come to their "aid" offering readymade candidates. In order to win elections, parties need money, so that parties come to depend upon domestic and foreign capital. Ultimately, the "people's representatives" turn out to be representatives of various financial groups that protect not the interests of the people at all, but the interests of those financiers that subsidize the party.

Democracy, as shown by the experience of its implementation (Italy before Fascism, the Weimar Republic before Hitler, France, the US), turns out to be the rule of the people only formally—it being "formal" since it is in fact a *pseudo-rule of the people*, a special form of "dictatorship of the plutocracy without a fatherland." Through parliaments, democratic states are enslaved by the international financial capital, the *Finintern*—the financial international. Democracy facilitates the global takeover by the Jews, which captures the driving force behind the "rule of the people"—money—and puts it into their own hands.

19. What Is Capitalism and What Does It Lead To?

Liberalism applied to the economy created the capitalist system. The capitalist system is built on the principles of the sacredness and inviolability of private property, and complete non-interference of the state in economic activity. Under capitalism, the state is only a mere "night-watchman," making sure that no one infringes on the sacrosanct private property. Economic life is built on full freedom of competition between entrepreneurs.

The view of private property as an inalienable right of the individual and the state as a night-watchman who cannot under any circumstance interfere in economic life turns the freedom of competition into freedom of exploitation; to the oppression of workers by capitalists and to the struggle between them, generating class discord. Capitalists seek to get their profits not only by increasing output and reducing the cost of production, but also by reducing the wages of workers.

Capitalism, to a certain extent, is a positive manifestation. However, the boundless exaltation of private property, in the end, turns against itself: in joint-stock companies, trusts, and enterprises, in essence, it turns capital into anonymous international capital.

Capitalism leads to capital overstepping national borders: instead of national production and trade capital, *there is international capital (interpeople's financial capital)*, which is almost entirely in Jewish hands, i.e., capitalism enslaves entire peoples under the rule of world Jewry.

The extremes of capitalism then give rise to spontaneous protests, such as socialism, which is also cleverly exploited by the same "fishers in troubled waters," the Jews.

20. What Is Socialism?

Socialism is a strain of socio-political thought that aims to eliminate all social injustices by decisively breaking up the entire existing system, destroying religion, nation, family, and property, and transferring the economy into the hands of society.

Socialism reached its greatest stage of development in Marxism, so-called "scientific socialism," the founder of which was Karl Marx (the Jew Mordechai Marx).

Marxism proceeded from the recognition that life is based on economic factors—the means to produce goods, which determines the character of the social system, the social division of society, etc. The history of the world, according to Marxists, is a constant struggle between classes. There is now a capitalist system—an economic power, and consequently, the political power resulting from it is in the hands of the capitalist class.

The capitalists own all the means of production, they exploit and oppress the proletariat, those workers who are forced to sell their labor to the capitalists in order not to starve to death. The capitalists live at the expense of the workers, without producing anything themselves. The capitalists rob the workers, using their power, giving them only a part of what they produce with their labor. The proletariat strives to free itself from oppression, so there is a constant struggle between capitalists and workers. The capitalist system is preparing its own destruction from within. It is built on complete freedom of economic activity: every capitalist, in pursuit of his own profit, strives to produce as much as possible. Therefore, overproduction occurs periodically, goods do not find buyers, and economic crises occur.

Economic crises are becoming more frequent and intensified. Eventually there will come a crisis that will prove disastrous for the capitalist system, and capitalism will be destroyed. All economic and political power will pass then into the hands of the proletariat.

This will be facilitated, on the one hand, by the fact that capital will be concentrated in a few hands, and the number of capitalists constantly decreasing, which results in a concentration of capital, and on the other hand, by the impoverishment of the working classes and the growth of their class consciousness, which manifests as hatred against capitalists.

After the overthrow of the capitalist system, the "dictatorship of the proletariat" is established—the rule of the proletariat, which, in the end, will lead to the establishment of the so-called "classless society" and a complete Communist order.

After the overthrow of the capitalist system, the economic well-being of the proletariat should improve many times over, since there will be no one to rob them, and all the means of production will go to them along with political power.

21. What Is the Cause of Socialism?

Marxism is entirely a product of Jewish psychology. Its creator and architect, Karl Marx, consciously or unconsciously reflected in Marxism the basic aspirations of Jewry.

In his teaching about the coming victory of the international proletarian class, he presented the proletariat as if it were one people who had fallen under the dependence of the rule of other peoples, thus identifying it with world Jewry, scattered all over the world and having no homeland of its own. The international proletariat is like a chosen people, a collective "messiah."

Marxism is a product of Jewish bitterness against the non-Jewish world. His main characteristic feature is the hatred that he incites in the masses. This hatred is expressed in the destruction and annihilation that the socialist movement brings to life, embodying the ideas of Marxism (for example, in Russia). Marxism is utterly devoid of any capacity to give any ground for creative work. All attempts by Marxists to move away from destruction to positive creation do not lead to anything. Marxism can only destroy. Its pathos is the pathos of blood and fire.

No wonder Karl Marx, so brilliant in his criticisms, is very weak in the part where he tries to paint a picture of the coming system that will replace the capitalist one, to point out the new ways. Here he confines himself to such airy phrases as "jumping from the realm of necessity to the realm of absolute freedom," etc.

At present, all the constructions of Marxism are breaking apart, all its ideas have been subjected to the most severe of criticisms.

The cornerstone of the entire Marxist theory is the doctrine of historical materialism. Marxism teaches that the way of producing material goods determines the nature of social, political, and intellectual life. In other words, the economic factor is at the heart of everything.

In reality, we do not observe such a picture at all. The economic factor is not at all the decisive factor determining everything else. All factors of social life are mutually dependent. This means that if the economy affects the social forms, the political system, and religion, then social forms, political relations, and people's religious beliefs affect the economy and economic relations. History gives us a whole series of vivid examples of people's behavior being determined by ideas that were far removed from the economy, regardless of and even at odds with their economic interests. Often a person sacrificed his personal economic interests for the good of his nation.

Marx, by defining the economic factor as a technique for the production of goods, is far from giving an exact definition of his understanding of a technique of production. If he understood technique in the narrow sense of the word, then he completely overlooked that the technique of production always presupposes a known idea, a creative thought that precedes the production process. Even a stonemason, before doing his work, develops a specific plan for how to carry it out with minimum costs.

If Marxism understands the technique of production as a whole as the general conditions of production, including geographical conditions, natural resources, etc., the theory turns out to be very vague, because the concepts of the general conditions can be extended indefinitely.

Marxism's doctrine of class struggle is also totally wrong. Marxism divides the world into two camps, putting the proletariat on the one hand and the capitalists on the other.

First of all, he is deeply mistaken in this construction. There are not two, but many classes in the world. What is understood by Marxists as one capitalist class is not really a whole, but a whole series of separate classes. Workers can also be divided into several distinct groups with pronounced opposing interests, primarily skilled workers and laborers. Within these there are classes such as: artisans, farmers, etc.

There are conflicts between all these classes that, far from bringing about the victory of the workers, will do nothing of the sort. Marx did not give an exact definition of class. This leads to the fact that, in practice, the proletarian class is understood as everyone supporting the socialist movement, regardless of their social origin, while the rest are considered capitalists. As a result of this, the "French" millionaire manufacturer Léon Blum is considered a proletarian, while a peasant in Russia who owns a couple of cows is considered "bourgeois."

Marxism teaches that, as the proletarian revolution approaches, the number of capitalists will decrease more and more, and all the wealth will eventually be concentrated in the hands of a small handful of capitalist aces. In parallel, the impoverishment of the proletariat will grow.

This statement is also incorrect: owners, as the facts show, do not decrease at all, but, on the contrary, as a result of the appearance of large joint-stock companies, and the distribution of shares in wide circles, their number increases. The number of landowners is also growing. The welfare of the proletariat has also, in general, improved compared to the time when Karl Marx's *Capital* was written.

The bankruptcy of Marxism is most clearly demonstrated by the Russian experience. The Russian experience also shows that the socialist movement has been hijacked by Jewish actors, who use it for their own Jewish purposes, far from the interests of the workers, for which the Marxists are officially fighting.

Marxists teach that every product is the result of physical labor, the value of a product, according to Marxism, being determined by the time spent on its production. They believe that all work is the result of physical labor, and forget that all labor is preceded by mental effort. Even the smallest and simplest labor is preceded by the creation of a specific work plan (for example: a person, before removing any stone, thinks how it is best and easiest to remove it). *All work consists of the cooperation of the brain and hands.*

By understanding labor as the result of purely manual efforts, Marxists believe that the owners of enterprises do not take any part in labor. Products in factories and plants are created by workers, but entrepreneurs keep a part of these manufactured products for themselves (surplus value), robbing the workers.

With the destruction of the capitalists according to Marxist theory, there will be no one else to rob, and therefore the situation of the workers should improve many times over. In Russia, entrepreneurs have been destroyed, but the situation of workers has not improved at all. On the contrary, it has only worsened many times over. Entrepreneurs interested in the productivity of production have been replaced by government officials who are completely uninterested in the productive process, and as a result of this, the economic devastation observed in Russia naturally follows.

The Communist Party in Russia is headed almost entirely by Jews, who care least of all about the interests of the proletariat, workers, and peasants, caring only about their own selfish interests, their personal well-being. They ultimately act, consciously or unconsciously, together with the rest of Jewry, which seeks the enslavement of Russia, the destruction of the Russian nation, as the first step towards its world domination.

22. Fascism as a Substitute for Liberalism and Socialism

Fascism opposes itself to both liberalism and socialism. It is a substitute for them.

Liberalism in both its forms, political and economic—in the form of democracy and in the form of capitalism—vividly demonstrates the discord of words and deeds, theory and life that exacerbates the contradictions between the individual and society. It gives rise to class struggle and class violence, it turns the state into a toy in the hands of various groups of financial capital, decomposing religion and the nation, until eventually it comes to a dead end, inciting social contradictions and suffering an ideological collapse.

Disillusioned with liberalism, the masses seek in socialism answers to the social questions tormenting them. Socialism, promising a solution to the social problem, in fact only leads to its exacerbation. The class struggle turns into class oppression. Instead of improving the lives of working people, it leads to their deterioration.

Currently, socialism has also lost all credit with the masses of the people. Humanity is looking for new ways, and finds them in fascism. Fascism is a new worldview, a new political and social order, a new movement, imperiously gaining new positions for itself, becoming the leading idea of all peoples.

23. How Does Fascism Differ from Liberalism and Marxism?

In contrast to the liberal idea of the individual and the Marxist idea of the class, fascism promotes the idea of the nation. The nation, as a national whole, is that social category which plays a decisive role in the social process. The individual and class exist only within the nation, and their interests are entirely subordinated to its interests.

Liberalism leads to the domination of materialism, while socialism asserts it and legitimizes it, as it were. Fascism proclaims the domination of spiritual principles—the cult of the spirit.

Liberalism leads to class struggle; socialism only ignites it and carries out class oppression, the domination of one class. Fascism strives for class solidarity, peace among the classes, the application of the interests of classes in the name of the nation.

Liberalism proclaims the sacredness and inalienable nature of private property. Socialism rejects it. Fascism recognizes limited private property, leaving property to the person, but demands that he manage his property without harming the interests of the state.

24. Why Are Fascists Hostile to the Jews?

Jews are the organic enemies of every nation-state.

Jews have not had their own state for a long time. They live among other nations. Scattered all over the world, they nevertheless are closely related to each other, representing a single international community due to their racial and cultural characteristics. In every nation in which they live, Jews strive to occupy a dominant position, to climb to the heights of society and eventually subordinate all nations to their influence, in order to establish a world Jewish rule.

The way for Jewry to seize power in the world is through the decomposition of other nations, to bring discord into their midst by means of its capital, its economic power. Therefore, all fascist movements (with the exception of the Italian Fascists, since there are barely any Jews in Italy) are resolutely fighting against Jewry, which always stands in the way of the national revival of individual countries.

25. Why Are Fascists Fighting Freemasonry?

Freemasonry is a secret international union of various secret societies united by a rite, a hierarchy, and a common goal.

Hiding behind various goals, mainly the goals of philanthropy, scholarship, mutual assistance, and fraternal love, these societies, *through the destruction of religion, the nation, the seizure of political and economic power in various states, through capitalism and revolution, through liberalism and socialism, are striving for power over the world.*

Freemasonry is led, as evidenced by numerous facts and documents, by Jews, being the agent of the Jewish plan for world domination, which is allegedly promised to the Jews by God.

Freemasonry is thus a Jewish instrument of the step-by-step conquest of the world mainly by non-Jewish hands.

The fight against Freemasonry is being waged in all fascist countries. Masonic lodges are banned in Italy and Germany.

Questions to Review:

1. List the main lines of political thought.
2. What is liberalism?
3. What are the dangers of liberalism?
4. What is democracy?
5. How is the supposed rule of the people accomplished in a democracy?
6. Why are political parties inevitable in a democracy?
7. Who actually rules in a democracy and how?
8. What is capitalism?
9. What is the role of the state under a capitalist system of economy?
10. What does capitalism lead to?
11. What is socialism?
12. What is Marxism and who is its founder?
13. Summarize the tenets of Marxism.
14. Why does Marxism express the basic aspirations of Jewry, how, and where?
15. Why are Marxists wrong in their doctrine of the superiority of the economic factor of technology of production over all other factors?
16. What is the fallacy of the Marxist doctrine of the class struggle and the coming victory of the proletariat?
17. What does the Russian experience tell us?
18. What is the fallacy of the Marxist understanding of labor?
19. What do the Jewish leaders of the Communist Party in Russia strive for?
20. Why does fascism replace liberalism and socialism?
21. What is the difference between fascism and liberalism and socialism?
22. Why are fascists hostile to the Jews?
23. In what ways does Jewry seek its world domination?
24. What is Freemasonry?
25. What is the connection between Freemasonry and Jewry?

Chapter III: The Situation in Russia

26. Why Are the Russian Fascists Fighting the Existing Power in the USSR?

The Russian Fascists declare a struggle against the Communist government because it is an anti-Russian power, hostile to the Russian people destroying the Russian nation—it is in fact a Jewish power, the power of international Jewry ruling over the Russian country, a power that is deceiving, oppressing and exploiting the Russian workers.

27. What Is the CPSU?

The CPSU—the Communist Party of the Soviet Union—is the dominant and sole party in the USSR (all other parties are prohibited). It is pursuing the Communist idea by officially carrying out the "dictatorship of the proletariat," while in reality being the dictatorship over the proletariat of its Jewish leadership—the CPSU is the true master of Russia.

28. Tell Us Briefly the History of the CPSU.

The CPSU originated initially in the form of the RSDLP (Russian Social Democratic Workers' Party) in the 1890s with the unification of the early Marxist circles in Russia. Among the founders were many Jews, some Russian nobles, and intellectuals, such as Zinoviev (Apfelbaum), Kamenev (Rosenfeld), Lenin (Ulyanov), Trotsky (Bronstein), Gotz, Dan, Plekhanov, Bukharin, Chicherin, etc.

In 1902, the RSDLP was split into the Mensheviks and Bolsheviks due to disagreements on tactical issues.

Since its establishment, the party has received more and more significant support from Jewish capital (mainly from the American banking house Kuhn, Loeb & Co.), as well as from some Russian capitalists. The Social Democrats, especially the Bolsheviks, have been developing vigorous work to involve Russian workers in their ranks and young people, organize secret circles, create a revolutionary professional movement, publish a great deal of propaganda literature, etc.

With the help of the Jewish capital of the RSDLP, it was not difficult in October 1917 to seize power in Russia with the so-called October Revolution.

In the same year, the RSDLP was renamed the RCP, or the Russian Communist Party (Bolsheviks), and in 1922 as the CPSU—the Communist Party of the Soviet Union (Bolsheviks).

29. What Is the Comintern?

The Comintern, or Communist International, is an international gathering of representatives of Communist parties from various countries.

The Comintern is closely connected to the Soviet People's Commissar of the USSR and the Politburo of the CPSU. Through the Comintern and by using Russia as a springboard, world Jewry is striving for world domination under the banner of the "world proletarian revolution," through the slogan—"workers of the world, unite!" The Comintern is also called the Third International, in contrast to the First International, founded by Marx in the 1860s, and the Second International, consisting of representatives of social democratic parties in Europe.

The second and third internationals, diverging on issues regarding tactics, demonstrated, as it were, a rivalry with each other. The formidable growth of fascism, however, forced them to discover a secret bond: on the basis of the struggle against fascism, both internationals united.

The executive body of the Comintern is called the ECCI (Executive Committee of the Communist International).

30. What Is the USSR?

The USSR or the Union of Soviet Socialist Republics, or in short, the Soviet Union, sometimes mistakenly called Soviet Russia abroad, is actually a Jewish state located in Russian territory. By seizing Russian wealth, they own the Russian people as slave owners and landlords.

The USSR is the domain of the CPSU, and therefore of world Jewry. The USSR should be distinguished from the enslaved Russia, which we call the "Second Russia" in contrast to the "First Russia" of the pre-revolutionary times, and the "Third Russia," the future fascist Russia.[246] Russia is included as the main component in the USSR, but it is in reality an oppressed, suppressed, destroyed component, not having any autonomous significance in the structure and life of the Soviet state.

31. Tell Us Briefly the History of the USSR.

The Judeo-Bolshevik seizure of power in October 1917 ended the existence of Russia, breaking up into a number of separate state formations that paved the way for a bloody civil war.

Russian patriots could not allow the death of Russia, and so the White movement arose, uniting the most heterogeneous of elements.

However, the ardent idealism of the White front proved powerless against world Jewry, which got support from the Bolsheviks not only in Moscow, but also in the rear of the White armies through the socalled "interventionists."

Intervention troops from France, England, the US, and elsewhere allegedly advanced to help the White movement. In fact, they only helped the Bolsheviks, (also because of the lack of a social program) and as such, the White movement collapsed.

Initially, the Communists proclaimed "self-determination of peoples," as a result of which the RSFSR, the Ukrainian SSR, the BSSR, the DDA, etc. appeared in place of Russia.

After the collapse of the White movement, Muscovite Jews found the facade no longer necessary. As a result, in 1922 the "unification" of all the "republics" into a single union state followed—the USSR, consisting formally of the RSFSR (Russian Soviet Federative Socialist Republic), the Ukrainian SSR (Ukrainian Soviet Socialist Republic), the TSFSR (Transcaucasian Socialist Federative Soviet Republic), the BSSR (Byelorussian Soviet Socialist Republic), and several other small republics.

32. What Is a Five-Year Plan?

In 1929, the five-year plan was announced: the "socialist reconstruction of industry," or "industrialization of the country" in five years. Noticing the emergence of new creative forces in the Russian people, the Communists channeled its course into one of its own. Once

---

[246] *подъяремный;* a word usually used by Communists meaning enslaved or subjugated under the yoke of the capitalist class. It was common for the Russian fascists and Rodzaevsky to adopt Communist rhetoric and language. (Translator's note)

again, Russian workers, this time mainly young workers, were deceived by the specter of a better life: "to catch up and overtake America."

The purpose of the five-year plan was a military one: under the pretext of the subsequent improvements in life, to strengthen the dictatorship of the CPSU by exhausting the people's energy and impotence, on the one hand, and by developing the military industry, on the other.

The Bolsheviks used up the first five-year plan for propaganda effect in four years, then failed in all areas of the five-year plan.

When it became too clear to everyone that the completion of the first five-year plan did not bring any life improvements, the Soviet Jews came up with a yet another five-year plan (from 1933 to 1937).

33. What Is Total Collectivization and What Are Its Results?

The five-year plan demanded "total collectivization," the transformation of Russia entirely into *kolkhozes*, collective farms instead of individual ones. Once the peasantry, realizing the ruinous effect of collective farming, refused to enter collective farms voluntarily, forced collectivization began—the total destruction of the peasantry as a class, under the pseudonym "destruction of the kulaks as a class on the basis of total collectivization." Peasants who did not agree to enter the collective farm were declared "kulaks," destroyed, and exiled (falling into the so-called "Lishenets").[247] This bloody massacre of the peasantry in the form of the "liquidation of the kulaks on the basis of total collectivization" was announced by the general party line of the CPSU.

The goal of collectivization—the destruction of the peasantry and the destruction of the agricultural base of Russia—clearly meant the artificial creation of hunger for the further weakening of the Russian people, and the destruction of "surplus population" on the way to turning Russia into a new Palestine for colonization by international Jewry.

The *kolkhozes* as collective farms should be distinguished from *sovkhozes* (Soviet farms), which are further stages of enslavement, where there is no longer a peasant at all, only an agricultural worker. A *kolkhoz* is a forced association of peasants for the conduct of general farming, with the transfer of all agricultural equipment into the hands of the *kolkhoz*.

The *sovkhozes* are an official state institution where peasants are simply wage laborers. In the collective farm, the peasant still retains

---

[247]*Лишенец*: A disenfranchised person in the USSR from 1918 to 1936, this included enemies of the revolution but could also include monks, clergy, merchants etc. (Translator's note)

the illusionary ownership of the land. In the state farm, however, he loses it completely, becoming an outright laborer.

34. Describe the Actual Situation in the USSR.

The USSR formally seems to be governed by workers. Officially in the USSR all power belongs to the soviets chosen by the population, i.e., there being a soviet power. In villages there are village councils, in cities, city councils. The highest bodies of the state are: the All-Union Congress of Soviets and the Council of Commissars, elected from the Central Executive Committee of the USSR, as well as the Council of People's Commissars, appointed by the Central Executive Committee.

Elections to the soviets are officially carried out by the population. In reality, thanks to the election system and the pressure of the GPU, all elections take place at the behest of the Communist Party.

The Soviet system in Russia is only a beautiful smokescreen, a gorgeous decoration, covering the undisputed dictatorship of the Communist Party.

It is not the people nor the workers who rule in Russia through the soviets, but Jewry through the Communist Party and the GPU, now renamed the People's Commissariat in order to fool the foreigners.

35. Describe the Mood of the Russian People.

At first, the Russian working people, succumbing to the clever provocation of the Marxists, supported the Bolshevik government; but as the true essence of their power became clear, discontent grew more and more among the people. This has now resulted in hatred of the Communist government and of Jewry, covering almost all the strata of the Russian population.

Now the Communist government is held almost exclusively with the help of the GPU, even those social groups that until recently were considered a faithful bulwark of the Communist dictatorship are beginning to retreat back out from it. The young Soviet generation, the *Komsomol*, began to become disillusioned with Communist ideas and switch sides to the opposition, becoming the most hostile element to the power at be. [248]

---

[248] The All-Union Leninist Young Communist League, was a political youth organization in the Soviet Union. It is worth noting that Rodzaevsky used to be part of this organization before fleeing to Manchuria, making this a personal statement. (Translator's note)

Hatred of the Communist government results in an active struggle against it: uprisings, riots, open opposition, insurrection, terror, etc. However, thanks to the presence of an organized apparatus of oppression in the hands of the Communist authorities, all open uprisings, which are mostly unorganized, are suppressed and all participants in them are subjected to severe reprisals.

The task of the Russian fascists is to give the Russian people a single idea, a single program and a single plan, and on the basis of these to create an organization and unity of action of all active forces of the enslaved Russia.

Questions to Review:

1. Why are Russian fascists fighting Communist power?
2. What is the CPSU?
3. What is the RSDLP?
4. Who was the founder of the RSDLP?
5. When did the RSDLP split into Bolsheviks and Mensheviks and why?
6. When was the RSDLP renamed the RCP and then the CPSU?
7. What is the Comintern?
8. When was the first International founded and by whom?
9. What is the USSR?
10. When did the Bolsheviks seize power?
11. Who tried to combat the Communists?
12. When was the Union of Soviet Socialist Republics founded?
13. How many republics are part of the USSR and which are they?
14. What was the first five-year plan?
15. What did the first five-year plan lead to?
16. Why did the Communists start the second five-year plan?
17. What is total collectivization?
18. What goals did the Communists pursue with the policy of collectivization of agriculture?
19. What are the *kolkhoz* and *sovkhoz*?
20. Who officially rules in the USSR?
21. Who truly rules the USSR?
22. Through what organs does the imaginary rule of the workers in the USSR take place?
23. What role does the Communist Party play?
24. How do Russian people treat Communists now?
25. Why can't the Russian people free themselves from the Communist power?
26. What should the Russian fascists do to help the Russian people free themselves from their Communist fetters?

PART TWO

Chapter I: Causes and Main Objectives of Russian Fascism

36. What Is the Ideology, Program, and Tactics of Russian Fascism?

The ideology of Russian fascism is a set of provisions defining the main ideas and ultimate goals of Russian fascism.

The program is a plan for bringing an ideology to life. The program of Russian fascism draws a draft of the political and social system that the Russian fascists are striving for: the state structure of the future Russia, the organization of the Russian national economy, the situation of individual social groups of the Russian people, etc.

The tactics of Russian fascism are methods (the means) of action chosen for the best and fastest achievement of the tasks set before Russian fascism.

The main difference between ideology and tactics is that ideology is not subject to change, while tactics change depending on the place, time, and location.

37. What Does the Failure of the White Movement Mean?

The failure of the White movement clearly shows that it is possible to fight the existing power in Russia only if there is a developed social program opposed to the destructive Communist program, and capable with its wide propaganda of attracting sympathy for the activation of the national-labor masses of the Russian people.

This program should reflect the demands of the enslaved Russian masses, mainly workers, peasants, and youth. It should be an expression of their aspirations and hopes.

The participants of the White movement were united only by their hatred of the Communist government and were totally indifferent to the future political, and most importantly, the social structure of the Russian state. They did not give concrete answers to the questions that they were bringing to Russian workers and peasants. With their complete inattention to social issues, they alienated the broad masses from themselves, who did not follow the White heroes, but the Communist demagogues, and ensured victory for the latter.

The absence of a program made it impossible to develop anti-Communist agitation on a large scale. The White armies fought only with bayonets, while the Bolsheviks' main means of struggle was the moral decomposition of the White fronts through Communist propaganda.

The lessons of the White movement bear witness to the destructiveness of a lack of resolution. The movement's failure shows that, to be able to destroy an idea, you have to oppose it with another idea. To combat propaganda, you have to neutralize it with yet another, stronger, more vital propaganda.

38. What Does the Experience of Italy and Germany Teach?

The experience of Germany and Italy confirms the importance of propaganda in the struggle against the Communist power. This experience also teaches that for the success of this struggle, it is necessary to have a *sacrificing and energetic national revolutionary party*, based on the support of the broad working masses.

Such a party can only be a fascist party, the party of an energetically innovative minority, which has set itself the goal of achieving national rebirth, not shying away from sacrifices or dangers.

Fascist parties are generally characterized by militant activism, a self-sacrificing and persistent struggle for the triumph of their idea. The activism of fascist parties stems from the very essence of the ideas of fascism. Fascism proceeds from the recognition that history is always created by an initiative minority, since in this minority the "majority of determination and will" (Hitler's words) is embodied.

39. The Situation in Emigration Before the Emergence of Russian Fascism

The situation among émigrés before the emergence of Russian fascism can be described as a state of almost complete apathy and passivity in the struggle with the Communist authorities.

The political thought of émigrés followed different paths: most of them remained with a lack of resolve; some, albeit a minority, remained faithful to the liberal democratic ideology; finally, many political groups of émigrés espoused restorationist sentiments. Individual manifestations of activism on the part of émigrés led to nothing, for they lacked an idea that appealed to the Russian population and the ability to mobilize an organized struggle against communism.

The totality of all this dictated the need for an organization to appear among émigrés, which would be based on an ideology and program reflecting the sentiments and will of the enslaved Russian population, and capable of transferring its idea and program to the territory of Russia for an active revolutionary struggle against communism.

The All-Russian Fascist Party, the bearer of the ideas of Russian fascism, aspires to become such an organization.

40. The Causes of Russian Fascism

Russian fascism was born as a result of the awakening of Russian émigrés from hibernation, the desire to actively express their nationalism and their love for the motherland. Russian fascism was the result of the disillusionment with the old emigrant ways: lack of resolve, liberalism and out of the denial of restorative aspirations.

Russian fascism is drawing a completely new path of revolutionary activism, the path of selfless struggle against the Judeo-Communist government.

41. What Is Russian Fascism?

Russian fascism is both an idea and a movement (a movement in the sense of an organization).

The materialism, anti-nationalism, and class antagonism of Marxism should be replaced with the holistic idea of Russian fascism, striving to build the life of the Russian people on the basis of religion, nation, and labor, striving to create a national labor state.

The Russian fascist movement should bring the idea of Russian fascism to life, giving the Russian people spiritual freedom, national freedom, and freedom as workers.

Russian fascism opposes the materialistic worldview with a religious worldview that requires a person to serve higher principles.

Russian fascism recognizes the nation as the highest social value, subordinating the individual and class to it. Russian fascism strives for the organized service of the Russian nation through a greater national-labor state.

Russian fascism evaporates class struggle and in return brings class solidarity and class cooperation based on the recognition of common national interests, self-organization of classes through the corporate system, and their comradery work for the benefit of the Russian state.

Russian fascism regards labor as the most sacred duty of all citizens, believing that the labor efforts of the members of the nation create national, material, and spiritual values. These, in turn, create a national culture and strengthen the national economy.

42. Why Is the Claim That Russian Fascists Copy Italian and German Fascism Unfounded?

The claim that Russian fascism is copying Italian and German fascism is baseless. There is a purely formal commonality between all fascist movements.

Italian, German, and Russian fascists strive to bring their basic ideas into reality, to create a state that has a spiritual and religious worldview, the principle of serving the nation, and a social system based on the recognition of the value of labor and class solidarity—this is common to all fascist movements. But each fascist movement in each country moves towards the realization of these ideals in its own purely national ways. Every country creates its own content in the fascist movement.

The inner essence of Russian fascism is determined by its desire to serve the Russian nation, to create a Russian national-labor state, the state of the Russian nation and the existing conditions and situation in Russia.

43. The Unique Elements of Russian Fascism

The main difference between Russian fascism and other fascist movements is that Russian fascism must replace Communism, whereas fascism in Italy and Germany replaced the liberal democratic state and the capitalist system. Therefore, Russian fascism in its practical policy should follow the path of emancipation, by providing the Russian people with a certain sphere of external freedom, concretely expressed in the recognition of private property, freedom of labor, freedom of religion, scientific creativity, and even, within certain limits, freedom of speech, press, etc.

All this is dictated by conditions existing in the USSR, where the people, suffocating in the terrible grip of the Communist dictatorship, bound up in all branches of life, long for freedom and emancipation.

Italian and German fascism went from liberalism to fascism, we are moving from communism to fascism, so it is as if we are moving toward the same goal from opposite sides.

44. The Connection of Russian Fascism with the Russian Historical Past

Russian fascism is not exclusively a new, post-revolutionary phenomenon. Russian fascism has deep roots in the Russian historical past.

We can observe separate manifestations of the ideas of Russian fascism, now crystallized and formed, throughout the entirety of Russian history.

The most complete fascist ideology manifested itself in the time of Tsar Alexei Mikhailovich, when the entire state system at the time represented nothing less than a prototype of a modern corporate system: the entire population of Russia was organized in ranks (classes)—corporate associations. The Zemsky Sobor, which expressed the people's will, was a meeting of representatives of individual ranks (classes), a modern body of representation in a corporate state.

45. Why Do We Call Ourselves "Fascists"?

We call ourselves "fascists" because this word fully expresses the essence of our movement, because it reflects our ideology, and because it is extremely popular in the USSR.

By calling himself a Russian fascist, the Russian patriot is already briefly formulating his beliefs.

Communists are currently shouting about fascism the most. The Soviet radio and the Soviet press present fascism as the main enemy of communism, thereby popularizing it in the eyes of the population dissatisfied with the Communist government.

The word "fascism" is now associated in the USSR with the idea of the only movement that can bring liberation to the Russian people.

Many are confused by the foreign origin of the word "fascism." The Russian language, as well as many other languages, has many words that have a foreign origin, but which eventually seem to have become part of the flesh and blood of the Russian language and have become widespread.

Among such words we can point out: "patriot," "monarchy," "legitimism," etc. To these words, in essence, the word "fascism" now belongs.

46. What Is the All-Russian Fascist Party?

The All-Russian Fascist Party is the avant-garde (vanguard) of the Russian fascist movement, as it most fully expresses the ideology of Russian fascism and is the most active organization that has set the goal of carrying out this ideology into existence.

Other organizations, which can be classified partially as representatives of Russian fascism, express it incompletely and have a number of incorrect points of view on certain issues, often completely distorting their fascist direction, killing their activism, or directing it to a completely unnecessary direction.

Similarly, you can point to the Union of Young Russians, which in its ideology is very close to Russian fascism, but its tactical line obliges its followers, in the event of war between the USSR and some other power, to take the side of the Comintern, taking the non-fascist path and thus betraying Russian fascism.

47. What Is the Russian National-Labor State?

When a group of people form a society settled on a certain territory, firmly organized under the leadership of a single supreme authority, then it is a state, but when members of a certain nation are united this way, then it is a national state.

The Russian national-labor state must unite the members of the Russian nation, and lead the organized service of their common Russian national interests.

The Russian national-labor state is at the same time a labor state, because it considers labor the sacred duty of all members of the Russian nation. The labor efforts of the members of the Russian nation create the spiritual and material value of the nation, national culture, and national wealth. The national-labor state sets itself the goal of coordinating the labor efforts of individual members of the nation, directing them to serve the common national good.

The Russian national-labor state, as a fascist state, is a corporate state. Through the corporate system, the unity of all members of the Russian nation, both politically and economically, is achieved.

The corporate system carries out the full cooperation of all members of the Russian nation and its individual social groups, classes in all areas of life: political, cultural, domestic, and economic.

Under the corporate system, the entire population is organized. Every citizen knows his place in the state, and his duties and rights.

The corporate system disciplines economic life without destroying personal interest. By recognizing private property, it introduces a certain system into the economy in a certain order, within which every citizen can exercise his private initiative.

48. What Is the Russian Nation?

The Russian nation is the spiritual unity of all the Russian people on the basis of the consciousness of a common historical destiny, a common national culture, traditions, etc.

Thus, the Russian nation includes not only Great Russians, White Russians, and Little Russians,[249] but also the other peoples of Russia: Georgians, Armenians, Tatars, etc.

49. Why Should the Russian Nation Include All the Peoples Inhabiting Russia?

Russian fascists believe that, although the main elements of the Russian nation were the Great Russians, Belarusians, and Little Russians who made the most valuable contribution to the Russian national culture and contributed more to the creation of the Russian national state, the Russian nation also includes other peoples of Russia who have participated in its historical life. The bond of these peoples with the central core of the Russian nation has been increasingly strengthened and reinforced over time.

The process of self-organization of the Russian nation proceeds on the basis of a long-term historical life within one state, and economic ties that closely connected all the peoples of the Russian nation.

Thus, all the peoples of Russia represent a single national organism, and our historical mission is to strengthen this organism in the future.

All the peoples of Russia should be part of a single Russian nation, because only in that case, if they are a closely knit family aware of the need for strong unity and cohesion, is it possible to create a powerful national state that can resist any external pressure, corrupting internal influences, all forms of Judeo-Masonic influence, and can ensure peace and prosperity for the entire nation as a whole, as well as the individual peoples included in it.

---

[249] The *Velikorossiya* (Russia), *Bielarus* (Belarus), and *Malorosiia* (Ukraine), respectively. (Translator's note)

50. The Task of the Russian Fascists in Relation to Russia

The Communist government has as its main goal the destruction of the Russian nation; for this goal, first of all, it seeks to introduce antagonism between the individual elements that make up the Russian nation: the individual peoples. They do this by maintaining national separatist aspirations: Ukrainian separatism, Belarusian, Caucasian, etc. In their destructive policy, the Communists have already achieved certain results, to a large extent indeed decomposing the Russian nation.

Therefore, the task of the Russian fascists is first of all, following the overthrow of the Communist power, the all-round propaganda of the ideas of a unified Russian nation. The task is to achieve the national unity of all the peoples of Russia on the basis of common historical ties through a national campaign to recreate the Russian national spirit uniting the entire Russian population.

51. What Does Russian Fascism Bring to the Individual Peoples of Russia?

All the peoples of Russia who will take part in the national revolution will receive cultural, administrative, and political autonomy.

Every nation in the Russian national-labor state will enjoy a certain degree of independence and self-sufficiency, since this independence will not run counter to national interests.

Cultural autonomy will enable each people to educate the younger generation in its own language, to produce literature in its native tongue, etc.

Thus, Russian fascists admit the possibility of organizing a Russian national-labor state on a federal basis, believing that a federal organization can be the most expedient form of political unification of the Russian Federation under existing conditions.

52. The Situation of Jews in the National-Labor State

Only those peoples that have become part of Russia with their own lands can become full members of the Russian nation, and since the Jewish land is located outside of Russia, in Palestine, the Jews do not have any rights granted to the individual peoples of Russia.

Russian fascists consider Jews to be the main culprits of the destruction of the Russian nation, and therefore they will tolerate them on the territory of Russia only as undesirable foreigners.

Russian fascists are supporters of an active struggle against Jewry. Taking into account that the Russian population is currently engulfed by anti-Semitism and hatred of Jewry, only the fascist resolution of the Jewish question can be accepted by the Russian people and unite them in the common struggle against the Communist government. In this way, it serves as a strong foundation for the further close cooperation in nation-building, the reconstruction of the Russian nation and its stronghold, the Russian state.

53. Obligations of Every Russian Citizen in Relation to the Russian National-Labor State

The Russian fascists are guided by the principle: "The good for the Fatherland is the supreme law." Therefore, they require every Russian citizen to serve the highest national interests.

Every citizen of the Russian national-labor state should take an active part in all branches of national life: political, economic and cultural.

How well each citizen fulfills his duties towards the nation will determine his value for the nation and determine his rights in the Russian national-labor state.

54. What Will the Russian National Labor State Give to Every Russian Citizen?

The Russian national-labor state gives every Russian citizen, first of all, national freedom and freedom as a worker.

National freedom is expressed in the right to participate in the political life of the country. Participation in political life through national councils is at the same time both a duty and a right.

Freedom with regards to work is expressed in the right to work freely, the ability to sustain oneself with one's own labor.

There should be neither exploitation nor oppression in the national-labor Russia. Only free labor can be creative, constructive, and fruitful for the national economy.

Every citizen has the right to own private property, to show his entrepreneurial abilities and talents, and to accumulate wealth—as long as this accumulation is not speculative, usurious, and thus harmful to the entire national economy.

The national labor state itself will provide every Russian citizen with a certain minimum of personal well-being and welfare. It will give him a well-fed and free life.

From the right to national freedom, the rights to be a full member of the Russian nation follow, within certain limits—freedom of speech, assembly, etc.

The national labor state also provides every Russian citizen with full freedom of conscience (to profess one religion or another at one's discretion), freedom of thought, etc.

55. The Role and Significance of the Family in the Future National Labor State

The family, from the point of view of fascism, is the main unit of state organization. The strength of this unit depends on the strength of the whole organism.

Therefore, the Russian fascists set the task of strengthening family values and concepts of morality in the Russian population in every possible way.

The Communists began the destruction of Russia with the destruction of the family. The Russian fascists will begin the creation of the Russian national labor state with the birth of strong family hearths.

For the protection of a strong family, special state laws will be issued, measures will be taken to encourage marriages through benefits from the state, etc.

Questions to Review:

1. What is the ideology, program, and tactics of Russian fascism?
2. What is the most important difference between ideology and tactics?
3. What do the failures of the White movement tell us?
4. What is necessary for a successful struggle against the Bolsheviks and why?
5. What do the lessons of Italy and Germany teach us?
6. Why does it take a sacrificial, energetic, national revolutionary party to successfully fight the Communists, and why can only a fascist party be such a party?
7. Describe the situation among émigrés prior to the emergence of Russian fascism.
8. Why was the Russian emigrant community not active in fighting the Bolsheviks?
9. What were the reasons for the emergence of Russian fascism?
10. What is Russian fascism and what is it fighting for?
11. Why is the claim that Russian fascism is a copy of Italian and German fascism unfounded?

12. What do Russian and foreign fascism have in common, and what are their differences?
13. Describe the unique elements of Russian fascism.
14. Why do Russian and foreign fascists pursue the same goal from different directions?
15. Specify examples of the manifestation of fascism in Russian history.
16. Why should we call ourselves "fascists"?
17. What is the All-Russian Fascist Party?
18. Why does RFP reflect the ideas of Russian fascism best and most fully, over against other Russian fascist organizations?
19. What is the Russian national-labor state?
20. Why is the Russian fascist state a labor state?
21. Why should the Russian national-labor state be based on the corporate system?
22. What is the Russian nation?
23. Why should the Russian nation include all the peoples of Russia?
24. What is the policy of the Bolsheviks towards the Russian nation?
25. What must Russian fascists do to recreate the Russian nation?
26. What does Russian fascism bring to the individual peoples of Russia?
27. Why do Russian fascists recognize the possibility of building a Russian state on federal grounds?
28. Why would Jews be considered foreigners in a Russian nation-state?
29. What are the duties of every Russian citizen to the Russian national-labor state?
30. What will the Russian national-labor state give to every Russian citizen?
31. Why do Russian fascists stand for a strong family?
32. The importance of the family to the state.

Chapter II: What Kind of State System Are the Russian Fascists Going to Build for the Russian People?

56. Basic Principles of the State Structure of the Future Fascist Russia

The state system of national-labor Russia should be a corporate system in which the entire populace, being the current generation of the nation, is organized into national unions (in Italy, these are called syndicates) and corporations. Through these bodies it participates in the political (governance of the country), economic (economy), and cultural life of the state.

The bodies of the (corporate) union state in the future fascist Russia will be national councils of representatives from national unions.

The corporate system provides state power with a supra-class character. Independent of class and personal influences, it alone can turn state power into a true guardian of the common national interests, the interests of the entire Russian nation.

57. What Is the Slogan "Russia for Russia"?

Communists consider the Russian territory, on which the USSR is now located, a springboard for the world revolution, the base of the Communist movement, which, in the end, should conquer the whole world. The anti-Russian essence of the Communist power is the basis of the Communist movement.

Communist power is anti-Russian power by its national composition; Communist power is Jewish power, for it is Jews that are at the head of the Communist Party and who rule the Soviet country, occupying the most important posts in the party and state apparatus.

The Russian slogan "Russia for Russia" means that *Russian fascists are striving to create a Russian state on the territory of Russia—a real Russian power that will take care of Russian national interests, the interests of the Russian nation, and has Russian power as its national composition! The Russian state should be run by the Russians themselves. The Russian state's economy should serve the interests of the Russian people, and its culture should be a historical Russian national culture.*

In practice, this can be realized only through a corporate system, in which only members of corporate associations, i.e., members of the Russian nation, will participate in the management of the country.

58. How Will the Corporate System Be Implemented in Russia?

The corporate system will be implemented in Russia through national unions, corporations and national councils. The Russian fascists will base the future national unions and soviets on the existing Communist trade unions and soviets, reforming them in the process of the national revolution (primarily by expelling Jews and Communists from them).

Russian fascists believe that at the time of a national revolution it is necessary to avoid, as much as possible, breaking down the existing institutions, so as to avoid anarchy. They must be adapted to new goals by taking them as the basic skeleton of the future corporate system and by introducing a completely new content into them and expelling the traitors to the nation and its workers: the Judeo-Communists of the Stalin-Kaganovich faction.

59. What Are National Unions and Their Differences from National Corporations?

A national union is an association of members of a nation based on common professional interests.

National unions are built on a professional basis. Further unification is based on production.

For example, every worker or employee of a particular factory or industry first enters the corresponding professional unit in his production: locksmiths in the unit of the union of metalworkers, laborers in the unit of the union of laborers, employees in the unit of the union of employees, engineers in the unit of the union of engineers, etc. Yet these units of workers and employees of this production together form a unit of the corresponding National Corporation of a given type of production.

Thus, units of workers of one profession of different enterprises form a national union; units of workers of different professions of one enterprise form a unit of a national corporation.

The union of national unions with conflicting interests (for example, workers and employers) of one particular branch of the national economy would form a national corporation.

National unions will be created by reforming the existing Communist trade unions through the expulsion of Communists and Jews, turning them into natural free associations of workers. For those classes of the population that did not have their own professional associations under the Communists, additional unions will be created (for example, unions of entrepreneurs).

60. Who in the National Labor State Will Be Considered a Worker?

Following the principle that workers are recognized as the creators of spiritual and material values, Russian fascists classify peasants, workers, professionals, entrepreneurs, army officers, clergy, etc. as labor. The activities of all the peoples inhabiting Russia will be recognized as valuable for the Russian national-labor state.

Thus, in the Russian national-labor state there will be national unions: workers and intellectuals of various professions, Cossacks, peasants, entrepreneurs of various professions, i.e., all workers.

61. Objectives of the National Union

Each national union will have the following tasks:
1. *Representation and protection of their interests.* Collective agreements between workers and entrepreneurs will be concluded on behalf of national unions, to determine working conditions, wages, etc. The national union will fully protect the interests of its members in all respects to the fullest extent possible.
2. *National and professional education of members.* In national unions, members of unions (Russian citizens) will be instilled with a national identity. A national spirit will be forged within them. Love for the motherland will be cultivated, for the Russian nation and for the state. National unions will also strive to supplement the professional knowledge of members, by setting up various kinds of schools, lectures, etc.

3. *Mutual assistance.* National unions will provide their members with full moral and material support. The national union is an association, which, first of all, is built on the principle of mutual assistance, close comradely unity.
4. *Arbitration.* National unions will participate in conciliatory elections on various conflicts between representatives of individual classes, protecting the interests of their members, in conciliatory corporate commissions (see below on corporations).
5. *The power of the workers.* National unions will send representatives to national councils, elections to which will be carried out through national unions.

62. What Is the National Council?

The existing Communist soviets in the USSR should be reorganized by expelling Jews and Communists from them and turning them into free organs of genuine popular representation.

Elections to national councils under the fascist system will be held by secret ballot, without any pressure from external forces, which will ensure that they are truly representative of the diverse interests of the people.

Elections will be held by unions, so that the entire population, organized by profession, are represented in the council.

National councils are organized on a territorial basis. The main units of the national-soviet system of fascism will be rural and urban national councils.

Each union sends a certain number of delegates, depending on its size and its significance.

63. What Is a National Corporation?

A national corporation is an association of national unions (e.g., workers and entrepreneurs) with opposing interests within a certain branch of the national economy.

Corporate units are created at every production facility, with corporations on a city, regional, provincial, and on an all-Russian scale.

The governing bodies of corporations include representatives of national unions united in corporations on a parity basis.

The main task of corporations is to reconcile the interests of the members of national unions united in a corporation. In addition, the corporation has the duty of general control over the branch of production of which it unites (e.g., the corporation of employers and workers in heavy industry). Corporations must promote the better organization of their industry, and may issue rules that are binding upon all workers in the industry for this purpose.

All disputes between national unions belonging to the national corporation are resolved in special conciliation commissions, which, also on a parity basis, include representatives of all interested unions.

If a dispute cannot be resolved by a lower corporation (for example, a city or regional corporation that unites workers and employers of a certain production), then the dispute is referred to a higher corporate association, up to a corporation of one or another production on an all-Russian scale.

64. How Will the Supreme State Power Be Organized?

The supreme constituent and legislative body of the Russian national-labor state will be the All-Russian National Council.

Elections to the All-Russian National Council will take place according to the principle of representation of individual national unions, i.e., on the same grounds as elections to rural and urban councils. The All-Russian National Council will present all categories of the Russian population, all its social groups, and all peoples of the Russian Federation.

The main difference between the supreme representative body of the people's interests in a fascist state and a democratic parliament is precisely that here what is represented is not an amorphous "people," i.e., such as the various groups of finance capital through political parties, but rather the individual parts of the nation doing this or that particular job (workers, intellectuals, peasants, entrepreneurs, the army, the clergy).

The All-Russian National Council approves the Russian national government.

65. The Role of the All-Russian Fascist Party in the State Life of the Future Fascist Russia

The Russian fascists maintain that the historical process is always created by an initiative minority. The All-Russian Fascist Party, today the vanguard of emigration, tomorrow the vanguard of the nation, should be such an initiative minority that will take on the task of liberating Russia and leading its national life.

The All-Russian Fascist Party should become the leading group of the Russian nation. In the Russian fascist state, the RFP should be the actual leader of the national-state, social, economic and cultural life.

All the most important leadership positions of the state, society, economy, and culture should be occupied by Russian fascists, carriers of the Russian national idea, and the party organization should permeate the entire state organization. The RFP should be represented in all state corporate bodies: national unions, councils, and corporations.

66. The Attitude of Fascists to the Form of Government

Russian fascists do not prejudge this or that form of government, believing that it does not play a significant role for the life of the state, because the social essence, the social nature of the state system is what is important, not the form.

It is important to guarantee all layers of the Russian people's participation in state power, and it does not matter at all how the supreme body of this power will be externally decorated or what title the head of state will bear.

States can have the same form of government, but by their social content and its internal essence, represent two opposite types of state. For example, you can point to Italy and England. Italy and England have a monarchical form of government, but in Italy we see a corporate fascist system, while England is a liberal capitalist state.

67. What Kind of Court Should Exist in National-Labor Russia?

In the Russian national-labor state, there should be a free and independent national court. The court of national-labor Russia absolutely cannot be an instrument of one or another particular group of the population as a means of oppressing some by others, it must be the best warden and caretaker of national and social justice, the guardian of all good in the Russian nation.

The national court will be the best defender of the interests of the population, protecting it from arbitrariness. If at present in Russia any citizen can be arrested and exiled without any court intervention, according to the decree of the People's Commissariat of Justice, then in the future Russia arrests of Russian citizens will be carried out only with the sanction of the judicial authorities. Only an impartial court authority can deprive a Russian citizen of freedom if it's to the benefit of the Russian national state.

Judges in the future Russia should be absolutely independent and stand above their position in terms of their moral character. Therefore, they could be removed from their post only by court order and for offenses provided by special legislative resolutions. Measures will be taken for the appropriate education of judicial figures, cultivating in them the spirit of impartiality, the spirit of service to the common national interests.

In order for all Russian citizens to always be aware of the court's work and follow the court proceedings directly, all judicial proceedings will be heard with open doors; everyone will be able to attend.

68. What Goals Will the Russian National-Labor State Pursue in the Matter of National Education and Enlightenment?

The task of educational activities of the future Russian national authorities will be the preparation of nationally productive citizens.

The school of the future Russia will have two tasks: the first, to provide the necessary knowledge of both general and special character; the second, to nurture and cultivate the national spirit in its students.

The latter task is especially important, and it is characteristic of the fascist state. In a fascist state, the school should, first of all, prepare the national elite, the leading selection of the nation. This selection should be an example of the fortitude of the national spirit and the strength of its national foundations.

69. What Does the Slogan "Make Way for Abilities and Talents" Mean?

This slogan means that the advancement on the social ladder, the occupation of this or that position in the Russian national-labor state, will be entirely determined only by the abilities and talents of the Russian people.

In the fascist state, no privileges related to descent, wealth, etc. are allowed.

Russian fascists proclaim the principle of full equality of opportunities. It will be up to each citizen as to how to use the opportunities provided to him.

In the Russian national-labor state, every poor, able-bodied citizen will be able to count on the same success in moving up the social ladder, engaging in one or another social position, as a citizen with material wealth. Poor, capable Russian citizens will be given the full opportunity to receive not only secondary, but also higher education: the state will come to their aid by providing degrees and material support, by providing them with a certain stipend from the state for the duration of their studies.

70. Religion in the Russian National Labor State

Russian fascists stand for complete religious freedom. The Orthodox religion, being the faith of the majority of the Russian people and the main creator of our spiritual culture, will be provided with all possible assistance and support.

Other religions, with the exception of fanatical sects, and Satanic, immoral, Judaizing pseudo-religions, will also enjoy the full support of the Russian national authorities.

Russian fascism proclaims the union of church and state for the moral and religious recovery of the Russian people.

Questions to Review:

1. On what principles will the state system of the future Russia be based?
2. What will the corporate system bring?
3. What does the slogan "Russia for Russians" mean?
4. How will the corporate system in Russia materialize?
5. Why should the future state system be based on the existing trade unions and councils?
6. How will the existing trade union and council system be reformed?
7. What is a national union?
8. Who will be part of the national unions?
9. Who in the Russian national-labor state would be considered laborers?
10. List and characterize the tasks of national unions.
11. What is a national council?
12. What is a national corporation?
13. What are the tasks of a national corporation?
14. What is the supreme state body of national-labor Russia?
15. What is the difference between an all-Russian national council and a democratic parliament?
16. Describe the role of the All-Russian Fascist Party in the state life of future Russia.
17. Why do Russian fascists not prejudge one form of government or another?
18. Why is the form of government in a state irrelevant in the modern world?
19. What kind of court should exist in a Russian national-labor state?
20. What are the tasks of the national court in relation to Russian citizens?

21. What will ensure the independence and impartiality of the national court?
22. What are the tasks of education and upbringing in the fascist Russia?
23. What is the meaning of the slogan, "make way for abilities and talents"?
24. Why do Russian fascists stand for complete freedom of religion?
25. What is the relationship between church and state in fascist Russia?

Chapter III: The National Economy and the Situation of Individual Classes in the Russian National Labor State

71. The Economic Policy of Russian Fascism

The economy of Russia should serve the interests of the Russian nation.

The basic principle behind the economic policy of the Russian fascists is the complete economic independence of Russia. The Russian economy should in no way depend on international and foreign capital in general.

The economic life of the Russian state should be determined exclusively by Russian interests and follow the path of recreating and strengthening the economic power of Russia.

The economy of Russia should be a harmonious whole, so each branch of the economy should develop depending on the needs of the population.

After the fall of the Communist regime, Russian fascists consider it necessary to pay special attention to light industry, the preparation of consumer goods, so that the basic needs of the Russian people are satisfied.

Therefore, every Russian citizen will be given full opportunity to enrich himself and improve his material well-being, for the well-being of the entire economy will depend on the degree of well-being of individual citizens. The national-labor state will ensure that the growth of welfare continues evenly, so that large fortunes are not concentrated in the hands of individuals at the expense of the rest of the population.

Russian fascists completely deny the possibility of accumulating wealth through speculation and other non-labor involving activities.

The economy of the national labor state should rest on an equal distribution of wealth among all segments of the population.

72. The Fascist Attitude Toward Private Property

Russian fascists stand for limited private property. Private property is the best incentive for fruitful economic activity, giving rise to personal investment in the outcome of one's work.

The best indicator of the value of personal interest can be the modern situation in Russia, where personal investment is completely destroyed, and the entire economy is in the hands of the state. The heads of industrial enterprises in the USSR are simple state officials, and as such treat their work like officials, the result of which is the wild anarchy and lack of direction that reigns in the economic life of the USSR.

Private interest plays a huge role in the fruitful development of the economy, but it must be limited. Otherwise, it works to the detriment of national interests, which we see in modern capitalist countries where the pursuit of profit has overshadowed everything here, pushing the welfare and the state into the background, subordinating them to the selfish interests of individual groups of financial capital.

Russian fascists stand for limited private property.

73. The Role of State Power in the Economy of the National-Labor State

Russian fascists stand for the involvement of state power in economic life. Providing a broad initiative for private interest, they limit this initiative within the framework of state regulation and planning, so that it does not harm the state or the nation. Russian fascists stand for regulation, control, and planning of the economy.

The economic life of the future Russia should follow a certain pre-developed plan. This plan, however, should be drawn up with the needs and interests of all groups of the population and the entire economy as a whole taken into account. Its difference from the Communist plan will be that it will establish only general milestones, indicating general paths, providing full opportunities for individual entrepreneurs to show their entrepreneurial talents.

Control over the economy will be carried out through special state bodies and corporations.

Each corporation of a particular industry should not only resolve conflicts of various workers in this industry, but also monitor the organization of production itself, improving it in every possible way. The corporation will be able to issue various kinds of rules related to the industry under its jurisdiction. Every entrepreneur of national-labor Russia should remember that the state, giving him the opportunity to manage his property, is providing him a loan, as it were—a loan he must repay to the state in full with his economic activities. In pursuing his personal interests, he must at the same time benefit the national economy.

74. How Will Private Entrepreneurs Be Attracted to Participate in the Economic Life of the National Labor State?

The Communist power has destroyed the class of private entrepreneurs in Russia. The Russian fascists consider it necessary to restore the economy and to direct it in a healthy direction to revive the entrepreneurial class.

Entrepreneurs of the future Russia should come from all strata of the population, representing the selection of the most energetic, most enterprising citizens. The state will come to the aid of the young Russian entrepreneurial class to facilitate the manifestation of private initiative by any means.

Recognizing the role and importance of private entrepreneurs and private entrepreneurial initiative, Russian fascists will nevertheless fight against the unlimited accumulation of wealth, the transformation of creative entrepreneurial capital into anonymous capital, with the formation of joint stock companies, trusts, syndicates, etc.

A number of sectors of the economy should gradually pass into the hands of private entrepreneurs, primarily domestic trade and light industry.

75. On What Grounds Will the Financial System of the National-Labor State Rest?

The financial system of the national labor state should rest on the principles of budgetary balance, i.e., the state expenses of the future Russia will be covered by state parishes.

The state revenues of the national-labor state will consist of taxes, duties, and income from the exploitation of state property and enterprises.

The Russian money market should be isolated from the foreign money market, and Russian banknotes should not be allowed to circulate in foreign countries. Paper money should have a solid, non-fluctuating, non-changing value within the country. The monetary currency of the national labor state must be firmly secured.

76. Trade in National-Labor Russia

The national-labor state brings full freedom of internal trade. Foreign trade that is in the interests of Russia will remain for the most part within the hands of the state.

Only then can we ensure an uninterrupted supply of everything necessary to meet all the needs of the population, when domestic trade is transferred to private hands.

In trade, the ability to adjust to the market is of great importance. A private trader who is interested in having more people buying from him will always adjust to the needs and interests of buyers, and will make sure that he always has a stock of everything necessary for the buyer, and in sufficient quantities.

The harm of trade, especially with consumer goods in state hands, is vividly demonstrated by the USSR, in cases where the seller is a government official not interested in the activity of his enterprise or in attracting new buyers, and does not consider the demands and market needs, showing a purely clerical and bureaucratic approach to the buyer.

In the USSR, the buyer is not supposed to buy what he wants, but what he is offered in government stores. The supply of government stores is least of all based on the principle of adjusting to the market, to the needs of customers.

Everyone knows examples from Soviet trade, when Soviet stores did not have the most basic consumer goods—clothes, shoes, etc.—and at the same time shelves bursting with useless things: vases, flowers, powder, etc. The Soviet consumer walked without shoes and was forced to purchase absolutely unnecessary items for himself.

Foreign trade will remain largely in the hands of the state, which is the best guarantee against the economy of the entire state falling under the influence of international capital. Due to the very fact of the monopoly of foreign trade of Russian citizens with foreigners, all trade relations with foreign countries can only be carried out through the state, and through state bodies directly controlled by it.

77. The Role of Individual Classes in the National Economy

A healthy development of the economy is conceivable only with the cooperation of all classes within the state. From the point of view of fascism, each class plays a certain role in the economic and productive process. The economic well-being of the state is created by the friendly joint creative work of all classes.

All classes are mutually dependent on each other: entrepreneurs depend on workers, workers on entrepreneurs, and all aforementioned on peasants, etc.

If the worker carefully performs his duties, takes an interest in business and manages his factory or plant, the peasant will receive all the industrial products necessary for him. If the peasant cultivates the land, industry will be provided with an adequate supply of raw materials, and the worker will have no difficulty acquiring the agricultural products he needs. For economic anarchy to set in, it is only necessary for one class to elude the performance of its functions in the economy.

A striking example: during the first years of the Communist regime, when the class of entrepreneurs was completely destroyed and therefore the industry went into complete ruin, the peasants refused to cultivate the land and supply the city with the necessary agricultural products, leading to spontaneous famine.

78. What Does Russian Fascism Give to Russian Workers?

The worker in the USSR is a beggar, a slave. He receives an officially high wage, but in reality, this wage barely enables him to live the most miserable existence; the Russian worker is naked and starving.

The slogan of the Bolsheviks, thrown out the window at the beginning of the revolution—"factories and factory workers"—turned out to be an impudent lie. The Russian worker, instead of owning the factories, was enslaved by them.

In the USSR, the reality is that a worker is bound to the production on which he works, without having the right to leave. The seven-hour working day of the Russian worker turned into a ten- or even eleven-hour day, thanks to the various kinds of competition and the toll it inflicts.

The Bolshevik government brought exploitation and oppression to the workers. Instead of the dictatorship of the proletariat, it gave the most hopeless, the most terrible of dictatorships over the proletariat: complete enslavement.

Russian fascism brings about the liberation of Russian workers from Communist exploitation. It seeks to create conditions under which the worker will be protected from capitalist exploitation.

Communism has turned the Russian worker into a slave. Russian fascism will make him the owner and the co-owner of the enterprise where he works. This will be achieved by creating a *special working part* in the capital of all enterprises, both private and public.

Participation in the profit making of the enterprise, being quite possible and a real thing, is only possible in a fascist state. The experience in this direction has already been done brilliantly in Germany. For example: Krupp plants (the biggest production plants in Germany) in 1934 received a profit of seven million marks, which was distributed among the workers of the enterprises.

A worker in fascist Russia will not only take part in the profit making of enterprises, he will also participate in the management of the enterprise with which he will work.

This will be achieved by creating a business council at each production facility, which will include representatives of workers. The participation of workers in business councils will give workers the opportunity to monitor the state of affairs at their enterprise, to control it. This will increase the consciousness of workers and will lead to the development of a sense of responsibility to the state for the conditions of their production.

The involvement of workers in the management of production has also been effectively implemented in Germany, which has brought enormous benefits to production, forcing workers to be interested in the conditions of production and to take care of its improvement.

The worker in the fascist conception is an employee of an enterprise who occupies the same position as the entrepreneur against the background of national labor.

The Russian fascists will strive for a real increase in the wages of workers. The Russian worker should be able to purchase with the wages he receives all that is necessary to lead a well-fed and free life.

Russian fascists will take care of the actual reduction of the working day.

The Workers' National Union will represent the workers who are in it in every possible way. Collective agreements will be concluded on behalf of the national union, and Russian workers will elect their representatives to state authorities through national unions.

National unions will send workers' representatives to corporate conciliation commissions.

The Workers' National Union is the real bulwark and protector of workers' interests!

Russian fascism carries the broadest social insurance: in case of death, injury, illness, unemployment, etc.

In a national-labor state, the work of minors will be completely prohibited. Women's work will be provided with special protection, special legislative resolutions.

79. What Does Russian Fascism Bring to Russian Peasants?

Forced collectivization led to the complete enslavement of the Russian peasantry. The Russian peasant is now effectively a farmhand in *kolkhozes* and *sovkhozes*.

In a *kolkhoz*, all land and inventory are considered the collective property of *kolkhoz*. With the exception of small plots remaining in the individual possession of peasants, they are all managed by the heads of the *kolkhoz*—representatives of the Communist Party—the apparatus of oppression of all Russian workers. Essentially, all agricultural products produced by the Russian peasantry are taken away from them under the guise of an exorbitantly high tax, grain procurement, forced sale of surplus to the state, etc. In the *sovkhozes*, an even greater enslavement of the peasantry takes place.

A striking indicator of the situation of the peasantry is the systematic famine in the USSR, from which, according to approximate estimates, about ten million peasants died in the last years.

Forced collectivization led to a spontaneous crop reduction, to the death of almost half of the working cattle. The cultivation of the land by agricultural machines did not bring any benefit due to their inept use. The deterioration of valuable machinery as soon as it arrived in the field acquired a spontaneous character in the USSR.

The Russian fascists strive for the emancipation of the peasantry. They repudiate the slogan of collectivization. All land belongs to the Russian peasantry for full, hereditary, inviolable, and indivisible use and ownership.

Every peasant now sitting on the land would receive a tract of land, of which he would be the complete steward. The Russian fascists stand for an individual farmstead, the creation of a strong and prosperous class for the Russian peasantry.

Acting as staunch enemies of collectivization, Russian fascists least of all seek to restore the pre-revolutionary form of land ownership, the commune, with the belief that the communal ownership has already outlived its age.

It is necessary to encourage the peasantry to take an interest in the cultivation their land, which is completely absent in the collective farms, while also being absent in a commune with temporary ownership of land.

The indivisibility of the peasant allotment is necessary in order to avoid the endless fragmentation of peasant land and the formation of such small plots, the exploitation of which will be completely unprofitable from the economic point of view, and not bring sufficient income to their owners.

The size of a peasant allotment is determined by the soil, climate, type of economy, availability of land, etc.

All land to the peasantry and only to the peasantry! Russian fascists are against the return of land to the former landlords. The Russian fascists will not allow a new class of landlords to form, resolutely fighting against land speculation, and mass purchase of land from the peasantry by private individuals.

In national-labor Russia, every peasant will have the opportunity of a comfortable existence, since he will be the complete administrator of the agricultural products produced by him, paying an extra significant agricultural tax to the state. The state will ensure the sale of agricultural products at an acceptable price for the peasantry, while also doing everything possible to combat speculation in this area.

The peasants in fascist Russia will be organized according to their peasant national unions for the joint protection of their peasant interests.

The organization of the Russian peasantry will best protect the peasantry from the arbitrary whims of other groups of the population who have economic relations with the peasantry. The duties of the peasant national unions will be the all-round protection of peasant interests, and their representation in all cases of a relationship of the peasantry with other groups of the population. Peasant national unions will strive to conclude better conditions for the sale of agricultural products. Through national unions, peasants will be able to purchase the necessary agricultural equipment (in particular expensive agricultural machinery) that individual peasants would not be able to. The national-labor state will wage a decisive struggle against shortages of land by organizing the systematic colonization of peasants to vacant land and helping them to settle in new places.

The Russian national-labor state will insure peasants against natural disasters, crop failures, etc.

Measures will be taken to provide the peasantry with proper medical, veterinary care, etc.

80. What Does Russian Fascism Bring to the Intelligentsia?

The intellectual labor class, specialists of various qualifications, representatives of liberal professions—teachers, doctors, journalists, clergy, etc.—are considered by fascists to be part of the working class, and everything said about the workers applies to them as well.

To the intelligentsia, *Russian fascism brings the possibilities of enormous creative work for the benefit of the people on all fronts of the industrial, agricultural, cultural, and spiritual life of the Russian nation.*

For the intelligentsia, Russian fascism brings complete religious and scientific freedom, freedom of cultural creativity, etc. Russian fascism strives for the most energetic, capable, and talented Russian people to emerge from among the rest of the mass of workers and peasants, and to select among them a new intelligentsia—the elite of the Third Russia.

Representatives of intelligent professions will form their own national unions.

Questions to Review:

1. On what grounds should the economic system of the future Russia rest?
2. To what industry will the Russian fascists pay special attention after the fall of Communist power?
3. How do Russian fascists view the healthy enrichment of Russian citizens?
4. How do fascists view private property?
5. Why is private property necessary?
6. Why must it be limited?
7. What will be the role of the state in relation to the economy in fascist Russia?
8. Through what organs would the control of production be exercised?
9. What is the attitude of Russian fascists toward entrepreneurs?
10. From what strata will the business class of fascist Russia emerge?
11. What should the financial system of the future Russia consist of?
12. Why do Russian fascists stand for complete freedom of domestic trade?
13. Why would Russian fascists seek to keep most foreign trade in the hands of the state?
14. What is the role of individual classes in the national economy?
15. Why are all classes mutually interested in each other?
16. What is the situation of the workers in fascist Russia?
17. How would the workers' participation in the profits of enterprises and their management be realized?
18. What will the workers of the Russian national union gain for the Russian workers?
19. Describe the situation of the Russian peasantry under Communist rule.
20. What does Russian fascism bring to the Russian peasantry?
21. Why do fascists stand for the de-collectivization of agriculture?
22. How do fascists view the restoration of the landlord class?
23. What will the peasant national union take care of?
24. What does Russian fascism bring to the Russian intelligentsia?

Chapter IV: Tactics of the All-Russian Fascist Party

81. Stages of the RFP's Work

There are three of these stages: the stage of the gathering of forces, the preparation; the stage of the offensive, the active struggle, which should culminate in a national revolution; and finally, the last stage, following the overthrow of the Communist government, it being that of national construction.

The first stage of gathering forces in the Far East can be considered fulfilled. Here in the ranks of the RFP, forces capable of actively fighting the Communist authorities have already been gathered. Now we are entering the second stage of our work—the deployment of forces, the offensive, the active struggle against Communism. In other organizations outside the Far East, the first stage is also coming to an end. The path of revolutionary activity is the propagation of our ideas and, based on them, the organization of internal Russian activists to deliver the last crushing blow to Communism for the national revolution.

Following the overthrow of the Communist government, the third stage of our mission will begin: nation-building, bringing our ideas and program to life.

82. What Is Our General Line and Our General Plan?

The general line determines the behavior of the entire party as a whole and of each Russian fascist individually. The general line of the party follows from the specific tasks set by the party, the national revolution and the subsequent nation-building, and from the surrounding situation and opportunities.

The master plan—our tactics—is a way to bring our ideology and our program to life.

The general plan of the RFP was developed and explained by the head of the RFP, K. V. Rodzaevsky, in the form of the fascist three-year plan, a three-year plan for the struggle against the Communist authorities.

The essence of the fascist three-year plan lies in the proclamation of the final stage of the anti-Communist struggle, for which all national forces must be prepared to deal a final blow to Communism, to carry out the goal of the national revolution.

The fascist three-year plan began on May 1st, 1935, and must be completed by May 1st, 1938. The RFP has set itself a general goal: in no more than three years, the Communist power must be overthrown. Russian fascists must fulfill this task or perish!

83. Ways to Implement the Three-Year Plan

The fascist three-year plan should be implemented through the maximum deployment of our internal Russian activity. For three years, the whole of Russia should be covered with networks of units unrelated to each other, which, at a given signal, in 1938, will provoke a temporary widespread uprising. This uprising will decide the fate of the Communist government and carry out a national revolution. Widespread self-organization of the oppressed Russian activists to fight the Communist government will also follow as a result of widespread propaganda of the ideas, programs, and tactics of Russian fascism.

Each newly emerged revolutionary unit in Russia will be assigned a striking task: to create several similar revolutionary units by distributing our revolutionary leaflets, oral propaganda, terror, insurrection, etc.

The idea of Russian fascism, which now unites the most active part of the Russian diaspora, should unite all the best elements of the Russian people, in order to become the leading idea of the reviving Russian nation.

84. What Are the Basic Principles of Our Revolutionary Work?

Our inner Russian revolutionary activity, by its very nature being a conspiratorial activity, rests firstly on the principle of its complete separation from the work in emigration, open work, and, secondly, on the principle of decentralization.

Only those who are directly involved know about the specifics of our conspiratorial activities. Only the guarantee of this principle can ensure the success of our revolutionary work, guaranteeing it from provocation and disclosure by Communist agents.

The principle of decentralization lies in the fact that our revolutionary units work completely independently from each other, and are not in any organizational connection between each other.

Under such conditions, it is absolutely impossible to disclose the entire network of our revolutionary units. It is possible to disclose only part of this network, dealing a partial blow to our internal Russian forces. All revolutionary units are united by a single idea, a single program and a single revolutionary plan.

85. The Tasks of the Party During the Implementation of the Fascist Three-Year Plan

Since the beginning of the fascist three-year plan, the All-Russian Fascist Party has become a national revolutionary party. Its main goal is to work on the revolutionary struggle against Communism. The activity of the party proceeds under the slogans "Everything is for Russia" and "all forces are for the national revolution."

The main work of the party during the fascist three-year plan takes place primarily on the territory of Russia and only secondarily abroad.

Work on the territory of Russia consists in preparing the ground for the national revolution by propagating the ideas of Russian fascism and switching the passive hatred of the enslaved Russian masses toward an active struggle against Communism.

For the work to be done on the Russian territory, we are currently attracting the best part of our forces, our biggest assets, the most persistent, the most strong-willed, ideological, and experienced of our associates. The rest of our party members must urgently prepare themselves for revolutionary work, forging national revolutionaries out of themselves for an immediate transition to this better part.

Work in emigration, therefore, should be reduced mainly to the training of national revolutionary cadres. Our internal Russian forces will always demand replenishment, and we must make this replenishment not only at the expense of sympathizers in Russia, but also at the expense of our foreign personnel.

In addition, for the last blow to the Communist government in 1938, it will take the combined efforts of the entire party organization, by the time the national revolution begins. All our fascist battalions must be drawn into battle.

The work of training personnel consists in raising the discipline of the party mass, its ideals, and its consciousness, teaching it the technique of revolutionary combat, forging revolutionary fighters, and creating a strong revolutionary organization as a reserve to the internal Russian activists.

86. What Is the Meaning and Role of Our Annual Tactical Slogans?

The proclamation of the fascist three-year plan assigns us the implementation of a number of separate specific tasks. Their content and the sequence of their implementation determine our tactical slogans for each year of our work.

In 1936, the party came out with the slogans: "Representation of Russia's enslaved," "From the selection—a select few," and the general slogan "Toward Russia."

The first slogan, "Representation of Russia's enslaved," means that the RFP should become, as it were, a representative of the enslaved Russian population, expressing its will, which the Russian population itself cannot reveal under the conditions of the current Soviet reality.

The slogan "From the selection—a select few" sets us with the task of creating a revolutionary group of activists in the ranks of the party, to make a selection based on the revolutionary readiness of each individual member.

The slogan "Toward Russia" denotes the common aspiration of our activities.

87. The Attitude of Fascists Toward Intervention

The RFP will welcome any invasion of the USSR by foreign troops, as long as this invasion is really aimed at overthrowing the Communist government and does not pursue any aggressive goals.

An external war can accelerate the overthrow of Communist power, force events to move at a faster pace, and bring us closer to the national revolution, shortening our fascist three-year plan.

88. The Attitude of Fascists Toward Japan

Russian fascists believe that the Japanese Empire is interested in the overthrow of the Comintern, and not in the dismemberment or weakening of the Russian state—Japan is interested in the revival of a friendly national Russia; Japan has its own national policy, independent of Masonic and Jewish influences. Japan, therefore, is interested in preventing the enslavement of Russia by international financial capital, since the creation of an American base in Siberia on the Asian mainland creates sources of constant unease for Japan.

There is a convergence of national Russian and Japanese interests, room for mutual understanding, rapprochement and friendship.

Japan, in the process of its historical growth, is now entering the mainland and is beginning a new era, the Renaissance of Asia, which again contrasts Japan with the Comintern and the Finintern.

Communism and Judeo-Freemasonry are the common enemy of Russian and Japanese nationalists: the necessary prerequisites for an alliance are obvious.

The union of the future Russian fascist state with the Japanese Empire will resolve the Pacific problem in the interests of both neighbors, to forever stop Anglo-American claims, to create a force that can dictate its will to the rest of the world.

Being in the vicinity of the Japanese for the most part, the Russian fascists must use their favorable position to get as close to them as possible.

89. The RFP's Attitude Toward Other Organizations

The RFP, aiming to unite in its ranks all the emigration activists, its most combat-ready elements, strives to establish full mutual understanding with other emigrant organizations.

The Bureau for Russian Emigrants in Manchukuo is considered as one emigrant center, a business association of emigrants joined on the basis of the protection and promotion of legal and economic interests, and actively promotes the RFP.

90. The Task of Each Individual Fascist

The task of each individual member of the party is to actively participate in the work of the party, in self-education and self-growth, in preparing themselves for national revolutionary activities, and the direct participation in such activities.

Every fascist should take part in the work of one or another organization of the party, in the area that he finds most suitable for himself.

Every fascist must carefully fulfill the duties assigned to him by the non-party charter and special provisions, and show a fascist initiative.

Every party member should strive to raise the party's funds, necessary for anti-Communist work, to sell our party literature, and to collect donations to the anti-Communist struggle fund.

Every fascist is also charged with conducting feasible propaganda and counterintelligence work, introducing the essence of the Russian fascist movement to all friends, protecting our party from attacks and complaints, and identifying GPU agents in the emigrant community.

To expose the work of Communists and Judeo-Masonry, report everything noticed to the relevant party bodies. Since the main work of the party should take place on the territory of Russia, get ready for this line of work. Prepare yourself to be a national revolutionary.

Every fascist is obliged to enrich his knowledge of the ideology, program, and tactics of Russian fascism, striving to increase the level of his political literacy. He must also study the situation in the USSR, remembering that knowing the enemy is the first guarantee of victory.

If you have organizational or campaigning abilities, improve them! Strive to raise discipline in your organization by setting an example of proper discipline and diligence to others.

Questions to Review:

1. What are the stages of the work of the All-Russian Fascist Party?
2. What defines the general line of the party?
3. What is the general plan of the RFP?
4. What is the Fascist three-year plan and by whom is it justified?
5. When did the Fascist three-year plan begin? When should it end?
6. What are our thoughts on the implementation of the Fascist three-year plan?
7. What should each revolutionary unit in Russia do?
8. Why do we stand for the complete separation of the open emigrant work from the conspiratorial work within Russia?
9. Why do we stand for the complete organizational independence of all revolutionary units?
10. What will unite all revolutionary units on the territory of Russia?
11. What are the tasks of the party for the time of the implementation of the Fascist triennium?
12. Whom do we now engage for domestic Russian work?
13. What should be our work in emigration?
14. What exactly does our work in emigration consist of?
15. Describe the significance of our annual tactical slogans.
16. Name the slogans for 1935 and explain their meaning.
17. How do Russian fascists feel about intervention?
18. What is our attitude toward the Japanese Empire?
19. Why should we seek an alliance between Russian nationalists and Japanese nationalists?
20. How does the RFP relate to other émigré organizations?
21. List the tasks of each individual Russian fascist.

Chapter V: Organization of Russian Fascism

91. What Is the Organization of Russian Fascism?

In order to achieve the great goals of Russian fascism, the overthrow of the Judeo-Communist dictatorship and the creation of a new national-labor Russia, it is necessary to have people ready and able to bring the ideology and program of Russian fascism into life. We must be ready and able to apply the means of implementing the ideology and program in life, the fascist tactics. Such people, i.e., Russian people who share the ideology, program, and tactics of Russian fascism, are called Russian fascists. For a successful struggle and victory, their joint work with each other is necessary. It is necessary that this work be organized. In other words, it is necessary to organize Russian fascism. Such an organization of Russian fascism is precisely the union of Russian people who have devoted themselves to the embodiment of the fascist ideology and program. The fascist tactic then is the All-Russian Fascist Party itself.

The All-Russian Fascist Party, therefore, can be defined as an organization of Russian fascism. The name of the party indicates that this union should first of all be a national selection: the union of the most courageous, the most fearless, the most selfless sons of the nation, of all the classes and all the peoples of Russia that are part of the Russian nation. Secondly, the name indicates that this union is the selection of the carriers of a given ideology, program, and tactics, namely the fascist ideology, program, and tactics. Thirdly, the name indicates that this selection is built in the form of a party that is based on the conscious discipline and independent activities of all its constituent units. Finally, the name indicates it is not an ordinary political party, but a fascist party claiming to be the one and only national elite. It combines the initiative of each individual member with the principles of sacrificial service to the motherland, the beginning of a party self-government. This is the basis of every political party. Starting with the principle of *Vozhdism*, it is necessary to give the party maximum revolutionary combat capability.[250]

The organization of Russian fascism is described in detail in the Charter of the RFP. The Charter of the RFP is the law regulating the life of the organization of Russian fascism, the life of the RFP. The Charter of the RFP regulates its goals and objectives, composition, structure, congresses, central and local leadership, duties and rights, and symbols of Russian fascism.

A detailed acquaintance with the Charter is required for every Fascist.

92. Territorial Distribution of RFP

The RFP should exist throughout Russia. But due to the occupation of Russia by International Jewry in the form of the Comintern, the RFP is currently scattered all over the world: in all considerably large centers of the Russian diaspora there are open or secret departments and centers of the party to join.

The headquarters of the organization of RFP is in Manchukuo, where the main group of RFP is located. In Manchuria, the RFP has departments in: Harbin, Iabloni, Handoahtzi, Imianpo, Hailar, Xinjing, Dairen, and districts and centers at all railway stations.

There are party departments in Japan (Tokyo and Yokohama), in Shanghai, and in Tianjin. There are a number of branches in a number of other locations in Japan and China, as well as in Persia, Java, and Syria.

In America, the RFP has departments in San Francisco, Seattle, New York, as well as a number of centers in Canada, Paraguay, and Brazil.

In Europe, representative offices, departments, and centers exist in Germany, Bulgaria, South Slavia, Italy, Switzerland, Estonia, England, France, Poland, Lithuania, Romania, and Finland.

There are also pockets in Africa and Australia.

In total, there are currently about 20,000 members in the ranks of the RFP.

93. Who Does the RFP Consist Of?

Admission into the RFP, the distribution of members into categories, and their promotion from one category to another is carried out based on the general mission facing the All-Russian Fascist Party, the

---

[250] Meaning "leader" in the Russian language, it serves as counterpart to the word *Führer* in German or *Duce* in Italian. (Translator's note)

national revolutionary struggle for the liberation of Russia from Communism. The main internal mission of the party, from national selection, is *to create strong revolutionary assets of ardent national revolutionaries.*

A member of the RFP may be any member of the Russian nation, regardless of their social status, their origin, or their past, who recognizes the charter and program of the RFP and is ready to obey the demands of party discipline.

Every person wishing to join the ranks of the party must first, after submitting the relevant application, stay at least six months in the category of sympathizer. Only after that, and after clarifying the political reliability of the person applying, the sincerity of his intentions to participate in the work of the party, and his commitment to serving the idea of Russian fascism, can he be accepted as a candidate and a full member of the party.

The main core of the party consists of those considered full members of the party. Only full members have the right to participate in the election of delegates to congresses and to be elected as such.

A full member must be infinitely devoted to the party, fully sharing its ideology, and sincerely willing to fight for the goals set by the party.

From the ranks of full members, another high category of party member stands out: *the party activist.* Enrollment in this class requires full psychological and technical readiness to fulfill any task. The most difficult job falls on the party's activists: the national revolutionary work. A member of the party's activists is a fully trained national revolutionary.

The condition of one or another associate in the category of a party activist is in complete secrecy. Women and girls make up a special section of the All-Russian Fascist Party: the Russian Women's Fascist Movement.

For the national education of youth under the RFP, there are special youth organizations: Union of the Avant-Garde (for boys ages ten to sixteen), Union of Young Fascists (for girls of the same age), and Union of Fascist Little Ones (children ages five to ten).

94. How Is the RFP Managed and Built?

The All-Russian Fascist Party is built on a combination of the principles of intra-party democracy in determining the main course of party policy (through congresses) and centralized leadership from above in its current line of work.

Intra-party democracy is carried out through Congresses of Russian Fascists, which are held every two years. Delegates to the

Congresses of the RFP are chosen by all full members of the party, according to individual party organizations at the rate of one delegate per fifty full members. Only full members can be elected to the Congress.

In the period between congresses, all power belongs to the head of the party, proclaimed by the Congress, and the central organs of the party. The Supreme Council, the Central Control Commission, and the Central Audit Commission are elected at the Congress.

The head of the party and its central bodies constitute the central leadership of the party, and lead the life and work of the party through the local and direct leadership (heads of individual organizations of the RFP) of the RFP throughout the world.

Local organizations: hearth, district, department are the constituent units from which the organization of the party of Russian fascism is built, the All-Russian Fascist Party.

95. Tell Us Briefly About the History of the Emergence and Development of the All-Russian Fascist Party

The first Russian fascist organization arose in 1925 on the initiative of a group of students of the Harbin higher educational institutions, and from the very first days of its existence it began to draw into its ranks the most active elements of the Harbin emigrant community and fugitives from the USSR, soon becoming the main center of all active anti-Communist work in the Far East.

At the beginning of 1927, in order to expand the fascist work on the initiative of K. V. Rodzaevsky, this fascist organization created the Union of National Syndicates of Russian Fascist Workers of the Far East, which developed even more vigorous activity. So, a number of branches of the CER line were opened. Waves of fascist propaganda poured into the USSR. All of the following years have passed under the sign of the widest propaganda work.

In 1931, the First Congress of Fascist Organizations, Unions, Syndicates, and Groups was convened in Harbin. This congress opened a new page in the history of Russian fascism. It was decided to merge all the Russian fascist streams of the Far East into a powerful single fascist stream in the form of the Russian Fascist Party, which included all of the hitherto independent fascist organizations. Its initiator, K. V. Rodzaevsky, was elected as General Secretary of the RFP. The Central Committee of the party was also elected, then renamed the Supreme Council. In the same year, the general line of the RFP's foreign policy was determined (even before Japan's speech on the mainland) towards rapprochement with Japan as the only real force taking up an active struggle against the Bolsheviks.

In 1932, the party began publishing the monthly magazine the *Nation*, and in 1932 the daily newspaper *Our Way*. From this moment, which coincided with the departure from the RFP of General V. D. Kosmin, begins the flowering of the Russian Fascist Party, quickly dominating in the emigrant community. The emigrant activists unite in its ranks.

In 1933, as a result of a meeting between the representatives of the RFP and the representatives of the All-Russian Fascist Organization in America, the Second Congress of All-Russian Fascists, the RFP united with the RFO into a single All-Russian Fascist Party. RFO Chairman A. A. Vonsiatsky was elected Chairman of the Central Executive Committee of the RFP and K. V. Rodzaevsky Deputy Chairman and General Secretary RFP. However, soon A. A. Vonsiatsky showed complete unfitness for the position of chairman of the CEC, and by bending the tactical line tried to create conflict between the RFP and its Far Eastern allies, as a result of which an extraordinary act of the CEC followed, removing him from the post of chairman of the CEC with his exclusion from the ranks of the party.[251]

Following his expulsion, Vonsiatsky tried to attract some of the members of the RFP to his side and create a parallel RFP organization with a similar name, but nothing came of this attempt: The vast majority of Russian fascists remain loyal to the party center in Harbin.

The party deploys the most extensive propaganda work, sending waves of anti-Communist literature into the USSR.

The publishing of our activities is also unfolding, and widespread propaganda work is being carried out in the emigrant community.

In July 1935, the Third Congress of Russian Fascists was held in Harbin, which was attended by the chairmen of all RFP organizations. More distant organizations (in America, Europe, and Africa) sent legates to Harbin's associates.

The Third Congress, at the unanimous request of all delegates, proclaimed the founder of the party, K. V. Rodzaevsky, the head of the party, approved the program and charter of the RFP, and authorized the removal and exclusion of Vonsiatsky.

The Third Congress also approved K. V. Rodzaevsky's master plan, the fascist three-year plan, and decided to direct all efforts towards its implementation.

The Third Congress marked a new stage in the development of the party's work, the stage of the maximum reduction of work in emigration while maximizing the expansion of work inside Russia, effecting

---

[251] *ЦИКа; Central Executive Committee.* Clearly inspired from the Soviet All-Union Central Executive Committee, showing further the parallels between the Soviet bodies and those of the Russian Fascist Party. (Translator's note)

the transformation of the party into a national-revolutionary party, the party of the national revolution.

The work of the party after the Third Congress seeks to implement the great decisions of that congress.

96. What Is the Meaning Behind the Party Symbolism?

A necessary element of the organization of the RFP is the party symbolism, which expresses the essence of Russian fascism through various symbols. Party symbols are the uniform, the party badge, the religious sign, the fascist greeting, the battle hymn, and the flag of the RFP.

97. What Composes the Party Uniform?

The fascist uniform in black colors expresses fascist self-denial and readiness to serve the motherland. The uniform is marked with the signs of the fascist hierarchy.

On the territory of Manchuria, the party uniform consists of a black shirt with pierced buttons with a swastika, a belt with a shoulder strap, galliffet trousers with an orange edging, and boots; an orange circle is worn on the left sleeve, surrounded by a white stripe, with a black swastika in the middle.

98. What Is the Party Badge and the Religious Sign of the RFP, What Do They Consist Of, and What Is Their Symbolism?

The political sign of the RFP consists of a two-headed eagle crowned with a cross and a swastika. The cross expresses the religious essence of Russian fascism, its striving for the primacy of spirit over matter.

The two-headed eagle expresses our national essence. It is the emblem of the Russian nation, showing that the main goal of Russian fascism is sacrificial service to the Russian nation.

The swastika speaks of our commonality with the fascist movements of other countries, indicating our united front in the fight against international forces of Communism, Freemasonry, and Jewry.

The political sign of the RFP is the graphic representation of our main slogan: "God, Nation, Labor."

The religious sign of the RFP is an image of Prince St. Vladimir Equal-to-the-Apostles with a raised cross.[252] This sign is worn together with the political sign and testifies to the devotion of the Orthodox members of the party to the religion of their ancestors, Christian Orthodoxy. Non-Orthodox party members (for example, Muslims) wear their own religious sign approved by the Supreme Council of the RFP.

99. What Does the Fascist Party Greeting and the Party Flag Mean?

The party greeting, raising the right hand towards the heavens, testifies to the primacy of spirit over matter. The exclamation "Glory to Russia," which the fascists exchange upon meeting, reflects the immense love of the fascists for the motherland. The desire to make it great and glorious.

The fascist party flag, which is a white field with an orange square, in which a black swastika is depicted, expresses the readiness of Russian fascists to fight against the world's evil, Judeo-Masonry.

The fascists unfold the party flag together with the national Russian tricolor flag, thus expressing the connection of the RFP with the Russian nation.

100. What Does the Fascist Battle Hymn Call For?

The fascist battle hymn, "Rise Up, Brothers, with Us," expresses the call of the Russian people to unite and awaken the Russian nation.

"The Fascist Anthem" (motif of the Preobrazhensky March):

Rise up, brothers, with us
Russian banners fly
Over hills, over valleys,
The Russian Truth soars!
With us all believers in God,
With us the Russian Soil!
We open the way
To the walls of the ancient Kremlin!

Strike harder, our Russian hammer,
And strike it like God's thunder. . . .
Let it fall, into ashes,
the satanic Sovnarkom[253]
Rise up, brothers, with us
The Russian banners fly
Over hills, over valleys,
The Russian Truth soars!

---

[252] St. Vladimir (d. 1015) was the first Christian ruler of the Kievan Rus and the patron saint of the RFP. (Translator's note)
[253] Sovnarkom: an abbreviation for the Soviet Councils of People's Commissars. (Translator's note)

Questions to Review:

1. What is necessary to overthrow Communist power and create a Russian national-labor fascist state?
2. What is the organization of Russian fascism?
3. What should the All-Russian Fascist Party represent?
4. What is the Charter of the RFP?
5. Where exist in the departments and hearths of the RFP at present?
6. Name the departments in Manchukuo.
7. List the departments and foci of the party in Japan and China.
8. State which countries have divisions and centers of the party in the Americas and Europe.
9. Approximately how many members are there in the RFP?
10. On what principle is the admission to the RFP, the categorization of members, and their advancement from one category to another?
11. The main intraparty objective of the party.
12. Into what category does a person wishing to join the party fall first?
13. List the categories of party members.
14. What organization do women and girls join?
15. What organizations exist for the national education of youth?
16. What principles underlie the organization of the party?
17. How is the principle of internal party democracy implemented?
18. Who has all the power between the congresses of the RFP?
19. Identify the local organizations of the RFP.
20. Give a brief history of the emergence and development of the party.
21. What is the meaning of the party symbols?
22. What does the uniform of the RFP consist of?
23. What do the RFP party badge and religious sign consist of and what is their symbolism?
24. What does the fascist party salute and party flag mean?
25. What does the fascist anthem call for?

THE PARTY PROGRAM OF THE ALL-RUSSIAN FASCIST PARTY

1. What Kind of State Does the All-Russian Fascist Party Fight For?

The All-Russian Fascist Party's main goal is: the overthrow of the Jewish Communist dictatorship over the Russian country; and the creation of a new National-Labor Great Russia, a Russia for Russians.

The overthrow of the Communist dictatorship that the RFP seeks to achieve implies: the removal from power of the party center of the CPSU, which has usurped the "dictatorship of the proletariat" in the interests of world Jewish capital; the expulsion of the Comintern, which has become a branch of the Finintern in the Russian territory; the dissolution of the All-Union Communist Party of Bolsheviks, led by the incompetent and saboteur leadership with their ideological and organizational bankruptcy; and the destruction of all those institutions which carry out arbitrariness and violence in the country, in particular the OGPU under all its guises, including that of the People's Commissariat for Internal Affairs.

The new Russia, for which the Russian Fascists are fighting, must be built on the principles of the motherland: nation and labor.

The new Russia we seek must be a free state, in which there is no place for the persecution of religion, in which everyone can freely believe, freely think, freely work.

The New Russia, which we want to create in place of the USSR, must be a real national state and a strong bulwark of the Russian nation, a common home for all Russians, built on a Russian foundation, by Russian hands, and for Russians above all.

The new Russia we want must be a labor state, an organized society of workers in which there is no place for exploiters and parasites, no place for non-laborers, no place for any privileged classes. No one is to have privileges.

The All-Russian Fascist Party fights for a fascist corporate Russia, in which the state power is independent and above class interests. It is a state which regards as its main duty the realization of national interests, the protection of freedom, labor, and the power of Russia, the unification of the peoples of Russia in the awareness of their common membership in the Great Russian nation, the protection of the products of national labor, the natural resources of Russia, and the integrity of Russian territory; in brief, the sacrificial service of the Nation: power is not a right, but a duty; power is not a master, but a servant—the guardian of the Nation.

In fascist Russia, every Russian should feel himself a member of one family—the Russian nation—subjecting his personal and class interests to the interests of the nation, bearing in mind that "the common good is to come before the private good" and that "the good of the fatherland is the supreme law."

In fascist Russia, there should be no class struggle, but class cooperation regulated by a supra-class state power: friendly creative work in the name of the nation.

2. What Does the RFP Bring to the Individual Peoples of Russia?

The All-Russian Fascist Party believes that the Russian Nation is an organism which unites all peoples of Russia on the basis of the unity of historical destiny, common culture, and awareness of common interests. Not only Great Russians, Ukrainians, and Belarusians, but also all the other peoples of Russia—Tatars, Armenians, Georgians, etc.—should be full citizens of Russia.

Every nation of Russia, participating in the national revolution and the coming national construction, should be granted the right to cultural, administrative, and political autonomy.

Since what is meant by the peoples of Russia includes those pertaining to the Russian nation with their own lands, and the Jews have their own land outside the Russian State, and are in addition responsible for the gravest troubles of the Russian people, the Jews in the future Russia are to be recognized as undesirable foreigners.

The RFP fights for a Great Russia, a fraternal union of all the peoples of Russia, preserving their cultural and everyday characteristics within the framework of a single Russian national-labor state.

3. What Kind of State System Does the RFP Seek to Establish?

Russian fascists leave the question of the form of government open, considering much more important the question of the state system, i.e., the social content that can essentially be infused into various forms.

The All-Russian Fascist Party does not call the Russian workers back to capitalism, but calls them forward to new national-labor forms of state, public, and social life.

The combination of the corporate system of fascism with the trade unions reformed in the process of the national revolution will provide the new national-labor system of fascist Russia.

The existing professional bodies in the USSR must be reorganized. Communists and Jews must be expelled from them. Through free elections, by closed ballot, the Communist trade unions should be transformed into Russian fascist national unions. Additionally, national unions should be organized for those professions without professional associations under the Communists.

National unions in fascist Russia must be organized in such a way as to encompass the entire population, so that not a single Russian would be left out of the corresponding union. No Lishenets! Fascist Russia will represent a society of freedom for workers organized into national unions, a single All-Russian Union of National Unions.

To the workers the fascists include all producers of material and spiritual values, i.e., the peasants, the army, the workers of physical and intellectual labor, professionals, entrepreneurs, the clergy, etc.

Similar unions with conflicting interests (e.g., the workers and employers of a single branch of the national economy) will unite to form national corporations with representatives of the unions concerned at the head. Corporations are created on a production scale (cells of various unions in production), as well as on a citywide, provincial, and all-Russian scale.

In a fascist national-labor state there must be a free and independent national court that is swift, right, and pious.

Judges may be removed only by court order.

Political crimes and crimes against the order of government are to be tried in common courts with popular representatives.

All courts without exception will convene in public. All citizens may attend.

No one can be arrested except by order of the judicial authorities.

The state power must be closely connected with all the living forces of the country. Representatives of national unions should constitute the bodies of rural and urban self-governments and national councils, the grassroots bodies of the administration and national economy, representing the diverse interests of the great Russian country.

The RFP fights for the reorganization of the existing city and rural councils into national councils, free of Communists and Jews. The councils must be based on unions. Elections to said councils must also be union-based. The councils also include representatives of the army, the youth, and the All-Russian Fascist Party.

The national councils, unlike the one-sided fictitious Communist councils, must be elected by secret ballot, by all workers (organized in national unions) without exception.

Similar to the grassroots soviets, district, provincial, territorial, and All-Russian National Unions are constructed on a district, provincial, territorial and All-Russian scale, exercising, together with the selection of Russian workers who rebelled against the Communists, power on a district, provincial, territorial and All-Russian scale.

4. What Does the RFP Seek to Accomplish in Industry and Agriculture?

The Russian fascists strive to create a national industry which would be in all areas completely independent of international foreign capital.

All products of all branches of industry must be produced in sufficient quantities to meet all the needs of the population.

Particular attention is given to the production of items of mass consumption, so that every citizen can purchase everything he needs at the lowest prices without any difficulty.

In industry a healthy private initiative must be widely encouraged: part of the machine-building industry, light industry, timber, food, and maritime and automobile transport will gradually be placed in the hands of private entrepreneurs or cooperative societies of Russian citizens.

Some ways of encouraging private initiative could be selling or leasing enterprises.

Should all industrial enterprises be subject to the state?

In order to concentrate state power on the construction of particularly important branches of industry connected with the defense of the country, as well as to influence the whole economic life of the country, to prevent the possibility of private monopolies, and to create a powerful cadre of workers and employees independent of the influence of private entrepreneurs, a number of branches of the national economy must remain in state hands. Namely, the mining industry (coal, oil, peat, ore, gold, platinum, etc.), metallurgy, some large machine-building, basic chemical, military, and aviation engineering, rail transport, large power stations, and mass communications.

To regulate the country's gross output and its distribution among individual enterprises in national construction, there must be state planning and an economic committee.

In the field of agriculture, the RFP should strive for the most rapid recovery of agriculture and its further prosperity.

Urgent measures should be taken to restore live and dead stock in agriculture as quickly as possible, through the development of the agricultural industry, the production and distribution of cheap mineral fertilizers, improved sowing seeds, improved livestock, and agricultural machinery should be promoted.

The RFP considers it necessary to establish a budget for research, training, and representative institutions serving the needs of agriculture, building an agricultural exhibition, excursions, courses, etc.

5. What Does the RFP Hope to Achieve in the Area of Finance?

One of the important tasks of the RFP in the future state structure of Russia is to create a financial system in which there would be a balanced budget, where expenditures are covered by state revenues.

The revenues of the state consist of: taxes and duties, revenues from the exploitation of state property, lands, and forests, from state enterprises, factories, and plants; exploitation of subsoil and extraction of metals, both precious and common, coal mining, operation of railroads, etc. The expenses of the state consist of expenses for defense, expenses for public education, social security expenses, and others.

The future monetary system should be organized on the conditions of isolation of the Russian money market from foreign markets, without the issue of Russian money for circulation in foreign countries.

Issued paper money should have inside the country a solid, non-fluctuating, and non-changing constant value. For this purpose, in addition to securing all the property of the state, they will be secured by establishing a fixed price for certain products or items of prime necessity, which will be released at fixed price from public warehouses and stores without fail.

In order to create a sufficient stock of money in gold for emergency needs, the state authorities must prohibit the export of gold from the country and the purchase of gold at a price fixed by the state, and take over the monopoly of certain foreign trades: bread, oil, metals, flax, etc.

All the money coming from this trade form the necessary gold reserve for emergency and unforeseen needs.

The RFP fights for taxes that are affordable to the people.

Down with forced loans!

6. What Is the RFP's Program in the Field of Trade?

The RFP believes that all citizens of the Russian national-labor state should be allowed to engage freely in domestic trade.

Foreigners engaged in trade shall be subject to special regulations to be issued to protect Russian citizens from foreign competition.

In order to prevent malignant speculation, trade in the necessities of life must be controlled and regulated in the general interest of the entire population.

Foreign trade in certain kinds of goods (coal, oil, metals, grain products, etc.) shall remain in the hands of the state.

No private enterprise companies can be allowed, and any that exist will be prosecuted under the law.

The state must give full support to small and medium-sized trading enterprises of Russian citizens and provide them with cheap credit.

7. What Will the RFP Accomplish in Education?

In education and upbringing, the RFP seeks to create religious, nationally conscious, socially productive people.

All education and upbringing of the younger generation has as its main goal the service of the nation. Hence the principle of sacrifice and duty is the goal of education, and the social utility of the individual is the foundation of education.

All educational institutions and schools are divided into three groups: lower, secondary, and higher.

Education in the lower school should be free and compulsory for all.

In secondary and higher education tuition is set only for the wealthy. The able-bodied but poor must be given a stipend.

Higher schools must admit only citizens of the Russian state, and foreigners only with special permission, and only if there are vacancies.

In secondary and lower schools, in addition to basic academic knowledge, great attention should be paid to physical development, national improvement, and practical labor (farming, carpentry, chauffeuring, mounter work, etc.).

8. What Does the RFP Seek for Religion?

The Orthodox religion, as the religion of the majority of the Russian nation, as the religion of the predominant creators of Russian culture and Russian history, enjoys the special patronage of the general state power.

By seeing religion as the basis of personal, family, and social life, the RFP imposes great responsibilities on the representatives of the Church in the religious and moral education of the entire population, especially of young people.

All other religions, with the exception of satanic and immoral pseudo-religions and Jewish sects, enjoy full freedom and support of the authorities.

9. What Does the RFP Bring to Russian Workers?

In the Russian national-labor state, the workers, as participants in the creation of national wealth, have their rightful place.

Russian fascism entails the destruction of Communist plunder and the prevention of capitalist exploitation.

Russian fascists seek:

- The creation of national-production trade unions to actually protect the interests of the working class.
- Workers' participation in the national control of production.
- The implementation of the resolution of conflicts between workers and entrepreneurs in the National Arbitration Commissions.
- The establishment of business councils in all enterprises, both private and public, to establish mutual understanding and business cooperation between workers and entrepreneurs.
- The shortening of the workday as much as possible.
- National compulsory insurance for workers against injury, sickness, old age, death.
- Free medical care and health counseling for workers and their families at government expense.
- Maternity protection in enterprises employing women workers.
- Prohibition of child labor, as well as shorter working hours for factory apprentices.
- Special labor protection legislation for industries that are especially hazardous to health.
- A real increase in wages and the payment of wages in cash in full and on firmly fixed terms.
- Participation of workers in the profits of the factory, by charging interest on wages to create a working part in the capital of private enterprises.
- Periodic leaves of absence with pay.

- The improvement of working and living conditions: a) hygienic and safe working conditions; b) hygienic and comfortable living conditions for workers; c) provision of cultural recreation, etc.
- Providing jobs for every physically fit citizen.

10. What Does the RFP Bring to the Russian Peasants?

The land to the peasants! All land, with the exception of state-owned land, must be given to the workers who personally cultivate it.

There will be no landlords in the future Russia.

All persons now sitting on the land and cultivating it by their own labor should receive it in full, inheritable, undisturbed, and indivisible labor possession and use.

Note: Indivisibility is understood in the sense of keeping indivisible a certain peasant allotment, the size of which is determined by the state, and varies depending on the soil, climate, type of farm, availability of land, etc.

Kolkhozes and *sovkhozes* are to be eliminated, and all their land is to be divided among the peasants. Each peasant gets his own plot of land.

Peasants, if they found it beneficial, could retain the collective farm form, but those who did not wish to retain that form will be granted the right to secede as an independent farm.

The state may establish large farms on vacant state lands for the prosperity of agriculture.

The peasants who have suffered under the Jewish Communist government are to receive help within the limits established by the state.

State insurance for peasants in case of death, crop failure, and natural disasters, free medical care, and free veterinary and sanitary assistance are to be introduced.

Peasants and national unions would be required to take care of loans and term loans to acquire title to land, buildings, and farm machinery.

Machine and tractor stations would be transferred to the peasant national unions of the districts they serve.

To combat landlessness of the peasantry, the state allocates special land for colonization and takes care to provide material assistance to the peasants in settling in their new homes.

11. The Army of the Future Russia

The national army and navy, which will be born in the fire of the national revolution, will exist to protect the coming Russian national-labor state. The national armed forces will have to rely on the entire Russian population. The Russian army and navy are the guardians of the national state.

During the war the entire population will have to take part in one way or another in the defense of the borders of the national-labor state, so the study of military affairs will be further regarded as the most important duty of every Russian citizen.

The permanent cadre of armed forces must be a school of military spirit, the guardians of the martial national traditions, and the breeding ground of military spirit. Therefore, they must consist of a considerable number of commanders who are strong in spirit and of a variable cadre of fighters with a short training period.

All those wounded in military service shall be provided with a state pension in the amount necessary for a comfortable livelihood.

Commanders who join the national forces during the national revolution are guaranteed the preservation of their official positions.

The Russian fascists are carrying out the destruction of the political directorates and political commissars in the army. In the national army, each commander will be at the same time a political educator, the leader of the national education of the fighters.

All special military units, such as the ChON and the units of the People's Commissariat of Internal Affairs, which had the task of maintaining the Communist dictatorship within the country, are to be disbanded.[254]

---

[254] *ЧОН:* Special armed formations, "Communist squads." (Translator's note)

ALL-RUSSIAN FASCIST PARTY DOCUMENTS

On the Party Greeting

1. The Russian Fascist Party greeting consists of raising the right hand from the heart to the sky with the cry in a loud voice, "Glory to Russia!"
2. The raising up of the hand symbolizes the aspiration of the soul of fascism to higher ideals, the primacy of the spirit over matter, while "Glory to Russia!" means the glorification of the former and future Russia.
3. When greeting, the arm is quickly and clearly stretched out to its full length with outstretched palm and fingers pressed together. "Glory to Russia!" is said loudly and clearly. If the salute is made while moving, the saluting officer stops with a "Ten-hut." Any careless salute is regarded as disrespectful to the All-Russian Fascist Party and to the Glory of Russia.
4. Greetings without a command are to be pronounced: a) at home, as a guest, in the street, in an institution, in a club, in a school, wherever a fascist meets another fascist—regardless of familiarity—with the subordinate greeting the superior first, or the man greeting the woman; b) at the entrance to a party room and to a party meeting. The greeting on command is pronounced at the entrance to the party meeting of the chief of the local RFP organization, at gatherings, demonstrations, parades, and in other specified cases.
5. Raising the hand to greet without shouting "Glory to Russia!" is called a salute; fascists salute each other instead of a full salute if their mouths are busy, or if "Glory to Russia!" cannot be said loudly in a given place. Fascists are to salute the national or party flag at the sight of the flag. Fascists salute at the playing of the fascist or national anthem, or the anthem of the sheltering country, with the senior fascist in the hierarchy proclaiming "Glory to Russia!" at the

end of the party anthem, to be picked up by all in attendance. The fascist salutes his superior and holds his hand up when reporting. Fascists salute any command "Ten-hut!" given for them, or to the military units in the area in question.

6. The RFP salute is also the common salute for the Russian Women's Fascist Movement, the Vanguard, the Union of Young Fascists, and the Union of Fascist Little Ones, and these rules are to apply fully to the members of these organizations as well.
7. The raising of hands by fascists in military service or in RFP training units are to be replaced by a salute, according to the Code of Order.
8. Failure to comply with these rules is considered a violation of party discipline and is punishable by the head of the local RFP organization according to the Disciplinary Statute.
9. These rules are binding not only on members, but also on those sympathetic to Russian Fascism.
10. These rules are announced in the Chancellery at the reception of an application to any RFP organization, and ignorance of these rules is not excusable.

On the Party Flag of the RFP

1. The party flag of the RFP is a black swastika on a yellow rhombus in the background on a white rectangular field. The flagstaff is decorated at the top with a double-headed eagle. The flag with the eagle also corresponds to the RFP party badge.
2. Also like the party badge, the RFP flag symbolizes the religious-national essence of Russian fascism—in the emblem of the Russian nation, the two-headed eagle—and the unity of various fascist movements in a common struggle against the world evil of Judaism, in the swastika.
3. All fascist premises, including the dwelling of every fascist, should be decorated with the party flag crossed with the national flag, to mark the inseparable link between the nation and the party.
4. When the national flag is hoisted, the party flag is hoisted behind it, to signify the same bond and the subordinate position of the party in relation to the nation: the RFP is a party of service to the nation, not of domination over the nation.
5. In every fascist procession, the party flag is to be carried before the national flag, to mark the same bond and role of the party as leader of the nation. The RFP is the vanguard in the awakening of the nation.
6. The flag is the fascist emblem, the most important element of fascist symbolism, and therefore it must be handled with care and due

respect. At the sight of the flag or at the encounter with the flag every fascist must salute it.
7. The flag of the RFP is also the flag of the Russian Women's Fascist Movement, the Vanguard, the Union of Young Fascists, the Union of Fascist Little Ones, as well as of other minor national organizations, training detachments, and all RFP special organizations.
8. Each RFP organization, in addition to the general party flag, may have its own special flag approved by the RFP Supreme Council. Special flags are also flown by the Russian Women's Fascist Movement, the Vanguard, the Union of Young Fascists, the Union of Fascist Little Ones, national minor organizations, training detachments, and special operation units.
9. These rules apply to all members of all RFP organizations, and violation of them is punishable by the head of the local RFP organization, in accordance with the Disciplinary Statute.
10. These rules are announced in the Chancellery at the reception of an application to any organization of the RFP and ignorance of these rules is not excusable.

On the National Flag and National Anthem

1. Russian fascists, as heirs and successors of Russia's glorious past, regard as their national flag the Russian tricolor, set up by Peter the Great as the flag of the Russian Empire.
2. The white-blue-red flag is regarded by Russian fascists as the flag of the Russian nation and of the coming New Russian Power. The white symbolizes a just national power, the blue symbolizes the native country, and the red symbolizes the blood shed by the peoples of Russia for the sake of the nation.
3. The national anthem the Russian fascists revere as the Russian *narodni*[255] anthem is the "God Save the Tsar!" with lyrics by Zhukovsky, and music by Lvov:

> God Save the Tsar! Strong and mighty,
> Reign for glory, for our glory!
> Reign in fear of our enemies! O Tsar of the Orthodox!
> God save the Tsar!

---

[255] *народный*: meaning the people of Russia; it is the counterpart of the German Volk. It stresses how the anthem is not just connected with the abstract concept of a Russian nation, but is intimately linked to the blood and peoples (the *narod*) of Russia. This is something worth noting upon reading the inaccurate English translation of "peoples" across this book. (Translator's note)

4. The sounds of "God Save the Tsar!" are regarded by Russian fascists as the anthem of the Russian nation and the coming Great Russia.
5. Every fascist must know the meaning and history of the national flag.
6. Every fascist must know the lyrics and music of the national anthem by participating in its common singing.
7. Every fascist premise, as well as every fascist's home, must be decorated with the national flag crossed with the party flag (left to right) in commemoration of the inseparable bond between the nation and the party.
8. When the party flag is hoisted, the national flag is to be hoisted in front of it, to mark the same connection and the subordinate position of the party in relation to the nation. The RFP is the party serving the nation, not the one dominating the nation.
9. In every fascist procession, the national flag follows the party flag, in commemoration of the same connection and role of the party as the leader of the nation: the RFP is the vanguard of the awakening nation.
10. The national flag is the national fascist emblem, the most important element of national and party symbols, and must therefore be treated with care and due respect. At the sight of the flag or when meeting the flag, every fascist must salute it.
11. The national anthem is sung at the opening of any meeting, gathering, celebration, after a prayer, or before the party anthem.
12. At the first sound of the national anthem, however distant, the fascist must stand "humbly" and extend his arm in salute.
13. It is forbidden to sing the anthem in inappropriate places and at inappropriate times, such as in cabarets, in dances, or in drunkenness.
14. The anthem of the country giving shelter to this RFP organization is sung on all occasions together with the national anthem, and these rules apply to it in full as well.
15. The flag of the country of shelter shall be placed in all cases with the national flag, and these rules apply in full to it.
16. These rules are binding on all members of all RFP organizations, and violation of them is punishable by the local RFP organization chief in accordance with the Disciplinary Statute.
17. These rules are announced in the Chancellery at the reception of a petition to any organization of the RFP; ignorance of these rules is not excusable.

On the Party Icon

1. Description of the badge of the RFP. The badge of the RFP is the Russian State Emblem (a golden two-headed eagle), fixed on the top of a square, so that the diameter of the emblem lies on the continuation of the diagonal of the square. The dimensions: the sides of the square are 0.7 inches, and along with that the diameter of the coat of arms. The square includes a white border one eighth of its side width. In the middle of the square a black swastika is depicted, the lines of which by its width are equal to one seventh of the side of the square, with the ends bent from left to right (clockwise). The field where the swastika is depicted is yellow.
2. Meaning of the RFP badge. The two-headed eagle is the symbol of the Russian nation, and the swastika the symbol of the active struggle with the world evil of communism and Judaism, which begat it.
3. The RFP badge is worn on the left side of the chest.
4. The right to wear the RFP badge is enjoyed by full members and candidates of the RFP. This right is also an obligation.
5. The RFP badge is issued by the head of the local organization in a solemn atmosphere, on behalf of the head of the party. The recipient of the badge makes a solemn pledge to serve the Russian Nation. The ceremonial presentation of the badge is worked out by the headquarters of the local organization depending on local conditions, and is approved by the Supreme Council of the RFP.
6. Payment of the cost of the badge is required in order to receive the badge.
7. Each badge has its own number under which it is inscribed to the owner.
8. Wearing the badge is mandatory. It is not necessary to wear a badge if specifically authorized by the head of the local RFP organization.
9. Everyone wearing an RFP badge is obliged to wear it with honor, keeping in mind the meaning of its emblems.
10. The wearer of the RFP badge must be a model of decency, morality, courage, fortitude, and good upbringing.
11. Everyone wearing the RFP badge, as well as any Russian fascist in general, must always and everywhere defend his dignity.
12. It is forbidden to wear the RFP badge if unauthorized, that is, without the permission and knowledge of the RFP.
13. It is forbidden to give one's RFP badge to another person (even if entitled to wear one).

14. It is forbidden to wear the RFP badge in all places, which by the nature of their activities cast a shadow on its dignity, such as cabarets, dancing, etc. It is equally prohibited to wear the RFP badge while engaged in the foxtrot and other immoral activities, while drunk, etc.
15. Persons who violate these rules will be deprived of the right to wear the badge RFP (temporarily or permanently) and will be subject to disciplinary penalties, up to exclusion from the RFP.
16. Deprivation of the right to wear the badge may also be followed by way of punishment, according to the Disciplinary Statute of the RFP.
17. These rules are communicated when the RFP badge is issued, and ignorance of these rules is not excusable.
18. In case of exclusion from the RFP, the badge is taken away without refund of the money paid for it.

On the Party Banner

1. The Party Banner of the All-Russian Fascist Party is a gold-colored cloth, on one side of which is an icon of the face of the Savior made without hands,[256] and on the other side is the image of Prince St. Vladimir. The edges of the cloth are bordered with a black strip on which on one side are the following inscriptions: "Let God arise and let his enemies be consumed," "God is with us, understand the tongues and obey." On the other side is inscribed "With God," "God, the Nation, and Labor," "For the Motherland," and "Glory to Russia." In the upper corners is an image of the double-headed eagle; in the lower corners is an image of a swastika.
2. The Party Banner of the All-Russian Fascist Party was consecrated in Harbin on May 24th, 1935, by Archbishop Nestor and Bishop Dimitriy during a prayer service at the parade on the occasion of the fourth anniversary of the RFP.
3. The party banner of the All-Russian Fascist Party is the party shrine, embodying the essence of Russian fascism, on which God's blessing rests.
4. The party banner of the All-Russian Fascist Party is kept by the head of the Supreme Council's chancellery in the office of the All-Russian Fascist Party's leader, folded up, in a black cover under the icon, before which a lamp is always lit.
5. The party banner of the All-Russian Fascist Party is on particularly solemn occasions to be carried during assemblies, meetings, processions, parades or other celebrations; three flag-bearers and

---

[256] *Acheiropoieta* (Translator's note)

assistants of specially distinguished fascists are appointed to carry the banner. This appointment goes by order of the head of the party.
6. A guard of honor is appointed to meet the banner.
7. Each fascist, upon meeting the banner, salutes it.
8. A fascist going on a job involving a risk to life takes an oath in private with the Head of the Party by the banner.
9. The party banner of the All-Russian Fascist Party is the common banner of all RFP organizations, and all members of all party organizations are obliged to treat it with the utmost respect and a sacred awe.
10. Disrespect for the banner is punishable by immediate expulsion from the RFP.
11. These rules are announced in the Chancellery at the reception of an application to any organization of the RFP, and ignorance of these rules is not excusable.

On the Party Uniform and Hierarchical Signs of the RFP

1. The RFP party uniform: a black shirt, black pants (galliffets)[257] with an orange edging, boots, a black cap with an orange edging and a swastika on a cockade in the middle. On the left arm, slightly above the fold, an orange circle with a black swastika in the middle is asserted. At the cuffs of the left arm the hierarchical signs are to be placed.
2. Party and religious badges, as well as national minor badges, orders, medals, college, academic, honorary and other extrinsic badges are worn on the left side of the chest, above the pocket and on the pocket.
3. Special designations may be allowed on the left arm above a circle with the swastika, with the approval of the head of the local RFP organization and the sanction of the Supreme Council.
4. The black color of the fascist uniform symbolizes our mourning for Russia and a fascist self-denial in the service of the nation.
5. RFP training detachments, units, organs, and organizations of the RFP of special assignment, national-minority RFP organizations, RFP organizations created for a special purpose, and RFP organizations in warm countries may have a special uniform approved by the Supreme Council of the RFP.
6. The Russian Women's Fascist Movement, the Vanguards, the Union of Young Fascists, and the Union of Fascist Little Ones have

---

[257] *галифе;* a style of military trousers in the uniform of the Soviet Army. (Translator's note)

their special uniforms, worked out by their governing centers and approved by the Supreme Council of the RFP.

7. The hierarchical insignia of the RFP, being a necessary addition to the uniform, is sewn on the cuff of the left arm of all but rank-and-file members, according to the attached table, and is an indication of the position held by a given fascist in the RFP hierarchy.
8. The Russian Women's Fascist Movement, the Vanguard, the Union of Young Fascists, and the Union of Fascist Little Ones have the same hierarchical insignia as RFP officials, but of lower degree.
9. The right to wear the uniform is enjoyed by all full members and candidates of the RFP; this right is also a duty.
10. It is absolutely compulsory to wear the uniform at all party celebrations, at public meetings, and at party activities, except with the special permission of the head of the local RFP organization.
11. Everyone wearing a uniform is obliged to wear it with honor, mindful of its significance, and the uniform must be clean, neatly ironed, and buttoned at all times.
12. It is forbidden to wear the uniform in places which do not conform to the fascist way of life, such as cabarets, at dances, and during immoral acts, such as when doing the foxtrot, in a state of drunkenness, etc.
13. Persons violating these rules are deprived of the right to wear the uniform (temporarily or permanently) by the head of the respective RFP organization, and are subject to disciplinary sanctions up to and including exclusion from the RFP. Deprivation of the right to wear the uniform can also follow the procedure of the RFP Disciplinary Statute.
14. These rules are communicated to the Chancellery upon receipt of an application to any RFP organization and ignorance of these rules is not excusable.

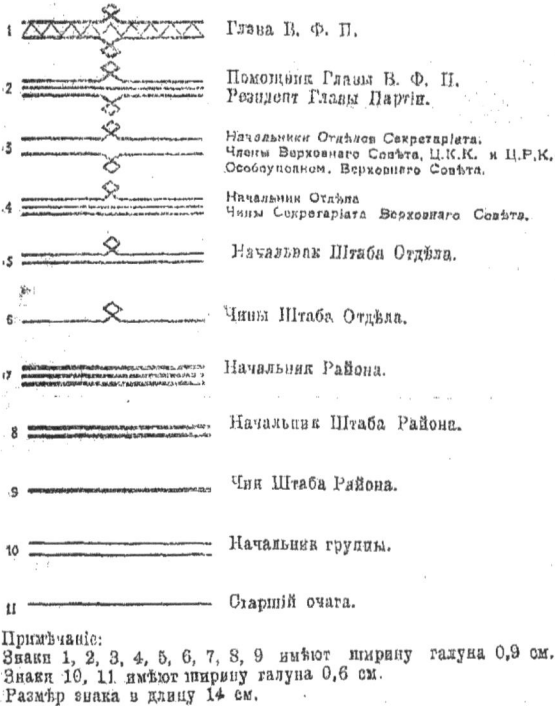

Translation of the table above:

1. Head of the RFP
2. Assistant to the head of the RFP
3. Main party president
4. Head of department of secretariat
5. Member of the Supreme Council, Central Committee, Central Committee Special Commissioner of the Supreme Council
6. Head of Department
7. Officials of the Secretariat of the Supreme Council
8. Chief of Staff of the Department
9. Headquarters Division Staff
10. District Manager
11. District Chief of Staff
12. District Headquarters rank member
13. Team leader
14. Senior hearth

Note: Ranks 1–9 have a lace with a width of 0.9 cm (0.035 in). Ranks 10 and 11 have a lace with a width of 0.6 cm (0.024 in). The size of the sign is of a length of 14 cm (0.55 in).

On the Religious Icon

1. Every fascist wears the religious badge of the religion to which he belongs. The religious badge of a national minority organization is drafted by its founders and is approved by the Supreme Council of the RFP.
2. The religious badge of the Orthodox Russian Fascists is an image of Prince St. Vladimir, Equal to the Apostles, on a shield with a blue background, framed with a Vladimir's ribbon (yellow-red-black).
3. The religious badge of the Orthodox Russian Fascist testifies to the fascist's loyalty to the religion of his fathers, the Orthodox faith, which is the foundation of the Russian nation.
4. The right to wear the religious badge is enjoyed not only by members of the RFP, but also by sympathizers and all Orthodox Russian people who wish to do so.
5. The badge is worn on the left side of the chest, first, next to the party badge.
6. The presentation of the badge takes place in a solemn atmosphere after its blessing by the clergy. The ceremonial presentation is worked out by the headquarters of the local RFP organization depending on local conditions.
7. Payment of the cost of the badge is required in order to receive the badge.
8. Each wearer of the badge, as in general every Russian Orthodox fascist, is obliged to defend his dignity and the Orthodox Church to which he belongs.
9. Each wearer of the badge is obliged to be a true faithful son of the Orthodox Church: to attend the Temple of God at holidays and feasts, not indulging at such a time in entertainment; to know the prayers, and to pray every day—morning and evening and before and after meals; to wear a pectoral cross; to have the Gospels at home and read them; to know Orthodox dogma, the history of the Orthodox Church, and the history of his saint; to lead a moral life; to fulfill the commandments of the Church; to help his fellow men; to belong to the corresponding parish.
10. It is forbidden to wear the badge in places that do not correspond to it in terms of morality, such as cabarets, dances, as well as during immoral activities such as the foxtrot, while in a state of drunkenness, etc.
11. Persons who have violated these rules, by the head of the relevant organization of the RFP are deprived of the right to wear the badge (temporarily or permanently), and are subject to disciplinary penalties up to exclusion from the RFP. Deprivation of the right to

wear the badge may also follow in accordance to the Disciplinary Statute of the RFP.
12. These rules are also valid for members of the Women's Russian Fascist Movement.
13. These rules are communicated when the badge is issued, and for those wearing it ignorance of these rules is not excusable.

SUPREME COURT OF THE RUSSIAN FEDERATION RULING NO. 043/46

Military Collegium of the Supreme Court of the Russian Federation

As part of: Colonel General of Justice N. A. Petukhov, presiding, and judges: Major General of Justice V. V. Homchik; Major General of Justice A. Y. Petrochenkov.

Examined on March 26th, 1998, the criminal case concerning the protest filed by the Deputy Prosecutor General of the Russian Federation, the Chief Military Prosecutor, against the judgment of the Military Board of the USSR Supreme Court of August 30th, 1946, in which were convicted:

Konstantin Vladimirovich Rodzaevsky, born in 1907, a native of the city of Blagoveshchensk, a journalist;

Alexei Proklovich Baksheev, born in 1873, a native of the village of Atamanovka in the Trans-Baikal Region, former lieutenant general of the White Army;

Lev Filippovich Vlasevsky, born in 1884, a native of the village of Pervy Chindant, Akshinsky district, Chita region, former lieutenant general of the White Army;

Boris Nikolaevich Shepunov, born in 1897, a native of the city of Yelenitopol, a former officer of the White Army.

Elizavetopol, a former White Army officer;

Ivan Andrianovich Mikhailov, born in 1891, in the village of Ust-Kara, Nerchinsk district, Chita region, former minister of the Kolchak government, on the basis of Art. 58-4, 58-6, part. 1, 58-8, 58-9, 58-10, Part 2, 58-11 of the Criminal Code of the RSFSR, to be shot and confiscation of property;

Lev Pavlovich Okhotin, born in 1911, in the city of Chita. Chita, serviceman; on the basis of Art. 58-4, 58-6, part. 1, 58-8, 58-9, 58-10 Part 2, 58-11 of the Criminal Code of the RSFSR to 15 years of hard labor, with confiscation of property;

Nikolai Alexandrovich Ukhtomsky, born in 1895, a native of Simbirsk, journalist; on the basis of Art. 58-4, 58-6, part. 1, 58-10 part 2, 58-11 of the Criminal Code of the RSFSR to 20 years of hard labor with confiscation of property.

The sentence was not subject to appeal and was carried out on the same day against Rodzaevsky, Baksheyev, Vlasyevsky, Shepunov, and Mikhailov.

Under the same case, Lieutenant General G. M. Semenev, former commander-in-chief of the Armed Forces of the Russian Eastern Province, was convicted. On April 4th, 1996, the Military Collegium of the Supreme Court of the Russian Federation overturned the sentence regarding his conviction under Article 58-10, part 2 of the RSFSR Criminal Code, and the case was dismissed for lack of evidence, the rest of the sentence was left unchanged.

Having heard the report of Major General of Justice A. Y. Petrochenkov and the speech of the senior military prosecutor of the department of the Chief Military Procuracy, Colonel of Justice E. A. Guranovich, who supported the protest, the Military Collegium established:

Rodzaevsky fled the USSR to Manchuria in 1925, and for twenty years was engaged in anti-Soviet activities. In 1926 he created the Russian Fascist Organization and was engaged in anti-Soviet propaganda. In 1931 in the city of Harbin he held a congress of Russian Fascists of the Far East. He collaborated with the Japanese command and prepared the Whites for a joint effort with the Japanese attack on the Soviet Union. He organized and participated in provocative incidents arranged by the Japanese as a pretext for the occupation of Manchuria. He published anti-Soviet newspapers and magazines, and trained spies and terrorists who were transferred to the Soviet Union. From 1943 he led anti-Soviet activities among the White Guards, and collaborated with German intelligence.

In 1918, Baksheyev and Vlasevsky voluntarily enlisted in the White Army of Ataman Semenov. At the same time Baksheyev, as a deputy of Semenov and chairman of the Cossack government of Transbaikalia, issued orders forcibly mobilizing the population into the White Guard units, was engaged in requisitioning food, forage, and horses from the civilian population, created punitive squads in villages to fight against guerrillas, and Vlasevsky, as head of the Cossack department of the White Army headquarters, led the formation of White Cossack units for armed combat with the Red Army.

Having fled to the territory of Manchuria in 1920, they continued their anti-Soviet activities. Baksheyev formed and led the Union of Cossacks in the Far East, which was being prepared for armed struggle against the USSR. In 1934, they created an anti-Soviet organization, the Bureau of Russian Emigrants in Manchuria, which trained terrorists, spies and saboteurs. In 1935, they led the Main Bureau for Russian Emigrants, and participated with the Japanese in the preparation of an armed attack on the USSR.

Shepunov, as part of the "Wild Division," participated in the counterrevolutionary Kornilov rebellion and attack on Petrograd, and then in the SR-Menshevik uprising in Ashkhabad. Later he joined the White Army of Semenov, in which he led the armed struggle against Soviet forces. Escaping in 1922 to Manchuria, he created the Monarchist Association, and then collaborated with anti-Soviet organizations, the Russian Militant Union, and the Russian Fascist Party. In 1932 he joined the Japanese detachment at the station in Pogranichnaya, where he conducted searches and investigated cases of persons arrested for activities against the Japanese, subjecting the arrested during interrogations to torture and beatings. By order of Japanese intelligence, he engaged in recruitment of spies and their transfer to the territory of the USSR, supplying those persons with anti-Soviet literature for distribution among the population. In 1938 he was appointed by the Japanese as head of the Bureau of Russian Emigrants in the city of Harbin, and carried out work to prepare the White Guards to participate in the war on the side of Japan. In 1941 he participated in the formation of the White Guard detachment intended for an armed attack on the Soviet Union.

From 1928, Okhotin was a member of fascist organizations created by the Japanese in Manchuria, and from 1937 he was a member of the Supreme Council of the Russian Fascist Union and an agent of Japanese intelligence, and later was appointed deputy chief of the Japanese intelligence school that trained spies and saboteurs who were sent to the Soviet Union for subversive activities. In 1940 he was appointed as a public official at the Japanese military mission in Harbin and, until the day of his arrest, participated in the training of spy personnel to fight against the USSR.

Mikhailov, as a minister of Kolchak's Siberian government, participated in the organization of the armed struggle against the Red Army. In 1920 Mikhailov and Ukhtomsky fled to Manchuria and together with Ataman Semenov participated in the preparation of a counterrevolutionary mutiny in Primorye and the creation of the so-called Amur Government.

During the period in Manchuria, Mikhailov organized the publication of anti-Soviet newspapers, while Ukhtomsky as a correspondent of the newspaper, posted slanderous articles about the Soviet Union and urged the White Guards to fight against the Soviet regime. In addition, Mikhailov from 1925 and Ukhtomsky from 1930 were agents of Japanese intelligence, and on its orders recruited agents to fight against the Soviet Union. They also provided espionage information about the USSR to other foreign intelligence agencies.

The objection raises the issue of dismissing the case against Rodzaevsky, Baksheyev, Vlasevsky, Shepunov, Mikhailov, Ukhtomsky, and Okhotin with respect to their conviction for the crime under Article 58-10, Part 2 of the RSFSR Criminal Code, and to leave the rest of the sentence unchanged, recognizing these individuals not to be rehabilitated.

Having examined the materials of the case and having discussed the arguments set out in the protest, the Military Collegium finds that the appeal is to be upheld on the following grounds.

The acts of Rodzaevsky, Baksheyev, Vlasyevsky, Shepunov, Mikhailov, Ukhtomsky, and Okhotin, expressed in the conduction of anti-Soviet propaganda, in accordance with paragraph "a" of Article 5 of the Law of the Russian Federation of October 18th, 1991, "On the rehabilitation of victims of political repressions," contain no public danger, and therefore are not criminally liable.

As for the accusation of these individuals in the commission of other criminal acts imputed by the sentence, it is fully confirmed both by their own testimony during the preliminary and court investigation, and by the testimony of witnesses questioned in the case, as well as by the contents of the written documents attached to the case.

On the basis of the above, guided by Articles 377, 378 of the RSFSR Criminal Procedural Code, and Article 10 of the RF Law of October 18th, 1991, "On the rehabilitation of victims of political repressions," the Military Chamber of the Russian Federation Supreme Court rules:

The verdict of the Military Collegium of the Supreme Court of the USSR of August 30th, 1946 against Konstantin Vladimirovich Rodzaevsky, Alexei Proklovich Baksheyev, Lev Philippovich Vlasyevsky, Boris Nikolayevich Shepunov, Ivan Andrianovich Mikhailov, Nikolai Alexandrovich Ukhtomsky, and Lev Pavlovich Okhotin to change, reversing it in part of their conviction under Article 58-10, Part 2 of the Criminal Code of the RSFSR, and dismissing the criminal case for lack of corpus delicti.

The rest of the verdict against Rodzaevsky, Baksheyev, Vlasyevsky, Shepunov, Mikhailov, Ukhtomsky, and Okhotin is to be left unchanged.

The presiding judge of the Military Collegium
of the Supreme Court of the Russian Federation,
Major-General of Justice A. Y. Petrochenkov

Secretary L. N. Korneyeva

www.ingramcontent.com/pod-product-compliance
Lightning Source LLC
Chambersburg PA
CBHW030243010526
44107CB00030B/1318/J